Lecture Notes in Artificial Inte

Edited by J. G. Carbonell and J. Siekmann

Subseries of Lecture Notes in Computer Science

Luc Lamontagne   Mario Marchand (Eds.)

Advances in Artificial Intelligence

19th Conference of the Canadian Society
for Computational Studies of Intelligence, Canadian AI 2006
Québec City, Québec, Canada, June 7-9, 2006
Proceedings

 Springer

Series Editors

Jaime G. Carbonell, Carnegie Mellon University, Pittsburgh, PA, USA
Jörg Siekmann, University of Saarland, Saarbrücken, Germany

Volume Editors

Luc Lamontagne
Mario Marchand
Université Laval
Département IFT-GLO, Pavillon Adrien-Pouliot
Québec, Canada, G1K 7P4
E-mail: {luc.lamontagne, mario.marchand}@ift.ulaval.ca

Library of Congress Control Number: 2006927048

CR Subject Classification (1998): I.2

LNCS Sublibrary: SL 7 – Artificial Intelligence

ISSN   0302-9743
ISBN-10   3-540-34628-7 Springer Berlin Heidelberg New York
ISBN-13   978-3-540-34628-9 Springer Berlin Heidelberg New York

This work is subject to copyright. All rights are reserved, whether the whole or part of the material is
concerned, specifically the rights of translation, reprinting, re-use of illustrations, recitation, broadcasting,
reproduction on microfilms or in any other way, and storage in data banks. Duplication of this publication
or parts thereof is permitted only under the provisions of the German Copyright Law of September 9, 1965,
in its current version, and permission for use must always be obtained from Springer. Violations are liable
to prosecution under the German Copyright Law.

Springer is a part of Springer Science+Business Media

springer.com

© Springer-Verlag Berlin Heidelberg 2006
Printed in Germany

Typesetting: Camera-ready by author, data conversion by Scientific Publishing Services, Chennai, India
Printed on acid-free paper   SPIN: 11766247   06/3142   5 4 3 2 1 0

Preface

This volume contains the papers presented at AI 2006, the 19th conference of the Canadian Society for the Computational Study of Intelligence (CSCSI). AI 2006 has attracted a record number of 220 paper submissions. Out of these, 47 high-quality papers were accepted by the Program Committee for publication in this volume. In addition, we have invited three distinguished researchers to give talks about their current research interests: Geoffrey Hinton from University of Toronto, Fred Popowich from Simon Fraser University, and Pascal Van Hentenryck from Brown University.

The organization of AI 2006 has benefited from the collaboration of many individuals. Foremost, we express our appreciation to the Program Committee members and the additional reviewers who provided thorough and timely reviews. We thank Dirk Peters for his technical assistance with Paperdyne: the conference management system used by AI 2006 to manage the paper submissions and reviews. Finally, we thank the Organizing Committee (Laurence Capus, Mamadou Koné, François Laviolette, Nicole Tourigny, and Hospitalité Québec) and the members of the CSCSI Executive Committee for all their efforts in making AI 2006 a successful conference.

June 2006

Luc Lamontagne and Mario Machand
Program Co-chairs, AI 2006

Guy Mineau
Conference Chair, AI 2006

Organization

AI 2006 was organized by the department of Computer Science and Software Engineering of Université Laval and CSCSI (the Canadian Society for the Computational Study of Intelligence).

Executive Committee

Conference Chair   Guy Mineau (Université Laval)

Program Co-chairs   Luc Lamontagne and Mario Marchand (Université Laval)

Local Organizers   Laurence Capus, Mamadou Koné, François Laviolette, Nicole Tourigny (Université Laval)

Program Committee

Esma Aïmeur (U. de Montral)
Massih Reza Amini (U. P&M Curie)
Caroline Barrière (NRC)
Shai Ben-David (U. of Waterloo)
Yosua Bengio (U. de Montréal)
Sabine Bergler (Concordia U.)
Michael Buro (U. of Alberta)
Cory Butz (U. of Regina)
Laurence Capus (U. Laval)
Nick Cercone (Dalhousie U.)
Brahim Chaib-draa (U. Laval)
Yllias Chali (U. of Lethbridge)
David Chiu (U. of Guelph)
Robin Cohen (U. of Waterloo)
Cristina Conati (UBC)
Lyne Da Sylva (U. de Montréal)
Douglas D. Dankel (U. of Florida)
Jim Delgrande (Simon Fraser U.)
Jörg Denzinger (U. of Calgary)
Chrysanne DiMarco (U. of Waterloo)
Renée Elio (U. of Alberta)
Michael Flemming (U. of N.B)
George Foster (NRC)
Richard Frost (U. of Windsor)

Scott Goodwin (U. of Windsor)
Jim Greer (U. of Saskatchewan)
Howard Hamilton (U. of Regina)
Bill Havens (Simon Fraser U.)
Robert Hilderman (U. of Regina)
Graeme Hirst (U. of Toronto)
Rob Holte (U. of Alberta)
Diana Inkpen (U. of Ottawa)
Nathalie Japkowicz (U. of Ottawa)
Howard Johnson (NRC)
Froduald Kabanza (U. de Sherbrooke)
Grigoris Karakoulas (U. of Toronto)
Vlado Keselj (Dalhousie U.)
Iluju Kiringa (U. of Ottawa)
Yves Kodratoff (U. Paris-Sud)
Greg Kondrak (U. of Alberta)
Mamadou Tadiou Koné (U. Laval)
Leila Kosseim (Concordia U.)
Philippe Langlais (U. de Montréal)
Guy Lapalme (U. de Montréal)
Kate Larson (U. of Waterloo)
François Laviolette (U. Laval)
Bernard Lefebvre (UQàM)
Hector Lévesque (U. of Toronto)

Alex Lopez-Ortiz (U. of Waterloo)
Choh Man Teng (U. of West Florida)
Shie Mannor (McGill)
Joel Martin (NRC)
Stan Matwin (U. of Ottawa)
Gord McCalla (U. of Saskatchewan)
Jean-Marc Mercantini (U. A-Marseille)
Bob Mercer (U. of Western Ontario)
Guy Mineau (U. Laval)
Bernard Moulin (U. Laval)
Eric Neufeld (U. of Saskatchewan)
Jian-Yun Nie (U. de Montréal)
Roger Nkambou (UQàM)
Gerald Penn (U. of Toronto)
Joelle Pineau (McGill)
Fred Popowich (Simon Fraser U.)
Pascal Poupart (U. of Waterloo)
Doina Precup (McGill)
Robert Reynolds (Wayne State U.)
Luis Rueda (U. of Windsor)
Marco Saerens (U. C. de Louvain)
Anoop Sarkar (Simon Fraser U.)

Abdul Sattar (Griffth U.)
Weiming Shen (NRC)
Finnegan Southey (U. of Alberta)
Bruce Spencer (NRC and UNB)
Rich Sutton (U. of Alberta)
Stan Szpakowicz (U. of Ottawa)
Ahmed Tawfik (U. of Windsor)
Nicole Tourigny (U. Laval)
Thomas Tran (U. of Ottawa)
Andre Trudel (Acadia U.)
Marcel Turcotte (U. of Ottawa)
Peter Turney (NRC)
Peter van Beek (U. of Waterloo)
Herna L. Viktor (U. of Ottawa)
Shaojun Wang (U. of Alberta)
Kay Wiese (Simon Fraser U.)
Dan Wu (U. of Windsor)
Yang Xiang (U. of Guelph)
Yiyu Yao (U. of Regina)
Jia You (U. of Alberta)
Nur Zincir-Heywood (Dalhousie U.)

Additional Reviewers

Maria-Luiza Antonie
Mohamed Aoun-allah
Amin Atrash
Erick Delage
Lei Duan
Chris Fawcett
Jie Gao
Wolfgang Haas
Sébastien Hélié
Svetlana Kiritchenko

Rob Kremer
Guohua Liu
Sehl Mellouli
Andrei Missine
David Nadeau
Nhan Nyguen
Laide Olorunleke
Vincent Risch
Saba Sajjadian
Elhadi Shakshuki

Tarek Sherif
Jelber Sayyad Shirabad
Pascal Soucy
James Styles
Petko Valtchev
Pinata Winoto
Bo Xu
Haiyi Zhang
Yan Zhao
M. Zimmer

Sponsoring Institutions

The Canadian Society for the Computational Study of Intelligence (CSCSI)
La Société Canadienne pour l'Étude de l'Intelligence par Ordinateur

Table of Contents

Agents

Bioinformatics

Constraint Satisfaction and Search

Knowledge Representation and Reasoning

Natural Language

Reinforcement Learning

Supervised and Unsupervised Learning

User Modeling

Integrating Information Gathering Interaction into Transfer of Control Strategies in Adjustable Autonomy Multiagent Systems

Michael Y.K. Cheng and Robin Cohen

School of Computer Science University of Waterloo
{mycheng, rcohen}@cs.uwaterloo.ca

Abstract. In this paper, we present a model that allows agents to reason about adjusting their autonomy in multiagent systems, integrating both full transfers of decision making control to other entities (users or agents) and initiations of interaction to gather more information (referred to as partial transfers of control). We show how agents can determine the optimal transfer of control strategy (which specifies which entities to transfer control to, and how long to wait for a response), by generating and evaluating possible transfer of control strategies. This approach extends earlier efforts in the field by explicitly demonstrating how information seeking interaction can be integrated into the overall processing of the agent. Through examples, we demonstrate the benefits of an agent asking questions, in order to determine the most useful transfers, or to improve its own decision making ability. In particular, we show how the model can be used to effectively determine whether or not it is beneficial to initiate interaction with users. We conclude with discussions on the value of the model as the basis for designing adjustable autonomy systems.

1 Introduction

Multiagent systems with the ability to adjust the autonomy of their agents, over time, are referred to as adjustable autonomy systems[4]. The need for adjustable autonomy systems has been reinforced by work such as that of Barber et al.[1] that show the value of dynamic levels of autonomy for agents, compared to static ones, for improving the performance of a system. Researchers in such application areas as space exploration (e.g. Martin et al.[7]) also emphasize how critical it is to allow for robots working with human users to have their autonomy adjusted, at times. Agent-based adjustable autonomy systems[6] are ones in which agents are provided with the ability to reason about adjusting their own autonomy. One promising approach for the design of these systems is that of Electric Elves (E-Elves)([9]: a model for agents to reason about whether to retain autonomy or to transfer decision-making control to another entity (user or agent).

In this paper, we present a new model that allows agents to initiate interactions with other entities, to gather more information, before ultimately selecting which entities to approach for transferring decision making control. With questions to entities included as possible actions from agents, the resulting model is in essence one of a *hybrid* transfer of control: either there is a full transfer of decision making control to another entity, or there is *partial* transfer of control, where input is obtained from another entity by

L. Lamontagne and M. Marchand (Eds.): Canadian AI 2006, LNAI 4013, pp. 1–12, 2006.
© Springer-Verlag Berlin Heidelberg 2006

asking a question, but the agent still retains decision making control. This approach therefore allows an agent to make use of run-time information (in the form of responses from entities) to drive the choice of which entities should be given decision making control, resulting in a more principled basis for deciding whether to adjust autonomy. This approach contrasts as well with those of researchers (e.g. Fleming and Cohen [3]) that have agents initiating interactions with other entities, but always retaining ultimate control over the decision making, themselves. We demonstrate the value of allowing an agent to reason about both decision making and interaction, towards the goal of maximizing the expected utility of its strategies.

2   Background

In the E-Elves model, which serves as the starting point for our work, the central notion is that of a *transfer-of-control strategy*, an agent's planned sequence of decision-making transfers, together with times indicating how long it should wait for the delegated entity to respond, before transferring control away to another entity, or perhaps back to itself. For example, the strategy $e_1(5), e_2(11), Agent$ denotes a strategy where the agent will first transfer control to entity e_1, and if e_1 hasn't responded with a decision by time point 5, then the agent will transfer control to entity e_2, which has until time point 11 to respond, before the agent gives up, and decides autonomously.

In E-Elves[9], each agent seeks to maximize the expected utility (EU) of its transfer-of-control strategy, by modeling two key factors for each entity in the system: the expected quality of a decision made by the entity, and the probability of the entity responding at a point in time to the delegation of decision making control[1]. The formula for evaluating potential agent strategies is the following: $EU = \int_0^\infty P_\mathsf{T}(t) \times (EQ_{e_c}^d(t) - W(t))dt$, where $P_\mathsf{T}(t)$ denotes the probability that the entity currently in control, e_c, will respond at time point t, $EQ_{e_c}^d(t)$ denotes the expected decision quality of the entity, e_c, for decision d at time point t, and $W(t)$ denotes the cost of waiting until time t to make a decision.

3   A Hybrid Transfer of Control Model

In our hybrid transfer-of-control model, we differentiate between two types of transfers-of-control (TOC), namely *full transfer-of-control* (FTOC), and *partial transfer-of-control* (PTOC). The transfers in the E-Elves [9] model are FTOCs, where the agent completely gives up decision-making control to some other entity. A PTOC denotes a new type of transfer where the agent queries another entity for information that can used in the problem solving process, while still retaining decision-making control.

Humans face problems of too much data and plans of too much complexity, while agents have the problem of under-specified domain information. As such, PTOCs are particularly useful in domains where neither the human user nor the agent are very

---

[1] In this paper, we factor out discussion of deadline delaying actions, which are also part of the E-Elves framework.

capable of making a good decision alone, while together they can. Another way PTOCs are useful is to make the overall strategy more flexible, to be better able to handle a dynamic (uncertain) environment. For example, an agent can query about a user's location, in order to determine whether or not it is still useful to transfer control to that user (in case the user changed locations and may no longer be responsive to transfers).

A critical difference between an FTOC and a PTOC is that a successful FTOC (i.e., the entity to whom control has been transferred to actually responds) means that a decision has been made, and so strategy execution ends. In contrast, a successful PTOC does not mean that a decision has been made, only that information has been gathered that can help lead to a good decision. As such, the strategy execution continues after a PTOC, with the agent performing other transfers.

The output of our model will be a *hybrid transfer-of-control (HTOC) strategy*, that the agent should follow to maximize overall expected utility. We use the term 'hybrid' to emphasize the fact that our agents can employ strategies containing both full transfers-of-control, and partial transfers-of-control. Visually, one can picture an HTOC strategy as a tree, with two types of nodes, *FTOC nodes* and *PTOC nodes*.

An FTOC node represents the agent fully transferring control to some entity at some time point t_i and waiting until time point t_{i+1} for a response. It is sequential in the sense that if the entity does not respond to the requested control transfer by time point t_{i+1}, then there is only one next step - i.e., execute the next node in the transfer-of-control strategy. For simplicity's sake, we will regard the case of the agent deciding autonomously as an FTOC to the agent itself. Note that for this special FTOC case, we do not need to plan for any transfers afterwards, since the decision will definitely have been made (i.e., the agent can be sure that it will respond to itself).

A PTOC node represents the agent partially transferring control by asking some entity a query at some time point t_i and waiting until time point t_{i+1} for a response. Each possible response to a query will be represented as a branch from the PTOC node to a strategy subtree (also referred to as a substrategy in this paper) representing what the agent should do when it receives that particular response. We will use the following terminology. Q_j denotes a particular query, and $r_{j,1}, r_{j,2}, ...r_{j,n}$ denote its possible answer responses. We also include "I don't know" as a valid response, denoted as $r_{j,?}$, and also allow for the 'no response' case, $r_{j,\neg resp}$, which occurs when the entity does not respond in time (i.e., by time t_{i+1}).

Figure 1 illustrates an example HTOC strategy where the agent is responsible for rescheduling a presentation meeting time. In this example, the agent is uncertain about which factor it should prioritize when selecting a meeting time. So, it does a PTOC to the group leader Bob, asking query Q_1 = "When rescheduling a meeting time, which factor should be prioritized?", with the possible answer responses being $r_{1,1}$ = "Prioritize having the meeting earlier", $r_{1,2}$ = "Prioritize having as many people being able to attend the meeting", and $r_{1,3}$ = "Prioritize having the meeting be convenient for the presenter". Depending on the response it gets back from Bob, the agent will do different things. For example, if the response is $r_{1,3}$, then the agent figures that the presenter, Ed, is much more capable to make a good decision and so does an FTOC to Ed, asking Ed to make the meeting time decision, and waiting until time T_2 for the response. If time T_2 arrives and Ed still hasn't responded back yet, then the agent will just decide itself (to

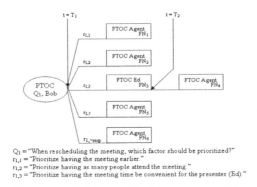

Q_1 = "When rescheduling the meeting, which factor should be prioritized?"
$r_{1,1}$ = "Prioritize having the meeting earlier."
$r_{1,2}$ = "Prioritize having as many people attend the meeting."
$r_{1,3}$ = "Prioritize having the meeting time be convenient for the presenter (Ed)."

Fig. 1. Example Hybrid TOC Strategy

avoid waiting around too long and not arriving at a decision). For the other responses, the agent decides to make the decision itself, either because it feels it is most capable (for responses $r_{1,1}$ and $r_{1,2}$) or because this is the best decision it can make. Note that the decision autonomously made by the agent will differ depending on the response it gets back from Bob. For example, if Bob's response were $r_{1,1}$, then the meeting time that the agent decides on may be different than if Bob's response were $r_{1,2}$.

An HTOC strategy extends the FTOC-only model of E-Elves [9], by allowing the agents to also perform PTOCs. It should be noted that E-Elves strategies are linear, in the sense that at any time point t_x, if the decision is not made yet, the agent knows in advance exactly who should have control. This contrasts with an HTOC strategy, since the entity given control depends on the responses received from earlier PTOCs. Note that it is important that the agent has a strategy, and reasons about future actions, since the best action to do at the moment often depends on what can be done afterwards. For instance, the usefulness of a PTOC depends on how the information obtained will affect the agent's later actions.

The procedure for an agent to find the optimal HTOC strategy will be a branch and bound search where the agent generates all possible strategies, of length up to a fixed number K, evaluates the generated strategies, and then selects the one with the highest expected utility value. As in E-Elves [9], we use bounds to restrict the number of strategies generated, but our procedure differs in order to generate and evaluate strategies containing PTOCs.

3.1 Strategy Generation

In the strategy generation phase, the agent generates all possible strategies from length 1 up to length K, where K is used to bound the length of strategies searched. Viewing a strategy as a tree, the length of the strategy is then the maximum depth of the tree.

Let Q be the set of all relevant queries and E the set of all relevant entities in the system (including the agent itself). Let FN be the set of all possible FTOC nodes, where each node (fn) identifies which entity $e \in E$ to fully transfer control to. Let PN be the set of all possible PTOC nodes, where the set consists of all possible pairings between a query $q \in Q$ and entity $e \in (E - \{agent\})$. So, each PTOC node (pn)

GenerateStrategy(int i) // where i denotes the length of strategies to generate

If (i = 1) // Base Case
    For each *fn*ε*FN* do
        create strategy of length 1 consisting of just *fn*
Else
    S_{i-1} := GenerateStrategy(i-1) // Get the set of strategies of length i-1
    For each *fn*ε*FN*- {*fn*_{agent}} and s_{i-1} ε S_{i-1} do
        create strategy by appending s_{i-1} to the end of *fn*
    For each *pn*ε*PN* do
        create strategy by appending strategies from S_{i-1} to branches of *pn*   (*)
        Repeat (*) for all combinations of S_{i-1} strategies and *pn* branches
Return set of all newly created strategies

// Note: *fn*_{agent} denotes FTOC where the agent decides autonomously

Fig. 2. Strategy generation algorithm

identifies which entity to ask which query. Also, each *pn* has branches for the possible responses to query *q*, and each of these branches will have an attached strategy subtree.

We present the basic strategy generation algorithm in Figure 2, and for brevity's sake, omitted the finer details/refinements. GenerateStrategy(K) will generate all strategies from length 1 to K.

3.2 Strategy Evaluation

In order to determine the optimal strategy s^*, we must first instantiate each generated strategy with the optimal timings of its transfers-of-control. For example, for a simple strategy consisting of an FTOC to Bob, then an FTOC back to the agent, we need to determine the optimal time point T that the agent should stop waiting for a response from Bob, and just decide by itself.

The optimal strategy is determined by evaluating the expected utility (EU) of each of the generated strategies and selecting the one with the highest EU value. The overall EU of strategy s is the sum of the EU of all the nodes in s:

$$EU(s) = \sum_{node \in s} EU(node) \tag{1}$$

The EU of a node depends on its type, which can be either an FTOC node, fn, or a PTOC node, pn.

[FTOC Node]. The expected utility of a FTOC node (fn_l), which denotes a full transfer-of-control to some entity e_i, is computed as follows:

$$EU(fn_l) = P_{trans}(fn_l) \times \int_{t_s}^{t_e} PR_{e_i}^d(t) \times (EQ_{e_i}^{d,\{info\}}(t) - W(t) - BC_{fn_l})dt \tag{2}$$

where t_s denotes the time point that the decision-making control is transferred to entity e_i, and t_e denotes the time point that the agent gives up, and transfers control away to some other entity. Or in other words, $[t_s, t_e]$ is the time duration of the FTOC node fn_l.

$PR_{e_i}^d(t) : \Re^+ \to \Re^+$ denotes the probability that entity e_i will respond with a decision d at time point t, given that the transfer-of-control to e_i occurred at time point t_s. Another way to look at this term is as P(e_i responds with a decision d at time point $t \mid e_i$ received decision-making control at time point( )$t_(s)$).

$EQ_{e_i}^{d,\{info\}}(t) : \Re^+ \to \Re$ denotes the expected quality of decision d made by entity e_i at time t, given that the agent has received the information $\{info\}$ from past PTOCs. It is important to make note of the $\{info\}$ term because the expected decision quality of an entity may differ depending on the information the agent gathers. For instance, it might be the case that the agent's decision making ability improves when it obtains the user's preference, i.e., $EQ_{agent}^{d,\{info\}} > EQ_{agent}^{d,\{\}}$.

$W(t) : \Re^+ \to \Re$ denotes the cost of waiting until time t to arrive at a decision.

BC_{fn_l} denotes the accumulated 'bother cost' to entities resulting from all the transfers-of-control that the agent has done up to (and including) FTOC node fn_l. For instance, looking back at Figure 1, the bother cost for FTOC node fn_3 is $BC_{fn_3} = BC_{Bob}^{Q_1} + BC_{Ed}^d$, where $BC_{Bob}^{Q_1}$ is the bother cost of asking Bob query Q_1 and BC_{Ed}^d is the bother cost of asking Ed to make the decision d. Asking queries thus incurs a cost, labelled here as the cost of bothering the entity being asked.

$P_{trans}(fn_l)$ is the probability that the agent will actually reach/execute node fn_l. For example, referring back to Figure 1, the probability of reaching/executing node fn_4 depends on the PTOC node to Bob giving back a response of $r_{1,3}$ and of the earlier FTOC node fn_3 (FTOC to Ed) failing, i.e., no decision response. So, $P_{trans}(fn_l)$ is computed as follows:

$$P_{trans}(fn_l) = \prod_{fn_{prev}} \left(1 - \int_{t_s}^{t_e} PR_{e_{prev}}^d(t)dt\right) \times \prod_{pn_{prev}} P_{e_{prev}}^{Q_j}(resp = r) \quad (3)$$

where the first product is iterated over all the previous FTOC nodes, and represents the probability that the decision was not made in an earlier FTOC node fn_{prev} (where fn_{prev} denotes a full transfer to entity e_{prev} for time frame $[t_s, t_e])^2$. The second product is iterated over all the previous PTOC nodes pn_{prev}, and represents the probability that for all the previously asked queries, the agent received the responses such that node fn_l will be reached/executed.

$P_{e_{prev}}^{Q_j}(resp = r)$ denotes the probability that asking entity e_{prev}^q query Q_j will result in a particular response r. The computation of this term will be described in a section further below.

As an example, referring back to Figure 1, we see that the probability of reaching/executing node fn_4 depends on the PTOC node to Bob giving back a response of $r_{1,3}$ and of the earlier FTOC node fn_3 (FTOC to Ed) failing. Mathematically then, $P_{trans}(fn_4) = P_{Bob}^{Q_1}(resp = r_{1,3}) \times (1 - \int_{T_1}^{T_2} PR_{Ed}^d(t)dt)$.

For an FTOC node fn_l to the agent itself (representing that the agent should decide autonomously), the calculation of EU is simplified to just $P_{trans}(fn_l) \times (EQ_{agent}^{d,\{info\}}(T) - W(T) - BC_{fn_l})$ where T denotes the time that the agent gets back control and decides itself. Following the original E-Elves [9] model, we assume that

---

[2] Note that the value of a product iterating over an empty set is 1.

an agent can always make a decision immediately; i.e., we do not need to factor in the probability of response[3].

[PTOC]. The expected utility of a PTOC node (pn_l) is just $EU(pn_l) = 0$. This is because a decision is never made in a PTOC (so there is no *direct* benefit to overall EU). The real benefit of PTOCs is *indirect*, and is reflected in the overall EU calculations as described above. The power of the PTOCs is that they allow agents to employ different branch strategies for different responses. To elaborate, different responses indicate different states of the world, which are modeled by different model parameter values for each branch. As an example, suppose that if the agent has no information, then it expects that $EQ_{Bob}^{d,\{\}} = EQ_{Ed}^{d,\{\}}$, but if it gathers some information (i.e., does a PTOC), it may find that for one response, $r_{1,1}$, *Bob* is the better decision maker, i.e., $EQ_{Bob}^{d,\{r_{1,1}\}} > EQ_{Ed}^{d,\{r_{1,1}\}}$ while for another response, $r_{1,2}$, *Ed* is the better decision maker. Different model parameter values may have different optimal strategies. So, continuing the earlier example, if the response from the PTOC was $r_{1,1}$, then the agent will do an FTOC to *Bob*, while if the response was $r_{1,2}$, then the agent will do an FTOC to Ed[4].

Here we will elaborate on the computation of $P_{e_i}^{Q_j}(resp = r_{j,k})$, the probability of getting a particular response $r_{j,k}$ when asking entity e_i query Q_j. The relevant entity characteristics are the $PEK_{e_i}^{Q_j}$ value, denoting the probability that entity e_i knows the answer to query Q_j, and the $PR_{e_i}^{Q_j}(t)$ value, denoting the probability distribution over time that e_i responds to Q_j at time point t. These two model parameters determine how much of the response probabilities will be 'shifted' from the answer responses to the "I don't know" and 'No response' case. The idea is that the probability of getting an answer response is contingent on e_i responding, and e_i knowing the answer. The three possible cases for how to compute the value of $P_{e_i}^{Q_j}(resp = r_{j,k})$, are as follows:

[No response]: $P_{e_i}^{Q_j}(resp = r_{j,\neg resp}) = (1 - \int_{t_s}^{t_e} PR_{e_i}^{Q_j}(t)dt)$

["I don't know"]: $P_{e_i}^{Q_j}(resp = r_{j,?}) = \int_{t_s}^{t_e} PR_{e_i}^{Q_j}(t)dt \times (1 - PEK_{e_i}^{Q_j})$

[Answer response]: $P_{e_i}^{Q_j}(resp = r_{j,a}) = \int_{t_s}^{t_e} PR_{e_i}^{Q_j}(t)dt \times PEK_{e_i}^{Q_j} \times PA(r_{j,a})$

where t_s is the time point at which the query was asked, and t_e is the time point that the agent will wait until for a response, and $PA(r_{j,a})$ denotes the probability that the answer to query Q_j is $r_{j,a}$. Note that $\int_{t_s}^{t_e} PR_{e_i}^{Q_j}(t)dt$ gives the probability of e_i responding to Q_j during time frame $[t_s, t_e]$.

4   Examples

We start with a simple example where an agent has to choose between fully transferring control to a user, or only partially transferring control. An agent is tasked with ordering

---

[3] If we want to be more precise about it, we can modify the waiting cost in the equation from $W(T)$ to $W(T + x)$ where x is the expected time for the agent to make a decision.

[4] This assumes that the agent will do an FTOC to a user, and that the other relevant user factors (e.g., probability of response) are the same between *Bob* and *Ed* (i.e., they are differentiated by the EQ value).

lunch for Bob. While the agent can make the decision by itself, it knows that Bob can make a much better decision (knowing what he likes to eat). On the other hand, by asking Bob (query $Q_1 = $ *"For lunches, do you prefer price or quality?"* and getting an answer, the agent can then make a good decision itself. Suppose the agent has the following three strategies available to it[5]: (i) s_1 where the agent immediately decides autonomously, (ii) s_2 where the agent first does an FTOC, fully transferring control to Bob until time point T, and then doing an FTOC back to itself if Bob does not respond in the time allotted, and (iii) s_3 where the agent first does a PTOC with query Q_1 until time T, to gather information from Bob, before deciding itself. Note that the optimal T value in s_2 will most likely be different than the optimal T value in s_3.

From history logs, the agent predicts that the probability that Bob prefers price is $PA(r_{1,1}) = 0.4$, and that the probability Bob prefers quality is $PA(r_{1,2}) = 0.6$. Since Bob knows his preferences, the probability that Bob knows the answer to Q_1 is $PEK_{Bob}^{Q_1} = 1$. The model parameters used will depend on the domain. Different users will have different response behaviour and bother reaction to transfers-of-control. For this sample scenario, we'll use $PR_{Bob}^{Transfer_j}(t) = \rho_j e^{-\rho_j t}$ to denote the probability of user Bob responding to a transfer-of-control of type $Transfer_j$ at time t. ρ_j controls how quickly Bob responds (the higher the ρ_j, the faster). Similarly, $BC_{Bob}^{Transfer_j}$ denotes the bother to Bob for a transfer-of-control of type $Transfer_j$. Since asking Bob a preference query is simpler (e.g., less cognitive effort required) than asking Bob to make the decision, we'll model $PR_{Bob}^{Q_1}(t)$ with $\rho_{Q_1} = 0.3$, $PR_{Bob}^d(t)$ with $\rho_d = 0.15$, $BC_{Bob}^{Q_1} = 3$, and $BC_{Bob}^d = 10$. For this example scenario, we model the waiting cost as $W(t) = t^{1.5}$. This reflects the fact that the longer it takes to make a decision, the longer Bob has to wait before eating (and Bob is getting hungry).

In this example scenario, we need to distinguish the EQ_{agent}^d values between the different branches in the strategies, since they will differ depending on the branch. To clarify, if an agent asks a query and gets an answer response, it will probably be able to make a decision that better suits Bob's preferences, and so EQ_{agent}^d will be higher than if the agent had no information. Suppose after looking at possible lunch options and factoring in possible user preferences, the agent arrives at the following expected decision quality values, $EQ_{Bob}^d(t) = 95$, $EQ_{agent}^{d,\{r_{1,1}\}}(t) = 90$, $EQ_{agent}^{d,\{r_{1,2}\}}(t) = 85$, $EQ_{agent}^{d,\{r_{1,?}\}}(t) = 60$, $EQ_{agent}^{d,\{r_{1,\neg resp}\}}(t) = 60$, $EQ_{agent}^{d,\{\}}(t) = 60$. This reflects the fact that Bob can make the best lunch decision, that the agent can improve its decision-making ability if it knows more about Bob's preferences (and that the agent has a slightly better chance of meeting Bob's preferences if his preference is price), and that the agent's expected decision quality is fairly low if it has no extra preference information to work on.

Computing the expected utility of the strategies at their optimal timings then, we get the following values: $EU(s_1) = 60$, $EU(s_2) = 63.38$, $EU(s_3) = 68.00$, with s_3 being the optimal strategy. For this particular example, it is worth it for the agent to perform a PTOC, and query Bob about his preference before deciding itself. When comparing

---

[5] In the strategy generation phase, the agent would have generated other (possibly more complex) strategies, such as a PTOC followed by another PTOC. For this example, we will focus only on these three strategies.

s_3 with s_1, the main differences are that s_1 has the advantage that the decision is made sooner and without bothering the user (so less wait and bother cost), but that s_3 allows for the agent to make better 'informed' decisions. When comparing s_3 with s_2, the main differences are that a successful FTOC results in a better decision being made by Bob, but that there is the penalty of a lower response rate and higher bother cost when compared to a PTOC. It is important to note that our model will select different strategies in different situations. For instance, if both bother costs were raised by 10 (i.e., Bob really does not like to be interrupted), then we'll have $EU(s_1) = 60$, $EU(s_2) = 53.38$, $EU(s_3) = 58.00$, with s_1, the strategy where the agent does not interact with Bob, being selected[6]. On the other hand, if the ρ_d value for the FTOC were increased to 0.20 (i.e., Bob does not take that long to make a decision), then $EU(s_1) = 60$, $EU(s_2) = 70.18$, $EU(s_3) = 68.00$, with s_2 being selected.

We now revisit the meeting example raised in Section 3 and expand the scenario. Ed, the presenter for an upcoming group meeting, has to cancel and the agent is tasked with rescheduling the meeting. Suppose the agent generates these strategies: (i) s_1 where the agent just autonomously makes a decision without doing any transfers to other entities (ii) s_2 where the agent gives up autonomy and fully transfers control to Ed until time point T, after which if Ed hasn't responded with a decision, then the agent will take back control and decide autonomously (iii) s_3 where the agent asks group leader Bob query Q_1 until time point T, after which the agent will decide itself (iv) s_4 (see Fig.1) which is in some sense, a hybrid of s_2 and s_3, where the agent first asks Bob query Q_1 until time point T_1, after which if the response is: $r_{1,3}$ (i.e., prioritize presenter convenience), then the agent will execute a substrategy that is just like s_2 (i.e., fully transfer control to Ed until time point T_2, and if no response, then take back control and make the decision) or if the response is $r_{1,1}, r_{1,2}, r_{j,?}$, or $r_{j,\neg resp}$, then the agent just decides itself. Suppose we have the following model parameter values:

- $EQ_{agent}^{d,\{\}} = EQ_{agent}^{d,\{r_1,?\}} = EQ_{agent}^{d,\{r_1,\neg resp\}} = 45$, $EQ_{agent}^{d,\{r_1,1\}} = 80$, $EQ_{agent}^{d,\{r_1,2\}} = 75$, $EQ_{agent}^{d,\{r_1,3\}} = 35$, $EQ_{Ed}^{d,\{\}} = 65$, $EQ_{Ed}^{d,\{r_1,3\}} = 80$. Note the difference between $EQ_{Ed}^{d,\{\}}$ and $EQ_{Ed}^{d,\{r_1,3\}}$ to reflect that if the agent knows that the presenter's convenience is prioritized, then Ed's expected decision quality is better than if the agent does not know the meeting priority, in which case, Ed's decision (which most likely favors his own convenience), may not be a very good decision, since other factors may have priority. When the priority is to value earlier meetings (i.e., $r_{1,1}$), then the agent is quite capable (hence the higher EQ value). Similarly for $r_{1,2}$.
- $PA(r_{1,1}) = 0.35$, $PA(r_{1,2}) = 0.4$, $PA(r_{1,3}) = 0.25$
- $PEK_{Bob}^{Q_1} = 1$ (since Bob is certain to know the answer to the query).
- $BC_{Ed}^d = 10$, $BC_{Bob}^{Q_1} = 3$ (it's much less bothersome to answer a query than to consider a lot of facts/constraints and make a decision about the meeting time).
- $W(t) = t^{1.5}$, and this reflects the cost of waiting to arrive at decision (e.g., less time for group members to plan to attend rescheduled meeting, etc.).
- For this example, we assume that we derived the probability of response functions ($PR_{Bob}^d(t_i), PR_{Ed}^d(t_i), PR_{Bob}^{Q_1}(t_i)$) empirically, instead of analytically, and so we have a discretized time step function with the following probability of response values.

---

[6] This strategy can also be optimal in scenarios where the agent is already quite capable of making the decision itself.

Timestep	1	2	3	4	5	6	7	8	...
Probability of Response	0.3	0.35	0.15	0.1	0.01	0.01	0.01	0.01	...

With the expected utility formulation and the model parameter values, the agent is able to evaluate the generated strategies. As part of the evaluation, the agent needs to determine the optimal timings of the transfers-of-control. In this case, it can use a brute-force approach where it tries all possible time instantiations and uses the time instantiation which gives the highest expected utility for the strategy[7].

Then, the evaluation of the strategies given these model parameters are: $EU(s_1) = 45$; $EU(s_2) = 49.33$ with $T = 4$; $EU(s_3) = 54.20$ with $T = 3$; $EU(s4) = 59.10$ with $T_1 = 3$ and $T_2 = 7$. So in this case, we see that doing a FTOC to Ed (s_2) or doing a PTOC to Bob (s_3) is better than the agent just deciding immediately (s_1). Furthermore, we can improve upon s_3 by having the agent do different actions depending on Bob's response. While the agent is quite capable at making the decision when told to prioritize for an early meeting or more attendees, it is much less capable at prioritizing for the presenter's convenience. As such, it makes sense to let Ed have decision-making control when Bob's response is $r_{1,3}$. As can be seen, s_4 has a higher expected utility value than s_3, and is in fact, the optimal strategy for this example. Note, however, that the optimal strategy may differ when model parameters change.

5   Discussion and Related Work

In this paper, we presented a domain-independent decision-theoretic adjustable auton- omy model that enables an agent to reason about the trade-offs between three different levels of autonomy, namely deciding autonomously; querying another entity for in- formation while still retaining decision-making control; and fully giving up autonomy to get a decision from another entity. Rather than restricting to only full transfers-of- control (as in E-Elves [9]) or to interaction without any transfers of decision-making control (as in Fleming [3]), our hybrid model allows agents to initiate information seek- ing interaction to determine the best transfer of decision-making control.

We extend the E-Elves [9] work by introducing the concept of a *partial transfer- of-control*, whereby an agent can gather information as part of its strategy. This infor- mation can be used by the agent to improve its own decision making ability (thereby reducing the need for full transfers-of-control to other entities), or to help reduce its uncertainty when reasoning about which full transfers-of-control to perform. An im- portant advantage is that while the E-Elves model requires the model parameter values (e.g., EQ, $PR(t)$) to remain more or less static in order to perform well, our model can still perform well in a dynamically changing world because agents can always query for information to obtain an up-to-date view of the world (i.e., reduce uncertainty). In our model, an agent checks to see if an entity is still available to accept decision-making control, before actually transferring control to that entity. Essentially, we are no longer

---

[7] For the curious, it took roughly 1.2 milliseconds to evaluate the expected utility of strategy s_4 (including finding the optimal timings of the strategy). Also, the evaluation code was unopti- mized (i.e., not efficient) so it probably takes even less time than that.

locked into a single strategy, but rather, we are more flexible and can use whichever strategy is best at the time, given the information gathered. In addition, we incorporate the concept of a bother cost, in order to model the very real costs of interrupting an entity when a transfer-of-control occurs, limiting the transfers-of-control to those that really add more benefit. As well, for possible entity responses to a PTOC, we allow a response of "I don't know", differentiated from the 'no response' case because for certain domains, there may be different information inferred.

It is important to note that since the FTOC-only strategies in E-Elves [9] are also generated and evaluated by our model, the strategy selected by our model as optimal must be better than or equal to the strategy selected by the E-Elves model, in terms of EU. Or in other (more mathematical) words, let S_{EE} denote the set of strategies generated by the E-Elves model, and let S_H denote the set of strategies generated by our hybrid model. Since $S_{EE} \subseteq S_H$, it must be the case that $\max EU(s)_{s \in SEE} \leq \max EU(s)_{s \in S_H}$. However, since we are generating and evaluating more strategies (namely those involving PTOCs), our model will require more computation time. As with the E-Elves model presented in [9], our model bounds the length of strategies searched by a value K. For most domains, the bother cost and waiting cost will eventually overwhelm the benefit of repeatedly transferring control, and so K can be kept fairly small.

In addition to extending the E-Elves model, we compare favourably with other approaches for the design of adjustable autonomy systems. Myers and Morley's work [8] involves allowing user-based adjustable autonomy [6], based on a user setting *permission requirements* and *consultation requirements* for decision making. Agents will only act autonomously in the absence of one of these conditions. Although our model is one of agent-based adjustable autonomy, it can incorporate elements of user-based control. Agents can now ask the user about his/her preferences, before making a decision. Even more importantly, the agent will explicitly weigh the benefits of asking a query against the costs of doing so. Thus, we begin to address the aim expressed in [6] of integrating aspects of user-based and agent-based adjustable autonomy within one model.

Braynov & Hexmoor [2] suggest that an agent's decision autonomy is in part a function of its knowledge of the user's preferences. Since our model provides a mechanism for acquiring more accurate knowledge of the user's preferences as part of the agent's reasoning about decision making (namely, allowing for queries to be asked), it clearly indicates how that information gathering process can be integrated with the agent's reasoning about decision making. Mac Mahon et al. [5] also emphasize the importance of providing for interaction, for the application of route planning decision making by robots. This reinforces the need for a framework to reason about interaction as part of the adjustable autonomy process.

The research being conducted at NASA ([7]) demonstrates the importance of agents operating with teams of users, reasoning about both collaboration and interaction. Their solution includes the use of proxy agents for users to facilitate the interaction and coordination. Our model can in fact support multiple users, with the agent reasoning not only about when to initiate interaction but also about which entity to select for the interaction, in an effort to perform the strategy which maximizes expected utility. The model, moreover, integrates reasoning about both decision making and interaction as part of the selection of the optimal strategy.

6 Conclusions

In this paper, we presented a hybrid transfer-of-control model for agents to reason about adjustable autonomy. This domain-independent decision-theoretic model allows an agent to reason about three levels of autonomy: (i) full autonomy, where the agent just decides by itself without the user's intervention, (ii) no autonomy, where the agent gives up autonomy and transfers the decision-making control to some other entity, and (iii) partial autonomy, where the agent queries another entity for information that determines how the decision should be made. By introducing the concept of a partial transfer-of-control, we allow for the human user and the agent to collaborate and arrive at a decision together. In essence, it allows for partial involvement of the user, without putting the heavy burden on the user to make the decision by him/herself. This middle ground approach is especially vital in domains where neither the human user nor the agent alone are capable of making a good decision, while together they can. As well, since the model is domain-independent, it can be used in any system with autonomous agents that could benefit from adjustable autonomy. This hybrid approach to reasoning about adjustable autonomy allows more informed decision making about transfers-of-control and provides more opportunities for agents to retain their autonomy, even if initially uncertain, once additional information has been provided. We are currently working on a set of heuristics to reduce the number of strategies to be evaluated by an agent, investigating how best to acquire various model parameters and developing more specific models of bother cost to users.

References

1. K. Barber, A. Goel, and C. Martin. Dynamic adaptive autonomy in multi-agent systems. *Journal of experimental and theoretical artificial intelligence*, 12(2):129–148, 2000.
2. S. Braynov and H. Hexmoor. *Book Agent Autonomy Chapter 4: Relative Autonomy in Multi-agent Interaction*. Kluwer, 2003.
3. M. Fleming and R. Cohen. A decision procedure for autonomous agents to reason about interaction with humans. In *Proceedings of the AAAI 2004 Spring Symposium on Interaction between Humans and Autonomous Systems over Extended Operation*, pages 81–86, 2004.
4. H. Hexmoor, R. Falcone, and C. Castelfranchi, editors. *Agent Autonomy*. Kluwer, 2003.
5. M. MacMahon, W. Adams, M. Bugajska, D. Perzanowski, A. Schultz, and S. Thomas. Adjustable autonomy for route-direction following. In *Proceedings of AAAI'04 Spring Symposium on Interaction Between Humans and Autonomous Systems over Extended Operation*, pages 23–28, 2003.
6. R.T. Maheswaran, M. Tambe, P. Varakantham, and K. Myers. Adjustable autonomy challenges in in personal assistant agents: A position paper. In *Proceedings of Autonomy'03*, 2003.
7. C. Martin, D. Schreckenghost, P. Bonasso, D. Kortenkamp, T. Milam, and C. Thronesbery. Helping humans: Agents for distributed space operations. In *Proceedings of the 7th International Symposium on Artificial Intelligence, Robotics and Automation in Space*, 2003.
8. K.L. Myers and D.N. Morley. Directing agent communities: An initial framework. In *Proceedings of the IJCAI-01 Workshop Autonomy, Delegation and Control: Interacting with Autonomous Agents*, 2001.
9. P. Scerri, D.V. Pynadath, and M. Tambe. Why the elf acted autonomously: Towards a theory of adjustable autonomy. In *Proceedings of AAMAS'02*, 2002.

A Pruning-Based Algorithm for Computing Optimal Coalition Structures in Linear Production Domains

Chattrakul Sombattheera and Aditya Ghose

Decision Systems Lab,
School of IT and Computer Science, Faculty of Informatics,
University of Wollongong, NSW 2500, Australia
{cs50, aditya}@uow.edu.au

Abstract. Computing optimal coalition structures is an important research problem in multi-agent systems. It has rich application in real
world problems, including logistics and supply chains. We study computing optimal coalition structures in linear production domains. The
common goal of the agents is to maximize the system's profit. Agents
perform two steps: *i*) deliberate profitable coalitions, and *ii*) exchange
computed coalitions and generate coalition structures. In our previous
studies, agents keep growing their coalitions from the singleton ones in
the deliberation step. This work takes opposite approach that agents
keep pruning unlikely profitable coalitions from the grand coalition. It
also relaxes the strict condition of coalition center, which yields the minimal cost to the coalition. Here, agents merely keep generating profitable
coalitions. Furthermore, we introduce new concepts, i.e., *best coalitions*
and *pattern*, in our algorithm and provide an example of how it can
work. Lastly, we show that our algorithm outperforms exhaustive search
in generating optimal coalition structures in terms of elapsed time and
number of coalition structures generated.

1 Introduction

Coalition formation is an important area of research in multi-agent systems.
It studies the process and criteria that lead to cooperation among agents. The
process involves two main inter-related activities: *i*) negotiation in order to exchange information among agents, and *ii*) deliberation in order to decide with
which agents should they cooperate. Coalition formation research has its roots
in the theory of cooperative game [1, 2] in which a characteristic function assigns
each coalition a *coalition value*. A coalition value is often economical value, such
as money, that is assumingly created jointly by the coalition. Such a value will be
distributed as *payoffs* among coalition members. The focus of the study is on *i*)
what the agents' payoff should be, that leads to *ii*) what coalitions would form.
Agents in such a setting are self-interested: they try to form coalition when they
foresee an opportunity to increase their payoffs. Most of the studies in the theory
of cooperative game operate in superadditive environment in which merging of

L. Lamontagne and M. Marchand (Eds.): Canadian AI 2006, LNAI 4013, pp. 13–24, 2006.
© Springer-Verlag Berlin Heidelberg 2006

two coalitions yields a new coalition value of at least as equal to the sum of the two coalition values.

However, the assumption of characteristic function is somewhat impragmatic that it leads to the ignorance of the process of forming coalitions. Also, the assumption of superadditive environment is not always true in various real world settings, taking into account multiple factors, including the cost of coalition. Coalition formation research in multi-agent systems [3, 4, 5, 6, 7] leaves such assumptions but takes into account reality. This usually involves various factors and a large number of agents. Thus coalition formation becomes a very complex process. There is a large number of messages to be sent across while negotiating and there is a large number of coalitions to be considered while deliberating. A strategy to reduce such complication in negotiation is that agents focus on deliberation: generate a list of potential coalitions, yet to be agreed upon by agents, that are likely to be formed [7]. Most of coalition formation studies in multi-agent systems involves self-interested agents and are highly successful [3, 4, 5, 6, 7].

Coalition formation among fully-cooperative agents is also an important, yet to receive more attention, area of research in multi-agent systems. The common goal of agents is to maximize the system's utility–agents are to form coalitions such that the sum of the coalition values is maximal. This problem is known as *finding optimal coalition structure* (see section 2.2). It has rich application in real world settings, including logistics and supply chains, grid computing systems, and composite web services. These settings usually involve a large number of agents that makes the problem intractable for even a small number of agents (see section 2.2). A handful of previous studies assume the existence of characteristic function [3, 8]. Although they have achieved high performance algorithms, they still rely heavily on the existence of characteristic function. This makes the algorithms impragmatic as mentioned above. For a system of m agents, generating all coalition values (due to the non-existence of characteristic function) of m agents is exponentially complex, i.e., 2^m, and can also be intractable for even a reasonably small number of m—let alone the problem of finding optimal coalition structures.

To our knowledge, our previous work [9, 10] is the only attempt to tackle the problem of finding optimal coalition structure with realistic assumption, i.e., agents have to compute their coalition values and the environment is non-superadditive. They propose a deliberation algorithm that helps reduce the number of coalitions generated. Each agent generates profitable coalitions. From its singleton coalition, it keeps adding profitable members based on existing resources of the coalition. The coalition grows until it cannot produce profit anymore. This work is different in various ways. Firstly, it takes the opposite approach: each agent keeps pruning least profitable agents from its grand coalition. Secondly, it relaxes the strict condition of *coalition center* [9] that agents merely keep generating profitable coalitions. Thirdly, we introduce pattern into coalition structure generation. Lastly, we propose a concrete algorithm in for generating coalition structures. We also provide an example of how it can work.

The outline of this paper is as follows. We restate the problem domains and discuss about related issues in optimal coalition structure. We then discuss the deliberation, coalition structure generation and example. Then we discuss about the experiment, show empirical results. Lastly, we discuss related work which followed by conclusion and future work.

2   Coalition Framework

2.1   Coalition in Linear Production Domains

We remodel Owen's work [11] as in our previous work. For the sake of completeness, we restate our model below. Let $A = \{a_1, a_2, \ldots, a_m\}$ be a set of agents, whose goals are to maximize the system's profit. Let $R = \{r_1, r_2 \ldots, r_n\}$ be the set of resources and $G = \{g_1, g_2, \ldots, g_o\}$ be a set of goods. Resources themselves are not valuable but they can be used to produce goods. The *linear technology matrix* $L = [\alpha_{ij}]_{n \times o}$, where $\alpha_{ij} \in \mathbb{Z}^+$, specifies the units of each resource $r_i \in R$ required to produce a unit of the good $g_j \in G$. The goods can be sold to generate revenue for the system. The price of each unit of goods produced is specified by the vector $P = [p_j]_{1 \times o}$. Each agent $a_k \in A$ is given a resource bundle $b^k = [b^k_i]_{n \times 1}$. In this setting, agents try to cooperate, i.e. form coalitions, in order to pool their resources, thus increase revenue for the system. A coalition $S \subseteq A$ has a total of $b^S_i = \sum_{k \in S} b^k_i$ of the ith resource. Each coalition S can use their resources to produce any vector $x = \langle x_1, x_2, \ldots, x_o \rangle$ of goods that satisfies the constraint:

$$\sum \alpha_{ij} x_i \leq b^S_i$$

and

$$x_j \geq 0$$

The cooperation cost among agents is specified by the matrix $C = [c_{kl}]_{m \times m}$, which assigns a cooperation cost between each pair (a_k, a_l) of agents such that $c_{kl} \in \mathbb{R}^+$ if $k \neq l, \in \{0\}$ otherwise. Agents in the coalition S have to find a vector x to maximize the revenue accruing to a coalition. Let

$$P_S = \sum_{l=1}^{o} p_l x_l.$$

be the maximal revenue the coalition can generate. Here, we introduce *virtual coalition center*. Each agent $a_k \in S$ can assume itself a coalition center and computes the virtual coalition cost.

$$C^k_S = \sum_{l \in S} c_{kl}.$$

The virtual coalition value v^k_S computed by a_k is

$$v^k_S = P_S - C_S.$$

Each agent then can exchange the virtual coalition value. The maximal virtual coalition value is, of course, the coalition value, v_S. Any agent a_k who yields the maximal virtual coalition value can be a coalition center.

2.2 Optimal Coalition Structures

Once agents agree to form coalitions, they can be viewed as a set has been partitioned into mutually disjoint proper subsets. Each subset is a coalition, $S \subset A$. The largest coalition is formed when all agents agree to cooperate. This set of all agents itself is called the *grand coalition*. Since a coalition is merely a set, we shall use the term *cardinality* to refer to the size of the coalition. Each instance such a partition is known as a *coalition structure*, CS. In our setting, the coalition value is independent of the actions of other agents outside the coalition. The *value* of each coalition structure

$$V(CS) = \sum_{S \in CS} v_S$$

indicates the system' utility yielded by that partitioning. Let L be the set of all coalition structures. The goal of cooperative agents in coalition formation [3, 8] is to maximize the system's utility. That is agents are to find at least a coalition structure CS^* such that

$$CS^* = argmax_{CS \in L} V(CS)$$

In the literature, coalition structures are laid down into m layers. Each layer L_κ, where $1 \leq \kappa \leq m$, is composed if coalition structures, whose number of coalition are equal to κ. We shall call the of number of coalitions within each coalition structure the *size* of the coalition structure. The number of coalition structures within each layer L_κ is known as the *Stirling number of the Second Kind* [8]:

$$S(m, \kappa) = \frac{1}{\kappa!} \sum_{\iota}^{\kappa-1} (-1)^\iota \binom{\kappa}{\iota} (\kappa - \iota)^m$$

Hence, the number of all coalition structure is

$$|L| = \sum_{\kappa=1}^{m} S(m, \kappa)$$

Computing the optimal coalition structures in a non-superadditive environment is non-trivial [3]. Sandholm et. al. show that it is NP-hard [3]. Due to the large search space, existing algorithms [3, 8] can *generate* coalition structures which are within a certain bound from optimal and will get closer as the algorithms proceed. This work assumes non-superadditive environment and non-existence of characteristic function. Each coalition value is not known a priori. Thus agents have to compute all coalition values first. Given a set of m agents, there are 2^m possible subsets, hence the complexity of computing all coalition structures is substantially worse.

2.3 Best Coalition and Coalition Structure Pattern

In previous studies [3, 8], coalition structures are generated based on the size of coalition structures and the cardinality of the coalitions. It appears that the search space is very large. Here, we try to reduce the search space. For each cardinality, each agent tries to do local search for a small number of coalitions. Firstly, we define the agent a_k's *best coalition* for the cardinality κ the coalition S_k^κ, whose members include a_k, that is found from a search within a given time and yields the maximal v_S. Within the same cardinality, the next coalition that yields the second highest coalition value is *second* best coalition, and so on.

We introduce the *pattern* of generating coalition structures. A pattern of a coalition structure describes the number of coalitions and their cardinalities in the coalition structure. It is written in the form

$$B_1 + B_2 + \ldots + B_\kappa, \text{ where } B_\iota \in \mathbb{Z}^+ \text{ and } \sum_{\iota=1}^{\kappa} B_\iota = m$$

This work proposes coalition structure pattern in breaking manner as the followings. Given a set of 6 agents, for example, the first pattern is 6 in layer L_1. There can be just one coalition, which is the grand coalition, whose cardinality is 6. In the next layer, L_2, the grand coalition will be broken into 2 coalitions by splitting a member from the grand coalition into the new coalition. Hence the pattern is $5 + 1$. The next pattern is 4+2 and 3+3. The pattern in each layer cannot grow once the difference between each pair of coalitions' cardinalities is ≤ 1. Then the pattern breaks into the next layer, i.e., $4 + 1 + 1$, $3 + 2 + 1$, $2 + 2 + 2$. The last pattern is obviously $1 + 1 + 1 + 1 + 1 + 1$. The pattern breaking process for 6 agents is shown below:

No. of coalitions	1	2	3	4	5	6
Patterns	6	5 + 1	4 + 1 + 1	3+1+1+1	2+1+1+1+1	1+1+1+1+1+1
		4 + 2	3 + 2 + 1	2+2+1+1		
		3 + 3	2 + 2 + 2			

Agents can use best coalitions to generate coalition structures by following these patterns. By using the best coalitions alone, agents will achieve some coalition structures whose best one will be close to the optimal one. Using more coalitions, i.e., the second, third best and so on, coalition structure values can be improved.

3   Algorithm for Generating Coalition Structure

Each agent has to do two steps of deliberation: *i*) Pruning: deliberate over what coalitions it might form by deleting unprofitable coalition members from the grand coalition, and *ii*) Generating: exchange coalitions generated and use the breaking pattern to generate coalition structures. The sets of such coalitions are at least close to the optimal coalition structures. The main goal of the algorithm is to reduce search space for finding the optimal coalition structures. This can be achieved by reducing the number of coalitions to be considered.

3.1   Deliberating Process

We take opposite approach our previous algorithms [9, 10] for agents' deliberation. Firstly, we explain the ranking trees that are used as infrastructure in the early stage of the deliberation. Each agent ranks other agents based on their suitability to be coalition members. Then we will explain the extended part where each agent tries to shrink its coalitions.

In the following, we will identify a coalition by the identifier of agent a_k. Thus the coalition S^k refers to a coalition being consider by agent a_k. Hence b^S represents the resource vector of S^k. Given a coalition S^k, let G^k refer to the set of goods whose resource requirements are fully or partially satisfied by b^S, the resources available in S^k (excluding goods whose resource requirement might be trivially satisfied because these are 0). For each good $g_j \in G^k$, the coalition center agent a_k ranks agents not currently in its coalition on a per good basis. For each resource r_i of good g_j, agent a_k ranks non-member agents by computing for each $a_l \notin S^k$, whose $b_i^l > 0$, the value π_i^j—its *proportional contribution* to the profit of the good (using its fraction of the resource requirements for that good provided by the a_l) minus the (pair-wise) collaboration cost between a_l and a_k, i.e.,

$$\pi_i^j = \frac{b_i^l}{\alpha_{ij}} p_j - c_{kl}.$$

The agent a_k uses this proportional contribution π_i^j to construct a binary tree for each g_j. The only child of the root g_j is the first resource α_{1j}, whose left child is the second resource α_{2j}, and so on. For each α_{ij}, its right child is either i) null if $\alpha_j^i = 0$, or ii) the agent $a_{1st}^{r_i}$, whose π_i^j value is the greatest. The right child of $a_{1st}^{r_i}$ is the agent $a_{2nd}^{r_i}$, whose π_i^j value is the second greatest, and so on. Agent a_k can use these trees to eliminate surplus agents.

The agent a_k uses b^S to determine surplus resources not used to produce additional units of a good g_j. For each $g_j \in G^k$ and resource r_i,

$$\beta_i^j = b_i^S - I(\alpha_{ij}),$$

where $I \in \mathbb{Z}^+$ is the smallest integer such that $\beta_i^j > 0$, represents the surplus amount of r_i that coalition S^k does not use to produce good g_j, provided the amount is non-negative ($\beta = 0$ otherwise). The *indicative vector*, $\beta^j = [\beta_i^j]_{1 \times n}$, represents surplus units of each resource r_i of good g_j.

In this work, the agent a_k creates the grand coalition and tries to shrink it by pruning least profitable members. The agent utilizes indicative vectors β^js and the the tree T^j in order to locate the agent who is the least useful to its present coalition. For each good, the positive value of β_i^j in the indicative vector indicates surplus resource that the agent who possesses the equivalent resource should be eliminated from the present coalition. The agent a_k create a trial coalition S' for each good. The surplus agents will be eliminated from S for the next smaller quantity of the good possible. Each trial coalition will be inserted into the pruning members S^-. The sub-algorithm for selecting profitable members is shown in algorithm 1.

In the main algorithm, the agent a_k considers itself a virtual coalition center of the grand coalitin. at the beginning of deliberating. It create the ranking tree T^G of all agent for each good. At this point, it is root and the only member of the profitable-coalition tree,L^-. It prunes the pruning agents S^- from the coalition.

Algorithm 1. Select the most profitable members

Require: A coalition S
Require: ranking trees T^G
  set highest profit $v^* = 0$
  set pruning members $S^- = S$
  for all $g_j \in G$ **do**
    if S is not capable of producing g_j **then**
      continue
    end if
    get surplus agents S'
    set trial coalition $S'_j = S \cup S'_j$
    compute trial coalition's profit $v_{S'_j}$
    set $S^- = S^- \leftarrow S'_j$
  end for
  return S^-

Each $S'_j \in S^-$ will be added as the children of the base coalition. Among all S'_js, the most profitable agents S^* are those that provide the highest additional profit v^* and are kept as the base for the further shrinking coalitions. The coalition keeps shrinking in this fashion until there are no prunable members left in T^G. Then the next profitable sibling of the base S'_j will be the new base. This repetition goes on until it cannot find the new base. The number of coalitions each agent a_k has to maintain is also much smaller compared to that of the exhaustive search. The main algorithm is shown in algorithm 2.

Algorithm 2. Main

---

  set $L^- = N$
  create ranking trees T^G for all goods
  collect pruning members S^-
  while $S^- \neq \emptyset$ **do**
    locate $S^* \in S^-$
    set $A' = A' - S^*$
    set $S = S \cup S^*$
    set $L^- = L^- \cup S$
    collect pruning members S^+
    if $S^+ = null$ **then**
      set $S^* =$ the next profitable sibling of S^*
    end if
  end while

3.2   Generating Coalition Structure

Once each agent finishes its deliberation in the first stage, it exchanges all the coalitions generated with all other agents. It then uses the pattern to generate coalition structures. Start with the best coalitions, it follows the patterss layer by layer from left to right and from top to bottom in each layer. For each pattern, the agent will choose a combination of its own best coalitions and those it received from other agents to generate coalition structures. For example, with a pattern of $4 + 3 + 2$, the agent will place its best coalition of cardinality 4 as the first coalition of that coalition structure. One of the best coalitions of cardinality 3, whose members are not in the first coalition, will be placed as the second coalition. One of the best coalitions of cardinality 2, whose member is not in the first two coalitions will be placed as the coalition structure as the last coalition. In the case the agent can not find appropriate coalitions to fit in, it places an empty set instead. The coalition structure value is the sum of those coalition values. In each round of proceeding through all patterns, agent can extend the scope of best coalitions involved one by one. It, for example, generates the coalition structure using only the best coalitions in the first round. It then use the best plus the second best coalitions for the second round, and so on. The following is the algorithm for generating coalition structures is shown in algorithm 3:

Algorithm 3. Generating Coalition Structures

---

exchange best coalitions with all other agents
sort coalitions for each cardinality by their coalition values in descending order
generate patterns for each layer
set bestcoal to 1
while time is available **do**
    insert the bestcoal coalitions for each CScardinality
    for all layers **do**
        for all patterns **do**
            generate combinations of best coalitions in CScardinality
        end for
    end for
    increase bestcoal by 1
end while

3.3   Example

This section gives an example of how this algorithm works. Let the system is composed of a set of four agents: $A = \{a_1, a_2, a_3, a_4\}$. After the first deliberation process, all the coalition values are computed and sent across. Their values are as the followings:

$$v_1 = 8 \quad v_{12} = 13 \; v_{123} = 21 \; v_{1234} = 22$$
$$v_2 = 12 \; v_{13} = 16 \; v_{124} = 23$$
$$v_3 = 13 \; v_{14} = 10 \; v_{134} = 16$$
$$v_4 = 6 \quad v_{23} = 18 \; v_{234} = 19$$
$$v_{24} = 20$$
$$v_{34} = 15$$

After exchanging the coalitions generated among each other, each agent can select for each cardinality its best coalition. Let assume that agents only operate on the best coalitions. Agents' best coalitions are as the followings:

Cardinality	a_1	a_2	a_3	a_4
1	v_1 8	v_2 12	v_3 13	v_4 6
2	v_{13} 16	v_{24} 20	v_{23} 18	v_{24} 20
3	v_{124} 23	v_{124} 23	v_{123} 21	v_{124} 23
4	v_{1234} 22	v_{1234} 22	v_{1234} 22	v_{1234} 22

For the system of 4 agents, the breaking patterns of coalitions are as the followings:

No. of coalitions	1	2	3	4
Patterns	4	3 + 1 2 + 2	2 + 1 + 1	1+1+1+1

Using the algorithm in the second deliberation process, each agent's coalition structures computed are shown below. Each agent will achieve the same optimal coalition structure whose value is 41.

a_1	a_2
$CS_{1234} = 22$	$CS_{1234} = 22$
$CS_{124,3} = 23 + 13 = 36$	$CS_{124,3} = 23 + 13 = 36$
$CS_{1,234} = 8 + 0 = 8$	$CS_{2,134} = 12 + 0 = 12$
$CS_{13,24} = 16 + 20 = 36$	$CS_{24,13} = 20 + 16 = 36$
$CS_{13,2,4} = 16 + 12 + 6 = 34$	$CS^*_{24,1,3} = 20 + 8 + 13 = 41$
$CS_{1,23,4} = 8 + 18 + 6 = 32$	$CS_{2,13,4} = 12 + 16 + 6 = 34$
$CS_{1,2,34} = 8 + 12 + 0 = 20$	$CS_{2,3,14} = 12 + 13 + 0 = 23$
$CS^*_{1,3,24} = 8 + 13 + 20 = 41$	$CS_{2,1,34} = 12 + 8 + 0 = 20$
$CS_{1,2,3,4} = 8 + 12 + 13 + 6 = 39$	$CS_{1,2,3,4} = 8 + 12 + 13 + 6 = 39$

a_3	a_4
$CS_{1234} = 22$	$CS_{1234} = 22$
$CS_{123,4} = 21 + 6 = 27$	$CS_{124,3} = 23 + 13 = 39$
$CS_{3,124} = 13 + 23 = 26$	$CS_{4,123} = 6 + 21 = 27$
$CS_{23,14} = 18 + 0 = 18$	$CS_{24,13} = 20 + 16 = 36$
$CS_{23,1,4} = 18 + 8 + 6 = 32$	$CS^*_{24,1,3} = 20 + 8 + 13 = 41$
$CS^*_{3,1,24} = 13 + 8 + 20 = 41$	$CS_{4,13,2} = 6 + 16 + 12 = 32$
$CS_{3,2,14} = 13 + 12 + 0 = 25$	$CS_{4,23,1} = 6 + 18 + 8 = 32$
$CS_{1,2,3,4} = 8 + 12 + 13 + 6 = 39$	$CS_{1,2,3,4} = 8 + 12 + 13 + 6 = 39$

4   Experiment

We conduct experiment by simulating agents executing our algorithm against exhaustive search within the range of $10 - 50$ agents due the the limitation to run exhaustive search. We compare the performance of both algorithms in terms of number of partitions generated and elapsed time of generating best coalition structures. In each round, the agents number increases by 5. The number of goods and resources are equal, begins from 3 and increases by 1 in every 2 rounds. The technology matrix, agents' resources and cooperation costs among agents are randomly generated with uniform distribution. The number of each resource α_{ij} in the technology matrix is in the range $0 - 10$. The prices of the goods are in the range of $10 - 20$ while the cooperation costs are in the range of 0 and the number of agents in that round, e.g., $10, 15, \ldots$ We test our algorithm down to the 5th best coalitions only. As our algorithm deals with non-superadditive environments, this setting tends to increase the cooperation cost of a coalition as its size grows. Hence it forces agents to work harder to form profitable coalitions and to achieve optimal coalition structures. Both algorithms uses the Simplex algorithm to find the optimal solution for each coalitions. Figure 1 compares the performance of our algorithm against that of exhaustive search. The left x-axis is the number of coalition structures generated while the right x-axis is the elapsed time spent for generating optimal coalition structures in milliseconds. Since the data used is randomly generated, we present average values from various runs which constantly show signficant difference between results of the two algorithms. The empirical results show that our algorithm performs significantly better than exhaustive search. We experienced that exhaustive algorithm hardly make progress after the number of agents is larger than 40. As shown in the figure, the number of coalition structures generated by exhaustive algorithm is much larger than that of our algorithm. Furthermore, the elapsed time for generating optimal coalition structures of exhaustive search is also much larger than that of our algorithm.

5   Related Work

Shehory et. al [7] propose an algorithm to allocate tasks to agents in distributed problem solving manner, i.e., agents try to maximize the utility of the system. They consider a domain where a task composed of multiple subtasks, each of which requires specific capacity. These tasks have to be carried out by agents who have specific capacities to carry out tasks. Each agent prepares its list of candidate coalitions and proposes to other agents. Shehory et. al. [5] study overlapping coalition formation in distributed problem solving systems in non-superadditive environments. Although agents can belong to multiple coalitions at the same time, agents execute one task at a time. The task allocation process is completed prior to the execution of the tasks. Agents are group-rational, i.e., they form coalition to increase the system's payoff. Sandholm et. al. [4] analyze coalition formation among self-interested agents who are bounded-rational. They consider deliberation cost in terms of monetary cost. The agents' payoffs

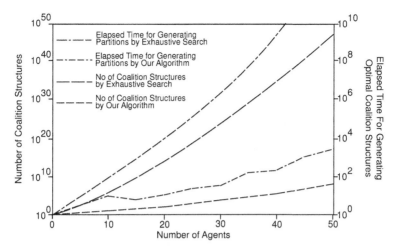

Fig. 1. This graph shows the number of coalition structures generated and elapsed time for generating the coalition structures of our algorithm against those of exhaustive search

are directly affected by deliberation cost. In their work, agents agree to form coalition and each of the agents can plan to achieve their goals. Soh et. al. [6] propose an integrated learning approach to form coalition in real time, given dynamic and uncertain environments. This work concentrates on finding out potential coalition members by utilizing learning approach in order to quickly form coalitions of acceptable quality (but possibly sub-optimal.) Sandholm et. al. [3] study the problem of coalition structure generation. Since the number of coalition structures can be very large for exhaustive search, they argue whether the optimal coalition structure found via a partial search can be guaranteed to be within a bound from optimum. They propose an anytime algorithm that establishes a tight bound withing a minimal amount of search.

6   Conclusion and Future Work

We propose an algorithm for computing optimal coalition structure for linear programming domains among fully-cooperative agents. Our algorithm tries generate best coalitions by pruning the least profitable agents from the grand coalition. Then the coalitions generated will be exchanged among agents. Lastly, agents use coalitions exchanged to generate coalition structure. The empirical results show that our algorithm help generate the coalition structures much faster than exhaustive search. Our algorithm dramatically reduces the number of coalitions generated hence reducing the number of coalition structures. As a result, the elapsed time of generating the coalition structures is relatively small.

Although this algorithm helps reduce number of coalitions involved in generating coalition structures, there is always room to improve. We want to further improve our algorithm for larger number of agents, for example, up to 1000 agents. Lastly, we want to study this problem in related domains, e.g., non-linear programming.

References

1. Kahan, J.P., Rapoport, A.: Theories of Coalition Formation. Lawrence Erlbaum Associates, Hillsdale, New Jersey (1984)
2. Neumann, J.V., Morgenstern, O.: Theory of Games and Economic Behaviour. Princeton University Press, Princeton, New Jersey (1953 (1963 printing))
3. Sandholm, T., Larson, K., Andersson, M., Shehory, O., Tohm, F.: Coalition structure generation with worst case guarantees. Artif. Intell. **111** (1999) 209–238
4. Sandholm, T., Lesser, V.: Coalition Formation among Bounded Rational Agents. 14th International Joint Conference on Artificial Intelligence (1995) 662–669
5. Shehory, O., Kraus, S.: Formation of overlapping coalitions for precedence-ordered task-execution among autonomous agents. In: ICMAS-96. (1996) 330–337
6. Soh, L.K., Tsatsoulis, C.: Satisficing coalition formation among agents. In: Proceedings of the first international joint conference on Autonomous agents and multiagent systems, ACM Press (2002) 1062–1063
7. Shehory, O., Kraus, S.: Task allocation via coalition formation among autonomous agents. In: Proc. of IJCAI. (1995) 655–661
8. Dang, V.D., Jennings, N.R.: Generating coalition structures with finite bound from the optimal guarantees. In: Third International Joint Conference on Autonomous Agents and Multiagent Systems - Volume 2 (AAMAS'04), pp. 564-571. (2004)
9. Sombattheera, C., Ghose, A.: A distributed algorithm for coalition formation in linear production domain. In: Proceedings of ICEIS 06. (2006)
10. Sombattheera, C., Ghose, A.: A distributed branch-and-bound algorithm for computing optimal coalition structures. In: Proceedings of the 4th Hellenic Conference on Artificial Intelligence. (2006)
11. Owen, G.: On the core of linear production games. Mathematical Programming 9 (1975) 358-370 (1975)

A Smart Home Agent for Plan Recognition

Bruno Bouchard[1], Sylvain Giroux[1], and Abdenour Bouzouane[2]

[1] Université de sherbrooke, 2500, boul. de l'Université,
Sherbrooke, Québec, Canada J1K2R1
{Bruno.Bouchard, Sylvain.Giroux}@usherbrooke.ca
[2] Université du Québec à Chicoutimi, 555, boul. de l'Université,
Chicoutimi, Québec, Canada G7H2B1
abdenour_bouzouane@uqac.ca

Abstract. Assistance to people suffering from cognitive deficiencies in a smart home raises complex issues. Plan recognition is one of them. We propose a formal framework for the recognition process based on lattice theory and action description logic. The framework minimizes the uncertainty about the prediction of the observed agent's behaviour by dynamically generating new implicit extra-plans. This approach offers an effective solution to actual plan recognition problem in a smart home, in order to provide assistance to persons suffering from cognitive deficits.

1 Introduction

Recent developments in information technology and increasing problems in the health field, including population ageing and medical staff shortages, have opened the way to a whole set of new and promising research avenues, most notably, work on smart homes. A growing literature [3][6][8][11] has explored the process by which cognitive assistance, inside a smart home, is provided to occupants suffering from cognitive deficiencies such as Alzheimer's disease and schizophrenia, for the performance of their Activities of Daily Living (ADL). One of the major difficulties inherent to cognitive assistance is to identify the on-going inhabitant ADL from observed basic actions. This problem is known as *plan recognition* in the field of artificial intelligence [7].

The problem of plan recognition can be basically synthesized by the need "...to take as input a sequence of actions performed by an actor and to infer the goal pursued by the actor and also to organize the action sequence in terms of a plan structure" [15]. Thus, the main objective is to predict the behaviour of the observed agent. In the context of cognitive assistance, these predictions are used to identify the various ways a smart home (observer agent) may help its occupants (patients). An important assumption underlying this problem is that the observed agent is rational, i.e. that all his performed actions are coherent with his intentions. However, for patients suffering from cognitive deficiencies, rationality might indeed be a strong assumption. The purpose of this paper is then to initiate the development of a generic approach to plan recognition for a smart home, that could be applied to people with cognitive impairments.

L. Lamontagne and M. Marchand (Eds.): Canadian AI 2006, LNAI 4013, pp. 25–36, 2006.
© Springer-Verlag Berlin Heidelberg 2006

The literature related to plan recognition [1][3][7], in particular the logical approaches [10][17], share a significant limitation in that they do not take into account intra-dependencies between the possible plans in the recognition process. These intra-dependencies result from the fact that, even if possible plans might seem connected, the intentions concerning two distinct observations are not necessarily related. In fact, Kautz [10] has pointed out this problem in his work. Hence, taking into account of this intra-dependency factor should be a solution to the issue of completing the observer's plans library. Our approach addresses this problem and relies on lattice theory and action description logic [5]. We define algebraic tools allowing to formalize the inferential process of plan recognition in a model of reasoning by classification through a lattice structure. This interpretation model defines a recognition space. This space will not only serve to characterize the uncertainty in the prediction of a future action. It will also serve to determine the appropriate time when the assisting agent could be brought in to increase his autonomy in order to perform an assistance action in the habitat by taking over the ADL patient control.

The paper is organized as follows. Section 2 presents our model of plan recognition based on lattice theory. Section 3 shows how the model is implemented to address the ADL recognition problem that we encounter in the DOMUS project. Section 4 presents an overview of previous works in the field of plan recognition. Finally, Section 5 presents our conclusion and future work.

2   Recognition Space Model

For an observer agent, the process of plan recognition consists in finding a recognition space (model of interpretation), based on the set of possible plans. This space allows the observer to interpret the set of the observed actions, performed by a human or another observed agent in action, with the aim of predicting his future actions and thus the plausible plans that would enable us to explain his behaviour. Let $A = \{a, b, \ldots\}$ be the set of actions that an observed agent is able to perform and let $P = \{\alpha, \beta, \ldots\}$ be the set of known plans of the observer (his knowledge base). Let O be the set of observations such that $O = \{o \mid \exists a \in A \rightarrow a(o)\}$. The assertion $a(o)$ means that observation o corresponds to an a-type action. The definition of a possible plan α that would explain the observation o is expressed as follows:

Definition 1. A plan α is a possible plan for an action $a(o)$ if and only if $a \in \alpha$. The action $a(o)$ is a component of the sequence α.

Consequently, the set of all possible plans for the observations O can be defined by $P_s^o = \{\alpha \in P \mid \exists (a, o) \in \alpha \times O \rightarrow a(o)\}$. Starting with this set of plans, we can deduce that the agent will at least perform one of them. However, its intentions can go beyond the set of possible plans. For instance, considering a well-known Kautz's example given in [10], we see that if we observe two actions *GetGun* and *GotoBank*, then we cannot automatically conclude that the observed agent wants to rob a bank, or deduce a disjunction of possible plans $Hunt$ or $RobBank$ as proposed by Kautz's theory. The fact is that his intentions can be to go on a hunting trip and to cash a check on the way, knowing that the initial set of possible plans were $RobBank$ and $Hunt$. Therefore, the model that we designed formally structures the recognition process to take this reality into account. In order to algebraically define our recognition model, we need first to show an overview of the action model on which it is based. This action model is described in great detail in [5].

2.1 Action Model Overview

Our approach to the formalization of the actions follows the lines of Description Logic (DL) [2]. We draw on the state-transition action model to develop a theoretical model of the action [5]. An action a over a set of states of the world W is a binary relation $a(w) = \{e|(w,e) \in W \times W\}$ where w and e are respectively the current and next states. The actions operate on the conceptual and assertion formulas that are used to describe facts about a state of the world (the patient's environment). The set of states where an action a may be performed is given by the domain $Dom(a) = \{w \in W| w \models pre(a)\}$, where $pre(a)$ is the precondition of a, defined as a conjunction of assertion formulas concerning the conceptual objects as well as the roles that bind these objects. The co-domain is given by $CoDom(a) = \{e \in W| e \models pos(a)\}$, where $pos(a)$ expresses the effect of $a(w)$, defined by a set assertions formulas that change the interpretation of concepts and roles involved in an action $a(w)$. The following definition, described in [5], defines the subsumption relationship between action concepts:

Definition 2. Let a and b designate two actions. If $Dom(a) \subseteq Dom(b)$ and $CoDom(a) \subseteq CoDom(b)$, then b subsumes a and we denote $a \prec_p b$.

Based on our action model in DL, a plan structure α may be defined as a sequence of actions $a_1, \ldots, a_n$, denoted $\alpha(a_n \circ a_{n-1} \circ \cdots \circ a_1)$ where $\circ$ is a sequence operator and $\alpha(w_0) = a_n(a_{n-1}(\cdots (a_1(w_0)) \cdots))$, allowing the transition from an initial state w_0 to a final state w_n. We now need to introduce a new concept of a variable plan to characterize the uncertainty in the predictions.

2.2 Variable Plan

Let $V = \{x, y, z, \ldots\}$ be the set of the action variables. An action variable x in a plan α corresponds to a variable for which we may substitute any sequence of actions included in its substitution domain $Sub(x) \subseteq 2^A$. A variable plan is then defined as a plan that contain at least one action variable in is sequence. This kind of plan corresponds to an intention schema, for which the instantiation allows to generate new implicit extra-plans that are not preestablished in the plans library. We define a substitution $\sigma : V \mapsto 2^A$ as a set of variable-actions pairs: $\sigma = \{x \leftarrow a_1, y \leftarrow a_2 \circ a_3, \ldots\}$, where $\sigma(\alpha) = (a_n, \ldots, \sigma(x), \ldots, \sigma(y), \ldots, a_1)$ corresponds to an instantiation of α, computed by substituting each action variable in α by the corresponding action sequence specified in σ. The only possible substitution for an action a is itself such that: $\forall a \in A$ then $\sigma(a) = a$.

Definition 3. $\alpha(a_n \circ \cdots \circ x \circ \cdots \circ a_1)$ is a variable plan if and only if there exists a substitution $\sigma(x) \in 2^A$ such that $\alpha(a_n \circ \cdots \circ \sigma(x) \circ \cdots \circ a_1)$ is a consistent plan.

We note that the consistency properties will be defined in the next section. An action variable will be introduced inside a new plan, resulting from the computation of the lower bound between a pair of incomparable possible plans. Incomparable plans mean that both contain at some i-*th* position of their sequence two actions that cannot both be subsumed by any common action. In such a case, an action variable whose substitution domain is equal to the composition of these two incompatible actions will be introduced. For instance, we can refer to Kautz's example and suppose that we have two incomparable possible plans $RobBank(GotoBank \circ GetGun)$ and $Hunt(GotoWood \circ GetGun)$. The actions $GotoBank$ and $GotoWood$ are incomparable and a variable plan $(x \circ GetGun)$ will result from the computation of the lower bound of these two plans. The substitution domain of the variable x would then be $Sub(x) = \{GotoBank \circ GotoWood, GotoWood \circ GotoBank\}$. From there, we can define the subsumption relationship that organizes plans into a taxonomy.

Proposition 1. Let α, β be two plans. We have $\alpha \prec_p \beta$ if there is a substitution $\sigma = \{x \leftarrow a_i, y \leftarrow b_j, \ldots\}$ such that $\forall i \in [1, |\beta|], (a_i, b_i) \in \alpha \times \beta$ then $\sigma(a_i) \prec_p \sigma(b_i)$, where $|\beta|$ is the cardinality of plan.

Proof 1. The proof directly follows from that of Definition 2 and the definition of plans subsumption. Let $Dom(\sigma(a_i)) = \{w \in W| \ w \models pre(\sigma(a_i))\}$. If $Dom(\sigma(a_i)) \subseteq Dom(\sigma(b_i))$, then $\forall (w, e) \in Dom(\sigma(a_i)) \times CoDom(\sigma(a_i))$, we have $(w, e) \in Dom(\sigma(b_i)) \times CoDom(\sigma(b_i))$. Therefore $w \models pre(\sigma(b_i))$ *and* $e \models pos(\sigma(b_i))$. If action $b_i \in \beta$ may be performed in every state where action $a_i \in \alpha$ is executable, then action b_i subsumes action a_i. Therefore, $\alpha \prec_p \beta$.   ◇

With these basic formal elements, the issue then is how to adequately refine the set of possible plans partially ordered by this subsumption relation. The solution we propose is to organize them into a taxonomy and make explicit the extra-plans that are implicit (induced by the existing intra-dependencies) by applying the composition and the disunification operation on each pair of incomparable possible plans.

2.3   Plans Composition

Let $\alpha, \beta \in P_s^o \times P_s^o$ be two possible plans interpreting a sequence of observed actions O at a specific time t. By composition, one seeks to determine all consistent combinations between the future actions succeeding the observations in the possible plans. The result of the composition of plans α and β, denoted $\alpha \oplus \beta$, is a set of extra-plans satisfying the following consistency properties:

1. Stability: each extra-plan in $\alpha \oplus \beta$ is formed by: (i) a set of partial plans included in the knowledge base P of the observer, (ii) at least one action common to plan α and to plan β, and (iii) a composition of actions that are component of α or component of β. There is no possibility of introducing other external actions.

2. Closure: each extra-plan in $\alpha \oplus \beta$ must admit an upper bound $\alpha \nabla \beta$ and a lower bound $\alpha \Delta \beta$. Hence, the extra-plans must be included in the interval $[\alpha \Delta \beta, \alpha \nabla \beta]$.

We note that the composition of a plan α with itself gives the same plan α. Now, let us reconsider Kautz's example where $GetGun$ is the observed action. The set of possible plans according to this observation is $P_s^{GetGun} = \{RobBank(GotoBank \circ GetGun), Hunt(GotoWood \circ GetGun)\}$. The composition of the plans $RobBank$ and $Hunt$ is $(RobBank \oplus Hunt) = \{(GotoBank \circ GotoWood \circ GetGun), (GotoWood \circ GotoBank \circ GetGun)\}$. These new extra-plans are dynamically computed according to the observed action $GetGun$. One can ask a question regarding the computational complexity of this composition operation. The answer is that the combination of the incomparable possible plans is not done blindly. First, we only consider the consistent possible plans, which satisfy the stability and closure criteria (first filter). Second, the possible plans that we consider are those which are in the lattice structure bounded by the upper and lower bounds (second filter). Finally, for each pair of incomparable plausible plans, we combine them by using the disunification operation (third filter), which will be defined in the next section. These filters allow us to reduce and control the computational complexity of the composition operation.

2.4   Disunification for Recognition Space Lattices

We define the set of plausible plans P_l^o as the union of the composition pairs of possible plans, according to the set of observed actions O, such that:

$$P_l^o = \bigcup_{\alpha, \beta \, \in \, P_s^o} \alpha \oplus \beta$$

We consider P_l^o as an interpretation model for O if P_l^o forms a lattice structure ordered by the subsumption relation of plans and if each couple of incomparable possible plans admits an upper bound ∇ and a lower bound Δ.

Proposition 2. The set of plausible plans P_l^o ordered by the subsumption relation $\prec_p$, forms a lattice[1] structure, denoted $\Re_o = <P_l^o, \prec_p, \Delta, \nabla>$.

This recognition space is the interpretation model of the observed agent behaviour, where the infimum of the lattice corresponds to the schema of minimal intention. It is defined as a plan that can contain action variables serving to characterize not only the uncertainty in the prediction of a future action but also

---

[1] The proof is available in $http://www.brunobouchard.com/proposition2\_proof.pdf$

the appropriate moment where the observer assisting agent could be brought to increase its autonomy to perform an assistance action in the habitat.

Definition 4. Let $\alpha(a_n \circ \cdots \circ a_1), \beta(b_m \circ \cdots \circ b_1) \in P_l^o$ interpret the observed actions O, where $|O| = k$. The upper bound $\alpha \nabla \beta$ is the least common partial plan subsumer $\pi(c_r \circ \cdots \circ c_1)$, such that $\forall i \in [1, r]$, with $k \leq r \leq min(n, m), \forall o_j \in [1,k], \forall (a_i, b_i) \in \alpha \times \beta$, then $c_j(o_j), o_j \in O, a_i \prec_p c_i$ and $b_i \prec_p c_i$.

The symbol π represents the result of the upper bound computation between two plans α and β, including the observations. Consequently, the upper bound cannot be empty as it is minimally composed of the observations. According to the previous example, the least common partial subsuming plan between the possible plans $RobBank$ and $Hunt$ is $(RobBank \nabla Hunt) = (GetGun(o_1))$, where $o_1 \in O$ is the only observation corresponding to the action type $GetGun$. The lower bound of two incomparable possible plans consists of the observed actions, followed by the predictions related to the future actions which are represented by action variables. The interest on computing this lower bound is to find a new intention schema by disunifying the possible plans using the first-order logic disunification operation $DisU$ [9]. Thereafter, this intention schema is used to reunify the possible plans through the composition operation previously defined to generate new implicit extra-plans.

Definition 5. Let $\alpha(a_n \circ \cdots \circ a_1), \beta(b_m \circ \cdots \circ b_1) \in P_l^o$ interpret the observed actions O, with $|O| = k$. The lower bound $\alpha \Delta \beta$ is the most common partial plan subsumed, given as follows:

$$\alpha \Delta \beta = \begin{cases} b_m \circ \ldots \circ b_{n+1} \circ DisU(a_n, b_n) \circ \ldots \circ DisU(a_{k+1}, b_{k+1}) \circ o_k \circ \ldots \circ o_1, \ if \ n \leq m \\ b_n \circ \ldots \circ b_{m+1} \circ DisU(a_m, b_m) \circ \ldots \circ DisU(a_{k+1}, b_{k+1}) \circ o_k \circ \ldots \circ o_1, \ if \ m \leq n \end{cases}$$

where $DisU$ is a disunification operation defined as an injective application: $A \cup V \times A \mapsto A \cup V$, on the set of incomparable actions of plans α, β:

$$DisU(a, b) = \begin{cases} c \quad iff \quad \exists c \in A \ : \ c \prec_p a \ and \ c \prec_p b \\ x \quad elsewhere, \ with \ Sub(x) = \{a \circ b, b \circ a\} \end{cases}$$

To summarize, the recognition process consists in finding a recognition space $\Re_o$, which is a minimal model of interpretation of the observations O that admits a supremum ∇_{sup}, corresponding to the most specific common subsumer of all possible plans, and that admits an infinimum Δ_{inf}, corresponding to the minimal intention schema predicting the future behaviour of the observed agent. This space $\Re_o = \{\delta \in P_l^o | \Delta_{inf} \prec_p \delta \prec_p \nabla_{sup}\}$ constitutes a very interesting tool to characterize and to control the recognition process. Of course, it is assumed that all the observed actions are related. Consequently, we build a lattice structure starting from the first observation that will be refined when new observations will be detected. This refinement will be computed by extracting a sub-lattice (a new refined recognition space) from the initial lattice structure, and so on.

3   Recognition of Activities in a Smart Home

The DOMUS [2] lab consists of a standard apartment with a kitchen, living room, dining room, bedroom, and bathroom that are equipped with sensors, smart tags (RFID), location and identification systems for objects and people, audio and video devices, etc. This smart home is used to explore ways to provide pervasive cognitive assistance to people suffering from cognitive deficiencies such as Alzheimer's disease, head traumas, and schizophrenia [11]. As we can see on Figure 1, the current infrastructure allows the connection of sensors (movement detectors, lighting system, pressure mats, etc.) to services that generate low-level information (for instance, basic actions and localization) [16]. In the current implementation, most of devices (sensors and effectors) are monitored and controlled through a Crestron-based infrastructure. Basic events are generated by sensors and are directly sent to the agents. Consequently, our low-level activity recognition (LAR) agent can register as an event listener, though a Java interface, in order to get the inputs sent by the sensors. This agent transforms low-level inputs into low-level actions that can be analyzed by higher level-agents. These inputs will then be used as a starting point from high-level recognition process.

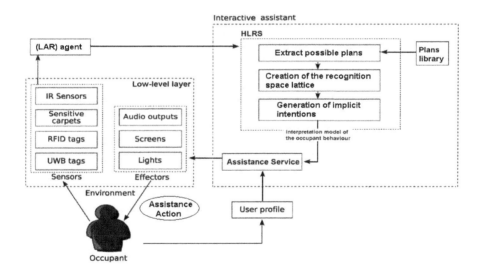

Fig. 1. Achitecture of the system

The LAR agent owns a virtual representation of the habitats environment encoded in a description logic knowledge base described with the PowerLoom system [13]. This terminological base is composed of a set of conceptual and assertional objects that synthesize the elements of the environments. In other

---

[2] The DOMUS lab is sponsored by the Natural Sciences and Engineering Research Council of Canada (NSERC) and by the Canadian Foundation for Innovation (CFI).

words, this knowledge base serves to define the current state of the environment. When new inputs are received from hardware sensors, the LAR agent updates the state of the world and creates an action structure, representing the changes that happened to the environment, according to our model of action described in [5]. This action structure is then classified according to a taxonomy of low-level actions to identify its conceptual type. Thereafter, the LAR agent notifies the cognitive assistant that a new low-level action is detected and it sends the actions type. Actually, we suppose that the low-level sensors give us correct inputs. Another DOMUS team is working on detection and isolation of sensors failure, in order to relax this strong assumption and to minimize low-level uncertainty.

3.1 High-Level Recognition Service

The assistant agent is equipped with a high-level recognition service (HLRS), which provides an interpretation model of the occupant behaviour as input to assistance service. We now discuss a simple assistance example that illustrates the principles of our high-level plan recognition process. Let us assume the case of Peter, a person with Alzheimer's disease at level 3 (mild cognitive decline) by referring to the global scale of the deterioration stages of the primary cognitive functions of an individual [14]. In the morning, Peter gets out of bed and moves towards the kitchen. The pressure mat located at the base of Peter's bed has detected his awakening and has activated the recognition system. The movement detector located at the kitchen entrance indicates that Peter has entered that room. The low-level action recognition system receives the sensors inputs, given by the Crestron infrastructure, and then conceptualizes the changes that have just occurred in the environment in an action structure that it classifies through its taxonomy to identify the observed action *GoToKitchen*. While referring to the knowledge base of the smart home, the observed action may be performed for several purposes, that is, to prepare a cup of tea in the kitchen or to wash a dish. To be able to plan a future assistance task, the agent must initially understand Peter's intentions by building a minimal interpretation model describing the plausible plans that can explain his behaviour at this specific moment. This model takes the form of a lattice built following our recognition model, as shown in Figure 2. On the left of the figure, one may see the description of low-level actions (top left) and the high-level activities (bottom left) that has been recognized by the system. On the top right, one can see a graphical tool built in SVG[3] (here showing the kitchen) that allows us to simulate the activation of the various environment sensors by clicking on the corresponding graphical objects. On the bottom right, one can see the recognition space lattice resulting from the high-level recognition.

The set $P = \{$ *WashDish(StartWashing ∘ GoToKichen), PrepareTea(GetWater ∘ GoToKitchen), WatchTv(TurnOnTv ∘ GoToLivingRoom), Drink(GetWater)*$\}$ constitutes the knowledge base of the assistant agent and includes all the

---

[3] Scalable Vector Graphics. Language for describing two-dimensional graphics in XML. See SVG web page http://www.w3.org/Graphics/SVG/

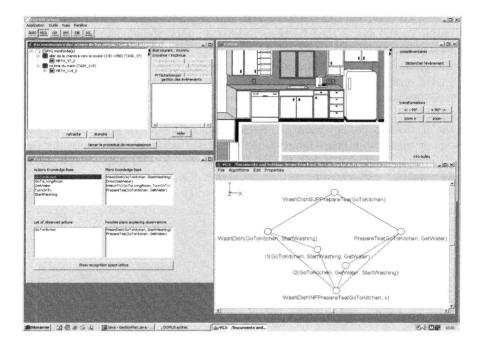

Fig. 2. DOMUS application of activities recognition

plans (ADL) of the occupant. The set O contains all the observed actions o_1 detected by the system, in this case, only one action of the $GoToKitchen$ type, such as $O = \{GoToKitchen(o_1)\}$. The set P_s^o contains all the known plans including, in their decomposition, the observed action that is the plans $PrepareTea$ and $WashDish$. The lattice supremum corresponds to the smallest common subsumer of the set of possible plans P_s^o which is the partial plan made up solely by the observation. The lattice infimum corresponds to the minimal intention schema of the occupant, as shown on the bottom left of Figure 2. The action variable x, obtained by the disunification operation, characterizes uncertainty in the prediction of the next action. The substitution domain of this variable is $Sub(x) = \{StartWashing \circ GetWater, GetWater \circ StartWashing\}$. The minimal intention schema enables us to generate, by the substitution process of the action variables, two new coherent extra-plans that did not exist beforehand in P, that is I_1 and I_2, as shown in Figure 2. These extra-plans are the result of the disunification and the composition of the possible incomparable plans according to their intra-dependencies. Extra-plans I_1 and I_2 are consistent, according to the consistency criteria defined in Section 2.3, as there is a decomposition of partial plans where each one subsumes a known plan included in P. The recognition space $\Re_o$ is composed of all the plans that can be classified between the lattice infimum and supremum, such as $\Re_o = \{WashDish, PrepareTea, WashDish \triangledown PrepareTea, WashDish \triangle PrepareTea, I_1, I_2\}$. These set constitute the whole plausible plans that can explain the behaviour of the occupant. Now, let us suppose that a second observation $GetWater(o_2)$ was detected. The new interpretation model would then be the sub-lattice upper bounded by $PrepareTea$ and lower bounded by $WashDish\Delta PrepareTea$, as shown in Figure 2. Let us now suppose that the assistant agent has detected that the inhabitant remains still for a certain period of time. In such a case, the assistant agent will have to increase his autonomy level by taking control of the home using the intention schema of the inhabitant, defined by the infimum $\Delta_{inf} = (x \circ GoToKitchen)$ of the lattice, to predict what the person wanted to do. In our example, the occupant wishes to prepare tea or pursues two distinct goals represented by the extra-plan I_1, that is $WashDish$ and $DrinkWater$. In this context, the smart home would be authorized to perform an action of assistance, like reminding the occupant of the procedure to achieve his inferred goals in the event of a memory lapse (i.e. Alzheimer's disease).

4   Related Works

Several approaches have been explored to seek solutions to plan recognition, such as the probabilistic approaches [1][6][7], the learning approaches [3][12] and the logical approaches [10][17]. The probabilistic methods, primarily based on the on the Markovian model [6], Bayesian networks [1] and on the Dempster-Shafer theory [7], use a set of probabilistic rules which enable to update the probability attributed to each plausible hypothesis following an observation. The conclusion drawn from the recognition process by the system is simply the hypothesis having the highest probability. For instance, Boger *et al.* [6] used such approach in the development of the COACH system; a cognitive aide for patients with dementia based on a partially observable Markov decision process (POMDP). This system aims to monitor a cognitively impaired user attempting a handwashing task, and to offer assistance in the form of task guidance (e.g. prompts or reminders). The weakness of the probabilistic approaches stems from the heuristic methods used to compute the probability of each competing hypothesis, which are highly dependent on the context [7]. The learning techniques seek to identify patterns from the observed actions in order to build a probabilistic predictive model of the observed agent behaviour. They have been used by [12] in order to develop the *Activity Compass* system; a cognitive assistant for early-stage Alzheimer's patients. It is based on a Bayesian learning model of a patient moving through a transportation network. The main limitation of this kind of approaches is due to the fact that the generalization learned rule might lead to infer inconsistent behaviour and also to a very large amount of training data. Moreover, these techniques cannot make useful predictions when novel events occur. The logical approaches of Kautz [10] and Wobke [17] are closer to our work. In these two theories, the observer agent starts with a plan library expressed with first-order axioms forming an abstraction/decomposition hierarchy. Kautz proposes a set of hypotheses (exhaustiveness, disjointedness, component/use, minimum cardinality), based on McCarthy's circumscription theory, that serves to extract a minimal covering model of interpretation from the hierarchy, based on a set of observed actions. The weakness of Kautz's approach is that all plans inferred as possible through the covering model are considered equiprobable. Wobke has proposed a solution to this limitation using situation theory [4]. His proposal, based on Kautz's work, consists in defining a partial order relation organizing hierarchy's elements by level of plausibility. A significant limitation of Wobke's work is created by the situation semantics (a particular case of possible worlds semantics), which is too complex to make operational in a real context. Finally, these previously explored approaches assume that the observer have a complete knowledge of the domain and thus, they cannot recognize plans that are not included in the plans library.

In contrast, our approach defines algebraic tools that allow to exploit the existing relations between possible plans in order to dynamically generate new plausible extra-plans that were not preestablished in the knowledge base. Consequently, our work partially addresses the problem of completing the plans library, which indeed cannot be complete in any domain. Another promising improvement of our model would be to organize the result of the recognition process into a structured interpretation model, which takes the form of a lattice, rather than a simple disjunction of possible plans without any classification. Therefore, our approach minimizes the uncertainty related to observed patient's behaviour by bounding the plausible recognition plans set. Moreover, we notice that the computational complexity of our recognition process is decreasing as the number of observations increases. This performance is due to the refinement process, which, instead of creating a whole new lattice, extracts a refined sub-lattice from the first one created.

5   Conclusion

In this paper, we proposed a non-quantitative approach, based on lattice theory and action description logic, for re-examining the main issues surrounding the problem of formalizing plan recognition. This approach provides a viable solution to plan recognition problems by minimizing uncertainty about the prediction of the observed agent's behaviour. This is achieved by dynamically generating implicit extra-plans resulting from intra-dependencies existing between possible plans. It should be emphasized that this initial framework is not meant to bring exhaustive answers to the issues raised by the multiple problems related to plan recognition. However, it can be considered as a first step towards developing a complete formal plan recognition theory, based on the classification paradigm. It should bring effective solutions to concrete problems such as plan recognition in a smart home. For further work, we plan to extend our logical model by attributing a probability to each plausible plan according to contextual information, such as the time of the day, and according to the inhabitant's specific profile, such as the learned patient's habits. Such hybrid approach will address the equiprobability problem of the possible plans characteristics to logical recognition models and thus, it will offer a means to favour one explanation over another in the lattice recognition space.

References

1. Albrecht D.W., Zukerman I., Nicholson A.: Bayesian Models for Keyhole Plan Recognition in an Adventure Game, User Modelling and User-Adapted Interaction, (1998), (8) 5-47.
2. Baader F., Calvanese D., McGuiness D., Nardi D., Patel-Schneider P.: The Description Logic Handbook: Theory, Implementation, and applications. Cambridge University Press, United Kingdom, (2003).
3. Bauchet J., Mayers A.: Modelisation of ADL in its Environment for Cognitive Assistance, In: Proc. of the 3rd International Conference on Smart homes and health Telematic, ICOST'05, Sherbrooke, Canada, (2005), 3-10.
4. Barwise J., Perry J.: Situations and Attitudes, MIT press, Cambridge, MA, (1983).
5. Bouzouane A.: Towards an Authority Sharing Based on The Description Logic of Action Model, In Proceeding of the Fifth IEEE International Conference on Intelligent Agent Technology (IEEE-IAT'05), September 19-22, Compigne, France, (2005), 277-280.
6. Boger J., Poupart P., Hoey J., Boutilier C., Fernie G. and Mihailidis A.: A Decision-Theoretic Approach to Task Assistance for Persons with Dementia. In Proc. of the International Joint Conference on Artificial Intelligence (IJCAI'05), pages 1293-1299, Edinburgh, Scotland, 2005.
7. Carberry S.: Techniques for Plan Recognition, User Modeling and User Adapted-Interaction, (2001), (11) 31-48.
8. Fatiha L., Lefebvre B.: A cognitive system for a smart home dedicated to people in loss of autonomy, In: Proc. of the 3rd International Conference on Smart homes and health Telematic, ICOST'05, Sherbrooke, Canada, (2005), 245-254.
9. Huet G., Oppen D.C.: Equations and Rewrite Rules: A Survey, In: Formal Language Theory: Perspectives and Open Problems, Academic Press, (1980), 349-405.
10. Kautz H.: A Formal Theory of Plan Recognition and its Implementation, Reasoning About Plans, Allen J., Pelavin R. and Tenenberg J. eds., Morgan Kaufmann, San Mateo, C.A., (1991), 69-125.
11. Pigot H., Mayers A., Giroux S.: The intelligent habitat and everyday life activity support, In: Proc. of the 5th International conference on Simulations in Biomedicine, April 2-4, Slovenia, (2003), 507-516.
12. Patterson D., Etzioni O., Fox D., Kautz H.: Intelligent ubiquitous computing to support alzheimers patients: Enabling the cognitively disabled. In Proc. of the 1st Int. Workshop on Ubiquitous Computing for Cognitive Aids, (2002), 12.
13. PowerLoom: Knowledge Representation System, ISI, University of Southern California, http://www.isi.edu/isd/LOOM/PowerLoom/index.html, (2002).
14. Reisberg B, Ferris S.H., Leon M.J., Crook T.: The Global Deterioration Scale for assessment of primary degenerative dementia, AM J Psychiatry, (1982), 1136-1139.
15. Schmidt C.F., Sridharan N.S., Goodson J.L.: The plan recognition problem: an intersection of psychology and artificial intelligence, Artificial Intelligence, (1978), 45-83.
16. Vergnes D., Giroux S., Chamberland D.: Interactive Assistant for Activities of Daily Living, In: Proc. of the 3rd International Conference on Smart homes and health Telematic, ICOST'05, Sherbrooke, Canada, (2005), 229-236.
17. Wobke W.: Two Logical Theories of Plan Recognition, Journal of Logic Computation, Vol. 12 (3), (2002), 371-412.

Using Multiagent Systems to Improve Real-Time Map Generation

Nafaâ Jabeur[1,2], Boubaker Boulekrouche[1,2], and Bernard Moulin[1,2]

[1] Computer Science Department, Laval University, Ste-Foy, G1K 7P4 Québec, Canada
[2] Geomatic Research Center, Laval University, Ste-Foy, Québec G1K 7P4, Canada
{nafaa.jabeur, bernard.moulin}@ift.ulaval.ca,
boubaker.boulekrouche.1@ulaval.ca

Abstract. Thanks to new technological advances, geospatial information is getting easier to disseminate via Internet and to access using mobile devices. Currently, several mapping applications are providing thousands of users worldwide with web and mobile maps generated automatically by extracting and displaying pre-processed data which is stored beforehand in specific databases. Though rapid, this approach lacks flexibility. To enhance this flexibility, the mapping application must determine by itself the spatial information that should be considered as relevant with respect to the map context of use. It must also determine and apply the relevant transformations to spatial information, autonomously and on-the-fly, in order to adapt it to the user's needs. In order to support this reasoning process, several knowledge-based approaches have been proposed. However, they did not often result in satisfactory results. In this paper, we propose a multiagent-based approach to improve real-time web and mobile map generation in terms of personalization, data generation and transfer. To this end, the agents of our system compete for space occupation until they are able to generate the required map. These agents, which are assigned to spatial objects, generate and transfer the final data to the user simultaneously, in real-time.

1 Introduction

Nowadays, users worldwide can readily access spatial data via Internet or using mobile devices. However, this data, which is increasingly available thanks to new advances in communication technologies, development standards and information storing and handling techniques [1], does not always matches users' requirements. Consequently, spatial transformations must often be applied in order to generate new data that meets users' needs. These transformations, which enable a given system to generate new data during a scale reduction process, correspond to the so-called *cartographic generalization process*. Currently, several mapping applications, such as *MapQuest*, *YahooMaps*, and *Google Earth*, apply transformations to geographic objects in a pre-processing mode. They provide maps to users by extracting and displaying the pre-processed data which is stored beforehand in specific databases. In spite of its rapidity, this automatic map generation approach lacks flexibility especially since data was produced once for all at predefined scales. In order to enhance the automatic web and mobile map generation process, the mapping

L. Lamontagne and M. Marchand (Eds.): Canadian AI 2006, LNAI 4013, pp. 37–48, 2006.
© Springer-Verlag Berlin Heidelberg 2006

application must determine by itself which spatial information should be considered as relevant with respect to the map context of use. It must also autonomously determine and apply the relevant transformations to spatial objects in order to adapt the content of the map to the user's expectations and display screen. When the user expects to get the required map immediately, the map generation process is said to be *on-the-fly*[1], otherwise, it is said to be *on-demand*. Several knowledge-based approaches, using case-based reasoning and rule-based systems, have been proposed to generate maps for web and mobile users on-the-fly. However, they were limited and unable to fully automate the web and mobile map generation process.

In this paper, we propose a new multiagent-based approach to improve on-the-fly web and mobile map generation. The idea is to assign a software agent to every spatial object. Due to the reduced sizes of screens, agents are regarded as competing for space occupation during the generation of the required maps. During this competition, they must cope with several types of constraints. Section 2 presents these constraints in the context of web and mobile mapping services. Section 3 outlines the knowledge-based approaches that addressed the on-the-fly map generation process. Section 4 focuses on the use of multiagent systems for on-the-fly web and mobile map generation. Section 5 deals with the interactions of our agents during the map generation process. It discusses the types of interactions that seem suitable to real-time map generation. Section 6 presents the architecture of the multiagent system that we propose in order to tackle important problems related to map personalization, generation, and transfer. Finally, Section 7 presents examples of web and mobile maps generated, on-the-fly, by the SIGERT system in which our multiagent-based approach is implemented.

2   Constraints of Web and Mobile Map Generation

On-the-fly web and mobile map generation is a challenging task. It has to deal with four kinds of constraints: *technical constraints*, *spatial data constraints*, *user constraints* and *spatial processing constraints* (Fig. 1):

- Technical constraints are independent of the approach used to generate the required map. In a web context, these constraints result from limitations, opportunities and characteristics of the web such as downloading time and data transfer rates. They also result from the limitations of displaying maps on the web such as color depth and quality as well as screen sizes and resolution [2]. These constraints, which cannot be controlled by map makers due to the variety of client systems, are also present in a mobility context in which tracking users is an additional constraint.
- Spatial data constraints are related to data modeling, availability and retrieval. A well structured spatial data helps to speed up the extraction of the required spatial datasets especially when an efficient spatial data indexation mechanism is available.

---

[1] On-the-fly web and mobile map generation can be defined as the real-time creation and the immediate delivery of a new map upon a user's request and according to a specific scale and purpose.

- Users' constraints result from users' requirements, preferences, cultural backgrounds, contexts and spatial reading and reasoning abilities.
- Spatial processing constraints are related to the challenging task of choosing the relevant spatial transformations, their particular implementation algorithms and identifying the best sequence to apply them. They are also related to the efficient use of spatial data and the real-time adaptation of the contents of maps in order to support users and technical constraints. During this adaptation, spatial conflicts may appear between cartographic objects, especially because screen sizes are often very limited. The resolution of spatial conflicts should comply as much as possible with several constraints such as graphical, topological, structural, and aesthetic constraints.

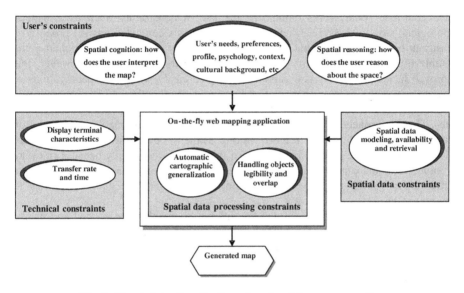

Fig. 1. Constraints of on-the-fly web and mobile map generation

Due to the large number of constraints and the time-consuming character of spatial processing, it is important to prioritize the issues to be tackled. In the scope of this paper, we are particularly interested in finding ways to improve on-the-fly web and mobile map generation in terms of personalization and data generation and transfer.

3 Knowledge-Based Approaches for On-the-Fly Map Generation

For a long time, new maps used to be generated automatically from existing data using algorithmic approaches that apply independent transformations to spatial objects. These transformations, which are particularly important during a scale reduction process, were generally applied without taking into account the immediate environment of spatial objects as well as users' expectations. In addition, they were often applied according to specific sequences that are not always suitable to process current space configurations. For these reasons, algorithmic approaches were not always able to generate new maps having a satisfactory quality. To enhance map quality, cartographers rely on their expertise and know-how. However, when it comes to the automatic map generation process, the mapping application should be able to determine and retrieve the relevant objects to be displayed on the final map with respect to the user's needs. It should also be able to determine and apply the suitable transformations to cartographic objects in order to adapt the content of the map to its context of use.

In order to take advantage of cartographers' expertise, several knowledge-based approaches have been proposed. Case-based reasoning approaches were set up using several types of knowledge, such as: geometric knowledge, procedural knowledge, and structural knowledge [5]. These types of knowledge may result in conflicts when choosing the suitable transformations to apply to spatial data. In order to minimize these conflicts, some works emphasize the use of constraints, such as graphical, topological, structural, and aesthetic constraints. In this context, Ruas [6] proposed a constraint-based approach that gives to every object the capacity to choose the suitable transformation to carry out with respect to its current state. However, this approach lacked flexibility and cannot be adapted easily when the specifications of the map generation process change. Furthermore, several authors [7,8] proposed rule-based approaches to formalize the decisions of cartographers into a set of formalized rules. These approaches resulted in interesting solutions for automatic map generation process. However, up to now, it has been impossible to develop a large enough set of rules to model all the potential situations of this process, especially because rules are in competition and cannot be applied to any case. In addition, these rules are related to cartographers' skills and do not take into account users' needs and abilities to interpret maps.

The existing knowledge-based and algorithmic approaches are limited and unable to fully automate the map generation process. In addition, they still lack autonomy and intelligence to decide by themselves what to do, when to do and how to do the relevant processing during map generation. This autonomy may be obtained using the multiagent paradigm [10].

4   Use of Multiagent Systems for On-the-Fly Map Generation

The use of multiagent systems in the field of automatic map generation results in multiple advantages that further motivate investigations of their application to improve on-the-fly web and mobile map generation. As mentioned in previous works [11,12,13] these advantages are: their flexibility in solving complex problems [12]; their dynamic adaptation to environment changes [13], and their ability to successfully model the entire process of automatic map generation, during which objects are added, merged, symbolized, or eliminated [11]. Furthermore, in contrast to expert systems, a multiagent-based approach supports the holistic nature of on-the-fly map generation process.

The use of multiagent systems in the field of automatic map generation is not new. Baeijs [14] used agents to solve spatial conflicts during the map generation process. Duchêne [15] used agents in order to generate automatically new data using predefined sequences of spatial transformations. Other authors proposed a web-based map information retrieval technique to search for geographical information using agents [16]. However, the main research work that investigated the automatic map generation process using multiagent systems was the AGENT[2] project. The general approach used in this project [6,11] consisted in transforming the geographic objects contained in the database into agents. The goals of these agents are to satisfy their cartographic constraints as much as possible. They choose and apply transformations which are adapted to the current configuration of space. They assess and control the evolution of their states with respect to performed actions.

Previous research works based upon multiagent systems were used to support the automatic generation of maps without addressing constraints related to on-the-fly map generation. In addition, they did not take into account users' needs. Nevertheless, we are convinced that multiagent systems are suitable to improve real-time web and mobile map generation thanks to their multiple advantages. In order to prove this, we addressed several questions, such as which geographic entities should be modeled as agents? Which kinds of interactions should exist between agents? And how can agents improve the personalization, generation, and transfer of maps?

5   Agents' Interactions

A map expresses a geographic reality, according to a specific scale and purpose. This reality cannot be accurately represented when the scale of the map is reduced (Fig. 2). Indeed, scale reduction often diminishes the map's legibility which then requires some modifications in order to be improved. Due to a limited display space, spatial objects and symbols may be regarded as competing for the occupation of this space. In order to carry out this competition, we propose to assign an agent to every spatial object. Since the importance of a given object depends on the user's query and the map's context of use, we assign a priority to every agent that follows from the importance of the object it is assigned to. Using these priorities, we propose to categorize, on-the-fly, the initial data into several datasets according to the importance of data to the user. We call these datasets *layers of interest*. Each layer of interest contains all the objects that have the same degree of importance for the user. Consequently, the automatic map generation process is driven by cartographic rules as well as by users' expectations.

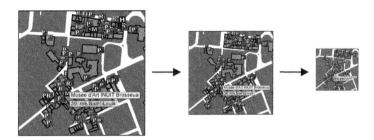

Fig. 2. Decrease of map legibility as a result of a zoom out operation

---

[2] AGENT stands for Automated Generalisation New Technology.

Our agents compete in order to generate the required maps autonomously. The use of classical multiagent systems' techniques (coalition formation, negotiation, etc.) during competition is interesting, but not realistic in the context of real-time map generation, especially because these techniques require the exchange of too many messages between agents, which would result in an extra time that slows down the system. In addition, attempts to form coalitions or to negotiate do not always mean that an agreement will be reached. Therefore, a user might wait indefinitely the map that may not be generated if the agents are not able to find solutions to solve their conflicts. In this case, we should better impose rules that restrict the autonomy of agents and lead them during their interaction. These rules are particularly important since on-the-fly map generation process is time-critical. In this paper, we limit the agent interactions to negotiation and cooperation. During these interactions, objects may be displaced, scaled-down, exaggerated, merged, or eliminated. At every map generation step, every agent checks the changes of its environment. If one or more spatial conflicts are detected, the agent verifies the results that it may obtain by the different actions it is able to carry out. Then, it chooses the best action to perform.

In order to facilitate the understanding of the map and adapt its content to users' expectations, we propose to emphasize the objects which are important to the user by using multiple representations: graphic, semantic, and geometric representations (Fig. 3). Thus, the goal of every agent is to guarantee legible representations of the object it is assigned to. When attempting to reach this goal, conflicts may appear due to the lack of space. In order to shorten the negotiation time necessary to solve these conflicts, we propose the following conflict resolution pattern (Fig. 4): when a spatial conflict occurs between two agents, the agent having the lower priority does the first attempt to solve the conflict. This attempt does not necessarily result in the application of a specific action. If the conflict remains, the agent with the higher

Fig. 3. Use of multiple representations: geometric (left), geometric-graphic (middle), and geometric-graphic-semantic (right)

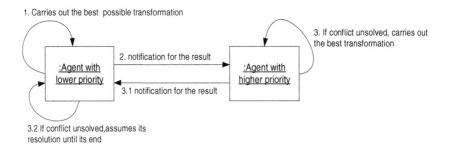

Fig. 4. Agents' negotiation pattern

priority tries to solve the conflict. If no solution can be found by this latter agent, the agent with the lower priority becomes responsible for the resolution of the conflict until its end. In some cases, this end may be reached by the elimination of the object handled by this agent.

This negotiation pattern enables us to process data according to its importance. As soon as a layer of interest is generated, it is transferred and superimposed on layers of interest already transmitted to the user's terminal. Meanwhile, the processing of the remaining data goes on. Our simultaneous generation and transfer of maps is an innovative approach. Indeed, existing approaches either focus on the generation of maps or on their transmission. In fact, they deal with each process separately. Our approach improves the automatic web and mobile map generation. Indeed, since the user can stop the map generation process whenever he finds the requested information from the data sets already transmitted, his waiting time is reduced. In addition, in a mobility context, his costs are reduced since data is reused on the client side.

6 Architecture of Our Multiagent System

In order to generate, on-the-fly, the required web and mobile maps, we propose a multiagent system that consists of two main modules: a *control module* and a *spatial data processing module* (Fig. 5). The control module contains a coordinator agent which is responsible for the communications with client applications. This agent analyzes the user's query and extracts relevant datasets from the *users database* (which stores information to authenticate users and parameters which are used to personalize maps' contents) and the *spatial database* (which stores spatial data in GML[3] files). It categorizes these datasets into several layers of interest and sends them to the spatial processing module. As soon as the coordinator agent receives the final GML file of a given layer of interest from the spatial processing module, it carries out a final adaptation of this layer in order to improve its personalization, and transfers it to the user's terminal in order to be displayed. This adaptation consists in transforming the GML data file into a new format which can be displayed by the user terminal such as SVG[4], SVG Tiny, or SVG Basic respectively if the user uses a desktop, a PDA or a SmartPhone. The transformation of GML files into SVG files is done using XSL (eXtensible Stylesheet Language) transformations.

The spatial processing module is composed of three layers. The first layer is the *federation layer* which contains several *Type agents*. Each *Type agent* is assigned to a specific layer of interest issued form data categorization. It creates and assigns an agent (called *instance agent*) to each spatial object of its type. The second layer of the spatial processing module is called the *spatial processing layer*. It contains all the *instance agents* created by the different *Type agents*. The *instance agents* are responsible for the generation of the required maps and the adaptation of their contents according to users' needs and the characteristics of their display terminals. They compete for space occupation as described in Section 5. The third layer of the spatial processing module is the *control layer*. It is composed of *container agents*.

---

[3] GML: Geography Markup Language.
[4] SVG: Scalable Vector Graphics.

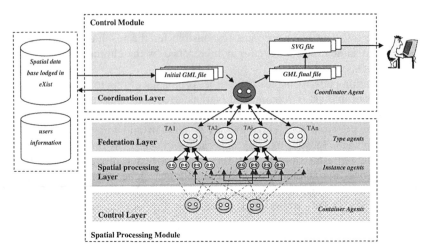

Fig. 5. Multi-layer architecture of our Multiagent system

A *container agent* is one that controls the generation of a group of objects that should be aggregated in the map at a scale inferior to the scale of the map required by the user. The importance of *container agents* lies in the acceleration they give to the map production process. Indeed, when *instance agents* are not able to solve their spatial conflicts due to lack of space, the *container agents* intervene in order to impose an arbitration solution and solve bottlenecks.

7   Application: The SIGERT System

The SIGERT system [17] was designed in order to provide maps for web and mobile users on the basis of cartographic generalization and multiple representations of geographic objects. It aims at creating software tools which can provide on-the-fly personalized maps to users according to their preferences and to the visualization characteristics of their terminals (desktop, PDA, mobile phone, etc.). The SIGERT system is based on a Client/Server architecture (Fig. 6). The Client side enables users to log in the system and specify their queries. It provides an orientation map that helps users to select their areas of interest. The Server side generates the required maps according to users' queries. These maps are generated and transferred to users at the same time by our multiagent system which was developed using Java and the Jade platform [18].

In order to get a map, a web user or a mobile user first logs in the SIGERT system. Then, he selects an area of interest on the orientation map displayed on his terminal. Using SIGERT's client interface, the user can indicate his destination or choose specific elements (buildings, lakes, etc.) he is looking for. When the SIGERT's server receives the user's query, the multiagent system analyzes it and retrieves the required datasets from the *spatial database* and from the *users database*. Next, the multiagent system stores these datasets in a GML file which will be processed automatically in

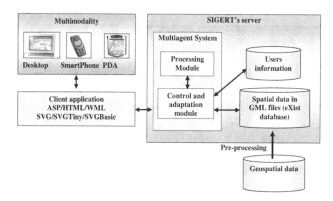

Fig. 6. SIGERT's Architecture

order to create a map which fits the user's needs and profile. As soon as a given layer of interest is generated, the multiagent system sends it to the user's terminal where it will be superposed on the data which was already transferred.

The current application of the SIGERT system addresses the tourist domain. It uses a dataset of a part of Quebec City at the scale 1:1000. This dataset was enriched by multiple representations of spatial objects. According to its importance to users, spatial data is categorized, on-the-fly, into *explicitly required objects (ERO), landmark objects (LMO), road network (RN)* and *ordinary objects (OO).* Currently, two user interfaces have been developed, one for desktops and one for PDAs using *ASP.NET* and *ASP.NET Mobile* respectively. Figure 7 and 8 are examples of a web and a mobile mapping service provided by the SIGERT prototype. When a web user moves the mouse over an important object, the SIGERT prototype displays its textual description. The user can get the address of this object by clicking on it (Fig. 7, right). A mobile

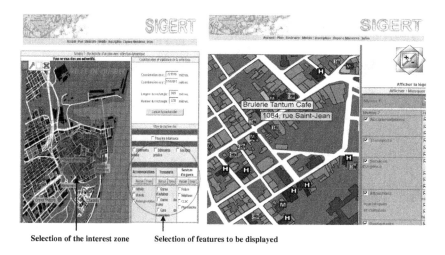

Selection of the interest zone   Selection of features to be displayed

Fig. 7. (left) Selection of the zone and features to be displayed, (right) Web map provided by the SIGERT prototype

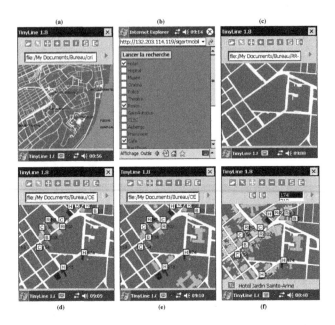

Fig. 8. (a) Selection of the interest zone, (b) Selection of features to be displayed, (c) RN layer, (d) RN and ERO layers, (e) RN, ERO and LMO layers, (f) Map provided by the SIGERT prototype to the mobile user

user can have the description and the address of any important object by selecting its reference which appears on the map from a scroll-down list on the top of the user interface (Fig. 8f). An example of results given to mobile users by the progressive transmission of layers of interest is illustrated in Figure 8: First, the user selects the area that interests him (Fig. 8a), then he specifies the features he is looking for (Fig. 8b). The SIGERT's server gets the user's query, generates, and transfers the required map layer by layer. In our prototype, the user's terminal gets first the RN layer (Fig. 8c). Next, it

Fig. 9. Maps respectively generated by Google Earth, MapQuest and SIGERT

gets and superimposes the ERO layer (Fig. 8d). Then, it gets and superposes the LMO layer (Fig. 8e). Finally, it gets and superposes the OO layer (Fig. 8f).

Furthermore, in order to make a comparison between our maps and those generated by existing web mapping application, we present in Figure 9 the maps respectively provided by *Google Earth*, *MapQuest* and SIGERT in response to a query looking for the address "*1084, rue Saint-Jean, Québec Canada*". The *Google Earth* map is a satellite image on which the road network is superimposed. The *MapQuest* map shows the road network as well as the requested location. However, in addition to the requested location, our map emphasizes important objects to the users.

8 Conclusion

In this paper we presented a multiagent-based approach to improve the on-the-fly web and mobile map generation process in terms of personalization, generation and transfer. In terms of personalization, our approach emphasizes objects which are importance to the user. Indeed, in addition to their geometric representations, these objects may be represented using graphic and semantic representations. In terms of map generation and transfer, our approach is based on an innovative approach that generates and transfers the required map to the user simultaneously. To this end, the initial data is categorized by layers of interest, on-the-fly, according to its importance to the user and map's context of use. As soon as a layer of interest is generated, it is transferred to the user and superimposed on the other layers which are already transmitted. This approach is interesting since the user may find the requested information from the data sets already transmitted. In this case, he is not obliged to wait until the entire map is downloaded. Our approach is particularly interesting in a mobile context since it reuses the already transferred data. Indeed, it reduces the costs of a mobile user who pays the amount of data transferred to its device.

Our approach was tested in a tourist domain but can be extended and used in other domains in order to generate maps for other needs such as military applications and emergency management. However, our prototype is still slow with respect to acceptable delays of real-time map generation. For example, our prototype generates and transmits a map whose size is 930ko in nearly 46 and 48 seconds to web and mobile users respectively. This is due to several factors: the slowness of the Java language and of Jade platform; the time required to parse GML files and the fact that we can optimize our code further. Moreover, our prototype is slow compared to other existing commercial web and mobile mapping system since we carry out a real-time map generalization process which is not supported by any other existing system. Our future works will focus on the improvement of the performance of our system in terms of processing time and data visualization. In addition, we can expect that the performance of our system will benefit from the technological advances of platform hardware and processing speed, as well as from the improvement of the performance of wireless communication that will occur in the coming years. In addition, our future works will focus on the enhancement of map personalization. To this end, we are planning to conduct a survey in order to determine users' needs and preferences.

Acknowledgments. This work is part of the GEMURE project which was funded by GEOIDE (Canadian Network of Centers of Excellence in Geomatics) and supported by the Ministry of Natural Resources of Québec, the Center of Research of Defense at Valcartier (Québec), the Center of Topographic Information at Sherbrooke (CITS) and Intergraph Canada. The first and second authors have respectively benefited from scholarships provided by the government of Tunisia and the company SONATRAC (Algeria).

References

1. Jabeur, N., Moulin, B.: A multiagent based approach for the resolution of spatial conflicts. European Workshop on Multi-Agent Systems (EUMAS), pp. 333-343, Barcelona (2004)
2. Arleth, M.: Problems in Screen Map Design. In: Proceedings of the 19th ICA/ACI Conference, pp. 849-857. Ottawa (1999)
3. Amstrong, M.P.: Knowledge classification and organization. In: Buttenfield B.P.,McMaster R.,Freeman H., Map generalization : making rules for knowledge representation. New York NY: Wiley, Harlow, Essex, England Longman Scientific & Technical, pp. 86-102 (1991)
4. Ruas, A.: Modèle de généralisation de données géographiques à base de contraintes et d'autonomie. Thèse de doctorat. Sciences de l'Information Géographique, Université de Marne La Vallée (1999)
5. Nunes, A., Caetano, M.R., Santos, T.G.: Rule-based generalization of satellite-derived raster thematic maps. Remote Sensing for Environmental Monitoring, GIS Applications and Geology II. Edited by Manfred Ehlers. Proceedings of the SPIE, Vol. 4886, pp. 289-297 (1999)
6. Sester, M., Klein A.: Rule Based Generalization of Buildings for 3D-Visualization. *In:* Proceedings of the 19th International Cartographic Conference of the ICA, pp. 214–224, Ottawa, Canada (1999)
7. Weiss, G.: Multiagent Systems. A Modern Approach to Distributed Artificial Intelligence, (Ed) Weiss G., The MIT Press, Cambridge, Massachusetts (1999)
8. Lamy, S., Ruas, A., Demazeau, Y., Jackson, M., Mackaness, W., Weibel, R.: The application of Agents in Automated Map Generalisation. In proceedings of 19th ICA meeting, pp. 160-169, Ottawa (1999)
9. Jabeur, N., Moulin B., Gbei, E.: Une approche par compétition d'agents pour la résolution de l'encombrement spatial lors de la généralisation automatique des cartes. Journées Francophones des Systèmes Multiagents JFSMA-2003, pp. 161-173, Tunis (2003)
10. Galanda M., Weibel R.: An Agent-Based Framework for Polygonal Subdivision Generalization. In: Richardson D. and van Oosterom P.(eds.): Advances in Spatial Data Handling. 10th International Symposium on Spatial Data Handling, Springer-Verlag Berlin Heidelberg (2002) 121-136
11. Baeijs, C.: Systèmes Multi-agents Hybrides pour la Généralisation Cartographique. *Conférence invitée Rencontres des Jeunes Chercheurs en Intelligence Artificielle, RJCIA'2000,* France (2000).
12. Duchêne, C. : Coordination multi-agents pour la généralisation automatique. Bulletin d'information de l'IGN, numéro 74, (2003/3) (2003)
13. Maozhen, L., Sheng, Z., Jones, Ch.: Multi-agent Systems for Web-Based Map Information Retrieval. In: M. J. Egenhofer and D.M. Mark (Eds.): GIScience, Springer-Verlag Berlin, pp. 161-180, (2002)
14. Gbei, E., Moulin B., Cosma I., Jabeur N., Delval, N. : Conception d'un prototype de service Web géolocalisé appliqué à l'industrie récréo-touristique. Revue internationale de géomatique (2003). Vol. 13, pp. 375-395
15. Jade, JADE Project Home Page. Available at http://sharon.cselt.it/projects/jade, last access 10-12-2005 (2005).

An Efficient Resource Allocation Approach in Real-Time Stochastic Environment

Pierrick Plamondon[1], Brahim Chaib-draa[1], and Abder Rezak Benaskeur[2]

[1] Computer Science & Software Eng. Dept, Laval University
{plamon, chaib}@damas.ift.ulaval.ca
[2] Decision Support Systems Section, Defence R&D Canada — Valcartier
Abderrezak.Benaskeur@drdc-rddc.gc.ca

Abstract. We are interested in contributing to solving effectively a particular type of real-time stochastic resource allocation problem. Firstly, one distinction is that certain tasks may create other tasks. Then, positive and negative interactions among the resources are considered, in achieving the tasks, in order to obtain and maintain an efficient coordination. A standard Multiagent Markov Decision Process (MMDP) approach is too prohibitive to solve this type of problem in real-time. To address this complex resource management problem, the merging of an approach which considers the complexity associated to a high number of different resource types (i.e. Multiagent Task Associated Markov Decision Processes (MTAMDP)), with an approach which considers the complexity associated to the creation of task by other tasks (i.e. Acyclic Decomposition) is proposed. The combination of these two approaches produces a near-optimal solution in much less time than a standard MMDP approach.

1   Introduction

Resource allocation problems are known to be NP-Complete [12]. Since resources are usually constrained, the allocation of resources to one task restricts the options available for other tasks. The action space is exponential according to the number of resources, while the state space is exponential according to the number of resources and tasks. The very high number of states and actions in this type of problem coupled with the time constraint makes it very complex, and here a reduction in the computational burden associated to the high number of different resource types is proposed. Many approximations and heuristics have been proposed ([2], [10], [1]). However, all these cited authors do not consider positive and negative interactions between resources. These interactions mean that a resource efficiency to realize a task is changed when another resource is used on the same task. Their approaches are consequently not very suitable to the type of problem tackled in this paper, since in many real applications there are positive and negative interactions between resources. An effective approach, as considered in the current paper, is to plan for the resources separately as proposed by Wu and Castanon [10]. Wu and Castanon formulates a policy for each resource and a greedy global policy is produced by considering each resource

L. Lamontagne and M. Marchand (Eds.): Canadian AI 2006, LNAI 4013, pp. 49–60, 2006.
© Springer-Verlag Berlin Heidelberg 2006

in turn, producing an approximate policy. Their coordination rules are sometime very specific to the problem's characteristics.

Since resources have local and global resource constraints on the number that can be used, the problem here can be viewed as a constrained Markov Decision Process ([2], [11]). In this context, dynamic programming [2] or linear programming [11] may be used to obtain a policy. Much work has been done in this field, but none of it considers positives and negative interactions among resource, as well as creation of tasks by other tasks.

This paper combines two approaches in a synergic manner to reduce the planning time. In the first approach, a planning agent manages each specific resource. These planning agents are coordinated together during the planning process by a *central* agent, and produce a near-optimal policy. On the other hand, the second approach is a decomposition technique which solves the problem efficiently by grouping cyclic states in separate components. The results obtained by the merging of these two approaches are very satisfying. The policy is near-optimal, while the convergence time is very small compared to a standard Multiagent Markov Decision Process (MMDP) [3] approach on the joint action and state space of all agents. The problem is now formulated in more detail.

2   Problem Formulation

An abstract resource allocation problem is described in Figure 1 (a). In this example, there are four tasks (t_1, t_2, t_3, and t_4) and three types of resources (res_1, res_2, and res_3) each type of resource being constrained by the number that may be used at a given time (local constraint), and in total (global constraint). The Figure shows the resource allocation to the tasks in the current state. An action is considered as the resource allocation to a group of tasks. In this problem, a state represents a conjunction of the particular state of each task, and the available resources. Indeed, when the state of the tasks changes, or when the number of available resources change, then the resource allocation usually changes also. The solution of this type of problem is called a policy. A policy π maps all states s into actions $a \in A(s)$ to maximize the expectation of realizing all tasks. The realization of a task is associated with a reward r. Thus, a policy maximizes the expected reward. The modelling of this type of problem is now detailed.

2.1   Multiagent Task Associated Markov Decision Process (MTAMDP)

Since resource allocation problems are known to be NP-Complete [12], one may decompose the previous problem into multiple planning agents. To do so, Multi-Agent Markov Decision Processes (MMDP) [3] may be a very suitable modelling framework. In an MMDP the individual actions of many planning agents interact so that the effect of one agent's actions may depend on the actions taken by others. Indeed, an MMDP is like a Markov Decision Process (MDP), except that the probability of reaching a state by executing an action now refers to

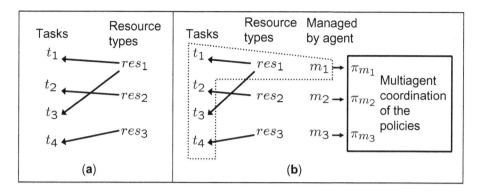

Fig. 1. Resource Allocation Problem

the probabilities of joint actions. An abstract schematization of the approach proposed by Plamondon et al. [7], which extends MMDP, to solve efficiently a resource allocation problem is described in Figure 1 (b). This in an extension of Figure 1 (a) where each planning agent (m_1, m_2, and m_3) manages one type of resource to accomplish the tasks. The dotted line in the Figure represents agent m_1 which manages resource type res_1 to accomplish all tasks. This way, each agent can compute a local policy (π_{m_1}, π_{m_2}, π_{m_3}). The policies of the agents are needs to be coordinated for two reasons. First of all, positive and negative interactions among resource have to be considered as the expectation of realizing a certain task t_1 by resource res_1 is changed when allocating another resource res_2 simultaneously on task t_1. The second reason why the planning agents should coordinate is because an efficient allocation divides the resources between the tasks. Thus, coordination should be considered in the case of simultaneous actions on a given task.

Multiagent Task Associated Markov Decision Processes (MTAMDP) [7] proposes to coordinate the different agents at each iteration of the planning algorithm considering positive and negative interactions, and simultaneous actions. Indeed, all existing algorithms to solve an MDP are iterative, thus the approach presented here should be pretty extensible. Figure 2 (a) describes this process. For example, if n iterations are needed for each planning agent to converge, then n coordination activities are made. MTAMDP is now formally described.

A Multiagent Task Associated Markov Decision Process (MTAMDP) [7] is defined as a tuple $\langle Res, Ag, T, S, A, P, W, R, \rangle$, where:

- $Res = \{res\}$ is a finite set of resource types available for the global planning process. The planning process has Res resource types of res number of resources. Each resource type has a local resource constraint L_{res} on the number that may be used on a single step, and a global resource constraint G_{res} on the number that may be used in total.
- $Ag = \{m\}$ is a finite set of agents. In an MTAMDP, a planning agent manages one or many resources which are used to accomplish its tasks. In this paper, a planning agent for each resource, and a $mNoop$ planning agent for

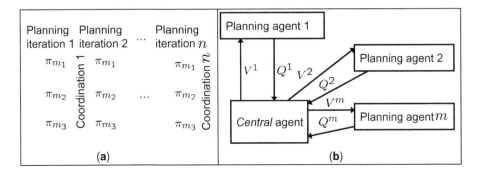

Fig. 2. The iterative coordination process

the *noop* (no operation) action are considered. The expected value of the *noop* action has to be considered since it may achieve tasks.

- $T = \{t\}$ is a finite set of tasks to be accomplished by the planning agents.
- $S = \{s^m\}$ is a finite set of states available for each planning agent. A state $s^m \in S$, represents a conjunction of the particular state s_t^m, which is the characteristic of each task t in the environment, and the available resources for the planning agent m. Also, S contains a non empty set $G \subseteq S$ of goal states.
- $A = \{a^m\}$ is a finite set of actions available for each planning agent. The actions $A^m(s^m)$ applicable in a state is the combination of all resource assignments that a planning agent m can execute, according to the state s^m. Thus, a^m is simply an allocation of resources to the current tasks, and a_t^m is the resource allocation to task t. The possible actions are limited by L_{res} and G_{res}.
- Transition probabilities $P_a^m(s'^m|s^m)$ for $s^m \in S$ and $a^m \in A^m(s^m)$.
- $W = [w_t]$ is the relative weight of each task, as described in [6].
- State rewards $R = [r_s] : \sum_{t=1}^{nbTasks} r_{s_t}$. The relative reward of the state of a task r_{s_t} is the product of a real number $\Re$ by the weight factor w_t. The rewards are not related to any specific planning agent, since they are only associated to the tasks, and not the resources.

The solution of an MTAMDP is a policy π^m for each planning agent in the environment. In particular, $\pi_t^m(s_t^m)$ is the action (i.e. resources to allocate) that should be executed on task t by agent m, considering the specific state s_t^m. As in reinforcement learning, the notion of Q-value is used for a planning agent m in the MTAMDP approach:

$$Q^m(a^m, s^m) = R(s^m) + \sum_{s'^m \in S^m} P_{a^m}(s'^m|s^m)V^m(s'^m(Res^m/\{a^m\})) \quad (1)$$

Let's consider $Q_t^m(a_t^m, s^m)$ as the part of $Q^m(a^m, s^m)$ related to task t. This part is called task-Q-value. A task-Q-value is not a decomposition, it simply means that the specific Q-value of a task within the global Q-value is referred to. Each

Q-value is subjected to the local resource constraints for each state task s_t of a global state s at a particular step. Furthermore, a Q-value is constrained on the total amount of resource that may be used by a planning agent m.

In this paper, the agents are coordinated through a *central* agent. Figure 2 describes the coordination process between the different planning agents and the *central* agent. At each iteration of an MDP algorithm, for example, value iteration, the planning agents send their Q-values to the *central* agent. With these Q-values, the *central* agent computes the global value of all action combinations. A description is made in the following sections how the central agent calculates the value of a global action, with a set of Q-values in hand. Afterwards, once the *central* agent knows the maximum value of a state, it assigns the value of each agent to its respective contribution (or to their adjusted Q-value as will be defined in the next section). The Algorithm 1 (MTAMDP-VI(states S, error ϵ)) gives a more formal description of this approach, which uses the following functions: ADJUST-I(action a), ADJUST-SA(action a), and GLOBAL-VALUE().

2.2   The MTAMDP Functions

Adjusting Considering Interactions. The ADJUST-I(*action a*) function [7] adjusts all task-Q-values of each planning agent m in a global state s according to the interactions among the actions of each other planning agent m'. In brief, this function uses an interaction parameter which quantifies the degree of interaction among two resources. For example an interaction of 0.5 means that the efficiency of a given resource is half its normal one when another resource is used simultaneously. In the case when the interaction is negative, the task-Q-value $Q_t^m(a_t^m, s)$ of an agent m is adjusted as follow:

$$Q_t^m(a_t^m, s) = null_{a_t^m} + ((Q_t^m(a_t^m, s) - null_{a_t^m}) \times inter(a_t^m, s|a_t'^{m'})), \quad (2)$$

where $null_{a_t^m} = Q_t^m(noop_{a_t^m}, s(Res_t^m/\{a_t^m\}))$ represents the value of an action which has an interaction of 0. The intuition is that doing nothing ($noop_{a_t^m}$), and subtracting the resource used by the action, has the same value as doing an action which is sure of not realizing its purpose. $inter(a_t^m, s|a_t'^{m'})$ is the value of the interaction between the action of the planning agents m with another agent m'.

Furthermore, to adjust the value in the case of a positive interaction (i.e. interaction > 1), an upper bound on the Q-value is needed. The heuristic used to determine the upper bound for a state s, and action a_t^m, by agent m, is the highest value of a possible state transition. A possible state transition is considered as, a state for which $P_{a_t^m}(s'|s) > 0$. This way, the upper bound overestimates the possible value of a state since it is very improbable that an action would guarantee reaching the upper bound. This upper bound provides an approximation of sufficient quality to address the problem at hand. Better approximations remain possible and scheduled for future work.

Adjusting Considering Simultaneous Actions. The ADJUST-SA (*action a*) function [7] adjusts all task-Q-values of each planning agent m in a global state s according to the simultaneous actions of all other planning agents m'. An upper bound on the Q-value that an agent may obtain is also used when adjusting considering simultaneous actions. This function reduces in a formal way the Q-value of two agents planning their resource simultaneously as exemplified in Section 2.1. To do so, the algorithm calculates two main terms: the *sum* and *val*. Firstly, the *sum* term computes the global value gain the agents make by planning independently. Then, the *val* term, computes the maximum gain the agents may have globally, considering the other agents actions, and the upper bound. Then all Q-value of the agents are "adjusted" by multiplying the initial gain to plan for this action by the ratio *val/sum*. An equation which summarizes the ADJUST-SA (*action a*) function is as follow:

$$\sum_{m \in Ag} Q_t^m(a_t^m, s) = null_{a_t^m} + ((Q_t^m(a_t^m, s) - null_{a_t^m}) \times$$

$$\frac{\sum_{m \in Ag} val = val + (((bound - noopG) - val) \times (\frac{Q_t^m(a_t^m, s) - null_{a_t^m}}{UpBound_s^{a_t^m} - null_{a_t^m}}))}{sum = \sum_{m \in Ag} Q_t^m(a_t^m, s) - null_{a_t^m}}), \quad (3)$$

where $val = 0$ and $sum = 0$ a priori. $UpBound_s^{a_t^m}$ is the upper bound of an action by an agent in a state. *bound* is the maximum upper bound of all planning agents. *noopG* is $null_{a_t^m}$ for the agent which has the highest upper bound.

Global Q-Value. To determine the action to execute in a state, the *central* agent has to calculate a global Q-value, considering each planning agent Q-values. This is done in a precise manner by considering the task-Q-values. Before introducing the algorithm, we recall that a planning agent for each resource type, and a $mNoop$ planning agent for the *noop* (no operation) action are considered. The *noop* action has to be considered since this action may modify the probability to achieve certain tasks in a state. The global Q-value $Q(a, s)$ of a state is:

$$\sum_{t \in T} Q(a, s) = Q(a, s) + val \sum_{m \in Ag} val = max(Q_t^m(a_t^m, s), val + ((1 - val) \times$$

$$Q_t^m(a_t^m, s) - Q_t^{mNoop}(a_t^{mNoop}))), \quad (4)$$

where $Q(a, s) = 0$ a priori. $val = 0$ every time the $m \in Ag$ loop is entered. The main function that the *central* agent uses to coordinate the planning agent in a near-optimal manner at each iteration is now described.

2.3 Value Iteration for MTAMDPs

The value iteration MTAMDP algorithm is presented in Algorithm 1. In Lines 6 to 9 of this algorithm, a Q-value is computed for all task-state-action tuples for each planning agent. The agents are limited by L_{res} and G_{res} while planning their respective policies. Afterwards, in Lines 13 and 14, the *central* agent adjusts the value of all action combinations, in all possible states using the ADJUST-I(*action a*) and ADJUST-SA(*action a*) functions. When the adjusted value of each action is determined, the global value $V'(s)$ is computed in Line 15. If this global Q-value is the maximum one at present, the value of each planning agent is assigned to the adjusted Q-value (i.e. $V'^m(s^m) = Q^m(a^m, s^m)$ in Line 18). The new value of the state is also assigned to the global value obtained by GLOBAL-VALUE() (i.e. $V'(s) = Q(a, s)$ in Line 19). When the global value function has converged, this policy is used for execution. All the performed experiments (Section 3) resulted in a convergence. This paper does not present a formal theorem to prove the convergence, or the near-optimality of the algorithm. These proofs are for future work.

Algorithm 1. MTAMDP-VALUE-ITERATION from [7].

1: **Fun** MTAMDP-VI(states S, error ϵ)
2: **returns** a value function V
  {Planning agents part of the algorithm}
3: **repeat**
4:   $V \leftarrow V'$
5:   $\delta \leftarrow 0$
6:   **for all** $m \in Ag$ **do**
7:     $V^m \leftarrow V'^m$
8:     **for all** $s^m \in S^m$ **and** $a^m \in A^m(s)$ **do**
9:       $Q^m(a^m, s^m) \leftarrow R(s^m) + \sum\limits_{s'^m \in S^m} P_{a^m}(s'^m|s^m) V^m(s'^m(Res^m/\{a^m\}))$
  {*Central* agent part of the algorithm}
10:   **for all** $s \in S$ **do**
11:     $V'(s) \leftarrow R(\neg s)$
12:     **for all** $a \in A(s)$ **do**
13:       ADJUST-I(a)
14:       ADJUST-SA(a)
15:       $Q(a, s) \leftarrow$ GLOBAL-VALUE()
16:       **if** $Q(a, s) > V'(s)$ **then**
17:         **for all** $m \in Ag$ **do**
18:           $V'^m(s^m) \leftarrow Q^m(a^m, s^m)$
19:         $V'(s) \leftarrow Q(a, s)$
20:     **if** $|V'(s) - V(s)| > \delta$ **then**
21:       $\delta \leftarrow |V'(s) - V(s)|$
22: **until** $\delta < \epsilon$
23: **return** V

An important characteristic of the resource allocation problem in this paper is that tasks may create other tasks. The task transitions in global are acyclic since these transitions always result in a group of tasks that were never visited previously, thus implying a partial order on the set of tasks. The acyclic decomposition algorithm [6] to effectively consider this characteristic is now described.

2.4   Acyclic Decomposition Algorithm

An efficient decomposition technique generally tries to regroup cyclic states. In the same sense, it is known that a planning problem which may be represented with an acyclic graph, instead of a cyclic one, is generally easier to solve. We recall that an acyclic graph is one where all state transitions always result in states that were never previously visited, thus implying a partial order on the set of states. On the other hand, a cyclic graph may visit certain states many times, which is not computationally efficient. The idea here is to transform our problem into an abstract acyclic one, which contains many cyclic components. A component corresponds to a group of tasks, and the graph contains a component for each possible task combination. On the other hand, the acyclic graph represents the possible task transitions. One may use Tarjan's [9] linear algorithm to detect the *strongly-connected components* of a directed graph to create the acyclic graph. Figure 3 shows the acyclic graph when task t_1 (a) or t_1 and t_2 (b), are in the environment. t_1 may create task t_3, and t_2 may create task t_4. So, task t_3 and t_4, which are leafs, may produce dire consequences for an executing agent. All nodes represent a cyclic component. This graph supposes that a task may create one other task at maximum. The significance of a link in Figure 3, simply means that the planning agent has a different group of tasks to achieve. Thus, it has a task transition meaning. Once the abstract acyclic graph is formed, it is solved using a backward approach just like in the AO* algorithm [5]. Algorithm 2 describes how the value V_c of each cyclic component c of an acyclic graph AcG is calculated.

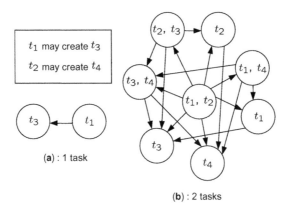

Fig. 3. The acyclic graph of cyclic components

Algorithm 2. Acyclic decomposition from [6].

1: **Function** ACYCLIC-DEC(error, ϵ, graph AcG)
2: **while** $AcG \neq null$ **do**
3:    Remove from AcG a component c, such that no descendent of c is in AcG
4:    $V_c \leftarrow$ MDP-ALGO(c, ϵ)

This algorithm solves each component, using an MDP algorithm ("MDP-ALGO(c)"), from the leaf to the root of the graph. This way, each component may only transit to a solved component, and thus each component has to be solved once. "MDP-ALGO(c)" may be any algorithm to solve an MDP, such as standard approaches like value iteration or policy iteration. For example, in Figure 3 (b), one can choose to remove whichever of t_3 or t_4, and solve it using MDP-ALGO(c). Then, if t_3 is removed in the first iteration, we may now remove t_4, or vice versa. When both t_3 and t_4 are removed, t_1 and t_2 may be removed. Components are removed in this order, until the component t_1, t_2 is removed and solved. In [6] the optimality of the acyclic decomposition algorithm is proved.

2.5   Merging the Acyclic Decomposition and MTAMDP Approaches (MTAMDP Decomposition)

The merging of the acyclic decomposition and the MTAMDP approaches is pretty straightforward. Indeed the line $V_c \leftarrow$ MDP-ALGO(c, ϵ) in Algorithm 2 is now $V_c \leftarrow$ MTAMDP-VI(c, ϵ). The fact that only this simple change is needed demonstrates the flexibility and extensibility of both these approaches.

3   Discussion and Experimentations

Modelling a stochastic resource allocation problem using the MTAMDP decomposition approach allows reducing the number of actions to consider in a given state. In particular, the difference in complexity between MMDPs and MTAMDPs resides in the reduction of the computational complexity from using the complex Bellman equation, in contrast to using the ADJUST-I(*action a*), ADJUST-SA(*action a*), and GLOBAL-VALUE() functions when computing the value of each action combination.

The domain of the experiments is a naval platform which must counter platforms, which may launch incoming missiles (i.e. tasks) by using its resources (i.e. weapons, movements). The different resources have their efficiency modified when used in conjunction on a same task, thus producing positive and negative interactions among resources. In this kind of problem, a platform may create a missile, but not vice versa, thus the task transition is acyclic. Thus the acyclic decomposition algorithm may be employed efficiently. For the experiments, 100 randomly resource allocation problems for all combinations of number of tasks and different number of resources, where one agent manages each resource type were generated. There are three types of states, firstly transitional states where no action is possible to modify the transition probabilities. Then, action states, where actions modify the transition probabilities. Finally, there are final states. The state transitions are all stochastic because when a platform or a missile is in a given state, it may always transit in many possible states.

We have compared four different approaches. The first one is the MMDP approach as described briefly in Section 2.1. MMDP is computed as a traditional "flat" MDP on the joint action and state spaces of all agents. The second

approach is the MTAMDP as described in Algorithm 1. The third one is the
"*one step* MTAMDP" where the adjustment of the Q-values is made only at the
last iteration for the planning agents. Thus, when each planning agent have converged, their Q-values are adjusted, and used for execution. The fourth approach
is the "*no coordination*" where each planning agent plans their resource completely independently of each other. We have compared these four approaches in
both the standard (no acyclic decomposition), and acyclic decomposition mode,
to efficiently consider the creation of tasks by other tasks.

We compare the MTAMDP approach with an MMDP approach in Figure 4,
where each agent manages a distinct resource type. The acyclic decomposition
algorithm further reduces the planning time for the four different approaches as
presented in Figure 5. The results are very encouraging. For instance, it takes
51.64 seconds to plan for an acyclic decomposition MMDP approach with five
agents. The acyclic decomposition MTAMDP approach solves the same type of
problem in an average of 0.72 seconds.

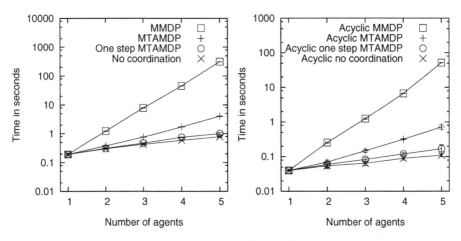

Fig. 4. Planning time using no acyclic
decomposition

Fig. 5. Planning time using the acyclic
decomposition

Table 1 details how far the expected value of the MTAMDP, *one step*
MTAMDP, and *no coordination* approaches are from an optimal MMDP approach. With one agent, all approaches are optimal since no coordination is
needed. This result suggests that the GLOBAL-VALUE() function is optimal.
All the tests performed with two agents resulted in an optimal policy for the
MTAMDP approach. This result suggests that the GLOBAL-VALUE() function is optimal, and a formal theorem to proof that is for future work. One can
also observe that when the agents do not coordinate, the resulting policy is far
from the optimal, which is not the case for the MTAMDP coordination approach.
The one step MTAMDP could be a viable approach in certain critical situations,

Table 1. The percentage of the optimal obtained with the different approaches

	MTAMDP	One step MTAMDP	No Coordination
1 agent	100%	100%	100%
2 agents	100%	99.89%	97.48%
3 agents	99.84%	99.63%	94.20%
4 agents	99.79%	99.55%	91.63%
5 agents	99.67%	99.41%	89.37%

since the solution is produced much faster than the MTAMDP approach while providing a near-optimal policy.

4   Conclusion and Future Work

The Multiagent Task Associated Markov Decision Process (MTAMDP) framework has been introduced to reduce the computational burden induced by the high number of different resource types. The acyclic decomposition approach aims at reducing the computational leverage burden associated to the state space in a problem where tasks create other tasks. The merging of these two approaches gives an efficient, and novel way to tackle the planning problem for resource allocation in a stochastic environment.

A way to improve the MTAMDP consists of coordinating the agents using the efficient Partial Global Planning (PGP) [4] approach instead of the *central* agent. The PGP approach solves the bottleneck effect induced by the *central* agent. Furthermore, the coordination will be less complex, as only interacting agents will coordinate with each other. The Q-decomposition approach proposed by Russell and Zimdars [8] may enable to approximate efficiently the resource allocation problem considered here. Indeed, the Q-decomposition would decompose the problem in tasks, and the MTAMDP method decomposes the problem in resources. This would permit two degrees of decomposition.

References

1. D. Aberdeen, S. Thiebaux, and L. Zhang. Decision-theoretic military operations planning. In *Proceedings of the International Conference on Automated Planning and Scheduling*, Whistler, Canada, 3–7 June 2004.
2. D. Bertsekas. Rollout algorithms for constrained dynamic programming. Technical report 2646, Lab. for Information and Decision Systems, MIT, Mass., USA, 2005.
3. C. Boutilier. Sequential optimality and coordination in multiagent systems. In *Proceedings of the Sixteenth International Joint Conference on Artificial Intelligence (IJCAI-99)*, pages 478–485, Stockholm, August 1999.
4. K. S. Decker and V. R. Lesser. Generalizing the partial global planning algorithm. *International Journal of Intelligent Cooperative Information Systems*, 1(2):319–346, 1992.
5. N. J. Nilsson. *Principles or Artificial Intelligence*. Tioga Publishing, Palo Alto, Ca, 1980.

6. P. Plamondon, B. Chaib-draa, and A. Benaskeur. Decomposition techniques for a loosely-coupled resource allocation problem. In *Proceedings of the IEEE/WIC/ACM International Conference on Intelligent Agent Technology (IAT 2005)*, September 2005.

7. P. Plamondon, B. Chaib-draa, and A. Benaskeur. A multiagent task associated mdp (mtamdp) approach to resource allocation. In *AAAI 2006 Spring Symposium on Distributed Plan and Schedule Management*, March 2006.

8. S. J. Russell and A. Zimdars. Q-decomposition for reinforcement learning agents. In *ICML*, pages 656–663, 2003.

9. R. E. Tarjan. Depth first search and linear graph algorithm. *SIAM Journal on Computing*, 1(2):146–172, 1972.

10. C. C. Wu and D. A. Castanon. Decomposition techniques for temporal resource allocation. Technical report: Afrl-va-wp-tp-2004-311, Air Force Research Laboratory, Air force base, OH, 2004.

11. J. Wu and E. H. Durfee. Automated resource-driven mission phasing techniques for constrained agents. In *Proceedings of the Fourth International Conference on Autonomous Agents and Multiagent Systems (AAMAS 2005)*, pages 331–338, August 2005.

12. W. Zhang. Modeling and solving a resource allocation problem with soft constraint techniques. Technical report: Wucs-2002-13, Washington University, Saint-Louis, Missouri, 2002.

Satisfaction Equilibrium: Achieving Cooperation in Incomplete Information Games*

Stéphane Ross and Brahim Chaib-draa

Department of Computer Science and Software Engineering, Laval University,
Québec (Qc), Canada, G1K 7P4
{ross, chaib}@damas.ift.ulaval.ca
http://www.damas.ift.ulaval.ca

Abstract. So far, most equilibrium concepts in game theory require that the rewards and actions of the other agents are known and/or observed by all agents. However, in real life problems, agents are generally faced with situations where they only have partial or no knowledge about their environment and the other agents evolving in it. In this context, all an agent can do is reasoning about its own payoffs and consequently, cannot rely on classical equilibria through deliberation, which requires full knowledge and observability of the other agents. To palliate to this difficulty, we introduce the satisfaction principle from which an equilibrium can arise as the result of the agents' individual learning experiences. We define such an equilibrium and then we present different algorithms that can be used to reach it. Finally, we present experimental results that show that using learning strategies based on this specific equilibrium, agents will generally coordinate themselves on a Pareto-optimal joint strategy, that is not always a Nash equilibrium, even though each agent is individually rational, in the sense that they try to maximize their own satisfaction.

1 Introduction

Game theory provides a general framework for decision making in multi-agent environments, though, general game models assume full knowledge and observability of the rewards and actions of the other agents. In real life problems, however, this is a strong assumption that does not hold in most cases.

One game model proposed by Harsanyi [1] considering incomplete information are Bayesian games. These games allow the modelling of unknown information as different agent types and a Nature's move that selects randomly each agent's type according to some probability distribution before each play. The agent must choose the action that maximizes its reward considering the probabilities it associates to each of the other agents' types and the probabilities it associates to the actions of the other agents when they are of a certain type. However, the

---

* This research was supported in part by the Natural Science and Engineering Council of Canada (NSERC).

L. Lamontagne and M. Marchand (Eds.): Canadian AI 2006, LNAI 4013, pp. 61–72, 2006.
© Springer-Verlag Berlin Heidelberg 2006

concept of Nash equilibrium in these games can be troublesome if not all agents have the same common beliefs about the probability distribution of all agents' types. Furthermore, a Nash equilibrium requires that each agent knows the exact strategy of the other agents, which is not always the case when an agent faces unknown agents[1].

Another recent approach based on Bayesian games is the theory of learning in games which relaxes the concept of equilibrium. Instead of considering an equilibrium as the result of a deliberation process, it considers an equilibrium as the result of a learning process, over repeated play, and it defines the concept of self-confirming equilibrium [2] as a state in which each agent plays optimally considering its beliefs and history of observations about the other agents' strategies and types. However, they showed that if an agent does not observe the other agents' actions, then the set of Nash equilibria and self-confirming equilibria may differ. While self-confirming equilibrium is a very interesting concept and worth consideration, we note that when an agent faces unknown agents and does not observe the other agents' actions, thinking rationally on possibly false beliefs may after all, not be optimal.

In order to address this problem, we consider here that an equilibrium is the result of a learning process, over repeated play, but we differ in the sense that we pursue an equilibrium that arises as the result of a learning mechanism, instead of rational thinking on the agent's beliefs and observations. To make this equilibrium possible, we introduce the satisfaction principle, which stipulates that an agent that has been satisfied by its payoff will not change its strategy, while an unsatisfied agent may decide to change its strategy. Under this principle, an equilibrium will arise when all agents will be satisfied by their payoff, since no agent will have any reason to change its strategy. From now on, we will refer to this equilibrium as a *satisfaction equilibrium*.

We will show that if the agents have well defined satisfaction constraints, Pareto-optimal joint strategies that are not Nash equilibria can be satisfaction equilibria and that henceforth, cooperation and more optimal results can be achieved using this principle, instead of rational thinking.

In this article, we will first introduce the game model we will use to take into account the constrained observability of the other agents' actions and rewards and we will also present the different concepts we will need to analyze a game in terms of satisfaction. Afterward, we will present different algorithms that converge towards satisfaction equilibria with experimental results showing their strengths and drawbacks in some specific games. Finally, we will conclude with future directions that can be explored in order to achieve better results.

2   Satisfaction Equilibrium

In this section, we will introduce the game model we will use to formalize a game where the agents do not know nor observe the actions and rewards of the other

---

[1] By "unknown agents", we mean that an agent does not know strategies, actions, outcomes, rewards, etc. of other agents.

agents. Afterward, we will formally define the satisfaction equilibrium based on the satisfaction function of the different agents.

2.1   Game Model

The game model we will consider will be a modified repeated game in which we introduce an observation function and a modified reward function in order to let the agents observe their rewards but not the other agents' actions.

Formally, we define the game as a tuple $(n, A, \Omega, O, R_1, R_2, \ldots, R_n)$; where n defines the number of agents, A defines the joint action space of all agents, i.e., $A = A_1 \times A_2 \times \ldots \times A_n$ and where A_i represents the set of actions agent i can do, Ω is the set of possible outcomes in the game observed by the agents, O the observation function $O : A \rightarrow \Omega$ which returns the observed outcome by the agents associated to the joint action played and finally R_i the reward function $R_i : \Omega \rightarrow \mathbf{R}$, which defines the reward of agent i given the outcome it observed. Each agent participating in the game only knows its own action set A_i and its reward function R_i. After each play, each agent is given the outcome $o \in \Omega$, corresponding to the joint action played, to compute its own reward. However, since the agents do not know the observation function O, they do not know which joint action led to this outcome.

2.2   Satisfaction Function and Equilibrium

To introduce the satisfaction principle in the game model previously introduced, we add a satisfaction function $S_i : \mathbf{R} \rightarrow \{0, 1\}$ for each agent i, that returns 1 if the agent is satisfied and 0 if the agent is not satisfied. Generally, we can define this function as follows:

$$S_i(r_i) = \begin{cases} 0 \text{ if } r_i < \sigma_i \\ 1 \text{ if } r_i \geq \sigma_i \end{cases}$$

where σ_i is the satisfaction constant of agent i representing the threshold at which the agent becomes satisfied, and r_i is a scalar that represents its reward.

Definition 1. *An outcome o is a satisfaction equilibrium if all agents are satisfied by their payoff under their satisfaction function and do not change their strategy when they are satisfied.*

$$(i) \ \ S_i(R_i(o)) = 1 \ \forall i$$
$$(ii) \ s_i^{t+1} = s_i^t \qquad \forall i, t : S_i(R_i(o_t)) = 1$$

s_i^{t+1} defines the strategy of agent i at time $t + 1$, s_i^t its strategy at time t and o_t the outcome observed at time t. Condition (i) states that all agents must be satisfied by the outcome o, and condition (ii) states that the strategy of an agent i at time $t + 1$ must not change if it was satisfied at time t. This is necessary in order to have an equilibrium. As a side note, this definition requires deterministic payoffs, because if $R_i(o)$ can be higher and lower than σ_i for the same observation o, then o will not be an equilibrium.

	C	D
C	-1,-1	-10,0
D	0,-10	-8,-8

$\sigma_i = -1$
$\Longrightarrow$

	C	D
C	1,1	0,1
D	1,0	0,0

Fig. 1. Prisoner's dilemma game matrix (left) and its satisfaction matrix (right)

We can now represent a satisfaction matrix by transforming a normal form game matrix with the satisfaction function of each agents. For example, the figure 1 shows the prisoner's dilemma game matrix with its transformed satisfaction matrix when both agents have a satisfaction constant set to -1.

While the game matrix and satisfaction matrix are not known to the agents, the satisfaction matrix is a useful representation to analyze the game in terms of satisfaction. Here, we can easily see that the only satisfaction equilibrium is the joint strategy (C, C), which is a Pareto-optimal strategy of the original game. This was the case in this example because we set both satisfaction constants to -1, which was the reward of the Pareto-optimal joint strategy of each agent. From this, we can conclude the following theorem 1.

Theorem 1. *In any game containing a Pareto-optimal joint strategy s, the outcome $O(s)$ and its equivalent outcomes[2] are the only satisfaction equilibria if $\sigma_i = R_i(O(s)) \forall i$.*

Proof. see [3].

Therefore, we see that a major part of the problem of coordinating the agents on a Pareto-optimal joint strategy is to define correctly the satisfaction constants of each agent. While we have assumed so far that these constants were fixed at the beginning of the learning process, we will show an algorithm in the last section that tries to maximize the satisfaction constant of an agent such that it learns to play its optimal equilibrium under the other agents' strategies.

2.3   Satisfying Strategies and Other Problematic Games

Similarly to the concept of dominant strategies, we can define a satisfying strategy as a strategy s_i for agent i such that it is always satisfied when it plays this strategy. The existence of a satisfying strategy in a game can be problematic if by playing such a strategy, no satisfaction equilibrium is possible. Furthermore, other games with some specific payoff structure can also be troublesome. For example, we will consider the following 2 games presented in figure 2.

In the first game (left), we see that the row agent has a satisfying strategy A. Therefore, if row agent starts playing strategy A, then column agent will be forced to accept an outcome corresponding to joint strategy (A, A) or (A, B). This is problematic since none of these outcomes are satisfaction equilibria. In the second game (right), there exists a unique Pareto-optimal joint strategy

---

[2] We consider that an outcome o' is equivalent to another outcome o if the rewards of all agents are the same in o and $o' : R_i(o) = R_i(o') \forall i$.

	A	B
A	1,0	1,0
B	1,1	0,0

	A	B	C
A	1,1	0,1	0,1
B	1,0	1,0	0,1
C	1,0	0,1	1,0

$\sigma_i = 1$
$\Longrightarrow$

	A	B	C
A	1,1	0,1	0,1
B	1,0	1,0	0,1
C	1,0	0,1	1,0

Fig. 2. A game containing a satisfying strategy (left) and a problematic game (right)

	B	F
B	2,1	0,0
F	0,0	2,1

$\sigma_i = 1$
$\Longrightarrow$

	B	F
B	1,1	0,0
F	0,0	1,1

Fig. 3. Battle of sexes game matrix (left) and its satisfaction matrix (right)

(A, A). With the satisfaction constants set to 1 for both agents, the corresponding satisfaction matrix is the same as the original game matrix. But, what we can see in this example is that we can never reach the satisfaction equilibrium (A, A) unless both agents starts with strategy A. Effectively, if one of the agent plays A but the other agent plays B or C, then the agent playing A will never be satisfied until it changes its strategy to B or C. This problem comes from the fact that an agent playing B or C will always be satisfied when the other agent plays A, and therefore, it will never change its strategy to A when the other agent plays A. Also, there is no joint strategy where both agents are unsatisfied that could allow a direct transition to joint strategy (A, A). From this, we conclude that if both agents do not start at the point of equilibrium (A, A), they will never reach an equilibrium since there exists no sequence of transitions that leads to this equilibrium. The effects of such payoff structures on the convergence of our algorithms will be showed with experimental results in the next sections.

2.4   Games with Multiple Satisfaction Equilibria

In some games, more than one satisfaction equilibrium can exist depending on how the satisfaction constants are defined. For example, we can consider the battle of sexes, presented in figure 3 with satisfaction constants set to 1. What will happen when more than one satisfaction equilibrium exists is that both agents will keep or change their strategy until they coordinate themselves on one of the satisfaction equilibrium. From there, they will keep playing the same action all the time.

2.5   Mixed Satisfaction Equilibrium

In some games, such as zero sum games in which each agent either get the maximum or minimum reward, it is impossible to find a satisfaction equilibrium in pure strategy, unless we set the satisfaction constant to the minimum reward. However, higher expected rewards could be obtained by playing mixed strategies. This can be achieved by playing a mixed satisfaction equilibrium.

Definition 2. *A mixed satisfaction equilibrium is a joint mixed strategy p such that all agents are satisfied by their expected reward under their satisfaction function and do not change their strategy when they are satisfied.*

$$(i)\ \ S_i(E_i(p)) = 1\ \forall i$$
$$(ii)\ p_i^{t+1} = p_i^t \qquad \forall i, t : S_i(E_i(p^t)) = 1$$

$E_i(p)$ represents the expected reward of agent i under the joint mixed strategy p. Condition (ii), as in definition 2.5, ensures that an agent keeps the same mixed strategy when it is satisfied at time t. This more general definition of the satisfaction equilibrium is also applicable in the case of stochastic payoffs, contrary to definition . However, the only way an agent will have to compute its expected reward will be to compute the average of the past n rewards it obtained under its current strategy, since it does not know the strategy of the other agents.

3   Learning the Satisfaction Equilibrium

We now present an algorithm that can be used by agents to learn over time to play the satisfaction equilibrium of a game.

3.1   Pure Satisfaction Equilibrium with Fixed Constants

The most basic case we might want to consider is the case where an agent tries to find a pure strategy that will always satisfy its fixed satisfaction constant.

Our algorithm 1 (called PSEL for Pure Satisfaction Equilibrium Learning) implements the satisfaction principle in the most basic way: if an agent is satisfied, it keeps its current action, else it chooses a random action in its set of actions to replace its current action.

Algorithm 1. PSEL: Pure Satisfaction Equilibrium Learning

Function PSEL(σ_i, K)
  $s_i \leftarrow ChooseAction()$
  for $n = 1$ **to** K **do**
    Play s and observe outcome o
    if $R_i(o) < \sigma_i$ **then**
      $s_i \leftarrow ChooseAction()$
    end if
  end for
  return s_i

In this algorithm, the constant K defines the allowed number of repeated plays and the *ChooseAction* function chooses a random action uniformly within the set of actions A_i of the agent. Under this learning strategy, once all agents are satisfied, no agent will change its strategy and therefore all agents reach an equilibrium. Once the agent has played K times, it returns its last chosen strategy. Evidently, in games where there exists no satisfaction equilibrium under the agents' satisfaction constants, those agents will never reach an equilibrium. Furthermore, if agent i has a satisfying strategy s_i, then we are not sure to reach a satisfaction equilibrium if s_i does not lead to an equilibrium (see figure 2 for an example).

3.2   Using an Exploration Strategy

While we have considered in our previous algorithm 1 that the *ChooseAction* function selects a random action within the set of actions of the agent, we can also try to implement a better exploration strategy such that actions that have not been explored often could have more chance to be chosen. To achieve this, the agent can compute a probability for each action, that corresponds to the inverse of the times it has chosen them, and then normalize the probabilities such that they sum to 1. Finally, it chooses its action according to the resulting probability distribution[3]. The results presented in section 3.3 will confirm that using this exploration strategy, instead of a uniform random choice, offers a slight improvement in the average number of plays required to converge to a satisfaction equilibrium.

3.3   Empirical Results with the PSEL Algorithm

We now present results obtained with the PSEL algorithm in different games. We have used 2 standard games, i.e. the prisoner's dilemma with satisfaction constants set to -1 for both agents (see figure 1 for the corresponding satisfaction matrix) and the battle of sexes with satisfaction constants set to 1 for both agents (see figure 3 for the corresponding satisfaction matrix). We also tested our algorithm in a cooperative game and a bigger game to verify the performance of our algorithm when the joint strategy space is bigger. These games are presented in figure 4. Finally, we also present results with the 2 problematic games introduced in sections 2.3.

In the cooperative game, the satisfaction constants were set to 3 for both agents such that the only satisfaction equilibrium is joint strategy (C, C). In the big game, they were set to 5 for both agents and therefore, the only satisfaction equilibrium is joint strategy (E, D).

For each of these 6 games, we ran 5000 simulations, consisting of 5000 repeated plays per simulation, varying the random seeds of the agents each time. In table 1, we present for each of these games the number of possible joint strategies, the number of satisfaction equilibria (SE), the convergence percentage to a SE and a comparison of the average number of plays required to converge to such an equilibrium (with 95% confidence interval) with the random and exploration strategies presented.

---

[3] A detailed presentation of this algorithm is available in [3].

	A	*B*	*C*
A	0,0	1,1	0,0
B	2,2	0,0	0,0
C	0,0	0,0	3,3

	A	*B*	*C*	*D*	*E*	*F*	*G*	*H*
A	0,0	0,0	-1,4	0,0	2,-2	0,0	3,0	0,0
B	1,2	0,0	0,0	3,0	0,0	0,0	0,3	1,1
C	0,0	3,3	0,0	1,1	0,0	0,0	2,2	0,0
D	4,4	0,0	5,1	0,2	2,2	1,4	0,0	0,0
E	0,1	0,0	0,0	5,5	0,0	0,0	2,1	0,0
F	0,4	2,2	0,2	0,0	0,0	3,3	0,0	4,4
G	0,0	5,3	3,0	0,0	-1,3	0,0	2,-1	0,0
H	0,0	2,4	1,1	0,0	0,0	-3,2	0,0	0,0

Fig. 4. Cooperative game matrix (left) and big game matrix (right)

Table 1. Convergence percentage and plays needed to converge to a SE in different games with the PSEL algorithm

Game	$\|A\|$	n_{SE}	conv. %	Random Avg. plays	Exploration Avg. plays	Improvement[4]
Prisoner's Dilemma	4	1	100%	8.67 ± 0.23	6.72 ± 0.18	22.49%
Battle of Sexes	4	2	100%	1.97 ± 0.04	1.95 ± 0.04	1.02%
Cooperative Game	9	1	100%	8.92 ± 0.23	7.82 ± 0.19	12.33%
Big Game	64	1	100%	67.95 ± 1.89	61.51 ± 1.65	9.48%
Problematic Game	9	1	10.88%	-	-	-
Game with satisfying strategy	4	1	33.26%	-	-	-

In each of these games, the *SE* were corresponding to Pareto-optimal joint strategies and the satisfaction constants were set according to theorem 1. In all non problematic games, we always converged to a *SE* within the allowed 5000 repeated plays. Therefore, we see from these results that, in non problematic games, when the satisfaction constants are well defined, we seem to eventually converge toward a Pareto-optimal satisfaction equilibrium[5] (*POSE*). However, in the problematic games, we see that the convergence percentage of the *PSEL* algorithm is dramatically affected. We note that in such games, the convergence of the algorithm is highly dependant on the initial joint action chosen by the agents, since some initial choices can never reach a SE. This is not the case of the other non problematic games where a SE is always reachable by doing a certain sequence of joint strategy transitions.

3.4 Convergence of the PSEL Algorithm

While we have already showed that the *PSEL* algorithm does not work in all games, there is a specific class of games where we can easily define the convergence probability of the *PSEL* algorithm according to theorem 2.

---

[4] The improvement corresponds to the percentage of gain in average plays required to converge to a SE with the exploration strategy : $\frac{Avg(Random)-Avg(Exploration)}{Avg(Random)} * 100\%$.

[5] We define a Pareto-optimal satisfaction equilibrium as a joint strategy that is a satisfaction equilibrium and also Pareto-optimal.

Theorem 2. *In all games where all agents have the same satisfaction in all outcomes, i.e. $(S_i(R_i(o)) = S_j(R_j(o))\forall i, j, o)$, the PSEL algorithm, using a uniform random exploration, will converge to a SE within K plays with probability $1 - q^K$ where $q = 1 - n_{SE}/|A|$ and the expected number of plays required to converge is given by $|A|/n_{SE}$.*

Proof. see [3].

Here, $|A|$ represents the joint action space size and n_{SE} is the number of SE in the game. This theorem will always be applicable to identical payoffs games[6] if we use the same satisfaction constant for all agents. In this case, since all agents have the same rewards and satisfaction constants, they will always have the same satisfaction in all outcomes. From theorem 2, we can conclude that in such games, as $K \to \infty$, the convergence probability will tend toward 1. In practice, for the cooperative game (figure 4) where theorem 2 applies, we see that the the expected number of plays required to converge is 9 and the probability to converge within 50 plays is around 99.7%.

4   Learning the Satisfaction Constant

While the *PSEL* algorithm has showed interesting performance in some games, it has the disadvantage that the satisfaction constant must be correctly set in order to achieve good results. To alleviate this problem, we present a new learning strategy that tries to maximize the satisfaction constant while staying in a state of equilibrium.

4.1   Limited History Satisfaction Learning (LHSL) Algorithm

In order to achieve this, we present an algorithm (called *LHSL* for Limited History Satisfaction Learning) that implements the strategy of increasing the satisfaction constant when the agent is satisfied and decreasing the satisfaction constant when it is unsatisfied. We also decrease the increment/decrement over time in order to converge to a certain fixed satisfaction constant. This will be achieved by multiplying the increment by a certain factor within the interval $]0, 1[$ after each play. Moreover, we keep a limited history of the agent's experience in order to prevent it from overrating its satisfaction constant, by checking whether it was unsatisfied by its current strategy in the past when its satisfaction constant was higher than a certain threshold. We will see in the results, that this technique really helps the convergence percentage of the algorithm compared to the case where we do not prevent this, as in the special case where the history size will be 0.

   In this algorithm, the satisfaction constant σ_i is initialized to the minimum reward of agent i and the constant δ_i is used to increment/decrement this satisfaction constant. More precisely, δ_i is decremented over time, such that it tends

---

[6] An identical payoffs game is a game where all agents have the same reward function.

Algorithm 2. LHSL : Limited History Satisfaction Learning

Function LHSL(δ_i, γ_i, n_i)
$\sigma_i \leftarrow min(r_i)$; $s_i \leftarrow ChooseAction()$
$S[0..|A_i| - 1, 0..n - 1] \leftarrow$ a matrix initialized with true values
$\Sigma[0..|A_i| - 1, 0..n - 1] \leftarrow$ a matrix initialized with $min(r_i)$ values
while $\delta_i > \epsilon_i$ **do**
    Play s_i and observe outcome o
    $lastStrategy \leftarrow s_i$; $satisfied \leftarrow (R_i(o) \geq \sigma_i)$; $tmp \leftarrow 0$
    if not $satisfied$ **then**
        $s_i \leftarrow ChooseAction()$; $tmp \leftarrow -\delta_i$
    else if always satisfied playing s_i with $\sigma_i \leq \sigma_i + \delta_i$ in history **then**
        $tmp \leftarrow \delta_i$
    end if
    If $n > 0$ add $satisfied$ and σ_i in history of $lastStrategy$ and remove oldest values
    $\sigma_i \leftarrow \sigma_i + tmp$; $\delta_i \leftarrow \delta_i \cdot \gamma_i$
end while
return (s_i, σ_i)

---

toward 0, by multiplying it by the constant $\gamma_i \in]0, 1[$ after each play. The matrix S keeps a history of the last n states of satisfaction for each action and the matrix Σ keeps, for each action, a history of the last n satisfaction constants when the agent played these actions. This history is used to check, before incrementing the satisfaction constant, whether or not the agent was unsatisfied by its current strategy in the past when its satisfaction constant was below its new satisfaction constant. Finally, after each play, we update the history of the agent. We consider that the algorithm has converged to the optimal satisfaction constant when δ_i is lower than a certain constant $\epsilon_i \simeq 0$. At this point, the algorithm returns the satisfaction constant and the last strategy chosen by agent i. When all agents have converged, if they are all satisfied by their strategy, then we have reach a satisfaction equilibrium since their satisfaction constant will be stable[7]. While we are not guaranteed to converge toward a *POSE*, we will see that in practice, this algorithm yields a convergence percentage of almost 100% toward the *POSE* in any non problematic games.

4.2   Empirical Results with the LHSL Algorithm

To test the *LHSL* algorithm, we have used the same 6 games we have presented for the results with the *PSEL* algorithm and we now try to learn the *POSE* without giving a priori its value to set accordingly the satisfaction constant. The results were obtained over 5000 simulations and we show the convergence percentage to the *POSE* obtained with the best γ_i value and history sizes we

---

[7] The satisfaction constants become stable when the floating point precision is insufficient to account for the change caused by the addition of δ_i. Therefore, we must choose ϵ_i such that $\sigma_i \pm \delta_i = \sigma_i$ when $\delta_i \leq \epsilon_i$. In fact, we could use $\sigma_i \pm \delta_i = \sigma_i$ as our convergence criteria.

Table 2. Convergence percentage to a POSE in different games with the LHSL algorithm

Game	$|A|$	With history			Without history	
		conv. %	γ_i	n_i	conv. %	γ_i
Prisoner's Dilemma	4	100%	0.99	64	89.96%	0.90
Battle of Sexes	4	100%	0.90	16	97.60%	0.80
Cooperative Game	9	99.66%	0.995	128	97.62%	0.95
Big Game	64	99.66%	0.995	16	93.88%	0.99
Problematic Game	9	9.86%	0.95	128	7.88%	0.50
Game with satisfying strategy	4	98.06%	0.95	128	38.78%	0.95

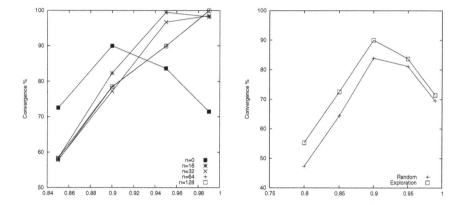

Fig. 5. Convergence percentage to a *POSE* in the prisoner's dilemma under different γ values, history sizes and exploration strategies

have tested[8]. We also compare these results to the special case where we do not use a history, i.e., $n = 0$. In all cases, δ_i was set to 1 and the convergence threshold ϵ_i was set to 10^{-20}.

In all cases, the best results, showed in table 2, were obtained with the exploration strategy we have presented in section 3.2. In most games, except the problematic game (figure 2), we were able to get a convergence percentage near 100%. We can also see that the use of a history offers a significant improvement over the results we obtain without a history. As a side note, the convergence percentage of the *LHSL* algorithm seems to vary a lot depending on the history sizes and gamma values. This is illustrated in figure 5.

The first graphic in figure 5 compares the results with different history sizes and γ values. We can see that the bigger the history size, the closer to 1 γ must be in order to achieve better performances. While, in general, the more slowly we decrement δ and the bigger the history size is, the better are the results, we see that small histories can also lead to very good results when γ is well defined. Since

---

[8] In these results, γ_i, δ_i, ϵ_i, σ_i and the history size were the same for all agents.

the closer γ is to 1, the more repetition will be needed for δ to reach ϵ, we can conclude that if we have only a few plays to learn the equilibrium, than it is better to use a small history, since it can achieve better convergence percentage when γ is smaller, and consequently, when the number of allowed repeated play is small. In the second graphic, we compare the convergence percentage of the 2 different exploration approaches under different γ values for the prisoner's dilemma, in the case where no history was used ($n = 0$). This graphic confirms that the exploration strategy presented in section 3.2 improves slightly the convergence percentage of the *LHSL* algorithm.

5   Conclusion and Future Works

While this article covered a lot of new concepts, it laid out only the basic theoretical foundations of the satisfaction equilibrium. The algorithms we have presented have shown great performance in practice, but we have seen some games with specific payoff structures that could pose problems or render impossible the convergence to a satisfaction equilibrium. We have identified possible solutions, such as allowing mixed satisfaction equilibrium and trying to maximize the satisfaction constant, that could sometimes palliate these problems. Although, what we may discover is that in some games it might not always be possible to converge to a satisfaction equilibrium, or to a *POSE*. What we might want to do in these games is to converge toward a Nash equilibrium. If convergence to a Nash equilibrium is always possible, then we may try to find an algorithm that converges in the worst case to a Nash equilibrium, and in the best case, to a Pareto-optimal satisfaction equilibrium. In order to achieve this goal, the next step will be to develop an algorithm that can converge to a Pareto-optimal mixed satisfaction equilibrium. Also, a lot of theoretical work needs to be done to prove and/or bound the efficiency of the presented algorithms and identify clearly in which cases the algorithms will converge or not to a satisfaction equilibrium. Afterward, another long term goal is to apply the satisfaction equilibrium to stochastic games in order to allow agents to learn a Pareto-optimal joint strategy without knowing anything about the other agents in these type of games.

References

1. Harsanyi, J.: Games of incomplete information played by bayesian players. Management Science **14** (1967) 159–182, 320–334, and 486–502
2. Dekel, E., Fudenberg, D., Levine, D.K.: Learning to play bayesian games. Games and Economic Behavior **46** (2004) 282–303
3. Ross, S., Chaib-draa, B.: Report on satisfaction equilibria. Technical report, Laval University, Department of Computer Science and Software Engineering, http://www.damas.ift.ulaval.ca/~ross/ReportSatisfactionEquilibria.pdf (2005)

How Artificial Intelligent Agents Do Shopping in a Virtual Mall: A 'Believable' and 'Usable' Multiagent-Based Simulation of Customers' Shopping Behavior in a Mall

Walid Ali[1,2] and Bernard Moulin[1,2]

[1] Computer Science and Software Engineering Department, 3904 Pav. Pouliot,
Laval University, Ste Foy, Québec G1K 7P4, Canada
[2] Research Center on Geomatics, Laval University, Ste Foy, Quebec G1K 7P4, Canada
{walid.ali, bernard.moulin}@ift.ulaval.ca

Abstract. Our literature review revealed that several applications successfully simulate certain kinds of human behaviors in spatial environments, but they have some limitations related to the 'believability[1]' and the 'usability[2]' of the simulations. This paper aims to present a set of requirements for multiagent-based simulations in terms of 'believability' and 'usability'. It also presents how these requirements have been put into use to develop a multiagent-based simulation prototype of customers' shopping behavior in a mall. Using software agents equipped with spatial and cognitive capabilities, this prototype can be considered sufficiently 'believable' and 'usable' for end-users, mainly mall managers in our case. We show how shopping behavior simulator can support the decision-making process with respect to the spatial configuration of the shopping mall.

1 Introduction

This paper deals with *multiagent-based simulation* and focuses on the *simulation of human behaviors in spatial environments*. This kind of simulation represents an interesting and powerful research method to advance our understanding of human spatial cognition and the interactions of human beings with their spatial environment. MultiAgent Systems (MAS) provide a computing paradigm which has been recently used to create such simulations [6]. Our literature review revealed that several researchers used this paradigm to develop applications that simulate different kinds of human behaviors in spatial environments ([13], [6], [5], [8], [11], etc.). These applications successfully simulated certain kinds of behaviors, but they limited by two aspects: the 'believability' [9] and the 'usability' [7].

In this context, the limitations of the applications which simulate human behaviors in spatial environments are related to:

---

[1] In this paper, the term 'believability' means the fidelity to the real behavior to be simulated and the real simulation environment.

[2] In this paper the term 'usability' means the fidelity to the end-user's goals.

L. Lamontagne and M. Marchand (Eds.): Canadian AI 2006, LNAI 4013, pp. 73–85, 2006.
© Springer-Verlag Berlin Heidelberg 2006

(1) the '*believability*' of the simulation: we noticed a noteworthy lack in the cognitive/spatial capabilities of the agents used in the simulation (perception, memorization, decision-making process, etc.); and

(2) the '*usability*' of the simulation: we found that the majority of simulations presented in the literature are only used to visualize and display on screens the behaviors to be simulated. They do not generate output data which can be used by end-users in order to make decisions. To sum up, the majority of these applications are used as animations and not as decision-making tools.

Developing 'Believable' and 'usable' simulations of behaviors in space is a challenging area of computer science. Many of the problems related to the creation of lifelike animated models have been solved, but the difficulty now lies in creating simulation applications of behaviors that are believable [14] and usable so that they can be effectively used by decision-makers (end-users). In this paper, we show how to improve the '*believability*' and the '*usability*' of simulation applications of human behaviors in spatial environments by using *intelligent agents with advanced cognitive/spatial capabilities* and *real/empirical input data that feed the simulation models*. As an illustration, we present a multiagent-based simulation prototype that simulates, in real-time, the shopping behavior in virtual geographic environment representing a mall. What's more, this prototype uses empirical data collected from real shoppers during a week long survey. This paper also presents how this prototype can be used by end-users, which are mainly mall managers, to support decisions about the spatial configuration of their mall.

This paper is organized as follows: In Section 2, we discuss the previous works dealing with multiagent-based simulation of human behaviors in spatial environments. We also propose some requirements which need to be satisfied by a multiagent-based simulation to be 'believable' and 'usable'. In Sections 3 and 4, we present a multiagent-based simulation prototype that simulates the shopping behavior in a mall. In Section 5, we show why this prototype can be considered to be 'believable' and 'usable' and discuss the satisfaction of the requirements defined in Section 2. Finally, Section 6 concludes the paper and presents some future works.

2   Requirements for 'Believable' and 'Usable' Multiagent Simulation of Human Behaviors in Spatial Environments

2.1   Previous Research Works

Several researchers used a multiagent system approach to develop simulation applications that simulate different human behaviors in spatial environments (wayfinding behavior in an airport [13] [6], pedestrian movements in a mall [5], people movements in a large scale environment representing a town [8], pedestrian movement in a geographic environment [2], [17], [15], [3], etc.). These applications successfully simulated certain kinds of behaviors, but they have some limitations related to the capabilities of the agents used in the simulation. For example, the agents of [13] and [6] perceive their environment using the concept of information and affordance [6]. [5] and [8] use a message passing technique between the agents and their environment. These perception mechanisms (affordance, message passing, etc.)

are efficient to perceive non-spatial information in the environment but do not allow agents to perceive the spatial/geographic characteristics of the environment. This is a major limitation when the goal of an application is to plausibly simulate the spatial behaviors of agents in a geographic environment. Furthermore, in these applications the agents do not have a memorization capability to memorize the elements perceived in the environment. What's more, the majority of the aforementioned applications do not use real (or empirical): their data is generated randomly using specific algorithms.

In addition, some applications such as those of [13], [6], [5] and [8] are only used to display on screens the behaviors to be simulated. The applications of [2], [17], [15], [3] are only used for animation purposes. To be more usable, simulation applications should be used beyond the mere visualization function: They should generate simulation output data which can help users to make decisions.

2.2 Requirements for 'Believable' Simulation

[16] have provided some insight into building believable agents for simulation applications. Here we refine these requirements with respect to the spatial aspects of the simulation. We identify two main types of requirements for multiagent simulation of human behaviors in spatial environments:

- *Requirements concerning the simulation models*: These models are based on the agent paradigm. In order to benefit from the progress in the multiagent domain (autonomy, sociability, etc.), the main actors of the simulation can be represented using agents. In order to get a 'believable' simulation, the structure of such agents may involve variables which represent various kinds of characteristics: psychological, sociological, demographic, etc [14]. What's more, the agents should be equipped with advanced cognitive and spatial capabilities. As mentioned in [16] here are some examples of these capabilities:
  - *perceive the environment*: Using this ability, the agent can perceive the elements of its environment.
  - *memorize the elements* belonging to the environment.
  - *make decisions and reason*: The agent can make complex non-spatial and spatial reasoning (e.g. make decisions about where to go in the spatial environment), perform spatial and temporal reasoning, etc.).
  - *act in and affect the environment* (e.g., navigate, communicate, etc.) taking into account the physical limitations of the environment (e.g., obstacles) and those of the human body simulated by the agent.
  - *hold multiple goals and interleave their achievement*.
  - *react to the changing spatial environment* and to interleave pursuing goals and reacting to the spatial environment.
  - *interact with other agents* in the simulation.

- *Requirements concerning the simulation data*: In order to enhance the believability of a simulation and to get meaningful and credible results from such simulation, one must use relevant and correct data. This data can be collected respectively from the observation of the phenomena to be simulated (human behaviors) and from its spatial environment. It is important to mention that relevant and credible data are needed to feed the simulation models, to calibrate them, and to verify and validate these models.

2.3 Requirements for 'Usable' Simulation

Simulation applications are generally used to support decision making [1]. In the literature, there exist several applications that simulate human behaviors in spatial environments. Unfortunately, these simulation applications are usually limited to display on screens the behaviors to be simulated (they play the role of computer animations). To be more usable, simulation applications should be used beyond the mere visualization function [1]. In this paper, 'usable simulation' means a simulation that can:

- visualize on the screen the course of the simulation;
- allow end-users to control the simulation time of the simulation, to parameterize the simulation models, to parameterize the visualization modes (e.g., zoom in, zoom out, etc.), ton change the configuration of the spatial environment, etc.;
- generate output data that can be used by the users for decision-making purposes. Since we deal with simulation in spatial environments, a large part of output data has a spatial dimension.
- analyze and explore non-spatial and spatial output data in order to support end-users' decision-making.

Sections 3 and 4 aim to illustrate the application of these requirements thanks to a multiagent prototype that simulates the shopping behavior in a mall. In Section 5, we discuss the aspects that make this prototype 'believable', while in the Section 6 discusses its usability.

3   A *'Believable'* Agent-Based Geosimulation Prototype: The Case of the Square One Shopping Mall (Toronto)

Before presenting the simulation prototype which aims to simulate the shopping behavior in a mall, we present the platform which is used to develop it. This platform is called MAGS (MultiAgent GeoSimulation) and presented in the next sub-section.

3.1   The MAGS: The MultiAgent GeoSimulation Platform

The shopping behavior simulation prototype is developed using a simulation platform called MAGS (MultiAgent Geo-Simulation) [11]. It is a generic platform that can be used to simulate, in real-time, thousands of knowledge-based agents navigating in a 2D or 3D virtual spatial environment. MAGS agents have several knowledge-based capabilities such as perception, navigation, memorization, communication and objective-based behavior which allow them to display an autonomous behavior within a 2D-3D geographic virtual environment. The agents in MAGS are able to perceive the elements contained in the environment, to navigate autonomously inside it and react to changes occurring in the environment. These agents have several knowledge-based capabilities.

- *The agent perception process*: In MAGS agents can perceive (1) terrain characteristics such as elevation and slopes; (2) the elements contained in the landscape surrounding the agent including buildings and static objects; (3) other mobile agents navigating in the agent's range of perception; (4) dynamic areas or volumes whose shape changes during the simulation (ex.: smoky areas or zones having pleasant odors); (5) spatial events such as explosions, etc. occurring in the agent's vicinity; (6) messages communicated by other agents [11].

- *The agent navigation process*: In MAGS agents can have two navigation modes: *Following-a-path-mode* in which agents follow specific paths which are stored in a bitmap called ARIANE_MAP or *Obstacle-avoidance-mode* in which the agents move through open spaces avoiding obstacles. In MAGS the obstacles to be avoided are recoded in specific bitmap called OBSTACLE_MAP.

- *The memorization process*: In MAGS the agents have three kinds of memory: *Perception memory* in which the agents store what they perceive during the last few simulation steps; *Working memory* in which the agents memorize what they perceive in one simulation and *Long-term memory* in which the agents store what they perceived in several simulations [12]. Unfortunately, the agents in MAGS can also memorize some elements of the simulation environment and do not have learning capabilities.

- *The agent's characteristics*: In MAGS an agent is characterized by a number of variables whose values describe the agent's state at any given time. We distinguish *static states* and *dynamic states*. A static state does not change during the simulation and is represented by a variable and its current value (ex.: gender, age group, occupation, marital status). A dynamic state is a state which can possibly change during the simulation (ex.: hunger, tiredness, stress). A dynamic state is represented by a variable associated with a function which computes how this variable changes values during the simulation. The variable is characterized by an initial value, a maximum value, an increase rate, a decrease rate, an upper threshold and a lower threshold which are used by the function. Using these parameters, the system can simulate the evolution of the agents' dynamic states and trigger the relevant behaviors [11].

- *The objective-based behavior*: In MAGS an agent is associated with a set of objectives that it tries to reach. The objectives are organized in hierarchies which are is composed of nodes that represent composite objectives and leaves that represent elementary objectives which are associated with actions that the agent can perform. Each agent owns a set of objectives corresponding to its needs. An objective is associated with rules containing constraints on the activation and the completion of the objective. Constraints are dependent on time, on the agent's states, and the environment's state. The selection of the current agent's behavior relies on the priority of its objectives. Each need is associated with a priority which varies according to the agent's profile. An objective's priority is primarily a function of the corresponding need's priority. It is also subject to modifications brought about by the opportunities that the agent perceives or by temporal constraints [11].

- *The agent communication process*: In MAGS agents can communicate with other agents by exchanging messages using mailbox-based communication.

The spatial characteristics of the environment and static objects are generated from data stored in Geographic Information System and in related databases. The spatial characteristics of the environment are recorded in raster mode which enables agents to access the information contained in various bitmaps that encode different kinds of information about the virtual environment and the objects contained in it. The

AgentsMap contains the information about the locations of agents and the static objects contained in the environment. The *ObstaclesMap* contains the locations of obstacles, the *ArianeMap* contains the paths that can be followed by mobile agents, the *HeightMap* represents the elevations of the environment, etc. The information contained in the different bitmaps influences the agent's perception and navigation. In MAGS the simulation environment is not static and can change during the simulation. For example, we can add new obstacles, or gaseous phenomena such as smoke, dense gases and odors which are represented using particle systems, etc. [11].

3.2   The Mall-MAGS Prototype: A Multiagent-Based Simulator of the Shopping Behavior in a Mall

a.   Creating Agent-Based Models with Complex Structures and Advanced Capabilities

In order to create believable shopping behavior simulation models we carried out an in-depth literature review related to several disciplines dealing with such behavior (consumer behavior, marketing, shopping behavior, etc.). Based on this literature review, we developed rich conceptual models representing the shopping behavior in a mall. The first part of these models represents the shopper. In this part, we integrated the majority of factors that influence the shopping behavior within a mall (e.g., demographic factors (age, gender, occupation, marital status, etc.), cultural factors (culture, sub-culture), psychological factors (emotions), etc.) as well as the processes that compose it (e.g., perception, memorization, alternatives evaluation, decision-making, displacement, buying, consumption, etc.). The second part of these conceptual models represents the environment (i.e. the mall) and contains the main elements that influence the shopping behavior (stores, kiosks, colors, music, etc.). Then, based on these conceptual models, we developed specific agent models.. We specified two categories of agents:

(1) The shopper agent: This type of agent corresponds to the main actor of the simulation. It represents the real shopper in the simulation. The structure of this agent contains several attributes which are demographic (age, gender, occupation, marital status, etc.), psychological (perception memory, short- and long- term memories), cultural (culture, sub-culture), etc. The behavior of this agent focuses on the shopping activities and contains the following processes (perception, memorization, reasoning, decision-making, action, navigation, etc.).

(2) The agents representing the environment' elements: In this category we find the agents representing stores, kiosks, doors, corridors, etc.

b.   Collecting Real Data About the Shopping Behavior in a Mall

To feed the agent-based simulation models related to the shoppers with real data we carried out a survey in October 2003 and collected 390 30-pages questionnaires completely filled by real shoppers in the *Square One* shopping mall (in Toronto area). This data belongs to two main categories: non-spatial data such as demographic information (gender, age group, marital status, occupation, preferences, habits, etc.) and spatial data such as preferred entrance and exit doors, habitual itineraries, well-known areas in the mall, etc.

The data concerning the simulation environment (the mall) is stored in a geographic information system (GIS) of the Square One shopping mall. It is proven in the literature, that GIS is a better mean to store meaningful geographic data about a spatial environment.

c. Developing the Simulation Prototype

Using the MAGS platform we developed the multiagent simulation prototype that simulates customers' shopping behavior in a mall. As a case of study we used the *Square One shopping mall*. Using the MAGS platform we benefit from the advanced cognitive and spatial capabilities of its agents when developing the agents of our shopping behavior prototype: perceive, memorize, make complex decisions, reason about distances, navigate autonomously, etc.

In Fig. 1a and Fig. 1b we display 2D and 3D screenshots of a simulation that involved 390 software Shoppers agents navigating in the virtual shopping mall.

Fig. 1a. The 2D simulation in MAGS platform (Square One mall)

Fig. 1b. The 3D simulation in MAGS platform (Square One mall)

In the simulation prototype a Shopper agent comes to the mall in order to visit a list of specific stores or kiosks that are chosen before the simulation on the basis of the agent's characteristics. It enters by a particular door and starts the shopping trip. Based on its position in the mall, its knowledge (memorization process) and on what it perceives in the mall (perception process), it makes decision about the next store or kiosk to visit (decision-making process). When it chooses a store or kiosk, it moves in its direction (navigation process). Sometimes, when it is moving to a chosen store or kiosk, the agent may perceive another store or kiosk (perception process) that is in its shopping list and that it did not know it before. In this case, the Shopper agent moves to this store or kiosk and memorizes its location (memorization process) for its next shopping trips. The Shopper agent accomplishes this behavior continually until it visits all the stores or kiosks on its list or until it has not enough time left for the shopping trip. If the Shopper agent has still time for shopping and some stores or kiosks of its list are in locations unknown by the agent, it starts to explore the shopping mall to search for these stores or kiosks. When the Shopper agent reaches the maximum time allowed to the shopping trip, it leaves the mall.

A Shopper agent can also come to the mall without a specific list of stores or kiosks to visit: This corresponds to a real person coming to the mall to explore it, to see people, or to make exercise, etc. In the exploration mode the Shopper agent takes its preferred paths in the shopping mall. In this mode the moving action of the Shopper agent to the stores, kiosks, music areas, odor areas, lighting areas, is directed by its habits and preferences. For example, if the Shopper agent likes *cars* and it passes in front of a car exhibition, it can move to this exhibition. To extend our simulation prototype, we can simulate the Shopper reactions to the mall's atmosphere. We can insert special agents that broadcast music, lighting or odor. If the shopper agent is in the exploration mode and likes the music or the lighting or the odor broadcasted by these special agents, it may move toward them and possibly enter the associated store.

During its shopping trip a Shopper agent can feel the need to eat or to go to the restroom (simulated by a dynamic variable reaching a given threshold). Since these needs have a higher priority than the need to shop or to play, the agent suspends temporarily its shopping trip and goes to the locations where it can eat something or to restrooms. In our geosimulation prototype the priorities of the activities of the shopping behavior are defined based on Maslow's hierarchy of needs [10].

d. Verifying and Validating the Simulation Prototype

Our simulation prototype is intended to be used by end-users as a decision making tool about the simulated system. In order to increase the users' confidence in the simulation models of the prototype, it is important to verify and validate these models. According to literature, verification and validation of human behaviors are extremely complex. The complexity of the shopping behavior in a mall to verified and validated leads us to make some choices and define some limits concerning the simulation models and especially the shopper's one. First, we are more interested to verify and validate the shopper agent's decision-making process. Second, we focus on some specific shopping situations in order to evaluate the movement decisions made by the shopper agent inside the virtual mall. Finally, we focus only on some shopping activities during the shopping situations (e.g., go to a shop, go to a snack bar, go to a restaurant, leave the mall, etc.). For each shopping activity in a specific situation, we observe if the shopper agent behaves (or make decision) like real shopper when he does the same activity in the same situation. Comparisons between decisions made by real shoppers and those made by software shopper agents give us idea about the credibility of the simulation model (decision-making process) in our prototype.

4 A 'Usable' Agent-Based Geosimulation Prototype: The Case of the Square One Shopping Mall (Toronto)

In Section 2, we presented some requirements to be satisfied by a simulation to be usable. In this section we aim to present the shopping behavior prototype from a usability point of view. Before showing the use of the prototype by end-users, we present how we collect output data from the simulation using observer agents. This output data, as well as analyses results on it, serve as a basis to the end-users in order to make efficient decisions about the shopper agent's behavior of the shopper agents or about the spatial configuration of the mall.

4.1   Collecting Simulation Outputs Using Intelligent Agents

The simulation output data is collected using specific software agents called *Observers*. The mission of an observer agent is to gather non-spatial and spatial data about the course of the simulation, and more especially about shopper agents which enter its perception field. Observer agents have capabilities that allow them to collect relevant non-spatial and spatial data during the simulation execution. The collected data is recorded in files and analyzed after the simulation. The analysis results are, then, used by end-users in order to make decisions in relation to the shopping behaviors of the agents and the spatial configuration of the simulation environment (mall).

4.2   The Use of the Mall_MAGS Prototype

A shopping mall manager can change the spatial configuration of the shopping mall (change a store location, close a door or a corridor, etc.) and create different simulation scenarios. For each scenario the manager can launch the simulation and collect the results. By comparing the results of different scenarios he can assess the impact of spatial changes in the mall.

To illustrate the use of our shopping behavior geosimulation tool we used 2 simulation scenarios. In the first one we launch a simulation with a set of input data about the shopping mall (GIS) (see Fig. 2a) and about a population of 390 shoppers. For this first scenario the system generates output data about the itineraries that the Shoppers agents take in the shopping mall. In scenario 2 we exchange the location of two department stores: *Wal-Mart* and *Zellers* (Fig. 2b), we launch the simulation again and the observer agents generate the output data about the itineraries of the same population of Shoppers agents. By comparing the output data of the two scenarios we notice the difference of the paths that the Shopper agents followed to attend the department stores *Wal-Mart* and *Zellers* stores. For example, the simulation output analysis shows us that corridor X is less frequented in scenario 2 than in scenario 1 (Fig. 3a). However, corridor Y is more frequented in scenario 2 than in scenario 1 (Fig. 3b). In these figures the flow of the agents Shoppers which pass through a corridor is represented by a line which is attached to this corridor. The width and the color of this line are proportional to the flow of Shoppers agents that pass through the corridor. If this flow grows, the width of the line grows and its color becomes darker. By a data analysis on the attributes of the Shopper agent (e.g., gender, age, etc.) we can see that in scenario 2, most of the Shoppers agents that go through corridor Y are female and they come to the mall to visit female cloth stores. If the mall manager chooses the mall configuration of scenario 2, he may think of renting the spaces along corridor Y to female cloth stores.

It is important to note that:

- The simulation output data are generated using software agents called *Observers*.

- The data analysis of the geosimulation output (non-spatial and spatial data) is implemented in an analysis tool that we developed using *Microsoft Visual basic 6.0*. This user-friendly tool uses the data generated by the *Observers* agents in order to make non-spatial and spatial analysis. The data generated from the shopping behaviour geosimulation can be also analyzed and explored using a tool called SOLAP (Spatial On Line Analytical Processing) [4]. An example of using the SOLAP

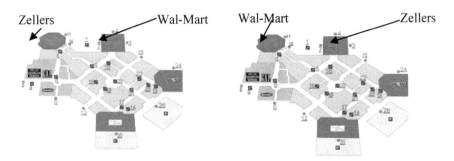

Fig. 2a. The simulation environment in Scenario 1

Fig. 2b. The simulation environment Scenario 2

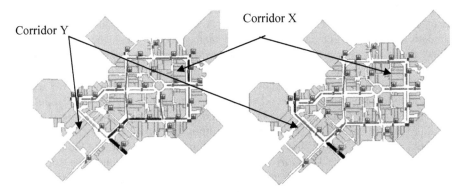

Fig. 3a. The spatial data analysis in Scenario 1   **Fig. 3b.** The spatial data analysis in Scenario 2

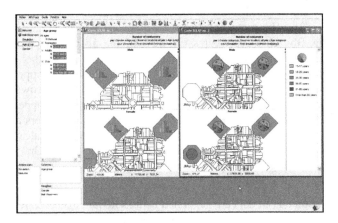

Fig. 4. Geosimulation output data analysis using SOLAP tool [4]

tool to explore geosimulation output data is presented in Fig. 4. In Fig. 4 the user can see the percentage of shopper agents (by age and gender) which visit three big stores in Square One mall (Wall-Mart, Zellers, and The Bay).

5 Satisfying the Requirements

Based on the requirements defined in Section 3 of this paper, we think that our shopping behavior simulation prototype is:

- 'believable' because:
    - it benefits from the advanced capabilities of the agents offered by the MAGS platform. The agents in the prototype exhibit believable shopping behaviors and capabilities, in the sense that they can perceive, memorize, make decisions, reason, act, navigate, etc. They also have complex structure that integrates different types of variables: demographic, psychological, social, etc.;
    - it uses non-spatial and spatial real data related to the shopping behavior (which are collected from real shoppers using questionnaires) and data related to the simulation environment (mall) (which are stored in geographic information systems (GIS)).
- 'usable' because:
    - it can visualize on screen the simulation in 2D and 3D modes;
    - it allows the user to control the simulation (the time, the visualization modes, etc.);
    - it can generate output data (non-spatial and spatial) using agents called 'observer agents'. This output data can be used by end-users for decision-making purposes;
    - it can be easily combined with analysis tools that can analyze and explore non-spatial and spatial data generated by the simulation in order to support decision-making.

6 Conclusion and Future Works

In this paper we presented some simulation applications that aim to simulate human behaviors in spatial environments. We also presented the main limitations of these applications in terms of 'believability' and 'usability'. Then, we presented some requirements for the agent-based simulations in order to be more 'believable' and 'usable'. After that, we presented an agent-based simulation prototype of customers' shopping behavior in a mall and, we discussed how this prototype can be 'believable' and 'usable' for end-users. The main contributions of our work are the following:

- The development of 'believable' agent-based simulation prototype of shopping behavior in a mall. The rich structure and behavior of the shopper agents, and empirical data used in the simulation, make these agents enough believable to simulate the shopping behavior of real shoppers in a mall.
- The development of a 'usable' agent-based simulation prototype that helps end-users (mall managers) to assess different spatial configurations of their mall.
- The coupling of the shopping behavior prototype with spatial analysis tools (our tool and the SOLAP one) in order to better analyze and explore output data generated from the geosimulation.

As future works we plan: (1) to enhance our prototype and especially the spatial cognitive capabilities of the intelligent agents in order to simulate more complex customers' shopping behavior in a mall (entertainment behaviors, social and groups behaviors, etc.); (2) to extend the usage of the simulator in order to help mall managers to make decisions about marketing strategies related to the changes of music or odor in a corridor, change of temperature, or wall colours in certain areas, etc. For each change they would execute the simulation and collect results. By comparing these results they can make decisions about the optimal marketing strategy to adopt. How to propose a systematic way to carry out these comparisons is still an open research area; and (3) to validate our geosimulation models, document our prototype and deliver a final version of the Mall_MAGS prototype to the managers of the *Square One* shopping mall in Toronto.

Acknowledgements

This research is supported by GEOIDE, the Canadian Network of Centers of Excellence in Geomatics. Many thanks to the Square One management who allowed our team to carry out the survey and use data. The development of the MAGS platform has been funded by the Defence (RDDC Valcartier). Many thanks to the MAGS team and especially, W. Chaker, J. Hogan, J. Perron and F. Belafkir for their work on various aspects of the MAGS platform.

References

1. Anu, M.: Introduction to modeling and simulation. Proceedings of the 29th Conference on Winter Simulation, December 07-10, Atlanta, Georgia (1997) 7-13.
2. Bandinin, S., Manzoni, S., Simone, C.: Heterogeneous agents situated in heterogeneous spaces. Applied Artificial Intelligence. 16 (9-10) (2002) 831-852.
3. Batty, M.: Agent-Based Pedestrian Modeling. CASA UCL Working papers series 61 (2003).
4. Bédard, Y., Rivest S., Proulx, M.J.: Spatial On-Line Analytical Processing (SOLAP): Concepts, Architectures and Solutions from a Geomatics Engineering Perspective. Book chapter in: Data Warehouses and OLAP: Concepts, Architectures and Solutions, Idea Group Publishing, In Press (2005).
5. Dijsktra, J., Harry, J-P., Bauke, U.: Virtual reality-based simulation of user behavior within the build environment to support the early stages of building design. In M. Schreckenberg and S.D. Sharma (ed.): *Pedestrian and Evacuation Dynamics*. Springer-Verlag, Berlin (2001) 173-181.
6. Frank, A.U., Bittner, S., Raubal, M.: Spatial and cognitive simulation with multi-agent systems, in D. Montello (edt.), *Spatial information Theory: Foundations for Geographic Information Science*, Springer Verlag, LNCS 2205 (2001) 124-139.
7. ISO/IEC.: 9241-14 Ergonomic requirements for office work with visual display terminals (VDT)s- Part 14 Menu dialogues, ISO/IEC 9241-14 (1998).
8. Koch, A.: Linking Multi-Agent Systems and GIS- Modeling and simulating spatial interactions-. Department of Geography RWTH Aachen. Angewandte Geographische Informationsverarbeitung XII, Beiträge zum AGIT-Symposium Salzburg 2000, Hrsg.: Strobl/Blaschke/Griesebner, Heidelberg (2001) 252-262.
9. Loyall, A.B.: *Believable Agents*, Ph.D. Thesis (Tech report CMU-CS-97-123), Carnegie Mellon University, Pittsburgh, Pennsylvania (1997).

10. Abraham, M.: *Motivation and Personality*, 2nd ed., Harper & Row, 1970.
11. Moulin, B., Chaker, W., Perron, J., Pelletier, P., Hogan, J.: MAGS Project: Multi-agent geosimulation and crowd simulation. In the proceedings of the COSIT'03 Conference, Ittingen (Switzerland), Kuhn, Worboys and Timpf (edts.), *Spatial Information Theory*, Springer Verlag LNCS 2825 (2003) 151-168.
12. Perron, J., Moulin, B.: Un modèle de mémoire dans un système multi-agent de géo-simulation. *Revue d'Intelligence Artificielle*, Hermes (2004).
13. Raubal, M.: Agent-Based Simulation of human wayfinding. A perceptual model for unfamiliar building. PhD thesis. Vienna University of Technology. Faculty of Sciences and Informatics (2001).
14. Rymill, S.J., and Dodgson, N.A.: A psychologically-based simulation of human behaviour. In Lever L., and McDerby M. (ed.): EG UK theory and Practice of Computer Graphics (2005).
15. Sung, M., Gleicher, M., Chenny, S.: Scalable behaviours for crowd simulation. Computer graphics Forum 23, 3 (2004).
16. Tambe, M., Jones, R.M., Laird, J.E., Rosenbloom, P.S., Schwamb, K.: Building believable agents for simulation environments: Extended abstract. In J. Bates (editor), *Working Notes of the AAAI Spring Symposium on BelievableAgents*. AAAI, Stanford, CA (1994) 82-85.
17. Ulicny, B., Thalmann, D.: Crowd Simulation for interactive virtual environments and VRtraining systems. Proceedings of Eurographics workshop on Animation and Simulation. Springer-Verlag (2001) 163-170.

A New Profile Alignment Method for Clustering Gene Expression Data

Ataul Bari[1] and Luis Rueda[2]

[1] School of Computer Science, University of Windsor
401 Sunset Avenue, Windsor, ON, N9B 3P4, Canada
bari1@uwindsor.ca
[2] Department of Computer Science, University of Concepción
Edmundo Larenas 215, Concepción, Chile
lrueda@inf.udec.cl

Abstract. We focus on clustering gene expression temporal profiles, and propose a novel, simple algorithm that is powerful enough to find an efficient distribution of genes over clusters. We also introduce a variant of a clustering index that can effectively decide upon the optimal number of clusters for a given dataset. The clustering method is based on a profile-alignment approach, which minimizes the mean-square-error of the first order differentials, to hierarchically cluster microarray time-series data. The effectiveness of our algorithm has been tested on datasets drawn from standard experiments, showing that our approach can effectively cluster the datasets based on profile similarity.

1 Introduction

Grouping (or clustering) genes based on the similarity of their temporal profiles is important to researchers as genes with similar expression profiles are expected to be functionally related or co-regulated [3][4][6]. Many unsupervised methods for gene clustering based on similarity (or dissimilarity) of their microarray temporal profiles have been proposed in the past few years [1][6][12]. These methods have used different kinds of distance measures to group genes based on similarity (or dissimilarity) among the microarray time-series profiles. The most commonly used distance measures are the Euclidean distance, the Mahalanobis distance, the Manhattan distance and its generalization, the Minkowski distance [5]. One of the methods for clustering microarray time-series data is based on a hidden phase model (similar to a hidden Markov model) to define the parameters of a mixture of normal distributions in a Bayesian-like manner, which are estimated by using the expectation maximization algorithm [2]. This model has been recently introduced and, to the best of our knowledge, has only been tested on synthetic data. On the other hand, some authors have proposed linear-correlation methods for clustering genes using microarray time-series data [3][7]. The method proposed in [3] requires computing the mean expression levels of some candidate

L. Lamontagne and M. Marchand (Eds.): Canadian AI 2006, LNAI 4013, pp. 86–97, 2006.
© Springer-Verlag Berlin Heidelberg 2006

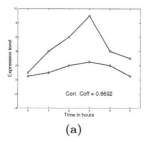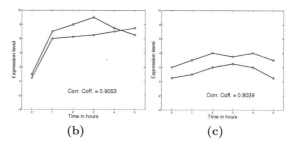

(a)   (b)   (c)

Fig. 1. (a) Two genes that are likely to be clustered as in [10]. (b) Two genes with different profiles that are likely to be clustered together by linear-correlation methods. (c) Two genes with similar profiles in terms of level of expression ratio changes between different time points.

profiles using some pre-identified, arbitrarily selected profiles. The authors of [7] proposed a method for clustering microarray time-series data employing a jack-knife correlation coefficient with or without using the seeded candidate profiles. Clustering using the correlation distance may not always group genes that are closer in terms of their temporal profiles. For example, as shown in Fig. 1, using the correlation distance, genes in Fig. 1(b) are most likely to be clustered together (as it has the largest value for the correlation coefficient among all three, which is 0.9053), but if the prime interest is to cluster genes according to the variation of their expression level at different time points, then, genes from Fig. 1(c) would be better candidates to be clustered together than the genes in Fig. 1(a) and (b). However, the value of the correlation coefficient between the pairs of genes in Fig. 1(c) is the minimum (0.8039) among all three pairs of genes shown in Fig. 1.

In [10], the authors proposed a method to select and cluster genes using the ideas of order-restricted inference, where estimation makes use of known inequalities among parameters. Although their method does not require arbitrarily selected genes to specify candidate profiles, it is necessary to specify the candidate profiles *a priori*. Also, as shown in Fig. 1 (a) and (c), by following this procedure, genes from Fig. 1(a) are more likely to be clustered together as they show similar profiles in terms of direction of the changes of expression ratios (e.g. up-up-up-down-down), even though, for one gene, the expression ratio increases sharply between the first three time points and decreases sharply between time points 3 and 4, whereas such increments/decrements are much softer for the second gene. However, in reality, it may be more desirable to cluster genes of Fig. 1(c) in the same group as they differ only a little amount of increase/decrease between the time points 2 and 3 and the time points 3 and 4.

In this paper, we propose a mean-square-error profile alignment approach to cluster temporal gene expression data. We propose to use a profile-alignment algorithm, which minimizes the mean-square-error of the first order differentials, to hierarchically cluster microarray time-series data. The alignment algorithm is also used to define a variant of a well-known clustering validity index that optimizes the number of clusters.

2   Minimum-Square-Error Profile Alignment

Consider a dataset $\mathcal{D} = \{x_1, x_2, ..., x_n\}$, where $x_i = [x_{i_1}, x_{i_2}, ..., x_{i_m}]^t$ is an m-dimensional feature vector that represents the expression level of gene i at m different time points. The aim is to partition $\mathcal{D}$ into k disjoint subsets $\mathcal{D}_1, \mathcal{D}_2, ..., \mathcal{D}_k$, where $\mathcal{D} = \mathcal{D}_1 \cup \mathcal{D}_2 \cup ... \cup \mathcal{D}_k$, and $\mathcal{D}_i \cap \mathcal{D}_j = \emptyset$, for $\forall i, j, i \neq j$, in such a way that a similarity (dissimilarity) cost function $\phi : \{0,1\}^{n \times k} \to \Re$ is maximized (minimized). We propose an efficient algorithm that takes two features vectors, and produces two new vectors in such a way that the mean-square-error difference between "aligned" vectors is minimized. Let $x_1, x_2 \in \mathcal{D}$ be two feature vectors. The aim is to find two new vectors x_1 and $x_2' = x_2 - a$ (e.g. to find a scalar a) such that, $f(a) = \|x_2 - a - x_1\|^2$ is minimized. The value of a that minimizes $f(a)$ is given by $a = \frac{1}{m} \sum_{i=1}^{m}(x_{2_i} - x_{1_i})$ (see [11]). Using the latter expression to obtain the value of a, i.e. the scalar that minimizes $f(a)$, we align two vectors by following the procedure given in Algorithm *Profile-Alignment*. The algorithm takes two feature vectors from the *original* space as input (which are two temporal gene expression data in this case) and outputs two feature vectors in the *transformed* space after aligning them in such a way that the mean-square-error is minimized.

Using the *Profile-Alignment* algorithm and a conventional distance function, we define a new distance function, namely $d_{MSE}(x_1, x_2)$, which aligns x_1 and x_2, and invokes a conventional metric [11]. In [11], it has been shown that the *Profile-Alignment* algorithm used in conjunction with any metric d is also a metric. Let $d : \Re^d \times \Re^d \to \Re$ be a metric and let $d_{MSE}(x_1, x_2)$ be the result of *Profile-Alignment* and d, with input (x_1, x_2), then:

1. $d_{MSE}(x_1, x_2) \geqslant 0$
2. $d_{MSE}(x_1, x_2) = d_{MSE}(x_2, x_1)$
3. $d_{MSE}(x_1, x_3) \leqslant d_{MSE}(x_1, x_2) + d_{MSE}(x_2, x_3)$

Note that once the *Profile-Alignment* algorithm is applied, any metric d can be used. In our experiments, we have used the Euclidean distance.

An example of temporal profile alignment for two genes (those of the example shown in Fig. 1) is given in Fig. 2, which shows the same gene profiles from Fig. 1 after aligning them using the *Profile-Alignment* algorithm. A simple visual

---

Algorithm 1. *Profile-Alignment*

Input: Two vectors, $x_1 = [x_{1_1}, x_{1_2}, ..., x_{1_m}]$ and $x_2 = [x_{2_1}, x_{2_2}, ..., x_{2_m}]$.
Output: Two vectors y_1 and y_2 such that the mean-square error is minimized.
begin

$\quad y_1 \longleftarrow x_1 - x_{1_1}$
$\quad a \longleftarrow \frac{1}{m} \sum_{i=1}^{m}(x_{2_i} - y_{1_i})$.
$\quad y_2 \longleftarrow x_2 - a$

end
return y_1, y_2

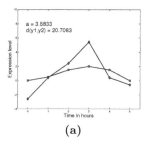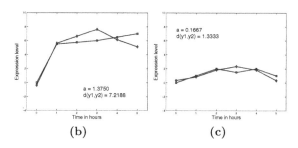

(a)   (b)   (c)

Fig. 2. (a) Result after aligning the two genes from Fig.1(a). (b) Result after aligning two genes from Fig.1(b). (c) Result after aligning two genes from Fig.1(c). As expected, the distances after applying the profile-alignment algorithm to the genes of Fig. (a) and (b) are larger than that of Fig.(c).

inspection shows that the genes in Fig. 2(c) are closer to each other compared to the genes from the other two figures, Fig. 2(a) and (b). Therefore their distance after alignment will be smaller compared to the distance of the other pair of genes, and hence, these two genes are more likely to be grouped together, as we will presently observe.

3   Hierarchical Agglomerative Clustering

In our clustering model, we have used *complete linkage* hierarchical clustering [4] with the profile alignment and a conventional distance, as discussed in Section 2. The generalized algorithm for *hierarchical agglomerative clustering* was slightly modified to obtain the desired number of clusters and is given in Algorithm 2. The algorithm receives two parameters as input, a complete microarray temporal dataset, $\mathcal{D}$, and the desired number of clusters, k, and returns the dataset after partitioning it into k clusters. The decision rule is based on the *furthest-neighbor* distance between two clusters [4], which is computed using $d_{MSE}(\boldsymbol{x_1}, \boldsymbol{x_2})$. The latter involves the alignment of each pair of profiles before applying a conventional (the Euclidean in our case) distance function.

4   Optimizing the Number of Clusters

Finding the optimal number of clusters is a well known open problem in clustering. For this, it is desirable to validate the number of clusters that is the best for a given dataset using a validity index. For the validity purpose of our clustering, we have used a variant of the $\mathcal{I}$-index [9]. Although this index has been found to work well in many cases, we have encountered that it is not appropriate for the time-series microarray data clustering due to a few reasons [11].

One of them is that, if finding differentially expressed genes is important, which, in many cases, are better to form clusters containing only one or two genes. Since this is penalized by the $\mathcal{I}$-index (also in the case of other indices found in the literature [9]), we propose the following variant of the $\mathcal{I}$-index:

Algorithm 2. *Agglomerative-Clustering*

Input: The complete dataset, $\mathcal{D} = \{x_1, x_2, ..., x_n\}$, and k, the desired number of
clusters.

Output: k disjoint subsets $\mathcal{D}_1, \mathcal{D}_2, ..., \mathcal{D}_k$.

begin

    Create n clusters, $\mathcal{D}_1, \mathcal{D}_2, ..., \mathcal{D}_n$, where $\mathcal{D}_i = \{x_i\}$

    $\mathcal{D}_{currentClustersSet} \longleftarrow \{\mathcal{D}_1, \mathcal{D}_2, ..., \mathcal{D}_n\}$

    for $q \longleftarrow n$ **down to** k **do**

        Find two clusters $\mathcal{D}_i, \mathcal{D}_j \in \mathcal{D}_{currentClustersSet}$, where, $i \neq j$, such that the
furthest-neighbor distance between $\mathcal{D}_i$ and $\mathcal{D}_j$ is the minimum among all such
distances, $d_{MSE}(.,.)$, between all pair of clusters.

        $\mathcal{D}_{mergedClusters} \longleftarrow \{\mathcal{D}_i \cup \mathcal{D}_j\}$

        $\mathcal{D}_{currentClustersSet} \longleftarrow \{\mathcal{D}_{currentClustersSet} \cup \mathcal{D}_{mergedClusters}\} - \{\mathcal{D}_i, \mathcal{D}_j\}$

    end

end

return $\mathcal{D}_{currentClustersSet}$

$$\mathcal{I}_{MSE}(k) = \left(\frac{1}{k}\right)^q \times \left(\frac{E_1}{E_k} \times D_k\right)^p, \tag{1}$$

where, $E_k = \sum_{i=1}^{k} \sum_{j=1}^{n} u_{ij} \|x_j - \mu_i\|$, $D_k = max_{i,j=1}^{k} \|\mu_i - \mu_j\|$, n is the total
number of samples in the dataset, $\{u_{ij}\}_{k \times n}$ is the partition (or membership)
matrix for the data, μ_i is the center of cluster $\mathcal{D}_i$, and k is the number of clusters.
The partition matrix $\{u_{ij}\}$ is defined as a membership function such that $u_{ij} = 1$, if x_j belongs to cluster $\mathcal{D}_i$, and zero otherwise. The best number of clusters is
the value of k that maximizes $\mathcal{I}_{MSE}(k)$. Note, however, that the implementation
of index $\mathcal{I}_{MSE}(k)$ is not straightforward. It includes the mean and scatter for
each cluster, and we meant these two to include the profile alignment concept
that we have introduced. For the mean, we use algorithm *Cluster-Mean*, given
in Algorithm 3, and once the *Cluster-Mean* is defined, we use it to compute the
scatter of a cluster. For this, we introduce the algorithm *Within-Cluster-Scatter*,
given in Algorithm 4.

Algorithm 3. *Cluster-Mean*

Input: A cluster $\mathcal{D}_i$ with n_i samples $\mathcal{D}_i = [x_{i_1}, x_{i_2}, ..., x_{i_{n_i}}]$.

Output: The mean of cluster $\mathcal{D}_i$, μ_i.

begin

    $\mu_i \longleftarrow x_{i_1}$

    for $j \longleftarrow 2$ **to** n_i **do**

        $[y_1, y_2] \longleftarrow d_{MSE}(\mu_i, x_{i_j})$

        $\mu_i \longleftarrow \frac{1}{2}(y_1 + y_2)$

    end

end

return μ_i

Algorithm 4. *Within-Cluster-Scatter*

Input: A cluster $\mathcal{D}_i$ with n_i samples, $\mathcal{D}_i = [\boldsymbol{x}_{i_1}, \boldsymbol{x}_{i_2}, \ldots, \boldsymbol{x}_{i_{n_i}}]$, and its mean, $\boldsymbol{\mu}_i$.
Output: The sum of the distances of each gene from the cluster mean, E_i.
begin
 $E_i \longleftarrow \mathbf{0}$
 for $j \longleftarrow 1$ **to** n_i **do**
  $E_i \longleftarrow E_i + d_{MSE}(\boldsymbol{\mu}_i, \boldsymbol{x}_{i_j})$
 end
end
return E_i

---

5 Experimental Results

We have tested the performance of our clustering method that consists of mean-square-error profile-alignment and hierarchical clustering (MSEHC) on a real-life dataset obtained from the experimental data [8], on the transcriptional response of cell cycle-synchronized human fibroblasts to serum. These experiments have measured the expression levels of 8,613 human genes after a serum stimulation at twelve different time points, at 0 hr. 15 min. 30 min. 1 hr. 2 hrs. 3 hrs. 4 hrs. 8 hrs. 16 hrs. 20 hrs. and 24 hrs. From these 8,613 gene profiles, 517 profiles were separately analyzed, as their expression ratio has changed substantially at two or more time points. Our experiments and analysis have focused on this dataset[1].

First, we applied our method to 260 gene profiles, arbitrarily selected from the dataset of 517 gene profiles. It is well known that, in general, the best number of clusters for any real-life detaset is usually less than or equal to $\sqrt{n}$, where n is the number of samples in the dataset [9]. However, we encountered that some useful clusters contain one or two differentially expressed genes. Thus, we considered a range for potential numbers of clusters, which includes values of k that lie between $\left\lceil \sqrt{\frac{1}{2}n} \right\rceil$ and $\left\lfloor \sqrt{\frac{3}{2}n} \right\rfloor$. We have, thus, run our algorithm on this experimental dataset for $k = 12$ to 20. The values of the $\mathcal{I}_{MSE}$-index were computed for each of these values of k, and for each k, the $\mathcal{I}_{MSE}$-index was computed using values of q from 0.3 to 1.0 (a table with all values of $\mathcal{I}_{MSE}$-index can be found in [11]). We have picked $q = 0.6$ for which the value of the index reaches to a maximum level when $k = 13$. Therefore, we have taken the value of $k = 13$ as the optimal number of clusters and plotted the profiles, as clustered using the MSEHC method. The plots are shown in Fig. 3. The x-axis in each plot represents the time in hours and the y-axis represents the expression ratio. Each plot represents a cluster. To compare our results with another method, we have clustered these 260 gene temporal profiles into 13 clusters, using the correlation distance and the same hierarchical agglomerative clustering method, applied to the original data, resulting in the 13 clusters (Fig. 4). Visual inspection

---

[1] Expression data for this subset were obtained from the website: http://genome-www.stanford.edu/serum/

of the figures reveal that genes placed in the same cluster in Fig. 3 contain closer
temporal profiles as compared to those of Fig. 4. For example, cluster 5 in Fig. 3
(indicated by $i = 5$) shows the temporal profiles for three genes IDs 488488,
359769 and 470008 belong to cluster 5, obtained using the MSEHC method.
Visual inspection justifies the clustering of these genes in a single group, as the
profiles are closely aligned all the way. Clustering using the correlation distance
also placed them into a single cluster (Fig. 4, $i = 5$), but along with some other
genes. The difference in the level and rate of expression ratio changes between
these genes and the rest of the genes in the cluster is apparent from the figure.
Also, gene ID 320355 was placed alone in cluster 1 by the MSEHC method
(Fig. 3, $i = 1$), whereas this gene was placed in cluster 4 by the correlation
method. Compared to the other profiles placed in cluster 4 (Fig. 4, $i = 4$), it
is obvious that the gene has a completely different temporal profile. Therefore,
we argue that this gene is better to be left alone in a single cluster, which is
clearly done by the MSEHC method. Also, the correlation method has produced
two clusters containing a single gene each, (IDs 112179 and 40630 in Fig. 4,
$i = 1$ and 2, respectively). These genes were placed in cluster 13 by MSEHC
(Fig. 3, $i = 13$). But it is visually clear that these genes are closely aligned to
the other genes placed in cluster 13 as they are not easily distinguishable within
the cluster.

Then, we have applied our method to the complete dataset (all 517 gene
profiles). This time, we have computed the values of the $\mathcal{I}_{MSE}$-index for $k = 16$

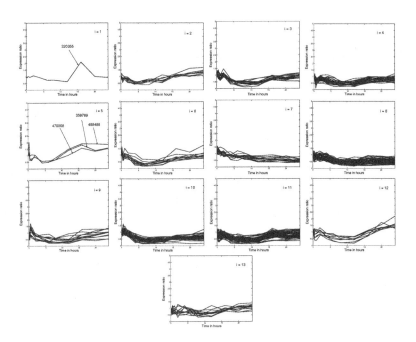

Fig. 3. Different clusters obtained using the MSEHC on the 260 gene temporal expression profiles, where $k = 13$

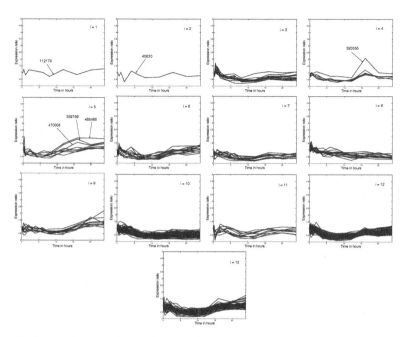

Fig. 4. Different clusters obtained using the correlation distance on the 260 gene temporal expression profiles, where $k = 13$

Table 1. Values of the $\mathcal{I}_{MSE}$ index for 517 genes, where $k = 16$ to 27 and $q = 0.3$ to 1.0

k	$q=0.3$	$q=0.4$	$q=0.5$	$q=0.6$	$q=0.7$	$q=0.8$	$q=0.9$	$q=1.0$
16	17344.58	13144.73	9961.84	7549.67	5721.58	4336.14	3286.18	2490.46
17	18791.87	14155.50	10663.02	8032.21	6050.49	4557.70	3433.21	2586.16
18	18685.75	13995.33	10482.28	7851.07	5880.32	4404.27	3298.73	2470.70
19	27333.00	20361.60	15168.29	11299.55	8417.55	6270.62	4671.27	3479.84
20	27169.35	20136.14	14923.59	11060.39	8197.23	6075.25	4502.58	3337.02
21	29057.98	21431.06	15805.99	11657.35	8597.61	6340.97	4676.64	3449.15
22	29577.07	21712.65	15939.35	11701.14	8589.86	6305.85	4629.15	3398.28
23	29554.55	21599.89	15786.24	11537.35	8432.05	6162.55	4503.89	3291.66
24	29493.69	21463.87	15620.21	11367.52	8272.65	6020.38	4381.29	3188.46
25	29981.57	21730.04	15749.49	11414.91	8273.29	5996.32	4346.01	3149.90
26	30081.89	21717.39	15678.71	11319.13	8171.76	5899.54	4259.13	3074.85
27	29959.90	21547.85	15497.71	11146.31	8016.69	5765.79	4146.89	2982.54

to 27, while keeping the range of values for q the same (from 0.3 to 1.0). These values for the $\mathcal{I}_{MSE}$-index for the corresponding values of k and q are shown in Table 1. Each row in the table corresponds to each value of k, each column corresponds to a value of q, and each cell shows the value of the index for the corresponding values of k and q. For $q = 0.6$, we found that the value of the index

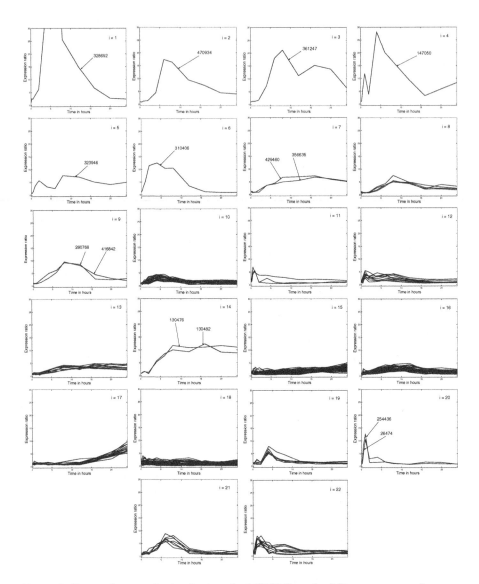

Fig. 5. Different clusters obtained using the MSEHC on the 517 gene temporal expression profiles, where $k = 22$

reaches to a maximum level when $k = 22$, and decreases when $k > 22$ or $k < 22$. Therefore, we have taken the value of $k = 22$ as the optimal number of clusters and plotted the profiles, as clustered using the MSEHC method corresponding to $k = 22$. The plots are shown in Fig. 5. Then, similar to the first experiments, we have clustered the complete dataset into 22 clusters using the correlation distance and the same hierarchical agglomerative clustering method, applied to the original data, resulting in 22 clusters as shown in Fig. 6.

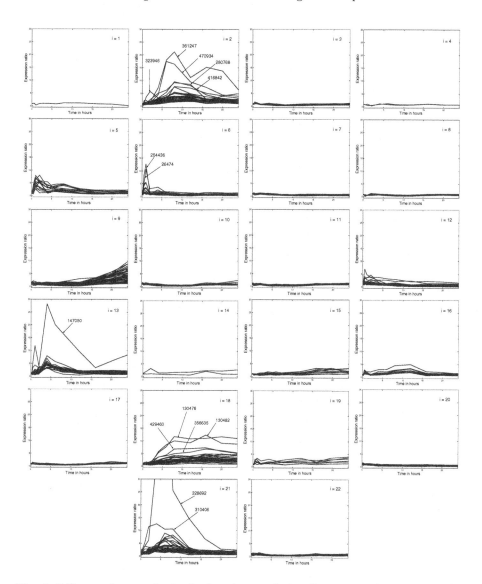

Fig. 6. Different clusters obtained using the correlation distance on the 517 gene temporal expression profiles, where $k = 22$

The comparison among the plots from Figs. 5 and 6, again, reveal the effectiveness of the MSEHC method. For example, the MSEHC method left clusters 1 to 6 containing a single gene each (IDs 328692, 470934, 361247, 147050, 323946 and 310406, respectively in Fig. 5). The correlation method, however, placed these genes in clusters 21, 2, 2, 13, 2 and 21, respectively (Fig. 6). Again, by visual inspection of all the temporal expression profiles, we noticed that these genes are *differentially expressed* and should be left alone in separate clusters, which is clearly done by the MSEHC method. Also, as shown in Fig. 5, the MSEHC method produced four clusters containing only two profiles each, clusters 7 (IDs 356635 and 429460), 9 (IDs 280768 and 416842), 14 (IDs 130476 and 130482) and 20 (IDs 26474 and 254436). The correlation method clustered these genes as follows: 356635 and 429460 in cluster 18, 280768 and 416842 in cluster 2, 130476 and 130482 in cluster 18, and 26474 and 254436 in cluster 6 (Figs. 5 and 6). Although the correlation method placed each pair of genes in the same cluster, it also placed some other genes with them. By looking at the plots of the profiles of the clusters produced by the correlation method (Fig. 6) and comparing them to the plots of the clusters of the corresponding genes produced by the MSEHC method (Fig. 5), it is clear that these pairs of genes are differentially expressed. Therefore, the gene profiles placed in the same cluster by the MSEHC method are more similar than those of the correlation method.

6   Conclusions

We have proposed a novel method to cluster gene expression temporal profile microarray data. On a sample and a complete real-life dataset, we have demonstrated that using hierarchical clustering with our method for similarity measure produces superior results when compared to that of the linear correlation similarity measure. We have introduced a variant of the $\mathcal{I}$-index that can make a trade-off between minimizing the number of useful clusters and keeping the distinctness of individual clusters.

The MSEHC method can be used for effective clustering of gene expression temporal profile microarray data. Although we have shown the effectiveness of the method in microarray time-series datasets, we are planning to investigate the effectiveness of the method as well in dose-response microarray datasets, and other time-series microarray data.

Acknowledgments. This research has been supported by the Natural Sciences and Engineering Research Council of Canada, the Canadian Foundation for Innovation, the Ontario Innovation Trust, and the Chilean National Council for Technological and Scientific Research, FONDECYT grant No. 1060904.

References

1. A. Brazma and J. Vilo. Gene expression data analysis. *FEBS Lett.*, 480:17–24, 2000.
2. L. Bréhélin. Clustering Gene Expression Series with Prior Knowledge. In *Lecture Notes in Computer Science*, volume 3692, pages 27–38, October 2005.
3. S. Chu, J. DeRisi, M. Eisen, J. Mulholland, D. Botstein, P. Brown, and I. Herskowitz. The transcriptional program of sporulation in budding yeast. *Science*, 282:699–705, 1998.
4. S. Drăghici. *Data Analysis Tools for DNA Microarrays*. Chapman & Hall, 2003.
5. R. Duda, P. Hart, and D. Stork. *Pattern Classification*. John Wiley and Sons, Inc., New York, NY, 2nd edition, 2000.

6. M. Eisen, P. Spellman, P. Brown, and D. Botstein. Cluster analysis and display of genome-wide expression patterns. In *Proc. Natl Acad. Sci.*, volume 95, pages 14863–14868, USA, 1998.

7. L. Heyer, S. Kruglyak, and S. Yooseph. Exploring expression data: identification and analysis of coexpressed genes. *Genome Res.*, 9:1106–1115, 1999.

8. V. Iyer, M. Eisen, D. Ross, G. Schuler, T. Moore, J. Lee, J. Trent, L. Staudt, Jr. J. Hudson, and M. Boguski. The transcriptional program in the response of human fibroblasts to serum. *Science*, 283:83–87, 1999.

9. U. Maulik and S. Bandyopadhyay. Performance Evaluation of Some Clustering Algorithms and Validity Indices. *IEEE Transactions on Pattern Analysis and Machine Intelligence*, 24(12):1650–1654, 2002.

10. S. Peddada, E. Lobenhofer, L. Li, C. Afshari, C. Weinberg, and D. Umbach. Gene selection and clustering for time-course and dose-response microarray experiments using order-restricted inference. *Bioinformatics*, 19(7):834–841, 2003.

11. L. Rueda and A. Bari. Clustering Microarray Time-Series Data Using a Mean-Square-Error Profile Alignment Algorithm. *Submitted for publication.* Electronically available at http://www.inf.udec.cl/~lrueda/papers/ProfileMSE-Jnl.pdf.

12. G. Sherlock. Analysis of large-scale gene expression data. *Curr. Opin. Immunol.*, 12:201–205, 2000.

A Classification-Based Glioma Diffusion Model Using MRI Data

Marianne Morris, Russell Greiner, Jörg Sander,
Albert Murtha[1], and Mark Schmidt

Department of Computing Science, University of Alberta,
Edmonton, AB, T6G 2E8, Canada
{marianne, greiner, joerg, schmidt}@cs.ualberta.ca
[1] Department of Radiation Oncology, Cross Cancer Institute,
11560 - University Ave, Edmonton, AB, T6G 1Z2, Canada

Abstract. Gliomas are diffuse, invasive brain tumors. We propose a
3D classification-based diffusion model, CDM, that predicts how a glioma
will grow at a voxel-level, on the basis of features specific to the patient,
properties of the tumor, and attributes of that voxel. We use Supervised
Learning algorithms to learn this general model, by observing the growth
patterns of gliomas from other patients. Our empirical results on clinical
data demonstrate that our learned CDM model can, in most cases, predict
glioma growth more effectively than two standard models: uniform radial
growth across all tissue types, and another that assumes faster diffusion
in white matter.

1 Introduction

Primary brain tumors originate from a single glial cell in the nervous system,
and grow by invading adjacent cells, often leading to a life-threatening condition. Proper treatment requires knowing both where the tumor mass is, and
also where the occult cancer cells have infiltrated in nearby healthy tissue. Some
conventional treatments implicitly assume the tumor will grow radially in all
directions — *e.g.*, the standard practice in conformal radiotherapy involves ir-
radiating a volume that includes both the observed tumor, and a uniform 2cm
margin around this border [6, 7]. Swanson's model [16] claims the tumor growth
rate is 5 times faster in white matter, versus grey matter. Our empirical evidence,
however, shows that neither model is particularly accurate.

We present an alternative approach to modeling tumor growth: use data from
a set of patients to *learn* the parameters of a diffusion model. In particular,
given properties of the patient, tumor and each voxel (based on MRI scans; see
Fig. 1[a–g]) at one time, our CDM system predicts the tumor region at a later time
(Fig. 1[h]). This model can help define specific treatment boundaries that would
replace the uniform, conventional 2cm margin. It can also help find regions where
radiologically occult cancer cells concentrate but do not sufficiently enhance on
the MRI scan. Therefore, the model can help define the appropriate radiation
doses to deliver to the relevant regions adjacent to the visible tumor.

L. Lamontagne and M. Marchand (Eds.): Canadian AI 2006, LNAI 4013, pp. 98–109, 2006.
© Springer-Verlag Berlin Heidelberg 2006

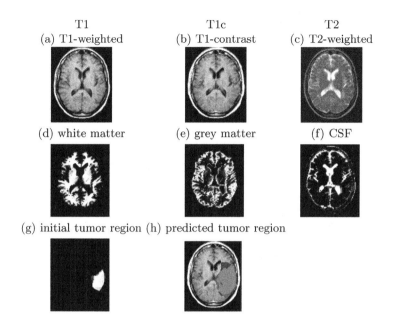

Fig. 1. Axial slices of brain tumor patient: (a) T1-weighted scan; (b) T1-weighted scan using gladolinium contrast; (c) T2-weighted scan; (d) white matter; (e) grey matter; (f) CSF — cerebrospinal fluid; (g) segmented patient tumor; (h) predicted patient tumor, after adding $30,000$ voxels in 3D, overlaid on T1c (light grey represents the true positives, dark grey the false positives and black the false negatives)

Section 2 reviews standard glioma diffusion models, and Section 3 formally defines the diffusion models we are considering. Finally, Section 4 describes our experiments testing CDM, comparing it with two other models: naïve uniform growth and tissue-based diffusion. Additional details are in [1, 12].

2   Related Work

In recent decades, glioma growth modeling has offered important contributions to cancer research, shedding light on tumor growth behaviour and helping improve treatment methods. In this section, we describe two types of tumor modeling: volumetric at the macroscopic level, and models based on white matter invasion.

2.1   Macroscopic and Volumetric Modeling

Mathematical modeling of gliomas at the macroscopic level has represented the traditional framework in predicting glioma diffusion, using growth and proliferation parameters. We review three of these models:

Kansal *et al.* [9] simulate the *gompertzian growth*, which views the tumor as a population of cells and the growth as a dynamic process where proliferating and inactive classes of cells interact. Kansal *et al.* use cellular automata to model the different states of tumor cells, from dividing cells at the periphery, to non-proliferating, and finally to the necrotic state at the centre of the tumor. This model is designed to predict the growth of glioblastoma multiforme (GBM), the most aggressive, grade IV gliomas. The model does not account for various tumor grades, brain anatomy, nor the infiltrating action of cancer cells in tissue near the tumor.

Tabatabai et al. [19] simulate asymmetric growth as in real tumors and accommodate the concept of increasing versus decreasing tumor radii (due to treatment effects), but do not account for various clinical factors involved in malignant diffusion. Instead, their model describes tumors as self-limited systems, not incorporating the interactions between healthy and cancer cells at the tumor border and the competition of cells inside the tumor. This is not a realistic representation of clinical cancer diffusion.

Zizzari's model [21] describes the proliferation of GBMs using tensor product splines and differential equations, the solutions of which give the distribution of tumor cells with respect to their spatio-temporal coordinates. Zizzari extends his growth model to introduce a treatment planning tool that incorporates a supervised learning task. However, his growth predictions are based only on geometric issues, and do not consider biological factors nor patient information.

2.2   Glioma Modeling Based on White Matter Invasion

The trend in glioma research is to study biological and clinical factors involved in cancer diffusion through healthy tissue. Recent models provide a more promising direction, which can also help provide more effective treatment. In this section, we review models that incorporate the heterogeneity of brain tissue and histology of cancer cells.

Swanson et al. [16] develop a model based on the differential motility of glioma cells in white versus grey matter, suggesting that the diffusion coefficient in white matter is 5 times that in grey matter. This model was extended to simulate virtual gliomas [18] and to assess the effectiveness of chemotherapy delivered to different tissue types in the brain [17]. This modeling is different from our CDM system as we do not a priori assume the cancer diffusion rates in different tissue types, but rather our system can learn glioma diffusion behaviour from clinical data.

Price et al. [14] use T2-weighted scans and Diffusion Tensor Imaging (DTI) to determine whether DTI can identify abnormalities on T2 scans. Regions of interest particularly include white matter adjacent to the tumor, and areas of abnormality on DTI that appeared normal on T2 images. Results demonstrated further glioma invasion of white matter tracts near the observed tumor.

Clatz et al. [3] propose a model that simulates the growth of GBM based on an anatomical atlas that includes white fibre diffusion tensor information. The model is initialized with a tumor detected on the MRI scan of a patient, and results are evaluated against the tumor observed six months later. However, model results are reported for only one patient, leaving in question how it performs on a variety of patients, and with various tumor types.

2.3   Discussion

Each of the glioma diffusion models presented above describes the geometrical growth of gliomas as evolving objects. Few of these models use the biological complexity of cancerous tumors, the heterogeneity of the human brain anatomy, or the clinical factors of malignant invasion. Moreover, none of these earlier systems attempts to *learn* general growth patterns from existing data, nor are they capable of predicting growth of various tumor grades (as opposed to methods specifically designed to predict GBM growth only).

The literature does suggest that the following factors should help us predict how the tumor will spread — *i.e.*, whether the tumor is likely to infiltrate to a new voxel:

- *Anatomical features of the brain*: regions that represent pathways versus brain structures that act as a boundary to the spreading action of the malignant cells.
- *Properties of the tumor*: the grade of the tumor (as high-grade gliomas grow much faster than low-grade ones); the location of the tumor within the brain (as the shape of the tumor depends on surrounding anatomical structures).
- *Properties of the voxels* (at the periphery of the tumor where there can be interaction between malignant and normal cells): its tissue type — grey versus white matter; whether it currently contains edema[1].

We incorporate these diffusion factors as learning features into our 'general' diffusion model, CDM. The remainder of this paper describes the diffusion models we implemented, presents the experiments, and evaluates the performance of the three models given our dataset of MRI scans.

3   Diffusion Models

In general, a diffusion model (Fig. 2) takes as input an image whose voxels are each labeled with: the current "voxel label", VL, which is "1" if that voxel is *currently* a tumor and "0" otherwise (see Fig. 1[g])[2] as well as general information $\mathbf{e} = \mathbf{e}_{Patient} \cup \mathbf{e}_{Tumor} \cup \{\mathbf{e}_i\}_i$ about the patient $\mathbf{e}_{Patient}$, the tumor $\mathbf{e}_{Tumor}$ and the individual voxels $\mathbf{e}_i$ (see Section 3.1). The third input is an integer s that tells the diffusion model how many additional voxels to include. See line 1 of Fig. 2. The output is the prediction of the next s additional voxels that will be incorporated into the tumor, represented as a bit-map over the image. For example, if the tumor is currently 1000 voxels and the doctor needs to know where the tumor will be, when it is 20% larger — *i.e.*, when it is 1200 voxels — he would set $s = 200$.

---

[1] Swelling due to accumulation of excess fluid.

[2] Here, expert radiologists have manually delineated the "enhancing regions" of tumors based on their MRI scans. Note this does not include edema, nor any other labels. We then spatially interpolate each patient image to fill inter-slice gaps and to obtain voxels of size 8mm^3.

1. Diffusion(VoxelLabel: VL; GeneralInfo: e; int: s)
    % VL[i, j, k]=1 if position $\langle i, j, k \rangle$ is a tumor
    % Initially VL corresponds to current tumor
    % When algorithm terminates, VL will correspond to tumor containing "s" additional voxels
2.   total_count := 0
3.   Do forever:
4.   Compute $N := \left\{ \langle x, y, z \rangle \; \middle| \; VL[x, y, z] = 0 \;\&\; \begin{pmatrix} VL[x+1, y, z] &=& 1 & \vee \\ VL[x-1, y, z] &=& 1 & \vee \\ &\vdots& \\ VL[x, y, z-1] &=& 1 \end{pmatrix} \right\}$
5.   For each location $v_i \in N$
6.   *Determine if v_i becomes a tumor*
7.   If so,
8.   Set VL[v_i] := 1
9.   total_count++;
10.   If (total_count == s), return

Fig. 2. Generic Diffusion Model

A diffusion model first identifies the set of voxels N just outside the border of the initial tumor; see line 4 of Fig. 2. In the following diagram

(1)

(where each **X** cell is currently a tumor), N would consist of the voxels labeled v1 through v5, but not v6 nor v7 (as we are not considering diagonal neighbors). In the 3D case, each voxel will have 6 neighbors.

The diffusion model then iterates through these candidate voxels, $v_i \in N$. If it decides that one has become a tumor, it then updates VL (which implicitly updates the tumor/healthy border) and increments the total number of "transformed voxels"; see lines $5-9$ of Fig. 2. After processing all of these neighbors (in parallel), it will then continue transforming the neighbors of this newly enlarged boundary. If a voxel is not transformed on one iteration, it remains eligible to be transformed on the next iteration. When the number of transformed voxels matches the total s, the algorithm terminates, returning the updated VL assignment (Fig. 2, line 10).

The various diffusion models differ only in how they determine if v_i has become tumor — line 6 of Fig. 2. The *uniform growth* model, UG, simply includes every "legal" voxel it finds (where a voxel is legal if it is part of the brain, as opposed to skull, eye, etc.). The *tissue-based* model, GW, assumes the growth rate for white matter is 5 times faster than for grey matter [16], and 10 times faster than other brain tissue. Here, whenever a neighboring voxel v_i is white matter, it is immediately included. If v_i is grey matter (other tissue), its count is incremented by 0.2 (resp., 0.1). GW does not allow diffusion into the skull. This is easy to determine as the e_i part of the GeneralInfo e specifies the tissue type of each v_i voxel, as computed by SPM [5] (see Fig. 1[d–f]).

3.1   CDM **Diffusion Model**

Our CDM model is more sophisticated. First, its decision about each voxel depends on a number of features, based on:

the patient, $e_{Patient}$: the age (which may implicitly indicate the tumor grade).
the tumor, e_{Tumor}: volume-area ratio, edema percentage, and volume increase.
each individual voxel $\{e_i\}_i$: various attributes for every voxel v_i — spatial coordinates, distance-area ratio, minimum euclidean distance from the tumor border, whether the voxel is currently in an edema region, white matter, grey matter, or CSF (automatically determined by SPM [5]), and image intensities of T1, T1-contrast and T2 axial scans [2] (obtained both from the patient's scan and a standard template[3] [8] — after normalization and registration using SPM [4]).
neighborhood of each voxel $\{e_i\}_i$: attributes of each of the 6 neighbors of the voxel — whether a neighbor voxel n_j is edema, white matter, grey matter, or CSF, and image intensities from the template's T2 and T1-contrast.

(The webpage [1] provides more details about each of these features, as well as some explicit examples.)

CDM then uses a probabilistic classifier to compute the probability q_i that one tumor neighbor v_i of a tumor voxel will become tumorous, $q_i = P_\Theta(\ell(v_i) = \text{Tumor} \mid e_{Patient}, e_{Tumor}, e_i)$. Some voxels can have more than *one* such tumor-neighbors; *e.g.*, in diagram (1), the voxels v1, v2 and v5 each have a single tumor-neighbor, while v3 and v4 each have 2. Each tumor-neighbor of the voxel v_i has a q_i chance to transform this v_i; hence if there are k such neighbors, and each acts independently, the probability that v_i will be transformed on this iteration is $p_i = 1 - (1 - q_i)^k$. CDM will then transform this voxel to be a tumor with probability p_i. We then assign it to be a tumor if $p_i > \tau$ using a probability threshold of $\tau = 65\%$.[4] CDM performs these computations in parallel — hence on the first iteration, even if v3 is transformed, v4 still has only 2 tumor-neighbors (on this iteration). We discuss below how CDM learns the parameters Θ used in $P_\Theta(\cdot)$.

4   Experiments

We empirically evaluated the three models, UG, GW and CDM, over a set of 17 patients. For each patient, we had two sets of axial scans R_1 and R_2 taken at different times, each with known tumor regions. Let s_i refer to the size of the tumor in scan R_i. For each patient, we then input that patient's initial scan (R_1) to each model, and asked it to predict the next $s = s_2 - s_1$ voxels that would be

---

[3] Several images of a normal brain of an individual, averaged and registered to the same coordinate system.
[4] We experimented with several thresholds, and chose this $\tau = 0.65$ value as it provided the best observed accuracy.

transformed. We then compare the predicted voxels with the truth — *i.e.*, the tumor region of the second scan, R_2.

To measure the quality of each model, let "nt" be a set of tumor cells for the patient that are actually transformed (*i.e.*, this is the "truth", associated with R_2) and "pt_χ" be the cells that the χ model predicts will be transformed. We then use the standard measures: "precision" of χ (on this patient) is $\frac{|nt \cap pt_\chi|}{|pt_\chi|}$ and "recall" is $\frac{|nt \cap pt_\chi|}{|nt|}$. In our case, as our diffusion models stop when $|pt_\chi| = |nt| = s$, the precision and recall values will be the same[5] (see tables in [1, 12]). We report results in terms of the "F-measure" $= \frac{2 \times precision \times recall}{precision + recall}$ [20], where F-measure = precision = recall, for each patient.

While UG and GW are completely specified, CDM must first be trained. We use a "patient level" cross-validation procedure: That is, we trained a learner (*e.g.*, Logistic Regression [11] or SVM [13]) on 16 patients, then tested on the 17th. Each training instance corresponded to a single voxel v_i around the initial tumor in the first scan R_1, with features $\mathbf{e}_{Patient}$, $\mathbf{e}_{Tumor}$, and $\mathbf{e}_i$, and with the label of "1" if this voxel was in the tumor in R_2, or "0" otherwise. Training voxels represent the set difference between the tumor in R_1 and R_2 for each patient (*i.e.*, the region that a 'perfect' diffusion model would consider), in addition to a 2-voxel border around the tumor in R_2 to account for the segmentation error margin at the tumor border. The total number of training voxels was approximately $\frac{1}{2}$ million for the 17 patients. Notice this training is at the voxel level, and is only implicitly based on the diffusion approach (in that this is how we identified the specific set of training voxels).

Results appear in Fig. 3 and in [1, 12]. Below we analyze these results in terms of best, typical, and special cases; describe system performance versus tumor grade; and statistically assess of the three models.

4.1 Feature Selection

Here, we consider finding the best subset of the 75 features described in Section 3.1, called S_0. We first computed the Information Gain (IG) of each feature, then ranked the features based on their IG scores. We observed that patient-specific tissue features have the lowest IG scores (likely due to SPM's segmentation errors and the presence of tumors in patients' scans). We formed two subsets of features based on the IG scores and the feature type (*e.g.*, tumor-specific, tissue-based features, spatial coordinates, etc.). The first subset S_1 contains 28 features only; it excluded all patient-specific tissue features since these have lower IG scores (see [1, 12]), as well as spatial coordinates and template-specific tissue features, to help generalize the learned tumor growth model (*i.e.*, without making any assumptions about the spatial location of the tumor). The second subset S_2 contains 47 features, excluding only CSF features as these are associated with the lowest IG scores, likely due to errors in SPM's tissue

---

[5] In some patients, precision and recall can be slightly different if the algorithm terminates prematurely, *i.e.*, before reaching the target size of the tumor.

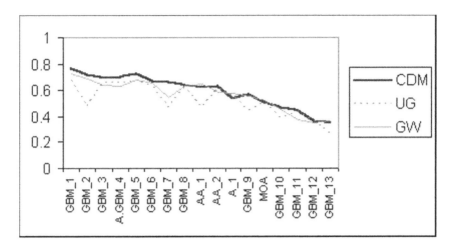

Fig. 3. Empirical Results

The F-measure for the three Models with 17-fold "patient-level" CV
(Note F-measure = precision = recall, for each patient — see Section 4).
Results correspond to the output of a logistic regression classifier, learned with feature
set S_1. The name of each patient identifies their tumor grades — Astrocytoma grade I
(A) and grade II (A.GBM) that progressed into GBM, Mixed Oligo-astrocytoma grade
II (MOA), Anaplastic astroyctoma grade III (AA), and the most common GBM.

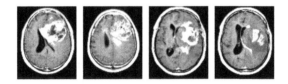

Fig. 4. Tumor-induced pressure deforms the ventricles in patients $A.GBM\_4$ and
GBM_12 (two image slices for each patient)

segmentation process. (Note tumors do not grow into CSF regions, *e.g.*, ventricles[6], but induced tumor pressure can deform them, which allows tumors to
appear in a region that *had* been ventricles, etc.)

By excluding tissue-based features from S_1, we allow the model to perform
more accurately for subjects whose tumors have altered the basic brain anatomy
— *e.g.*, tumors that have deformed the ventricles, such as patients $A.GBM\_4$ and
GBM_12 (see Fig. 4). But accuracy slightly decreased for scenarios that rely on
specific training information (*i.e.*, voxel locations and tissue information). Since
S_2 includes spatial and tissue information, classifiers that used these features
performed almost the same as S_0. Fig. 3 reports results obtained when training
on S_1 feature set only. Results with the other feature sets appear in [1, 12].

---

[6] Cavities in the brain filled with cerebrospinal fluid (CSF).

4.2   Tumor Growth Patterns Learned from the Data

Here, we considered training voxels a perfect diffusion algorithm will consider over our 17 patients — these are the voxels that were normal in the first scan but tumor in the second. Of the voxels that went from normal to tumor, 45% were edema, 23% had T2 $\geq$ 0.75, 42% had T1 $<$ 0.5, 45% were grey matter, and 32% white matter. Of the remaining voxels that stayed normal, we observed 25%, 15%, 51%, 39%, and 24%, respectively. (Generally, white matter voxels are more likely to become tumor than grey matter.) $P(class(v) = \text{'tumor'} \mid edema(v) = 1,\ T2(v) \geq 0.75,\ tissue(v) = w) = 86\%$. We then ran Logistic Regression, training on 16 patients, and testing on GBM_7, the conditional probability was 99.9% .

These probabilities confirm our assumption that voxels located in edema regions (bright on T2, dark on T1 scans) and in the grey or white matter (the last being a diffusion pathway for tumor cells) are likely to become diseased. See [1] for other patterns we found in the data.

4.3   Typical, Best, and Special Case Results

Patients GBM_1, GBM_2, and GBM_3 represent typical case results, where CDM performs more accurately than UG and GW by at least a small percentage. In these cases, the tumor tends to grow along the edema as glioma cells have already infiltrated into the peritumoral edema regions. These diffuse occult cells did not enhance at first on T1-contrast images as these cells may exist only in very low concentration. But on the next scan of the patient, enhancing tumors appeared in these regions as glioma cells built up into detectable masses.

Infiltration of glioma cells in edema regions is particularly more obvious on the MRI scans for patient GBM_7 (Fig. 5), which represents the best case results as CDM models tumor diffusion more accurately than UG and GW, by 20% and 12% respectively (see Fig. 3 and tables in [1, 12]).

In typical and best case scenarios, the prediction is based on what the classifier recognizes as 'tumor', which are often voxels located in edema regions. Glioma cell infiltration in peritumoral edema may be even more detectable if the truth volume was obtained from a patient scan before that patient underwent a surgical procedure or received radiation treatment.

Patients GBM_10, GBM_12, and GBM_13 are examples of special tumor growth cases where tumors do not follow usual diffusion patterns (*e.g.*, the tumor shrinks due to treatment and recurs a few months later in regions near the original mass). In these cases, CDM performed the same as the standard models. The effect of treatment is present in all of our data, but is more prominent in these patients.

4.4   Model Performance Versus Tumor Grade

Our dataset consists of four different glioma grades ranging from low-grade astrocytomas to the most invasive GBM. GBMs are the most common among

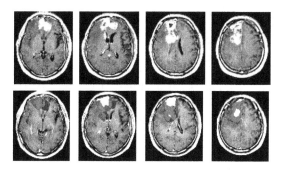

Fig. 5. Top: MR T1-contrast images of Patient *GBM_7*, showing lower to higher axial brain slices from left to right, corresponding to the "truth" volume (R_2). Bottom: the initial images (R_1) augmented with shades of grey corresponding to results from CDM model: initial tumor volume is colored white, true positives are light grey, false positives are dark grey, and false negatives are black (see color version in [1]).

glioma patients, and represent $\frac{2}{3}$ of our data. Because CDM is a general learning model, it is not restricted to predicting a particular tumor grade, but it requires a fair representation of various tumor types in training data. Currently, low-grade tumors are under-represented in our data since they are less common among glioma patients.

Also, CDM's prediction is based on probabilities assigned by classifiers to the unlabeled voxels. High-probability tumor voxels are likely to be located in peritumoral edema regions (edema features have the highest IG scores), particularly more pronounced in high-grade, larger tumors (*e.g.*, patients *GBM_1*, *GBM_3*, and *GBM_7*). This is because peritumoral edema regions harbour diffuse malignant cells that infiltrated through tissue near the visible tumor. These malignant cells form detectable tumor masses over time.

4.5   Statistical Evaluation of the Three Models

Over the 17 patients, the average leave-one-out recall ($\equiv$ precision) values for the CDM, UG and GW models are 0.598, 0.524 and 0.566 respectively. We ran a *t*-test [15] for paired data to determine if these average values are statistically significant from one another, at the 95% confidence interval (*i.e.*, $p < 0.05$).

- Comparing CDM versus UG, the *t* value is 4.14 meaning the probability of the null hypothesis (*i.e.*, values are not significantly different) is 0.001. In this case, we reject the null hypothesis and conclude that the average recall obtained with CDM and UG are significantly different.
- Comparing CDM versus GW, the *t* value is 3.61 meaning the probability of the null hypothesis is 0.002, which suggests that the average recall obtained with CDM and GW are significantly different as well.

Given the above *t*-test results, we conclude that our CDM model is performing more accurately, in general, than either of UG and GW.

4.6 Computational Cost of the Three Models

CDM requires several preprocessing steps of the MRI scan followed by feature extraction (which require approximately one hour). Given a segmented tumor, and a learned classifier (*e.g.*, Logistic Regression), CDM produces its prediction of tumor growth in 10 minutes on average[7]. UG and GW require the same data processing, and produce their predictions in 1 and 10 minutes on average, respectively. Note UG performs the fewest number of iterations.

5 Contributions and Future Work

Our team has produced a system that can automatically segment tumors based on their MRI images [1]; we are currently using this system to produce tumor volume labels for hundreds of patients, over a wide variety of tumor types and grades. We plan to train our diffusion model on this large dataset. We will also experiment with other learning algorithms, including Conditional and Support Vector Random Fields [10], as these may better account for neighborhood interpendencies between tumor and normal voxels. We will also investigate other attributes, *e.g.*, estimated tumor growth rate, and features from other types of data such as Magnetic Resonance Spectroscopy. We may also incorporate diagonal neighbors in the diffusion algorithm, which may help improve the accuracy, and will also help decrease the number of iterations required to grow the tumor, making the algorithm more efficient.

Contributions. This paper has proposed a classification-based model, CDM, to predict glioma diffusion, which *learns* 'general' diffusion patterns from clinical data. (To the best of our knowledge, this is the first such system.) We empirically compare CDM with two other approaches: a naïve uniform growth model (UG) and a tissue-based diffusion model (GW), over pairs of consecutive MRI scans. Our results, on real patient data (as opposed to simulating virtual tumors [18]), show statistically that CDM is more accurate. See [1] for more details.

References

1. Brain Tumor Growth Prediction: http://www.cs.ualberta.ca/~btgp/ai06.html
2. Brown M., and Semelka R., MRI Basic Principles and Applications (2003) Wiley, Hoboken, NJ, USA
3. Clatz O., Bondiau P., Delingette H., *et al.*, In Silico Tumor Growth: Application to Glioblastomas. *MICCAI 2004, LNCS 3217* (2004) 337–345
4. Friston K., Ashburner J., Frith C., Poline J., Heather J., and Frackowiak R., Spatial Registration and Normalization of Images Human Brain Mapping **2** (1995) 165–189
5. Friston K., and Ashburner J., Multimodal Image Coregistration and Partitioning — a Unified Framework **6** (1997) NeuroImage 209–217

---

[7] This average is computed over our set of 17 patients, characterized by a wide variety of tumor sizes, including a few that require a very large number of additional voxels to grow, and were therefore more computationally costly.

6. Halperin E., Bentel G., and Heinz E., Radiation Therapy Treatment Planning in Supratentorial Glioblastoma Multiforme, Int. J. Radiat. Oncol. Biol. Phys. **17** (1989) 1347–1350
7. Hochberg F., and Pruitt A., Assumptions in the Radiotherapy of Glioblastoma, Neurology **30** (1980) 907–911
8. Holmes C., Hoge R., Collins L., *et al.*, Enhancement of MR images using registration for signal averaging. *J Comput Assist Tomogr*, **22**(2) (1998) 324–333
9. Kansal A., Torquato S., Harsh G., *et al.*, Simulated brain tumor growth dynamics using a three-dimensional cellular automaton. *J Theor Biol.* **203** (2000) 367–382
10. Lee C.H., Greiner R., and Schmidt M., Support Vector Random Fields for Spatial Classification (2005) *PKDD 2005*
11. le Cessie S. and van Houwelingen J., Ridge Estimators in Logistic Regression. *Applied Statistics*, **41**(1) (1992) 191–201
12. Morris M., *Classification-based Glioma Diffusion Modeling.* MSc Thesis, University of Alberta (2005)
13. Platt J., Fast Training of Support Vector Machines using Sequential Minimal Optimization. *Advances in Kernel Methods — Support Vector Learning*, eds., Schoelkopf B., Burges C., and Smola A. (1998) MIT Press
14. Price S., Burnet N., Donovan T., *et al.*, Diffusion tensor imaging of brain tumorss at 3T: a potential tool for assessing white matter tract invasion? *Clinical Radiology*, **58** (2003) 455–462
15. Student, The Probable Error of a Mean. *Biometrika*, **6** (1908) 1–25
16. Swanson K., Alvord E., Murray J., A Quantitative Model for Differential Motility of Gliomas in grey and White Matter, *Cell Prolif*, **33** (2000) 317–329
17. Swanson K., Alvord E., Murray J., Quantifying efficacy of chemotherapy of brain tumors with homogeneous and heterogeneous drug delivery. *Acta Biotheor*, **50**(4) (2002) 223–237
18. Swanson K., Alvord E., Murray J., Virtual brain tumors (gliomas) enhance the reality of medical imaging and highlight inadequacies of current therapy, *British Journal of Cancer*, **86** (2002) 14–18
19. Tabatabai M., Williams D. and Bursac Z., Hyperbolastic growth models: theory and application. *Theor Biol Med Model*, **2**(1) (2005), 14
20. Van Rijsbergen C. J., *Information Retrieval* (1979) second edition, London, Butterworths.
21. Zizzari A., *Methods on Tumor Recognition and Planning Target Prediction for the Radiotherapy of Cancer* (2004) PhD Thesis, University of Magdeburg

Bayesian Learning for Feed-Forward Neural Network with Application to Proteomic Data: The Glycosylation Sites Detection of the Epidermal Growth Factor-Like Proteins Associated with Cancer as a Case Study

Alireza Shaneh[1] and Gregory Butler[1]

[1] Research Laboratory for Bioinformatics Technology,
Department of Computer Science and Software Engineering, Concordia University,
1515 St-Catherine West, Montreal, Quebec H3G 2W1, Canada
{a_dariss, gregb}@cs.concordia.ca
http://www.cs.concordia.ca

Abstract. There are some neural network applications in proteomics; however, design and use of a neural network depends on the nature of the problem and the dataset studied. Bayesian framework is a consistent learning paradigm for a feed-forward neural network to infer knowledge from experimental data. Bayesian regularization automates the process of learning by pruning the unnecessary weights of a feed-forward neural network, a technique of which has been shown in this paper and applied to detect the glycosylation sites in epidermal growth factor-like repeat proteins involving in cancer as a case study. After applying the Bayesian framework, the number of network parameters decreased by 47.62%. The model performance comparing to One Step Secant method increased more than 34.92%. Bayesian learning produced more consistent outcomes than one step secant method did; however, it is computationally complex and slow, and the role of prior knowledge and its correlation with model selection should be further studied.

1 Introduction

Proteomic data are huge, sparse and redundant, and dealing with these characteristics is a challenge and requires powerful methods to infer knowledge. Soft computing techniques have been extensively used to mine and extract as much necessary information as possible from a large set of protein sequences. Generally speaking, the soft computing methods used to solve optimization problems are divided into computational, statistical, and metaheuristic frameworks. Computational approaches optimize the learning algorithm by predicting the future state of a solution based on the past evaluation of data in both supervised and unsupervised ways. Artificial neural networks are obvious examples of such methods. Statistical learning theory emphasizes on the statistical methods used for automated learning; for example, kernel-based methods such as support vector machines [24] find an optimal separating hyperplane by mapping data to a higher dimensional search space. Metaheuristic algorithms are

L. Lamontagne and M. Marchand (Eds.): Canadian AI 2006, LNAI 4013, pp. 110–121, 2006.
© Springer-Verlag Berlin Heidelberg 2006

usually used to find a best solution through other combinatorial optimizers; in fact, metaheuristic approaches suggest a framework for other heuristic frameworks. Fuzzy systems and genetic algorithms are examples of metaheuristic methods [25, 9].

In this paper, we have employed a statistical approach (Bayesian learning) in order to find a better structure for a computational learning tool (feed-forward network); consequently, it is possible to manipulate the proteomic data more intelligently. A Bayesian regularization neural network (BPROP-BRNN) takes the large weights into account to regularize and measure the complexity of the network [20]. A similar approach has been applied in this study to examine the consistency of Bayesian learning for the large proteomic data set.

Protein glycosylation [19] is the molecular process in which a protein attaches to a simple carbohydrate molecule and makes a protein-sugar complex called a *glycoprotein*. The attachment residue in protein is literally known as a *glycosylation site*. The glycoprotein is then sent out of the cell for performing its biological tasks, a mechanism called *secretion*. Secretion is crucial for intercellular interaction, cell growth, and protein folding [12, 13]. Abnormal increase of the number of glycosylation sites causes irreversible diseases such as brain and lung cancer [12]; as a result, study on the number of glycosylation sites is very essential. Furthermore, the proteins focused in this paper belong to the *epidermal growth factor-like* (EGFL) family [1, 8], which are glycosylated and important for cell adhesion and growth [15, 22]. In addition, to better analyze the three dimensional distribution of glycosylation sites in the future, it is necessary to focus on one superfamily of proteins. EGFL repeat proteins are well-studied in terms of glycosylation process, making them a good candidate for this research.

There are various studies about glycosylation sites detection or prediction using neural networks [17]. Hansen et al has launched a prediction website for a specific type of glycosylation which predicts the glycosylation sites between 65-90% of accuracy [14]. Gupta et al has revised the neural predictor of glycosylation sites using a majority vote for the collection of neural networks used in their approach [10]. Gupta and Brunak have developed a neural network method to infer the correlation between the function of proteins and glycosylation sites in human cells [11]. Cai et al has proposed a more specific application of neural network prediction to model the functionality of the enzyme responsible for attaching a sugar to a protein [7]. Nevertheless, none of those techniques specifically study the non-linear functionality between the number of glycosylation sites and the epidermal growth factor-like repeats based on statistical learning approaches such as Bayesian learning.

The objective of this study was to examine the response of the neural model when the size of the network decreases. This model was then applied to detect the glycosylation sites in EGFL protein data involving in cancer.

In section 2, the materials and methods will be discussed. Moreover, the algorithm applied for Bayesian regularization will be explained. Section 3 will cover the results and discussion, and the last section will review the objectives and lessons learned from the study; in addition, it will raise an open question, which could be carried out later during further studies.

2 Materials and Methods

2.1 Data Specification

Epidermal growth factor-like protein sequences were collected from biological web repositories such as PROSITE [16] and UniProt Knowledgebase (UniProtKB) [2]. The sequences we selected from the mammalian EGFL sequences stored in the repositories. Pfam's Hidden Markov Models [5] were run through the EGFL protein sequences, and the sequences with more than 80% of similarity were ignored to avoid the redundancy in the data. Furthermore, the sequences without signal peptides are not glycosylated, and those sequences were also removed. To build a more generalized classifier, it is necessary to feed control data to the classifier. Thus, 412 control sequences were used for training. Control data were the glycosylated sequences which did not participate in any form of carcinogenesis.

The test set consisted of 880 sequences, divided into 5 groups. The first 220 sequences were glycosylated ones, as indicated by "+" in Table 1. The second subset included the EGFL sequences not glycosylated. Non-glycosylated sites were assumed to be the ones which either had not been annotated or had been considered as the putative glycosylated sites. They tagged as negative sequences and marked "-". The third category was the same as the first subset and the fourth set, indicated by "*" in Table 1, corresponded to non-EGFL, glycosylated sequences. The last set represented noise to the data as a measure of reliability of the model. In fact, the noise sequences were any kind of not glycosylated, not EGFL protein sequences.

Target set was labeled as $\{0.1, 0.9\}^n$, where 0.9 and 0.1 represented the model response for glycosylated and not glycosylated sets respectively. n denotes the number of the underlying sequences. The labels were substituted for '0' and '1' since using binary set in sigmoid function shifts the function response to large values and significantly increases the weights of the network. This phenomenon, so-called *shifting effect*, leads to an unstable network; consequently, the target values are usually set to 0.1 and 0.9 instead of their respective binary counterparts.

Table 1. Data specification. Control set were glycosylated but not participated in any kind of malignancy. Glycosylated and not glycosylated sets are shown in + and − respectively. Noisy data are indicated as *. Target values were chosen to be [0.1,0.9] to avoid the shifting effect.

No. of Sequences	Description		Target Value
3400	Training set		0.9
412	Control set		0.1
880	Test Set:	220 – Glyco +	0.9
		220 – Glyco –	0.1
		220 – Glyco +	0.9
		175 – Glyco *	0.1
		45 – Noise	0.1

To study the effect of altering the number of inputs fed to back-propagation network, all sequences were divided into five different window frames around the glycosylation site with the size of 5, 11, 15, 19, and 29 amino acids (Table 2). Orthogonal encoding [18] was used as a scheme to preprocess the sequences before feeding into the network. In this scheme, only one amino acid has the binary value '1' while the rest of the residues in the sequence remain '0'. Although this technique is redundant and increases the number of weights in the neural network, it prevents the network to learn a false correlation between amino acids [23].

Table 2. Window frame specification. The sequences were divided into five classes: 5-, 11-, 15-, 19-, and 29-residue frames, each of which fed the Bayesian regularization neural network. The assumption made for encoding was orthogonal scheme. X is an arbitrary amino acid, and $X_{Glycosite}$ is the residue participating in glycosylation, i.e. Asparagine, Serine, or Threonine (glycosylation site). HU indicates the number of hidden units in the hidden layer.

Window Frame	Sequence Pattern	No. of Parameters in Networks	
		HU=5	HU=10
5	2(X)- $X_{GlycoSite}$-2(X)	511	1021
11	5(X)- $X_{GlycoSite}$-5(X)	1111	2221
15	7(X)- $X_{GlycoSite}$-7(X)	1511	3021
19	9(X)- $X_{GlycoSite}$-9(X)	1911	3821
29	14(X)- $X_{GlycoSite}$-14(X)	2901	5821

2.2 Neural Network Model

One hidden-layer feed-forward network was used in this study to restrict our approach to search in a moderate solution space rather than a complex one. One hidden layer, consisting of h hidden units for a sequence of length ℓ, according to the orthogonal encoding scheme, has $h(20\ell + 2) + 1$ parameters (weights and biases). For model selection, the networks with $h=5$ and $h=10$ were selected.

In terms of learning, the Levenberg-Marquardt algorithm was used along with a Bayesian automated regularization (BPROP-BRNN); Moreover, the back-propagation network was separately trained with One Step Secant (OSS) algorithm [4] along with a backtrack minimization approach as a line search function (BPROP-OSS) as a benchmark to Bayesian learning. One hidden layer with either 5 or 10 hidden units was also selected for BPROP-OSS, and it was validated using 10-fold cross validation.

2.3 Learning by Bayesian Inference

The non-linear functionality between the search space and the target set is inferred by a back-propagation network, and the model should cover the new unseen data as well. Consequently, it is not only necessary to estimate targets by minimizing the mean squared error of the model output, but also by including a regularized term as a cost term to penalize the large values of weights in the network. The regularization term applied was the squared sum of the weights of the neural network:

$$\varepsilon_T = \beta\varepsilon_D + \alpha\varepsilon_R = \frac{\beta}{2}\sum_{k=1}^{N}(y_k - t_k) + \frac{\alpha}{2}\sum_{i=1}^{M}w_i \cdot \tag{1}$$

where α and β are coefficients assigned to each term. The second term in (1) is sometimes called *weight decay*, as it guarantees that the weights of the network do not exceed than the total error of the network.

Instead of cross validation, the weights and biases of back-propagation network were assumed as the random variables with specific distribution and unknown variances [20, 21]. As a result, it is possible to estimate these parameters using Bayesian inference. This process maximizes the *posterior probabilities* of the parameters' distribution given the data:

$$p(\theta|D,\alpha,\beta) = \frac{P(D|\theta,\alpha,\beta)\,p(\theta|\alpha,\beta)}{P(D)}. \tag{2}$$

where θ is the network parameters along with regularization and mean squared error coefficient terms in (1). BPROP-BRNN first estimates the optimal weights of the networks, and then maximizes the posteriors by adjusting α and β. Therefore, the model automatically finds the best coefficients for each MSE and regularization terms in (1). To find a practical algorithm which could calculate (2), prior, likelihood and posterior probabilities were computed individually.

2.3.1 Prior Probability

Choosing a Gaussian distribution $N\left(0,\frac{1}{\alpha^2}\right)$ will simplify the calculation of all the prior probabilities associated with the weights:

$$P(W|\alpha) = \prod_{i=1}^{W}P(w_i|\alpha) = \frac{1}{Z_W(\alpha)}e^{(-\alpha E_W)} \tag{3}$$

$$Z_W(\alpha) = \left(\frac{2\pi}{\alpha}\right)^{\frac{W}{2}}; E_W = \frac{1}{2}\sum_{i=1}^{W}w_i^2$$

where W, E_W and $Z_W(\alpha)$ are the number of weights, weight decay and normalization factor respectively.

2.3.2 Likelihood Estimation

The likelihood expresses how data energy *is likely* to decay through the learning process. Hence, the following approach was used to reach at the model likelihood:

$$P(D|\vec{W},\beta) = \prod_{i=1}^{N} P(t_i|x_i,\vec{W},\beta) = \frac{1}{Z_D(\beta)}e^{-\beta E_D} \qquad (4)$$

$$Z_D(\beta) = \left(\frac{2\pi}{\beta}\right)^{\frac{N}{2}}; E_D = -\frac{\beta}{2}\sum_{i=1}^{N}[M(x_i)-t_i]^2$$

where $M(x_i)$, $Z_D(\beta)$ and E_D are model output given an input sequence, normalization factor and output error respectively.

2.3.3 Posterior Probability
Posterior probability is simply calculated from (2), (3), and (4):

$$P(W|D,\alpha,\beta) = \frac{1}{Z_s(\alpha,\beta)}e^{-(\beta E_D + \alpha E_W)} \qquad (5)$$

$$Z_s(\alpha,\beta) = \frac{1}{Z_W(\alpha)Z_D(\beta)P(D)}$$

Maximizing the posterior probability is easier by minimizing the total error of the network according to (5).

2.3.4 Updating α and β
It has been shown that the priors are reliable for every re-parameterization when they are proportional reciprocally to the parameters themselves [21], i.e., $P(\alpha) = \frac{1}{\alpha}$ and $P(\beta) = \frac{1}{\beta}$. By plugging these values in (2) and then expanding a Taylor-approximation of (5), one can get the following inference:

$$\ln P(\alpha,\beta) \propto \ln P(D|\alpha,\beta) + \ln P(\alpha,\beta) = -\alpha E_W^* - \beta E_D^* - \frac{1}{2}\ln\|H\| + \frac{W}{2}\ln\alpha +$$
$$\frac{N}{2}\ln\beta - \frac{N}{2}\ln(\beta) - \frac{N}{2}\ln(2\pi) - \ln\alpha - \ln\beta \qquad (6)$$

$$H = -\nabla\nabla\ln P(\vec{W}|D) \qquad (7)$$

where the starred parameters referred to optimized values of energies obtained from the last procedure. (7) is Hessian of (9) at optimized weights W^*.

The goal is to find the optimum energy parameters, which is done by calculating the partial derivatives of (6) with respect to α and β, and set the result equal to zero to find the optimum values for the parameters:

$$\alpha^* = \frac{\gamma}{2E_W^*}; \ \beta^* = \frac{n-\gamma}{2E_D^*}; \ \gamma = N - 2\alpha_{old}^* tr(H^*)^{-1} \qquad (8)$$

where N is the number of parameters and H^{*-1} is inverse of the Hessian matrix. Having obtained the updated parameters of energy function, one can simply implement an

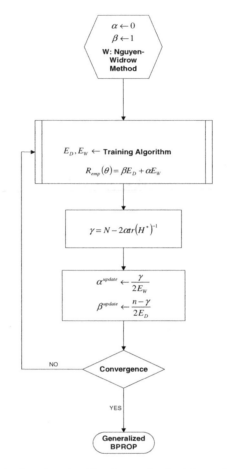

Fig. 1. The Bayesian learning algorithm for pruning feed-forward neural network

iterative algorithm embedded with any learning technique. Fig. 1 shows the flowchart of embedded Bayesian regularization to a learning algorithm.

2.4 Developing Environment

MATLAB was used as the developing environment. The Levenberg-Marquardt Algorithm along with Bayesian automated regularization was applied to the data sets. A general purpose cross validation code was developed, and its argument was set to perform a 10-fold cross validation over the BPROP-OSS network. Also, a general-purpose encoder was implemented to convert the protein sequences to orthogonal encoded sets. In addition, the routines for standard assessments such as precision, recall and correlation coefficient were implemented using Visual Studio .NET C++ 2003.

The average run time for each window frame using Bayesian learning was 30 minutes on a PC with Dual Processor Pentium 4 (3.99-2.99GHz) with 1GB of RAM.

3 Results and Discussion

According to the findings demonstrated in Table 4, after applying the Bayesian learning framework to the feed-forward neural network, the average size of the network

Table 3. Standard measurement for BPROP-BRNN and BPROP-OSS. WF indicates the window frame size. SPEC%, SENS% and MCC are specificity and sensitivity percentage as well as Matthews' Correlation Coefficient value respectively. The highest values for SPEC% and MCC are highlighted.

Window Name	Assess	BRNN	OSS
5-residue	SPEC%	66.37	38.91
	SENS%	69.22	51.00
	MCC	0.674	0.111
11-residue	SPEC%	70.99	47.11
	SENS%	68.17	54.83
	MCC	0.790	0.165
15-residue	SPEC%	66.25	43.29
	SENS%	75.23	55.17
	MCC	0.715	0.153
19-residue	SPEC%	75.16	**57.15**
	SENS%	70.19	60.90
	MCC	0.821	**0.341**
29-residue	SPEC%	**77.00**	50.11
	SENS%	76.19	49.35
	MCC	**0.851**	0.313

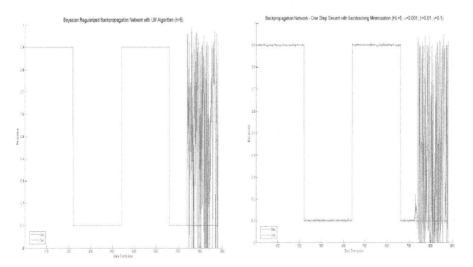

Fig. 2. The left figure shows the network response after applying Bayesian learning with Levenberg-Marquardt (LM) algorithm, and the right one is the network output for the quasi-Newton One Step Secant (OSS) learning algorithm with backtracking minimization parameters. Both networks had a hidden layer consisting of 5 hidden units, and they were applied to 29-residue window frame. The test set was 880 EGFL sequences, as described in Table 1.

Table 4. BRNN-BPROP Structure. The columns from l-r: window frame size, no. of hidden units, no. of total parameters, no. of effective parameters, and the network reduction factor.

WF	HU	$\Gamma_{BPROP-BRNN}$	γ_E	$\rho = \dfrac{\|\Gamma_{BPROP-BRNN} - \gamma_E\|}{\Gamma_{BPROP-BRNN}} \times 100$
5	1	106	66.95	36.84
	2	212	100.98	52.37
	3	318	156.97	50.64
	4	424	156.97	62.98
	5	530	156.97	70.38
	6	636	156.97	75.32
11	1	232	166.22	28.35
	2	464	342.25	26.24
	3	696	542.51	22.05
	4	928	763.64	17.71
	5	1160	811.00	30.09
	6	1392	811.00	41.74
	7	1624	811.00	50.06
15	1	316	22.93	92.74
	2	632	209.61	66.83
	3	948	794.15	16.23
	4	1264	826.00	34.65
	5	1580	826.00	47.72
	6	1896	826.00	56.44
	7	2212	826.00	62.66
19	1	400	258.99	35.25
	2	800	665.79	16.78
	3	1200	836.00	30.33
	4	1600	835.97	47.75
	5	2000	836.00	58.20
	6	2400	836.00	65.17
	7	2800	835.92	70.15
29	1	610	442.93	27.39
	2	1220	804.19	34.09
	3	1830	846.99	53.72
	4	2440	847.00	65.29
	5	3050	847.00	72.23

decreases by 47.62% which shows that this approach has been successfully reduced the number of unnecessary parameters of the neural network. Table 3 shows the situation of the network parameters for each window frame.

There are several assessment methods for proteomic data [3]; however, the specificity, sensitivity, and correlation of the data were measured through the following standard performance measurement for bioinformatics data:

$$Sensitivity\% = \frac{TP}{TP+FN} \times 100.$$

$$Specificity\% = \frac{TP}{TP+FP} \times 100. \tag{9}$$

$$MCC = \frac{TP \times TN - FP \times FN}{\sqrt{(TP+FN)+(TP+FP)+(TN+FP)+(TN+FN)}}.$$

where *TP, TN, FP,* and *FN* are true positives, true negatives, false positives, and false negative glycosylation sites respectively. *Matthews' Correlation Coefficient* (MCC) [3] was higher for longer frames. The exception was 15-residue window frame in which there was no evidence found for stability of the results. The results also showed a 62.22% in the maximum correlation coefficient using Bayesian automated regularization, which is a significant improvement for the neural network. BRNN could detect the true positive hits by 34.92% when 29-residue window frame was used. Fig. 2 shows that the response of the network is noisier in BPROP-OSS than BPROP-BRNN. This suggests that the Bayesian learning could lead to a stronger generalization than that of BPROP-OSS.

4   Conclusion

A Bayesian framework was applied to a feed-forward network to study the neural network structure and topology. The network was initially implemented by the maximizing the posterior probabilities. After that, the network parameters were pruned such that the less important weights and biases were neglected. As a benchmark, the performance of a quasi-Newton learning method, one step secant, was measured. Bayesian learning outperformed the semi Newton one in terms of both accuracy and consistency over the networks parameters as well as model response. The neural network with both Bayesian and semi Newton learning approaches was employed to detect the glycosylation sites of the epidermal growth factor-like repeat proteins. The true positive hits were much higher in the network trained with Bayesian learning. This would suggest applying this framework for knowledge inference from proteomic data. In fact, with enough prior information, it is possible to estimate the model parameters even with large number of protein sequences. Nonetheless, Bayesian learning is expensive and computationally complex. Using other encoding schemes such as adaptive encoding may suggest a solution to overcome that disadvantage of BPROP-BRNN. Furthermore, evolutionary-related EGFL sequences may affect the accuracy of the model due to an unavoidable similarity among those sequences. Removing the sequences with the same origin from the dataset introduces less prior knowledge to the model whereas keeping them may influence the model response. Therefore, the trade-off between keeping and removing evolutionary-related EGFL sequences is a challenging issue for further studies.

Although Bayesian regularized neural network significantly improved the model response, biologists should validate the results of this network to evaluate to what extend *in-silico* detection of glycosylation sites would provide them with worth studying protein sequences. Moreover, the validation procedure avoids the wrong analysis of outcomes of the model which may influence the biological interpretation of the results used, for example, in an analysis toward knocking out or silencing a gene.

Finally, Bayesian learning should be studied in terms of correlation between prior knowledge, which will be carried out through further studies.

References

1. Appella, E., Weber, I.T, Blasi, F.: Structure and Function of Epidermal Growth Factor-Like Regions in Proteins, FEBS Lett., Vol. 231. (1988) 1-4
2. Bairoch, A., Apweiler, R., Wu, C. H., Barker, W. C., Boeckmann, B., Ferro, S., Gasteiger, E., Huang, H., Lopez, R., Magrane, M., Martin, M. J., Natale, D. A., O'Donovan, C., Redaschi N., Yeh, L. S.: The Universal Protein Resource (UniProt). Nucleic Acids Res., Vol. 33. (2005) 154-159
3. Baldi, P., Brunak, S., Chauvin, Y., Andersen, C.A., Nielsen H.: Assessing the Accuracy of Prediction Algorithms for Classification: An Overview. Bioinformatics, Vol. 16. (2000) 412-24
4. Battiti, R.: First and Second Order Methods for Learning: Between Steepest Descent and Newton's Method. Neural Computation, Vol. 4. (1992) 141-166
5. Bateman, A., Coin, L., Durbin, R., Finn, R. D., Hollich, V., Griffiths-Jones, S., Khanna, A., Marshall, M., Moxon, S., Sonnhammer, E. L., Studholme, D. J., Yeats, C., Eddy, S. R.: The Pfam Protein Families Database. Nucleic Acids Res. Vol. 32. (2004) 138-141
6. Bishop, C., M.: Neural Network for Pattern Recognition, Oxford University Press (1995)
7. Cai, Y. D., Yu, H., Chou, K. C.: Artificial Neural Network Method for Predicting the Specificity of GalNAc-Transferase, J. Protein Chem., Vol. 16. (1997) 689-700
8. Davis, C.G.: The Many Faces of Epidermal Growth Factor Repeats. New Biol., Vol. 5. (1997) 410-419
9. Goldberg, D. E.: Genetic Algorithms in Search, Optimization, and Machine Learning, Addison-Wesley Pub. Co. (1989)
10. Gupta, R., Birch, H., Kristoffer, R., Brunak, S., Hansen, J. E.: O-GLYCBASE Version 4.0: A Revised Database of O-Glycosylated Proteins. Nuc. Acid. Res., Vol. 27. (1999) 370-372
11. Gupta, R., Brunak, S.: Prediction of Glycosylation across the Human Proteome and the Correlation to Protein Function, Pac. Symp. Biocomput., (2002) 310-322
12. Hakamori, S.: Glycosylation Defining Malignancy: New Wine in an Old Bottle. PNAS, Vol. 99. (2002) 10231-10233
13. Haltiwanger, R.S, Lowe, J.B.: Role of Glycosylation in Development. Annu. Rev. Biochem., Vol. 73. (2004) 491-537
14. Hansen, J.E., Lund, O., Nielsen, J.O., Brunak, S.: O-GLYCBASE: A Revised Database of O-glycosylated Proteins. Nuc. Acid. Res., Vol. 24. (1996) 248-252
15. Heitzler P, Simpson P.: Altered Epidermal Growth Factor-Like Sequences Provide Evidence for a Role of Notch as a Receptor in Cell Fate Decisions. Development, Vol. 117. (1993) 1113-23
16. Hulo N., Sigrist C.J.A., Le Saux V., Langendijk-Genevaux P.S., Bordoli L., Gattiker A., De Castro E., Bucher P., Bairoch A. Recent improvements to the PROSITE database, Nucl. Acids. Res., Vol. 32. (2004) 134-137

17. Julenius, K., Molgaard, A., Gupta, R., Brunak, S.: Prediction, Conservation Analysis, and Structural Characterization of Mammalian Mucin-Type O-Glycosylation Sites, Glycobiology, Vol. 15. (2005) 153-64
18. Lin, K., May, A. C. W., Taylor, W. R.: Amino Acid Encoding Schemes from Protein Structure Alignments: Multi-Dimensional Vectors to Describe Residue Types, J. Theor. Biol., Vol. 216. (2002) 361-365
19. Lis, H., Sharon, N.: Protein Glycosylation: Structural and Functional Aspects. Eur. J. Biochem., Vol. 218. (1993) 1-27
20. MacKay, D. J.: A Practical Bayesian Framework for Backprop Networks. Neural Computation, Vol. 4. (1992) 448—472
21. MacKay, D. J.: Bayesian Interpolation. Neural Computation, Vol. 4. (1992) 415-447
22. Marshall, R. D.: Glycoproteins. Annu. Rev. Biochem (1972) 673-702
23. Riis, S. K., Krogh, A.: Improving Prediction of Protein Secondary Structure Using Structured Neural Network and Multiple Sequence Alignments, J. Comp. Biol., Vol. 3. (1996) 163-183
24. Vapnik, V., N.: The Nature of Statistical Learning Theory, Springer, 1995
25. Zadeh, L., A.: Fuzzy Sets, Information and Control, Vol. 8. (1965) 338-353

Relaxation of Soft Constraints Via a Unified Semiring

Peter Harvey and Aditya Ghose

Decision Systems Laboratory
School of IT and Computer Science
University of Wollongong
NSW 2522 Australia

Abstract. The semiring framework for constraint satisfaction allows us to model a wide variety of problems of choice. Semiring constraint satisfaction problems are able to represent both classical consistency and optimisation problems, as well as soft constraint problems such as valued and weight CSPs. In this paper we pose and answer the question: how can we represent and 'solve' the relaxation of a semiring constraint satisfaction problem?

1 Introduction

Example 1. Consider the following marking scheme for artwork produced by students of an art class. Each artwork is given a mark of Platinum, Gold, Silver or Bronze for the 'colour brightness' and 'colour harmony' aspects of their work. The final mark is the *lowest* received for either aspect of the artwork. We want to find the top student to receive an award. Their component and final marks are presented below:

	Brightness	**Harmony**	**Final Mark**
Amy	Gold	Bronze	Bronze
Bob	Silver	Silver	Silver
Col	Bronze	Bronze	Bronze
Dan	Bronze	Silver	Bronze

None of the students scored well; perhaps our marking was too harsh? While Bob was the only student to receive a final mark of Silver, we cannot give him an award while admitting our marking was flawed. We need to investigate what happens if we relax our marking scheme...

The semiring framework [2, 3, 4] for constraint satisfaction allows us to model a wide variety of problems of choice. It generalises many other soft constraint satisfaction frameworks [1, 5], while retaining useful properties for algorithm development.

It is trivial to represent the marking scheme in this example as a semiring constraint satisfaction problem (SCSP). However, it is much more difficult to represent the ways in which the marking scheme can be adjusted, specifically *relaxed*, as a SCSP. We will describe a semiring constraint *relaxation* problem (SCRP) which extends a SCSP, providing optimal solutions under all attempts to relax the marking scheme. We will then pose the question: how can we represent a semiring constraint relaxation problem as a semiring constraint satisfaction problem?

L. Lamontagne and M. Marchand (Eds.): Canadian AI 2006, LNAI 4013, pp. 122–133, 2006.
© Springer-Verlag Berlin Heidelberg 2006

The concept of 'relaxation' introduced in this paper should not be equated with that of 'optimisation' or 'satisfaction' commonly found in the semiring constraint framework. A semiring constraint satisfaction problem involves finding the optimal assignment of values to variables, using constraints as measures of satisfaction. However, we work under the presumption that the original semiring constraints are themselves somehow flawed and too 'tight'. We will treat the constraints as representations that may be modified (in a consistent fashion!) to achieve some goal. In the above example, and in this paper, our goal is to find a better set of constraints for a given problem.

2   Constraint Relaxation with Two Semirings

We will define the semiring constraint relaxation problem by extending the semiring constraint satisfaction problem, with detailed examples to follow. First, we give a simplified description of semiring constraint satisfaction problems.

Definition 1. *A **c-semiring** is a tuple $\mathcal{A} = \langle A, +_{\mathcal{A}}, \times_{\mathcal{A}}, 0_{\mathcal{A}}, 1_{\mathcal{A}} \rangle$ satisfying (for $\alpha \in A$):*

- *A is a set with $0_{\mathcal{A}}, 1_{\mathcal{A}} \in A$*
- *$+_{\mathcal{A}}$ is a commutative, associative, and idempotent operator on A.*
- *$\times_{\mathcal{A}}$ is a commutative, associative, and binary operator on A.*
- *$\times_{\mathcal{A}}$ distributes over $+_{\mathcal{A}}$*
- *$\alpha +_{\mathcal{A}} 0_{\mathcal{A}} = \alpha$ and $\alpha +_{\mathcal{A}} 1_{\mathcal{A}} = 1_{\mathcal{A}}$*
- *$\alpha \times_{\mathcal{A}} 1_{\mathcal{A}} = \alpha$ and $\alpha \times_{\mathcal{A}} 0_{\mathcal{A}} = 0_{\mathcal{A}}$*

We can derive the partial ordering $\leq_{\mathcal{A}}$ from a c-semiring by $(\alpha \leq_{\mathcal{A}} \beta) \Leftrightarrow (\alpha +_{\mathcal{A}} \beta = \beta)$. As a result of this definition, $+_{\mathcal{A}}$ and $\times_{\mathcal{A}}$ are both monotone on $\leq_{\mathcal{A}}$, $\langle A, \leq_S \rangle$ is a complete lattice and $\alpha +_{\mathcal{A}} \beta = \text{lub}(\alpha, \beta)$. Note that we will often use the symbols Σ and $\prod$ to refer to the semiring operators in prefix notation. We forgo the subscripting of these for convenience; the precise operator to be used should be clear from the context.

Definition 2. *A **semiring constraint satisfaction problem** is a tuple $\mathcal{P} = \langle \mathcal{V}, \mathcal{D}, \mathcal{A}, \mathcal{C} \rangle$:*

- *$\mathcal{V}$ is a set of variables*
- *$\mathcal{D}$ is a set of values to be to assigned to variables.*
- *S denotes the set of all assignments, written as functions $s : \mathcal{V} \to \mathcal{D}$.*
- *$\mathcal{A}$ is a c-semiring used to evaluate each assignment.*
- *$\mathcal{C}$ is a set of constraints, written as functions $c_i : S \to \mathcal{A}$.*

Definition 3. *Given a semiring constraint satisfaction problem $\mathcal{P} = \langle \mathcal{V}, \mathcal{D}, \mathcal{A}, \mathcal{C} \rangle$, we define the **solution** as the function:*

$$sol(s) = \prod_{c_i \in C} c_i(s)$$

*and the **abstract solutions** as the set:*

$$\{ s \in S : \forall t \in S, sol(s) \not<_{\mathcal{A}} sol(t) \}$$

Definitions 1, 2, and 3 provide a shortened description of the semiring constraint satisfaction problem. We have deliberately left out details not used in this paper. For a more complete treatment of c-semirings and SCSP, and how they generalise many forms of constraint satisfaction and optimisation problems, see [3].

Using the above simplified definition of a semiring constraint satisfaction problem, we will now define a semiring constraint *relaxation* problem. Whereas the aim of an SCSP is to find the 'best' solutions satisfying some constraints, a SCRP aims to find the best solutions for any relaxation of those constraints.

We define a relaxation as being a set of uniform substitutions $a \Rightarrow a'$, where $a, a' \in A$. For example, in our introductory example we could relax the Harmony marks for all students by changing all Silver marks to Gold. We could *not* however change the Silver mark in Harmony for Bob and not change it for Dan. Therefore, with respect to SCSP, a 'relaxation' will be the modification of the value a constraint uses from a semiring, but not a modification of the way in which individual solutions are evaluated. This is an explicit but intuitive restriction we place on the concept of relaxations; we are relaxing the constraints, not arbitrarily rewriting the problem.

Definition 4. *Given a pair of c-semirings A and B, we define a **relaxation function** as a function $r : A \times A \to B$ satisfying (where $a_1, a_2, a_3, a_4 \in A$):*

- *if $a_1 \leq_A a_2$ and $a_3 \leq_A a_4$ then $r(a_2, a_3) \leq_B r(a_1, a_4)$*
- *if $a_1 \leq_A a_2$ then $r(a_2, a_1) = 1_B$*

A relaxation function measures the 'amount of relaxation' if one c-semiring value was to be substituted for another. The conditions imposed in this definition ensure that raising a c-semiring value further always requires a greater amount of relaxation. Also, leaving a c-semiring value unchanged (performing no substitution) involves no relaxation, and so is measured as 1_B.

Definition 5. *A **semiring constraint relaxation problem** is a tuple $Q = \langle V, D, A, C, B, R \rangle$:*

- *V is a set of variables*
- *D is a set of values to be assigned to variables*
- *S denotes the set of all assignments, written as functions $s : V \to D$.*
- *A and B are c-semirings, and either $\times_A$ is idempotent or $\leq_B$ is a total order.*
- *C is a set of constraints, written as functions $c_i : S \to A$.*
- *R is a corresponding set of relaxation functions $r_i : A \times A \to B$.*

The definition of a relaxation problem extends that of a satisfaction problem with a new c-semiring B and relaxation functions R. The relaxation functions are used to express preferences on the possible relaxations. The following definitions are all given with respect to a semiring constraint relaxation problem $Q = \langle V, D, A, C, B, R \rangle$.

Definition 6. *A sequence $\Delta \in A^{|C|}$ is an **r-delta**. An r-delta, when viewed in conjunction with a complete assignment $s \in S$, provides a replacement 'relaxed' value for each constraint in C. We can measure the total amount of relaxation for a complete assignment s and r-delta Δ by:*

$$\prod_{c_i \in C} r_i(c_i(s), \Delta_i)$$

Definition 7. *We will then define the **relaxed solution** of Q as the function (where $\prod \Delta$ denotes $\Delta_1 \times_{\mathcal{A}} \ldots \times_{\mathcal{A}} \Delta_{|C|}$ and $s \in \mathcal{S}$, $a \in A$):*

$$rsol(s,a) = \sum_{(\prod \Delta)=a} \left(\prod_{c_i \in C} r_i(c_i(s), \Delta_i) \right)$$

We can read this definition as "the minimum amount of relaxation required to change each constraint in such a way that the combined evaluation of s is a". We are then able to define the abstract solutions of a semiring constraint relaxation problem as those which require a minimal amount of relaxation for *any* relaxation target a.

Definition 8. *For a pair of assignments s,t we write $s \preceq t$ to mean $\forall a \in A, rsol(s,a) \leq_{\mathcal{B}} rsol(t,a)$. We will define the **abstract relaxed solutions** of Q as the set:*

$$\{s \in \mathcal{S} : \forall t \in \mathcal{S}, s \npreceq t\}$$

2.1 Example Satisfaction Problem

The original problem from our introductory example is: which student should receive an award? In this problem there exists only one variable; the student. The possible marks, in ascending order, are Bronze, Silver, Gold and Platinum. Two constraints (Brightness and Harmony) determine the marks for each student.

Formally, we have variables $\mathcal{V} = \{v\}$ with domain $\mathcal{D} = \{Amy, Bob, Col, Dan\}$, and a c-semiring $\mathcal{A} = \langle \{Bronze, Silver, Gold, Platinum\}, \max, \min, Bronze, Platinum \rangle$. The constraints $C = \{c_1, c_2\}$ represent the Brightness and Harmony marks respectively:

$s(v)$	$c_1(s)$	$c_2(s)$	$c_1(s) \times_{\mathcal{A}} c_2(s)$
Amy	Gold	Bronze	Bronze
Bob	Silver	Silver	Silver
Col	Bronze	Bronze	Bronze
Dan	Bronze	Silver	Bronze

The abstract solution is obviously 'Bob' as he received the highest final mark. However, as described in the introduction, we are not satisfied with the abstract solution and wish to relax out constraints.

2.2 Example Relaxation Problem

The relaxation problem from our introductory example is: which student should be awarded if we relax our constraints? The variables, domains, and constraints of our original problem are retained. However, we add an additional relaxation c-semiring $\mathcal{B}$ and set of relaxation functions $\mathcal{R}$. For simplicity we will use the same relaxation function for both constraints (so $r_1 = r_2 = r$), and the c-semiring $\mathcal{B} = \langle \mathbb{Z}^+ \cup \{\infty\}, \min, +, \infty, 0 \rangle$.

Within the context of our example, the relaxation function r can be said to measure the 'sacrifice' in our marking standards. One possible relaxation function is:

a_1	a_2	$r(a_1, a_2)$
Gold	Platinum	2
Silver	Platinum	4
Silver	Gold	1
Bronze	Platinum	5
Bronze	Gold	4
Bronze	Silver	1
All others		0

Note that r measures sacrifice for component marks (ie. the individual constraints) and *not* the final mark. To determine the sacrifice for changing a students final mark we must combine relaxation measures as per Definition 7:

- to change Amy's final mark to Gold would require changing the Bronze in Harmony to Gold, which amounts to $r(\text{Bronze}, \text{Gold}) = 4$.
- to change Bob's final mark to Gold would require changing the Silver in both constraints to Gold, which amounts to $r(\text{Silver}, \text{Gold}) + r(\text{Silver}, \text{Gold}) = 1 + 1 = 2$.
- to change Amy's final mark to Platinum would require changing the Bronze in Harmony and the Gold in Brightness, which amounts to $r(\text{Bronze}, \text{Platinum}) + r(\text{Gold}, \text{Platinum}) = 5 + 2 = 7$.
- to change Bob's final mark to Platinum would require changing the Silver in both constraints to Platinum, which amounts to $r(\text{Silver}, \text{Platinum}) + r(\text{Silver}, \text{Platinum}) = 4 + 4 = 8$.

We can tabulate the relaxation amounts for each student and each final mark, giving the 'relaxed solution' of Definition 7:

$s(v)$	Platinum	Gold	Silver	Bronze
Amy	7	4	1	0
Bob	8	2	0	0
Col	10	8	2	0
Dan	9	5	1	0

By inspection we can see that the two abstract relaxed solutions are 'Amy' and 'Bob'. If we wish to relax our marks to give a student Gold, then Bob is the best choice, requiring only a relaxation amount of 2. However, if we wish to relax our marks to give a student Platinum, then Amy is the best choice, requiring only a relaxation amount of 7. So depending on how far we wish to relax our constraints we may end up awarding different students. Note that we can never award Col or Dan under *any* relaxation.

2.3 Relaxing Other Solutions

As a sidenote, it is interesting also to consider how we might adjust final marks for *other* students if, for example, Amy receives a final mark of Platinum. To give Amy a final mark of Platinum requires a relaxation of 6, and the highest final mark Bob can receive with the same relaxation amount is Gold. Therefore it can be argued that if we relax our marking to assign Amy Platinum, we *should* also assign Bob Gold. Col and Dan should also be assigned at least Silver and Gold respectively. Following this reasoning we can determine the new final marks for different relaxations amounts:

Relaxation	Amy	Bob	Col	Dan
0	Bronze	Silver	Bronze	Bronze
1	Silver	Silver	Bronze	Silver
2	Silver	Gold	Silver	Silver
4	Gold	Gold	Silver	Silver
5	Gold	Gold	Silver	Gold
7	Platinum	Gold	Silver	Gold
8	Platinum	Platinum	Gold	Gold
9	Platinum	Platinum	Gold	Platinum
10	Platinum	Platinum	Platinum	Platinum

However, this reasoning assumes that we are trying to find 'a relaxed final mark for each student' and not 'a new relaxed marking scheme'. Note that, by the above table, to assign Amy Gold we must also assign Bob Gold, and this would supposedly require a relaxation amount of 4. However, these each require a *different* relaxation; to find a single marking scheme which gives them both Gold simultaneously may require a greater relaxation amount.

To find 'a relaxed final mark for each student' is subtly different to finding 'a relaxed marking scheme to achieve some goal'. They correspond to the tasks of 'exploring the possible outcomes of all relaxed SCSPs' and 'finding a single new relaxed SCSP'. Either is a valid task and achievable within our framework, but not simultaneously.

3   Constraint Relaxation with One Semiring

The two-semiring formulation of the semiring constraint relaxation problem obviously deviates from the usual semiring constraint satisfaction framework, making application of existing algorithms and results difficult. We wish to define a new c-semiring which unifies the two c-semirings, and appropriate constraints to model the semiring constraint relaxation problem as a semiring constraint satisfaction problem. In capturing the constraint relaxation problem as a regular semiring constraint satisfaction problem we also demonstrate the flexibility of the semiring framework in solving a wider variety of choice problems.

Let $Q = \langle \mathcal{V}, \mathcal{D}, \mathcal{A}, C, \mathcal{B}, \mathcal{R} \rangle$ be a semiring constraint relaxation problem. We wish to define a new semiring constraint satisfaction problem $\mathcal{P}' = \langle \mathcal{V}, \mathcal{D}, \mathcal{U}, \mathcal{E} \rangle$ such that the abstract solutions are the same as that of Q. We will define a unified c-semiring which captures all possible relaxations, and describe the adaptation of existing constraints. These definitions will then be demonstrated in a detailed worked example.

Definition 9. *Given a pair of c-semirings* $\mathcal{A}, \mathcal{B}$ *we define the* **unified c-semiring** $\mathcal{U} = \langle U, +_{\mathcal{U}}, \times_{\mathcal{U}}, 0_{\mathcal{U}}, 1_{\mathcal{U}} \rangle$ *as follows:*

- *U is the set of monotonic decreasing functions* $u : A \to B$, *where* $u(0_{\mathcal{A}}) = 1_{\mathcal{B}}$.
- *$0_{\mathcal{U}}(a_3) = 1_{\mathcal{B}}$ when* $a_3 = 0_{\mathcal{A}}$; *$0_{\mathcal{B}}$ otherwise*

- $1_{\mathcal{U}}(a_3) = 1_{\mathcal{B}}$
- $(u_1 +_{\mathcal{U}} u_2)(a_3) = u_1(a_3) +_{\mathcal{B}} u_2(a_3)$
- $(u_1 \times_{\mathcal{U}} u_2)(a_3) = \displaystyle\sum_{a_1 \times_{\mathcal{A}} a_2 = a_3} u_1(a_1) \times_{\mathcal{B}} u_2(a_2)$

Note that c-semiring values in U describe the level of relaxation required to be able to use each A-semiring value. Therefore we have defined the operators and elements of U as *functions* mapping A-semiring value to B-semiring values.

Also note that our intent with the c-semiring $\mathcal{U}$ is to capture the concept of 're-laxation functions mapping $A \to B$' within the c-semiring itself. As will be described later, we are able to develop new constraints e_i for $\mathcal{U}$ which, given a variable-value as-signment, return an element of U describing the amount of relaxation required for any choice of $a \in A$. Keeping this in mind, we will describe the formulation of $\times_{\mathcal{U}}$ and $+_{\mathcal{U}}$ in detail:

$u_1(a_3) +_{\mathcal{B}} u_2(a_3)$ A U-semiring value encapsulates all possible (relaxed) A-semiring values, with corresponding B-semiring (penalty for do-ing the relaxation) values. $u_1(a_1)$ may be read as 'the amount of relaxation required to change an original constraint to give a_1 for a particular variable-value assignment'. For the $+_{\mathcal{U}}$ oper-ator we wish to determine the minimum amount of relaxation given the *choice* between u_1 and u_2. Therefore, for each relaxed A-semiring value a_3 we choose the best possible amount of re-laxation: $u_1(a_3) +_{\mathcal{B}} u_2(a_3)$.

$u_1(a_1) \times_{\mathcal{B}} u_2(a_2)$ Whereas the $+_{\mathcal{U}}$ operator is defined to select between two U-semiring values, the $\times_{\mathcal{U}}$ operator must *combine* two U-semiring values. Again, a U-semiring value encapsulates all possible (relaxed) A-semiring values, with corresponding B-semiring (penalty for doing the relaxation) values. Therefore we read $u_1(a_1) \times_{\mathcal{B}} u_2(a_2)$ as 'the total amount of relaxation required to change a pair of distinct original constraints to give a_1 and a_2 for a particular variable-value assignment'.

$\displaystyle\sum_{a_1 \times_{\mathcal{A}} a_2 = a_3}$ Recall that we are attempting to minimise the penalty values (ie. find the minimal relaxation), and so the B-semiring value $(u_1 \times_{\mathcal{U}} u_2)(a_3)$ must be 'the *minimum* amount of relaxation re-quired to use the A-semiring value a_3'. To that end, we explore the combined amount of relaxation required for all pairs of val-ues a_1, a_2 such that $a_1 \times_{\mathcal{A}} a_2 = a_3$. This can be seen as 'consid-ering all possible relaxations of the pair of original constraints, and determining the total relaxation required in each case'. The $\sum$ operator (which is the basis for the $\leq_B$ ordering) then deter-mines the minimum amount of relaxation required.

Lemma 1. $+_{\mathcal{U}}$ *is a commutative, associative and idempotent operator on U, and* $\times_{\mathcal{U}}$ *is a commutative, associative, and binary operator on U*

Proof. All properties for $+_{\mathcal{U}}$ follow trivially from the matching properties of $+_{\mathcal{B}}$. Commutativity of $\times_{\mathcal{U}}$ follows from the symmetry in the definition of $\times_{\mathcal{U}}$ and the commutativity of the $+_{\mathcal{A}}, \times_{\mathcal{A}}$ and $\times_{\mathcal{B}}$ operators used. It is also evident that $\times_{\mathcal{U}}$ is binary. We must then prove that $\times_{\mathcal{U}}$ is associative. The following steps provide a simplification of $(u_1 \times_{\mathcal{U}} u_2) \times_{\mathcal{U}} u_3$ which, through symmetry, is obviously equal to $u_1 \times_{\mathcal{U}} (u_2 \times_{\mathcal{U}} u_3)$.

$$((u_1 \times_{\mathcal{U}} u_2) \times_{\mathcal{U}} u_3)(a_3) = \sum_{a_1 \times_{\mathcal{A}} a_2 = a_3} \left(\sum_{a'_1 \times_{\mathcal{A}} a'_2 = a_1} u_1(a'_1) \times_{\mathcal{B}} u_2(a'_2)) \right) \times_{\mathcal{B}} u_3(a_2)$$

$$[\text{by distributivity of} \times_{\mathcal{B}}] = \sum_{a_1 \times_{\mathcal{A}} a_2 = a_3} \left(\sum_{a'_1 \times_{\mathcal{A}} a'_2 = a_1} u_1(a'_1) \times_{\mathcal{B}} u_2(a'_2) \times_{\mathcal{B}} u_3(a_2) \right)$$

$$[\text{by associativity of} +_{\mathcal{B}}] = \sum_{a'_1 \times_{\mathcal{A}} a'_2 \times_{\mathcal{A}} a_2 = a_3} u_1(a'_1) \times_{\mathcal{B}} u_2(a'_2) \times_{\mathcal{B}} u_3(a_2)$$

Theorem 1. $\mathcal{U} = \langle U, +_{\mathcal{U}}, \times_{\mathcal{U}}, 0_{\mathcal{U}}, 1_{\mathcal{U}} \rangle$ *satisfies the requirements of a c-semiring.*

Proof. By the above lemmas, and inspection of the $1_{\mathcal{U}}$ and $0_{\mathcal{U}}$ elements, it is evident that all requirements of Definition 1 except distributivity are proven to be satisfied. We can prove distributivity as follows:

$$((u_1 +_{\mathcal{U}} u_2) \times_{\mathcal{U}} u_3)(a_3) = \sum_{a_1 \times_{\mathcal{A}} a_2 = a_3} (u_1(a_1) +_{\mathcal{B}} u_2(a_1)) \times_{\mathcal{B}} u_3(a_2)$$

$$[\text{by distributivity of} \times_{\mathcal{B}}] = \sum_{a_1 \times_{\mathcal{A}} a_2 = a_3} (u_1(a_1) \times_{\mathcal{B}} u_3(a_2)) +_{\mathcal{B}} (u_2(a_1) \times_{\mathcal{B}} u_3(a_2))$$

$$[\text{by associativity of} +_{\mathcal{B}}] = \sum_{a_1 \times_{\mathcal{A}} a_2 = a_3} (u_1(a_1) \times_{\mathcal{B}} u_3(a_2)) +_{\mathcal{B}}$$
$$\sum_{a_1 \times_{\mathcal{A}} a_2 = a_3} (u_2(a_1) \times_{\mathcal{B}} u_3(a_2))$$

$$[\text{by definition of} \times_{\mathcal{U}}] = (u_1 \times_{\mathcal{U}} u_3)(a_3) +_{\mathcal{B}} (u_2 \times_{\mathcal{U}} u_3)(a_3)$$
$$[\text{by definition of} +_{\mathcal{U}}] = ((u_1 \times_{\mathcal{U}} u_3) +_{\mathcal{U}} (u_2 \times_{\mathcal{U}} u_3))(a_3)$$

Using this unified c-semiring $\mathcal{U}$ we must now model each constraint/relaxation pair as a constraint. The following definition gives that transformation:

Definition 10. *Given a constraint c_i and a relaxation function r_i we can form a* **unified constraint** e_i *mapping variable-value tuples to a function in U. For any given variable-value assignment s we have $e_i(s) = u \in U$ where $u(a) = r_i(c_i(s), a)$ for all $a \in A$.*

This definition allows us to construct a new set of constraints $\mathcal{E}$ to replace the constraints and relaxations c_i, r_i of the semiring constraint relaxation problem. We are then able to construct a new semiring constraint satisfaction problem $\mathcal{P}' = \langle V, \mathcal{D}, \mathcal{U}, \mathcal{E} \rangle$ from the relaxation problem $Q = \langle V, \mathcal{D}, \mathcal{A}, C, \mathcal{B}, \mathcal{R} \rangle$. We must now prove that they are equivalent.

Theorem 2. *Given a semiring constraint relaxation problem $Q = \langle V, D, A, C, B, R \rangle$ and a matching semiring constraint satisfaction problem $P' = \langle V, D, U, E \rangle$ derived by the above definitions, then the relaxed solution of Q is equal to the solution of P'. Formally, $rsol(s,a) = sol(s)(a)$.*

Proof. By a sequence of algebraic substitutions we can prove that $rsol(s,a) = sol(s)(a)$.[1]

$$rsol(s,a) = \sum_{a=\prod\Delta} \left(\prod_{c_i \in C} r_i(c_i(s), \Delta_i) \right)$$

$$\text{[by definition of } e_i(s)\text{]} = \sum_{a=\prod\Delta} \left(\prod_{e_i \in E} e_i(s)(\Delta_i) \right)$$

$$\text{[by definition of } \times_U\text{]} = \left(\prod_{e_i \in E} e_i(s) \right)(a)$$

$$\text{[by definition of } sol(s)\text{]} = sol(s)(a)$$

The abstract solutions of P' are thus equal to the relaxed abstract solutions of Q due to the semantic equivalence of $\leq_U$ (derived from $+_U$) and $\preceq$ (from Definition 8).

3.1 Example

We are now able to reformulate our example semiring constraint relaxation problem Q as a semiring constraint satisfaction problem P'. First we construct the semiring U consisting of functions mapping A to B, as per Definition 9. Simple examples of the operators for U are presented below:

	Platinum	Gold	Silver	Bronze
u_1	5	3	2	0
u_2	8	2	1	0
$u_1 \times_U u_2$	13	5	3	0
$u_1 +_U u_2$	5	2	1	0

Note that each *row* of the above table corresponds to a value from U. For example, the first row describes a semiring value u_1 where $u_1(\text{Platinum}) = 5$ and $u_1(\text{Gold}) = 3$. We will use this table layout for values in U throughout the following example.

Using Definition 10 we are able to convert each constraint c_i and relaxation r_i of Q to a new constraint e_i for P'. We begin with the Brightness constraint:

---

[1] From the proof of Lemma 1 we have a general expression for combining $u_1, \ldots, u_n \in U$.
$$\left(\prod u_i \right)(a) = \sum_{a=\prod\Delta} \left(\prod u_i(\Delta_i) \right).$$

Combine c_1 with r_1 from the old semiring constraint relaxation problem...

$s(v)$	$c_1(s)$
Amy	Gold
Bob	Silver
Col	Bronze
Dan	Bronze

a_1	a_2	$r_1(a_1,a_2)$
Gold	Platinum	2
Silver	Platinum	4
Silver	Gold	1
Bronze	Platinum	5
Bronze	Gold	4
Bronze	Silver	1
All others		0

...to get constraint e_1 for the new semiring constraint satisfaction problem.

$s(v)$	\multicolumn{4}{c}{$e_1(s)$}			
	Platinum	Gold	Silver	Bronze
Amy	2	0	0	0
Bob	4	1	0	0
Col	5	4	1	0
Dan	5	4	1	0

Note well that e_1 remains a unary constraint mapping the assignment of v to a semiring value from $\mathcal{U}$. For example, if s represents the complete assignment in which Bob is selected as 'best student', then $e_1(s) = \{\langle \text{Platinum}, 4 \rangle, \langle \text{Gold}, 1 \rangle, \langle \text{Silver}, 0 \rangle, \langle \text{Bronze}, 0 \rangle\} \in \mathcal{U}$. We can perform the same transformation to obtain a new Harmony constraint:

Combine c_2 with r_2 from the old semiring constraint relaxation problem...

$s(v)$	$c_2(s)$
Amy	Bronze
Bob	Silver
Col	Bronze
Dan	Silver

a_1	a_2	$r_2(a_1,a_2)$
Gold	Platinum	2
Silver	Platinum	4
Silver	Gold	1
Bronze	Platinum	5
Bronze	Gold	4
Bronze	Silver	1
All others		0

...to get constraint e_2 for the new semiring constraint satisfaction problem.

$s(v)$	Platinum	Gold	Silver	Bronze
	\multicolumn{4}{c}{$e_2(s)$}			
Amy	5	4	1	0
Bob	4	1	0	0
Col	5	4	1	0
Dan	4	1	0	0

We then find the solution for each student by $sol(s) = e_1(s) \times_\mathcal{U} e_2(s)$. An example, showing the calculation of $sol(s)$ when $s(v) = $ Amy, is as follows:

	Platinum	Gold	Silver	Bronze
$e_1(s)$	2	0	0	0
$e_2(s)$	5	4	1	0
$sol(s)$	7	4	1	0

Once the solution has been generated, the abstract solutions can be assembled by use of $\leq_\mathcal{U}$. The complete calculation of solution and abstract solutions is presented below:

Compute *sol* **by** $e_1 \times_{\mathcal{U}} e_2$ to get the solution to the new semiring constraint satisfaction problem ...

$s(v)$	sol			
	Platinum	Gold	Silver	Bronze
Amy	7	4	1	0
Bob	8	2	0	0
Col	10	8	2	0
Dan	9	5	1	0

...and use $\leq_{\mathcal{U}}$ to obtain the abstract solutions.

$s(v)$	Platinum	Gold	Silver	Bronze
Amy	7	4	1	0
Bob	8	2	0	0

As found in the relaxed abstract solutions of Q, Amy and Bob are unable to be compared and no relaxation can make Col or Dan our best student. The difference between Q and $\mathcal{P}'$ is that we are able to use existing algorithms and results of semiring constraint satisfaction to solve $\mathcal{P}'$.

3.2   Notes on Efficiency and Correctness

Note that in our example the calculation of $\times_{\mathcal{U}}$ was quite trivial, requiring only simple application of $\times_{\mathcal{B}}$. This will always occur if $\times_{\mathcal{A}}$ is idempotent.

Theorem 3. *If* $\times_{\mathcal{A}}$ *is idempotent, then* $(u_1 \times_{\mathcal{U}} u_2)(a_3) = u_1(a_3) \times_{\mathcal{B}} u_2(a_3)$. *If* $\times_{\mathcal{B}}$ *is also idempotent, then* $\times_{\mathcal{U}}$ *is idempotent.*

Proof. Let $a_1, a_2, a_3 \in A$ be any values such that $a_1 \times_{\mathcal{A}} a_2 = a_3$ and so $a_3 \leq_{\mathcal{A}} a_1, a_2$. By Definition 9 we know that u_1 is monotonic decreasing, and so $u_1(a_1) \leq_{\mathcal{B}} u_1(a_3)$ and $u_2(a_2) \leq_{\mathcal{B}} u_2(a_3)$. Therefore $(a_1 \times_{\mathcal{A}} a_2 = a_3) \Rightarrow (u_1(a_1) \times_{\mathcal{B}} u_2(a_2) \leq_{\mathcal{B}} u_1(a_3) \times_{\mathcal{B}} u_2(a_3))$. Using this result we can show the following:

$$(u_1 \times_{\mathcal{U}} u_2)(a_3) = \sum_{a_1 \times_{\mathcal{A}} a_2 = a_3} u_1(a_1) \times_{\mathcal{B}} u_2(a_2)$$

$$[\text{by above results}] = u_1(a_1) \times_{\mathcal{B}} u_2(a_2), \text{ where } a_1 = a_2 = a_3$$

$$[\text{by substitution}] = u_1(a_3) \times_{\mathcal{B}} u_2(a_3)$$

Assuming that $\times_{\mathcal{B}}$ is also idempotent, then $(u_1 \times_{\mathcal{U}} u_1)(a_3) = u_1(a_3) \times_{\mathcal{B}} u_1(a_3) = u_1(a_3)$.

Note that when $\times_{\mathcal{A}}$ is *not* idempotent, the calculations may be non-trivial and involve the consideration of many pairs $a_1, a_2 \in \mathcal{A}$. However, by Definition 5 we know that if $\times_{\mathcal{A}}$ is not idempotent then $\leq_{\mathcal{B}}$ must be a total order. This restriction ensures that for each a_3 that there exists *some* a_1, a_2 such that $(u_1 \times_{\mathcal{U}} u_2)(a_3) = u_1(a_1) \times_{\mathcal{B}} u_2(a_2)$.

Without the ability to identify a specific a_1, a_2 for each a_3 the operator $\times_{\mathcal{U}}$ may be 'overly optimistic' and fail to identify a real relaxation. The idempotency of $\mathcal{A}$, or the total order of $\leq_{\mathcal{B}}$, ensure the correctness of $\times_{\mathcal{U}}$.

4   Applications

We have formally presented a concept of 'relaxation' for semiring constraint satisfaction problems. It has been deliberately limited, permitting less freedom than some alternative notions [6], but more than our previous work DBLP:conf/ausai/GhoseH02. However, we argue that little is lost and have shown how the resulting relaxation problem itself can be modelled as a semiring constraint satisfaction problem. In doing so we have extended the usefulness of SCSP, while retaining properties useful for algorithm development.

Although the example used is trivial (one variable, two unary constraints) it serves to demonstrate how relaxation can be performed on a semiring constraint satisfaction problem. The formulation of the operators has been made with few assumptions on the c-semirings or constraints themselves, ensuring applicability to many domains and generalisation of some existing work. For example:

– finding the optimal solutions of a semiring constraint satisfaction problem when subjected to different numbers of original constraints
– determining the most cost-effective upgrade to manufacturing machinery to permit a configuration with increased reliability (reliability measured with $\mathcal{A}$, cost to alter reliability measured with $\mathcal{B}$)

Note that the unified semiring approach generalises the example of constraint relaxation presented in [1]. For example, given any semiring $\mathcal{A}$ we can measure the number of constraints 'satisfied' with a simple integer-based $\mathcal{B} = \langle \mathbb{Z}^+ \cup \{\text{inf}\}, \min, +, \text{inf}, 0 \rangle$ and relaxation function r where $r(a_1, a_2) = 1$ iff $a_2 \not\leq_{\mathcal{A}} a_1$. The resulting SCSP with semiring $\mathcal{U}$ will have, as abstract solution, those value assignments which require discarding the least number of constraints to reach any threshold in $\mathcal{A}$.

References

[1] Stefano Bistarelli, Eugene C. Freuder, and Barry O'Sullivan. Encoding partial constraint satisfaction in the semiring-based framework for soft constraints. In *ICTAI*, pages 240–245. IEEE Computer Society, 2004.

[2] Stefano Bistarelli, Ugo Montanari, and Francesca Rossi. Constraint solving over semirings. In *IJCAI (1)*, pages 624–630, 1995.

[3] Stefano Bistarelli, Ugo Montanari, and Francesca Rossi. Semiring-based constraint logic programming. In *IJCAI (1)*, pages 352–357, 1997.

[4] Stefano Bistarelli, Ugo Montanari, and Francesca Rossi. Semiring-based constraint satisfaction and optimization. *J. ACM*, 44(2):201–236, 1997.

[5] Stefano Bistarelli, Ugo Montanari, Francesca Rossi, Thomas Schiex, Gérard Verfaillie, and Hélène Fargier. Semiring-based csps and valued csps: Frameworks, properties, and comparison. *Constraints*, 4(3):199–240, 1999.

[6] Louise Leenen, Thomas A. Meyer, and Aditya K. Ghose. Relaxations of semiring constraint satisfaction problems. In S. de Givry and W. Zhang, editors, *CP 2005 Workshop on Preferences and Soft Constraints - Soft-2005*, 2005.

Intelligent Information Personalization Leveraging Constraint Satisfaction and Association Rule Methods

Syed Sibte Raza Abidi and Yan Zeng

Faculty of Computer Science, Dalhousie University,
Halifax, B3H 1W5, Canada
{sraza, yzeng@cs.dal.ca}

Abstract. Recommender systems, using information personalization methods, provide information that is relevant to a user-model. Current information personalization methods do not take into account whether multiple documents when recommended together present a factually consistent outlook. In the realm of content-based filtering, in this paper, we investigate establishing the factual consistency between the set of documents deemed relevant to a user. We approach information personalization as a constraint satisfaction problem, where we attempt to satisfy two constraints—i.e. user-model constraints to determine the relevance of a document to a user and consistency constraints to establish factual consistency of the overall personalized information. Our information personalization framework involves: (a) an automatic constraint acquisition method, based on association rule mining, to derive consistency constraints from a corpus of documents; and (b) a hybrid of constraint satisfaction and optimization methods to derive an optimal solution comprising both relevant and factually consistent documents. We apply our information personalization framework to filter news items using the Reuters-21578 dataset.

1 Introduction

Information seekers are different in nature in that they manifest different information seeking behavior, therefore their information seeking experience and outcome should not only be unique but it should be tailored to their individual persona, purpose, interests, educational backgrounds, demographics and preferences. Information Personalization (IP) research purports strategies to either filter or adapt information items based on both the user's characteristics and information retrieval criterion [1, 2, 3]. The ensuing information personalization systems employ adaptive hypermedia, information retrieval and artificial intelligence methods to (a) formulate a user-model and (b) leverage this user-model to personalize the information to be recommended to an individual user. From an AI perspective, a variety of techniques have been employed for pursuing IP. Foltz used latent semantic indexing (LSI) to perform information personalization [4]; Mooney and Roy developed a book recommending system based on a Bayesian text classifier [5]; Malone et al built a rule-based system to filter e-mail messages [6]; Jennings and Higuchi helped users get better access to news service using neural-networks [7]; Desjardins and Godin use genetic algorithms

L. Lamontagne and M. Marchand (Eds.): Canadian AI 2006, LNAI 4013, pp. 134–145, 2006.
© Springer-Verlag Berlin Heidelberg 2006

for personalization [8]. However, pursuing IP as a constraint satisfaction problem is a novel approach.

Notwithstanding the efficacy of intelligent IP systems to determine the relevance of the recommended information item towards a user-model, it can nevertheless be argued that the underlying information personalization mechanism do not account for the factual consistency between the recommended information items—i.e. whether multiple recommended information items when presented together present a consistent outlook or inadvertently lead to a contradictory outlook. We believe that whilst two information items may be relevant to the user model, there may be instances when their simultaneous presentation to the user can potentially lead to a situation whereby one information item is stating a certain fact/recommendation whilst the other information item maybe contradicting the same fact/recommendation. Alternatively, users may seek information items that present divergent views in which case factually inconsistent information items need to be presented to the user. In each case, the requirement is to establish the factual similarity/dissimilarity between two information items.

We approach IP as a constraint satisfaction problem. Intuitively speaking, the problem of information personalization entails the satisfaction of two different constraints for each information item: (a) *relevancy constraints* to establish the relevance of the document to the user; and (b) *consistency constraints* to establish the factual consistency between the selected documents. Our approach to IP involves the satisfaction of the abovementioned constraints such that: (i) given a large set of documents we select only those documents that correspond to the user-model; (ii) given the selected user-compatible documents, we retain only those documents that cumulatively present a level of factually consistency as specified by the user; and (iii) we attempt to maximize the information coverage of the personalized information by selecting the largest possible set of documents that satisfy the above two constraints. In our work IP is achieved without deep content analysis, rather by leveraging the pre-defined classification of documents in terms of topics.

In this paper, we build on our previous work on IP [9, 10] by extending it in terms of (a) an automatic constraint acquisition method based on association rule mining [11] to derive consistency constraints from a corpus of documents. This current method eliminates the need for acquiring consistency constraints from domain experts which was previously viewed as a bottleneck; (b) adding more flexibility to the constraint satisfaction framework by solving IP as an Over-constrained CSP through a hybrid of partial constraint satisfaction and optimization methods; and (c) a user preference setting mechanism whereby users can set the personalization criteria, such as tolerance to inconsistency or degree of information comprehensiveness in line with their information needs. We demonstrate the working of our IP framework for news item selection for a personalized news delivery service using the Reuters-21578, Distribution 1.0 data-set.

2 Specification of an IP Problem

Computationally, constraint satisfaction methods allow the efficient navigation of large search spaces to find an optimal solution that entails the assignment of a value from its domain to every problem variable, in such a way that every constraint is satisfied. This may involve finding (a) just one solution with no preferences, (b) all solutions, or (c) an optimal solution given some objective function [12, 13, 14]. In our work, the problem of IP is specified as follows:

2.1 User-Model

The user-model characterizes the user in terms of: (a) user's *interests* represented as a list of topics, (b) user's *tolerance* towards inter-document inconsistency, and (c) user's *preference* towards the coverage of the solution—i.e. whether the solution should satisfy all user-interests or instead it should satisfy all consistency constraints.

2.2 Information Items

The information items (i.e. documents) comprise two sections: (a) *Content* section that contains the actual information; and (b) *Context* section that contains a list of topics categorizing the document. During the IP process, the topics in the context section are compared with the topics mentioned within user-model to determine the relevance of a document to a particular user.

2.3 Information Personalization Constraints

Two types of constraints are used to pursue IP: (a) *Relevancy constraints* to ensure that the selected documents are relevant to the user's interest as specified in the user-model; and (b) *Consistency constraints* to (i) ensure that the personalized information is factually consistent. This is achieved through *negative consistency constraints,* which define what pairs of topics cannot co-exist together. Negative consistency constraints are represented as the tuple *nc (topic1, topic2, degree)*, where *degree* is the degree of inconsistency between the two topics. Two documents cannot be simultaneously presented to the user if the topics they represent cannot coexist; and (ii) to maximize the coverage of the personalized information. This is achieved through *positive consistency constraints*, which define what topics' if simultaneously presented would likely be of interest to the user. Positive consistency constraints are represented as the tuple *pc (topic1, topic2, degree)*, where *degree* is the degree of similarity between the two topics. For example, recently in the news the topics *Ice-Skating* and *Winter Olympics 2006* appeared quite frequently, thus suggesting a positive consistency constraint between *Winter Olympics 2006* and *Ice-Skating.* Such a constraint can be used to recommend additional information about *Winter Olympics 2006* if the user is interested in *Ice-Skating* and vice versa.

2.4 Information Personalization Requirements

Given a user-model, a corpus of documents and a set of constraints, our solution to an IP problem needs to address the following requirements:

1. The personalized information should be relevant to the interests of the user. The user may choose the degree of relevance to include either all or a partial list of topics of interest.

2. The personalized information should be factually consistent—i.e. the set of documents being presented to the user should mutually satisfy the consistency constraint.
3. The IP process should attempt to find the largest set of consistent documents in terms of the coverage of topics defined in the user-model.

2.5 Defining IP as a Constraint Satisfaction Problem

In our constraint satisfaction approach for information personalization, the topics representing the user's interest are viewed as variables, and domains of the variables comprise any combination of available documents. Requirement 1 can be solved as a unary constraint to the variables and represented by constraint c_1. Requirement 2 can be represented by a unary constraint c_2 and a binary constraint c_3. Requirement 3 can be addressed through an objective function O. c_1, c_2, c_3 and O are explained below.

We define our IP problem as P (V, D, C, O).

- Variable set $V = \{v_1, v_2, \ldots, v_n\}$, where n is the number of topics of a user's interest; v_i, $1 \leq i \leq n$, represents the ith topic of a user's interest.
- Domain set $D = \{d_1, d_2, \ldots, d_n\}$; d_i, $1 \leq i \leq n$, represents the domain of v_i. Suppose $s = \{t_1, t_2, \ldots, t_m\}$ is a set consisting of all documents, then d_i is the power set of s without the empty set ø. E.g. If $\{t_1, t_2\}$ is the set of documents, the domain of the variable will be $\{\{t_1\}, \{t_2\}, \{t_1, t_2\}\}$.
- Constraint set $C = \{c_1, c_2, c_3\}$; $c_1 = rel(v_i)$, where $1 \leq i \leq n$, is a unary constraint, and means the value of v_i must be relevant to users' interest (Requirement 1). Suppose v_i represents the ith topic of a user's interest, and the domain of v_i is $\{\{t_1\}, \{t_2\}, \{t_1, t_2\}\}$. By checking the topics of t_1 and t_2, we know t_1 is relevant to the ith topic of the user's interest, but t_2 is not. To satisfy c_1, $\{t_2\}$ and $\{t_1, t_2\}$ will be removed from the domain of v_i. $c_2 = con1(v_i)$, where $1 \leq i \leq n$, is a unary constraint, and means the documents assigned to v_i must be consistent to each other (Requirement 2). Suppose the system is trying to assign $\{t_1, t_2\}$ to v_1. To decide whether c_2 is satisfied or not, we can check the consistency between t_1 and t_2. Suppose t_1 presents topics 'acquisition' and 'stocks', and t_2 presents topics 'acquisition' and 'gold'. We take one topic from t_1 and t_2 respectively to form pairs of topics ordered alphabetically. Then we get four pairs - *(acquisition, acquisition), (acquisition, gold), (acquisition, stocks)* and *(gold, stocks)*. We check these four pairs against the effective negative consistency constraints, and find that *(acquisition, gold)* triggers a negative constraint. So we know c_2 is violated and the assignment fails. $c_3 = con2(v_k, v_j)$, where $k \neq j$ and $1 \leq k, j \leq n$, is a binary constraint, and means the value of v_k and v_j must be consistent to each other (Requirement 2). When checking c_3, we take a document from the value of both variables to form pairs of documents. If any pair is inconsistent, c_3 is violated.
- $O = \Sigma_i (n_i * weight_i)$ is the objective function, where i is a member of the set of satisfied positive consistency constraints--S. n_i is the time the constraint i is satisfied. $weight_i$ is the correlation value of the constraint i. The target is to find a complete valuation that maximizes the objective function. This function will be used in step3 (coverage maximization) of our CSP process solving.

- From the above specification, it can be seen that our IP problem is an Over-constrained CSP (OCSP)—i.e. a complete valuation that satisfies all hard constraints cannot be guaranteed—because the settings of the user's information personalization preferences may lead to the non-satisfaction of the negative consistency constraints. In this case, (a) if a user prefers *maximum coverage of the topics of interest* then the solution that covers the largest possible number of topics of interest whilst violating the least number of negative consistency constraints will be selected, and (b) If the user prefers a certain degree of *consistency in the adapted information* then the solution will allow only the corresponding violation of negative consistency constraints. In order to address OCSP, we have modified our CSP as follows: (i) add the empty set ϕ to the domain of variables; and (ii) add a collection of constraints, $c_4 = \{no\_empty(v_i), 1 \leq i \leq n\}$. It means the empty set is a variable's last choice. Now the constraint set $C = \{c_1, c_2, c_3, c_4\}$.

3   Constraint Satisfaction Based IP Framework

Our IP framework performs two related functions: (a) given a corpus of documents it automatically finds the consistency constraints; and (b) given a user-profile it generates an information personalization solution. The functional steps (in shaded boxes) and the technical methods used in our IP framework are illustrated in Figure 1.

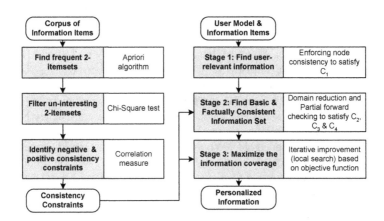

Fig. 1. The functional steps and the corresponding methods used in our IP framework

Our information personalization strategy works in three main stages: (1) Find all the information items relevant to the user-model; (2) Find a simplified solution whereby each user interest is accounted for by a single information item, whilst ensuring factual consistency between the selected information items; (3) Use the simplified solution as the basis to maximize the scope of the solution by including more information items that satisfy both relevance and consistency constraints.

3.1 Our Approach for Consistency Constraint Acquisition

One problem that we faced in our previous work was the acquisition of consistency constraints from domain experts. The literature is inconclusive in this regard. Padmanabhuni et al [15] suggest a framework for learning only positive constraints for discrete domain; O'Sullivan et al [16] use an interactive approach to acquire constraints from users by searching through a 'hypothesis space' of constraints.

In our current work, we addressed this problem by acquiring consistency constraints directly from the given corpus of information items (with pre-assigned topics) by using the association rule-mining approach [5]. The premise of the approach is that when information is composed it entails some inherent relationships between discussion topics that can meaningfully co-occur within a given document. Such relationships between topics are largely determined by the authors' working knowledge. We leverage these intrinsic relationships between topics to establish consistency constraints such that the frequency of co-occurrence of information topics may reflect the degree of consistency between the topics. We treat topics as items in the *Apriori* rule association method to find 2-itemsets [5]. We select the 2-itemsets with high support value and calculate the correlation between the two items as $corr(A,B) = \dfrac{p(AB)}{p(A)p(B)}$. The correlation value is used to distinguish between positive and negative consistency constraints as follows:

- If $0 < corr(A, B) < 1$, A and B are correlated negatively it means these two topics are inconsistent to each other, so a *negative consistency constraint* can be established between these two topics.
- If $corr(A, B) > 1$, A and B are positively correlated, and they encourage the co-occurrence of each other, so a *positive consistency constraint* is found between these two topics.
- If $corr(A, B) = 1$, A and B are independent to each other.

After our experiments with the Reuters-21578 dataset, we acquired 913 frequent 2-itemsets We used the Chi-Square statistical significance test to measure the interestingness of the 2-itemsets [17], where the Chi-Square significance level was set

Table 1. Illustration of some 2-itemsets and their selection as consistency constraints

Topic1	Topic2	Frequency	Correlation	Chi_Square	Action
crude	natural-gas	81	11.171	803.615	**Positive Constraint**
rice	wheat	20	11.089	189.774	**Positive Constraint**
livestock	soy-meal	3	11.079	.345	Removed
...	...	...	...	...	...
grain	trade	20	.657	3.984	**Negative Constraint**
...	...	...	...	...	...
coffee	crude	3	.371	3.433	Removed
acquisition	natural-gas	10	.357	14.914	**Negative Constraint**
...	...	...	...	...	...
acquisition	money-fx	1	5.797E-03	233.783	**Negative Constraint**

to 95% and we acquired a smaller-sized but high quality set of consistency constraints. The consistency constraints were sub-divided into positive and negative consistency constrains based on their correlation values (as shown in Tables 1 and 2).

Table 2. Final distribution of the consistency constraints

Positive/Negative	2-item rules	Interesting 2-item rules
Positively correlated	768	120
Negatively correlated	145	57
TOTAL	913	177

3.2 Solving the Constraint Satisfaction Problem for Information Personalization

We highlighted earlier that our information personalization is an OCSP, and hence its solution can be viewed as a partial constraint satisfaction problem (PCSP) in which a complete valuation is made with some constraints unsatisfied, and the valuation with the smallest distance is selected as the final solution. The distance can be defined as the number of constraints violated by a valuation [18]. Our strategy to solve the PCSP is explained using an exemplar user profile (in Table 3) and dataset (in Table 4).

Table 3. User profile used in the working example

Component	Value
Interests	Acquisition, Gas, Income, Jobs
Tolerance	20% factual inconsistency
Preference	Satisfy all consistency constraints

Table 4. Dataset used for the example

News Item	Topics	News Item	Topics
t_1	acquisition	t_9	jobs
t_2	acquisition, crude, nat-gas	t_{10}	bop, cpi, gnp, jobs
t_3	acquisition, gold, lead, silver, zinc	t_{11}	jobs, trade
t_4	gas	t_{12}	gnp, jobs
t_5	CPI, crude, fuel, gas, nat-gas	t_{13}	acquisition
t_6	fuel, gas	t_{14}	fuel, gas
t_7	crude, gas	t_{15}	jobs, trade
t_8	GNP, income, ipi, retail, trade		

From the user's interests we get four variables, each representing a topic of the user's interest. We refer to these variables as v_{acq}, v_{gas}, v_{income} and v_{jobs}. The domain of these four variables is the power set of the 15 news items that are shown in Table 4.

Step 1: Filter User-Relevant Information
The first step involves finding all the documents that correspond to the user's interest as per requirement 1of the information personalization specification. This involves the

satisfaction of the relevancy constraint by enforcing node consistency to satisfy the unary constraint $c_1 = rel(v_1)$ by comparing the topics of the various documents against a user's interest as noted in the user-model. The node representing the variable v in a constraint graph is node consistent if for every value x in the current domain of v, each unary constraint on v is satisfied. Functionally, if the variable v_{acq} has a value (i.e. news item) that is not equal to the topic '*acquisition*' (one of the four interests of the user) then the value will be filtered out from v_{acq}'s domain. The same process is repeated for v_{gas}, v_{income} and v_{jobs} in case of our working example. At the end of step one we get user-relevant news items for each variable as shown in the second column of Table 5. For example, the relevant set of v_{acq} is found to be $\{t_1, t_2, t_3, t_{13}\}$ and for v_{gas} the relevant set is $\{t_4, t_5, t_6, t_7, t_{14}\}$. After step1, the domain of a variable is the power set of its relevant set, i.e. the domain of v_{acq} is the power set of $\{t_1, t_2, t_3, t_{13}\}$.

Table 5. User relevant items for the variables

Variable	Retained Relevant item	Removed Relevant item	Variable	Retained Relevant item	Removed Relevant item
v_{acq}	t_1, t_2, t_3	t_{13}	v_{income}	t_8	
v_{gas}	t_4, t_5, t_6, t_7	t_{14}	v_{jobs}	$t_9, t_{10}, t_{11}, t_{12}$	t_{15}

Step 2: Find the Basic Information Set

At the end of stage 1, the size of the set of user-relevant items is typically quite large, and likewise the resulting power set is quite large. We feel that in such a situation it is unwise to use systematic methods to solve OCSP because we will probably just be able to find a partial solution for the problem, whereas there may exist the possibility to completely solve the problem—i.e. the adapted information is imperfect and does not meet a user's requirements as perfectly as it is possible. In order to personalize the information with respect to all the constraints in the constraint set C, we attempt to solve a simplified version of the original problem in order to find out: (a) whether the problem can be satisfied completely or not? If not, what is the least number of violated constraints? and (b) what feasible solutions can be used as the starting point for the optimization process in order to maximize the coverage of the personalized information. To answer the above questions, we pursue domain reduction—i.e. eliminate some elements from the domain of variables to make it feasible to search the solution space systematically to find a *basic information set*. A solution is called *basic information set* if (i) each user interest is assigned at most one information item; and (ii) it violates the least number of consistency constraints; and (iii) least number of user-interests have no information item. Domain reduction is done in three steps.

First, we delete duplicate items from the set of user-relevant documents. If a document represents a group of topics that are also represented exactly by other documents, then we keep one document and remove the others.

Second, we delete values with multiple elements from the domain of variables because values with multiple elements can unnecessarily violate more consistency constraints. This enables the domain size of a variable with k relevant items to be reduced from 2^k to $k+1$.

Third, we delete dominating values (sets) from the domain. If the topic set of item t_1 is a subset of the topic set of item t_2, we say t_2 dominates t_1, and t_2 is a dominating item. If a value contains only dominating items, it is a dominating value. Since a dominating item comprises extra topics it offers a stronger likelihood to violate more consistency constraints as compared to the item that it dominates. It may be noted that if t_2 dominates t_1 and t_1 is inconsistent with t_3, t_2 is inconsistent to t_3 too. Hence, if we have checked the consistency between the value of $\{t_1\}$ and $\{t_3\}$, we do not need to check the consistency between $\{t_2\}$ and $\{t_3\}$ any more. So we can eliminate all dominating values from the domain without changing the characteristics of the problem. Here, we just show for v_{acq} the details of deleting multi-elements and dominating values in Table 6, and the resulting domain of the four variables is shown in Table 7.

Table 6. Deleting multi-element and dominating values

Retained	Removed (dominating)	Removed (multi-elements)
$\emptyset, \{t_1\}$	$\{t_2\}, \{t_3\}$	$\{t_1, t_2\}, \{t_1, t_3\}, \{t_2, t_3\}, \{t_1, t_2, t_3\}$

Table 7. The domain of the variables

Variable	Domain	Variable	Domain
v_{acq}	$\{\emptyset, \{t_1\}\}$	v_{income}	$\{\emptyset, \{t_8\}\}$
v_{gas}	$\{\emptyset, \{t_4\}\}$	v_{jobs}	$\{\emptyset, \{t_9\}\}$

Step 3: Establish Factual Consistency of User-Relevant Information

This step involves establishing the factual consistency between the selected information. After domain reduction we have managed to simplify the solution space to apply a variant of *branch and bound method*—i.e. Partial Forward Checking (PFC)—that systematically searches for the solutions by satisfying the constraints c_2, c_3 and c_4. PFC being a variant of forward checking has been shown to perform better than most systematic methods used to solve PCSP [12]. It may be noted that in comparison with step1, which can be realized quite efficiently, and step4, which can be terminated at any time according to the availability of resources, step3 involves a systematic search and hence is the key to the success of the whole process of information personalization. To ensure this we conducted compared variants of PFC.

We apply PFC algorithm to our PCSP using two different distances: (i) the number of variables assigned to the empty set (violating c_4), referred to as d_{empty} and (ii) the number of times the negative consistency constraints are violated, referred as $d_{violation}$. If a user's preference is 'Satisfy all topics of interest', $d_{violation}$ will be used; otherwise, d_{empty} will be used. For our example, the results of using PFC is shown in Table 8.

Table 8. Factually consistent solutions after domain reduction

Solution	acquisition	gas	income	jobs
1	$\{t_1\}$	$\{t_4\}$	$\emptyset$	$\{t_9\}$
2	$\emptyset$	$\{t_4\}$	$\{t_8\}$	$\{t_9\}$

It may be noted that $\{t_1\}$ and $\{t_8\}$ are inconsistent to each other because of the effectiveness of nc(acquisition, trade, 0.034). For both solutions, the distance is

$d_{empty} = 1$. It means there is one topic of interest left empty. And this calculated distance is the minimum distance that solutions to the original problem can achieve.

Step 4: Maximize Information Coverage

In this step we attempt to maximize the information coverage of the solution obtained in step 3. Note that the solution at this stage contains at most one information item for every topic defined in the user's interest. This condition is in line with requirement 3 of our information personalization specification. We use local search based optimization techniques to improve the solution by assigning values with more elements (information items) to variables (topics of a user's interest) whilst maintaining the factual consistency.

The iterative improvement method [19] used works as follows: First, it sets the solution at step 3 as the current solution and then searches the current solution's neighborhood for a better solution. If there is such a solution, the current solution is set to this 'improved' solution, and the search goes on. Else, the current solution is returned as the result of optimization. The neighborhood of the current solution consists of all solutions whose difference from the current solution is just the value of one variable. Two criteria are used to determine which solution is better: (1) higher value of the objective function, i.e. a higher sum of degrees of the satisfied positive consistency constraints. The positive consistency constraints are checked in the same way the negative consistency constraints are checked, i.e. first construct item pairs from assigned values, then construct topic pairs from item pairs, and finally check topic pairs against positive consistency constraints. The optimization round using this criterion is called *positive consistency round*; and (2) higher number of information items. The optimization round using this criterion is called *cardinality round*.

For optimization purposes, the non-null variables in the factually consistent solution (i.e. Table 8) are restored with their original domain representing information items corresponding to the user's interests (as shown in Table 5). For instance, the domain of v_{acq} is restored to be the power set of $\{t_1, t_2, t_3\}$.

The optimization results (shown in Table 9) lead to two solution—i.e. solution3 and solution4. However, solution4 has the higher objective function value and hence is designated as the final optimized solution. Finally, the information items comprising solution4 will be presented to the user as the information personalization solution based on his/her user-model.

Table 9. Final optimized solutions

Solution	acquisition	gas	income	jobs	Objective function
3	$\{t_1\}$	$\{t_4, t_6\}$	NULL	$\{t_9, t_{10}, t_{12}\}$	45.28
4	NULL	$\{t_4, t_6\}$	$\{t_8\}$	$\{t_9, t_{10}, t_{11}, t_{12}\}$	121.65

4 Evaluations of Variants of Partial Forward Checking

In general, variable and value ordering heuristics are effective in improving efficiency of systematic search methods. In this section we compare the performance of partial forward checking (basic_pfc), partial forward checking with variable ordering (order_pfc), partial forward checking with variable and value ordering (full_pfc) in terms of the number of constraint checks that is a standard measure of efforts for CSP algorithms. The basic branch and bound method was tested to compare it against PFC. The variable ordering heuristic used in this evaluation is the smallest-domain heuristic [20]. The value ordering heuristic used in this evaluation is to select first the value with minimal inconsistency count [20].

For Reuters-21578 dataset and a list of topics of a user's interest, we compare the performance of these algorithms by varying the user's preference (Fig. 2) and tolerance (Fig. 3). From our experiments we note that any variant of PFC performs better than branch and bound method. Furthermore, the full_pfc always gave the best performance which vindicates are decision to use PFC in step 3 for establishing factual consistency.

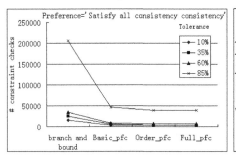

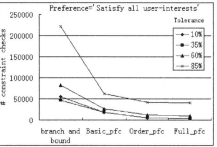

Fig. 2. Performance of algorithms (satisfying all consistency constraints)

Fig. 3. Performance of algorithms (satisfying all user-interests)

5   Concluding Remarks and Future Work

Viewing information personalization as a constraint satisfaction problem offers an interesting AI based perspective to an information retrieval issue. We have demonstrated the successful application of a hybrid of constraint satisfaction methods that offer personalized information that is based on user's interests and personalizetion preferences. Our information personalization strategy makes it possible to find better sub-optimal solutions by combining systematic search and local search for the information personalization problem, and we believe this approach can be applied to other fields as well. In this work, we additionally addressed the core issue of constraint acquisition from the domain knowledge as opposed from domain experts. Our current association rule based approach works with the a priori defined classification of the documents. In future we plan to analyze the content of the document, as opposed to meta-level topics, to establish richer consistency constraints using automated text categorization techniques involving learning mechanisms.

References

1. Belkin N.J., Croft W.B. Information personalization and information retrieval: Two sides of the same coin? *Communications of the ACM*, 35(12), 1992, 29-38.
2. Baeza-Yates, R., Ribeiro-Neto, B. *Modern Information Retrieval*, Addison-Wesley, 1999.
3. Hanani, U., Shapira, B., Shoval, P. Information Filtering: Overview of Issues, Research and Systems. *User Modeling and User-Adapted Interaction,* 11, 2001, 203-259.
4. Foltz, P.W. Using latent semantic indexing for information filtering. In *ACM SIG-OIS*, 1990, 40-47.
5. Mooney, R.J., Roy, L. Content-based book recommending using learning for text categorization. In *Proceedings of the 5th ACM Conference on Digital Libraries*, June 2000, San Antonio, Texas, USA. 195-204.
6. Malone, T.W., Grant, K.R., Turbak, F.A., Brobst, S.A., Cohen, M.D. Intelligent information sharing systems. *Communications of the ACM*, 30(5), 1987, 390-402.
7. Jennings, A., Higuchi, H. A personal news service based on a user model neural network. *IEICE Transactions on Information and Systems.* E75-D(2) 198-210.
8. Desjardins G, Godin R. Combining relevance feedback and genetic algorithms in an Internet information personalization engine. *RIAO'2000 Conference Proceedings.* Vol.2, 2000, Paris, France.
9. Abidi, S.S.R., Han, C. Constraint Satisfaction Methods for Information Personalization. In *A. Tawfik, S. Goodwin (Eds.) Lecture Notes in Artificial Intelligence 3060, 17tth Canadian Conference. on Artificial Intelligence,* London, Ontario, 2004.
10. Abidi, S.S.R., Han, C. An Adaptive Hypermedia System for Information Customization via Content Adaptation. *IADIS International Journal of WWW/Internet,* 2(1), 2004, 79-94
11. Han, J.W., Kamber, M. *Data Mining: Concepts and Techniques.* Morgan Kaufmann Publishers, 2000.
12. Tsang E, Foundations of constraint satisfaction. Academic Press, London, UK. 1993.
13. Barták, R. Constraint programming: In pursuit of the holy grail. *Proceedings of the Week of Doctoral Students (WDS99),* Part IV, MatFyz Press, Prague, 1999, 555-564.
14. Torrens, M., Faltings, B. SmartClients: Constraint satisfaction as a paradigm for scaleable intelligent information systems. *Workshop on Artificial Intelligence on Electronic Commerce, AAAI-99,* 1999, Florida, USA.
15. Padmanabhuni, S., You, J.H., Ghose, A. A framework for learning constraints. *Proc. of the PRICAI Workshop on Induction of Complex Representations,* August 1996.
16. O'Sullivan, B., Freuder, E.C.., O'Connell, S. Interactive Constraint Acquisition. In *Workshop on User-Interaction in Constraint Satisfaction, Seventh International Conference on Principles and Practice of Constraint Programming* - CP 2001, 2001.
17. Brin, S., Motwani, R., Silverstein, C. Beyond Market Baskets - Generalizing Association Rules to Correlations. In *Proceedings of the ACM SIGMOD*, 1997.
18. Freuder, E., Wallace, R. Partial Constraint Satisfaction. *Artificial Intelligence*, Vol. 58, 1992, 21-70.
19. Aarts, E., Lenstra, J.K., eds. *Local search in combinatorial optimization.* Princeton University Press, Princeton, NJ, 2003.
20. Meseguer, P., Bouhmala, N., Bouzoubaa, T., Irgens, M., Sanchez, M. Current Approaches for Solving Over-Constrained Problems. *Constraints*, Vol. 8, 2003, 9-39.

On the Quality and Quantity of Random Decisions in Stochastic Local Search for SAT

Dave A.D. Tompkins and Holger H. Hoos

Department of Computer Science, University of British Columbia
2366 Main Mall, Vancouver, BC, V6T 1Z4, Canada
{davet, hoos}@cs.ubc.ca

Abstract. Stochastic local search (SLS) methods are underlying some of the best-performing algorithms for certain types of SAT instances, both from an empirical as well as from a theoretical point of view. By definition and in practice, random decisions are an essential ingredient of SLS algorithms. In this paper we empirically analyse the role of randomness in these algorithms. We first study the effect of the quality of the underlying random number sequence on the behaviour of well-known algorithms such as Papadimitriou's algorithm and Adaptive Novelty$^+$. Our results indicate that while extremely poor quality random number sequences can have a detrimental effect on the behaviour of these algorithms, there is no evidence that the use of standard pseudo-random number generators is problematic. We also investigate the amount of randomness required to achieve the typical behaviour of these algorithms using derandomisation. Our experimental results indicate that the performance of SLS algorithms for SAT is surprisingly robust with respect to the number of random decisions made by an algorithm.

1 Introduction

The Propositional Satisfiability Problem (SAT) is the prototypical $\mathcal{NP}$-complete problem and a prominent hard combinatorial decision problems. Some of the best known methods for solving certain types of SAT instances are Stochastic Local Search (SLS) algorithms; these are typically incomplete, i.e., they cannot determine that a formula is unsatisfiable, but they often find models of satisfiable formulae surprisingly effectively. Many SLS algorithms are probabilistically approximate complete (PAC) and will solve a soluble instance with arbitrarily high probability when allowed to run long enough [1].

A typical SLS algorithm for SAT consists of an initialisation phase, in which a truth value is assigned to each variable, and a search phase, during which the values of individual, heuristically selected variables are changed in an attempt to reach a satisfying assignment. The search phase is a sequence of search steps known as *flips* because in each step typically one variable's assignment is changed *(or flipped)*. Stochastic (random) decisions are typically used in both phases, and in the following we describe the most common ways SLS algorithms for SAT make use of random decisions:

Variable initialisation is heavily randomised in most SLS algorithms for SAT; typically, the initial variable assignment is obtained by assigning each variable a truth value $\{\top, \bot\}$ chosen uniformly and independently at random.

Heuristic tie-breaking occurs when a choice needs to be made between several alternatives that are ranked identically by a given heuristic evaluation function; many SLS algorithms for SAT break these ties randomly.

L. Lamontagne and M. Marchand (Eds.): Canadian AI 2006, LNAI 4013, pp. 146–158, 2006.
© Springer-Verlag Berlin Heidelberg 2006

Variable selection often includes randomised choices; examples include the noise mechanisms in Novelty and variable selection in Simulated Annealing.

Neighbourhood selection occurs when an algorithm narrows the list of flip candidates to a subset of all the variables. For example, in the WalkSAT algorithms, in each step an unsatisfied clause is selected uniformly at random, and then only variables in occurring in this clause are considered as flip candidates.

Random walk steps involve flipping randomly selected variables; they can help to increase search diversification, to avoid stagnation, and to render an algorithm PAC. In a uniform random walk all variables can be selected with uniform probability. In a conflict-directed random walk only variables occurring in currently unsatisfied clauses can be selected, such as in Papadimitriou's algorithm [2] and WalkSAT [3].

Random restarts cause an algorithm to randomly re-initialise all variables; most SLS algorithms for SAT, including algorithms of purely theoretically interest, such as Schöning's algorithm [4], perform periodic random restarts.

Search control mechanisms can also make use of randomised decisions; examples include the probabilistic smoothing mechanism in the SAPS algorithm [5] and the random selection of the tabu tenure parameter in Robust Tabu Search [6].

The prominent use of random decisions in many components of SLS algorithms raises some interesting questions: Why are most algorithms so heavily randomised? How important are those random decisions? How important is the quality of the underlying random numbers? How much randomness is necessary? Can randomness be eliminated altogether? In this paper, we attempt to shed light on some of these questions.

Some of these questions have been addressed in previous work. Gent and Walsh investigated the role of random decisions in GSAT [7]. They found that random decisions were neither important in the initialisation phase nor for tie breaking, and that deterministic substitutions could be made in both cases. Much of their analysis revolved around the ability of the algorithm to diversify the search during re-initialisation. They did not study the impact of the quality of random decisions, and it is not clear to which extent their observations apply to more powerful SLS algorithms for SAT that do not require restart mechanisms and their application to a broad range of SAT instances.

There has been a large body of work dedicated to the quest for increasingly higher quality random number generators. In the Monte Carlo simulation literature, there has been evidence that even *good* random number generators can produce very undesirable errors in their results [8, 9]. In work related to this paper, Ribeiro *et al.* recently surveyed random number generators to find a good candidate for randomised algorithms [10]. In our previous work [11] we investigated the role of random decisions in the SAPS algorithm, which we will develop further in Section 4.

The remainder of this paper is structured as follows: In Section 2 we briefly introduce the algorithms and problem instances used in our computational experiments reported later. In Section 3 we investigate how important the quality of the random decisions are, while in Section 4 we explore the quantity of random decisions required to achieve the typical behaviour of these algorithms. Finally, Section 5 contains a brief discussion of our main findings and points out some directions for future work.

2 Preliminaries

The first algorithm we consider in this work is conflict-directed random walk (CR-WALK). After randomly initialising all variables, in each search step this algorithm selects a currently unsatisfied clause and flips a randomly chosen variable from that clause. This algorithm was first studied by Papadimitriou, who proved that it solves 2-SAT in expected quadratic time [2]. Extending it with a simple periodic restart mechanism leads to Schöning's algorithm, whose run-time on 3-SAT instances was proven to be bounded from above by $O(1.334^n)$ [4]. More recently, Iwama and Tamaki's have extended Schöning's algorithm to improve this bound to $O(1.324^n)$ [12].

We chose to include CRWALK in our study because it is a prominent, yet very simple algorithm that is purely based on random decisions. Originally, we had decided to include Schöning's algorithm in our study because of its provably excellent worst-case behaviour, but in preliminary experiments on a large set of instances from SATLIB we found no empirical evidence for any differences between its behaviour and that of CRWALK (which, given well-known empirical results on the behaviour of WalkSAT algorithms [13, 1] is not surprising). As will also be apparent from the results reported later in this paper, CRWALK performs quite poorly when compared against high-performance SLS algorithms for SAT, because it completely lacks heuristic guidance.

The two other algorithms we used in this study, Adaptive Novelty$^+$ (ANOV$^+$) [14] and SAPS [5] are amongst the best performing SLS algorithms for SAT currently known. ANOV$^+$, a member of the WalkSAT family, placed first in the random category of the 2004 SAT competition [15]. In addition to random initialisation it uses randomised neighbourhood selection, randomised heuristic variable selection, and conflict directed random walk steps. ANOV$^+$ employs a deterministic mechanism for adapting its noise setting p during the search and therefore requires no parameter tuning.

Scaling and Probabilistic Smoothing (SAPS) changes the space it is searching by dynamically modifying penalty weights associated with the clauses of the given CNF formula [5]. In addition to random initialisation it uses randomised heuristic tie-breaking, randomised search control mechanisms, and uniform random walk steps. SAPS shows performance that is competitive with ANOV$^+$. We mainly included it in this study because (as we will discuss in more detail later) in long search trajectories SAPS approaches deterministic behaviour [11]. In all experiments reported in this study we used the default parameters for SAPS ($\alpha = 1.3$, $\rho = 0.8$, $P_{smooth} = 0.05$, $wp = 0.01$).

All three algorithms (CRWALK, ANOV$^+$ and SAPS) are available as part of the UBCSAT software package [16] which is available for download from the UBCSAT website[1]. Unless otherwise stated (as in Section 3) all experiments have been conducted using the default random number generator in UBCSAT, Mersenne Twister [17].

For our experiments, we have used individual satisfiable instances obtained from SATLIB [18]. We provide brief descriptions here, while more detailed information is available from the SATLIB website[2]. The uniform random 3-SAT instance sets (ufN-*) are all randomly generated with N variables at the phase transition. The hardest, median and easiest instance from these sets are referred to as -hard, -med and

---

[1] http://www.satlib.org/ubcsat
[2] http://www.satlib.org

-easy, respectively. The flatN-* instances are encodings of randomly generated flat graph 3-colouring problems with N vertices; these instances share structure induced by the SAT-encoding. The ii and ssa instances are from the DIMACS challenge set, and are a formulation of Boolean function synthesis problem and encodings from circuit fault analysis, respectively. The bw instances are encodings of a blocks world planning problem and have been popular instances in the literature. The ferry instances are from the SAT 2003 competition industrial category. The anov10M-struct set contains over two thousand instances and includes all structured (non-random) instances currently available on SATLIB where ANOV$^+$ has a median run-time between 1 000 and 10 000 000 steps.

3   The Quality of Random Decisions

When implementing SLS algorithms, all random decisions are realised using a random number generator (RNG). In principle, a true random number generator (TRNG), which obtains a sequence of random numbers from a truly random source could be used. Hardware implementations of TRNGs that obtain random data from physical phenomae, such as atmospheric noise or radioactive decay, are available and are popular in applications such as gambling[3] and cryptography [19]. However, most computer implementations use pseudo-random number generators (PRNG) instead. A PRNG is a finite state machine with memory, and performs deterministic mathematical operations on the state information to generate a sequence of numbers. Once a PRNGs is initialised with a numerical *seed*, it will produce a series of numbers that may have the appearance of being random, but in fact can all be deterministically calculated from the seed. The quality of a PRNG is solely determined by the mathematical operations it performs. Ideally, sequences will be uniform and unbiased (*i.e.*, equal fractions of numbers from the sequence should fall into equal intervals), uncorrelated (*i.e.*, the numbers in the sequence should be statistically independent of one another), and have long periods (because the state information in a PRNG is finite, all PRNGs will eventually cycle, but the period between cycles should be very large) [1].

Because of the importance of high quality random numbers in cryptography and other applications, tests have been developed that measure the quality of a sequence of random data. The American National Institute of Standards and Technology (NIST) has produced a document [20] with companion software[4] to test the quality of random data. The NIST software includes 16 groups of tests that cover a wide variety of statistical properties. Another popular software tool for quickly analysing the quality of random numbers is known as ent and was developed by John Walker at Fourmilab[5].

There are numerous PRNGs available that use a wide variety of mathematical methods. We have selected a few characteristic PRNGs to test, in addition to data generated by a TRNG. The following are brief descriptions of the RNGs we used:

True Random Data. This data was obtained from random.org and was generated by a hardware device measuring atmospheric noise.

---

[3] http://www.first.fraunhofer.de/owx_download/keno-engl.pdf
[4] http://csrc.nist.gov/rng
[5] http://www.fourmilab.ch/random

Table 1. Randomness quality tests on 160MB of data generated by various RNGs. The Bias value is the average value of all bits (the ideal value is 0.5). The χ^2 analysis from ent shows the distribution value and a percentage which indicates how frequently a TRNG would have a larger distribution value, where values $> 95\%$ or $< 5\%$ are highly suspect. The Monte Carlo π analysis from ent gives an estimated value of π and the respective error. For the NIST tests, we report the overall percentage of the tests passed by the respective data, where each of the 16 groups of tests was weighted equally.

	Bias	χ^2 Analysis	Monte Carlo π	NIST %
True random	0.5000290	235.9 (75%)	3.14094 (0.021%)	97.80
Unix C random()	0.4999988	224.6 (90%)	3.14148 (0.004%)	99.50
LCG	0.5000000	0.0 (99.99%)	3.14123 (0.011%)	93.53
LFG	0.5000129	237.3 (75%)	3.14139 (0.007%)	96.69
MT	0.5000204	278.5 (25%)	3.14203 (0.014%)	98.37
Random: Skewed 1.25:1	0.5554831	2165538.1 (0.01%)	2.76998 (11.829%)	16.39
Random: Cycled 16k	0.5000086	4327.3 (0.01%)	3.14631 (0.150%)	59.18

'C' random(). We chose the linux gcc 'C' `random()` function because it is the default PRNG for many programmers, and is also currently the default PRNG for the original WalkSAT software package by Kautz [3] when compiled under Linux. We used gcc v3.3.3 on SuSE Linux v9.1.

LCG. The Linear Congruential Generator (LCG) we chose was based on the ANSI 'C' specification: $I_{j+1} = (I_j \times 1103515245 + 12345)$ except that only one byte (bits 11-18) of random data was collected per iteration, a common practice to improve the quality of this particular PRNG.

LFG. The Lagged Fibonacci Generator (LFG) we chose was from the book by Knuth [21], and the source code is available from his website[6].

MT. The Mersenne Twister (MT) we chose is the MT19937 algorithm [17], which has an astounding period of $(2^{19937} - 1)$. This is the default PRNG in the current release of the UBCSAT software package [16].

In Table 1 we examine the relative quality of the some of these RNGs. There is little difference between the results for the PRNGs and the TRNG, with the exception of LCG, which is clearly the worst of the tested PRNGs. It is often the case that individual sequences of TRNGs fail more tests than individual sequences of PRNGs [20]. The bottom two rows of Table 1 will be discussed later.

We now investigate to which extent the quality of the source of randomness affects SLS behaviour. Intuitively, bias in the random number sequence can be expected to have a negative impact on SLS performance for the following reason. For most random decisions made within an SLS algorithm, there are more bad choices (that increase the length of the current run) than good choices. Most forms of bias would therefore tend to increase the relative probability of making a bad choice. However, note that even when using a TRNG with extreme bias, as long as the probability of generating 0 or 1 at any position of the sequence is greater zero, the PAC property of a given SLS algorithm

---

[6] http://www-cs-faculty.stanford.edu/~knuth/programs/rng.c

Table 2. The effect of different types of random data streams on the CRWALK algorithm. For the true random data, the mean number of search steps (run-length) required to find a solution is given, while for all other sources the mean search steps is given as a fraction of the number required for the true random source. The *c.v.* is calculated as the standard deviation divided by the mean ($\sigma/\bar{x}$). Note that $c.v. = 1$ characterises an exponential run-length distribution, which is typical for high-performance SLS algorithms for SAT. All experiments results are based on 500 runs with a maxiumum run-length of 2^{32} (4.3B) steps. For the cycled streams with a reported ∞ mean, we confirmed cyclic behaviour by examining the respective search trajectories.

	ii8c2		ssa7552-159		flat50-med		uf100-med		uf50-hard	
	$\bar{x}/\bar{x}_{rand}$	c.v.	$\bar{x}/\bar{x}_{rand}$	c.v.	$\bar{x}/\bar{x}_{rand}$	c.v.	$\bar{x}/\bar{x}_{rand}$	c.v.	$\bar{x}/\bar{x}_{rand}$	c.v.
True random	300k	0.99	2.21M	0.97	631k	0.97	76.1M	0.94	372k	0.97
Unix C random()	1.13	0.94	1.02	0.91	0.96	0.93	1.10	0.99	1.10	0.99
LCG	1.13	1.02	1.02	1.00	0.95	0.98	1.02	0.96	1.02	0.96
LFG	1.15	0.99	1.05	1.02	0.94	1.03	0.98	0.97	0.98	0.97
MT	0.97	0.95	0.99	0.98	0.90	0.93	0.93	0.96	0.93	0.96
Skewed 1.25:1	0.48	0.97	3.39	1.08	0.93	0.97	0.97	1.03	0.97	1.03
Skewed 1.5:1	0.29	0.92	**15.27**	0.97	0.85	1.04	1.10	0.96	1.10	0.96
Skewed 2:1	0.13	0.94	> **368**	0.97	0.93	1.03	1.03	0.99	1.03	0.99
Skewed 4:1	**0.06**	1.00	> **2 000**	0.02	0.88	1.02	0.96	1.05	0.96	1.05
Cycled 16k	1.28	0.86	0.66	0.96	0.92	0.87	0.82	1.16	0.82	1.16
Cycled 4k	1.23	0.85	0.82	1.15	0.89	0.83	0.61	1.11	0.61	1.11
Cycled 1k	0.89	0.76	2.17	0.91	0.55	0.83	0.52	1.00	0.52	1.00
Cycled 512	0.68	1.22	∞	**0**	0.10	0.75	0.63	1.12	∞	**0**
Cycled 256	2.38	0.56	∞	**0**	0.41	0.70	0.41	0.69	∞	**0**

would remain intact, since the required sequence of 'correct decisions' would still occur (albeit with much lower probability).

The effect of correlation in the random number sequence, as long as it does not involve deterministic dependencies, would be very similar for analogous reasons. (Note that correlation, in this context, corresponds to bias for certain subsequences.)

Deterministic cycles in the random number sequence, on the other hand, could easily lead to a loss of the PAC property, because in combination with the finite state information held by the algorithm (which in addition to the search position may include search control variables, such as tabu status information or dynamic penalty weights), they could cause cycles in the search trajectory that do not include any solutions to the given problem instance. Note that all PRNGs are periodic; whether or not this leads to observable stagnation of a given SLS algorithms depends on the period of the PRNG as well as on the amount and nature of state information used by the SLS algorithm.

In order to empirically study the effect of poor quality RNGs on SLS algorithms, we generated some intentionally bad random number sequences by manipulating the data we had from the TRNG. First, we introduced a skew s in our data by converting 32-bits of our random data to obtain fixed-point binary values in the range [0,1), generating a 1 if the value was greater than $s/(s+1)$. Next, we generated cycled data where we simply truncated the random data at a fixed number of bytes and repeated the same sequence. We ran our new poor streams through the same tests we performed on the PRNGs, and from Table 1 it is clear that our poor RNGs do not meet very high standards of quality.

Table 3. The effect of different sources of random data streams on the ANOV$^+$ algorithm *(above)* and the SAPS algorithm *(below)* on the same instances. See Table 2 for details.

Random Data	uf100-med		uf250-hard		bw-large.c		ferry9u	
	$\overline{x}/\overline{x}_{rand}$	c.v.	$\overline{x}/\overline{x}_{rand}$	c.v.	$\overline{x}/\overline{x}_{rand}$	c.v.	$\overline{x}/\overline{x}_{rand}$	c.v.
Random Source	998	0.63	3.00M	0.96	10.0M	0.99	880k	0.88
Skewed 1.25:1	1.17	0.61	1.29	1.06	0.91	1.05	0.57	0.87
Skewed 2:1	1.61	0.65	4.16	1.01	0.99	0.95	0.68	0.90
Skewed 4:1	3.02	0.76	**96.31**	0.62	1.30	1.00	**> 3 122**	0.75
Cycled 16k	1.06	0.80	0.85	0.95	0.93	1.17	0.98	0.40
Cycled 512	1.26	0.50	∞	**0**	0.13	1.61	1.03	0.80
Cycled 256	0.33	0.79	∞	**0**	0.66	1.33	∞	**0**
Random Source	1.06k	1.01	304k	1.07	14.6M	0.99	1.92M	1.01
Skewed 1.25:1	1.31	0.97	1.33	1.01	0.54	1.04	0.39	0.97
Skewed 2:1	1.89	1.16	**3.03**	1.08	0.34	0.97	0.26	0.97
Skewed 4:1	**2.37**	1.09	**5.45**	1.04	**0.42**	1.02	**0.11**	0.90
Cycled 16k	1.10	0.99	0.99	1.00	0.95	0.97	0.78	0.90
Cycled 512	0.55	0.72	0.96	0.49	0.88	1.18	2.18	0.89
Cycled 256	1.39	0.89	1.44	0.83	1.26	0.99	0.39	1.23

In what follows, we made the streams progressively worse, and so the data in Table 1 can be considered the best of the bad streams we generated.

To examine the effects of different RNGs on our selected algorithms, we ran CR-WALK, ANOV$^+$ and SAPS with the different sources of random data, and present the results in Tables 2, 3 (top), and 3 (bottom) respectively. We provided the PRNG comparison for CRWALK, and we can see the algorithm was very robust *w.r.t.* the selection of the PRNGs; analogous observations were made for ANOV$^+$ and SAPS.

For the skewed data, the data streams had an increasing amount of ones, and we shall consider what effect it would have on the specific implementations of the algorithms. For CRWALK, the bias would be toward arbitrarily specific clauses and literals. For the ANOV$^+$ algorithm, the same bias would exist for clause selection, but more importantly the frequency of random walk steps and noisy heuristic decisions would decrease. For SAPS, the only significant change is a decrease in the smoothing frequency. Not all of the changes were negative, and in some cases such as the CRWALK algorithm on the ii8c2 instance, the skew greatly improved the performance of the algorithm.

For the cycled data, we continued to shorten the length of the cycles and thereby increased the likelihood that the algorithms would cycle. In Tables 2 and 3 we present results from situations where both the CRWALK and the ANOV$^+$ algorithm became stuck in endless loops. Note that although CRWALK and ANOV$^+$ are both PAC, our empirical results show that these algorithms can become essentially incomplete when using cyclic random number streams. The fact that all finite PRNGs eventually cycle suggests that *no conventional implementation* of an SLS algorithm is truly PAC. (An implementation may be PAC for a given instance, but with a countably infinite number of SAT instances there is no hope of guaranteeing that an implementation will be PAC for any arbitrary instance.)

Given this conclusion, it might seem wise to implement algorithms with TRNGs. If efficient TRNGs were readily available it would be an ideal solution. However, TRNGs are far from efficient when compared to PRNGs. We must add perspective to this discussion and consider how incredibly unlikely the aforementioned circumstances are with a good PRNG. For example, the Mersenne Twister PRNG has a period of $(2^{19937} - 1)$, which makes it very unlikely to ever encounter cycling behaviour in practice. Rather, if cyclic behaviour is observed for an algorithm using a PRNG of this type, the cyclic behaviour is far more likely due to a design flaw, an implementation error, or simply because (even when using true random numbers) the algorithm is not PAC.

When implementing an SLS algorithm and selecting a PRNG, there are several factors to be considered. To assess the quality of a given PRNG, one of the many available test suites can be used; however, any reasonable PRNG will have sufficient quality *w.r.t.* bias and correlation to render impacts on the performance of typical SLS algorithms very unlikely. However, in order to minimise the chance of encountering cycling behaviour of an SLS algorithm in practice, it is generally advisable to chose a PRNG with a large period. Another potentially important factor is the efficiency of a PRNG; this is particularly relevant in the context of highly randomised SLS algorithms that make random decisions in every (or almost every) search step. Finally, especially in the context of scientific research, the use of platform-independent PRNGs makes it possible to reproduce unusual algorithm behaviour exactly across different hardware and operating systems. The previously mentioned Mersenne Twister has *all* of the qualities that are desirable for a PRNG and overall appears to be the best choice in the context of implementing SLS algorithms.

4   Quantity of Randomness

In the previous section, we examined how the quality of random numbers can affect SLS behaviour. In this section, we will study the quantity of random decisions made by SLS algorithms, and consider how many random decisions are truly required. We first investigate random decisions in the SAPS algorithm and give a quick review of our previous work [11]. It has been observed that high-performance dynamic local search algorithms, such as ESG or SAPS, become essentially deterministic after an initial search phase [22]. Intuitively, the clause penalties become unique after numerous scaling and smoothing steps, and so there is no heuristic tie breaking necessary. To further investigate the role of randomness in these algorithms, we have previously created and studied a mostly derandomised variant of SAPS known as SAPS/NR [11].

SAPS/NR does not perform any random walk steps at local minima, uses periodic smoothing after every ($\lfloor 1/P_{smooth} \rfloor$) local minima, and breaks all ties by selecting the variable with the smallest index. At first glance, it may seem that SAPS/NR is completely deterministic, but we must emphasise that the initialisation of SAPS/NR is identical to the initialisation in SAPS, and consequently the initial starting position for each run of SAPS/NR is completely random. In Figure 1 we compare the performance differences between SAPS and SAPS/NR. The `ferry9u` instance is one of the few cases in which we have found significant performance differences; in the overwhelming majority of cases, both algorithms show no significant performance differences.

Instance	SAPS		SAPS/NR	
	Mean	*c.v.*	Mean	*c.v.*
uf100-med	1 075	0.95	1 041	1.01
uf250-hard	287 907	0.98	292 488	0.96
bw-large.c	13 413 962	0.98	14 510 361	1.05
ferry9u	1 883 606	1.03	3 179 808	1.06

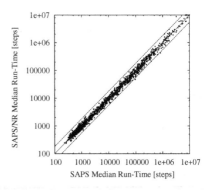

Fig. 1. Performance comparison of SAPS and SAPS/NR. *Left:* For each instance, SAPS and SAPS/NR were run 1000 times. For a description of the *c.v.*, see Table 2. *Right:* Correlation of median run-time over 100 runs on each instance of set `anov1OM-struct`. Using the Mann-Whitney U-test with sample size 100, performance ratios below 1.8 (corresponding to data points inside the band drawn around the main diagonal of the plot) are not statistically significant at standard significance and power levels [1].

After restricting all of the random decisions to the initialisation phase, we will next consider what happens when we remove the random decisions from the initialisation phase as well. If we deterministically initialise the variable assignments, SAPS/NR will always take the same number of steps to solve an instance, reducing the variability in the run-time to zero, which can be seen in Figure 3 *(left)* as a vertical line. The deterministic initialisation method we used was a simple greedy approach: for each variable, if the positive literal appears more frequently than the negative, the variable is assigned a value of $\top$, otherwise $\bot$. When variables with an equal number of positive and negative literals are encountered, they are deterministically assigned $\top$ or $\bot$, alternating between variables.

We next consider what happens if between the initialisation and the search phase we select one variable uniformly at random and flip it [7]. Remarkably, as can be seen in Figure 3 *(left)*, the variability introduced by just that one random decision is close to the full variability seen by the regular, fully randomised version of SAPS. Because this instance has 250 variables, there are 250 discrete levels in the curve, corresponding to each of the 250 variables that could have been flipped. It is quite remarkable and rather counter-intuitive that flipping just one variable between the initialisation and search phase could have such a dramatic effect on the run-time behaviour of the algorithm. We note that this phenomenon is very reminiscent of the extremely sensitive dependence on initial conditions found in chaotic dynamic systems.

Next, we consider similar derandomisations for CRWALK and ANOV$^+$, two algorithms that depend on random decisions to a much greater extent than SAPS. It should be noted that the derandomised versions of these algorithms described in the following were chosen for their simplicity rather than for their performance or their exceptionally strong correlation to the original algorithms. We did not invest time in tuning and engineering our algorithms with different derandomisation strategies to meet higher quality

---

[7] Parameters `-varinitgreedy -varinitflip 1` in UBCSAT.

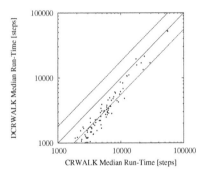
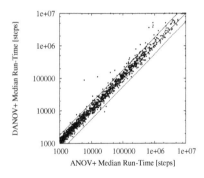

Fig. 2. Comparison of *left:* CRWALK and DCRWALK and *right:* ANOV$^+$ and DANOV$^+$. Instance sets *left:* `flat30-*` and *right:* `anov10M-struct`. For each instance, 100 runs were performed. See Figure 1 for further details.

standards. Our goal was to illustrate that our simple, straightforward approach works reasonably well for most instances.

Recall that CRWALK uses random decisions to select unsatisfied clauses and to decide which variable in a selected clause is to be flipped. To implement clause selection in DCRWALK, our deterministic version of CRWALK, we keep track of the number of times each clause has been selected (count) and the number of steps that each clause has been unsatisfied (unsat) and we simply select the clause that has the smallest (count: unsat) ratio, breaking ties by selecting the clause with the smallest index. This method ensures that clauses are selected in a uniform, fair, and deterministic manner. For literal selection, we simply keep a counter for each clause, selecting the first literal the first time the clause is selected, the second literal the second time, and so on, returning to the first literal when all have been exhausted. Thus, DCRWALK removes all of the randomness from the heuristic search phase, while still allowing for random decisions at the initialisation phase. Note that our approach differs substantially from some of the published theoretical methods for derandomising Schöning's algorithm [23], which use Hamming balls to eliminate randomness from the initialisation phase and depart from traditional SLS by using backtracking in the local search phase.

To derandomise the ANOV$^+$ algorithm, we need to replace three types of random decisions: clause selection, random walk steps, and noisy variable selection. For clause selection, we maintain a list of the currently false clauses and simply step through that list, selecting the clause in the list that is the current search step number modulo the size of the list. Instead of random walk steps, every ($\lfloor 1/wp \rfloor$) steps a variable is selected to be flipped using the same variable selection scheme used by DCRWALK. For the noisy variable selection, we use two integer variables n and d. If the ratio ($\frac{n}{d}$) is less than the current noise setting p a noisy decision is made and n is incremented, conversely, if ($\frac{n}{d}$) is greater than p the greedy decision is made and d is incremented. Whenever the adaptive mechanism modifies the noise parameter p, the values of n and d are reinitialised to $\lfloor 256 \cdot p \rfloor$ and $(256 - n)$, respectively.

In Figure 2 we compare the performance of DCRWALK and DANOV$^+$ with their fully randomised versions. In general, we do not see the same tight correlation observed for SAPS/NR, however, for the most part our derandomised algorithms show very

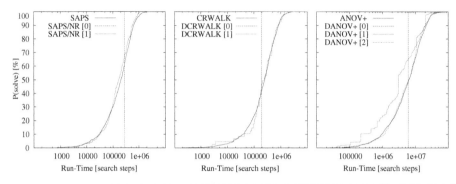

Fig. 3. A run-length distribution comparison of *left:* SAPS and SAPS/NR, *centre:* CRWALK and DCRWALK and *right:* ANOV$^+$ and DANOV$^+$ (with [N] total random decisions per run) based on 1000 runs. See the text for the deterministic initialisation method used for the derandomised algorithms. The vertical bar ([0]) reflects when *all* random decisions have been replaced, while the [1] curve shows the behaviour when one single random variable has been flipped after the deterministic initialisation in each run. Instances are *left:* uf250-hard, *centre:* uf50-hard and *right:* bw-large.c.

similar behaviour. Our DCRWALK algorithms seems to outperform CRWALK for the vast majority instances, possibly because the clause selection scheme is fair and un-biased. Gent and Walsh observed similarly improved behaviour for a fair deterministic version of GSAT [7]. Our DANOV$^+$ algorithm suffers from slightly worse performance on average, and there are significant outliers that indicate some inherent problems with our derandomisation approach on some specific instances, but for most instances the performance of DANOV$^+$ resembles that of ANOV$^+$.

In Figure 3 we see evidence that the same 'chaotic' behaviour observed for SAPS/NR is also present for DCRWALK and DANOV$^+$. Using the same deterministic initiali-sation as in SAPS/NR, we obtain the same behaviour: with just one simple random decision in DCRWALK and two in DANOV$^+$, the full variability found in the run-time distributions of the original, heavily randomised versions of these algorithms is achieved. What makes this observation remarkable is not so much that in principle, the amount of random decisions can be drastically reduced without any substantial effect on the behaviour of the algorithm (after all, any implementation of an SLS algorithm using a PRNG is fully deterministic), but rather that it can be done using very simple derandomisation schemes.

5   Conclusions

In this paper we have investigated the role of random decisions in SLS algorithms for SAT. Most of these algorithms heavily use various types of random decisions, and we have argued that from a theoretical point of view, their performance can be expected to be severely compromised by some of the features associated with poor-quality random number sequences. Nevertheless, our our empirical results indicate that in practice, the behaviour of these algorithms is remarkably robust with respect to the quality of the

RNG used to implement these random decisions. This is in contrast to some other types of randomised algorithms, such as algorithms used for Monte Carlo simulations. As a consequence, there is no reason to consider the use of true random number generators (which have the disadvantage of typically being rather slow), or to worry about minor differences in the quality of readily available pseudo-random number generators, especially if their period is high. Because of its extremely high period, efficiency and platform-independent availability, we recommend to use the Mersenne Twister PRNG for the implementation of SLS algorithms.

We have also found that at least the three prominent SLS algorithms for SAT we studied (SAPS, $ANOV^+$, CRWALK) can be almost completely derandomised using very simple mechanisms to replace the random decisions without significantly changing their behaviour. In particular, versions of these algorithms that use only a single random decision during intialisation exhibit basically the full variability in the run-time required to solve a given SAT instance as the original, fully randomised algorithms. Eliminating this last random decision leads to completely deterministic algorithms which may often perform similarly well as their fully randomised versions on average. At the same time, these deterministic algorithms can no longer benefit from easy and efficient parallelisation by means of performing multiple independent tries in parallel [1]. Additionally, at least for the deterministic version of $ANOV^+$ we observed substantially degraded performance on a very small number of instances. Therefore, we see no practical advantages in using completely or partially derandomised SLS algorithms.

Overall, our results are fully consistent with the widely held view that the role of random decisions in SLS algorithms is primarily to provide search diversification. Therefore, neither the quality of the RNG nor the quantity of random decisions used by an SLS algorithm is of crucial importance to its behaviour.

In future work, it would be interesting to conduct a detailed empirical analysis on the implementation costs of various PRNGs and the difference in run-time behaviour between randomised and derandomised algorithms. With respect to the quantity of random decisions, more algorithms can be tested for straightforward derandomisation, and more robust derandomisation methods should be explored. For individual instances on which derandomised algorithms are found to perform poorly (*i.e.* ferry9u for SAPS/NR), it would be interesting to further explore the reasons underlying the loss of performance, and to investigate which specific type of derandomisation is causing the problem; this information could be used to help identify how to use random decisions more effectively. Finally, it would be very worthwhile to extend our methods to other combinatorial problem domains (*e.g.*, constraint satisfaction or travelling salesperson problems) to test the generality of our observations.

References

1. Hoos, H.H., Stützle, T.: Stochastic Local Search: Foundations and Applications. Morgan Kaufmann (2004)
2. Papadimitriou, C.H.: On selecting a satisfying truth assignment. In: Proc. of the 32nd Symp. on Foundations of Computer Science. (1991) 163–169
3. Selman, B., Kautz, H.A., Cohen, B.: Noise strategies for improving local search. In: Proc. of the 12th Nat'l Conf. on Artificial Intelligence (AAAI 94). (1994) 337–343

4. Schöning, U.: A probabilistic algorithm for k-SAT and constraint satisfaction problems. In: Proc. of the 40th Symp. on Foundations of Computer Science. (1999) 410–414
5. Hutter, F., Tompkins, D.A., Hoos, H.H.: Scaling and probabilistic smoothing: Efficient dynamic local search for SAT. In: Proceedings of CP-02. (2002) 233–248
6. Éric D. Taillard: Robust taboo search for the quadratic assignment problem. Parallel Computing **17** (1991) 443–455
7. Gent, I.P., Walsh, T.: Towards an understanding of hillclimbing procedures for SAT. In: Proc. of the 11th Nat'l Conf. on Artificial Intelligence (AAAI 93). (1993) 28–33
8. Ferrenberg, A.M., Landau, D.P., Wong, Y.J.: Monte Carlo simulations: Hidden errors from "good" random number generators. Physical Review Letters **69** (1992) 3382–3384
9. Bauke, H., Mertens, S.: Pseudo random coins show more heads than tails. Journal of Statistical Physics **114** (2004) 1149–1169
10. Ribeiro, C.C., Souza, R.C., Vieira, C.E.C.: A comparative computational study of random number generators. Pacific Journal of Optimization **1** (2005) 565–578
11. Tompkins, D.A.D., Hoos, H.H.: Warped landscapes and random acts of SAT solving. In: Proc. of the 8th Symp. on Artificial Intelligence and Mathematics. (2004)
12. Iwama, K., Tamaki, S.: Improved upper bounds for 3-SAT. In: Proc. of the 15th ACM-SIAM Symp. on Discrete algorithms (SODA 04). (2004) 328–328
13. Parkes, A.J., Walser, J.P.: Tuning local search for satisfiability testing. In: Proc. of the 13th Nat'l Conf. on Artificial Intelligence (AAAI 96). (1996) 356–362
14. Hoos, H.H.: An adaptive noise mechanism for WalkSAT. In: Proc. of the 18th Nat'l Conf. on Artificial Intelligence (AAAI 02). (2002) 655–660
15. Le Berre, D., Simon, L.: 55 solvers in Vancouver: The SAT 2004 competition. In: Proc. of 7th Conf. on Theory & Applications of Satisfiability Testing (SAT 04). (2005) 321–345
16. Tompkins, D.A.D., Hoos, H.H.: UBCSAT: An implementation and experimentation environment for SLS algorithms for SAT and MAX-SAT. In: Proc. of (SAT 04). (2005) 305–320
17. Matsumoto, M., Nishimura, T.: Mersenne twister: a 623-dimensionally equidistributed uniform pseudo-random number generator. ACM Modeling & Comp. Simulation **8** (1998) 3–30
18. Hoos, H.H., Stützle, T.: SATLIB: An online resource for research on SAT. In: SAT2000: Highlights of Satisfiability Research in the year 2000. (2000) 283–292
19. Bagini, V., Bucci, M.: A design of reliable true random number generator for cryptographic applications. In: Workshop Cryptographic Hardware & Embedded Syst. (1999) 204–218
20. Rukhin, A., Soto, J., Nechvatal, J., Smid, M., Barker, E., Leigh, S., Levenson, M., Vangel, M., Banks, D., Heckert, A., Dray, J., Vo, S.: A statistical test suite for random and pseudorandom number generators for cryptographic applications. Technical Report 800-22, NIST (2000)
21. Knuth, D.E.: The Art of Computer Programming, Volume 2. Addison-Wesley (1969)
22. Schuurmans, D., Southey, F., Holte, R.C.: The exponentiated subgradient algorithm for heuristic boolean programming. In: Proc. of (IJCAI 01). (2001) 334–341
23. Dantsin, E., Goerdt, A., Hirsch, E.A., Schöning, U.: Deterministic algorithms for k-SAT based on covering codes & local search. In: Automata, Languages & Prog. (2000) 236–247

Simple Support-Based Distributed Search

Peter Harvey, Chee Fon Chang, and Aditya Ghose

Decision Systems Laboratory
School of IT and Computer Science
University of Wollongong
NSW 2522 Australia

Abstract. Distributed Constraint Satisfaction Problems provide a natural mechanism for multiagent coordination and agreement. To date, algorithms for Distributed Constraint Satisfaction Problems have tended to mirror existing non-distributed global-search or local-search algorithms. Unfortunately, existing distributed global-search algorithms derive from classical backtracking search methods and require a total ordering over agents for completeness. Distributed variants of local-search algorithms (such as distributed breakout) inherit the incompleteness properties of their predecessors, or depend on the creation of new communication links between agents. In [5, 4] a new algorithm was presented designed explicitly for distributed environments so that a global ordering is not required, while avoiding the problems of existing local-search algorithms. This paper presents a significant improvement on that algorithm in performance and provability.

1 Introduction

Constraint Satisfaction Problems (CSPs) have proven applicable in a wide variety of domains. A CSP is classically defined by a set of variables $\mathcal{V}$, a domain for each variable $\mathcal{D}_v$, and a set of constraints $\mathcal{C}$. A *solution* to a CSP is a complete assignment of values to variables which satisfies every constraint.

A Distributed CSP (DisCSP) is formed when the description and solution procedure of a CSP are separated amongst multiple agents. The distributed environment extends the applicability of CSPs to domains such as distributed scheduling and resource contention. Of particular interest is the use of DisCSPs as models for solving other multiagent problems, with DisCSP algorithms defining a protocol for agent communication. Common examples of such problems include scheduling, task assignment, and limited forms of negotiation where simple decision(s) must be made per agent. A DisCSP can be constructed by representing each of the agents decisions as a variable, with constraints describing any inter-agent relationships.

A DisCSP can be solved by distributed variants of existing global-search or local-search algorithms. However, local-search algorithms [12] are incomplete in both the distributed and non-distributed case. Distributed variants of global-search [1, 3, 8, 10] presented to date make use of a total order over variables.

L. Lamontagne and M. Marchand (Eds.): Canadian AI 2006, LNAI 4013, pp. 159–170, 2006.
© Springer-Verlag Berlin Heidelberg 2006

We argue that any total order impacts the characteristics of backtracking-style search in undesirable ways for use in many multiagent problems. For example, an agent which has a 'higher' rank in the ordering has more 'authority' and is therefore less likely to change its value than a 'lower' ranking agent. In an anytime environment this results in higher-ranked agents being granted more stable answers. While some problems may desire such behaviour our concern lies with those problems which do not.

We also argue that, when using a total order, it is difficult to add constraints between two previously independent DisCSPs. To do so would require a re-computation of the variable ordering and/or an arbitrary decision that one DisCSP ranks higher than the other. If a problem is frequently altered by the addition of groups of variables, as is likely to occur in large DisCSP networks, global re-computation will become increasingly difficult. If variable ordering is instead made arbitrarily (for example, ordering by variable identifier) the problem of stability is exacerbated.

We have previously demonstrated these arguments [5, 4] by reference to large-scale meeting scheduling systems. In such systems, it is expected that the solution will be accessed and the constraint network modified at any time by distributed users. The relationship between users, agents and variables also ensures that fairness in frequency of variable assignment is also important. The specific difficulties of large-scale distributed meeting scheduling motivated us to develop an algorithm which:

- has no need for 'authority' between variables, effectively avoiding the need for a total order on variables.
- provides fairness in the level of stability for variables.
- does not add links between variables, avoiding the eventual need for 'broadcasting' assignments.
- addresses the risk of cyclic behaviour exhibited by local search algorithms.

Section 2 will present a model of a simple meeting scheduling problem as a DisCSP, and present how *arguments* can form the basis of communication between agents. Section 3 will describe the internal decision processes of each agent to handle arguments in an appropriate manner. Section 4 will present analysis of the algorithm.

2   Modelling Arguments

Example 1. Consider the following small distributed constraint satisfaction problem. Alice, Bob, Carla and Dennis must organise meeting times:

- Bob must meet with Carla.
- Bob must meet with Alice before his meeting with Carla.
- Dennis must meet with Alice.
- Bob, Carla and Dennis must have a separate group meeting.
- Available times are 1pm, 2pm and 3pm.

To find the solution they state arguments (proposals and rejections) in turn, providing further detail if two arguments are contradictory or if they need to alter a previous argument:

Alice to Dennis	⇒	I propose a 1pm meeting
Dennis to Carla	⇒	I propose a 2pm group meeting
Dennis to Bob	⇒	I propose a 2pm group meeting
Carla to Bob	⇒	I propose a 1pm meeting
Alice to Bob	⇒	I propose a 2pm meeting
Bob to Alice	⇒	I have a group meeting at 2pm, so I propose a 1pm meeting instead
Bob to Carla	⇒	I completely reject your proposal, so I propose a 3pm meeting instead
Alice to Dennis	⇒	I now have another meeting at 1pm, so I propose a 3pm meeting instead

Example 1 demonstrates how a distributed constraint satisfaction problem can be solved through arguments. We will describe a formal model of this problem with corresponding notation able to represent the dialogue. This transformation will then lead us to a simple distributed constraint satisfaction algorithm called Support-based Distributed Search.

To construct a distributed constraint satisfaction problem we translate the time of attending a meeting for each person into a variable. Equality constraints are used to ensure meeting times are agreed to by all users. For example, a pair of variables a and b may represent the scheduled time of the meeting between Alice and Dennis. The constraint $a = b$ is interpreted as 'the time Alice decides to meet with Dennis must be the same as the time that Dennis decides to meet with Alice'. Inequality constraints ensure that meetings occur at distinct times.

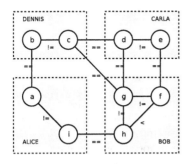

$$\mathcal{V} = \{a, b, c, d, e, f, g, h, i\}$$

$$\mathcal{D} = \{1\text{pm}, 2\text{pm}, 3\text{pm}\}$$

$$\mathcal{C} = \left\{ \begin{array}{llll} a = b & b \neq c & c = d \\ c = g & d \neq e & d = g \\ e = f & f \neq g & f > h \\ g \neq h & h = i & a \neq i \end{array} \right\}$$

Note that there is significant redundancy in the constraints and variables. This occurs as the constraints upon one person are not automatically known to others. Relaxing this requirement would generate a simpler constraint graph, but would conflict with our aim to solve in a distributed manner. Using this constraint model as an example, we will now define suitable notation for representing the dialogue.

Definition 1. *An **isgood** is an ordered partial assignment for a sequence of connected variables, and so represents a 'proposal'.*

Consider the argument in Example 1 where Bob says to Alice: "I already have a group meeting at 2pm, so I propose a 1pm meeting for us instead". This is a proposal, and so can be written as an ordered partial assignment or 'isgood':

$$\langle (g, 2\text{pm}), (h, 1\text{pm}) \rangle$$

This isgood is read as "variable g took on value 2pm, and so h took on value 1pm". Note that variables in an isgood must be connected to their immediate predecessor, and therefore $\langle (d, 2\text{pm}), (h, 1\text{pm}) \rangle$ is *not* an isgood. Also note that we use the operator $+$ to represent the appending of a variable assignment to an isgood. For example, $\langle (g, 2\text{pm}), (h, 1\text{pm}) \rangle + (i, 1\text{pm}) = \langle (g, 2\text{pm}), (h, 1\text{pm}), (i, 1\text{pm}) \rangle$.

Note that this definition of an isgood has an important difference from that presented in [5, 4], in that no measure of 'strength' is defined. We address the lack of such a measure within the algorithm itself, described later.

Definition 2. *A **nogood** is an unordered partial assignment which is provably not part of a solution, and so represents a 'rejection'.*

Consider the argument in Example 1 where Bob says to Carla: "I reject your proposal, and I propose a 3pm meeting for us instead" This is a rejection (he must meet Carla before Alice, so 1pm is not a possible meeting time) followed by a proposal, which written in sequence are:

$$\{(e, 1\text{pm})\} \quad \text{and} \quad \langle (f, 3\text{pm}) \rangle$$

They are read as "variable e cannot take value 1pm" and "variable f took on value 3pm" respectively. As demonstrated in Example 1 a nogood is usually accompanied by an isgood.

3   Solving with Arguments

Using the above notation, and the dialogue of Example 1 as a guide, it is possible to construct a distributed search algorithm in which agents will:

- send and receive proposals (isgoods) and rejections (nogoods)
- convince neighbours to change by progressively longer proposals
- reject a proposal from a neighbour if it is inconsistent
- justify their variable assignment by the proposal of just one neighbour
- communicate only with agents for which they share a constraint

To achieve this, each agent records the most recent proposals sent/received by neighbouring agents and an unbounded nogood store. Unlike other distributed algorithms, SBDS does not regard all information from neighbours as a consistent 'agent view'. Instead, the isgood received from just one neighbour is chosen as justification for our current assignment and combines to form our 'agent view'. Formally, the information stored by each agent is:

- *sent(v)* - last isgood sent to each neighbour v, initially empty
- *recv(v)* - last isgood received from each neighbour v, initially empty
- *nogoods* - set of all nogoods ever received, initially empty
- *support* - the neighbour chosen for our 'agent view'
- *view* - current agent view (*recv(support)* extended by an assignment to our own variable)

The *main* loop of our algorithm processes all messages before choosing *support* and *view* and sending new isgoods. Incoming isgoods are stored in *recv(v)* by the

---

Procedure 1. *main* ()

1: **while** true **do**
2:    **for all** received nogoods N (in fifo order) **do**
3:       *receive-nogood*(N)
4:    **for all** received isgoods I (in fifo order) **do**
5:       *receive-isgood*(I)
6:    *select-support*()
7:    **for all** neighbours v **do**
8:       *send-isgood*(v)
9:    wait until at least one message in the queue

Procedure 2. *receive-isgood* (I)

1: **let** v be the variable which sent I
2: **set** *recv(v)* to I
3: **if** no choice of value is consistent wrt *recv(v)* **then**
4:    *send-nogood(v)*

Procedure 3. *receive-nogood* (N)

1: **if** N in *nogoods* **then**
2:    **break**, as this nogood was already known
3: add N to *nogoods*
4: **if** no value is consistent **then**
5:    terminate algorithm
6: **for all** neighbours v **do**
7:    **if** no choice of value is consistent wrt *recv(v)* **then**
8:       *send-nogood(v)*

Procedure 4. *select-support* ()

1: *update-view* ()
2: **if** our current value is inconsistent wrt some *recv(v)* and $|recv(v)| \geq |view|$ **then**
3:    **set** *support* to a neighbour u, maximising $|recv(u)|$
4: *update-view* ()

Procedure 5. *update-view* ()

1: **let** *view'* be *recv*(*support*) extended by a consistent
   assignment to self, and maximal with respect to $\prec$
2: **let** v be the first variable assigned in *view'*
3: **if** *scope*(*view*) $\neq$ *scope*(*view'*) **or** *view* $\prec$ *view'* **or**
   the assignment of v is equal in *view'* and *recv*(v) **or**
   the assignment of v is unequal in *view* and *recv*(v) **then**
4:    **set** *view* to *view'*

Procedure 6. *send-nogood* (v)

1: **let** N be an inconsistent subset of *recv*(v)
2: **send** N to v
3: **set** *recv*(v) to $\langle \rangle$
4: **if** *support* = v **then set** *support* to *self*

Procedure 7. *send-isgood* (v)

1: **if** our current value is consistent wrt *recv*(v) **and**
   sent(v) $\sqsubseteq$ *view* **then**
2:    **break**, as a new isgood is not necessary
3: **lock** communication channel with v
4: **if** there are no unprocessed isgoods from v **then**
5:    **let** R be the longest isgood such that $R \sqsubseteq$ *view* and $v \notin scope(R)$
6:    **let** L be $\max(|recv(v)|, |sent(v)|) + 1$
7:    **let** I be the isgood such that $I \sqsubseteq R$ and $|I| = \min(L, |R|)$
8:    **send** I to v
9:    **set** *sent*(v) to I
10: **unlock** communication channel with v

---

receive-isgood procedure. If no assignment to our own variable is consistent with respect to the new isgood and current known nogoods, the procedure *send-nogood* is called to derive and send a nogood. Similarly the *receive-nogood* procedure handles an incoming nogood; each *recv*(v) is re-tested for consistency, and *send-nogood* is called if appropriate.

The *select-support* procedure determines which neighbouring variable will be considered as our support for this iteration. A new support must be chosen if a received isgood from a neighbour is longer than our current *view* and conflicts with our current value.

The *update-view* procedure refreshes the current *view* according to the isgood *recv*(*support*). In most cases *update-view* will replace *view* by selecting and appending a consistent assignment for our variable to the tail of *recv*(*support*). As our algorithm is asynchronous, and agents can determine their assignments simultaneously, there is the possibility of cyclic behaviour. As in [5, 4], we make use of orderings for isgoods defined over the same set of variables to pause the algorithm when a cycle is deemed likely.

Formally, let $scope(I)$ be the sequence of variables in the isgood I. For example, with $I = \langle (c, 1\text{pm}), (b, 2\text{pm}) \rangle$ we have $scope(I) = \langle c, b \rangle$. We assume an ordering $\prec$ is known to all agents and is total for isgoods of the same *unordered* scope. We will not replace a *view* with *view'* if each of the following is true:

- *view'* is easily demonstrated to be out-of-date, but *view* is not
- *view'* and *view* are defined over the same cycle in the constraint network
- *view'* is lower in the ordering than *view*

This scheme causes an agent to postpone changing its value if its new view would be out-of-date, would propagate a cycle, and the old view is regarded as 'superior' by the ordering. As the definition of the ordering is uniform across all agents, any cyclic behaviour will quickly resolve in favour of a single view. Theorem 1 contains a formal statement and proof of this result.

The *send-nogood* procedure generates and sends an appropriate nogood when a received isgood is found to be inconsistent. The *send-isgood* procedure constructs the strongest possible isgood to send to agent v while satisfying certain 'minimality' requirements. To prevent trivial cycles we dot not sent an isgood to a neighbour v if there are unprocessed isgoods in the communication channel.

To avoid more complex cycles of oscillating agent values in inconsistent problems, we increase the length of successive arguments which are sent. As any cycle must be finite, eventually the arguments (isgoods) being transmitted will contain the cycle itself. If the cycle is formed from inconsistent values it will generate a nogood and break the cycle; otherwise the cycle-breaking mechanism of *update-view* will take effect.

4   Results

In the introduction we have described desirable properties of an algorithm for distributed constraint satisfaction. The fact that we do not add links between variables is evident from the algorithm itself. Similarly, we note the absence of any total ordering over the variables, which avoids any notion of 'authority'.

We can provide empirical evidence that no variables change value significantly more often than any other. Figure 1 presents the number of value changes per variable while using our algorithm to solve a randomly constructed problem of 100 variables, 300 constraints and domain size of 5. Each graph plots the frequency of value change for each variable, sorted in ascending order, and a line of best fit. When using constraint tightness of 0.3 (easy to solve), 0.325 (hard to solve) and 0.35 (unsolvable) we observe the same results; no variable is forced to change value significantly more often than most others.

We have also provided a novel method to address cyclic behaviour which plagues distributed local search algorithms [12]. Below we present proof that cyclic behaviour has been eliminated:

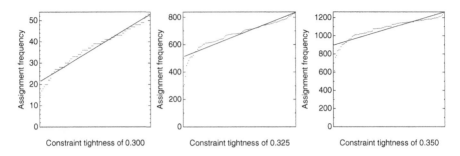

Fig. 1. Frequency of assignment changes per variable, for a random problem of 100 variables, 300 constraints, domain size of 5, and constraint tightness of 0.3 (easy), 0.325 (hard) and 0.35 (unsolvable)

Lemma 1. *Eventually no new nogoods will be generated.*

Proof. Each agent keeps all nogoods it ever receives. A nogood is sent when a received isgood is found to be inconsistent, ensuring that the isgood will never be received twice from the same source. As the set of possible isgoods must be finite, eventually no new nogoods will be generated.

Note that it appears possible to use a nogood-deletion policy derived from that of Dynamic Backtracking [2], though caution must be taken. Dynamic Backtracking has just one single variable ordering at any one time, allowing for nogoods to be deleted while guaranteeing that some information is always retained. It is common for SBDS to have multiple conflicting variable orderings and to contain cycles, and so information can be lost permanently if a nogood is deleted. To prevent information loss, it is possible to annotate a nogood with the variable ordering that was in use at the time of the nogood construction. Using this annotation it is possible to apply the nogood-deletion policy of Dynamic Backtracking safely, though the impact on algorithm performance has not been tested.

Lemma 2. *If no new nogoods are generated, then eventually the length of view will become stable for each agent.*

Proof. If no new nogoods are generated, the length of *view* becomes monotonic increasing, with one exception. If an agent chooses a new *support* that forms a cycle, then the length of arguments for agents in the cycle may be limited (line 5 of *send-isgood*), causing a decrease in *view* for those (and other) variables.

However, within the set of variables that are affected by such a choice, we can guarantee that the minimum length of *view* increases. As the length of *view* is bounded above, we are guaranteed that the length of *view* will become stable for each agent.

The above proof is best illustrated with an instance of our meeting scheduling example. Consider the following table showing possible *view*s for each variable.

A diagram showing the direction of the *support* relation is also provided. In the diagram, c has chosen b as support, d has chosen c as support, etc.

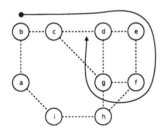

Example *view* held by each variable

b: $\langle (b, 1\text{pm}) \rangle$
c: $\langle (b, 1\text{pm}), (c, 2\text{pm}) \rangle$
d: $\langle (b, 1\text{pm}), (c, 2\text{pm}), (d, 2\text{pm}) \rangle$
e: $\langle (b, 2\text{pm}), (c, 1\text{pm}), (d, 1\text{pm}), (e, 2\text{pm}) \rangle$
f: $\langle (b, 2\text{pm}), (c, 1\text{pm}), (d, 1\text{pm}), (e, 2\text{pm}), (f, 2\text{pm}) \rangle$
g: $\langle (c, 1\text{pm}), (d, 1\text{pm}), (e, 2\text{pm}), (f, 2\text{pm}), (g, 1\text{pm}) \rangle$

In the above table, b, c and d have recently changed value, so the *view* held by g is contradictory to that held by d. However, g can provide a longer argument to d in the form of an isgood $\langle (e, 2\text{pm}), (f, 2\text{pm}), (g, 1\text{pm}) \rangle$. As the argument provided by g is longer, and contradicts the current *view* of d, it forces d to choose g as a new *support* and update it's *view* accordingly. Following this choice, and after a few iterations, we can have the following situation:

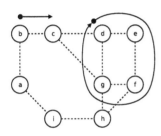

Example *view* held by each variable

b: $\langle (b, 1\text{pm}) \rangle$
c: $\langle (b, 1\text{pm}), (c, 2\text{pm}) \rangle$
d: $\langle (e, 2\text{pm}), (f, 2\text{pm}), (g, 1\text{pm}), (d, 1\text{pm}) \rangle$
e: $\langle (f, 2\text{pm}), (g, 1\text{pm}), (d, 1\text{pm}), (e, 2\text{pm}) \rangle$
f: $\langle (g, 1\text{pm}), (d, 1\text{pm}), (e, 2\text{pm}), (f, 2\text{pm}) \rangle$
g: $\langle (d, 1\text{pm}), (e, 2\text{pm}), (f, 2\text{pm}), (g, 1\text{pm}) \rangle$

The *view* held by each of d, e, f and g were affected by d's choice. Importantly, the length of *view* for f and g decreased. However, the minimum $|view|$ for affected variables has increased from 3 to 4. This demonstrates in a concrete way that mechanism described in the proof of Lemma 2.

Note that, in the above table, the *view* held by c is shorter and contradictory to that held by d and g. Therefore c and subsequently b would change their choice of *support* and *view*, giving us the following:

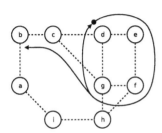

Example *view* held by each variable

b: $\langle (g, 1\text{pm}), (c, 1\text{pm}), (b, 2\text{pm}) \rangle$
c: $\langle (e, 2\text{pm}), (f, 2\text{pm}), (g, 1\text{pm}), (c, 1\text{pm}) \rangle$
d: $\langle (e, 2\text{pm}), (f, 2\text{pm}), (g, 1\text{pm}), (d, 1\text{pm}) \rangle$
e: $\langle (f, 2\text{pm}), (g, 1\text{pm}), (d, 1\text{pm}), (e, 2\text{pm}) \rangle$
f: $\langle (g, 1\text{pm}), (d, 1\text{pm}), (e, 2\text{pm}), (f, 2\text{pm}) \rangle$
g: $\langle (d, 1\text{pm}), (e, 2\text{pm}), (f, 2\text{pm}), (g, 1\text{pm}) \rangle$

While we do not argue that these examples provide any theoretical results, they do illustrate the proof of Lemma 2. A formal proof of soundness and termination (completeness) is presented below.

Theorem 1. *The algorithm is sound, and will terminate.*

Proof. The algorithm uses sound nogood derivation techniques and will terminate with 'no solution' only if the empty nogood is derived. Inversely, each agent ensures that its neighbours know its current value, and will continue to communicate if an inconsistency exists. Therefore the algorithm will not terminate unless it has a correct answer, and so is sound.

By Lemmas 1 and 2 we know that eventually no new nogoods will be generated and the length of *view* will become stable for each agent. Therefore the *support* for each agent will also become stable, and so value selection for each variable will become dependant only upon information from its *support*. In such a situation the algorithm will only fail to terminate if there exists some directed tour of agents $v_1, \ldots, v_n$ which are 'supporting' each other and oscillating between candidate solutions. However, each candidate solution has the same unordered scope, and so by the postponement scheme outline above we know that solutions ranked lower by $\prec$ will be removed until the oscillating stops and the algorithm terminates.

5   Comparisons

A number of centralised and distributed algorithms have been used as inspiration in the construction of SBDS. Many contain similar elements, such as dynamic distributed variable ordering [13], nogood construction [8, 2, 1], and heuristic search [7, 6, 12]. There are however, some differences in the way the techniques from this previous work have been used.

As noted in the introduction, most algorithms that rely on variable ordering require that ordering to be total, though it may be a preorder as in [9]. In SBDS, each isgood describes an order over variables within only a local context. The purpose of the ordering in this instance is to provide support for nogoods in the style of Dynamic Backtracking [2, 1]. The combination of these local orders does not necessarily end in the construction of a total order over variables, and may contain cycles. Permitting cycles clearly distinguishes SBDS from previous algorithms.

In our own previous work [5, 4] we attempted to limit the progressive lengthening of isgoods by a complicated measure of 'strength'. To minimise the rate of growth of L, and to increase performance, we have replaced this measure in implementation with a min-conflict heuristic. To ensure completeness we use iteration limits to revert to provably complete search.

Finally, Figure 2 presents a comparisons of SBDS and Distributed Breakout, each using a min-conflict heuristic. We compare with Distributed Breakout as it is simple to implement, and is often very fast on feasible problem instances. We ran each on approximately 13000 feasible random binary problem instances, with an upper limit of 10000 iterations per instance. We also ran SBDS on approximately 350 infeasible random problem instances generated in the same way.

We have plotted each random problem instance found feasible by SBDS, comparing the number of iterations taken for each algorithm. We also present the percentage of completed problems for Distributed Breakout and SBDS within iteration bounds. As can be seen, the vast majority of problems are more easily solved by SBDS than by Distributed Breakout. Given a 4000-iteration limit, SBDS is able to solve 98% of problems, whereas Distributed Breakout can solve only 50%, and just 55% within 10000 iterations.

Note that we have not used the stochastic variant of Distributed Breakout [11], and we are not measuring communication cost. Future work will involve further comparisons to other algorithms, and investigation of compression techniques for isgoods. In our experiments the majority of isgoods involved changes to just one or two variables; using a delta-compression scheme would significantly reduce any communication costs.

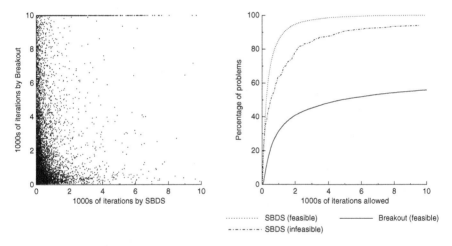

Fig. 2. Comparison of SBDS and Distributed Breakout for feasible random problems with 200 variables and 400 constraints, domain size of 5, and constraint tightness of 0.4

6   Conclusion

Distributed Constraint Satisfaction Problems provide a natural mechanism for multiagent coordination and agreement. To date, algorithms for Distributed Constraint Satisfaction Problems have tended to mirror existing non-distributed global-search or local-search algorithms. However, there exist natural examples of DisCSPs for which a total variable ordering and/or linking of variables is not desired. If we are to solve such DisCSPs we must develop new algorithms designed specifically for distributed environments.

In this paper we have presented one such algorithm. Key to the success of the algorithm is the use of argumentation as a model for agent operation. This technique avoids fixed ranks for agents and the resultant behaviour which is undesirable in natural problems such as meeting scheduling. The placing of a total order over solutions for subsets of variables also provides a novel approach to solving the issue of cyclic behaviour in local search algorithms. This paper also represents a significant simplification, with formal proof results and better performance, of the algorithm presented in [5, 4].

References

[1] C. Bessière, A. Maestre, and P. Meseguer. Distributed dynamic backtracking. In T. Walsh, editor, *CP*, volume 2239 of *Lecture Notes in Computer Science*, page 772. Springer, 2001.

[2] M. L. Ginsberg. Dynamic backtracking. *J. Artif. Intell. Res. (JAIR)*, 1:25–46, 1993.

[3] Y. Hamadi. Interleaved backtracking in distributed constraint networks. *International Journal on Artificial Intelligence Tools*, 11(2):167–188, 2002.

[4] P. Harvey, C. F. Chang, and A. Ghose. Practical application of support-based distributed search. In *ICTAI*. IEEE Computer Society, 2005.

[5] P. Harvey, C. F. Chang, and A. Ghose. Support-based distributed search. In *Proc. 6th Intern. Workshop on Distributed Constraint Reasoning (DCR-05)*, pages 45–59, July, 2005.

[6] K. Hirayama and M. Yokoo. The distributed breakout algorithms. *Artif. Intell.*, 161(1-2):89–115, 2005.

[7] P. Morris. The breakout method for escaping from local minima. In *AAAI*, pages 40–45, 1993.

[8] M. Yokoo. Asynchronous weak-commitment search for solving distributed constraint satisfaction problems. In U. Montanari and F. Rossi, editors, *CP*, volume 976 of *Lecture Notes in Computer Science*, pages 88–102. Springer, 1995.

[9] M. Yokoo. Asynchronous weak-commitment search for solving large-scale distributed constraint satisfaction problems. In V. R. Lesser and L. Gasser, editors, *ICMAS*, page 467. The MIT Press, 1995.

[10] M. Yokoo and K. Hirayama. Algorithms for distributed constraint satisfaction: A review. *Autonomous Agents and Multi-Agent Systems*, 3(2):185–207, 2000.

[11] W. Zhang, G. Wang, Z. Xing, and L. Wittenburg. Distributed stochastic search and distributed breakout: properties, comparison and applications to constraint optimization problems in sensor networks. *Artif. Intell.*, 161(1-2):55–87, 2005.

[12] W. Zhang and L. Wittenburg. Distributed breakout revisited. In *AAAI/IAAI*, pages 352–, 2002.

[13] R. Zivan and A. Meisels. Dynamic ordering for asynchronous backtracking on discsps. In *Proc. 6th Intern. Workshop on Distributed Constraint Reasoning (DCR-05)*, pages 15–29, July, 2005.

Modeling Causal Reinforcement and Undermining with Noisy-AND Trees

Y. Xiang and N. Jia

University of Guelph, Canada

Abstract. When data are insufficient to support learning, causal modeling, such as noisy-OR, aids elicitation by reducing probability parameters to be acquired in constructing a Bayesian network. Multiple causes can reinforce each other in producing the effect or can undermine the impact of each other. Most existing causal models do not consider their interactions from the perspective of reinforcement or undermining. We show that none of them can represent both interactions. We present the first explicit causal model that can encode both reinforcement and undermining and we show how to use such a model to support efficient probability elicitation.

1 Introduction

A Bayesian network (BN) [7] encodes concisely probabilistic knowledge about a large problem domain. But when a variable has many parent variables in the BN, acquisition of the corresponding conditional probability table (CPT) is exponential on the number of parents. The CPT may be acquired through learning. However, in a given problem domain, there may be insufficient data to support learning, but experts are available for elicitation. Hence, how to elicitate the CPT from them efficiently is still a practical need.

To support such elicitation, Pearl pioneered idea of a noisy-OR model [7]. Henrion [5] added to the noisy-OR model a leaky probability. Diez [1] and Srinivas [9] extended noisy-OR from binary to multi-valued variables. Heckerman and Breese [4] analyzed a collection of causal independence relations that allows efficient acquisition of conditional probability tables in BNs. Recently, Lemmer and Gossink [6] proposed the recursive noisy-OR model.

When multiple causes are present, they can reinforce each other in producing the effect or they can undermine the impact of each other. Unlike [6], previous work do not consider causal interactions among variables from the perspective of reinforcement or undermining, and model parameters are limited to probabilities of single cause events. All previously proposed causal models, including noisy-OR, recursive noisy-OR, noisy-MAX, noisy-AND and noisy-addition, are limited to represent either reinforcement or undermining, but not both.

In this work, we present an noisy-AND tree model that represents arbitrary causal interactions among a set of causes, some of them are reinforcing and others are undermining. Reinforcement and undermining are encoded explicitly

L. Lamontagne and M. Marchand (Eds.): Canadian AI 2006, LNAI 4013, pp. 171–182, 2006.
© Springer-Verlag Berlin Heidelberg 2006

to support probability elicitation and probabilities for multi-cause events can be incorporated as model parameters if so desired.

In Section 2, we introduce the terminology and define formally reinforcement and undermining. Section 3 presents how reinforcement and undermining can be modeled uniformly using noisy-AND gates. Section 4 proposes the noisy-AND tree model and how to use it to obtain causal probability is described in Section 5. We present, in Section 6, how to use noisy-AND trees to model causal interaction when default independence assumptions do not hold. We demonstrate elicitation of CPTs with noisy-AND trees in Section 7. Section 8 compares related causal models with noisy-AND trees.

2   Background

We aim to assess a conditional probability distribution of a variable x conditioned on a set of variables Y based on their causal relation. The causes that we consider are uncertain causes. Following Lemmer and Gossink [6], an *uncertain cause* is a cause that can produce an effect but does not always do so. We denote a set of binary cause variables as $X = \{c_1, ..., c_n\}$ and their effect variable (binary) as e. For each c_i, we denote $c_i = true$ by c_{i1} and $c_i = false$ by c_{i0}. Similarly, we denote $e = true$ by e_1 and $e = false$ by e_0.

We refer to the event that a cause c_i causes an effect e to occur as a *causal event*. We denote this causal event by $e_1 \leftarrow \{c_{i1}\}$ or simply $e_1 \leftarrow c_{i1}$, and we denote its negation that c_i does not cause e as $e_1 \not\leftarrow c_{i1}$. Note that causal event $e_1 \leftarrow c_{i1}$ is not just the concurrence of c_{i1} and e_1. With the above notation, c_i is an uncertain cause of e if and only if $0 < P(e_1 \leftarrow c_{i1}) < 1$.

We denote the causal event that a set $X = \{c_1, ..., c_n\}$ of causes causes e by $e_1 \leftarrow \{c_{11}, ..., c_{n1}\}$, or simply $e_1 \leftarrow c_{11}, ..., c_{n1}$ or $e_1 \leftarrow \mathbf{x_1}$. When the cause set is indexed, such as $W_i = \{c_1, ..., c_n\}$, the causal event may be denoted $e_1 \leftarrow \mathbf{w_{i1}}$. We allow broad interpretations of causal event by a set of causes, as will be seen in later sections. For instance, we are not limited to the interpretation in [6]: *the effect is caused by at least one of the causes.*

Pearl [7] regards a cause as an event whose occurrence always results in an effect. He encodes the causal uncertainty using an uncertain inhibitor. The conjunction of a certain cause and an inhibitor in his formulation is equivalent to an uncertain cause.

When modeling a domain with a BN, the set of all causes of an effect variable e is its parents. We denote the set of all causes of e by C. To capture causes that we do not wish to represent explicitly, we include a leaky cause variable in C (as one of c_1 through c_n).

Probability of causal event can be used to assess CPT $P(e|C)$. For example, if $C = \{c_1, c_2, c_3, c_4\}$, then $P(e_1|c_{11}, c_{20}, c_{31}, c_{41}) = P(e_1 \leftarrow c_{11}, c_{31}, c_{41})$. Note that only cause variables of value *true* are included in the right-hand side of the causal probability.

When multiple causes are present, they may reinforce each other in producing the effect. That is, their combined influence is greater than that from only some of them. Alternatively, multiple causes may undermine each other in producing the effect. Below, we define reinforcement and undermining formally.

Definition 1. *Let $R = \{W_1, W_2, ...\}$ be a partition of a set X of causes, R' be a proper subset of R, and Y be the union of elements in R'. Sets of causes in R are said to* **reinforce** *each other, if for every subset $R' \subset R$, it holds that*

$$P(e_1 \leftarrow \mathbf{y_1}) \leq P(e_1 \leftarrow \mathbf{x_1}).$$

Otherwise, sets of causes in R are said to **undermine** *each other.*

When each R_i is a singleton, *reinforcement* corresponds to *positive causality* in [6] and *undermining* corresponds to *inhibition*. Hence, reinforcement and undermining are more general. They allow modeling of reinforcement of sets of causes when causes in some set are undermining. Similarly, they allow modeling of undermining of sets of causes when causes in some set are reinforcing. This will become more clear in Section 4.

3   Noisy-AND Gates for Reinforcement and Undermining

We propose to model reinforcement as well as undermining uniformly based on AND gate, which we refer to as *noisy-AND gate*. It builds on previous work with noisy-OR [7] and noisy-AND [2], but takes a different perspective from reinforcing and undermining interactions among uncertain causes.

We assume that, *by default*, sets of reinforcing causes $R = \{W_1, ..., W_m\}$, where W_i and W_j are disjoint for all i and j, satisfy *failure conjunction*:

$$(e_1 \nleftarrow \mathbf{w_{11}}, ..., \mathbf{w_{m1}}) = (e_1 \nleftarrow \mathbf{w_{11}}) \wedge ... \wedge (e_1 \nleftarrow \mathbf{w_{m1}}). \tag{1}$$

That is, sets of reinforcing causes fail to produce effect if each set of causes has failed to produce the effect. We also assume that, *by default*, sets of reinforcing causes satisfy *failure independence*:

$$P(e_1 \nleftarrow \mathbf{w_{11}}, ..., \mathbf{w_{m1}}) = P(e_1 \nleftarrow \mathbf{w_{11}}) \ ... \ P(e_1 \nleftarrow \mathbf{w_{m1}}). \tag{2}$$

That is, failure events $e_1 \nleftarrow \mathbf{w_{11}}$, ..., $e_1 \nleftarrow \mathbf{w_{m1}}$ are independent of each other.

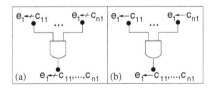

Fig. 1. Noisy-AND gate

We model the default reinforcing interaction graphically with the noisy-AND gate in Fig. 1 (a), where each $W_i = \{c_i\}$ is a singleton, $m = n$, failure conjunction is expressed by the AND gate, and failure independence is expressed by lack of direct connection between individual failure events. The following Lemma confirms their reinforcement. Due to space limit, we omit proofs for all formal results.

Lemma 1. *Let* $R = \{W_1, W_2, ...\}$ *be a partition of a set* X *of uncertain causes of effect* e *and sets in* R *satisfy Eqns (1) and (2). Then, interaction among sets of causes in* R *is reinforcing.*

When each W_i is a singleton, Eqn (2) can be alternatively written as

$$P(e_1 \leftarrow c_{11}, ..., c_{n1}) = 1 - \prod_{i=1}^{n}(1 - P(e_1 \leftarrow c_{i1})), \tag{3}$$

which is the noisy-OR model [7]. Therefore, Lemma 1 also formalizes relation between noisy-OR and reinforcement. We refer to the noisy-AND gate in Fig. 1 (a) as the default model for reinforcement. The default model represents only one possible reinforcement among sets of causes. We present representation for different reinforcements in Section 6.

Next, we consider undermining. We assume that, *by default*, sets of undermining causes satisfy *success conjunction*:

$$e_1 \leftarrow \mathbf{x_1} = (e_1 \leftarrow \mathbf{w_{11}}) \wedge ... \wedge (e_1 \leftarrow \mathbf{w_{m1}}). \tag{4}$$

That is, when sets of undermining causes succeed in causing the effect *in undermining way*, each set of causes must have been effective. We emphasize that the success occurs in an undermining way. If any set of causes has occurred but has failed to be effective, it would not undermine the other sets of causes. We also assume that, *by default*, sets of undermining causes *succeed independently*, i.e.,

$$P(e_1 \leftarrow \mathbf{x_1}) = P(e_1 \leftarrow \mathbf{w_{11}}) ... P(e_1 \leftarrow \mathbf{w_{m1}}). \tag{5}$$

The following lemma confirms their undermining interaction, whose proof is straightforward.

Lemma 2. *Let* $R = \{W_1, W_2, ...\}$ *be a partition of a set* X *of uncertain causes of effect* e *and sets in* R *satisfy Eqns (4) and (5). Then, interaction among sets of causes in* R *is undermining.*

Again, the default model represents only one possible undermining interaction among sets of causes. We describe representation of other undermining interactions in Section 6.

4   Noisy-AND Trees

Consider two sets X and Y of causes that reinforce each other. It is possible that causes within X undermine each other, and so do causes within Y. In general, such interplay of causal interactions of different natures can form a hierarchy. In this section, we present a graphical representation to model such a hierarchy. It is based on noisy-AND gates and has a tree topology. We term it *noisy-AND tree*. We assume that a domain expert is comfortable to assess reinforcing and undermining interactions among causes according to some partial order and is able to articulate the hierarchy.

For example, consider a patient in the process to recover from a disease D. Taking medicine M helps recovery and so does regular exercise. Patient's normal diet contains minerals that facilitate recovery but taking with medicine M reduces effectiveness of both.

The causes and effect involved are defined as follows:

- e_1 : Recovery from disease D within a particular time period.
- c_{11}: Taking medicine M.
- c_{21}: Regular exercise.
- c_{31}: Patient takes his/her normal diet.

For the purpose of prognosis, one needs to assess $P(e_1 \leftarrow c_{11}, c_{21}, c_{31})$. To ease the task, a physician may consider first undermining interaction between c_1 and c_3. (S)he then considers reinforcing interaction between sets $\{c_1, c_3\}$ and $\{c_2\}$. Thus, the physician has articulated an order for stepwise assessment. In addition, the physician also assesses

$$P(e_1 \leftarrow c_{11}) = 0.85, P(e_1 \leftarrow c_{21}) = 0.8, P(e_1 \leftarrow c_{31}) = 0.7.$$

If this is all the information that the physician can provide, the causal interaction can be modeled as the noisy-AND tree in Fig. 2 (a).

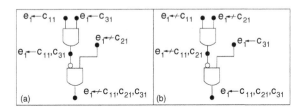

Fig. 2. (a) Noisy-AND tree model of disease example. (b) Alternative model.

From the upper AND gate and Eqn (5), we derive $P(e_1 \leftarrow c_{11}, c_{31}) = 0.595$, an effect of undermining. The output of the upper AND gate is negated (shown by the white oval) before entering the lower AND gate and the corresponding event has probability $P(e_1 \not\leftarrow c_{11}, c_{31}) = 0.405$. From the lower AND gate and Eqn (2), we derive

$$P(e_1 \not\leftarrow c_{11}, c_{21}, c_{31}) = P(e_1 \not\leftarrow c_{11}, c_{31})P(e_1 \not\leftarrow c_{21}) = 0.081,$$

and $P(e_1 \leftarrow c_{11}, c_{21}, c_{31}) = 0.919$. The following defines a noisy-AND tree in general.

Definition 2. *Let e be an effect and* $X = \{c_1, ..., c_n\}$ *be a set of uncertain causes that is known to have occurred. An* noisy-AND tree *for modeling causal interaction among elements of* X *is a directed tree where the following holds:*

1. *There are two types of nodes on the tree. An* event *node is shown as a black oval and a* gate *node is shown as an AND gate. Each event node has an in-degree* ≤ 1 *and an out-degree* ≤ 1. *Each gate has an in-degree* ≥ 2 *and an out-degree* 1.
2. *Every link connects an event node with a gate node. There are two type of links:* forward *links and* negation *links. Each link is directed from its* tail *node to its* head *node consistently along the input-to-output stream of gates. A forward link is shown as a line and is implicitly directed. A negation link is shown as a line with a white oval at the head and is explicitly directed.*
3. *All terminal nodes are event nodes and each is labeled by a causal event in the form* $e_1 \leftarrow \mathbf{y}$ *or* $e_1 \nleftarrow \mathbf{y}$. *Exactly one terminal node, called the* leaf, *is connected to the output of a gate and has* $\mathbf{y} = \mathbf{x_1}$. *Each other terminal node is connected to the input of a gate and is a* root. *For each root,* $\mathbf{y}$ *is a proper subset of* $\mathbf{x_1}$, *it holds* $\bigcup_i \mathbf{y_i} = \mathbf{x_1}$ *with* i *indexing roots, and for every two roots with* $\mathbf{y_j}$ *and* $\mathbf{y_k}$, *it holds* $\mathbf{y_j} \cap \mathbf{y_k} = \emptyset$.
4. *Multiple inputs of a gate g must be in one of the following cases:*
   (a) *Each is either connected by a forward link to a node labeled with* $e_1 \leftarrow \mathbf{y}$, *or by a negation link to a node labeled with* $e_1 \nleftarrow \mathbf{y}$. *Output of g is connected by a forward link to a node labeled with* $e_1 \leftarrow \cup_i \mathbf{y_i}$.
   (b) *Each is either connected by a forward link to a node labeled with* $e_1 \nleftarrow \mathbf{y}$, *or by a negation link to a node labeled with* $e_1 \leftarrow \mathbf{y}$. *Output of g is connected by a forward link to a node labeled with* $e_1 \nleftarrow \cup_i \mathbf{y_i}$.

Degree restriction in Condition 1 ensures that an event represents the output of no more than one gate and is connected to the input of no more than one gate. Condition 4 ensures that inputs to each gate either all corresponds to causal events in the form of $e_1 \leftarrow \mathbf{y}$, or all corresponds to causal events in the form of $e_1 \nleftarrow \mathbf{y}$. Semantically, 4 (a) corresponds to undermining sets of causes and 4 (b) corresponds to reinforcing sets.

5   Noisy-AND Tree Evaluation

A noisy-AND tree can be used to evaluate $P(e_1 \leftarrow \mathbf{x_1})$ given $P(e_1 \leftarrow \mathbf{y})$ or $P(e_1 \nleftarrow \mathbf{y})$ for each root node. The computation can be performed recursively by decomposing the noisy-AND tree into subtrees. The following lemma shows that such decomposition is valid.

Lemma 3. *Let T be a noisy-AND tree, the leaf of T be v, and the gate connected to v be g. Let v and g be deleted from T, as well as the links incoming to g. In the remaining graph, each component is either an isolated event node or a noisy-AND tree.*

A noisy-AND tree can be evaluated according to the following algorithm.

Algorithm 1. *GetCausalEventProb(T)*
Input: A noisy-AND tree T.

denote leaf of T by v and gate connected to v by g;
for each node w directly connected to input of g, do
   if probability $P(w)$ for event at w is not specified,
     denote sub-AND-tree with w as the leaf by T_w;
     $P(w) = GetCausalEventProb(T_w)$;
   if (w, g) is a forward link, $P'(w) = P(w)$;
   else $P'(w) = 1 - P(w)$;
$P(v) = \prod_w P'(w)$;
return $P(v)$;

The following theorem establishes soundness of GetCausalEventProb. We define the *depth* of a noisy-AND tree to be the maximum number of gate nodes contained in a path from a root to the leaf.

Theorem 1. *Let T be a noisy-AND tree where probability for each root node is specified in the range $(0, 1)$ and $P(v)$ be returned by GetCausalEventProb(T). Then $P(v)$ is a probability in the range $(0, 1)$ and it combines given probabilities according to reinforcement or undermining specified by the topology of T.*

Note that the topology of T is a crucial piece of knowledge. For the above example, suppose the physician articulates a different order, which is shown in Fig. 2 (b). The physician feels that reinforcing interaction between c_1 and c_2 should be considered first. The undermining interaction between sets $\{c_1, c_2\}$ and $\{c_3\}$ should then be considered. Applying GetCausalEventProb, we obtain $P(e_1 \nleftarrow c_{11}, c_{21}) = 0.03$ and $P(e_1 \leftarrow c_{11}, c_{21}, c_{31}) = 0.679$.

6   Relaxing Default Assumptions

A noisy-AND tree assumes, by default, failure independence for reinforcing sets of causes and success independence for undermining sets of causes. For given sets of causes, the expert may disagree with such assumptions. This may manifest in terms of disagreement of the expert with output event probability of a noisy-AND gate. When this occurs, noisy-AND tree representation allows easy modification by deleting the corresponding AND gate from the tree. In particular, let g be the gate in question and its output be connected to node v. If the expert disagrees with the event probability computed for node v, the entire subtree with v as the leaf can be discarded by deleting the link (g, v). Node v remains in the resultant new noisy-AND tree as a root node. The expert can then specify a proper event probability for v.

For instance, with the noisy-AND tree in Fig. 2 (a), suppose that the expert disagrees with $P(e_1 \leftarrow c_{11}, c_{31}) = 0.595$. Instead, (s)he feels that 0.4 is more appropriate. Note that this assignment is consistent with the undermining interaction between c_1 and c_3, but the degree of undermining is different from what the default assumption dictates. We can then remove root nodes labeled by $e_1 \leftarrow c_{11}$ and $e_1 \leftarrow c_{31}$ as well as the gate that they are connected to. As the result, node $e_1 \leftarrow c_{11}, c_{31}$ becomes a root node and $P(e_1 \leftarrow c_{11}, c_{31}) = 0.4$ can be assigned to it. Applying GetCausalEventProb to the new noisy-AND tree, we obtain $P(e_1 \leftarrow c_{11}, c_{21}, c_{31}) = 0.88$.

This flexibility of noisy-AND tree allows it to be used interactively, increasing its expressive power as a tool for probability elicitation: An expert can start by articulating a noisy-AND tree where each root is labeled by a single cause c_i. The default assumptions on failure and success independence now allow computation of probability for each non-root causal event. This can be viewed as the first approximation of the expert's subjective belief. The expert can then examine each computed event probability and decide if it is consistent with his/her belief.

Upon identification of disagreement over a node v connected to the output of a gate g, the expert can trace backward to input events connected to g. The expert will decide whether (s)he disagrees with the probabilities of any input events. If no such disagreement is identified, then the expert must be disagreeing with the degree of reinforcement or undermining implied by the assumption on failure or success independence. (S)he can then assess a probability for the output event as we illustrated above. Note that this assessment, with the computed probability as reference, is easier than an assessment to be made from vacuum. On the other hand, if disagreement with the probability of an input event is identified, the processing continues by tracing further back towards root nodes.

It is possible that as the expert traces disagreements, makes modifications to event probabilities, and deletes subtrees, a deep noisy-AND tree started with becomes shallow in the end. Many root node labels now consist of a subset of causes, instead of a single one at the start. The resultant noisy-AND tree becomes topologically very different. This does not mean that the original noisy-AND tree was wrong. It has disappeared after serving its useful role in elicitation.

7   Elicitation of CPTs with Noisy-AND Trees

We demonstrate how to use noisy-AND trees to elicit CPTs in BNs with an example [1]. Consider an effect (child) variable e with a set of seven causes (parents) in a BN: $c_1, ..., c_7$. Suppose that a domain expert identifies the following three subsets of causes and interaction within each subset:

- Subset s_1: c_1 and c_2 are undermining each other.
- Subset s_2: c_2, c_3 and c_4 are reinforcing each other.
- Subset s_3: c_6 and c_7 are reinforcing each other.

The expert assesses that interaction between subsets s_1 and s_2 is also undermining and, together as a group, they reinforce s_3. Without further quantitative information, these assessments produce the noisy-AND tree in Fig. 3 (a). Suppose that the following probabilities for single-cause events are also provided:

---

[1] To demonstrate in a more general setting, we use here an example that is more challenging than the medical example used above.

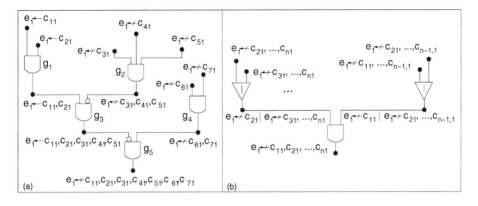

Fig. 3. (a) An example noisy-AND tree. (b) Graphical model for recursive noisy-OR.

$$P(e_1 \leftarrow c_{11}) = 0.65, P(e_1 \leftarrow c_{21}) = 0.35, P(e_1 \leftarrow c_{31}) = 0.8,$$

$$P(e_1 \leftarrow c_{41}) = 0.3, P(e_1 \leftarrow c_{51}) = 0.6, P(e_1 \leftarrow c_{61}) = 0.75, P(e_1 \leftarrow c_{71}) = 0.55.$$

To assess $P(e_1|c_{11}, ..., c_{71})$, we apply GetCausalEventProb to obtain

$$P(e_1|c_{11}, ..., c_{71}) = P(e_1 \leftarrow c_{11}, ..., c_{71}) = 0.912.$$

To assess $P(e_1|c_{11}, c_{21}, c_{30}, c_{41}, c_{51}, c_{61}, c_{71})$, eliminate node $e_1 \nleftarrow c_{31}$ from Fig. 3 (a) and modify output labels for g_2, g_3 and g_5. The evaluation gives

$$P(e_1|c_{11}, c_{21}, c_{30}, c_{41}, c_{51}, c_{61}, c_{71}) = P(e_1 \leftarrow c_{11}, c_{21}, c_{41}, c_{51}, c_{61}, c_{71}) = 0.906.$$

We have used the same noisy-AND tree to assess both probabilities above. This is not necessary. That is, noisy-AND trees do not require that different causal probabilities to be assessed using the same tree. If the expert feels that a particular combination of a subset of causes follows a different pattern of interaction, a distinct noisy-AND tree can be used, without producing invalid CPT. Commonly, we expect that one tree can be used for assessment of all probabilities in a CPT. If the expert is happy with the result, the complexity of his/her assessment task is only $O(n)$, where n is the number of causes.

Suppose that the expert believes that 0.906 is too high for $P(e_1|c_{11}, c_{21}, c_{30}, c_{41}, c_{51}, c_{61}, c_{71})$ and (s)he attributes to the output from gate g_4 $P(e_1 \nleftarrow c_{61}, c_{71})$ = 0.113 as too low. Instead, (s)he believes 0.2 is a better assessment. In response, we remove the subtree with g_4 as the leaf and specify 0.2 as the probability for the new root event node $e_1 \nleftarrow c_{61}, c_{71}$. GetCausalEventProb now generates $P(e_1|c_{11}, c_{21}, c_{30}, c_{41}, c_{51}, c_{61}, c_{71}) = 0.833.$

8   Related Models of Causal Interaction

We compare noisy-AND trees with related models of causal interaction. As we have defined reinforcement and undermining under the binary context, the following analysis is restricted to such context if appropriate.

Some models of causal interaction are limited to represent either reinforcement or undermining but not both. Noisy-MAX model [1] becomes noisy-OR model when variables are binary. Therefore, from Lemma 1, when domain is binary, noisy-MAX represents only reinforcing interaction.

Similarly, noisy-MIN model [2] becomes noisy-AND when variables are binary. Hence, according to Lemma 2, when domain is binary, noisy-MIN represents only undermining interaction.

Lemmer and Gossink [6] proposed RNOR to model reinforcement. To assess effect probability due to a set of causes, RNOR model can combine causal probabilities due to subsets of causes, where each subset may not be singleton. Their combination at subset level has influenced our thinking in formulation of noisy-AND trees. According to RNOR, for a set of causes $X = \{c_1, ..., c_n\}$, if $P(e_1 \leftarrow c_{11}, ..., c_{n1})$ is not provided by the expert, it is estimated as

$$P(e_1 \leftarrow c_{11}, ..., c_{n1}) = 1 - \prod_{i=1}^{n} \frac{1 - P(e_1 \leftarrow c_{11}, ..., c_{i-1,1}, c_{i+1,1}, ..., c_{n1})}{1 - P(e_1 \leftarrow c_{11}, ..., c_{i-1,1}, c_{i+2,1}, ..., c_{n1})} \quad (6)$$

as long as causes in X are reinforcing. However, if causes in X are undermining, the result from the equation may not be a valid probability.

No graphical representation of RNOR was proposed in [6]. We present a graphical model which reveals the independence assumption underlying RNOR. Using failure events, we rewrite Eqn (6) below:

$$P(e_1 \nleftarrow c_{11}, ..., c_{n1}) = \prod_{i=1}^{n} \frac{P(e_1 \nleftarrow c_{11}, ..., c_{i-1,1}, c_{i+1,1}, ..., c_{n1})}{P(e_1 \nleftarrow c_{11}, ..., c_{i-1,1}, c_{i+2,1}, ..., c_{n1})} \quad (7)$$

$$= \prod_{i=1}^{n} \frac{P((e_1 \nleftarrow c_{i+1,1}) \wedge (e_1 \nleftarrow c_{11}, ..., c_{i-1,1}, c_{i+2,1}, ..., c_{n1}))}{P(e_1 \nleftarrow c_{11}, ..., c_{i-1,1}, c_{i+2,1}, ..., c_{n1})} \quad (8)$$

$$= \prod_{i=1}^{n} P(e_1 \nleftarrow c_{i+1,1} | e_1 \nleftarrow c_{11}, ..., c_{i-1,1}, c_{i+2,1}, ..., c_{n1}) \quad (9)$$

Fig. 3 (b) shows the graphical model of RNOR based on Eqn (7) and Eqn (9). A gate representing "conditioning" has been introduced and is shown as a triangle with a vertical bar in the center. We refer to the gate as a COND gate. The output of a COND gate is the event of its left input event conditioned on its right input event. Note that $e_1 \nleftarrow c_{i+1,1} | e_1 \nleftarrow c_{11}, ..., c_{i-1,1}, c_{i+2,1}, ..., c_{n1}$ is a well defined event. Each input event to a COND gate is associated with a real *potential*. Its output event is assigned a potential defined by the division of the two input potentials (the one in the left divided by that in the right). For the AND gate, its output event is assigned a potential defined by the product of potentials of its inputs. Inputs of each gate are not connected in any path other than through the gate.

Eqn (9) and Fig. 3 (b) reveal that RNOR model assumes that conditional failure event denoted by $e_1 \nleftarrow c_{i+1,1} | e_1 \nleftarrow c_{11}, ..., c_{i-1,1}, c_{i+2,1}, ..., c_{n1}$ (where i runs from 1 to n) is independent of each other. This is not surprising as RNOR is derived from rewriting Eqn (3) and it assumes failure independence among all causes. However, when RNOR is used recursively by replacing default probabilities on input of some COND gates, the independence assumption is invalidated, while the topology of the graphical model and the rule of probability combination (Eqn (6)) remain and do not reflect such invalidation.

On the other hand, independence assumptions made in noisy-AND trees are local to each gate. Assumption made relative to a gate governs only the probability combination at the output of the gate and is independent of the assumptions made at other gates. When the default probability produced by a gate is replaced and the corresponding subtree removed, it does not invalidate any independence assumptions at other gates in the remaining noisy-AND tree. That is, modification of a noisy-AND tree does not invalidate the coherence of the underlying independence assumptions.

Noisy-addition [3] can represent neither reinforcement nor undermining. Consider a noisy-adder with two binary causes c_1 and c_2 whose domains are $\{0, 1\}$. It has the following DAG model, where i_1 and i_2 are intermediate variables and effect $e = i_1 + i_2$:

$$c_1 \longrightarrow i_1 \longrightarrow e \longleftarrow i_2 \longleftarrow c_2$$

The model assumes $P(i_j = 0|c_j = 0) = 1$ and $0 < P(i_j = 1|c_j = 1) < 1$ for $j = 1, 2$. For simplicity, we assume $P(i_1 = 1|c_1 = 1) = P(i_2 = 1|c_2 = 1)$ and denote their value by q. Note that $P(e = 1|c_1 = 1) = P(i_1 = 1|c_1 = 1)$. To decide whether this model can represent reinforcement or undermining, $P(e = 1|c_1 = 1, c_2 = 1)$ should be compared with q. We derive the following:

$$P(e = 1|c_1 = 1, c_2 = 1)$$
$$= P(i_1 = 0, i_2 = 1|c_1 = 1, c_2 = 1) + P(i_1 = 1, i_2 = 0|c_1 = 1, c_2 = 1)$$
$$= P(i_1 = 0|c_1 = 1)P(i_2 = 1|c_2 = 1) + P(i_1 = 1|c_1 = 1)P(i_2 = 0|c_2 = 1)$$

Denoting $P(e = 1|c_1 = 1, c_2 = 1)$ by r, we have $r = 2q(1-q)$. If $q < 0.5$, then $r > q$. If $q > 0.5$, then $r < q$. By Definition 1, if a causal model is reinforcing, then no matter what value $P(e_1 \leftarrow \mathbf{y_1})$ is, the relation $P(e_1 \leftarrow \mathbf{y_1}) \leq P(e_1 \leftarrow \mathbf{x_1})$ must hold and reverse of the inequality must hold for undermining. Being unable to maintain the inequality across the entire range of values for $P(e_1 \leftarrow \mathbf{y_1})$ implies that noisy-addition is unable to represent either reinforcement or undermining.

Noisy-AND trees differ from those considered in [4] in that the amechanistic model has essentially a star topology and other three models (decomposable, multiply decomposable and temporal) are essentially binary trees. When the binary tree is instantiated according to noisy-OR, noisy-AND, noisy-MAX, noisy-MIN, noisy-addition, it inherits limitations of these models as discussed above. In these models, each root node must be a single cause variable, while noisy-AND trees allow a root node to represent a causal event of multiple causes.

Pearl [8] analyzed causation using functional causal models. Our work is consistent with his functional approach and in particular proposes noisy-AND trees as a useful boolean functional model.

9   Conclusions

Causal interactions may be reinforcing or undermining. Their distinction can facilitate causal modeling and CPT elicitation in constructing Bayesian networks. We have shown that existing causal models can model either only one type of interactions (such as noisy-OR, noisy-AND, noisy-MAX, noisy-MIN and recursive noisy-OR) or none of them (such as noisy-addition). We present the first explicit causal model, termed noisy-AND trees, that can encode both reinforcement and undermining. Furthermore, existing causal models, except recursive noisy-OR, limit model parameters to probabilities of single cause events. Recursive noisy-OR introduces inconsistent dependence assumptions when probabilities of multi-cause events are integrated through recursion. On the other hand, noisy-AND trees integrate probabilities of both single cause events and multi-cause events coherently. Therefore, noisy-AND trees provide a simple yet powerful new approach for knowledge elicitation in probabilistic graphical models.

Acknowledgements

The financial support from National Sciences and Engineering Research Council (NSERC) of Canada through Discovery Grant to the first author is acknowledged.

References

1. F.J. Diez. Parameter adjustment in Bayes networks: The generalized noisy or-gate. In D. Heckerman and A. Mamdani, editors, *Proc. 9th Conf. on Uncertainty in Artificial Intelligence*, pages 99–105. Morgan Kaufmann, 1993.
2. S.F. Galan and F.J. Diez. Modeling dynamic causal interactiosn with Bayesian networks: temporal noisy gates. In *Proc. 2nd Inter. Workshop on Causal Networks*, pages 1–5, 2000.
3. D. Heckerman. Causal independence for knowledge acquisition and inference. In D. Heckerman and A. Mamdani, editors, *Proc. 9th Conf. on Uncertainty in Artificial Intelligence*, pages 122–127. Morgan Kaufmann, 1993.
4. D. Heckerman and J.S. Breese. Causal independence for probabilistic assessment and inference using Bayesian networks. *IEEE Trans. on System, Man and Cybernetics*, 26(6):826–831, 1996.
5. M. Henrion. Some practical issues in constructing belief networks. In L.N. Kanal, T.S. Levitt, and J.F. Lemmer, editors, *Uncertainty in Artificial Intelligence 3*, pages 161–173. Elsevier Science Publishers, 1989.
6. J.F. Lemmer and D.E. Gossink. Recursive noisy OR - a rule for estimating complex probabilistic interactions. *IEEE SMC, Part B*, 34(6):2252–2261, 2004.
7. J. Pearl. *Probabilistic Reasoning in Intelligent Systems: Networks of Plausible Inference*. Morgan Kaufmann, 1988.
8. J. Pearl. *Causality: Models, Reasoning, and Inference*. Cambridge University Press, 2000.
9. S. Srinivas. A generalization of noisy-or model. In D. Heckerman and A. Mamdani, editors, *Proc. 9th Conf. on Uncertainty in Artificial Intelligence*, pages 208–215. Morgan Kaufmann, 1993.

An Improved LAZY-AR Approach to Bayesian Network Inference

C.J. Butz and S. Hua

Department of Computer Science,
University of Regina
Regina, SK, S4S 0A2, Canada
{butz, huash111}@cs.uregina.ca

Abstract. We propose LAZY arc-reversal with variable elimination (LAZY-ARVE) as a new approach to probabilistic inference in Bayesian networks (BNs). LAZY-ARVE is an improvement upon LAZY arc-reversal (LAZY-AR), which was very recently proposed and empirically shown to be the state-of-the-art method for exact inference in discrete BNs. The primary advantage of LAZY-ARVE over LAZY-AR is that the former only computes the actual distributions passed during inference, whereas the latter may perform unnecessary computation by constructing irrelevant intermediate distributions. A comparison between LAZY-AR and LAZY-ARVE, involving processing evidence in a real-world BN for coronary heart disease, is favourable towards LAZY-ARVE.

1 Introduction

Bayesian networks (BNs) [1, 2, 10, 14] are an established framework for uncertainty management in artificial intelligence. A BN consists of a *directed acyclic graph* (DAG) and a corresponding set of *conditional probability tables* (CPTs). The *probabilistic conditional independencies* (CIs) [15] encoded in the DAG indicate the product of CPTs is a joint probability distribution. Exact inference algorithms in BNs can be broadly classified into two categories. One approach is *join tree propagation* (JTP), which systematically passes messages in a *join tree* (JT) constructed from the DAG of a BN. The classical JTP methods were proposed by Lauritzen and Spiegelhalter [5], Shafer and Shenoy [14], and Jensen et al. [3]. Madsen and Jensen [7] suggested a JTP algorithm, called LAZY propagation, and empirically demonstrated a significant improvement in efficiency over the traditional JTP methods. A second approach to BN inference is *direct computation* (DC), which performs inference directly in a BN. The classical DC algorithms are variable elimination (VE) [17, 18, 19], arc-reversal (AR) [9, 13] and symbolic probabilistic inference (SPI) [6, 12]. The experimental results provided by Zhang [17] indicate that VE is more efficient than the classical JTP methods when updating twenty or less non-evidence variables, given a set of twenty or fewer evidence variables.

Very recently, Madsen [8] examined hybrid approaches to BN inference. Inference is still conducted in a JT, but DC computation is utilized to perform

L. Lamontagne and M. Marchand (Eds.): Canadian AI 2006, LNAI 4013, pp. 183–194, 2006.
© Springer-Verlag Berlin Heidelberg 2006

the physical computation. Of the three hybrid approaches tested, LAZY arc-reversal (LAZY-AR) was empirically shown to be the state-of-the-art method for exact inference in discrete BNs [8]. When a JT node is ready to send its CPT messages to a neighbour, the LAZY-AR approach eliminates all variables not appearing in the neighbour node. In particular, eliminating variable v may require directed edges (arcs) to be reversed in the DAG (defined by the CPTs at the sending JT node) in order to make v *barren* [13]. Such arc reversals are useful, since it is well-known that barren variables can be exploited for more efficient inference [7]. The missing CPTs of the newly constructed DAG are physically built from the existing CPTs. We point out that the LAZY-AR approach is sometimes wasteful as it can construct intermediate CPTs that are immaterial.

In this paper, we propose LAZY arc-reversal with variable elimination (LAZY-ARVE) as a new approach to BN inference. As the name suggests, our method is based upon the LAZY-AR approach. Whereas LAZY-AR iterates between semantic modeling and physical computation, LAZY-ARVE performs semantic modeling and physical computation separately. More specifically, LAZY-ARVE first performs semantic modeling in order to identify those CPT messages to be sent to a neighbour JT node. LAZY-ARVE next physically constructs the distributions of the passed CPTs using the VE inference algorithm. There are important advantages to uncoupling the independent tasks of semantic modeling and physical computation. By treating these two tasks as dependent, LAZY-AR can construct intermediate CPTs that will neither be sent to a neighbour, nor needed in the construction of the propagated CPTs. Physically constructing these irrelevant intermediate CPTs not only wastes computation but also the time required to build these distributions. As the screen shot in Fig. 5 illustrates, we have implemented the AR approach to identify the CPTs to be propagated. Using a real-world BN for *coronary heart disease* (CHD) [2], we compared our approach of applying VE to build only the propagated CPTs with the state-of-the-art method. The results in Table 1, in which roughly eighteen percent of the BN variables are instantiated as evidence variables, show promise.

This paper is organized as follows. Section 2 contains background knowledge. In Section 3, we discuss a new approach to probabilistic inference. Related works are provided in Section 4. The conclusion is presented in Section 5.

2   Background Knowledge

Here we review Bayesian networks, probabilistic inference and the AR method.

2.1   Bayesian Networks

Let $U = \{v_1, v_2, \ldots, v_n\}$ denote a finite set of discrete random variables. Each variable v_i is associated with a finite domain, denoted $dom(v_i)$, representing the values v_i can take on. For a subset $X \subseteq U$, we write $dom(X)$ for the

Cartesian product of the domains of the individual variables in X. Each element $x \in dom(X)$ is called a *configuration* of X. A *potential* [2] on $dom(X)$ is a function ϕ on $dom(X)$ such that $\phi(x) \geq 0$, for each configuration $x \in dom(X)$, and at least one $\phi(x)$ is positive. For brevity, we refer to a potential as a probability distribution on X rather than $dom(X)$, and we call X, not $dom(X)$, its domain [14]. A *joint probability distribution* (JPD) [14] on U, denoted $p(U)$, is a potential on U that sums to one. Given $X \subset U$, a *conditional probability table* (CPT) [14] for a variable $v \notin X$ is a distribution, denoted $p(v|X)$, satisfying the following condition: for each configuration $x \in dom(X)$, $\sum_{c \in dom(v)} p(v = c \mid X = x) = 1.0$.

A *Bayesian network* (BN) [10] on U is a pair (D, C). D is a *directed acyclic graph* (DAG) on U. C is a set of CPTs defined as: for each variable $v_i \in D$, there is a CPT for v_i given its parents P_i in D. Based on the *probabilistic conditional independencies* [15] encoded in D, the product of the CPTs in C is a JPD $p(U)$.

Example 1. The DAG of one real-world BN for *coronary heart disease* (CHD) [2] is shown in Fig. 1. The corresponding CPTs are not pertinent to our discussion. For pedagogical reasons, we have made the following minor adjustments to the DAG: edge (a, f) has been removed; edges (c, f) and (g, i) have been replaced with edges (c, d), (c, e), (d, f), (e, f) and (g, j), where d and e are dummy variables.

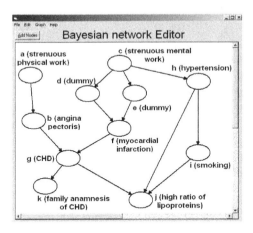

Fig. 1. The *coronary heart disease* (CHD) BN [2] in Example 1

We will use the terms BN and DAG interchangeably if no confusion arises. The *family* F_i of a variable v_i in a DAG is $\{v_i\} \cup P_i$. A numbering $\prec$ of the variables in a DAG is called *ancestral* [1], if the number corresponding to any variable v_i is lower than the number corresponding to each of its children v_j, denoted $v_i \prec v_j$.

In the CHD BN in Fig. 1, we will always use the fixed ancestral numbering as $a \prec b \prec \ldots \prec k$.

2.2 Probabilistic Inference

In this paper, we only consider exact inference in discrete BNs. Probabilistic inference (or query processing) means computing $p(X)$ or $p(X|E = e)$, where X and E are disjoint subsets of U. The *evidence* in the latter query is that E is instantiated to configuration e, while X contains *target* variables. Barren variables can be exploited in inference [7]. A variable is *barren* [13], if it is neither an evidence nor a target variable and it only has barren descendants. Probabilistic inference can be conducted directly in the original BN [6, 9, 12, 13, 17, 18, 19]. It can also be performed in a join tree [3, 5, 7, 8, 14].

Shafer [14] emphasizes that *join tree propagation* (JTP) is central to the theory and practice of probabilistic expert systems. A *join tree* (JT) [10, 14] is a tree with sets of variables as nodes, with the property that any variable in two nodes is also in any node on the path between the two. The *separator S* between any two neighbour nodes N_i and N_j is $S = N_i \cap N_j$. The task of transforming a DAG into a JT has been extensively studied in probabilistic reasoning literature. Note that constructing a minimal JT is NP-complete [16]. For example, recall the CHD BN in Fig. 1. One possible JT with nodes $\{ab, bfg, cdefgh, ghij, gk\}$ is depicted in Fig. 2 (ignoring the messages at the moment).

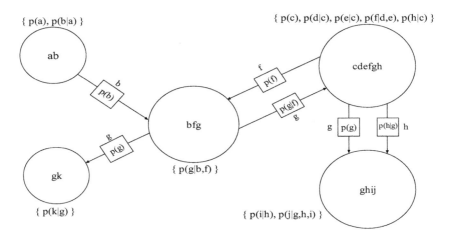

Fig. 2. A JT for the CHD BN in Fig. 1

Unlike traditional JTP approaches [3, 5, 14], LAZY propagation [7] maintains structure in the form of a multiplicative factorization of potentials at each JT node and each JT separator. Maintaining a decomposition of potentials offers LAZY the opportunity to exploit barren variables and independencies induced by evidence. Doing so improves the efficiency of JTP remarkably as the experimental results in [7] clearly emphasize.

2.3 Arc Reversal

The basic idea of *Arc-reversal* (AR) [9, 13] is to make a variable barren via a sequence of arc reversals prior to eliminating it. Suppose variable v_i is to be eliminated and arc (v_i, v_j) needs to be reversed. The arc (v_i, v_j) is graphically reversed as (v_j, v_i) by setting the new parents of v_i as $P_i \cup F_j - \{v_i\}$, while making $P_i \cup P_j - \{v_i\}$ the new parents of v_j. Note that AR uses an ancestral numbering $\prec$ of the given BN to avoid creating directed cycles. Hence, a DAG structure is maintained after eliminating a variable by applying AR [4, 8]. The next example illustrates how AR reverses arcs when eliminating variables during inference not involving evidence.

Example 2. Consider how node $cdefgh$ sends the CPT messages $\{p(g), p(h|g)\}$ to node $ghij$ in the JT in Fig. 2. Node $cdefgh$ collects the CPT $p(g|f)$ sent from bfg. A DAG in Fig. 3 (i) is defined on the set $C = \{p(c), p(d|c), p(e|c), p(f|d, e), p(g|f), p(h|c)\}$ of CPTs at $cdefgh$. Applying AR to eliminate variables $\{c, d, e, f\}$ gives the sub-DAG in Fig. 3 (ii). For pedagogical purposes, let us eliminate the variables in the order d, c, e, f. To eliminate d, arc (d, f) needs to be reversed. Here, $v_i = d$, $P_i = \{c\}$, $v_j = f$, $P_j = \{d, e\}$ and $F_j = \{d, e, f\}$. The reversed arc (f, d) is created by setting $P_i' = \{c, e, f\}$ and $P_j' = \{c, e\}$, as shown in Step 1 of Fig. 4 (i). Variable d becomes barren and can be removed. The remaining sub-DAG under consideration is illustrated in Step 2 of Fig. 4 (i). For variable c, arcs (c, e), (c, f) and (c, h) need to be reversed. According to $\prec$ of the CHD BN in Fig. 1, arc (c, e) will be reversed first. Here, $v_i = c$, $P_i = \emptyset$, $v_j = e$, $P_j = \{c\}$ and $F_j = \{c, e\}$. The reversed arc (e, c) is created by setting $P_i' = \{e\}$ and $P_j' = \emptyset$, as shown in Step 1 of Fig. 4 (ii). In a similar manner, arcs (c, f) and (c, h) are reversed as shown in Step 2 and Step 3 of Fig. 4 (ii), respectively. Variable c becomes barren and can be removed giving the sub-DAG in Step 4

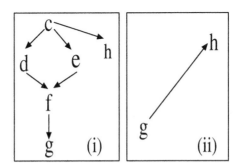

Fig. 3. (i) The initial DAG for Example 2. (ii) Applying AR to eliminate $\{c, d, e, f\}$ yields this sub-DAG.

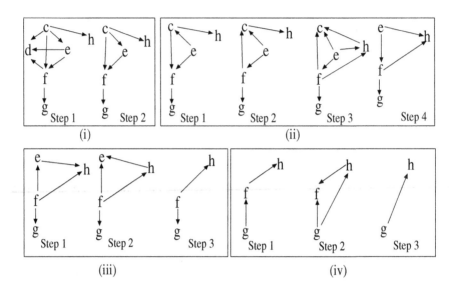

Fig. 4. Illustrating Arc-Reversal (AR) by eliminating variables d (i), c (ii), e (iii) and f (iv) from the initial DAG in Fig. 3 (i). The final DAG is shown in Fig. 3 (ii).

of Fig. 4 (ii). Similarly, variables e and f are removed via the arc reversals as shown in Fig. 4 (iii) and (iv), respectively.

3   New Approach LAZY-ARVE for BN Inference

In this section, we introduce LAZY Arc-Reversal with Variable Elimination (LAZY-ARVE) as a new algorithm for BN inference. LAZY-ARVE is built upon the AR Message Identification (ARMI) and VE [17, 18, 19] algorithms. First, the sub-algorithm ARMI applies AR for the graphical identification of the propagated CPTs. Next, VE is applied to compute only the propagated CPTs.

Algorithm 1. LAZY-ARVE(C, X)
Input: a set C of CPT distributions at a JT node,
       the set X of variables to be eliminated from C.
Output: the set C of CPT distributions sent from a JT node to a neighbour.
begin
1. Call ARMI to identify the labels of the propagated CPTs.
2. **for** each CPT label $p(v|X)$ output from Step 1
    Call VE to physically construct the actual distribution.
3. **return** the physical distributions output from Step 2
end

The sub-algorithm ARMI applies AR to *identify* the labels of the actual CPT messages to be sent from a JT node to a neighbour.

Algorithm 2. ARMI $(C,X,\prec)$

Input: a set C of CPT labels at a JT node,

the set X of variables to be eliminated from C,

an ancestral numbering $\prec$ of the variables in the BN.

Output: the set C of CPT labels sent from a JT node to a neighbour.

begin

Construct the DAG $G = (V, E)$ defined by C.

for each variable v_i in X

{

   Let $Y = \{v_1, \ldots, v_k\}$ be the set of all children of v_i in G, where $v_1 \prec \ldots \prec v_k$.

   for $j = 1, \ldots, k$

   {

$$P_i' = P_i \cup F_j - \{v_i\}$$
$$P_j' = P_i \cup P_j - \{v_i\}$$
$$C = C \cup \{ p(v_i|P_i'), p(v_j|P_j') \} - \{ p(v_i|P_i), p(v_j|P_j) \}$$

   }

   Remove barren variable v_i from G and its CPT from C.

}

return(C)

end

After identifying the CPT labels to be sent from a JT node, the VE [17, 18, 19] algorithm is called to physically *compute* the propagated CPTs. To compute $p(X|Y = Y_0)$, VE calls the sub-algorithm sum-out to eliminate variables outside $X \cup Y$ from a list of factors one by one, according to an elimination ordering σ.

Algorithm 3. [19] VE$(\mathcal{F}, X, Y, Y_0, \sigma)$

Input: $\mathcal{F}$ - the list of conditional probabilities in a BN,

X - a list of query variables,

Y - a list of observed variables,

Y_0 - the corresponding list of observed values,

σ - an elimination ordering for variables outside $X \cup Y$.

Output: the physical distribution of $p(X|Y = Y_0)$.

begin

Set the observed variables in all factors to their corresponding observed values.

While σ is not empty,

{

   Remove the first variable z from σ,

   $\mathcal{F} = $ sum-out$(\mathcal{F},z)$.

}

Set $h = $ the multiplication of all the factors on $\mathcal{F}$.

Return $p(X|Y = Y_0) = h(X)/\sum_X h(X)$.

end

Algorithm 4. [19] sum-out$(z,\mathcal{F})$

Input: $\mathcal{F}$ - a list of factors,

z - a variable.

Output: another list of factors.

begin
Remove from $\mathcal{F}$ all the factors, say $f_1, \ldots, f_k$, that contain z.
Add the new factor $\sum_z \prod_{i=1}^{k} f_i$ to $\mathcal{F}$.
Return $\mathcal{F}$.
end

The next example illustrates our LAZY-ARVE inference algorithm.

Example 3. Recall Fig. 3 (i). In Step 1, ARMI returns the CPT labels $\{p(g),$ $p(h|g)\}$, as depicted in Fig. 3 (ii), to be sent from node $cdefgh$ to $ghij$ in the JT in Fig. 2. In Step 2, LAZY-ARVE calls VE to compute the physical distributions for $p(g)$ and $p(h|g)$.

Consider physically computing $p(h|g)$. Here, $\mathcal{F} = \{p(c), p(d|c), p(e|c),$ $p(f|d, e), p(g|f), p(h|c)\}$, $X = h$, $Y = g$ and $Y_0 = \emptyset$. Suppose the elimination ordering σ is $\{d, c, e, f\}$. The first variable d in σ is removed by calling sum-out, which computes $\phi(c, e, f) = \sum_d p(d|c) \cdot p(f|d, e)$ and then sets $\mathcal{F} = \{p(c), \phi(c, e, f), p(e|c), p(g|f), p(h|c)\}$. Next, sum-out removes variable c as $\phi(e, f, h) = \sum_c p(c) \cdot \phi(c, e, f) \cdot p(e|c) \cdot p(h|c)$ leaving $\mathcal{F} = \{\phi(e, f, h), p(g|f)\}$. It can be verified that $\mathcal{F} = \phi(g, h)$ after removing $\{e, f\}$. Lastly, VE computes $p(h|g)$ by normalizing $\phi(g, h)$, i.e., $p(h|g) = \phi(g, h)/\sum_h \phi(g, h)$. The CPT $p(g)$ can be similarly constructed.

The important point to remember is that LAZY-ARVE uses AR to maintain CPT structure during the elimination of variables, yet applies VE to physically compute only those CPTs propagated in the JT.

4   Related Works

This section compares the computation work required by LAZY-ARVE with LAZY-AR, the state-of-the-art algorithm recently proposed by Madsen [8] for exact inference in discrete BNs. Our comparison is conducted in the real-world CHD BN of Fig. 1. Since the work for identification of the passed CPTs is the same for both algorithms, we only contrast the physical computation.

LAZY-AR implements arc-reversal (AR) as the engine for performing inference in LAZY propagation with impressive experimental results [8]. Roughly speaking, LAZY-AR maintains a sub-BN at a JT node after eliminating a variable by applying AR and constructing the corresponding CPTs of the sub-BN. The following outline draws from [4, 8]. Let variable v_i be eliminated and arc (v_i, v_j) needs to be reversed. Assume v_i has parents $P_i = X_m \cup X_n$ and variable v_j has parents $P_j = \{v_i\} \cup X_n \cup X_k$, where $X_m \cap X_n = X_m \cap X_k = X_n \cap X_k = \emptyset$ such that $X_m = P_i - P_j$ are the parents of v_i but not v_j, $X_n = P_i \cap P_j$ are parents of both v_i and v_j, and $X_k = P_j - F_i$ are the parents of v_j but not v_i and its parents. Arc (v_i, v_j) is reversed by setting $P_i = X_m \cup X_n \cup X_k \cup \{v_j\}$ and $P_j = X_m \cup X_n \cup X_k$. Next, new CPTs for v_i and v_j in the modified DAG are physically constructed as follows:

$$p(v_j \mid X_m, X_n, X_k) = \sum_{v_i} p(v_i \mid X_m, X_n) \cdot p(v_j \mid v_i, X_n, X_k), \qquad (1)$$

$$p(v_i \mid v_j, X_m, X_n, X_k) \;=\; \frac{p(v_i \mid X_m, X_n) \cdot p(v_j \mid v_i, X_n, X_k)}{p(v_j \mid X_m, X_n, X_k)} \,. \qquad (2)$$

Note that it is not necessary to perform the last invocation of Equation (2) when the last arc from v_i is reversed, since v_i will be eliminated as a barren variable.

The next example shows how LAZY-AR physically constructs a sequence of intermediate CPTs by applying Equations (1) and (2).

Example 4. Recall Example 2. Let us show the physical computation performed by LAZY-AR to construct the propagated CPTs $p(g)$ and $p(h|g)$ from the JT node $cdefgh$ to the JT node $ghij$. In Step 1 of Fig. 4 (i), the two new CPTs are $p(d|c, e, f)$ and $p(f|c, e)$. While the former need not be computed as d is barren, the latter is constructed by Equation (1) as:

$$p(f|c, e) \;=\; \sum_d p(f|d, e) \cdot p(d|c) \,.$$

In Step 4 of Fig. 4 (ii), computing three new CPTs $p(e)$, $p(f|e)$ and $p(h|e, f)$ after elimination of c requires the construction of five intermediate CPTs:

$$p(e) \;=\; \sum_c p(c) \cdot p(e|c),$$
$$p(c|e) \;=\; p(c) \cdot p(e|c)/p(e),$$
$$p(f|e) \;=\; \sum_c p(c|e) \cdot p(f|c, e),$$
$$p(c|e, f) \;=\; p(c|e) \cdot p(f|c, e)/p(f|e),$$
$$p(h|e, f) \;=\; \sum_c p(c|e, f) \cdot p(h|c).$$

To eliminate e and f, LAZY-AR needs to construct six intermediate CPTs:

$$p(f) \;=\; \sum_e p(e) \cdot p(f|e), \qquad (3)$$
$$p(e|f) \;=\; p(e) \cdot p(f|e)/p(f), \qquad (4)$$
$$p(h|f) \;=\; \sum_e p(e|f) \cdot p(h|e, f), \qquad (5)$$
$$p(g) \;=\; \sum_f p(f) \cdot p(g|f), \qquad (6)$$
$$p(f|g) \;=\; p(f) \cdot p(g|f)/p(g), \qquad (7)$$
$$p(h|g) \;=\; \sum_f p(f|g) \cdot p(h|f) \,. \qquad (8)$$

The next example illustrates that LAZY-AR physically constructs intermediate CPTs that will neither be passed during inference, nor required in the construction of those CPTs actually passed in the JT.

Example 5. In Example 4, after variables d and c are removed, variable e can be simply eliminated as follows:

$$\sum_e p(e) \cdot p(f|e) \cdot p(h|e,f). \tag{9}$$

On the contrary, by reversing (e,f) as (f,e), LAZY-AR eliminates e as:

$$\sum_e p(f) \cdot p(e|f) \cdot p(h|e,f), \tag{10}$$

which requires the physical construction of $p(f)$ and $p(e|f)$ in Equations (3) and (4), respectively. By substituting Equation (3) into Equation (10), we obtain

$$\sum_e [\ \sum_e p(e) \cdot p(f|e)\ ] \cdot p(e|f) \cdot p(h|e,f). \tag{11}$$

By substituting Equation (4) into Equation (11), we have

$$\sum_e [\ \sum_e p(e) \cdot p(f|e)\ ] \cdot \frac{p(e) \cdot p(f|e)}{p(f)} \cdot p(h|e,f). \tag{12}$$

By Equation (3), we can rewrite Equation (12) as

$$\sum_e p(e) \cdot p(f|e) \cdot p(h|e,f) \cdot \frac{\sum_e p(e) \cdot p(f|e)}{\sum_e p(e) \cdot p(f|e)}. \tag{13}$$

During its physical computation, Equation (13) indicates that LAZY-AR multiplies and divides the same term

$$\sum_e p(e) \cdot p(f|e).$$

By comparing Equations (9) and (13), it is explicitly demonstrated that LAZY-AR performs unnecessary computation by physically constructing intermediate CPTs that will neither be passed during inference, nor required in the construction of the actual propagated CPTs. Although intermediate CPTs are useful for message identification, they are not necessarily needed for message construction. Any redundant work will delay the construction of the actual CPTs required for BN inference.

Similar to the comparisons made by Schmidt and Shenoy [11], we conclude this section by providing the following comparison between LAZY-AR and LAZY-ARVE. Approximately eighteen percent of the CHD BN variables are instantiated as evidence variables, such as was done for the largest BN used in the experimental results of [7].

Example 6. Given $b = 0$ and $g = 0$ as collected evidence in the CHD JT in Fig. 2. The screen shot of our implemented system in Fig. 5 shows all identified CPT messages. Table 1 shows the work needed by our LAZY-ARVE approach and LAZY-AR to physically construct the CPT messages $p(b = 0)$, $p(f)$, $p(g = 0|b = 0)$, $p(g = 0|b = 0, f)$, and $p(h|b = 0, g = 0)$ in Fig. 5.

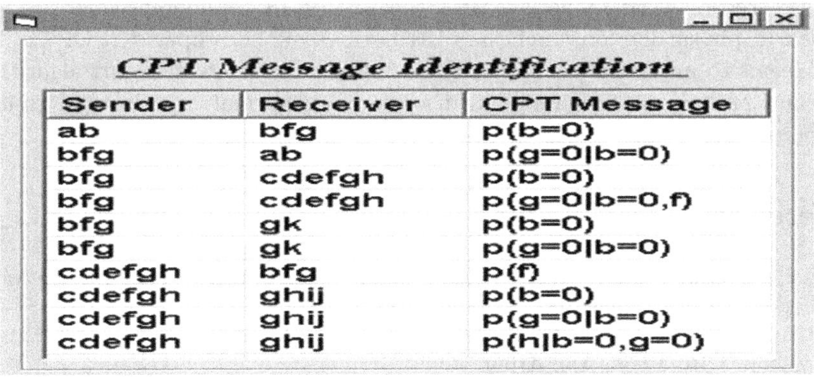

CPT Message Identification		
Sender	**Receiver**	**CPT Message**
ab	bfg	p(b=0)
bfg	ab	p(g=0|b=0)
bfg	cdefgh	p(b=0)
bfg	cdefgh	p(g=0|b=0,f)
bfg	gk	p(b=0)
bfg	gk	p(g=0|b=0)
cdefgh	bfg	p(f)
cdefgh	ghij	p(b=0)
cdefgh	ghij	p(g=0|b=0)
cdefgh	ghij	p(h|b=0,g=0)

Fig. 5. In the CHD JT in Fig. 2, given evidence $b = 0$ and $g = 0$, our implemented system identifies the CPT messages to be propagated

Table 1. Given evidence $b = 0$ and $g = 0$, the computation needed in LAZY-AR versus LAZY-ARVE to physically construct the CPTs passed in the CHD JT

CPT	LAZY-AR			LAZY-ARVE		
message	$+$	$\times$	$\div$	$+$	$\times$	$\div$
$p(b = 0)$	1	2	0	1	2	0
$p(f)$	14	36	8	11	20	2
$p(g = 0\|b = 0)$	13	34	8	11	24	1
$p(g = 0\|b = 0, f)$	0	0	0	0	0	0
$p(h\|b = 0, g = 0)$	29	80	22	19	44	2

The results in Table 1 suggest that our LAZY-ARVE has promise. In fact, the LAZY-ARVE can be fine-tuned by re-using some calculations. For instance, some work required to build $p(h|g)$ in Example 3 can be utilized when computing $p(g)$. Formal experimental results consisting of running times for exact inference in large, discrete, real-world BNs will be presented in a forthcoming paper.

5   Conclusions

In this paper, we propose LAZY-ARVE as a new approach to probabilistic inference in BNs. LAZY-ARVE is an improvement upon LAZY-AR, which was very recently proposed and empirically shown to be the state-of-the-art method for exact inference in discrete BNs [8]. However, intermediate CPTs computed by LAZY-AR may be irrelevant to BN inference. The reason for this unnecessary computation is that LAZY-AR iterates between semantic modeling and physical computation. Although intermediate CPT labels are useful for semantic modeling, the corresponding distributions do not necessarily have to be physically computed. We suggest separating these two independent tasks. Semantic computation is carried out first by implementing AR only to graphically identify the

CPTs passed between JT nodes. Next, the VE [17, 18, 19] inference algorithm is applied to physically construct the distributions of the propagated CPTs. Table 1 seems to imply that LAZY-ARVE could be the state-of-the-art algorithm for exact probabilistic inference in discrete BNs. Formal experimental results will be presented shortly.

References

1. E. Castillo, J. Gutiérrez and A. Hadi, Expert Systems and Probabilistic Network Models, Springer, New York, 1997.
2. P. Hájek, T. Havránek and R. Jiroušek, Uncertain Information Processing in Expert Systems, CRC Press, Ann Arbor, 1992.
3. F.V. Jensen, S.L. Lauritzen and K.G. Olesen, Bayesian updating in causal probabilistic networks by local computations, Comp. St. Q., 4, pp. 269-282, 1990.
4. U. Kjaeulff and A.L. Madsen, Probabilistic Networks - An Introduction to Bayesian Networks and Influence Diagrams, 133 pages, Unpublished, 2005.
5. S.L. Lauritzen and D.J. Spiegelhalter, Local computations with probabilities on graphical structures and their application to expert systems, J. Roy. Statistical Society, B, 50(2), pp. 157-224, 1988.
6. Z. Li and B. D'Ambrosio, Efficient inference in Bayes networks as a combinatorial optimization problem, Internat. J. Approx. Reason., 11(1), pp. 55-81, 1994.
7. A.L. Madsen and F.V. Jensen, LAZY propagation: A junction tree inference algorithm based on lazy evaluation, Artif. Intell., 113 (1-2), pp. 203-245, 1999.
8. A.L. Madsen, An empirical evaluation of possible variations of lazy propagation, in: Proc. 20th Conference on Uncertainty in Artificial Intelligence, 2004, pp. 366-373.
9. S. Olmsted, On representing and solving decision problems, Ph.D. thesis, Department of Engineering Economic Systems, Stanford University, Stanford, CA., 1983.
10. J. Pearl, Probabilistic Reasoning in Intelligent Systems: Networks of Plausible Inference, Morgan Kaufmann, 1988.
11. T. Schmidt and P.P. Shenoy, Some improvements to the Shenoy-Shafer and Hugin architectures for computing marginals, Artif. Intell., 102, pp. 323-333, 1998.
12. R. Shachter, B. D'Ambrosio and B. Del Favero, Symbolic probabilistic inference in belief networks, in Proc. 8th National Conference on Artificial Intelligence, 1990, pp. 126-131.
13. R. Shachter, Evaluating inflence diagrams, Oper. Res., 34(6), pp. 871-882, 1986.
14. G. Shafer, Probabilistic Expert Systems, Society for Industrial and Applied Mathematics, 1996.
15. S.K.M. Wong, C.J. Butz and D. Wu, On the implication problem for probabilistic conditional independency, IEEE Trans. Syst. Man Cybern., A, 30(6), pp. 785-805, 2000.
16. M. Yannakakis, Computing the minimal fill-in is NP-complete, SIAM J. of Algebraic Discrete Methods, 2, pp. 77-79, 1981.
17. N.L. Zhang, Computational properties of two exact algorithms for Bayesian networks, Appl. Intell., 9 (2), pp. 173–184, 1998.
18. N.L. Zhang and D. Poole, A simple approach to Bayesian network computations, In: Proc. 10th Canadian Conference on Artificial Intelligence, 1994, pp. 171-178.
19. N.L. Zhang and D. Poole, Exploiting causal independence in Bayesian network inference, J. Artif. Intell. Res., 5, pp. 301-328, 1996.

Four-Valued Semantics for Default Logic*

Anbu Yue, Yue Ma, and Zuoquan Lin

Department of Information Science, Peking University, Beijing 100871, China
{yueanbu, mayue, lz}@is.pku.edu.cn

Abstract. Reiter's default logic suffers the triviality, that is, a single contradiction in the premise of a default theory leads to the only trivial extension which everything follows from. In this paper, we propose a default logic based on four-valued semantics, which endows default logic with the ability of handling inconsistency without leading to triviality. We define four-valued models for default theory such that the default logic has the ability of nonmonotonic paraconsistent reasoning. By transforming default rules in propositional language $\mathcal{L}$ into language $\overline{\mathcal{L}}^+$, a one-to-one relation between the four-valued models in $\mathcal{L}$ and the extensions in $\overline{\mathcal{L}}^+$ is proved, whereby the proof theory of Reiter's default logic is remained.

1 Introduction

Reiter's default logic [1] is an important nonmonotonic logic. It has been studied widely for its clarity in syntax as well as strong power in reasoning. In the default logic, a set of formulae W and a set of default rules D form a default theory (W, D). Reiter's default logic is supposed to reason with consistent knowledge: even a single contradiction presented in W will lead to the unique trivial extension which includes everything.

One way to make default logic handle inconsistent knowledge is to resolve the contradictions in the premise of a default theory. The signed system [2] decomposes the connection between positive atoms and negative ones by formulae transformation and then restores a consistent set of formulae by default logic. The set of formulae transformed from the original one is consistent and it is used as W in a default theory. It follows that all extensions are nontrivial. Roughly speaking, the signed system does not aim at handling inconsistencies in a nonmonotonic logic, since the default rules are not used in knowledge representation. In the bi-default logic [3], all parts of default rules are transformed in the same way, and then default theories are transformed into the bi-default theories. Because of the differences between its proof theory and that of default logic, it will take much effort to implement the bi-default logic.

The systems listed above have a similar character, that is they provide procedures of two steps: transforming and then computing. However, they lack semantics. Also it is hard to point out the direct connections between the inconsistent default theory and its conclusions.

Some nonmonotonic paraconsistent logics (see [4, 5] among others) have been proposed by directly introducing nonmonotonicity into paraconsistent logics, especially

---

* This work was partially supported by NSFC (grant numbers 60373002 and 60496322) and by NKBRPC (2004CB318000).

L. Lamontagne and M. Marchand (Eds.): Canadian AI 2006, LNAI 4013, pp. 195–205, 2006.
© Springer-Verlag Berlin Heidelberg 2006

Belnap's four-valued logic [6, 7]. However, at the level of computing, there are challenges in implementing effective theorem provers for them.

Our main contribution in this paper is to provide the four-valued semantics for default logic whereby we gain a nonmonotonic paraconsistent logic, named four-valued default logic, in which we can reason under a nice semantics but by a classical proof theory. So the semantics works as an interface of nonmonotonic paraconsistent reasoning, and the procedure of transforming and computing just serves as a tool to compute the models of default theories. This novel reasoning method makes the four-valued default logic applicable in commonsense reasoning. Inheriting the proof theory of Reiter's default logic and equipped with semantics of Belnap's four-valued logic, our four-valued default logic is a paraconsistent version of the former and a nonmonotonic extension of the latter.

We develop our work in the following steps. First of all, four-valued models are defined as semantics of default logic. As we know, an extension of a default theory is a minimal set satisfying both W and D in the context expressed by the extension itself. We adopt the similar approach. A four-valued model of a default theory is minimal in the sense of "information" and satisfies both W and D in the context expressed by the model itself. Similarly, our method can be extended to any other minimalities.

Secondly, we propose a uniform procedure to compute four-valued models in the context of Reiter's default logic. A transformation of default rules is provided with which default theories in $\mathcal{L}$ are transformed into those in $\overline{\mathcal{L}}^+$, and then the computation of models is converted to that of extensions. The reason we can do this is that we have gotten the one-to-one relation between the four-valued models in $\mathcal{L}$ and the extensions in $\overline{\mathcal{L}}^+$. Consequently, the four-valued semantics for default logic can be easily implemented by classical reasoning systems for the original default logic [8].

The logic DL3 presented in [9] also combines default logic with a multi-valued logic, Lukasiewicz three-valued logic. But DL3 also suffers the triviality. On the other hand, the proof theory of Reiter's default logic is modified in DL3 unlike that of the four-valued default logic. Comparison details appear in Section 6.

By briefly reviewing Reiter's default logic and Belnap's four valued logic in Section 2 and 3 respectively, we focus on the k-minimal model in Section 4, its computation and the transformation of default theories in Section 5. Finally, we compare our work with some others in Section 6 and conclude this paper in Section 7.

2   Default Logic

Let $\mathcal{L}$ be a propositional language. A theory is a set of formulae, and $Th(\cdot)$ denotes the consequence operator on propositional logic.

A *default theory* is a pair (W, D), where W is a theory of $\mathcal{L}$ and D is a set of *default rules* of the form: $\frac{\alpha:\beta}{\gamma}$. The formulae α, β, γ of $\mathcal{L}$ are called *prerequisite, justification* and *conclusion* respectively. For the sake of simplicity, we assume that there is one and only one justification in a default rule, and this restriction is not essential (see [10]). We denote the prerequisite, justification and conclusion of a default rule δ as $Preq(\delta)$, $Jus(\delta)$ and $Cons(\delta)$ respectively. A default theory may have none, a single or multiple *extensions* defined by a fixed point of the following definition.

Definition 1 ([1]). *Let* $T = (W, D)$ *be a default theory. For any set* S *of formulae, let* $\Gamma(S)$ *be the smallest set that satisfies:*

(D1) $\Gamma(S) = Th(\Gamma(S))$;
(D2) $W \subseteq \Gamma(S)$;
(D3) *if* $\frac{\alpha:\beta}{\gamma} \in D, \alpha \in \Gamma(S)$ *and* $\neg\beta \notin S$, *then* $\gamma \in \Gamma(S)$.

A set E *is an extension of* T *iff* $\Gamma(E) = E$.

An extension represents a possible belief set expressed by the default theory.

The next theorem provides a more intuitive characterization of extensions of a default theory.

Theorem 1 ([1]). *If* $T = (W, D)$ *is a default theory, then a set* E *of formulae is an extension of* T *iff* $E = \bigcup_{i=0}^{\infty} E_i$, *where*

$$E_0 = W, \text{ and for } i \geq 0$$

$$E_{i+1} = Th(E_i) \cup \{\gamma \mid \frac{\alpha : \beta}{\gamma} \in D, \text{ where } E_i \vdash \alpha \text{ and } \neg\beta \notin E\}$$

Proposition 1 (Minimality of Extensions [1]). *If* E *and* F *are extensions of a default theory* (W, D) *and* $E \subseteq F$ *then* $E = F$.

Reiter's default logic can not deal with inconsistencies:

Proposition 2 ([1]). *A default theory* $T = (W, D)$ *has an inconsistent extension iff* W *is inconsistent, and it is the only extension of* T.

3 Four-Valued Logic

As four truth-values in Belnap's logic [6,7,5], $FOUR = \{t, f, \top, \bot\}$ (also written as $(1, 0), (0, 1), (1, 1)$ and $(0, 0)$ respectively) intuitively represent truth, falsity, inconsistency and lack of information respectively. The four truth-values form a *bilattice* $(FOUR, \leq_t, \leq_k)$ named $\mathcal{FOUR}$, where the partial orders are defined as the following rules: for every $x_1, x_2, y_1, y_2 \in \{0, 1\}$,

$$(x_1, y_1) \leq_t (x_2, y_2) \text{ iff } x_1 \leq x_2 \text{ and } y_1 \geq y_2;$$
$$(x_1, y_1) \leq_k (x_2, y_2) \text{ iff } x_1 \leq x_2 \text{ and } y_1 \leq y_2.$$

Intuitively, the partial order $\leq_t$ reflects differences in the amount of *truth*, while $\leq_k$ reflects differences in the amount of *information*. The first element x of the truth-value pair (x, y) stands for a formula and the second against it.

It follows the operators of $\mathcal{FOUR}$: $\neg(x, y) = (y, x)$, $(x_1, y_1) \wedge (x_2, y_2) = (x_1 \wedge x_2, y_1 \vee y_2)$, $(x_1, y_1) \vee (x_2, y_2) = (x_1 \vee x_2, y_1 \wedge y_2)$, $(x_1, y_1) \supset (x_2, y_2) = (\neg x_1 \vee x_2, x_1 \wedge y_2)$, and $(x_1, y_1) \rightarrow (x_2, y_2) =_{df} \neg(x_1, y_1) \vee (x_2, y_2)$.

In four-valued logic, *internal implication* is interpreted as operator $\supset$ and *material implication* is interpreted as operator $\rightarrow$ in $\mathcal{FOUR}$. We use the same symbols to denote connectives in $\mathcal{L}$ and operators on $\mathcal{FOUR}$.

A *four-valued valuation* v is a function that assigns a truth value from $FOUR$ to each atom in $\mathcal{L}$. Any valuation is extended to complex formulae in the obvious way. A valuation v is a *four-valued model* of (or *satisfies*) a formula ψ if $v(\psi) \in \{t, \top\}$.

Definition 2 ([5]). *Let Σ be a set of formulae and ψ a formula in $\mathcal{L}$. Denote $\Sigma \models^4 \psi$, if every four-valued model of Σ is a four-valued model of ψ.*

Let v and u be four-valued valuations, denote $v \leq_k u$ if $v(p) \leq_k u(p)$ for every atom p. Given a formulae set Σ in $\mathcal{L}$, the minimal elements w.r.t. $\leq_k$ in all models of Σ are called the *k-minimal models* of Σ.

Definition 3 ([5]). *Let Σ be a set of formulae and ψ a formula in $\mathcal{L}$, Denote $\Sigma \models_k^4 \psi$ if every k-minimal model of Σ is a model of ψ.*

4   Four-Valued Default Logic

Let $\mathcal{L}$ be a propositional language that does not contain constants t, f, $\top$ and $\bot$. All logic connectives in $\mathcal{L}$ are $\neg$, $\vee$, $\wedge$, $\rightarrow$ and $\supset$, where $\rightarrow$ is defined by $\neg$ and $\vee$ in the usual way. Suppose Δ is a set of models, we denote $\Delta(\phi) \in truthSet$ if $\forall M \in \Delta, M(\phi) \in truthSet$, where $truthSet$ is a subset of $FOUR$ and ϕ is a formula in $\mathcal{L}$.

In Reiter's default logic, a single (classical) model cannot represent beliefs. One of the reasons is that a single model cannot differentiate "being false" and "not being true". By deductive closed theory, which is equal to a set of (classical) models, we can say that ϕ is false if $\neg\phi$ is in that theory, and that ϕ is not known (i.e. "not being true" and "not being false") if both ϕ and $\neg\phi$ are not in the theory. In the case of four-valued logics, we can distinguish them by non-classical truth values. So, we can use one single four-valued model to represent beliefs expressed by default theories.

A default theory may have none, a single or multiple k-minimal models defined by:

Definition 4. *Let $T = (W, D)$ be a default theory in $\mathcal{L}$. For any four-valued valuation N on $\mathcal{L}$, let $\Gamma_k(N)$ be the biggest set of four-valued valuations on $\mathcal{L}$ satisfying that:*

(Ax) *If $N' \in \Gamma_k(N)$ then N' is a four-valued model of W.*
(K-min) *If $N' \in \Gamma_k(N)$ then $N' \leq_k N$.*
(Def) *If $\frac{\alpha:\beta}{\gamma} \in D$, $\Gamma_k(N)(\alpha) \in \{t, \top\}$ and $N(\beta) \in \{t, \bot\}$, then $\Gamma_k(N)(\gamma) \in \{t, \top\}$.*

A valuation M is a k-minimal model of T iff $\Gamma_k(M) = \{M\}$.

Example 1. Let $W = \{p\}$, $D = \{p : q/r\}$, $T = (W, D)$. In Reiter's default logic, T has its unique extension: $E = Th(p, r)$. And T has a unique k-minimal model M such that $M(p) = t, M(q) = \bot, M(r) = t$.

In Definition 4, a singleton is required in the condition $\Gamma_k(M) = \{M\}$, because any other model in the set $\Gamma_k(M)$ includes less information than the context M does and it should be eliminated when reconstructing the context. The condition K-min indicates that all information achieved should be restricted by the context.

Definition 5. *We say a model M' satisfies a default theory T in the context of M, if*

- *M' is a four-valued model of W, and*
- *If $\frac{\alpha:\beta}{\gamma} \in D$, $M'(\alpha) \in \{t, \top\}$ and $M(\beta) \in \{t, \bot\}$, then $M'(\gamma) \in \{t, \top\}$.*

It is easy to show that M satisfies T in the context of M itself, if M is a k-minimal model of $T = (W, D)$, and what's more, M is the $\leq_k$-minimal one:

Theorem 2. *If M is a k-minimal model of a default theory $T = (W, D)$, then M is a $\leq_k$-minimal model that satisfies T in the context of M.*

Example 2. Let $W = \{p, \neg p\}$, $D = \{\frac{p:r}{q}\}$, $T = (W, D)$. W has four models that assign r the value $\perp$: $M_1(q) = t$, $M_2(q) = f$, $M_3(q) = \top$, $M_4(q) = \perp$ and they all assign p the value $\top$. If N is a model of W and $N(r) \neq \perp$, there exists a model $M_i \in \Gamma_k(N), 1 \leq i \leq 4$. Since $\Gamma_k(M_1) = \{M_1\}$, $\Gamma_k(M_2) = \Gamma_k(M_4) = \emptyset$, and $\Gamma_k(M_3) = \{M_1, M_2, M_3, M_4\}$, M_1 is the only k-minimal model of T.

In this example, from an inconsistent prerequisite p, we inferred that q is "consistent" true. But in practice, we may expect that the conclusion is also inconsistent or we do not want any conclusions at all, given that the prerequisite is inconsistent. The next example shows how these things can be represented in the four-valued default logic.

Example 3. Let $W = \{p, \neg p\}$, $D_1 = \{\frac{p:p \wedge r}{q}\}$. $T_1 = (W, D_1)$ has only one k-minimal model M_1 s.t. $M_1(p) = \top, M_1(q) = \perp, M_1(r) = \perp$. Let $D_2 = \{\frac{p:r}{q}, \frac{p \wedge \neg p:r}{q \wedge \neg q}\}$. $T_2 = (W, D_2)$ has only one k-minimal model M_2 s.t. $M_2(p) = \top, M_2(q) = \top, M_2(r) = \perp$.

Notice that, when we replace W by the set $\{p\}$, each default theory in the above examples has only one k-minimal model M s.t. $M(p) = t, M(q) = t, M(r) = \perp$.

Some contradictions introduced by default rules can also be handled "properly":

Example 4. Let $T = (\emptyset, \{\frac{:p}{q}, \frac{:p}{\neg q}\})$. T lacks extensions, while T has one k-minimal model: $M(p) = \perp, M(q) = \top$.

Example 5. Let $T = \{\{p\}, \{\frac{:q}{\neg p}\}$. T lacks extensions, while T has a unique k-minimal model M such that $M(p) = \top, M(q) = \perp$.

Example 6 (Tweety dilemma). A representation in four-valued logic is given as follows (see [5]):

$$W_0 = \begin{cases} bird\_Tweety \rightarrow fly\_Tweety \\ penguin\_Tweety \supset bird\_Tweety \\ penguin\_Tweety \supset \neg fly\_Tweety \end{cases}$$

$W = W_0 \cup \{bird\_Tweety\}$, $W' = W_0 \cup \{penguin\_Tweety\}$.

The k-minimal four-valued models of W and W' are shown in Table 1.

Table 1. k-minimal models of W and W'

		$bird\_Tweety$	fly_Tweety	$penguin\_Tweety$
W	M_1	t	t	$\perp$
	M_2	$\top$	$\perp$	$\perp$
W'	M_3	$\top$	f	t
	M_4	t	$\top$	t

When all we know about Tweety is that it is a bird, we can not draw the reasonable conclusion that Tweety can fly by four-valued logic (in its k-minimal reasoning). When knowing more about Tweety that Tweety is a penguin, we are confused with whether Tweety is a bird (for we have the negative knowledge that Tweety is not a bird).

In the four-valued default logic, we can get an alternative representation:

$$T_0 = \begin{cases} p \wedge \neg p \\ penguin\_Tweety \supset bird\_Tweety \\ penguin\_Tweety \supset \neg fly\_Tweety \\ bird\_Tweety : fly\_Tweety/fly\_Tweety \end{cases}$$

where $(p \wedge \neg p)$ stands for any contradiction. Denote $T_0 = (W_1, D)$, $W_2 = W_1 \cup \{bird\_Tweety\}$, $T = (W_2, D)$ and $W' = W_2 \cup \{penguin\_Tweety\}$, $T' = (W', D)$.
The k-minimal models of T and T' are shown in Table 2.

Table 2. k-minimal models of T and T'

		bird_Tweety	fly_Tweety	penguin_Tweety	p
T	M_1'	t	t	$\perp$	$\top$
T'	M_2'	t	f	t	$\top$

Just as expected, when what we know about Tweety is only that it is a bird, we think it can fly. After knowing that Tweety is a special bird: a penguin, we revise our beliefs and claim that it can't fly without being confused.

In Example 6, because of the presence of contradictions in p, Reiter's default logic will collapse, but in the four-valued default logic, the inconsistencies are successfully localized and do not do any harm to reason about Tweety.

Definition 6. *Let $T = (W, D)$ be a default theory and ϕ be a formula in $\mathcal{L}$. Denote $T \models^k \phi$, if for any k-minimal model M of T, $M(\phi) \in \{t, \top\}$ holds.*

Theorem 3. $W \models_k^4 \phi$ *iff* $(W, \emptyset) \models^k \phi$.

Theorem 3 shows that the four-valued default logic in its k-minimal reasoning pattern can be viewed as an extension of four-valued logic in k-minimal reasoning. And as a consequence, only the skeptical consequence relation (defined in Definition 6) is suitable for the four-valued default logic.

The next theorem provides a more intuitive characterization of k-minimal models of a default theory.

Theorem 4. *If $T = (W, D)$ is a default theory in $\mathcal{L}$, then a four-valued valuation M is a k-minimal four-valued model of T iff $\bigcap_{i=0}^{\infty} \overline{M}_i = \{M\}$, where*

$$\overline{M}_0 = \{N \leq_k M \mid N \text{ is a four-valued model of } W\}$$

$$\overline{M}_{i+1} = \{N \in \overline{M}_i \mid N(\gamma) \in \{t, \top\}, \frac{\alpha : \beta}{\gamma} \in D,$$

$$where \ \overline{M}_i(\alpha) \in \{t, \top\} \ and \ M(\beta) \in \{t, \perp\}\}$$

The four-valued default logic has some nice properties shown in the following.

Theorem 5. *Let M be a four-valued valuation in $\mathcal{L}$ and define $F = \{\alpha \supset \gamma \mid \frac{\alpha:\beta}{\gamma} \in D, M(\beta) \in \{t, \bot\}\}$. M is a $\leq_k$-minimal valuation that satisfies T in the context of M iff M is a k-minimal model of $(W \cup F)$.*

Corollary 1. *If M is a k-minimal model of T then M is a k-minimal model of $(W \cup F)$, where $F = \{\alpha \supset \gamma \mid \frac{\alpha:\beta}{\gamma} \in D, M(\beta) \in \{t, \bot\}\}$.*

Definition 7. *Suppose $T = (W, D)$ is a default theory and M is a k-minimal model of T. The set of generating defaults for M w.r.t. T is defined to be $GD(M, T) = \{\frac{\alpha:\beta}{\gamma} \in D \mid M(\alpha) \in \{t, \top\}, M(\beta) \in \{t, \bot\}\}$.*

Theorem 6. *Suppose $T = (W, D)$ is a default theory. If M is a k-minimal model of T then M is a k-minimal model of $(W \cup Cons(GD(M, T)))$.*

Theorem 7 (Minimality of k-minimal models). *Let $= (W, D)$ be a default theory, where $Jus(D)$ does not include the internal implication $\supset$. Suppose that M and N are k-minimal models of T. If $M \leq_k N$ then M and N are identical.*

Theorem 7 indicates that sometimes we need restrict the occurrences of internal implication in $Jus(D)$ to achieve nice properties, but we also need internal implication in W, $Preq(D)$, and $Cons(D)$ to strengthen the expressive power.

5 Computing k-Minimal Models of Default Theories

Let $\overline{\mathcal{L}}^+$ be the objective language of formulae transformation satisfying that $\mathcal{L} \cap \overline{\mathcal{L}}^+ = \emptyset$ and $\mathcal{A}(\overline{\mathcal{L}}^+) = \{p^+, p^- \mid p \in \mathcal{A}(\mathcal{L})\}$, where operator $\mathcal{A}(\mathcal{L})$ denotes all atoms in $\mathcal{L}$. And $\overline{\mathcal{L}}^+$ only includes logic connectives: $\neg, \vee, \wedge$ and $\rightarrow$. Notice that the internal implication and the material implication coincide in the classical logic.

5.1 Transformation of Formulae

In [11, 12, 2, 3], the technique of transformation has been proved very useful. In this subsection, we show this method in a convenient way.

Definition 8. *For every formula ϕ in $\mathcal{L}$, $\overline{\phi}^+$ in $\overline{\mathcal{L}}^+$ is a transformation of ϕ if:*

1. $\overline{\phi}^+ = p^+$, *where* $\phi = p, p \in \mathcal{A}(\mathcal{L})$
2. $\overline{\phi}^+ = p^-$, *where* $\phi = \neg p, p \in \mathcal{A}(\mathcal{L})$
3. $\overline{\phi}^+ = \overline{\varphi}^+ \vee \overline{\psi}^+$, *where* $\phi = \varphi \vee \psi$
4. $\overline{\phi}^+ = \overline{\varphi}^+ \wedge \overline{\psi}^+$, *where* $\phi = \varphi \wedge \psi$
5. $\overline{\phi}^+ = \neg\overline{\varphi}^+ \vee \overline{\psi}^+$, *where* $\phi = \varphi \supset \psi$
6. $\overline{\phi}^+ = \overline{\psi}^+$, *where* $\phi = \neg\neg\psi$
7. $\overline{\phi}^+ = \overline{\neg\varphi}^+ \wedge \overline{\neg\psi}^+$, *where* $\phi = \neg(\varphi \vee \psi)$

8. $\overline{\phi}^+ = \overline{\neg\varphi}^+ \vee \overline{\neg\psi}^+$, where $\phi = \neg(\varphi \wedge \psi)$
9. $\overline{\phi}^+ = \overline{\varphi}^+ \wedge \overline{\neg\psi}^+$, where $\phi = \neg(\varphi \supset \psi)$

In the rest of the paper, we denote $\overline{\Sigma}^+ = \{\overline{\phi}^+ \mid \phi \in \Sigma\}$.

Theorem 8. $\overline{W}^+$ is (classical) consistent for any theory W.

We call a theory E complete if it contains p or $\neg p$ for every atom $p \in \mathcal{A}(E)$.

Definition 9. Let E^+ be a theory in $\overline{\mathcal{L}}^+$, define a map v_{E+} on $\mathcal{L}$ w.r.t. E^+ as:

$$
v_{E+}(\phi) = \begin{cases}
\top = (1,1) & \overline{\phi}^+ \in E^+, \overline{\neg\phi}^+ \in E^+ \\
t = (1,0) & \overline{\phi}^+ \in E^+, \overline{\neg\neg\phi}^+ \in E^+ \\
f = (0,1) & \overline{\neg\phi}^+ \in E^+, \overline{\neg\phi}^+ \in E^+ \\
\bot = (0,0) & \overline{\neg\phi}^+ \in E^+, \overline{\neg\neg\phi}^+ \in E^+
\end{cases}
$$

Obviously, the map v_{E+} is a valuation when E^+ is consistent and complete.

Theorem 9. If E^+ is a consistent and complete theory in $\overline{\mathcal{L}}^+$, then the map v_{E+} is a four-valued valuation on $\mathcal{L}$, i.e.: $v_{E+}(\neg\phi) = \neg v_{E+}(\phi)$, $v_{E+}(\phi \vee \psi) = v_{E+}(\phi) \vee v_{E+}(\psi)$, $v_{E+}(\phi \wedge \psi) = v_{E+}(\phi) \wedge v_{E+}(\psi)$, and $v_{E+}(\phi \supset \psi) = v_{E+}(\phi) \supset v_{E+}(\psi)$.

Definition 10. Let v be a valuation on $\mathcal{L}$, define the complete and deductive closed theory E_v^+ w.r.t. v in $\overline{\mathcal{L}}^+$ by:

$$
E_v^+ = Th\left(\{p^+ \mid p \in \mathcal{L}, v(p) \in \{t, \top\}\} \cup \{p^- \mid p \in \mathcal{L}, v(p) \in \{f, \top\}\} \right.
$$
$$
\left. \cup \{\neg p^+ \mid p \in \mathcal{L}, v(p) \in \{f, \bot\}\} \cup \{\neg p^- \mid p \in \mathcal{L}, v(p) \in \{t, \bot\}\}\right)
$$

Proposition 3. The theory E_v^+ w.r.t. v is (classical) consistent.

Theorem 10. Let E_v^+ be the theory w.r.t. a given valuation v, then

1. $\overline{\phi}^+ \in E_v^+$ if $v(\phi) \in \{t, \top\}$; $\overline{\neg\phi}^+ \in E_v^+$ if $v(\phi) \in \{f, \top\}$.
2. $\neg\overline{\phi}^+ \in E_v^+$ if $v(\phi) \in \{f, \bot\}$; $\overline{\neg\neg\phi}^+ \in E_v^+$ if $v(\phi) \in \{t, \bot\}$.

Thus the correspondence between consistent and complete deductive closed theories and four-valued valuations is built up completely.

Corollary 2. Let v be a valuation on $\mathcal{L}$ and E^+ be a consistent complete and deductive closed theory, then v is w.r.t. E^+ iff E^+ is w.r.t. v.

5.2   Relation Between Models and Extensions

From Definition 9, we can see that under the transformation it is reasonable to declare ϕ is true (or false) when $\overline{\phi}^+$ (or $\overline{\neg\phi}^+$) is present, while the presence of $\neg\overline{\phi}^+$ (or $\overline{\neg\neg\phi}^+$) states the lack of information of "being true (or false)". In the sense of information keeping, transformation is naturally extended to commit default rules:

Definition 11. $T(D) = \{\overline{\alpha}^+ : \neg\neg\overline{\beta}^+/\overline{\gamma}^+ \mid \alpha : \beta/\gamma \in D\}$

In Definition 11, the prerequisite and the justification are transformed in such different ways that we can easily distinguish different beliefs they stand for.

In order to minimize the statements drawn by the default theory, we explicitly import $\neg p^+$ and $\neg p^-$ by default to declare that we lack the information about whether p is true and false respectively.

Definition 12. $D^k = \{\frac{:\neg p^+}{\neg p^+}, \frac{:\neg p^-}{\neg p^-} \mid p \in \mathcal{A}(\mathcal{L})\}.$

Definition 13. *The k-minimal transformation of default theory T is defined by*

$$T^k(T) = (\overline{W}^+, T(D) \cup D^k).$$

Theorem 11. *All extensions of $T^k(T)$ are consistent and complete.*

The following example shows how our technique of transformation works:

Example 7. Suppose that $T = (\emptyset, \{\frac{:p}{q}, \frac{:p}{\neg q}\})$. T has no extensions. By transformation, we get that $T^k(T) = (\emptyset, \{\frac{:\neg p^-}{q^+}, \frac{:\neg p^-}{q^-}, \frac{:\neg p^+}{\neg p^+}, \frac{:\neg p^-}{\neg p^-}, \frac{:\neg q^+}{\neg q^+}, \frac{:\neg q^-}{\neg q^-}\})$, and $T^k(T)$ has a unique extension: $E^+ = Th(\{\neg p^+, \neg p^-, q^+, q^-\})$, which means that p is neither true nor false in E^+ and q is both true and false in E^+.

Theorem 12. *Let M be a four-valued model in $\mathcal{L}$, $\overline{M}_i$ is defined as in Theorem 4. Then E^+ w.r.t. M is an extension of $T^k(T)$ iff $E^+ = \bigcup_{i=0}^{\infty} E_i^+$, where $E_i^+ = \bigcap_{N \in \overline{M}_i} E_N^+$, and E_N^+ is the theory w.r.t. N.*

Theorem 13. *Let M be a k-minimal model of a default theory $T = (W, D)$. If E^+ is the theory w.r.t. M, then E^+ is an extension of $T^k(T)$.*

Theorem 14. *Let $T = (W, D)$ be a default theory in $\mathcal{L}$ and E^+ is an extension of $T^k(T)$. If M is the valuation w.r.t. E^+, then M is a k-minimal model of T.*

Corollary 3. *Let T be a default theory in $\mathcal{L}$ and $\phi \in \mathcal{L}$. Then $T \models^k \phi$ iff $\overline{\phi}^+$ is in every extension of $T^k(T)$.*

Thus we can get four-valued models of a default theory by computing extensions of its counterpart transformed from itself and vise versa as shown in Fig. 1.

Example 8. We can get the k-minimal model(s) of $T = (\emptyset, \{\frac{:p}{q}, \frac{:p}{\neg q}\})$ by:

1. Computing $T^k(T)$ (see Example 7).
2. Computing the extension of $T^k(T)$, that is: $E^+ = Th(\{\neg p^+, \neg p^-, q^+, q^-\})$.
3. By Definition 9, computing the model $M = v_{E^+}$, i.e. $M(p) = \bot, M(q) = \top$.

And M is the unique k-minimal model of T as shown in Example 4.

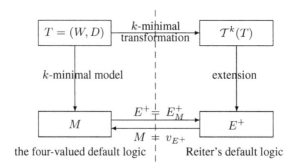

Fig. 1. The relationship between the four-valued default logic and Reiter's default logic

6 Related Work

The default logic in the signed system [2] is only used to restore contents from formulae in $\overline{\mathcal{L}}^+$, which are transformed from the original ones in $\mathcal{L}$. In this paper, we presented a paraconsistent variant of default logic.

In terms of proposing a variant and an extension of Reiter's default logic, one of the previous work is the bi-default logic [3]. The bi-default logic (or Reiter's default logic) is incomparable to the four-valued default logic in reasoning power. For example, the default theory in Example 4 has a k-minimal four-valued model but lacks bi-extensions (and extensions). But when there is no default rules present, the four-valued default logic may infer less conclusions than the bi-default logic (or default logic) does, which is based on classical logic. Secondly, although a map from the bi-extensions to $FOUR$ is given, we can not get four-valued models of a default theory. In fact, the map is even not a four-valued valuation, e.g. there is a map which gives both ϕ and ψ the same value $\top$ but assigns $\phi \wedge \psi$ the value f. But we explicitly defined four-valued models for default theory. Finally, in the four-valued default logic, the prerequisite and the justification of a default rule are transformed into different forms, unlike the case of the bi-default logic, in which the bi-extension is defined to justify whether a default rule is applicable. One advantage of our method is that the proof theory of Reiter's default logic is preserved.

In the method proposed in [11, 12], circumscription is used as a tool to calculate multi-valued preferential models in classical logic. But circumscription is weaker than default logic [13], so their method is also weaker than ours in expressive and reasoning power.

The three-valued default logic DL3 [9] is based on Lukasiewicz three-valued logic LUK3. By introducing modal like operators M and L, a formula can be declared to be "possibly" true or "certainly" true in DL3. Since LUK3 is not paraconsistent [14], DL3 also collapses whenever the premise is not consistent. Considering the adopted approaches, there are two main differences between DL3 and the four-valued default logic. First, we defined four-valued models for default theory instead of extensions done in DL3. Second, we can get all four-valued models of every default theory by computing extensions in standard default logic. But Radzikowska only discussed the proof theory limited to normal default theories in the original paper [9], by simulating that of Reiter's default logic.

7 Conclusion

In this paper, we proposed the k-minimal four-valued semantics for default theory. As an extension of Belnap's four-valued logic [6, 7, 5] and a paraconsistent version of Reiter's default logic [1], the four-valued default logic can handle inconsistencies and it still uses default theories in knowledge representation.

A novel technique was also provided to transform default theories into the ones without trivial extensions. The one-to-one correspondence between the extensions of default theory gained by transformation and the four-valued models of the original one was set up as shown in Fig.1. Thus, four-valued models of default theory can be computed by default logic theorem provers (e.g. [8]).

In this paper, we defined k-minimal models for default theory, and we confirmed that our method can be applied to other minimalities. The results of this paper are limited to propositional level, we will extend it to first-order case, as well as consider the applications of the four-valued default logic in commonsense reasoning in the future.

References

1. Reiter, R.: A logic for default reasoning. Artificial Intelligence **13** (1980) 81–132
2. Besnard, P., Schaub, T.: Signed systems for paraconsistent reasoning. Journal of Automated Reasoning **20** (1998) 191–213
3. Han, Q., Lin, Z.: Paraconsistent default reasoning. In: 10th International Workshop on Non-Monotonic Reasoning. (2004) 197–203
4. Lin, Z.: Paraconsistent circumscription. In: Canadian Conference on AI. (1996) 296–308
5. Arieli, O., Avron, A.: The value of the four values. Artificial Intelligence **102** (1998) 97–141
6. Belnap, N.D.A.: How computer should think. In Ryle., G., ed.: Contemporary Aspects of Philosophy. Oriel Press (1977) 7–37
7. Belnap, N.D.A.: A useful four-valued logic. In Dunn, J.M., G. Epstein, D.R., eds.: Modern uses of multiple-valued logic. Reidel (1977) 30–56
8. Cholewinski, P., Marek, V.W., Mikitiuk, A., Truszczynski, M.: Computing with default logic. Artificial Intelligence **112** (1999) 105–146
9. Radzikowska, A.: A three-valued approach to default logic. Journal of Applied Non-Classical Logics **6**(2) (1996) 149–190
10. Marek, V.W., Truszczynski, M.: Nonmonotonic logic – context-dependent reasoning. Springer, Berlin (1990)
11. Arieli, O., Denecker, M.: Modeling paraconsistent reasoning by classical logic. In: Foundations of Information and Knowledge Systems, Second International Symposium, Proceedings. (2002) 1–14
12. Arieli, O.: Paraconsistent preferential reasoning by signed quantified boolean formulae. In: 16th European Conf. on Artificial Intelligence (ECAI04). (2004) 773–777
13. Janhunen, T.: On the intertranslatability of non-monotonic logics. Annals of Mathematics and Artificial Intelligence **27** (1999) 79–128
14. da Costa, N.: Theory of inconsistent formal systems. Notre Dame Journal of Formal Logic **15** (1974) 497–510

Exploiting Dynamic Independence in a Static Conditioning Graph

Kevin Grant and Michael C. Horsch

Dept. of Computer Science, University of Saskatchewan,
Saskatoon, SK, S7N 5A9
{kjg658, horsch}@mail.usask.ca

Abstract. A conditioning graph (CG) is a graphical structure that attempt to minimize the implementation overhead of computing probabilities in belief networks. A conditioning graph recursively factorizes the network, but restricting each decomposition to a single node allows us to store the structure with minimal overhead, and compute with a simple algorithm. This paper extends conditioning graphs with optimizations that effectively reduce the height of the CG, thus reducing time complexity exponentially, while increasing the storage requirements by only a constant factor. We conclude that CGs are frequently as efficient as any other exact inference method, with the advantage of being vastly superior to VE and JT in terms of space complexity, and far simpler to implement.

1 Introduction

Recently, we proposed *conditioning graphs* (CGs) which are runtime representations of belief networks [6]. CGs have a number of important properties. First, they require only linear space, in terms of the size of the original network, whereas a join tree for example, requires space that is exponential in the width of the network. Second, a CG consists of simple node pointers and floating point values; no high-level elements of belief network computation are included. As well, inference algorithms for conditioning graphs are small recursive algorithms, easily implementable on any architecture, without requiring monolithic runtime libraries, or worse, the implementation of complex inference techniques such as variable elimination [15, 4] or junction tree propagation [9].

Conditioning graphs are a form of recursive factorization of belief networks. Recursive decomposition [10] and recursive conditioning [2] restrict the number of children at each internal node to two, and no restriction is made on the number of variables at each internal node. In contrast, conditioning graphs have exactly one variable at each internal node, and no restriction on the number of children. This difference simplifies the implementation of inference substantially.

Conditioning graphs are also related to Query-DAGs [3] in which simple formulae are precomputed and stored as DAGs. The evaluation engine for this approach is very lightweight, reducing system overhead substantially. However, the size of a Q-DAG may be exponential in the size of the network.

L. Lamontagne and M. Marchand (Eds.): Canadian AI 2006, LNAI 4013, pp. 206–217, 2006.
© Springer-Verlag Berlin Heidelberg 2006

Inference in belief networks allows the calculation of posterior probabilities while considering only essential information. Any information deemed irrelevant to the current query is ignored by certain inference algorithms (such as Variable Elimination (VE) [15]). Such pruning can provide enormous efficiency gain in application, both space and time-wise. The complexity of pruning is linear on the size of the network model, making it fast in comparison to inference.

Because precompiled structures like conditioning graphs must be general enough to allow any query, they do not inherently exploit the use of variables that are irrelevant for a given query. In previous work, we exploited certain domain-dependent observation variables for faster calculation [6]. In this paper, we show how to exploit irrelevant variables for a given query. We show that with a small amount of additional memory, we can achieve exponential speedup for inference using conditioning graphs. In some cases, the time complexity is very competitive with other exact methods such as VE and JTP, with the advantage of requiring only linear space, and being very simple to implement.

The remainder of this paper is as follows. Section 2 reviews conditioning graphs and their methods. Sections 3 and 4 present two improvements to the basic algorithm. Section 5 shows empirical analysis of these improvements over some well-known networks. Section 6 summarizes current and future research.

2   Elimination Trees and Conditioning Graphs

We denote a random variable with capital letters (eg. X, Y, Z), and sets of variables with boldfaced capital letters $\mathbf{X} = \{X_1, ..., X_n\}$. Each random variable X has an associated domain of size m_X, and can be assigned a value or *instantiated*. An instantiation of a variable is denoted $X = x$, or x for short, where $x \in \{0, ..., m_X - 1\}$. A *context*, or instantiation of a set of variables, is denoted $\mathbf{X} = \mathbf{x}$ or $\mathbf{x}$.

An *elimination tree* [6] over a belief network is a tree in which each leaf corresponds to a conditional probability table (CPT) in the network, and each non-leaf corresponds to a random variable from the network. The tree is structured such that for any non-leaf node N in the tree, the variable at N and its ancestor variables in the tree d-separate all variables of one subtree directly below N from all variables in another subtree below N. An elimination tree can be derived from an elimination ordering using a modified version of elimination [15] (see Grant & Horsch [6,7] for details). Figure 1(b) shows the elimination tree for the *Fire* example, shown in Figure 1(a)

An algorithm for computing probabilities in elimination trees is presented in Figure 2. At each internal node T, we condition over its variable (denoted by V_T), unless it is observed. To compute probability $P(e)$ from elimination tree T, we call $\mathcal{P}(T, e)$. The context is extended as the tree is traversed in a depth-first manner, and when a leaf node T is reached, its CPT (denoted by ϕ_T) is indexed by that context.

A conditioning graph [6] is a low-level representation of an elimination tree. The abstract algorithm in Figure 2 is given a compact efficient implementation

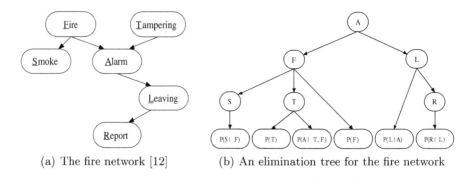

(a) The fire network [12]   (b) An elimination tree for the fire network

Fig. 1. Elimination tree construction

```
𝒫(T, c)
1.    if T is a leaf node
2.        return φ_T(c)
3.    elseif V_T is instantiated in c
4.        Total ← 1
5.        for each T' ∈ ch_T
6.            Total ← Total * 𝒫(T', c)
7.        return Total
8.    else
9.        Total ← 0
10.       for each v_T ∈ dom(V_T)
11.           Total ← Total + 𝒫(T, c ∪ {v_T})
12.       return Total
```

Fig. 2. Algorithm $\mathcal{P}$, for processing an elimination tree given a context

in terms of conditioning graphs, and primitive computational operations such as arithmetic and pointer manipulation.

An example of a conditioning graph is shown in Figure 3(a). Note that at each leaf, we store the CPT as an array of values, and an index as an integer variable, which we call *pos*. In each internal node, we store a set of primary arcs, a set of secondary arcs, and an integer representing the current value of the node's variable. The primary arcs are used to direct the recursive computation, and are obtained from the elimination tree. The secondary arcs are used to make the associations between variables in the graph and the CPTs that depend on them. The secondary arcs are added according to the following rule: *there is an arc from an internal node A to leaf node B iff the variable X associated with A is contained in the definition of the CPT associated with B.*

We implement $\mathcal{P}$ as a depth-first traversal. When we reach a leaf node, we need to retrieve the CPT parameter that corresponds to the context. To do this, we store each CPT as a linear array of parameters, as follows. Let $\{C_1, \cdots, C_k\}$ be the variables of the CPT ϕ, ordered according to the order of their depth in the tree. The index of $\phi(c_1, \cdots, c_k)$ is calculated as follows:

$$
\begin{aligned}
index([]) &= 0 \\
index([c_1, \cdots, c_k]) &= c_k + m_k \times index([c_1, \cdots, c_{k-1}])
\end{aligned}
\tag{1}
$$

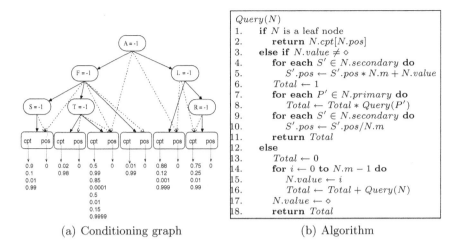

(a) Conditioning graph	(b) Algorithm

Fig. 3. Conditioning graph of the *Fire* example and the algorithm for computing probabilities from it

where m_i is the size of the domain of variable C_i. By choosing an ordering that is consistent with the path from root to leaf in the elimination tree, we can compute the CPT's index as the context is constructed, that is, while we traverse the tree.

Inference in a CG consists of summing out 'hidden' variables. Variables that are either being queried or used as evidence are instantiated in advance of calling $\mathcal{P}$. To do this, we maintain one global context over all variables, denoted g. Each variable V_i is instantiated in g to a member of $\mathcal{D}(V_i) \cup \{\diamond\}$). The symbol $\diamond$ (borrowed from Darwiche and Provan [3]) is a special symbol that means the variable is unobserved (we use -1 in our implementation). Initially, all nodes are assigned $\diamond$ in g, as no variables have been instantiated. To calculate $P(E_1 = e_1, \cdots, E_k = e_k)$, we set $E_i = e_i$ in g for $i = 1 \ldots k$. While performing the algorithm, when conditioning a node to $V_i = v_i$, we set $V_i = v_i$. To reset the variable (after conditioning on all values from its domain), we set $V_i = \diamond$ in g.

Figure 3(b) shows *Query*, the final low-level implementation of $\mathcal{P}$. We use dot notation to refer to the data members of the variables. For a leaf node N, we use $N.cpt$ and $N.pos$ to refer to the CPT and its current index, respectively. For an internal node N, we use $N.primary$, $N.secondary$, $N.value$, and $N.m$ to refer to the node's primary children, secondary children, variable value, and variable size, respectively. The variable's value represents the evidence, if any. To set the evidence $V = v_i$, the application would set $V.value = i$. It is assumed that a constant-time mapping exists between the variable and the node that contains it: such a mapping can be constructed during compilation of the graph.

To avoid confusion regarding the notions of parents and children in the various graphs and trees, we refer to the parents (children) of a variable in the belief network as its *network parents (children)*, while those in the conditioning graph will be *graph parents (children)*.

3   Optimizing Indexing

Conditioning graphs index CPTs as variables are instantiated using a depth-first traversal. For each variable that has been observed or conditioned, the indices for its CPTs (linked through secondary pointers) are updated (Line 4 and 5 of the *Query* algorithm). These values must be unset once the child values have been calculated (Line 9 and 10 of the *Query* algorithm). This linear-time indexing occurs once for each time the node is visited; the number of times a variable is visited in exponential in the depth of the variable in the elimination tree. This approach is simple to implement, but inefficient. We can dramatically improve the efficiency of indexing by precomputing some of parameters involved, at a small cost in terms of memory.

The function *index* takes a context over the variables of a CPT and returns a unique index for that context's entry in the CPT. We showed *index* in its Horner form (Equation 1), but we can also represent it as a linear function over its parameters. Let $M_i = \prod_{j=i+1}^{k} m_j$. This means that $index(c_1, \cdots, c_k) = \sum_{i=1}^{k} c_i M_i$. The cardinality of a variables never changes during inference, so M_i is a constant that can be calculated during the compilation of the conditioning graph. The commutativity of addition means that we can add the terms in the above equation in any order. Consequently, evidence values can be determined and their effect on the indexing computation is independent of any query. Furthermore, evidence only needs to be set once. This is in contrast to the original algorithm, where the evidence was factored into the index when an evidence variable was visited in the traversal, and evidence variables were reset when the traversal of the subtree was completed. Hence, the number of times the evidence is set and reset reduces from exponential to constant (per query). This decrease in the number of operations is exponential on the height of the tree, although this is not evident in terms of asymptotic complexity. If the evidence remains unchanged over multiple queries, then the savings propagates over these queries as well.

Figure 4 gives the new algorithm for updating evidence, and querying the graph. We represent the scalar value between a node N and a respective secondary child S using the function $scalar(N, S)$. Notice that the query algorithm does not compute over the secondary links for an observed variable.

4   Relevant Variables

When computing a posterior probability, the variables in the belief network can be classified into three sets.

1. The *query* variables, including the variable over which a posterior distribution is to be computed, as well as all the evidence variables.
2. The *relevant* variables, whose CPTs must be included.
3. The *irrelevant* variables, whose CPTs may be safely left out.

The irrelevant variables include *barren* variables [13] and *d-separated* variables [5]. Barren variables are variables whose marginalization would produce intermediate distributions full of 1s. Barren variables often comprise a considerable

```
SetEvidence(N, i)
1.      diff ← i − N.value {◇ = 0 in this equation}
2.      for each S' ∈ N.secondary do
3.          S'.pos ← S'.pos + scalar(N, S') * diff
4.      N.value ← i

Query2(N)
1.      if N is a leaf node
2.          return N.cpt[N.pos]
3.      else if N.value <> ◇
4.          Total ← 1
5.          for each P' ∈ N.primary do
6.              Total ← Total * Query2(P')
7.          return Total
8.      else
9.          Total ← 0
10.         for i ← 0 to N.m − 1 do
11.             SetEvidence(N, i)
12.             Total ← Total + Query2(N)
13.         SetEvidence(N, ◇)
14.         return Total
```

Fig. 4. Algorithms for setting evidence and querying, given that secondary scalar values are used

portion of the belief network, especially when the observations and queries are localized to a particular section of the network, and even more so when those observations/queries are shallow (closer to the root than the leaves). D-separated variables are variables in the belief network that are irrelevant to the current query given the current evidence. These variables can also be ignored.

Finding barren and d-separated variables requires traversal through the belief network, but the conditioning graph does not store the belief network in a convenient manner for this. Two possibilities are immediately apparent:

1. At each node, store two tertiary sets of pointers, that correspond to the original belief network. That is, node N storing variable V would have two sets, *parents* and *children*, that point to the nodes containing V's network parents and network children, respectively.

2. Make the secondary arcs bi-directional. In other words, each leaf node in the conditioning graph stores pointers up to its variables in the conditioning graph. As the leaf node stores a CPT for a variable V, and a CPT represents a relationship between V and its network parents, every leaf node has a distinguished arc to V (called a root arc), and a set of pointers to V's network parents (a non-root arc).

Tertiary pointers are more intuitive, and require only one step to traverse to a neighbour (rather than the two step process of traversing to a tree leaf first). However, including tertiary pointers is more space-expensive than making existing secondary arcs bidirectional. In a highly connected graph, the difference can be substantial. For simplicity, we will use the first option, but the algorithms are easily modified to use the second option if space is limited.

There exist several algorithms for finding nodes that are relevant to the query. One of the more recent ones, the Bayes-ball algorithm [14], finds both d-separated and barren variables simultaneously, and is a very good choice. However, since barren variables can be identified prior to the query, our algorithm performs these tasks separately: first non-barren variables are identified, and from these, the set of dependent variables are found.

The simplest definition of a barren variable is recursive: a variable in a belief network is barren if (a) it is not observed or part of the query and (b) either it is a leaf node, or all of its children are barren. For our algorithm, we maintain the collection of non-barren variables dynamically, as follows: whenever a barren variable becomes observed (or part of a query), then it becomes non-barren, and notifies its network parents of its non-barren state. This process continues in a recursive manner. Conversely, when a non-barren variable becomes unobserved, it checks whether or not its children are all barren. If they are, it becomes barren, and notifies its parents of its barren-ness. To accomplish this in a timely fashion, each internal node in the conditioning graph maintains an integer, *nonbarren*, that represents the number of *nonbarren* children that variable has in the network. When a variable becomes non-barren, it notifies its network parents, which update their *nonbarren* status by incrementing it. The opposite process occurs when a non-barren node becomes barren. A variable is barren if it is not observed and its *nonbarren* value is 0. Figure 5 shows *SetEvidence2*, our new evidence entry method that maintains barren variables. Note that *SetEvidence2* is called whenever the observed value of a variable changes, independent of any query.

```
SetEvidence2(N, i)
1.      SetEvidence(N, i)
2.      if i ≠ ◇
3.          ResetBarren(N)
4.      else
5.          SetBarren(N)

ResetBarren(N)
1.      if N.barren = true
2.          N.barren ← false
3.          for each Pa ∈ N.parents do
4.              Pa.nonbarren ← Pa.nonbarren + 1
5.              ResetBarren(Pa)

SetBarren(N)
1.      if N.barren = false AND N.nonbarren = 0 AND N.value = ◇
2.          N.barren ← true
3.          for each Pa ∈ N.parents do
4.              Pa.nonbarren ← Pa.nonbarren - 1
5.              SetBarren(Pa)
```

Fig. 5. Algorithm for setting the evidence, maintaining labeling of barren nodes

From the set of nonbarren variables, we can select the relevant information. The relevant information of a query in a belief network is information that is not independent of the query; it is not *d-separated* from the query [11]. Space precludes a detailed discussion on d-separation, however, it suffices to say that a query is *dependent* on a variable if there exists at least one (undirected) path between the query and that variable that is not blocked by the evidence.

A variable is *relevant* if its local distribution is relevant to the query. Given that all non-barren nodes have been identified, relevant variables can be identified recursively (we assume that a query variable is not observed), using the rules of d-separation [11]:

1. A query variable is marked as a relevant variable.
2. An unmarked barren variable is marked as an irrelevant variable.
3. Given a relevant variable, its unmarked, unobserved parents are relevant.
4. Given a relevant unobserved variable, its unmarked children are relevant.

It must be noted that the above definition of a relevant variable only applies if the barren variables are identified. This simple recursive definition allows us to write a depth-first search algorithm for marking the relevant nodes. This algorithm, *SetRelevant*, is given in Figure 6. To identify relevant variable, a boolean value *relevant* is attached to each node, and is given the value *true* for each graph node which contains a relevant variable.

```
SetRelevant(N)
1.    for each node N' in the conditioning graph
2.        N'.relevant ← N'.active ← false
3.    MarkRelevant(N,N)

MarkRelevant(N, Q)
1.    N.relevant ← true
2.    MarkActive(N.root)
3.    for each P ∈ N.pa s.t. P.barren = false AND P.relevant=false AND P.value= ◇ do
4.        MarkRelevant(P, Q)
5.    if N = Q OR N.value ≠ ◇
6.        for each C ∈ N.ch s.t. C.barren=false AND C.relevant=false do
7.            MarkRelevant(C, Q)

MarkActive(N)
1.    N.active ← true
2.    if N.parent.active = false
3.        MarkActive(N.parent)
```

Fig. 6. The *SetRelevant* algorithm, which marks the active part of the conditioning graph for processing a particular query

In addition to marking the relevance of each node, we need to mark the active paths through the conditioning graph. A leaf node is active if the query is dependent on its CPT. An internal node is active iff (a) the query is dependent on its variable or (b) it has a dependent primary child. Only the active nodes are traversed, the rest are ignored. In addition, the active nodes that are not dependent are treated as observed nodes: they are not conditioned over, they only combine results from their active children. We identify each active node in the conditioning graph by setting a value *active=true*. We use the *MarkActive* algorithm in Figure 6 to mark the active nodes in the graph as we identify relevant information. Note that *MarkActive* requires that each node N have a pointer to its parent node, which we identify as *N.parent* in the algorithm. As well, we denote N's root arc (described previously) as *N.root*.

```
Query3(N)
1.      if N is a leaf node
2.         return N.cpt[N.pos]
3.      else if N.value ≠ ◇ OR N.relevant = false
4.         Total ← 1
5.         for each P' ∈ N.primary s.t. P'.active = true do
6.            Total ← Total * Query3(P')
7.         return Total
8.      else
9.         Total ← 0
10.        for i ← 0 to N.m − 1 do
11.           SetEvidence(N, i)
12.           Total ← Total + Query3(N)
13.        SetEvidence(N, ◇)
14.        return Total
```

Fig. 7. The Query algorithm, utilizing active and relevant nodes (Lines 03 and 05)

Given that we have marked the active and relevant nodes in the conditioning graph (that is, we have called *SetRelevant* on the query node), *Query3* in Figure 7 shows the new query algorithm. The new query algorithm only traverses the active part of the network. It only conditions over relevant nodes. Each node now additionally stores pointers to the nodes containing its network parents and children, and maintains *nonbarren*, *relevant*, and *active* flags. These additions cumulatively contribute a constant factor to the current network storage.

5   Results

Conditioning graphs offer linear-space computation, and easy portability to any architecture. However, they have a worst-case time complexity that is exponential on the size of the network. Methods for balancing elimination trees have been developed [7], however, the subsequent heights are still a function of network size. Elimination methods, on the other hand, compute in time exponential on the tree-width of the network [4]. This value is typically small in comparison to the network size, so elimination methods will typically be quicker to answer queries than conditioning methods, but they require much more space. In this section, we show that the proposed optimizations provide considerable speedup in inference, and that the inference times are reasonable compared to elimination.

We refer to the height of a conditioning graph as its *actual height* h, while its height after ignoring irrelevant nodes will be its *effective height* h^*. We will refer to the *effective conditioning graph* as the conditioning graph with its irrelevant nodes ignored. To draw a comparison between conditioning graph methods and elimination methods, we compare the effective height h^* of the conditioning graph to the width w^* of the network generated using the min-fill heuristic [8]. By comparing the CG height to induced width, we are comparing the complexity of inference in CGs with the complexity of inference in VE and JTP, by looking at the exponent involved in the worst case analysis.

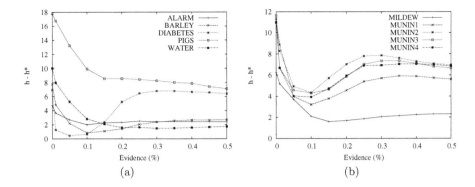

Fig. 8. Height difference between actual and relevant conditioning graph

We compared the approaches over ten well-known networks, obtained from the Bayesian network repository.[1] We tested the algorithms using different percentages of evidence variables (ranging from $0 - 50\%$ of the variables in the network). For each test, we generated 100 random sets of evidence, and tested 50 different query variables on for each set of evidence, for a total of 5000 runs *per evidence set size*, per network.

Figure 8 shows the difference $h - h^*$ for each network (for readability, we have presented the results in two graphs). The graphs show that ignoring the irrelevant information of the network offers a substantial speedup over computing over it. The speedup is most prominent when there is no evidence; there is also a tendency for the difference to increase when the amount of evidence is greater than 20%. An explanation for these results is offered below.

We next compare the height of the effective relevant graph to the width of the network (generated using the standard min-fill algorithm), i.e., $h^* - w^*$. Figure 9 shows the result of this comparison. While the actual height of the conditioning graph is typically much worse than the width of the network, the effective height of the relevant conditioning graph is not that much worse than the network width - in fact, it's typically *better* when the amount of evidence is greater than 20%. The curves are similar for all graphs: an initial growth, followed by a decline. This shows that in many cases, the complexity of recursive decompositions is within the width of the network, meaning that we obtain reasonable time while maintaining the benefits of conditioning graphs, namely, linear space implementation and portability.

The results for both sets of graphs are easily explained by considering where the hardest inference problems are in terms of amount of evidence. When a network has no evidence, the number of barren variables is typically high, so the complexity is low. As evidence is added, the number of barren variables declines, increasing the complexity. However, this increase in the number of variables is eventually offset by the number of d-separated variables, so the complexity begins

---

[1] http://www.cs.huji.ac.il/labs/compbio/Repository/

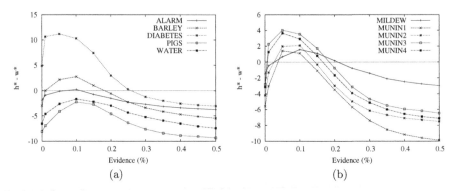

Fig. 9. Difference between relevant height of conditioning graph and network width

to decline. Hence, the hardest problems for inference in our example networks occur when the amount of evidence is greater than 0% and less than 20%.

6   Conclusions and Future Work

This paper presents two optimizations to conditioning graphs, to improve their efficiency while still maintaining linear space. The first optimization improved the efficiency of indexing in the CPTs of the conditioning graph. The second optimization demonstrated how to leave irrelevant variables out of the conditioning technique. These optimizations required simple extensions to the original code which are consistent with the original goal of CGs: easily implementable, making them universally portable. The optimizations attempt to avoid repeat calculation and irrelevant information. They take advantage of current model state.

The first optimization saves us an exponential number of arithmetic operations for a given query, and these savings can be realized across queries in cases where the evidence remains the same. For the second optimization, we measured its performance according to the effective height of the conditioning graph (the maximum number of *relevant* non-observed variables along any path). We observed that the effective height of the network is typically better than the actual height, which means an exponential speedup in the run-times of conditioning graphs. We also observed that this speedup allows conditioning graphs to be competitive in runtime to elimination algorithms in certain cases, especially when the percentage of observed nodes does not fall between 5% and 20%. Both of these optimizations increase the storage requirements of the algorithm by only a constant factor.

While these optimizations provide some speedup, providing caching of intermediate values at internal nodes ultimately produces the fastest recursive structures [2]. Caching is easily implemented in conditioning graphs (caches are indexed the same as distributions). However, naive caching seems to require exponential space. Darwiche et al. have provided good methods for optimal caching given limited space for d-trees [1]. We are currently investigating the most effective use of space in a conditioning graph.

References

1. D. Allen and A. Darwiche. Optimal time–space tradeoff in probabilistic inference. In *Proceedings of the 18th International Joint Conference on Artificial Intelligence (IJCAI-03)*, pages 969–975, 2003.
2. A. Darwiche. Recursive Conditioning: Any-space conditioning algorithm with treewidth-bounded complexity. *Artificial Intelligence*, pages 5–41, 2000.
3. A. Darwiche and G. Provan. Query dags: A practical paradigm for implementing belief network inference. In *Proceedings of the 12th Annual Conference on Uncertainty in Artificial Intelligence*, pages 203–210, 1996.
4. R. Dechter. Bucket elimination: A unifying framework for reasoning. *Artificial Intelligence*, 113(1-2):41–85, 1999.
5. D. Geiger, T. Verma, and J. Pearl. Identifying independence in Bayesian networks. *Networks*, 20:507–534, 1990.
6. K. Grant and M. Horsch. Conditioning Graphs: Practical Structures for Inference in Bayesian Networks. In *Proceedings of the The 18th Australian Joint Conference on Artificial Intelligence*, pages 49–59, 2005.
7. K. Grant and M. Horsch. Methods for Constructing Balanced Elimination Trees and Other Recursive Decompositions. *Proceedings of the the 19th International Florida Artificial Intelligence Research Society Conference (To Appear)*, 2006.
8. U. Kjaerulff. Triangulation of graphs - algorithms giving small total state space. Technical report, Dept. of Mathematics and Computer Science, Strandvejan, DK 9000 Aalborg, Denmark, 1990.
9. S. Lauritzen and D. Spiegelhalter. Local computations with probabilities on graphical structures and their application to expert systems. *Journal of the Royal Statistical Society*, 50:157–224, 1988.
10. S. Monti and G. F. Cooper. Bounded recursive decomposition: a search-based method for belief-network inference under limited resources. *Int. J. Approx. Reasoning*, 15(1):49–75, 1996.
11. J. Pearl. *Probabilistic Reasoning in Intelligent Systems: Networks of Plausible Inference*. Morgan Kaufmann Publishers Inc., 1988.
12. D. Poole, A. Mackworth, and R. Goebel. *Computational Intelligence*. Oxford University Press, 1998.
13. R. D. Shachter. Evaluating influence diagrams. *Oper. Res.*, 34(6):871–882, 1986.
14. R. D. Shachter. Bayes-ball: The rational pastime (for determining irrelevance and requisite information in belief networks and influence diagrams). In *Proceedings of the 14th Annual Conference on Uncertainty in Artificial Intelligence*, pages 480–487, 1998.
15. N. Zhang and D. Poole. A Simple Approach to Bayesian Network Computations. In *Proc. of the 10th Canadian Conference on Artificial Intelligence*, pages 171–178, 1994.

Probabilistic Melodic Harmonization

Jean-François Paiement[1], Douglas Eck[2], and Samy Bengio[1]

[1] IDIAP Research Institute, Rue du Simplon 4, Case Postale 592, CH-1920,
Martigny, Switzerland
{paiement, bengio}@idiap.ch
[2] Département d'Informatique et de recherche opérationnelle,
Université de Montréal, Pavillon André-Aisenstadt,
CP 6128, succ Centre-Ville, Montréal, QC, H3C 3J7, Canada
eckdoug@iro.umontreal.ca

Abstract. We propose a representation for musical chords that allows
us to include domain knowledge in probabilistic models. We then introduce a graphical model for harmonization of melodies that considers
every structural components in chord notation. We show empirically that
root notes progressions exhibit global dependencies that can be better
captured with a tree structure related to the meter than with a simple
dynamical HMM that concentrates on local dependencies. However, a
local model seems to be sufficient for generating proper harmonizations
when root notes progressions are provided. The trained probabilistic
models can be sampled to generate very interesting chord progressions
given other polyphonic music components such as melody or root note
progressions.

1 Introduction

Probabilistic models for analysis and generation of polyphonic music would be
useful in a broad range of applications, from contextual music generation to
on-line music recommendation and retrieval. However, modeling music involves
capturing long term dependencies in time series. This has proved very difficult
to achieve with traditional statistical methods. Note that the problem of long-
term dependencies is not limited to music, nor to one particular probabilistic
model [1]. This difficulty motivates our exploration of chord progressions and
their interaction with melodies. In its simplest definition, a chord is a group of
note names. Chord progressions constitute a fixed, non-dynamical structure in
time and thus can be used to aid in describing long-term musical structure in
tonal music. A harmonization is a particular choice of chord progression given
other components of tonal music (e.g. melodies or bass lines). In this paper,
we propose a graphical model to generate harmonizations given melodies based
on training data. In general, the notes comprising a chord progression are not
played directly. Instead, given that a particular temporal region in a musical
piece is associated with a chord, notes comprising that chord or sharing some
harmonics with notes of that chord are more likely to be present.

L. Lamontagne and M. Marchand (Eds.): Canadian AI 2006, LNAI 4013, pp. 218–229, 2006.
© Springer-Verlag Berlin Heidelberg 2006

Graphical models can capture the chord structures and their interaction with melodies in a given musical style using as evidence a limited amount of symbolic MIDI[1] data. One advantage of graphical models is their flexibility, suggesting that our models could be used either as an analytical or a generative tool to model chord progressions. Moreover, models like ours could be integrated into more complex probabilistic transcription models [2], genre classifiers, or automatic composition systems [3].

Cemgil [2] uses a somewhat complex graphical model that generates a mapping from audio to a piano-roll using a simple model for representing note transitions based on Markovian assumptions. This model takes as input audio data, without any form of preprocessing. While being very costly, this approach has the advantage of being completely data-dependent. However, strong Markovian assumptions are necessary in order to model the temporal dependencies between notes. Hence, a proper chord transition model could be appended to such a transcription model in order to improve polyphonic transcription performance. Raphael [4] use graphical models for labeling MIDI data with traditional Western chord symbols. Lavrenko and Pickens [5] propose a generative model of polyphonic music that employs Markov random fields. While being very general, this model would benefit from having access to more specific musical knowledge. For instance, we go a step further in this paper by including abstract chord representation in the model[2] as a smoothing technique towards better generalization. Allan and Williams [8] designed a harmonization model for Bach chorales using Hidden Markov Models (HMMs). While generating excellent musical results, this model has to be provided polyphonic music with specific 4 voice structure as input, restricting its applicability in more general settings. Our proposed model is more general in the sense that it is possible to extract the appropriate chord representation from any polyphonic music, without regard to specific labeling or harmonic structure. One can then use it to generate harmonization given any melody without regard to the musical style of the corpus of data at hand.

2   Graphical Models

Graphical models [9] are a useful framework to describe probability distributions where graphs are used as representations for a particular factorization of joint probabilities. Vertices are associated with random variables. A directed edge going from the vertex associated with variable A to the one corresponding to variable B accounts for the presence of the term $P(B|A)$ in the factorization of the joint distribution for all the variables in the model. The process of calculating probability distributions for a subset of the variables of the model given the joint distribution of all the variables is called *marginalization* (e.g. deriving $P(A, B)$ from $P(A, B, C)$). The graphical model framework provides efficient algorithms

---

[1] In our present work, we only consider notes onsets and offsets in the MIDI signal.

[2] The proposed model is defined using standard jazz chord notation as described in [6, 7].

for marginalization and various learning algorithms can be used to learn the parameters of a model, given an appropriate dataset.

The Expectation-Maximization (EM) algorithm [10] can be used to estimate the conditional probabilities of the hidden variables in a graphical model. This algorithm proceeds in two steps applied iteratively over a dataset until convergence of the parameters. First, the E step computes the expectation of the hidden variables, given the current parameters of the model and the observations of the dataset. Secondly, the M step updates the values of the parameters in order to maximize the joint likelihood of the observations and the expected values of the hidden variables.

Marginalization must be carried out in the proposed model both for learning (during the expectation step of the EM algorithm) and for evaluation. The inference in a graphical model can be achieved using the Junction Tree Algorithm (JTA) [9]. In order to build the junction tree representation of the joint distribution of all the variables of the model, we start by moralizing the original graph (i.e. connecting the non-connected parents of a common child and then removing the directionality of all edges) so that some of the independence properties in the original graph are preserved. In the next step (called triangulation), we add edges to remove all chord-less cycles of length 4 or more. Then, we can form clusters with the maximal cliques of the triangulated graph. The Junction Tree representation is formed by joining these clusters together. We finally apply a message passing scheme between the potential functions associated to each cluster of the Junction Tree. These potential function can be normalized to give the marginalized probabilities of the variables in that cluster. Given evidence, the properties of the Junction Tree allow these potential functions to be updated. Exact marginalization techniques are tractable in the proposed model given its limited complexity.

3   Interactions Between Chords and Melodies

Each note in a chord has a particular impact on the chosen notes of a melody and a proper polyphonic model should be able to capture these interactions. Also, including domain knowledge (e.g. A major third is not likely to be played when a diminished fifth is present) would be much easier in a model dealing directly with the notes comprising a chord. While such a model is somewhat tied to a particular musical style, it is also able to achieve complex tasks like melodic accompaniment.

3.1   Melodic Representation

A simple way to represent a melody is to convert it to a 12-dimensional continuous vector representing the relative importance of each pitch class over a given period of time t. We first observe that the lengths of the notes comprising a melody have an impact on their perceptual emphasis. Usually, the meter of a piece can be subdivided into small time-steps such that the beginning of any note in the whole piece will approximately occur on one of these time-steps. For instance, let t be the time required to play a whole measure. Given that a 4-beat piece (where each beat is a quarter note in length) contains only eight notes or longer notes, we could divide every measure into 8 time-steps with length $t/8$ and every notes of the piece would occur approximately on the onset of one of these time-steps occurring at times $0, t/8, 2t/8, \ldots, 7t/8$. We can assign to each pitch-class a perceptual weight equal to the total number of such time-steps it covers during time t.

However, it turns out that the perceptual emphasis of a melody note depends also on its position related to the meter of the piece. For instance, in a 4-beat measure, the first beat (also called the downbeat) is the beat where the notes played have the greatest impact on harmony. The second most important one is the third beat. We illustrate in Table 1 a way of constructing a weight vector assessing the relative importance of each time-step in a 4-beat measure divided into 12 time-steps with swing eight notes, relying on the theory of meter [11]. At each step represented by a row in the table, we consider one or more positions that have less perceptual emphasis than the previous added ones and increment all the values by one. The resulting vector on the last row accounts for the perceptual emphasis that we apply to each time-step in the measure.

Table 1. This table illustrates a way to construct a vector assessing the relative importance of each time-step in a 4-beat measure divided into 12 time-steps. On each row, we add positions that have less perceptual importance than the previous added ones, ending with a weight vector covering all the possible time-steps.

Beat 1	.	.	2	.	.	3	.	.	4	.	.
						.					
.						.					
.			.			.			.		
.		.	.		.	.		.	.		.
.	.	.	.	.	.	.	.	.	.	.	.
5	1	2	3	1	2	4	1	2	3	1	2

Although this method is based on widely accepted musicological concepts, more research would be needed to assess its statistical reliability and to find optimal weighting factors.

3.2 Modeling Root Note Progressions

One of the most important notes in a chord with regard to its interaction with the melody may be the root note[3]. For example, bass players play the root note of the current chord very often when accompanying other musicians in a jazz

---

[3] The root note of a chord is the note that gives its name to the chord. For instance, the root note of the chord Em7b5 is the note E.

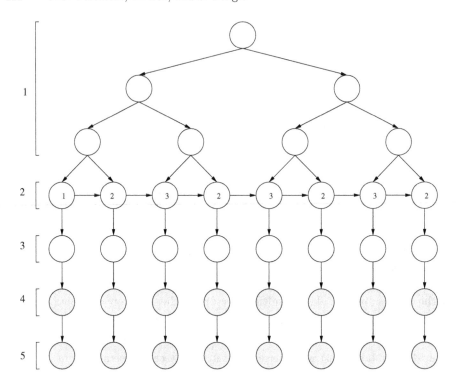

Fig. 1. A graphical model to predict root note progressions given melodies. White nodes are hidden random variables while gray nodes are observed.

context. Figure 1 shows a model that learns interactions between root notes (or chord names) and the melody.

Discrete nodes in levels 1 and 2 are not observed. The purpose of the nodes in level 1 is to capture global chord dependencies related to the meter [11, 12]. Nodes in level 2 are modeling local chord dependencies conditionally to the global dependencies captured in level 1. For instance, the fact that the algorithm is accurately generating proper endings is constrained by the upper tree structure.

Such a model is able to predict sequences of root notes given a melody, which is a non-trivial task even for humans. Nodes in level 1 and 2 are discrete hidden variables and play the same role than in previous models. Nodes in level 2 are tied according to the numbers shown inside the vertices. Probabilities of transition between levels 3 and 4 are fixed with probabilities of substitution related to psychoacoustic similarities between notes [13]. These random variables have 12 possible states corresponding to each possible root note. We thus model the probability of substituting one root note for one another. Nodes in level 3 are hidden while nodes in level 4 are observed. Discarding level 4 and directly observing nodes in level 3 would assign extremely low probabilities to unseen root notes in the training set. Instead, when observing a given chord on level 4 during learning, the probabilities of *every* root notes are updated with respect to the fixed probabilities of substitution. Nodes in level 5 are continuous 12-dimensional

Gaussian distributions that are also observed during training where we model each melodic observation using the technique presented in Section 3.1.

Evaluation of Root Notes Prediction Given Melody. In order to evaluate the model presented in Figure 1, a database consisting of 47 standard jazz melodies in MIDI format and their corresponding root note progressions taken in [6] has been compiled by the authors. Every sequence was 8 bar long, with a 4-beat meter, and with one chord change every 2 beats (yielding observed sequences of length 16). It was required to divide each measure into 24 time-steps in order to fit each melody note to an onset. The technique presented in Section 3.1 was used over a time span t of 2 beats corresponding to the chords lengths.

The proposed tree model was compared to an HMM (built by removing nodes in level 1) in terms of prediction ability *given* the melody. In order to do so, average negative conditional out-of-sample likelihoods of sub-sequences of length 4 on positions 1, 5, 9 and 13 have been computed. For each sequence of chords $\mathbf{x} = \{x_1, \ldots x_{16}\}$ in the appropriate validation set, we average the values

$$- \log P(x_i, \ldots, x_{i+3} | x_1, \ldots, x_{i-1}, x_{i+4}, \ldots, x_{16}). \qquad (1)$$

with $i \in \{1, 5, 9, 13\}$. Hence, the likelihood of each subsequence is conditional on the rest of the sequence taken in the validation set and the corresponding melody.

Double cross-validation is a recursive application of cross-validation [14] where both the optimization of the parameters of the model and the evaluation of the generalization of the model are carried out simultaneously. We let the number of possible states for random variables in levels 1 and 2 go independently from 2 to 15. This technique has been used to optimize the number of possible values of hidden variables and results are given in Table 2 in terms of average conditional negative out-of-sample log-likelihoods of sub-sequences. This measure is similar to perplexity or prediction ability. We chose this particular measure of generalization in order to account for the binary metrical structure of chord progressions, which is not present in natural language processing, for instance.

Table 2. Average conditional negative out-of-sample log-likelihoods of sub-sequences of root notes of length 4 on positions 1, 5, 9 and 13 *given* melodies. These results are computed using double cross-validation in order to optimize the number of possible values for hidden variables. The results are better (lower negative likelihood) for the tree model than for the HMM.

Model	Negative log-likelihood
Tree	6.6707
HMM	8.4587

The fact that results are better for the tree model than for the HMM tells us that non-local dependencies are present in root notes progressions [12]. Generated root notes sequences given out-of-sample melodies are presented in Section 3.4 together with generated chord structures.

3.3   Chord Model

Before describing a complete model to learn the interactions between complete chords and melodies, we introduce in this section a chord representation that allows us to model dependencies between each chord component and the proper pitch-class components in the melodic representation presented in Section 3.1.

The model that we present in this section is observing chord symbols as they appear in [6] instead of actual *instantiated* chords (i.e. observing directly musical notes derived from the chord notation by a real musician). This simplification has the advantage of defining directly the chord components as they are conceptualized by a musician. This way, it will be easier in further developments of this model to experiment with more constraints (in the form of independence assumptions between random variables) derived from musical knowledge. However, it would also be possible to infer the chord symbols from the actual notes with a deterministic method, which is done by most of the MIDI sequencers today. Hence, a model observing chord symbols instead of actual notes could still be used over traditional MIDI data.

Each chord is represented by a root note component (which can have 12 possible values given by the pitch-class of the root note of the chord) and 6 structural components detailed in Table 3. While it is out of the scope of this paper to describe jazz chord notation in detail [7], we just note that there exists a one-to-one relation between the chord representation introduced in Table 3 and chord symbols as they appear in [6].

We show in Table 4 the mappings of some chord symbols to structural vectors according to this representation. The fact that each structural random

Table 3. Interpretation of the possible states of the structural random variables. For instance, the variable associated to the 5th of the chord can have 3 possible states. State 1 corresponds to the perfect fifth (P), state 2 to the diminished fifth (b) and state 3 to the augmented fifth (#).

	Values			
Component 1	2	3	4	
3rd	M	m	sus	-
5th	P	b	#	-
7th	no	M	m	M6
9th	no	M	b	#
11th	no	#	P	-
13th	no	M	-	-

Table 4. Mappings from some chord symbols to structural vectors according to notation described in Table 3. For instance, the chord with symbol 7#5 has a major third (M), an augmented fifth (#), a minor seventh (m), no ninth, no eleventh and no thirteenth.

Symbol	3rd	5th	7th	9th	11th	13th
6	1	1	4	1	1	1
M7	1	1	2	1	1	1
m7b5	2	2	3	1	1	1
7b9	1	1	3	3	1	1
m7	2	1	3	1	1	1
7	1	1	3	1	1	1
9#11	1	1	3	2	2	1
m9	2	1	3	2	1	1
13	1	1	3	2	1	2
m6	2	1	4	1	1	1
9	1	1	3	2	1	1
dim7	2	2	4	1	1	1
m	2	1	1	1	1	1
7#5	1	3	3	1	1	1
9#5	1	3	3	2	1	1

variable has a limited number of possible states will produce a model that is computationally tractable. While such a representation may not look general for a non-musician, we believe that it is applicable to most of tonal music by introducing proper chord symbol mappings. Moreover, it allows us to directly model the dependencies between chord components and melodic components.

3.4   Chord Model Given Root Note Progression and Melody

Figure 2 shows a probabilistic model designed to predict chord progressions *given* root note progressions and melodies. The nodes in level 1 are discrete hidden nodes as in the root notes progressions model. The gray boxes are subgraphs that are detailed in Figure 3.

The H node is a discrete hidden node modeling local dependencies and corresponding to the nodes on level 2 in Figure 2. The R node corresponds to the current root note. This node can have 12 different states corresponding to the pitch class of the root note and it is always observed. Nodes labeled from 3rd to 13th correspond to the structural chord components presented in Section 3.3. Node B is another structural component corresponding to the bass notation (e.g. G7/D is a G seventh chord with a D on the bass). This random variable can have 12 possible states defining the bass note of the chord. All the structural components are observed during training to learn their interaction with root note progressions and melodies. These are the random variables we try to predict when using the model on out-of-sample data. The nodes on the last row labeled from 0 to 11 correspond to the melodic representation introduced in Section 3.1.

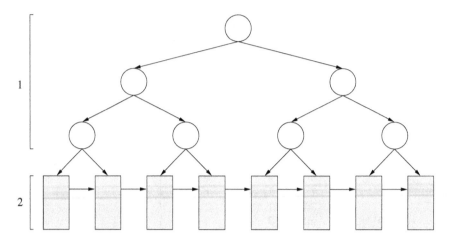

Fig. 2. A graphical model to predict chord progressions given root notes progressions and melodies. The gray boxes correspond to subgraphs presented in Figure 3.

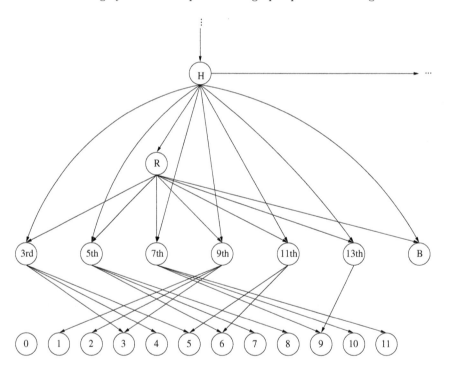

Fig. 3. Subgraph of the graph presented in Figure 2. Each chord component is linked with the proper melodic components on the bottom.

It should be noted that the melodic components are observed *relative* to the current root note. In Section 3.2, the model is observing melodies with absolute pitch, such that component 0 is associated to note C, component 1 to note C#, and so on. On the other hand, in the present model component 0 is associated to the root note defined by node R. For instance, if the current root note is G, component 0 will be associated to G, component 1 to G#, component 2 to A, and so on. This approach is necessary to correctly link the structural components to the proper melodic components as shown by the arrows between the two last rows of nodes on Figure 3.

Generation of Harmonization. It is possible to evaluate the prediction ability of the model for chord structures. We present in Table 5 the average negative conditional out-of-sample log-likelihoods of chord structures of length 4 on positions 1, 5, 9 and 13, given the rest of the sequences, the complete root note progressions and the melodies for the tree model and an HMM model built by removing the nodes in level 1 in Figure 2.

Table 5. Average negative conditional out-of-sample log-likelihoods of sub-sequences of chord structures of length 4 on positions 1, 5, 9 and 13, given the rest of the sequences and the complete root note progressions and melodies using double cross-validation

Model	Negative log-likelihood
Tree	9.9197
HMM	9.5889

Again, we used double cross-validation in order to optimize the number of hidden variables in the models. We observe that the HMM gives better results than the tree model in this case. This can be explained by the fact that the root note progressions are given in these experiments. This would mean that most of the contextual information would be contained in the root note progression, which make sense intuitively. Further statistical experiments could be done to investigate this behavior. Table 6 shows three different harmonizations of the last 8 measures of the jazz standard *Blame It On My Youth* [6] generated by the proposed model.

When observing the predicted structures given the original root notes progression, we see that most of the predicted chords are the same as the originals. When the chord differs, the musician will observe that the predicted chords are still relevant and are not in conflict with the original chords. It is more interesting to look at the sequence of chords generated by taking the sequence of root notes with the highest probability given by the root note progression model presented in Section 3.2 and then finding the most likely chord structures given this predicted root note progression and the original melody. While some chord change are debatable, most of the chords comply with the melody and we think that the final result is musically interesting. These results show that valid harmonization models for melodies that could learn different musical styles could be implemented in commercial software in the short term. More generated results from the models presented in this paper are available on http://www.idiap.ch/~paiement/canai.

Table 6. Three different harmonizations of the last 8 measures of the jazz standard *Blame It On My Youth*. Rows beginning with OC correspond to the original chord progression. Rows beginning with OR correspond to the most likely chord structures given the original root note progression and melody with respect to the model presented in Section 3.4. Finally, rows beginning with NH correspond to a new harmonization generated by the same model and the root note progression model presented in Section 3.2 when observing original melody only.

OC (1-8)	AbM7	Bb7	Gm7	Cm7	Fm7	Fm7/Eb	Db9#11	C7
OR	AbM7	Bb7	Gm7	C7	Fm7	Fm7	Db7	Cm7
NH	C7	C7	Gm7	Gm7	Fm7	Fm7	Bb7	Bb7

OC (9-16)	Fm7	Edim7	Fm7	Bb7	Eb6	Eb6	Eb6	Eb6
OR	Fm7	E9	Fm7	Bb7	Eb6	Eb6	Eb6	Eb6
NH	Edim7	Gm7	Fm7	Bb7	Eb6	Eb6	Eb6	Eb6

4   Conclusion

In this paper, we introduced a representation for chords that allows us to easily introduce domain knowledge in a probabilistic model for harmonization by considering every structural components in chord notation.

A second main contribution of our work is that we have shown empirically that chord progressions exhibit global dependencies that can be better captured with a tree structure related to the meter than with a simple dynamical HMM that concentrates on local dependencies. However, the local (HMM) model seems to be sufficient when root notes progressions are provided. This behavior suggest that most of the time-dependent information may already be contained in root note progressions.

Finally, we designed a probabilistic model that can be sampled to generate very interesting chord progressions given other polyphonic music components such as melody or even root note progressions.

Acknowledgments

This work was supported in part by the IST Program of the European Community, under the PASCAL Network of Excellence, IST-2002-506778, funded in part by the Swiss Federal Office for Education and Science (OFES) and the Swiss NSF through the NCCR on IM2.

References

[1] Bengio, Y., Simard, P., Frasconi, P.: Learning long-term dependencies with gradient descent is difficult. IEEE Transactions on Neural Networks **5** (1994) 157–166
[2] Cemgil, A.T.: Bayesian Music Transcription. PhD thesis, Radboud University of Nijmegen (2004)

[3] Eck, D., Schmidhuber, J.: Finding temporal structure in music: Blues improvisation with LSTM recurrent networks. In Bourlard, H., ed.: Neural Networks for Signal Processing XII, Proc. 2002 IEEE Workshop, New York, IEEE (2002) 747–756

[4] Raphael, C., Stoddard, J.: Harmonic analysis with probabilistic graphical models. In: Proceedings of ISMIR 2003. (2003)

[5] Lavrenko, V., Pickens, J.: Polyphonic music modeling with random fields. In: Proceedings of ACM Multimedia, Berkeley, CA (2003)

[6] Sher, C., ed.: The New Real Book. Volume 1. Sher Music Co. (1988)

[7] Levine, M.: The Jazz Piano Book. Sher Music Co./Advance Music (1990)

[8] Allan, M., Williams, C.K.I.: Harmonising chorales by probabilistic inference. In: Advances in Neural Information Processing Systems. Volume 17. (2004)

[9] Lauritzen, S.L.: Graphical Models. Oxford University Press (1996)

[10] Dempster, A.P., Laird, N.M., Rubin, D.B.: Maximum likelihood from incomplete data via the em algorithm. Journal of the Royal Statistical Society **39** (1977) 1–38

[11] Cooper, G., Meyer, L.B.: The Rhythmic Structure of Music. The Univ. of Chicago Press (1960)

[12] Paiement, J.F., Eck, D., Bengio, S., Barber, D.: A graphical model for chord progressions embedded in a psychoacoustic space. In: Proceedings of the 22nd International Conference on Machine Learning. (2005)

[13] Paiement, J.F., Eck, D., Bengio, S.: A probabilistic model for chord progressions. In: Proceedings of the 6th International Conference on Music Information Retrieval. (2005)

[14] Hastie, T., Tibshirani, R., Friedman, J.: The Elements of Statistical Learning. Springer series in statistics. Springer-Verlag (2001)

Learning Bayesian Networks in Semi-deterministic Systems

Wei Luo

School of Computing Science, Simon Fraser University, Vancouver, Canada
wluoa@cs.sfu.ca

Abstract. In current constraint-based (Pearl-style) systems for discovering Bayesian networks, inputs with deterministic relations are prohibited. This restricts the applicability of these systems. In this paper, we formalize a sufficient condition under which Bayesian networks can be recovered even with deterministic relations. The sufficient condition leads to an improvement to Pearl's IC algorithm; other constraint-based algorithms can be similarly improved. The new algorithm, assuming the sufficient condition proposed, is able to recover Bayesian networks with deterministic relations, and moreover suffers no loss of performance when applied to nondeterministic Bayesian networks.

1 Introduction

Learning Bayesian networks is an important topic in artificial intelligence. Earlier works by Spirtes, Glymour, Scheines [15], and Pearl [11] have shown that it is possible to recover Bayesian networks from observational data, if there exist no deterministic relations among variables. That is, it is assumed that every relation among variables is *inherently stochastic* or is a functional relation *with stochastic inputs* [11, Sect.1.4] [14, Ch.2]. In many applications (e.g., robotics, games, databases), however, some relationships are deterministic (functional, c.f., [13]). In such cases, the current algorithms (e.g., the Inductive Causation (IC) algorithm [11] and the PC algorithm [15]) may output erroneous Bayesian networks [6]. In this paper, we show that, assuming a sufficient condition introduced later, deterministic relations do not prevent us from recovering the correct Bayesian network, provided we correctly detect the deterministic relations.

In this section, we briefly review the assumptions and mechanisms underlying current constraint-based algorithms. In Section 2, we analyze how deterministic relations affect the identifiability of Bayesian networks. In section 3, we modify the IC algorithm so that we can recover a Bayesian network given a set of deterministic relations. We also discuss how to use association-rule miners to detect deterministic relations. The last section shows experimental results on a robotics dataset.

1.1 d-Separation, Stochastic Independence, and the Faithfulness Assumption

We employ notation and terminology from [11] and [15]. A **Bayesian network** is a directed acyclic graph (DAG) in which nodes represent random variables

L. Lamontagne and M. Marchand (Eds.): Canadian AI 2006, LNAI 4013, pp. 230–241, 2006.
© Springer-Verlag Berlin Heidelberg 2006

and edges represent dependence among variables. In this paper, we assume that every random variable is discrete. We use $E(G)$ to denote edges in a DAG G. A **path** in G is a sequence of nodes such that every two consecutive nodes in the sequence are adjacent in G. We shall use $X \rightarrow Y$ to denote a directed edge $(X, Y) \in E(G)$, and use $X - Y$ to denote the undirected edge.

Definition 1. *Let G be a directed graph and p be a path in G. Then a node X is a **collider** on p if X is an interior node on p and X's left and right neighbors on p both have edges pointing to X.*

Fig. 1 shows a Bayesian network from [11, p.15]. In this network, node `wet` is a collider on the path `sprinkler − wet − rain`; in contrast, node `wet` is not a collider on the path `sprinkler − wet − slippery`.

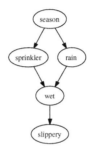

Fig. 1. The sprinkler example

Random variables A and B are **stochastically independent given** S in a distribution P, denoted by $(A \perp\!\!\!\perp B | S)_P$, if $P(A, B | S) \equiv P(A | S) \cdot P(B | S)$. A Bayesian network G **generates** a joint probability distribution P that satisfies the following condition.

Definition 2 (Markov Condition). *Let V be a set of variables, G a Bayesian network over V, and P a joint probability distribution over V. Then G and P satisfy the **Markov condition** if for every $X \in V$, variable X is stochastically independent of its non-descendants in G given its parents in G. (The notions* descendant *and* parent *carry the standard meaning as in graph theory.)*

Definition 3 (d-separation). *Let G be a Bayesian network over variables V. Two nodes X and Y are **d-separated** by a set of nodes $S \subseteq V \setminus \{X, Y\}$ if for every path p connecting X and Y,*

1. *there exists some collider Z on p such that S does not contain Z or any descendant of Z, or*
2. *set S contains a node in p which is not a collider on p.*

For example, in Fig. 1, nodes `sprinkler` and `rain` are d-separated by {`season`}, but `sprinkler` and `rain` are not d-separated by {`season`, `wet`}. In this paper, we use $(A \perp\!\!\!\perp B | S)_G$ to denote that A and B are d-separated by S in graph G.

The Markov condition tells us that, in a distribution P generated by a Bayesian network G, $(A \perp\!\!\!\perp B|S)_G$ implies $(A \perp\!\!\!\perp B|S)_P$. The current constraint-based methods for recovering Bayesian network also assume the converse: $(A \perp\!\!\!\perp B|S)_P$ implies $(A \perp\!\!\!\perp B|S)_G$. This is the so-called **faithfulness assumption** [15, p.13]. Hence given a sample generated by a Bayesian network, we can get the d-separation information through testing stochastic independence among variables. With the d-separation information, we can then reconstruct the topology of the Bayesian network. This is the theoretical basis of constraint-based algorithms. For example, the IC algorithm [11, p.50] is based on this idea.

1.2   Deterministic Relation and Stable Distribution

Definition 4 (deterministic relation). *Let V be a set of variables, and P be a distribution over V. A set of variables $S \subseteq V$ **determines** a variable $X \in V$ in P, denoted by $S \Rightarrow_P X$, if there exists a (partial) function f such that for every instantiation s of S, if $P(S = s) \neq 0$, then*

1. *$P(X = f(s)|S = s) = 1$, and*
2. *$P(X \neq f(s)|S = s) = 0$.*

Therefore the relation $S \Rightarrow_P X$ gives us a function from S to X.

A distribution P **satisfies** a set $\mathcal{D}$ of deterministic relations if every relation in $\mathcal{D}$ holds in P.

Definition 5 (stable distribution). *A distribution P generated by a Bayesian network G is **stable** with respect to a set of deterministic relations $\mathcal{D}$ if*

1. *P satisfies $\mathcal{D}$, and*
2. *every stochastic independence relation that holds in P also holds in other distributions generated by G that satisfy $\mathcal{D}$.*

Therefore when there exist no deterministic relations, a distribution is faithful to a Bayesian network if and only if it is stable.

2   How Deterministic Relations Affect Bayesian-Network Discovery

This section shows why deterministic relations are not allowed in the current constraint-based algorithms, by presenting an example where the IC algorithm fails because of deterministic relations.

2.1   An Example Where the IC Algorithm Fails

Pearl's IC algorithm is a typical constraint-based algorithm. The IC algorithm outputs a pattern of the target Bayesian network. Every Bayesian network G defines an equivalence class $\mathcal{C}_G$ of Bayesian networks that have the same set of d-separation relations. A **pattern** G' of G is a partially directed graph with the skeleton of G such that an arrow is in G' if and only if it is in every Bayesian network in $\mathcal{C}_G$.

The main steps of the IC algorithm are sketched in Fig. 2.

Input: A sample from a faithful distribution P generated by a Bayesian network G over variables V.

Output: The pattern of G.

Stage 1: *Form the skeleton of the graph.* For every pair of variables X and Y in V, connect $X - Y$ in G if X and Y are dependent conditional on every set $S \subseteq V \setminus \{X, Y\}$.

Stage 2: *Identify colliders.* For every pair of variables X and Y nonadjacent in the resulted graph and every common neighbor Z, if $(X \perp\!\!\!\perp Y | S)_P$ for some S not containing Z, then Z must be a collider on path $X - Z - Y$ and we can direct the edges as $X \rightarrow Z \leftarrow Y$.

Stage 3: Maximally complete the partial directed graph by the constraints that (1) a Bayesian network is *acyclic* and (2) no more unshielded collider should appear in any consistent DAG extension. (A collider on a path is **unshielded** if its left and right neighbors and itself do not form a clique in the graph.)

Fig. 2. Outline of the IC algorithm [11]

To see how the IC algorithm fails when deterministic relations exist, we first examine a simple example.

Example 1. Suppose the Bayesian network in Fig. 1 has no deterministic relation among variables, then, given a sample generated from the structure, the IC algorithm is expected to output a partially directed graph as shown in Fig. 3(a). Now impose a deterministic relation: the sidewalk is wet whenever it rains or the sprinkler is on, and not wet otherwise (i.e., `wet` = T $\iff$ `sprinkler` = $T \vee$ `rain` = T). With this seemingly harmless restriction on data, the IC algorithm fails to recover the Bayesian network. Actually, the IC algorithm outputs a partially directed graph as shown in Fig. 3(b). In this partially directed graph, `slippery` is shown to have no causal relation with any other variables, a claim which is not reasonable.

The IC algorithm outputs an incorrect Bayesian network because the faithfulness assumption fails when deterministic relations exists among variables. In this particular example, {`sprinkler`, `rain`} determines `wet`; therefore `wet` and `slippery` are stochastically independent given `sprinkler` and `rain` (i.e., (`wet` $\perp\!\!\!\perp$ `slippery`|{`sprinkler`, `rain`})$_P$). Hence the IC algorithm removes the edge between `wet` and `slippery` because of this stochastic independence (see Stage 1 of Fig. 2). But on the other hand, in Fig. 1, `wet` and `slippery` are not d-separated by other variables (in particular, ¬(`wet` $\perp\!\!\!\perp$ `slippery`|{`sprinkler`, `rain`})$_G$). Hence the edge between `wet` and `slippery` should not be removed.

2.2 Failure of Faithfulness Due to Deterministic Relations

We have seen in the previous section that deterministic relations may introduce stochastic independence relations which do not correspond to d-separations in a

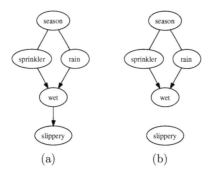

(a)   (b)

Fig. 3. Outputs of the IC algorithm. 3(a) is the output when there exists no deterministic relation; 3(b) is the output when {sprinkler,rain} determines wet.

Bayesian network. In this section, we try to characterize the additional independence relations introduced by deterministic relations so that we can distinguish them in our algorithm.

Lemma 1. *Let P be a distribution over variables V. Let $S \subseteq V$ and $X \in V$.*

1. *If $S \Rightarrow_P X$, then $U \Rightarrow_P X$ for every U such that $S \subseteq U \subseteq V$.*
2. *If $S \Rightarrow_P X$, then there exists a minimal set $W \subseteq S$ such that $W \Rightarrow_P S$.*

Proof. 1. Let $X = f(S)$ and π_S^U be the projection function from U to S. Then $f \circ \pi_S^U$ is a function that maps U into X.[1]
2. This is a direct consequence of S' being finite.   □

The following lemma shows how a deterministic relation introduces a set of stochastic independence relations.

Lemma 2. *Let P be a distribution over a set of variables V. Let $X \in V$ and $S \subseteq V$. If $S \Rightarrow_P X$, then $(X \perp\!\!\!\perp Y|W)_P$ for every $Y \in V$ and for every W such that $S \subseteq W \subseteq V$.*

Proof. Suppose $S \Rightarrow_P X$. Then $W \Rightarrow_P X$ by Lemma 1. Let $X = f(W)$; then

$$P(X = x|W = w) = \begin{cases} 1 & \text{if } x = f(w) \\ 0 & \text{otherwise.} \end{cases}$$

On the other hand

$$P(X = x, Y = y|W = w) = \begin{cases} P(Y = y|W = w) & \text{if } x = f(w) \\ 0 & \text{otherwise.} \end{cases}$$

Therefore $P(X = x, Y = y|W = w) \equiv P(X = x|W = w) \cdot P(Y = y|W = w)$. That is, $(X \perp\!\!\!\perp Y|W)_P$.   □

---

[1] Readers familiar with Armstrong's axioms may recognize that the statement follows from the augmentation rule and the decomposition rule [16, p. 218].

In Example 1, $\{\texttt{sprinkler}, \texttt{rain}\}$ is the minimum set that determines $\texttt{wet}$. Then the stochastic independencies introduced by this deterministic relation include $(\texttt{wet} \perp\!\!\!\perp \texttt{slippery} | \{\texttt{sprinkler}, \texttt{rain}\})_P$ and $(\texttt{wet} \perp\!\!\!\perp \texttt{season} | \{\texttt{sprinkler}, \texttt{rain}\})_P$. Therefore at Stage 1 of the IC algorithm, the edges $\texttt{wet} - \texttt{slippery}$ and $\texttt{season} - \texttt{wet}$ are removed.

We have seen that a deterministic relation $S \Rightarrow_P X$ introduces probability values 0 and 1, and hence a conditional independence relation $(X \perp\!\!\!\perp Y | W)_P$ for every $W \supseteq S$ and every $Y \in V \setminus (W \cup \{X\})$. We argue that no other conditional independence relations will be introduced in a *stable* distribution. Let P be a stable distribution generated by G. Suppose that $W \not\Rightarrow_P X$, $W \not\Rightarrow_P Y$, and $\neg(X \perp\!\!\!\perp Y | W)_G$. Then there exists x, y, and w such that $0 < P(X = x | W = w) < 1$ and $0 < P(Y = y | W = w) < 1$. Assume for contradiction that $P(X = x, Y = y | W = w) = P(X = x | W = w) \cdot P(Y = y | W = w)$. Then we can perturb distribution P such that $P(X = x, Y = y | W = w) \neq P(X = x | W = w) \cdot P(Y = y | W = w)$, which contradicts P's being stable. The perturbation can be achieved, for example, by perturbing the marginal distribution $P(X | \text{Pa}(X))$, where $\text{Pa}(X)$ contains all parents of X, provided $\text{Pa}(X) \not\Rightarrow_P X$. Such perturbation breaks the equality $P(X = x, Y = y | W = w) = P(X = x | W = w) \cdot P(Y = y | W = w)$ because on the one hand X and Y are not d-separated and on the other hand $P(X = x | W = w)$ and $P(Y = y | W = w)$ do not take extreme values 0 or 1.

3 Recover Bayesian Networks with Deterministic Relations

In this section, we discuss how to recover a Bayesian network if we already know all the deterministic relations. First we look at a problem that determinism may impose on a learning algorithm.

3.1 Statistical Indistinguishability Imposed by Determinism

We have seen that deterministic relations may introduce stochastic independence relations which do not correspond to d-separations in a Bayesian network. If we can remove just those *additional* independence relations, then we get a complete set of d-separations and hence can recover the Bayesian network. However, some stochastic independence relation can be explained by both a deterministic relation and a d-separation. Therefore, we may not know which stochastic independence relation is *additional*.

Example 2. In Fig. 4, we are asked to distinguish two Bayesian networks from a stably generated distribution P. Suppose that we know $\{\texttt{sprinkler}, \texttt{rain}\} \Rightarrow_P \texttt{wet}$, and hence expect to observe the stochastic independence $(\texttt{season} \perp\!\!\!\perp \texttt{wet} | \{\texttt{sprinkler}, \texttt{rain}\})_P$. Should there be an edge between $\texttt{season}$ and $\texttt{wet}$? Actually we cannot tell. If there exists no edge between $\texttt{season}$ and $\texttt{wet}$ (see Fig. 4(a)),

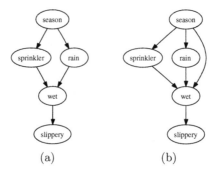

Fig. 4. Two possible structures with the same set of stochastic independence relations, when sprinkler and rain together determine wet

then the stochastic independence (season⊥⊥ wet|{sprinkler, rain})$_P$ can be explained by both the deterministic relation {sprinkler, rain} ⇒$_P$ wet and the d-separation (season⊥⊥ wet|{sprinkler, rain})$_G$. If there exists an edge between season and wet (see Fig. 4(b)), then the stochastic independence (season ⊥⊥ wet|{sprinkler, rain})$_P$ can still be explained by the deterministic relation {sprinkler, rain} ⇒$_P$ wet alone.

3.2   A Sufficient Condition for Identifiability

Example 2 shows a situation where deterministic relations prevent us from singling out the correct Bayesian network. Therefore, we need to find a subclass of problems in which we can avoid such situations. One observation from Example 2 is that {sprinkler, rain} is the only set that d-separates season and wet, and it also determines wet. This motivates the following condition.

Condition 1. *Let G be a Bayesian network and P be a stable distribution generated by G. For every pair of variables X and Y nonadjacent in G, there exists a set S such that the following three statements are satisfied:*

1. *S d-separates X and Y,*
2. *$S \not\Rightarrow_P X$,*
3. *$S \not\Rightarrow_P Y$.*

In Example 2, network G and distribution P do not satisfy Condition 1, since {sprinkler, rain}, the only set that d-separates season and wet, determines wet.

Condition 1 first guarantees that we can identify the skeleton of a Bayesian network.

Lemma 3. *If G and P satisfy Condition 1, then the adjacency between every pair of variables in G is identifiable from P, provided we know all deterministic relations in P.*

Proof. Let X and Y be two variables in G. We check if there exists a set S such that (*) $S \not\rightarrow_P X$, $S \not\rightarrow_P Y$, and $(X \perp\!\!\!\perp Y | S)_P$. If such an S is found, we know that X and Y are nonadjacent, since $(X \perp\!\!\!\perp Y | S)_G$ follows from (*) and P's being stable. If no such S is found, then by Condition 1, X and Y must be adjacent. □

Condition 1 also guarantees that we can identify the colliders on a Bayesian network, provided we have a correct skeleton.

Lemma 4. *Let G and P be satisfying Condition 1, and (X, Y) be a pair of nonadjacent nodes with a common neighbor Z. Then it is identifiable from P whether Z is a collider on the path $X - Z - Y$, provided we know all deterministic relations in P.*

Proof. Since G and P satisfy Condition 1, there exists a set S such that S d-separates X and Y, $S \not\rightarrow_P X$, and $S \not\rightarrow_P Y$. Suppose that Z is a collider on the path $X - Z - Y$. Then $Z \notin S$, otherwise X and Y are d-connected by path $X - Z - Y$. On the other hand, suppose that Z is not a collider on the path $X - Z - Y$. Then $Z \in S$, otherwise X and Y are d-connected by path $X - Z - Y$. In other words, Z is a collider if and only if $Z \notin S$. □

Proposition 1. *Let G be a Bayesian network and P be a stable distribution generated by G. If G and P satisfy Condition 1, then the pattern of G is identifiable from P.*

Proof. Theorem 1 in [17] states that a skeleton and a set of colliders on it uniquely define a pattern. Then the proposition follows directly from Lemma 3 and Lemma 4. □

3.3   Improved IC Algorithm

With Proposition 1, we are ready to introduce our algorithm.

If a Bayesian network and its stable distribution satisfy Condition 1, and if we abstain from relating the additional independencies to d-separations in the Bayesian network, then we can avoid the situation in Section 2.1. Fig. 5 shows a modest modification to the IC algorithm. Given an independence relation caused by deterministic relations, the algorithm simply ignores it. Proposition 1 guarantees that the algorithm returns a valid pattern under Condition 1.

3.4   Detecting Deterministic Relations

Given a set of deterministic relations, the algorithm described in Fig. 5 recovers the Bayesian network. But how can we get the deterministic relations in a dataset?

There are various ways to detect deterministic relations among variables. Here we only consider detecting deterministic relations using association-rule miners. The advantage of this choice is that there are many reliable and efficient association-rule mining algorithms (e.g., Apriori [1], Tertius [2]). Since we are

Input: A sample from a stable distribution P of G.
Output: A pattern of G.
Stage 1: *Form the skeleton of the graph.* For every pair of variables X and Y in V, connect $X - Y$ in G if X and Y are dependent conditional on every set $S \subseteq V \setminus \{X, Y\}$ such that $S \not\Rightarrow_P X$ and $S \not\Rightarrow_P Y$.
Stage 2: *Identify colliders.* For every pair of variables X and Y nonadjacent in the resulted graph and every common neighbor Z, if $(X \perp\!\!\!\perp Y | S)_P$ for some S not containing Z and $S \not\Rightarrow_P X$ and $S \not\Rightarrow_P Y$, then direct the edges as $X \rightarrow Z \leftarrow Y$.
Stage 3: Maximally complete the partial directed graph by the constraints that (1) a Bayesian network is acyclic and (2) no more unshielded colliders should appear in any consistent DAG extension.

Fig. 5. A modified IC algorithm

interested in only the rules with confidence equal to 100%, the execution of a miner is expected to be relative fast.

Given two sets of disjoint variables W and V, if for every possible instantiation w of W with nonzero support, there exists a rule "if $W = w$ then $V = v$" with confidence 100%, then we know that every variable in V is determined by W. We are interested in only the deterministic relations of singleton right-hand-side. For every pair of sets W and V, we then need to decompose V so that we have a set containing a deterministic relation $W \Rightarrow_P X$ for each $X \in V$.

4   Experimental Results

In this section, we evaluate our method with a dataset from the *University of Regina Artificial Life* (URAL) program [4, 5, 3, 6]. This dataset is about the interaction between a robot and environment. The robot moves around on an 8×8 square board. The location of the robot is described by coordinate variables x and y. The robot can take an action, denoted by a, to move left, right, up, or down. Food, denoted by f, is located somewhere on the board, and, if found by the robot, enables it to continue moving around. Each of the variables (x, y, f, and a) is measured at three consecutive times. Karimi used twelve variables to describe them: x_1, y_1, f_1, a_1, x_2, y_2, f_2, a_2, x_3, y_3, f_3, a_3. The system can be

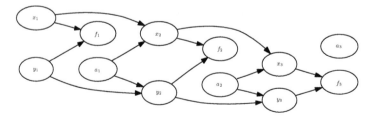

Fig. 6. The target Bayesian network

summarized as a Bayesian network in Fig. 6. In this system, we expect that a_1 and x_1 determine x_2, and a_1 and y_1 determine y_2. Similarly, a_2 and x_2 determine x_3, and a_2 and y_2 determine y_3.

The dataset contains 9998 examples sampled from the causal system. Karimi reported in his PhD thesis [4] that both the PC algorithm and the FCI algorithm from the Tetrad program [12] return incorrect Bayesian networks over this dataset. We replicate the experiment with an implementation of the PC algorithm in the Bayes Net Toolbox (BNT) for Matlab [9]. The structure returned by the PC algorithm is shown in Fig. 7(a). It shows that nodes f_2 and f_3 are isolated variables which do not have causal connections with other variables, which is certainly incorrect.

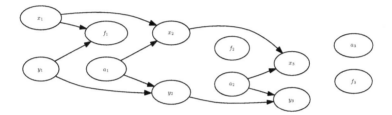

(a) The network returned by the original IC algorithm

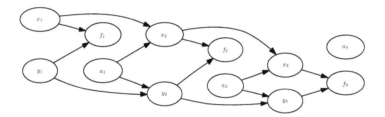

(b) The network returned by the modified IC algorithm

Fig. 7. Outputs from the IC algorithm and the modified IC algorithm

We use the association rule miner *Apriori* in Weka 3 [18] to discover deterministic relations. The returned rules include: $\{a_1, x_1\} \Rightarrow_P x_2$, $\{a_1, x_2\} \Rightarrow_P x_1$,

$\{a_1, y_1\} \Rightarrow_P y_2$, $\{a_1, y_2\} \Rightarrow_P y_1$,
$\{a_2, x_2\} \Rightarrow_P x_3$, $\{a_2, x_3\} \Rightarrow_P x_2$,
$\{a_2, y_2\} \Rightarrow_P y_3$, $\{a_2, y_3\} \Rightarrow_P y_2$.

The rules such as $\{a_1, x_2\} \Rightarrow_P x_1$ show that an event may functionally depend on another event that happened later. We initially failed to realize this; but the association rule miner effectively discovered this kind of deterministic relations.

We feed the discovered deterministic relations to the modified IC algorithm in Fig. 5. The returned Bayesian network is shown in Fig. 7(b); it is identical to the one in Fig. 6. Hence, by using the detected deterministic relations, we prevent the edges $y_2 - f_2$, $x_2 - f_2$, $y_3 - f_3$, and $x_3 - f_3$ from being removed, and recover the correct Bayesian network.

5   Discussion and Open Problems

In this paper, we have shown that the existence of deterministic relations does not necessarily prevent us from inferring Bayesian networks from observational data, as long as we can correctly identify those deterministic relations and a certain condition about the network and distribution is satisfied. Note that noise in data actually breaks deterministic relations; hence noise is not a special issue for our method compared to the IC algorithm.

Several open questions are worth pursuing. First, it would be interesting to know in what situations we can infer causal direction through deterministic relations. For example, suppose we have a partial order over variables such that a variable with lower order cannot be a cause of a variable with higher order. We know that A determines B, but not the other way around. If A has a higher order than B, can we infer that variables in A are direct causes of variables in B? In our robotics example, we have the deterministic relation $\{x_1, a_1\} \Rightarrow_P x_2$ and we know that x_2 is always realized after x_1 and a_1; then we may infer that x_1 and a_1 are direct causes of x_2. Mackie's INUS explanation of causality [8] may help here.[2] Second, compared to mining association rules, is there a more efficient way to detect deterministic relations? It is well known that the existence of deterministic relations may introduce an unusual Markov boundary [10]. We may be able to use Markov boundaries to infer deterministic relations.

Acknowledgments

This research was supported by a NSERC Discovery Grant. I am grateful to Oliver Schulte and Russ Greiner for their valuable advice. Howard Hamilton and Kamran Karimi kindly provided the dataset used in this paper. I would also like to thank anonymous referees for their comments and suggestions.

References

1. R. Agrawal and R. Srikant. Fast algorithms for mining association rules in large databases. In *Proc International Conference on Very Large Databases*, pages 478–499, Santiage, Chile, 1994. Morgan Kaufmann, Los Altos, CA.
2. P. A. Flach and N. Lachiche. Confirmation-guided discovery of first-order rules with tertius. *Machine Learning*, 42:61–95, 1999.
3. H.J. Hamilton and K. Karimi. The timers ii algorithm for the discovery of causality. In *Proceedings of 9th Pacific-Asia Conference on Knowledge Discovery and Data Mining (PAKDD 2005)*, pages 744–750, Hanoi, Vietnam, May 2005.

---

[2] Mackie argues that a cause to a phenomenon refers to an *insufficient* but *non-redundant* part of an *unnecessary* but *sufficient* condition. See also [7].

4. K. Karimi. *Discovery of Causality and Acausality from Temporal Sequential Data.* PhD thesis, University of Regina, 2005.
5. K. Karimi and H.J. Hamilton. Distinguishing causal and acausal temporal relations. In *Proceedings of the Seventh Pacific-Asia Conference on Knowledge Discovery and Data Mining (PAKDD'2003)*, pages 234–240, Seoul, South Korea, April/May 2003.
6. K. Karimi and Howard J. Hamilton. Discovering temporal/causal rules: A comparison of methods. In *Canadian Conference on AI*, pages 175–189, 2003.
7. J. L. Mackie. Causes and conditions. *American Philosophical Quarterly*, 2:245–264, 1966.
8. J. L. Mackie. *The cement of the universe: a study of causation.* Oxford : Clarendon Press, 1974.
9. K. P. Murphy. The bayes net toolbox for matlab. In *Computing Science and Statistics*, volume 33, pages 1–20, 2001.
10. J. Pearl. *Probabilistic Reasoning in Intelligent Systems.* Morgan Kauffmann, San Mateo, CA, 1988.
11. J. Pearl. *Causality: Models, Reasoning, and Inference.* Cambridge university press, 2000.
12. CMU Philosophy. Tetrad project. url: http://www.phil.cmu.edu/projects/tetrad/.
13. S. J. Russell. *Analogical and Inductive Reasoning.* PhD thesis, Stanford University, 1986.
14. R. Scheines, P. Spirtes, C. Glymour, C. Meek, and T. Richardson. *TETRAD 3:Tools for Causal Modeling – User's Manual.* CMU Philosophy, 1996.
15. P. Spirtes, C. Glymour, and R. Scheines. *Causation, prediction, and search.* MIT Press, 2000.
16. J. D. Ullman. *Principles of database systems.* 2. Computer Science Press, 1982.
17. T. S. Verma and J. Pearl. Equivalence and synthesis of causal models. In *Proceedings of the Sixth Conference on Uncertainty in Artificial Intelligence*, pages 220–227, Mountain View, CA, 1990.
18. I. H. Witten and E. Frank. *Data Mining: Practical Machine Learning Tools and Techniques.* Morgan Kaufmann, 2 edition, 2005.

Progressive Defeat Paths in Abstract Argumentation Frameworks

Diego C. Martínez, Alejandro J. García, and Guillermo R. Simari

Artificial Intelligence Research and Development Laboratory,
Department of Computer Science and Engineering, Universidad Nacional del Sur
Bahía Blanca - Buenos Aires - República Argentina
{dcm, ajg, grs}@cs.uns.edu.ar

Abstract. Abstract argumentation systems are formalisms for defeasible reasoning where some components remain unspecified, the structure of arguments being the main abstraction. In the dialectical process carried out to identify accepted arguments in the system some controversial situations may appear. These relate to the reintroduction of arguments into the process which cause the onset of circularity. This must be avoided in order to prevent an infinite analysis. Some systems apply the sole restriction of not allowing the introduction of previously considered arguments in an argumentation line. However, repeating an argument is not the only possible cause for the risk mentioned. A more specific restriction needs to be applied considering the existence of subarguments. In this work, we introduce an extended argumentation framework where two kinds of defeat relation are present, and a definition for *progressive defeat path*.

1 Introduction

Different formal systems of defeasible argumentation have been defined as forms of representing interesting characteristics of practical or common sense reasoning. The central idea in these systems is that a proposition will be accepted if there exists an argument that supports it, and this argument is regarded as acceptable with respect to an analysis performed considering all the available counterarguments. Therefore, in the set of arguments of the system, some of them will be *acceptable* or *justified* or *warranted* arguments, while others will be not. In this manner, defeasible argumentation allows reasoning with incomplete and uncertain information and is suitable to handle inconsistency in knowledge-based systems.

Abstract argumentation systems [1, 3, 12] are formalisms for defeasible reasoning where some components remain unspecified, being the structure of arguments the main abstraction. In this type of systems, the emphasis is put on elucidating semantic questions, such as finding the set of accepted arguments. Most of them are based on the single abstract notion of *attack* represented as a relation among the set of available arguments. From that relation, several *argument extensions* are defined as sets of possible accepted arguments.

L. Lamontagne and M. Marchand (Eds.): Canadian AI 2006, LNAI 4013, pp. 242–253, 2006.
© Springer-Verlag Berlin Heidelberg 2006

For example, the argumentation framework defined by Dung in [1] is a pair $(AR, attacks)$, where AR is a set of arguments, and $attacks$ is a binary relation on AR, i.e. $attacks \subseteq AR \times AR$. In Dung's approach several semantic notions are defined as argument extensions. For example, a set of arguments S is said to be *conflict-free* if there are no arguments $\mathcal{A}, \mathcal{B}$ in S such that $\mathcal{A}$ attacks $\mathcal{B}$. The set of accepted arguments is characterized using the concept of *acceptability*. An argument $\mathcal{A} \in AR$ is *acceptable* with respect to a set of arguments S if and only if every argument $\mathcal{B}$ attacking $\mathcal{A}$ is attacked by an argument in S. It is also said that S is defending $\mathcal{A}$ against its attackers, and this is a central notion on argumentation. A set R of arguments is a *complete extension* if R defends every argument in R. A set of arguments G is a *grounded extension* if and only if it is the least (with respect to set inclusion) complete extension. The grounded extension is also the least fixpoint of a simple monotonic function:

$$F_{AF}(S) = \{\mathcal{A} : \mathcal{A} \text{ is acceptable wrt } S\}.$$

In [1], theorems stating conditions of existence and equivalence between these extensions are also introduced.

Although the area of abstract argumentation has greatly evolved, the task of comparing arguments to establish a preference is not always successful. Having a preference relation in the set of arguments is essential to determine a defeat relation. In [5], an abstract framework for argumentation with two types of argument defeat relation are defined among arguments. In the dialectical process carried out to identify accepted arguments in the system, some controversial situations may be found, as previously presented in [10, 2]. These situations are related to the reintroduction of arguments in this process, causing a circularity that must be avoided in order to prevent an infinite analysis. Consider for example three arguments $\mathcal{A}, \mathcal{B}$ and $\mathcal{C}$ such that $\mathcal{A}$ is a defeater of $\mathcal{B}$, $\mathcal{B}$ is a defeater of $\mathcal{C}$ and $\mathcal{C}$ is a defeater of $\mathcal{A}$. In order to decide the acceptance of $\mathcal{A}$, the acceptance of its defeaters must be analyzed first, including $\mathcal{A}$ itself.

An *argumentation line* is a sequence of defeating arguments, such as $[\mathcal{A}, \mathcal{B}]$ or $[\mathcal{A}, \mathcal{B}, \mathcal{C}, \mathcal{A}]$ in the system above. Whenever an argument $\mathcal{A}$ is encountered while analyzing arguments for and against $\mathcal{A}$, a circularity occurs. Some systems apply a single restriction to argumentation lines: no previously considered argument is reintroduced in the process. In [10], the relation between circularity in argumentation and the comparison criteria used in the system is established. Arguments in such situations are called *fallacious arguments* and the circularity itself is called a *fallacy*. In somes systems such as [3, 4], these arguments are classified as *undecided* arguments: they are not accepted nor rejected.

In this work, we show that a more specific restriction needs to be applied, other than to the prohibit reintroduction of previous arguments in argumentation lines. In the next section, we define the extended abstract framework in order to characterize *progressive* argumentation lines.

2   Abstract Argumentation Framework

Our abstract argumentation framework is formed by four elements: a set of arguments, the subargument relation, a binary conflict relation over this set, and a function used to decide which argument is preferred given any pair of arguments.

Definition 1. *An abstract argumentation framework is a quartet $\langle AR, \sqsubseteq, \mathbf{C}, \pi \rangle$, where AR is a finite set of arguments, $\sqsubseteq$ is the subargument relation, $\mathbf{C}$ is a symmetric and anti-reflexive binary conflict relation between arguments, $\mathbf{C} \subseteq AR \times AR$, and $\pi : AR \times AR \longrightarrow 2^{AR}$ is a preference function among arguments.*

Here, arguments are abstract entities [1] that will be denoted using calligraphic uppercase letters. No reference to the underlying logic is needed since we are abstracting the structure of the arguments (see [6, 11, 8, 9, 2] for concrete systems). The symbol $\sqsubseteq$ denotes subargument relation: $\mathcal{A} \sqsubseteq \mathcal{B}$ means "$\mathcal{A}$ is a subargument of $\mathcal{B}$". Any argument $\mathcal{A}$ is considered a superargument and a subargument of itself. Any subargument $\mathcal{B} \sqsubseteq \mathcal{A}$ such that $\mathcal{B} \neq \mathcal{A}$ is said to be a non-trivial subargument. Non-trivial subargument relation is denoted by symbol $\sqsubset$. The following notation will be also used: given an argument $\mathcal{A}$ then $\mathcal{A}^-$ will represent a subargument of $\mathcal{A}$, and $\mathcal{A}^+$ will represent a superargument of $\mathcal{A}$. When no confusion may arise, subscript index will be used for distinguishing different subarguments or superarguments of $\mathcal{A}$.

Example 1. Let $\Phi = \langle AR, \sqsubseteq, \mathbf{C}, \pi \rangle$ be an argumentation framework, where: $AR = \{\mathcal{A}, \mathcal{B}, \mathcal{C}, \mathcal{D}, \mathcal{E}\}$, $\mathcal{B} \sqsubseteq \mathcal{A}, \mathcal{D} \sqsubseteq \mathcal{C}$, $\mathbf{C} = \{\{\mathcal{C}, \mathcal{B}\}, \{\mathcal{C}, \mathcal{A}\}, \{\mathcal{E}, \mathcal{D}\}, \{\mathcal{E}, \mathcal{C}\}\}^{1}$, $\pi(\mathcal{C}, \mathcal{B}) = \{\mathcal{C}\}$, and $\pi(\mathcal{E}, \mathcal{D}) = \{\mathcal{E}\}$ [2].

The conflict relation between two arguments $\mathcal{A}$ and $\mathcal{B}$ denotes the fact that these arguments cannot be accepted simultaneously since they contradict each other. For example, two arguments $\mathcal{A}$ and $\mathcal{B}$ that support complementary conclusions cannot be accepted together. Conflict relations are denoted by unordered pairs of arguments, and the set of all pairs of arguments in conflict on Φ is denoted by $\mathbf{C}$. Given a set of arguments S, an argument $\mathcal{A} \in S$ is said to be in conflict in S if there is an argument $\mathcal{B} \in S$ such that $(\mathcal{A}, \mathcal{B}) \in \mathbf{C}$. Given an argument $\mathcal{A}$ we define $Conf(\mathcal{A})$ as the set of all arguments $\mathcal{X} \in AR$ such that $(\mathcal{A}, \mathcal{X}) \in \mathbf{C}$. As stated by the following axiom, conflict relations have to be propagated to superarguments.

Axiom 1 (Conflict inheritance). *Let $\Phi = \langle AR, \sqsubseteq, \mathbf{C}, \pi \rangle$ be an argumentation framework, and let $\mathcal{A}$ and $\mathcal{B}$ be two arguments in AR. If $\mathcal{A}$ and $\mathcal{B}$ are in conflict, then the conflict is inherited by any superargument of $\mathcal{A}$ and $\mathcal{B}$. That is, if $(\mathcal{A}, \mathcal{B}) \in \mathbf{C}$, then $(\mathcal{A}, \mathcal{B}^+) \in \mathbf{C}$, $(\mathcal{A}^+, \mathcal{B}) \in \mathbf{C}$, and $(\mathcal{A}^+, \mathcal{B}^+) \in \mathbf{C}$, for any superargument $\mathcal{A}^+$ of $\mathcal{A}$ and $\mathcal{B}^+$ of $\mathcal{B}$.*

---

[1] When describing elements of $\mathbf{C}$, we write $\{\mathcal{A}, \mathcal{B}\}$ as an abbreviation for $\{(\mathcal{A}, \mathcal{B}), (\mathcal{B}, \mathcal{A})\}$, for any arguments $\mathcal{A}$ and $\mathcal{B}$ in AR.

[2] Note that only the relevant cases, those involving conflicting arguments, of function π are shown.

The constraints imposed by the conflict relation lead to several sets of possible accepted arguments. For example, if $AR = \{\mathcal{A}, \mathcal{B}\}$ and $(\mathcal{A}, \mathcal{B}) \in \mathbf{C}$, then $\{\mathcal{A}\}$ is a set of possible accepted arguments, and so is $\{\mathcal{B}\}$. Therefore, some way of deciding among all the possible outcomes must be devised. In order to accomplish this task, the function π is introduced in the framework along with the set of arguments and the conflict relation. The function π will be used to evaluate arguments, comparing them under a preference criterion.

Definition 2. *Given a set of arguments AR, an argument comparison criterion is a preference function $\pi : AR \times AR \longrightarrow 2^{AR}$, and $\pi(\mathcal{A}, \mathcal{B}) \in \wp(\{\mathcal{A}, \mathcal{B}\})$.*

Remark 1. *If $\pi(\mathcal{A}, \mathcal{B}) = \{\mathcal{A}\}$ then $\mathcal{A}$ is preferred to $\mathcal{B}$. In the same way, if $\pi(\mathcal{A}, \mathcal{B}) = \{\mathcal{B}\}$ then $\mathcal{B}$ is preferred to $\mathcal{A}$. If $\pi(\mathcal{A}, \mathcal{B}) = \{\mathcal{A}, \mathcal{B}\}$ then $\mathcal{A}$ and $\mathcal{B}$ are arguments with equal relative preference. If $\pi(\mathcal{A}, \mathcal{B}) = \emptyset$ then $\mathcal{A}$ and $\mathcal{B}$ are incomparable arguments. Observe that $\pi(\mathcal{A}, \mathcal{B}) = \pi(\mathcal{B}, \mathcal{A})$.*

Given an argumentation framework $\langle AR, \sqsubseteq, \mathbf{C}, \pi \rangle$ where $\mathcal{A}$ and $\mathcal{B}$ are in AR, and $(\mathcal{A}, \mathcal{B}) \in \mathbf{C}$, according to definition 2 there are four possible outcomes:

- $\pi(\mathcal{A}, \mathcal{B}) = \{\mathcal{A}\}$. In this case a *defeat* relation is established. Because $\mathcal{A}$ is preferred to $\mathcal{B}$, in order to accept $\mathcal{B}$ it is necessary to analyze the acceptance of $\mathcal{A}$, but not the other way around. It is said that argument $\mathcal{A}$ *defeats* argument $\mathcal{B}$, and $\mathcal{A}$ is a *proper defeater* of $\mathcal{B}$.
- $\pi(\mathcal{A}, \mathcal{B}) = \{\mathcal{B}\}$. In a similar way, argument $\mathcal{B}$ *defeats* argument $\mathcal{A}$, and therefore $\mathcal{B}$ is a *proper defeater* of $\mathcal{A}$.
- $\pi(\mathcal{A}, \mathcal{B}) = \{\mathcal{A}, \mathcal{B}\}$. Both arguments are equivalent, *i.e.* there is no relative difference of conclusive force, so $\mathcal{A}$ and $\mathcal{B}$ are said to be *indistinguishable* regarding the preference relacion π. No proper defeat relation can be established between these arguments.
- $\pi(\mathcal{A}, \mathcal{B}) = \emptyset$. Both arguments are *incomparable* according to π, and no *proper* defeat relation is inferred.

In the first two cases, a concrete preference is made between two arguments, and therefore a defeat relation is established. The preferred arguments are called *proper defeaters*. In the last two cases, no preference is made, either because both arguments are indistinguishable from each other or because they are incomparable. These cases are slightly different. If the arguments are indistinguishable, then according to π they have the *same* relative conclusive force. For example, if the preference criterion establishes that smaller[3] arguments are preferred, then two arguments of the same size are indistinguishable. On the other hand, if the arguments are *incomparable* then π is not able to establish a relative difference of conclusive force. For example, if the preference criterion states that argument $\mathcal{A}$ is preferred to $\mathcal{B}$ whenever the premises of $\mathcal{A}$ are included in the premises of $\mathcal{B}$, then arguments with disjoint sets of premises are incomparable. This situation seems to expose a limitation of π, but must be understood as a natural behaviour. Some arguments just cannot be compared.

---

[3] In general, the size of an argument may be defined on structural properties of arguments, as the number of logical rules used to derive the conclusion or the number of propositions involved in that process.

When two conflictive arguments are indistinguishable or incomparable, the conflict between these two arguments remains unresolved. Due to this situation and to the fact that the conflict relation is a symmetric relation, each of the arguments is *blocking* the other one and it is said that both of them are *blocking defeaters* [7, 11]. An argument B is said to be a *defeater* of an argument A if B is a blocking or a proper defeater of A.

Example 2. Let $\Phi = \langle AR, \sqsubseteq, \mathbf{C}, \pi \rangle$ be an argumentation framework, where: $AR = \{A, B, C, D\}$, $\mathbf{C} = \{\{A, B\}, \{B, C\}, \{C, D\}\}$ and $\pi(A, B) = \{A\}, \pi(B, C) = \{B\}$ and $\pi(C, D) = \{C, D\}$. Here, argument A is a proper defeater of argument B, while C is a blocking defeater of D and vice versa, D is a blocking defeater of C.

Abstract frameworks can be depicted as graphs, with different types of arcs. We use the arc (⋯⋯•) to denote the subargument relation. An arrow (⟶) is used to denote proper defeaters and a double-pointed arrow (⟷) connects blocking defeaters. In figure 1, a simple framework is shown. Argument C is a subargument of A. Argument B is a proper defeater of C and D is a blocking defeater of B and viceversa.

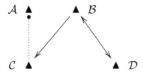

Fig. 1. Defeat graph

Some authors leave the preference criteria unspecified, even when it is one of the most important components in the system. However, in many cases it is sufficient to establish a set of properties that the criteria must exhibit. A very reasonable one states that an argument is as strong as its weakest subargument [12]. We formalize this idea in the next definition.

Definition 3 (Monotonic preference relation). *A preference relation π is said to be monotonic if, given $\pi(A, B) = \{A\}$, then $\pi(A, B) = \pi(A, B_i^+)$, for any arguments A and B in Φ.*

We will assume from now on that the criterion π included in Φ is monotonic. This is important because any argument A defeated by another argument B should also be defeated by another argument B^+.

In figure 2, a simple framework is depicted corresponding to example 2. Here argument C defeats B, but it should also be a defeater of A, because B is its subargument. The same holds for arguments $\mathcal{E}, C$ and D.

In figure 3, argument B is shown defeating argument A via its subargument A_i and two valid ways to depict this situation. The arrow denoting the defeat relation between B and A as shown in (a), may be omitted if subargument arcs are drawn in the graph, as in (b).

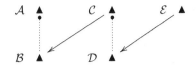

Fig. 2. An abstract framework

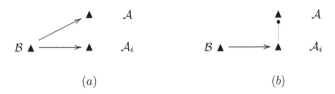

(a)   (b)

Fig. 3. Defeating subarguments

3   Argumentation Semantics

In [1], several semantic notions are defined. Other forms of clasifying arguments
as *accepted* or *rejected* can be found in [3, 4]. However, these concepts are applied to abstract frameworks with single attack relation, as the one originally
shown by Dung. It is widely accepted that defeat between arguments must be
defined over two basic elements: contradiction and comparison. The first one
states that when two arguments are contradictory and therefore cannot be accepted simultaneously. The second one determines which of these argument is
preferred to the other, using a previously defined comparison method. Due to the
possibility of lack of decision at comparison stage, the outcome of this process is
not always equivalent to an attack relation as in [1]. According to this situation,
our framework includes two kind of relations: proper defeat and blocking defeat.
We will focus in this section on the task of defining the structure of a well-formed
argumentation line, from an abstract point of view.

Definition 4 (Defeat path). *A* defeat path λ *of an argumentation framework*
$\langle AR, \sqsubseteq, \mathbf{C}, \pi \rangle$ *is a finite sequence of arguments* $[A_1, A_2, \ldots, A_n]$ *such that ar-*
gument A_{i+1} *is a defeater of argument* A_i *for any* $0 < i < n$. *The number of*
arguments in the path is denoted $|\lambda|$.

A defeat path is a sequence of defeating arguments. The length of the defeat
path is important for acceptance purposes, because an argument $\mathcal{A}$ defeated by
an argument $\mathcal{B}$ may be reinstated by another argument $\mathcal{C}$. In this case, it is said
that argument $\mathcal{C}$ *defends* $\mathcal{A}$ against $\mathcal{B}$. Note that three arguments are involved
in a defense situation: the attacked, the attacker and the defender.

Definition 5 (Defeat paths for an argument). *Let* $\Phi = < AR, \mathbf{C}, \pi >$ *be an*
argumentation framework and $\mathcal{A} \in AR$. *A defeat path for* $\mathcal{A}$ *is any defeat path*
starting with $\mathcal{A}$ $[\mathcal{A}, \mathcal{D}_1, \mathcal{D}_2, \ldots, \mathcal{D}_n]$. *With* $DP(\mathcal{A})$ *we will denote the set of all*
defeat paths for $\mathcal{A}$.

If the length of a defeat path for argument $\mathcal{A}$ is odd, then the last argument in the sequence is playing a *supporting* or *defender* role. If the length is even, then the last argument is playing an *interfering* or *attacker* role [10, 2].

Definition 6 (Supporting and interfering paths). *Let Φ be an argumentation framework, $\mathcal{A}$ an argument in Φ and λ a defeat path for $\mathcal{A}$. If $|\lambda|$ is odd then λ is said to be a* supporting *defeat path for $\mathcal{A}$. If $|\lambda|$ is even, then λ is said to be an* interfering *defeat path for $\mathcal{A}$.*

The notion of defeat path is very simple and only requires that any argument in the sequence must defeat the previous one. Under this unique constraint, which is the basis of argumentation processes, it is possible to obtain some controversial structures, as shown in the next examples.

Example 3. Let $\Phi = \langle AR, \sqsubseteq, \mathbf{C}, \pi \rangle$ an argumentation framework where

$AR = \{\mathcal{A}, \mathcal{B}, \mathcal{C}\}$,
$\mathbf{C} = \{\{\mathcal{A}, \mathcal{B}\}, \{\mathcal{B}, \mathcal{C}\}, \{\mathcal{A}, \mathcal{C}\}\}$ and
$\pi(\mathcal{A}, \mathcal{B}) = \{\mathcal{B}\}, \pi(\mathcal{B}, \mathcal{C}) = \{\mathcal{C}\}, \pi(\mathcal{A}, \mathcal{C}) = \{\}$

The sequence $\lambda = [\mathcal{A}, \mathcal{B}, \mathcal{C}, \mathcal{A}]$ is a defeat path in Φ, because $\mathcal{B}$ is a proper defeater of $\mathcal{A}$, $\mathcal{C}$ is a proper defeater of $\mathcal{B}$ and $\mathcal{A}$ and $\mathcal{C}$ are blocking defeaters of each other. The argument $\mathcal{A}$ appears twice in the sequence, as the first and last argument. Note that in order to analyze the acceptance of $\mathcal{A}$, it is necessary to analyze the acceptance of every argument in λ, including $\mathcal{A}$. This is a circular defeat path for $\mathcal{A}$.

Example 4. Let $\Phi = \langle AR, \sqsubseteq, \mathbf{C}, \pi \rangle$ an argumentation framework where

$AR = \{\mathcal{A}, \mathcal{B}, \mathcal{C} \, \mathcal{A}_1{}^-\}$
$\mathbf{C} = \{\{\mathcal{A}_1{}^-, \mathcal{B}\}, \{\mathcal{B}, \mathcal{C}\}, \{\mathcal{A}_1{}^-, \mathcal{C}\}\}$ and
$\pi(\mathcal{A}, \mathcal{B}) = \{\mathcal{B}\}, \pi(\mathcal{B}, \mathcal{C}) = \{\mathcal{C}\}, \pi(\mathcal{A}_1{}^-, \mathcal{C}) = \{\}, \pi(\mathcal{A}, \mathcal{C}) = \{\}$

In this framework a subargument of $\mathcal{A}$ is included. By Axiom 1 if $(\mathcal{A}_1{}^-, \mathcal{B}) \in \mathbf{C}$ then also $(\mathcal{A}, \mathcal{B}) \in \mathbf{C}$. The same is true for $(\mathcal{A}, \mathcal{C})$, due the inclusion of $(\mathcal{A}_1{}^-, \mathcal{C})$ in $\mathbf{C}$. According to this, the sequence $\lambda = [\mathcal{A}, \mathcal{B}, \mathcal{C}, \mathcal{A}_1{}^-]$ is a defeat path in Φ, because $\mathcal{B}$ is a proper defeater of $\mathcal{A}$, $\mathcal{C}$ is a proper defeater of $\mathcal{B}$ and $\mathcal{A}_1{}^-$ and $\mathcal{C}$ are blocking defeaters of each other. Note that even when no argument is repeated in the sequence, the subargument $\mathcal{A}_1{}^-$ was already taken into account in the argumentation line, as argument $\mathcal{B}$ is its defeater. This sequence may be considered another circular defeat path for $\mathcal{A}$.

Controversial situations are clear in examples 3 and 4. In the next example some piece of information is repeated in the sequence, but this is not a controversial situation.

Example 5. Let $\Phi = \langle AR, \sqsubseteq, \mathbf{C}, \pi \rangle$ an argumentation framework where

$AR = \{\mathcal{A}, \mathcal{B}, \mathcal{C} \, \mathcal{A}_1{}^-, \mathcal{A}_2{}^-\}$
$\mathbf{C} = \{\{\mathcal{A}_1{}^-, \mathcal{B}\}, \{\mathcal{B}, \mathcal{C}\}, \{\mathcal{A}_2{}^-, \mathcal{C}\} \ldots\}$ and
$\pi(\mathcal{A}, \mathcal{B}) = \{\mathcal{B}\}, \pi(\mathcal{B}, \mathcal{C}) = \{\mathcal{C}\}, \pi(\mathcal{A}_2{}^-, \mathcal{C}) = \{\}, \pi(\mathcal{A}, \mathcal{C}) = \{\}$

Again, because $(\mathcal{A}_1{}^-, \mathcal{B}) \in \mathbf{C}$ then $(\mathcal{A}, \mathcal{B}) \in \mathbf{C}$. Also $(\mathcal{A}, \mathcal{C}) \in \mathbf{C}$, because $(\mathcal{A}_1{}^-, \mathcal{B}) \in \mathbf{C}$. According to this, the sequence $\lambda = [\mathcal{A}, \mathcal{B}, \mathcal{C}, \mathcal{A}_2{}^-]$ is a defeat path in $\varPhi$, because $\mathcal{B}$ is a proper defeater of $\mathcal{A}$, $\mathcal{C}$ is a proper defeater of $\mathcal{B}$ and $\mathcal{A}_2{}^-$ and $\mathcal{C}$ are blocking defeaters of each other. In this case, a subargument $\mathcal{A}_2{}^-$ of $\mathcal{A}$ appears in the defeat path for $\mathcal{A}$. However, this is not a controversial situation, as $\mathcal{A}_2{}^-$ was not involved in any previous conflict in the sequence. Argument $\mathcal{B}$ is defeating $\mathcal{A}$ just because $(\mathcal{A}_1{}^-, \mathcal{B}) \in \mathbf{C}$, and is not related to $\mathcal{A}_2{}^-$. Defeat path λ is correctly structured.

Note that $[\mathcal{A}, \mathcal{C}]$ is also a defeat path for $\mathcal{A}$. In this case, as stated in example 4, $\mathcal{A}_2{}^-$ should not appear in the sequence.

The initial idea of restricting the inclusion of arguments previously considered in the sequence is not enough. The examples 3, 4 and 5 show that the characterization of well-formed argumentation lines requires more restrictions. Two main problematic situations must be taken into account, as shown in figures 4(a) and 4(b). The marked argument is reinserted in the defeat path. In the first case, it appears again as a defeater of $\mathcal{C}$. In the second case, $\mathcal{A}_i$ is indirectly reinserted by including a superargument in the sequence.

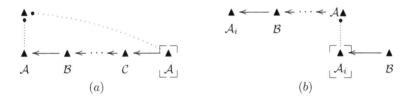

Fig. 4. (a) Direct reinsertion and (b) indirect reinsertion

Both situations are controversial and some well-formed structure must be devised. In the next section we explore these ideas.

4   Progressive Defeat Paths

In this section, we present the concept of progressive defeat paths, a notion related to *acceptable argumentation lines* defined for a particulary concrete system in [2]. This characterization of well-formed defeat path is introduced in the context of our abstract argumentation framework. First, we formalize the consequences of removing an argument from a set of arguments. This is needed because it is important to identify the set of arguments available for use in evolving defeat paths.

Suppose S is a set of available arguments used to construct a defeat path λ. If an argument $\mathcal{A}$ in S is going to be discarded in that process (*i.e.*, its information content is not taken into account), then every argument that includes $\mathcal{A}$ as a subargument should be discarded too.

Definition 7 (Argument extraction). *Let S be a set of arguments and A an argument in S. The operator $\triangle$ is defined as*

$$S \triangle A = S - Sp(A)$$

where $Sp(A)$ is the set of all superarguments of A.

In figure 5, the extraction of arguments is depicted: $S \triangle A$ excludes A and all of its superarguments.

Fig. 5. Argument extraction

Example 6. Let $S = \{A, A^+, B, B^-, C\}$ be a set of arguments. Then
$S \triangle A = \{B, B^-, C\}$ and
$S \triangle B = \{A, A^+, B^-, C\}$

As stated in Axiom 1, conflict relations are propagated through superarguments: if A and B are in conflict, then A^+ and B are also conflictive arguments. On the other hand, whenever two arguments are in conflict, it is always possible to identify conflictive subarguments. This notion can be extended to defeat relations. Let A and B be two arguments such that B is a defeater of A. Then both arguments are in conflict and $\pi(B, A) \neq \{A\}$. By axiom 1, there may exist a non-trivial subargument $A_i \sqsubset A$ such that $(B, A_i) \in \mathbf{C}$. It is clear, as π is monotonic, that $\pi(B, A_i) \neq \{A_i\}$, and therefore B is also a defeater of A_i. Thus, for any pair of conflictive arguments (A, B) there is always a pair of conflictive arguments (C, D) where $C \sqsubseteq A$ and $D \sqsubseteq B$. Note that possibly C or D are trivial subarguments, that is the reason for the existence of the pair to be assured.

Definition 8 (Core conflict). *Let A and B be two arguments such that B is a defeater of A. A core conflict of A and B is a pair of arguments (A_i, B) where*

- *$A_i \sqsubseteq A$,*
- *B is a defeater of A_i and*
- *there is no other argument $A_j \sqsubset A_i$ such that A_j is defeated by B.*

The core conflict is the underlying cause of a conflict relation between two arguments, due to the inheritance property. Observe that the core conflict is not necessarily unique. It is possible to identify the real disputed subargument, which is causing other arguments to fall in conflict.

In figure 6, argument C defeats A because it is defeating one of its subarguments B. The core conflict of A and C is B. In this case the defeat arc between the superarguments may not be drawn.

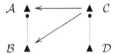

Fig. 6. Argument $\mathcal{B}$ is a core conflict

Definition 9 (Disputed subargument). *Let $\mathcal{A}$ and $\mathcal{B}$ be two arguments such that $\mathcal{B}$ is a defeater of $\mathcal{A}$. A subargument $\mathcal{A}_i \sqsubseteq \mathcal{A}$ is said to be a disputed subargument of $\mathcal{A}$ with respect to $\mathcal{B}$ if $\mathcal{A}_i$ is a core conflict of $\mathcal{A}$ and $\mathcal{B}$.*

The notion of *disputed subargument* is very important in the construction of defeat paths in dialectical processes. Suppose argument $\mathcal{B}$ is a defeater of argument $\mathcal{A}$. It is possible to construct a defeat path $\lambda = [\mathcal{A}, \mathcal{B}]$. If there is a defeater of $\mathcal{B}$, say $\mathcal{C}$, then $[\mathcal{A}, \mathcal{B}, \mathcal{C}]$ is also a defeat path. However, $\mathcal{C}$ should not be a disputed argument of $\mathcal{A}$ with respect to $\mathcal{B}$, as circularity is introduced in the path. Even more, $\mathcal{C}$ should not be an argument that *includes* that disputed argument, because that path can always be extended by adding $\mathcal{B}$ again.

The set of arguments available to be used in the construction of a defeat path is formalized in the following definition.

Definition 10 (Defeat domain). *Let $\Phi = \langle AR, \sqsubseteq, \mathbf{C}, \pi \rangle$ be an argumentation framework and let $\lambda = [\mathcal{A}_1, \mathcal{A}_2, \ldots, \mathcal{A}_n]$ be a defeat path in Φ. The function $D^i(\lambda)$ is defined as*

- $D^1(\lambda) = AR$
- $D^k(\lambda) = D^{k-1}(\lambda) \triangle \mathcal{B}_n$, *where $\mathcal{B}_n$ is the disputed subargument of $\mathcal{A}_{k-1}$ with respect to $\mathcal{A}_k$ in the sequence, with $2 \leq k \leq n$.*

The defeat domain discards controversial arguments. The function $D^k(\lambda)$ denotes the set of arguments that can be used to extend the defeat path λ at stage k, *i.e.*, to defeat the argument $\mathcal{A}_k$. Choosing an argument from $D^k(\lambda)$ avoids the introduction of previous disputed arguments in the sequence. It is important to remark that if an argument including a previous disputed subargument is reintroduced in the defeat path, it is always possible to reintroduce its original defeater.

Therefore, in order to avoid controversial situations, any argument $\mathcal{A}_i$ of a defeat path λ should be in $D^{i-1}(\lambda)$. Selecting an argument outside this set implies the repetition of previously disputed information. The following definition characterizes well structured sequences of arguments, called *progressive defeat paths*.

Definition 11 (Progressive defeat path). *Let $\Phi = \langle AR, \sqsubseteq, \mathbf{C}, \pi \rangle$ be an argumentation framework. A progressive defeat path is defined recursively in the following way:*

- *$[\mathcal{A}]$ is a progressive defeat path, for any $\mathcal{A} \in AR$.*
- *If $\lambda = [\mathcal{A}_1, \mathcal{A}_2, \ldots, \mathcal{A}_n]$, $n \geq 1$ is a progressive defeat path, then for any defeater $\mathcal{B}$ of $\mathcal{A}_n$ such that $\mathcal{B} \in D^n(\lambda)$, $\lambda' = [\mathcal{A}_1, \mathcal{A}_2, \ldots, \mathcal{A}_n, \mathcal{B}]$ is a progressive defeat path.*

Observe that defeat paths of examples 3 and 4 are not progressive. Progressive defeat paths are free of circular situations and guarantees progressive argumentation, as desired on every dialectical process. Note that it is possible to include a subargument of previous arguments in the sequence, as long as it is not a disputed subargument.

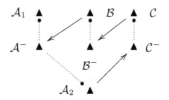

Fig. 7. Controversial Situation

In figure 7 a controversial abstract framework is shown. For space reasons we do not provide the formal specification, although it can be deduced from the graph. There are seven arguments $\mathcal{A}_1, \mathcal{A}_2, \mathcal{A}^-, \mathcal{B}, \mathcal{B}^-, \mathcal{C}, \mathcal{C}^-$. There exists an infinite defeat path $[\mathcal{A}_1, \mathcal{B}, \mathcal{C}, \mathcal{A}_2, \mathcal{B}, \mathcal{C}..]$ which is not progressive. Lets construct a progressive defeat path λ for argument $\mathcal{A}_1$. We start with $\lambda = [\mathcal{A}_1]$. The pool of arguments used to select a defeater of $\mathcal{A}_1$ is $D^1(\lambda) = \{\mathcal{A}_2, \mathcal{A}^-, \mathcal{B}, \mathcal{B}^-, \mathcal{C}, \mathcal{C}^-\}$. The only defeater belonging to $D^1(\lambda)$ is $\mathcal{B}$, with disputed subargument $\mathcal{A}^-$, so we add it to λ. Now $\lambda = [\mathcal{A}_1, \mathcal{B}]$ and the pool of available arguments is $D^2(\lambda) = \{\mathcal{B}, \mathcal{B}^-, \mathcal{C}, \mathcal{C}^-\}$, where $\mathcal{A}^-$ and its superarguments were removed. $\mathcal{C} \in D^2(\lambda)$ is a defeater of $\mathcal{B}$ so we add it to the path and now $\lambda = [\mathcal{A}_1, \mathcal{B}, \mathcal{C}]$. The potential defeater arguments are now in $D^3(\lambda) = \{\mathcal{C}, \mathcal{C}^-\}$. As there are no defeaters of $\mathcal{C}$ in $D^3(\lambda)$, then the path can not be extended. Thus, the resulting sequence $[\mathcal{A}_1, \mathcal{B}, \mathcal{C}]$ is a progressive defeat path.

5   Conclusions

Abstract argumentation systems are formalisms for argumentation, where some components remains unspecified, usually the structure of arguments. In the dialectical process carried out to identify accepted arguments in the system, some controversial situations may be found, related to the reintroduction of arguments in this process, causing a circularity that must be treated in order to avoid an infinite analysis process. Some systems apply a single restriction to argumentation lines: no previously considered argument is reintroduced in the process. In this work, we have shown that a more specific restriction need to be applied, taking subarguments into account in the context of an extended argumentation framework. We finally presented a new definition of *progressive defeat path*, based on the concept of *defeat domain*, where superarguments of previously disputed arguments are discarded.

References

1. Phan M. Dung. On the Acceptability of Arguments and its Fundamental Role in Nomonotonic Reasoning and Logic Programming. In *Proceedings of the 13th. International Joint Conference in Artificial Intelligence (IJCAI), Chambéry, Francia*, pages 852–857, 1993.
2. Alejandro J. García and Guillermo R. Simari. Defeasible logic programming: An argumentative approach. *Theory and Practice of Logic Programming*, 4(1):95–138, 2004.
3. Hadassa Jakobovits. Robust semantics for argumentation frameworks. *Journal of Logic and Computation*, 9(2):215–261, 1999.
4. Hadassa Jakobovits and Dirk Vermeir. Dialectic semantics for argumentation frameworks. In *ICAIL*, pages 53–62, 1999.
5. Diego Martínez, Alejandro J. García, and Guillermo R. Simari. An abstract argumentation framework with proper and blocking defeaters. In *Congreso Argentino de Ciencias de la Computación*, Buenos Aires, Argentina, 2004. CACIC, Universidad Nacional de La Matanza.
6. Donald Nute. Defeasible reasoning: a philosophical analysis in PROLOG. In J. H. Fetzer, editor, *Aspects of Artificial Intelligence*, pages 251–288. Kluwer Academic Pub., 1988.
7. John Pollock. Defeasible Reasoning. *Cognitive Science*, 11:481–518, 1987.
8. John Pollock. Oscar - A general purpose defeasible reasoner. *Journal of Applied Non-Classical Logics*, 6:89–113, 1996.
9. Henry Prakken and Giovanni Sartor. Argument-based logic programming with defeasible priorities. *J. of Applied Non-classical Logics*, 7(25-75), 1997.
10. Guillermo R. Simari, Carlos I. Chesñevar, and Alejandro J. García. The role of dialectics in defeasible argumentation. In *XIV International Conference of the Chilenean Computer Science Society*, pages 111–121, November 1994.
11. Guillermo R. Simari and Ronald P. Loui. A Mathematical Treatment of Defeasible Reasoning and its Implementation. *Artificial Intelligence*, 53:125–157, 1992.
12. Gerard A. W. Vreeswijk. Abstract argumentation systems. *Artificial Intelligence*, 90(1–2):225–279, 1997.

Parsing Korean Honorification Phenomena in a Typed Feature Structure Grammar

Jong-Bok Kim[1], Peter Sells[2], and Jaehyung Yang[3]

[1] School of English, Kyung Hee University, Seoul, Korea 130-701
[2] Dept. of Linguistics, Stanford University, USA
[3] School of Computer Engineering, Kangnam University, Kyunggi, 446-702, Korea

Abstract. Honorific agreement is one of the main properties of languages like Korean or Japanese, playing an important role in appropriate communication. This makes the deep processing of honorific information crucial in various computational applications such as spoken language translation and generation. We argue that, contrary to the previous literature, an adequate analysis of Korean honorification involves a system that has access not only to morpho-syntax but to semantics and pragmatics as well. Along these lines, we have developed a typed feature structure grammar of Korean (based on the framework of HPSG), and implemented it in the Linguistic Knowledge Builder (LKB). The results of parsing our experimental test suites show that our grammar provides us with enriched grammatical information that can lead to the development of a robust dialogue system for the language.

1 Basic Properties of Honorific Agreement

1.1 Subject Agreement

Honorification, one of the main features of spoken language in Korean, plays a key role in proper and successful verbal communication ([1, 2, 3]).[1] The Korean honorific system basically requires that when the subject is in the honorific form (usually with the marker *-nim*), the predicate also be inflected with the honorific form *-(u)si* as in (1):[2]

(1) a. sensayng-nim-i   wus-usi-ess-e.
         teacher-HON-NOM laugh-HON-PST-DECL
         'The teacher laughed.'
     b. #sensayng-nim-i wus-ess-e.

---

[1] We thank three anonymous reviewers for their helpful comments and suggestions. This work was supported by the Korea Research Foundation Grant funded by the Korean Government (KRF-2005-042-A00056).

[2] Abbreviations we use in the paper include ARG (argument), ACC (accusative), BAKGR (background), COMP (complementizer), CTXT (context), DECL (declarative), HON (honorific), IMPER (imperative), NOM (nominative), ORTH (orthography), PST (past), SYN (syntax), SEM (semantics), RELS (relations), and POS (part of speech).

L. Lamontagne and M. Marchand (Eds.): Canadian AI 2006, LNAI 4013, pp. 254–265, 2006.
© Springer-Verlag Berlin Heidelberg 2006

This type of agreement is often assumed to be purely pragmatic, mainly because certain contexts allow disagreeing cases between the subject and the verb: the utterance of (1b) can be felicitous when the speaker does not honor the referent of the subject (marked by #). The possibility of having such disagreement has often led to an assumption in the literature that the cooccurrence of -*nim* on the subject and -*si* on the verb is a matter of gradience and appropriateness rather than grammaticality (cf. [1, 4, 5]).

However, one often neglected fact is that this agreement constraint must be observed when the subject is non-human as in (2) (cf. [3]):

(2) a. cha-ka   o-(*si)-ess-e.
        car-NOM come-(*HON)-PST-DECL
        'The car came.'
     b. kwukhoy-ka pepan-ul simuy-ha-(*si)-ess-e.
        congress   bill   review-(*HON)-PST-DECL
        'The congress reviewed the bill.'

In both examples, the nonhuman subject does not allow the presence of the honorific marker -*si* in the verb. If we rely only on pragmatic information, we would have difficulty understanding why, in contrast to the disagreement in (1b), disagreement like that in (2) are rarely found in real language usages.

In addition, there exist agreement-sensitive syntactic phenomena such as auxiliary verb constructions. Consider examples with the negative auxiliary verb *anh-* 'not':

(3) a. sensayng-nim-i   nolay-lul pwulu-si-ci   anh-(usi)-ess-e.
        teacher-HON-NOM song-ACC sing-HON-COMP not-(HON)-PST-DECL
        'The teacher did not sing a song.'
     b. sensayngnim-i ton-ul   mo-(*si)-e   twu-si-ess-e.
        teacher-NOM money-ACC save-HON-COMP held-(*HON)-PST-DECL
        'The teacher saved money (for rainy days).'
     c. sensayng-nim-i   nolay-lul pwulu-si-na   po-(*si)-e.
        teacher-HON-NOM song-ACC sing-HON-COMP seem-(*HON)-DECL
        'The teacher seems to sing a song.

As noted here, even though the subject is honored in each case, the honorific marker on the main predicate in (3a) is optional with the auxiliary verb *anh-* 'not'; in (3b) the marker must appear only on the auxiliary verb *twu-* 'hold'; meanwhile in (3c) the marker cannot appear on the auxiliary *po* 'seem'. Such clear contrasts, we can hardly attribute to pragmatic factors.

1.2   Addressee Agreement

Matters become more complicated when we consider the agreement triggered by different types of verbal endings. Korean has at least two different endings depending on the honoring relationship between speaker and addressee (cf. [1]):

(4) a. haksayng-i   o-ass-e/o-ass-eyo.
        student-NOM come-PST-plain.DECL/come-PST-resp.DECL
        'The student came.'

  b. sensayng-nim-i o-si-ess-e/o-si-ess-eyo.
   teacher-HON-NOM come-HON-PST-plain.DECL
   'The teacher came.'

As noted here the verbal endings -*e* and -*eyo* are different with respect to addressee agreement. The 'respectful declarative (resp.DECL)' ending -*eyo* is used when the social status of the addressee is higher than that of the speaker. The data implies that not only the speaker but also the addressee plays a role in proper communication strategies with respect to the honorification system.

2 Honorification in a Typed Feature Structure Grammar

A closer look at the honorific phenomena of the language in the previous section suggests that an adequate theory of honorification aiming for integration into a proper communication system requires not just complex pragmatic information but also syntactic and semantic information. The basic framework of the grammar we adopt for modelling the language is the typed feature structure grammar of Head-Driven Phrase Structure Grammar. This framework, HPSG, seeks to model human languages as systems of constraints on typed feature structures. In particular, the grammar adopts the mechanism of a type hierarchy in which every linguistic sign is typed with appropriate constraints and hierarchically organized. This system then allows us to express cross-classifying generalizations about linguistic entities such as lexemes, stems, words, and phrases in the language (cf. [6, 7, 4]).

2.1 Lexicon and Subject Agreement

Our grammar, named KPSG (Korean Phrase Structure Grammar), first assumes that a nominal with -*nim* and a verbal with -*si* bear the head feature specification [HON +]. This is supported by the contrast in the following:

(5) a. [[haksayng-i manna-n] sensayng-**nim**-i] o-**si**-ess-e.
    student-NOM meet-MOD teacher-HON-NOM come-HON-PST-DECL
    'The teacher that the student met came.'
  b. [[sensayng-**nim**-i manna-si-n] haksayng-i] o-(*si)-ess-e.
    teacher-HON-NOM come-HON-MOD student-NOM come-(*HON)-PST-DECL
    'The student that the teacher met yesterday came.'

As seen here, it is the honorific information on the head noun *sensayng-nim* in (5a) that agrees with that of the verb.

  With this head feature information, the grammar builds the honorific nominal type (*n-hon*) from the basic lexeme (*n-lxm*) as represented in the following feature structures:[3]

---

[3] The information our grammar encodes for such lexeme entries is only the shaded part: all the other information is inherited from its supertypes defined in the grammar. For a more comprehensive system of morphology built within such a system, see [6, 7].

(6)

a.
$$
\begin{bmatrix}
n\text{-}lxm \\
\text{ORTH } \boxed{1}\langle\text{sensayng }\rangle \text{ 'teacher'} \\
\text{SYN | HEAD } \begin{bmatrix} \text{POS } noun \\ \text{HON } boolean \end{bmatrix} \\
\text{SEM } \boxed{2} \begin{bmatrix} \text{INDEX } i \\ \text{RELS } \left\langle \begin{bmatrix} \text{PRED teacher-rel} \\ \text{INSTANCE } i \end{bmatrix} \right\rangle \end{bmatrix}
\end{bmatrix}
$$

b.
$$
\begin{bmatrix}
n\text{-}hon \\
\text{ORTH } \boxed{1} + \langle\text{nim}\rangle \text{ 'teacher + HON'} \\
\text{SYN | HEAD } \begin{bmatrix} \text{POS } noun \\ \text{HON } + \end{bmatrix} \\
\text{SEM } \boxed{2}
\end{bmatrix}
$$

As seen in (6a), a nominal lexeme with no honorific marker -*nim* is underspecified for the HON feature.[4]

Meanwhile, the subject of an honorific verbal element carries the feature [HON +] in addition to the relevant pragmatic information:

(7)

$$
\begin{bmatrix}
v\text{-}lxm \\
\text{ORTH } \boxed{1} \\
\text{SYN | HEAD} \begin{bmatrix} \text{POS } verb \\ \text{HON } boolean \end{bmatrix} \\
\text{ARG-ST } \left\langle \text{NP}\begin{bmatrix} \text{INDEX } i \end{bmatrix}, \dots \right\rangle \\
\text{SEM } \boxed{2}
\end{bmatrix}
$$

$$
\begin{bmatrix}
v\text{-}hon \\
\text{ORTH } \boxed{1} + \langle\text{si}\rangle \\
\text{SYN | HEAD} \begin{bmatrix} \text{POS } verb \\ \text{HON } + \end{bmatrix} \\
\text{ARG-ST } \left\langle \text{NP}\begin{bmatrix} \text{HON } + \\ \text{INDEX } i \end{bmatrix}, \dots \right\rangle \\
\text{SEM } \boxed{2} \\
\text{CTXT} \begin{bmatrix} \text{C-INDICES | SPEAKER } p \\ \text{BAKGR} \left\langle \begin{bmatrix} \text{PRED } honoring \\ \text{ARG1 } p \\ \text{ARG2 } i \end{bmatrix} \right\rangle \end{bmatrix}
\end{bmatrix}
$$

The basic verbal lexeme type *v-lxm* in (7) does not carry any restriction on its subject. However, the *v-hon* type with the -*(u)si* suffix adds the information that its subject (the first element in the ARG-ST (argument structure)) is [HON +], in addition to the information that the speaker is honoring the subject referent as given in the CTXT value.

One of the key points in this system is that even though the [HON +] verb selects a [HON +] subject, the subject of a nonhonorific verb can be either in the honorific or nonhonorific form since its value is underspecified with respect

---

[4] The boxed number here is used as a way of showing that semantic value of the lexeme, *n-lxm* is identical with that of the honorific noun *n-hon*.

to the verb. This then correctly allows disagreeing examples like (1)b where the subject is [HON +] and the verb's HON value is 'boolean':

(1) a. sensayng-nim-i wus-ess-e. 'The teacher laughed.'

The nonhonorific verb combines with the honorific subject with no honoring intention from the speaker since the nonhonorific verb does not bear the pragmatic constraint that the speaker honors the referent of the subject.

Yet the grammar blocks disagreeing cases like (??) where an honorific verb combines a nonhonorific subject:

(2) a. *cha-ka o-si-ess-ta. 'The car came.'
     b. *kwukhoy-ka ku pepan-ul simuy-ha-si-ess-e.
        'The congress reviewed the bill.'

These are simply not parsed since the honorific verb here would combine with the [HON −] subject, violating the constraint in (6b). A noun like *sensayng* 'teacher' is [HON boolean], while *sensayng-nim* is [HON +], and canonical lexeme nouns are [HON −].[5]

2.2 Object and Oblique Agreement

While subject honorification has a productive suffixal expression, there are some lexically suppletive forms like *poyp-e* 'see.HON-DECL' and *mosi-e* 'take.HON-DECL', which require their object to be in the honorific form:

(8) a. John-i   Mary-lul   *poyp-ess-e/po-ass-e.
        John-NOM Mary-ACC *see.HON-PST-DECL/see-PST-DECL
        'John honorably saw Mary.'
     b. John-i   sensayng-nim-ul   poyp-ess-e.
        John-NOM teacher-HON-ACC see.HON-PST-DECL
        'John honorably saw the teacher.'

Our grammar lexically specifies that these suppletive verbs require the object to be [HON +] together with the pragmatic honoring relation. The following is the lexical information that a suppletive verb like this accumulates from the inheritance hierarchy:

(9)
$$
\begin{bmatrix}
\textit{v-lxm} \\
\text{ORTH } \langle \text{poyp-} \rangle \text{ 'HON.see'} \\
\text{SYN} \mid \text{HEAD } \boxed{1}[\text{HON } +] \\
\text{ARG-ST } \left\langle \text{NP[INDEX } i], \text{NP} \begin{bmatrix} \text{HON } + \\ \text{INDEX } j \end{bmatrix} \right\rangle \\
\text{SEM } \textit{see-rel} \\
\text{CTXT} \left[\text{BAKGR} \left\langle \begin{bmatrix} \text{PRED } \textit{honoring} \\ \text{ARG1 } i \\ \text{ARG2 } j \end{bmatrix} \right\rangle \right]
\end{bmatrix}
$$

---

[5] Nouns such as *taythonglyeng* ('president') are inherently [HON +] without the honorific marker *nim*.

Such lexical information can easily block examples like (8a) where the object is [HON −].[6]

Lexically suppletive forms like *tuli-e* 'give.HON-DECL' and *yeccup-e* 'ask.HON-DECL' require their oblique argument to be in the HON form (nonhonorific forms are *cwu-e* and *mwul-e*, respectively). This is why the non-honored oblique argument *haksayng-eykey* 'student-DAT' in (10b) is not acceptable here:

(10) a. John-i   sensayng-nim-eykey senmwul-ul   tuli-ess-e.
         John-NOM teacher-HON-DAT   present-ACC give.HON-PST-DECL
         'John gave the present to the teacher.'
    b. *John-i haksayng-eykey senmwul-ul tuli-ess-e.

Just like object agreement, our grammar assigns the HON restriction on its dative argument together with the pragmatic honoring constraint:

$$(11) \begin{bmatrix} v\text{-}lxm \\ \text{SYN} \,|\, \text{HEAD} \,|\, \text{HON} + \\ \text{ARG-ST} \left\langle [\text{INDEX } i], [\ ], \begin{bmatrix} \text{HON} + \\ \text{INDEX } k \end{bmatrix} \right\rangle \\ \text{CTXT} \,|\, \text{BAKGR} \left\langle \begin{bmatrix} \text{PRED } honoring \\ \text{ARG1 } i \\ \text{ARG2 } k \end{bmatrix} \right\rangle \end{bmatrix}$$

Once again the grammar rules out examples like (10b) in which the dative argument *haksayng-eykey* 'student-DAT' is nonhonorific. However, nothing blocks the grammar from generating examples like (12) where the dative argument *sensayng-nim-eykey* 'teacher-HON-DAT' is [HON +] even if the verb *cwu-* 'give' is in the nonhonorific (unspecified) form:

(12) John-i sensayng-nim-eykey senmwul-ul cwu-ess-e. ($\approx$(10)a)

2.3 Multiple Honorification

Given this system, we can easily predict that it is possible to have multiple honorific examples in which subject agreement cooccurs with object agreement:

---

[6] Notice here that unlike the case with subject agreement, here the pragmatic background information involves the honoring relationship between the subject and the object. This implies that if there is a situation where the speaker honors the object, a given example can be felicitous. In fact, we find a corpus example like the following from our test suites:

(i) *pro* chayk-ul   mosi-ko ...
    pro book-ACC attend.to.HON-COMP
    'He/she attends to the books ...

We leave the issue of dealing with such examples for future research.

(13) ape-nim-i   sensayng-nim-ul   poyp-(usi)-ess-e.
     father-HON-NOM teacher-HON-ACC HON.see-(HON)-PST-DECL
     'The father saw the teacher.'

The honorific suffix *-si* on the verb here requires the subject to be [HON +]
whereas the suppletive verb stem asks its object to be [HON +]. In such examples, the honorific marker in the verb can be optional or the verb can even be
replaced by the nonsuppletive form *po-* 'seem'. However, the grammar does not
generate cases like the following:

(14) a. *John-i   sensayng-nim-ul   poyp-usi-ess-e.
         John-NOM teacher-HON-ACC HON.see-HON-PST-DECL
         'John saw the teacher.'
     b. *ape-nim-i   John-lul   poyp-ess-e.
         father-HON-NOM John-ACC HON.see-HON-PST-DECL
         'The father saw the teacher.'

(14a) is ruled out since the HON form *-(u)si* requires the subject to be [HON
+] whereas (14b) is ruled out since the suppletive form *poyp-* selects a [HON +]
object. We also can see that oblique agreement can occur together with subject
agreement:

(15) a. eme-nim-i   sensayng-nim-eykey senmwul-ul   tuli-si-ess-e.
         mother-HON-NOM teacher-HON-DAT present-ACC give.HON-PST-DECL
         'Mother gave the teacher a present.
     b. #eme-nim-i sensayng-nim-eykey senmwul-ul tuli-ess-e.
     c. #eme-nim-i sensayng-nim-eykey senmwul-ul cwu-(si)-ess-e.
     d. *John-i sensayng-nim-eykey senmwul-ul tuli-si-ess-e.
     e. *eme-nim-i John-eykey senmwul-ul tuli-si-ess-e.

Since the nonhonorific verb places no restriction on the subject, the grammar
allows the disagreement in (15b) and (15c). However, (15d) and (15e) cannot be
generated: the former violates subject agreement and the latter violates object
agreement.

2.4   Agreement in Auxiliary Constructions

The present honorification system in the KPSG can offer us a streamlined way
of explaining the agreement in auxiliary verb constructions we noted in section 1.1. Basically there are three types of auxiliaries with respect to agreement
(see [8]):

Type I: In the construction with auxiliary verbs like *anh-* 'not', when the subject
is in the honorific form, the honorific suffix *-si* can optionally appear either on
the preceding main verb or on the auxiliary verb or on both:

(16) a. sensayng-nim-i o-si-ci   anh-usi-ess-e.
         teacher-NOM   come-HON-COMP not.HON-PST-DECL
         'The teacher did not come.'

    b.   sensayng-nim-i o-si-ci anh-ass-e.
    c.   sensayng-nim-i o-ci anh-usi-ess-e.
    d.   #sensayng-nim-i o-ci anh-ass-e.

Type II: When the head auxiliary verb is one like *po-* 'try', *twu-* 'hold', and *ci-* 'become', subject honorification occurs only on the auxiliary verb. That is, the preceding main verb with the specific COMP suffix form *-a/e* cannot have the honorific suffix *-si*:

(17) a. *sensayng-nim-i   John-ul   cap-usi-e   twu-si-ess-e.
            teacher-HON-NOM John-ACC catch-HON-COMP do-HON-PST-DECL
            'The teacher hold John for future.'
      b.   sensayng-nim-i John-ul cap-a twu-si-ess-e.
      c.   *sensayng-nim-i John-ul cap-usi-e twu-ess-e.
      d.   sensayng-nim-i John-ul cap-a twu-ess-e.

Type III: Unlike Type II, auxiliary verbs like *po-* 'see' and *kath-* 'seem' cannot have the honorific suffix *-si* even if the subject is in the honorific form:

(18) a. *sensayng-nim-i   chayk-ul   ilk-usi-na   po-si-ta.
            teacher-HON-NOM book-ACC read-HON-COMP seem-HON-DECL
            'The teacher seems to read a book.'
      b.   sensayng-nim-i chayk-ul ilk-usi-na po-ta.
      c.   #sensayng-nim-i chayk-ul ilk-na po-ta.
      d.   *sensayng-nim-i chayk-ul ilk-usi-na po-ta.

First, the agreement in Type I simply follows from the general assumption that this kind of auxiliary verbs acts like a raising verb whose subject is identical with that of the main verb:[7]

(19) a.
$$\begin{bmatrix} aux\text{-}v \\ \text{ORTH } \langle \text{anh-a} \rangle \text{ 'not-DECL'} \\ \text{SYN} \mid \text{HEAD} \mid \text{AUX } + \\ \text{ARG-ST } \left\langle \boxed{1}, \boxed{2}\begin{bmatrix} \text{LEX } + \\ \text{ARG-ST}\langle \boxed{1}, \dots \rangle \end{bmatrix} \right\rangle \\ \text{SEM } not\text{-}rel \end{bmatrix}$$

     b.
$$\begin{bmatrix} aux\text{-}hon\text{-}v \\ \text{ORTH } \langle \text{anh-usi-e} \rangle \text{ 'not-HON-DECL'} \\ \text{SYN} \mid \text{HEAD} \begin{bmatrix} \text{AUX } + \\ \text{HON } + \end{bmatrix} \\ \text{ARG-ST } \left\langle \boxed{1}[\text{HON } +], \boxed{2} \right\rangle \\ \text{SEM } not\text{-}rel \end{bmatrix}$$

---

[7] The semantic relation *not-rel* represents the predicate relation induced by the negative auxiliary verb *anh-*.

The negative auxiliary verb with or without the *-(u)si* suffix selects as its arguments a subject and a lexical complement whose subject is identical with the auxiliary's subject. This means when either one of the verbs requires an HON subject, then the combination of the main verb as a complex predicate will also require an HON subject.[8]

The verb in Korean cannot be an independent word without inflectional suffixes. The suffixes cannot be attached arbitrarily to a stem or word, but need to observe a regular fixed order. Reflecting this, the verbal morphology has traditionally been assumed to be templatic:

(20) V-base + (Passive/Causative) + (HON) + (TENSE) + MOOD

The absence of the HON on the main verb for the Type II AUX is due to the language's morphological constraints. Such an auxiliary verb forms a verbal complex together with a main verb that bears the COMP suffix *-a/e*: this suffix morphologically requires its verb stem to have no honorific *-(u)si* (cf. [6]). As can be seen from the above template, verb suffixes, attaching to the preceding verb stem or word, mark honorific, tense, and mood functions. COMP suffixes are classified depending on which slot they can occur here: for example the COMP suffix *a/e* occupies the HON slot:

(21) a. sensayng-nim-i sakwa-lul   tusi-e   po-si-ess-e.
         teacher-NOM   apple-ACC HON.eat-COMP try-HON-PST-DECL
         'The teacher tried to eat the apple.'
      b. sensayng-nim-i chayk-ul   ilk-(*usi)-e   po-si-ess-e.
         teacher-NOM   book-ACC read-(*HON)-COMP try-HON-PST-DECL
         'The teacher tried to read the book.'

Within the grammar we developed where each specific verb stem has its own type constraint, the stem value of the COMP suffix *-a/e* must be a verb lexeme with no suffix *-si*.

As for the Type III AUX, the grammar needs to rely on semantics: AUX verbs like *po-* 'seem' and *kath-* 'seem' select an event (*e1* or *e2*) as their semantic argument:

$$
(22) \begin{bmatrix} \langle \text{po-} \rangle \text{ 'see'} \\ \text{SYN} \mid \text{HEAD} \begin{bmatrix} \text{AUX} + \\ \text{HON} - \end{bmatrix} \\ \text{ARG-ST } \langle S[\text{INDEX } \boxed{2}e2] \rangle \\ \text{SEM} \begin{bmatrix} \text{INDEX } \boxed{1}e1 \\ \text{RELS} \left\langle \begin{bmatrix} \text{PRED } seem\text{-}rel \\ \text{ARG0 } \boxed{1}e1 \\ \text{ARG1 } \boxed{2}e2 \end{bmatrix} \right\rangle \end{bmatrix} \end{bmatrix}
$$

---

[8] This treatment assumes that the auxiliary verb combines with the preceding (main or auxiliary) verb and forms a complex predicate. See [6] for this line of treatment.

The honoring relation applies not to a proposition but to a human individual: it is such a semantic property that places a restriction on the HON value of the auxiliary verb.

2.5   Addressee Agreement

As noted in Section 1.1, Korean mood marking may also indicate an honoring relationship between the addressee and the speaker. Our grammar, in which the inflected verbal element is built from a basic verbal lexeme within a type hierarchy system (cf. [6]), systematically allows addition of this honoring relationship in the lexical information:

(23)

a.
$$
\begin{bmatrix}
\textit{v-plain-decl} \\
\text{ORTH } \langle \text{o-si-ess-e} \rangle \text{ 'come-HON-PST-plain.DECL'} \\
\text{SYN } \boxed{1} \,|\, \text{HEAD} \,|\, \text{HON } + \\
\text{ARG-ST } \left\langle \text{NP} \begin{bmatrix} \text{HON } + \\ \text{INDEX } i \end{bmatrix} \right\rangle \\
\text{SEM } \boxed{3} \\
\text{CTXT} \begin{bmatrix}
\text{C-INDICES} \begin{bmatrix} \text{SPEAKER } p \\ \text{ADDRESSEE } q \end{bmatrix} \\
\text{BAKGR} \left\langle \begin{bmatrix} \text{PRED } \textit{honoring} \\ \text{ARG1 } p \\ \text{ARG2 } i \end{bmatrix}, \begin{bmatrix} \text{PRED } \textit{soc-higher} \\ \text{ARG1 } p \\ \text{ARG2 } q \end{bmatrix} \right\rangle
\end{bmatrix}
\end{bmatrix}
$$

b.
$$
\begin{bmatrix}
\textit{v-resp-decl} \\
\text{ORTH } \langle \text{o-si-ess-eyo} \rangle \text{ 'come-HON-PST-resp.DECL'} \\
\text{SYN } \boxed{1}[\text{HEAD} \,|\, \text{HON } +] \\
\text{ARG-ST } \left\langle \text{NP} \begin{bmatrix} \text{HON } + \\ \text{INDEX } i \end{bmatrix} \right\rangle \\
\text{SEM } \boxed{3} \\
\text{CTXT} \begin{bmatrix}
\text{C-INDICES} \begin{bmatrix} \text{SPEAKER } p \\ \text{ADDRESSEE } q \end{bmatrix} \\
\text{BAKGR} \left\langle \begin{bmatrix} \text{PRED } \textit{honoring} \\ \text{ARG1 } p \\ \text{ARG2 } i \end{bmatrix}, \begin{bmatrix} \text{PRED } \textit{soc-higher} \\ \text{ARG1 } q \\ \text{ARG2 } p \end{bmatrix} \right\rangle
\end{bmatrix}
\end{bmatrix}
$$

The plain declarative ending adds the information that the speaker is higher than the addressee whereas the respective one the opposite relation. The treatment of address agreement follows the same vein as subject/object agreement.

3   Testing the Feasibility of the Analysis

In testing the performance and feasibility of the grammar, we implemented our grammar in the LKB (Linguistic Knowledge Builder) (cf. [9]). The test suites we used consist of the SERI Test Suites '97 ([10]), the Sejong Corpus, and sentences from the literature on honorification. The SERI Test Suites ([10]), designed to evaluate the performance of Korean syntactic parsers, consists of a total of 472 sentences (292 test sentences representing the core phenomena of the language and 180 sentences representing different types of predicate). Meanwhile, the Sejong Corpus has 179,082 sentences with about 2 million words. We randomly selected 200 simple sentences (the average number of words in each sentence is about 5) from the corpus. These sentences are classified according to their honorification types (agreement target × predicate) and the ratio of parsed sentences:[9]

(24)

(target)× (predicate)	# of Sentences	# Parsed Sentences
nonHON (tgt) × nonHON (pred)	514 (76.4%)	455 (88.5%)
HON (tgt) × HON (pred)	64 (9.5%)	58 (90%)
HON (tgt) × nonHON (pred)	90 (13.3%)	82 (91%)
nonHON (tgt)× HON (pred)	4 (0.05%)	0 (0%)
Total	672	595 (88.5%)

In addition to these sentences, we selected 100 sentences (including the ones given in the paper) from the literature on Korean honorification: 51 sentences with -*si* marked verbs, 31 with auxiliary verb constructions, and 18 with suppletive verb forms. We obtained similar results: the grammar parsed a total of 96 sentences.[10] Among the total of 691 parsed sentences, we checked the meaning representations (minimal recursion semantics: MRS) and the pragmatic representations of 100 randomly selected sentences, and could see that the representations contain the correct information that the grammar is designed for. We believe that the enriched deep processing of grammatical honorific information that the grammar successfully composed in the parsing process can well function for the proper understanding of natural data.

---

[9] The four nonHON × HON sentences are cases where the nominals are not in the honorific form. One way to accept such examples is to remove the [HON +] restriction on the object of such verbs while keeping the pragmatic honoring relationship between the subject and object.

[10] The failed sentences are due to the unwritten parts of our grammar. For example, the current version of our grammar does not cover postposing, floating quantifiers, gapping, and so forth.

4   Conclusion

Honorification, one of the most salient features of the language, involves various grammatical levels of information: morphology, syntax, semantics, and pragmatics. It is thus necessary for a parser to have not only shallow but also deep processing of the honorific information, so that we can check that a given sentence is felicitous. Such deep processing is a prerequisite to the success of dialogue processing, zero pronominal/anaphoric resolution, and so forth.

The grammatical architecture we adopt is a typed feature structure grammar, based on HPSG, that allows us to handle morpho-syntactic, semantic, and also pragmatic information. The implementation of this grammar in the LKB system proves that a typed feature structure grammar can provide us with a proper deep processing mechanism for Korean honorification that opens doors for promising applications in such areas as machine translation and dialogue systems.

References

1. Chang, S.J.: Korean. John Benjamins, Amsterdam (1996)
2. Lee, D.Y.: Information-based processing of Korean dialogue with reference to English. Thaehak Publishing, Seoul (1998)
3. Sohn, H.M.: The Korean Language. Cambridge University Press, Cambridge (1999)
4. Pollard, C., Sag, I.A.: Head-Driven Phrase Structure Grammar. University of Chicago Press, Chicago (1994)
5. Lee, I., Ramsey, R.: The Korean Language. State University of New York Press (2000)
6. Kim, J.B., Yang, J.: Projections from morphology to syntax in the korean resource grammar: implementing typed feature structures. In: Lecture Notes in Computer Science. Volume 2945. Springer-Verlag (2004) 13–24
7. Kim, J.B.: Korean Phrase Structure Grammar. Hankwuk Publishing, Seoul (2004) In Korean.
8. Sells, P.: Structural relationships within complex predicates. In Park, B.S., Yoon, J., eds.: The 11th International Conference on Korean Linguistics, Seoul, Hankwuk Publishing (1998) 115–147
9. Copestake, A.: Implementing Typed Feature Structure Grammars. CSLI Publications, Stanford (2002)
10. Sung, W.K., Jang, M.G.: Seri test suites '95. In: Proceedings of the Conference on Hanguel and Korean Language Information Processing. (1997)

Unsupervised Named-Entity Recognition: Generating Gazetteers and Resolving Ambiguity

David Nadeau[1,2], Peter D. Turney[1], and Stan Matwin[2,3]

[1] Institute for Information Technology
National Research Council Canada
{david.nadeau, peter.turney}@nrc-cnrc.gc.ca
[2] School of Information Technology and Engineering, University of Ottawa
{dnadeau, stan}@site.uottawa.ca
[3] Institute for Computer Science, Polish Academy of Sciences

Abstract. In this paper, we propose a named-entity recognition (NER) system that addresses two major limitations frequently discussed in the field. First, the system requires no human intervention such as manually labeling training data or creating gazetteers. Second, the system can handle more than the three classical named-entity types (person, location, and organization). We describe the system's architecture and compare its performance with a supervised system. We experimentally evaluate the system on a standard corpus, with the three classical named-entity types, and also on a new corpus, with a new named-entity type (car brands).

1 Introduction

This paper builds on past work in unsupervised named-entity recognition (NER) by Collins and Singer [3] and Etzioni *et al.* [4]. Our goal is to create a system that can recognize named-entities in a given document without prior training (supervised learning) or manually constructed gazetteers. (We use the term *gazetteer* interchangeably with the term *named-entity list*.)

Collins and Singer's [3] system exploits a large corpus to create a generic list of proper names (named-entities of arbitrary and unknown types). Proper names are collected by looking for syntactic patterns with precise properties. For instance, a proper name is a sequence of consecutive words, within a noun phrase, that are tagged as NNP or NNPS by a part-of-speech tagger and in which the last word is identified as the head of the noun phrase. Like Collins and Singer, we use a large corpus to create lists of named-entities, but we present a technique that can exploit diverse types of text, including text without proper grammatical sentences, such as tables and lists (marked up with HTML).

Etzioni *et al.* [4] refer to their algorithm as a named-entity *extraction* system. It is not intended for named-entity *recognition*. In other words, it is used to create large lists of named-entities, but it is not designed for resolving ambiguity in a given document. The distinction between these tasks is important. It might seem that having a list of entities in hand makes NER trivial. One can extract city names from a given document by merely searching in the document for each city name in a city list.

L. Lamontagne and M. Marchand (Eds.): Canadian AI 2006, LNAI 4013, pp. 266–277, 2006.
© Springer-Verlag Berlin Heidelberg 2006

However, this strategy often fails because of ambiguity. For example, consider the words "It" (a city in Mississippi State and a pronoun) and "Jobs" (a person's surname and a common noun). The task addressed by Etzioni *et al.* could be called *automatic gazetteer generation*. Without ambiguity resolution, their system cannot perform robust, accurate NER. This claim is supported by the experiments we present in Section 3.

In this paper, we propose a named-entity recognition system that combines named-entity extraction (inspired by Etzioni *et al.*[4]) with a simple form of named-entity disambiguation. We use some simple yet highly effective heuristics, based on the work of Mikheev [9], Petasis *et al.* [13], and Palmer and Day [12], to perform named-entity disambiguation. We compare the performance of our unsupervised system with that of a basic supervised system, using the MUC 7 NER corpus [1]. We also show that our technique is general enough to be applied to other named-entity types, such as car brands, or bridge names. To support this claim, we include an experiment with car brands.

The paper is divided as follows. First, we present the system architecture in Section 2. Then, we compare its performance with a supervised baseline system on the MUC 7 NER corpus in Section 3. Next, we show that the system can handle other type of entities, in addition to the classic three (person, location, and organization), in Section 4. We discuss the degree of supervision in Section 5. We conclude in Section 6 by arguing that our system advances the state-of-the-art of NER by avoiding the need for supervision and by handling novel types of named-entities. The system's source code is available under the GPL license at http://balie.sourceforge.net.

2 Unsupervised Named-Entity Recognition System

The system is made of two modules. The first one is used to create large gazetteers of entities, such as a list of cities. The second module uses simple heuristics to identify and classify entities in the context of a given document (i.e., entity disambiguation).

2.1 Generating Gazetteers

The task of automatically generating lists of entities has been investigated by several researchers. In Hearst [6], lexical patterns are studied that can be used to identify nouns from the same semantic class. For instance, a noun phrase that follows the pattern "the city of" is usually a city. In Riloff and Jones [14], a small set of lexical patterns and a small set of entities are grown using mutual bootstrapping. Finally, Lin and Pantel [7] show how to create large clusters of semantically related words using an unsupervised technique. Their idea is based on examining words with similar syntactic dependency relationships. They show they can induce semantic classes such as car brands, drugs, and provinces. However, their technique does not discover the labels of the semantic classes, which is a common limitation of clustering techniques.

The algorithm of Etzioni *et al.* [4] outperforms all previous methods for the task of creating a large list for a given type of entity or semantic class; the task of automatic gazetteer generation. Nadeau [11] shows that it is possible to create accurate lists of cities and car brands in an unsupervised manner, limiting the supervision to a seed of four examples. In the remainder of this section, we summarize how to generate a list of thousands of cities from a seed of a few examples, in two steps (repeated if necessary).

2.1.1 Retrieve Pages with Seed

The first step is information retrieval from the Web. A query is created by conjoining a seed of k manually generated entities (e.g., "Montreal" AND "Boston" AND "Paris" AND "Mexico City"). In our experience, when k is set to 4 (as suggested by Etzioni *et al.* [4]) and the seed entities are common city names, the query typically retrieves Web pages that contain many names of cities, in addition to the seed names. The basic idea of the algorithm is to extract these additional city names from each retrieved Web page.

The same strategy can be applied to person names, company names, car brands, and many other types of entities. Although it is outside of the scope of this paper, we should mention that we successfully applied this technique to more than 50 named-entity types.

2.1.2 Apply Web Page Wrapper

A Web page wrapper is a rule-based system that identifies the location of specific types of information within a Web page. For example, a wrapper for identifying the location of news headers on the Web site *radio-canada.ca* might contain the rule, "A header is an HTML node of type <a>, with text length between 10 and 30 characters, in a table of depth 5 and with at least 3 other nodes in the page that satisfy the same rule."

The gazetteer generation algorithm proceeds by learning rules that identify the locations of positive examples. For each page found in 2.1.1, a Web page wrapper is trained on the k positive examples that are known to appear in the page, but only if they are strictly contained in an HTML node (e.g., <td> Boston </td>) or surrounded by a small amount of text inside an HTML node (e.g., <td> Boston hotel </td>). The remaining HTML nodes in the page are treated as if they were negative examples, but we only include in the negative set the nodes with the same HTML tags as the positive examples [11]. For instance, if the k positive nodes are tagged as bold (i.e., "<b>"), then the negative examples will be restricted to the remaining bold text in the Web page. The Web page wrapper we used is similar to Cohen and Fan's [2] wrapper, in terms of the learning algorithm and the feature vector.

As described above, Web page wrapping is a classification problem. A supervised learning algorithm is used to classify unknown entities in the current Web page. In this application, the training set and the testing set are the same. The learning algorithm is trained on the given Web page and then the learned model is applied to reclassify the text in the same Web page. The idea is to learn rules, during training, that identify the locations of the known entities (the seed entities) and can be applied, during testing, to identify entities appearing in similar contexts, which may be further positive examples.

Two main problems make this task difficult. First, there is noise in the class labels in the training data, because everything except the seed words are initially labeled as negative. If the page contains more than k entities of the desired type, the very nodes we want to extract were labeled as negative. The second problem is the class imbalance in the data. Along with the k positive examples, there are usually hundreds or thousands of negative examples. These two problems are handled by noise filtering and cost-sensitive classification, respectively.

At this point, our technique goes beyond the system of Etzioni *et al.* [4], which uses a simple Web page wrapper, consisting of hand-crafted rules. To handle the problem of noise in the class labels, we use a filtering approach inspired by Zhu *et al.* [16]. The noise filtering strategy is to simply remove any instance similar to a positive instance. We say that two nodes are similar when their feature vectors are identical, except for the text length feature. (Refer to Cohen and Fan [2] for a description of the Web page wrapper's features.) Using this filter, an average of 42% of the examples that are initially labeled as negative are removed from the training set. These examples are left in the (unlabeled) testing set. When the trained model is later applied to the testing set, some of the removed examples may be classified as positive and some may be classified as negative.

To handle the class imbalance problem, we use a cost-sensitive supervised learning system. Using the original unbalanced dataset, the wrapper is almost incapable of extracting new entities. It mainly guesses the majority class (negative) and only extracts the initial seed from Web pages. To discourage the learning algorithm from using the trivial solution of always guessing the majority class, a high cost is assigned to misclassification errors in which a positive example is classified as negative. This cost-sensitive approach over-samples the positive examples to rebalance the dataset. This rebalancing must be done for each individual Web page, to take into account the imbalance ratio of each wrapper. Rebalancing is performed automatically, by randomly choosing HTML nodes to add to the dataset, up to the desired ratio of positive to negative examples.

Past research suggests that supervised learning algorithms work best when the ratio is near 1:1 [8]. We hypothesized that the wrapper would work best when we rebalanced the dataset by duplicating positive instances until the ratio reached 1:1. To verify this hypothesis, we studied the behavior of the wrapper with different ratios on a set of 40 Web pages. As expected, we found that the wrapper performance is optimal when the ratio is 1:1. We therefore use this ratio in the experiments in Sections 3 and 4.

2.1.3   Repeat

The two steps above (2.2.1, 2.2.2) are repeated as needed. Each iteration brings new entities that are added to the final gazetteer. At each iteration, k new randomly chosen entities are used to refresh the seed for the system. Entities are chosen from the gazetteer under construction. Preference is given to seed entities that are less likely to be noise, such as those appearing in multiple Web pages.

2.2   Resolving Ambiguity

The *list lookup strategy* is the method of performing NER by scanning through a given input document, looking for terms that match a list entry. The list lookup strategy suffers from three main problems: (1) entity-noun ambiguity errors, (2) entity boundary detection errors, and (3) entity-entity ambiguity errors. Due to these three problems, the gazetteer generating module presented in Section 2.1 is not adequate, by itself, for reliable named-entity recognition. We found heuristics in the literature to tackle each of these problems.

2.2.1 Entity-Noun Ambiguity

Entity-noun ambiguity occurs when an entity is the homograph of a noun. The plural word "jobs" and the surname "Jobs" is an example of this problem. To avoid this problem, Mikheev [9] proposes the following heuristic: In a given document, assume that a word or phrase with initial capitals (e.g., "Jobs") is a named-entity, unless (1) it sometimes appears in the document without initial capitals (e.g., "jobs"), (2) it only appears at the start of a sentence or at the start of a quotation (e.g., "Jobs that pay well are often boring."), or (3) it only appears inside a sentence in which all words with more than three characters start with a capital letter (e.g., a title or section heading).

2.2.2 Entity Boundary Detection

A common problem with the list lookup strategy is errors in recognizing where a named-entity begins and ends in a document (e.g., finding only "Boston" in "Boston White Sox"). This can happen when a named-entity is composed of two or more words (e.g., "Jean Smith") that are each listed separately (e.g., "Jean" as a first name and "Smith" as a last name). It can also happen when an entity is surrounded by unknown capitalized words (e.g., "New York Times" as an organization followed by "News Service" as an unlisted string). Palmer and Day [12] propose the longest match strategy for these cases. Accordingly, we merge all consecutive entities of the same type and every entity with any adjacent capitalized words. We did not, however, merge consecutive entities of different types, since we would not have known the resulting type.

The rule above is general enough to be applied independently of the entity type. We found that other merging rules could improve the precision of our system, such as "create a new entity of type organization by merging a location followed by an organization". However, we avoided rules like this, because we believe that this type of manual rule engineering results in brittle, fragile systems that do not generalize well to new data. Our goal is to make a robust, portable, general-purpose NER system, with minimal embedded domain knowledge.

2.2.3 Entity-Entity Ambiguity

Entity-entity ambiguity occurs when the string standing for a named-entity belongs to more than one type. For instance, if a document contains the named-entity "France", it could be either the name of a person or the name of a country. For this problem, Petasis et al. [13], among others, propose that at least one occurrence of the named-entity should appear in a context where the correct type is clearly evident. For example, in the context "Dr. France", it is clear that "France" is the name of a person.

We could have used cues, such as professional titles (e.g., farmer), organizational designators (e.g., Corp.), personal prefixes (e.g., Mr.) and personal suffixes (e.g., Jr.), but as discussed in the preceding section, we avoided this kind of manual rule engineering.

Definitions.

D = a given input document.

$A = \{a_1,...,a_n\}$ = the set of all sets of aliases in the document D.

$a_i = \{e_1,...,e_m\}$ = a set of aliases = a set of different entity instances, referring to the same actual entity in the world.

$e = \langle D, s, p \rangle$ = a unique instance of a named-entity, consisting of a string s in document D at position p.

overlap(e_i, e_j) = a Boolean function; returns **true** when $e_i = \langle D, s_i, p_i \rangle$ and $e_j = \langle D, s_j, p_j \rangle$ and the strings s_i and s_j share at least one word with more than three characters; returns **false** otherwise.

Algorithm.

Let $A = \{\}$.

For each instance of a named-entity e in document D:

If there is exactly one alias set a_i with a member e_j such that overlap(e, e_j), then modify A by adding e to a_i.

If there are two or more alias sets a_i, a_j with members e_k, e_l such that overlap(e, e_k) and overlap(e, e_l), then modify A by creating a new alias group a_p that is the union of a_i, a_j, and $\{e\}$, add a_p to A, and remove a_i and a_j from A.

Otherwise, create a new alias set a_q, consisting of $\{e\}$, and add a_q to A.

Fig. 1. Simple alias resolution algorithm

Instead, we applied a simple alias resolution algorithm, presented in Figure 1. When an ambiguous entity is found, its aliases are used in two ways. First, if a member of an alias set is unambiguous, it can be used to resolve the whole set. For instance, "Atlantic ocean" is clearly a location but "Atlantic" can be either a location or an organization. If both belong to the same alias set, then we assume that the whole set is of type *location*. A second way to use the alias resolution is to include unknown words in the model. Unknown words are typically introduced by the heuristic in Section 2.2.2. If an entity (e.g., "Steve Hill") is formed from a known entity (e.g., "Steve") and an unknown word (e.g., "Hill"), we allow occurrences of this unknown word to be added in the alias group.

3   Evaluation with the MUC-7 Enamex Corpus

In the Message Understanding Conferences (MUC), the Named-Entity Recognition (NER) track focuses on the three classical types of named-entities: person, location, and organization. These three types of named-entities are collectively called *Enamex*.

In this section, we compare the performance of our system with a baseline supervised system, using the Enamex corpus from MUC-7. For this experiment, a portion of the corpus is given to the supervised system in order to train it. Our unsupervised system simply ignores this portion of corpus.

The same baseline experiment was conducted on MUC-6 and MUC-7 by Palmer and Day [12] and Mikheev et al. [10] respectively. Their systems work as follows. A training corpus is read and the tagged entities are extracted and listed. Given a testing corpus, the lists are used in a simple lookup strategy, so that any string that matches a list entry is classified accordingly.

Table 1 presents the results of Mikheev on MUC-7 (in the "Learned lists" columns). There is also a comparison with a system that uses hand-made lists of common entities (in the "Common lists" columns). The "Combined lists" columns are based on a combination of both approaches. These results are from Mikheev's published experiments [10].

In Table 1, "re" is the recall, "pr" is the precision, and "f" is the f-measure (the harmonic mean of precision and recall), expressed as percentages.

Table 1. Results of a supervised system on MUC-7

	Learned lists			Common lists			Combined lists		
	re	Pr	f	re	pr	f	re	pr	f
organization	49	75	59	3	51	6	50	72	59
person	26	92	41	31	81	45	47	85	61
location	76	93	84	74	94	83	86	90	88

For the purpose of comparison, we ran our system on MUC-7 using gazetteers that we generated as described in Section 2.1. We generated gazetteers for some of the subtypes of named-entities given by Sekine [15]. The generated gazetteers are described in Table 2. We also used a special list of the months of the year, because we noticed they were an abnormally important source of noise on the development (dry run) set.[1] Many months are also valid as personal first names.

List size depends on the performance of the Web page wrapper at extracting entities. Nadeau [11] showed that lists have a precision of at least 90%. We did not restrict the web mining to a specific geographic region and we did not enforce strict conditions for the list elements. As a result, the "state / province" list contains elements from around the world (not only Canada and the U.S.) and the "first name" list contains a multitude of compound first names, although our algorithm is designed to capture them by merging sequences of first names, as explained in Section 2.2.2.

---

[1] It can be argued that the month list is a form of manual rule engineering, contrary to the principles discussed in Section 2.2.2. We decided to use it because most of the noise was clearly corpus-dependent, since each article contains a date header. For results without the month list, subtract 5% from the precision for the person type.

Table 2. Type and size of gazetteers built using Web page wrapper

Gazetteer	Size
Location: city	14,977
Location: state / province	1,587
Location: continent / country / island	781
Location: waterform	541
Location: astral body	85
Organization: private companies	20,498
Organization: public services	364
Organization: schools	3,387
Person: first names	35,102
Person: last names	3,175
Person: full names	3,791
Counter-examples: months	12

Table 3 shows the result of a pure list lookup strategy, based on our generated gazetteers (in the "Generated lists" columns). For comparison, Table 3 also shows the best supervised results from Table 1 (in the "Mikheev combined lists" columns). The results we report in Tables 1, 3, 4, and 5 are all based on the held-out formal corpus of MUC-7.

Table 3. Supervised list creation vs. unsupervised list creation techniques

	Mikheev combined lists			Generated lists		
	Re	pr	f	re	pr	f
organization	50	72	59	70	52	60
person	47	85	61	59	20	30
location	86	90	88	83	31	45

We believe the comparison in Table 3 gives a good sense of the characteristics of both approaches. The supervised approach is quite precise but its recall is lower, since it cannot handle rare entities. The unsupervised approach benefits from large gazetteers, which enable higher recall at the cost of lower precision.

The case of locations is interesting. There is evidence that there is a substantial vocabulary transfer between the training data and the testing data, which allows the supervised method to have an excellent recall on the unseen texts. Mikheev's lists get a high recall with a list of only 770 locations. The supervised method benefits from highly repetitive location names in the MUC corpus.

These results are slightly misleading. The MUC scoring software that produces these measures allows partial matching. That means, if a system tags the expression "Virgin Atlantic" when the official annotated key is "Virgin Atlantic Group", it will be credited with a success. In Table 4, we provide another view of the system's performance, which may be less misleading. Table 4 gives, for our system, the precision and recall of all entity types at the level of *text*; that is, the performance on finding exact string matches.

Table 4. Generated list performance on text matching

	Generated lists		
	re	pr	f
text	61	29	39

The next step in our evaluation consists in adding the heuristics presented in Sections 2.2.1 to 2.2.3. These heuristics are designed to be unsupervised; that is, they require no training (unlike n-gram contexts, for example) and they are not deduced from our domain knowledge about a specific entity type. Table 5 shows the contribution of each heuristic. The "Generated lists" columns are copied from Tables 3 and 4, to show the performance of the list lookup strategy without disambiguation (i.e., Section 2.1 without Section 2.2).

Table 5. Performance of heuristics to resolve named-entity ambiguity

	Generated lists			H1 (Entity-noun ambiguity)			H1 + H2 (Entity boundary)			H1 + H2 + H3 (Entity-entity ambiguity)		
	re	pr	f	re	pr	f	re	pr	f	re	pr	f
org.	70	52	60	69	73	71	69	74	71	71	75	73
per.	59	20	30	58	53	55	66	63	64	83	71	77
loc.	83	31	45	82	69	75	81	77	79	80	77	78
text	61	29	39	61	57	59	72	72	72	74	72	73

The contribution of each heuristic (H1, H2, H3) is additive. H1 (Section 2.2.1) procures a dramatic improvement in precision with negligible loss of recall. The main source of ambiguity is entity-noun homographs such as "jobs", "gates", and "bush".

Heuristic H2 (Section 2.2.2) gives small gains in precision and recall of individual entity types (the first three rows in Table 5). As explained, these scores are misleading because they count partial matches and thus these scores are not sensitive to the boundary detection errors that are corrected by H2. However, the performance of text matching is greatly improved (last row in Table 5). We noticed that most corrected boundaries are attributable to person entities composed of a known first name and an unlisted capitalized string standing, presumably, for the surname.

H3 (Section 2.2.3) mainly increases precision and recall for named-entities of the person type, due to the the alias resolution algorithm. An occurence of a full person name is usually unambiguous and thus can help with annotating isolated surnames, which are often either ambiguous (confused with organization names) or simply unlisted strings.

4   Evaluation with Car Brands

There are many more types of named-entities than the three classical types in Enamex. Sekine *et al.* [15] propose a hierarchy of 200 types of named-entities. Evans

[5] proposes a framework to handle such wide variety. His approach is based on lexical patterns, inspired by Hearst [6]. He paired this technique with a heuristic for handling ambiguity in capitalized words. Our system is similar, but it is based on a method proven to give better recall at finding entities [4].

In this section, we show how the system performs on the task of recognizing car brands. Intuitively, it seems that this type is easier to handle than a type such as persons that has an almost infinite extension. However, recognizing car brands poses many difficulties. Car brands can be confused with common nouns (e.g., Focus, Rendez-Vous, Matrix, Aviator) and with company names (e.g., "Ford" versus "Ford Motor Company"). Another difficulty is the fact that new car brands are created every year, so keeping a gazetteer of car brands up-to-date is challenging.

We created a small pilot corpus composed of news specifically about cars from some popular news feeds (CanWest, National Post, and The Associated Press). We use eight documents, for a total of 5,570 words and 196 occurrences of car brands.

The Web-page wrapper technique was used to generate a list of 5,701 car brands and the heuristics of sections 2.2.1 to 2.2.3 were applied without any modifications. Table 6 reports the results.

Table 6. System performance for car brand recognition

	Generated list			H1, H2 and H3		
	Re	pr	f	re	pr	f
cars	86	42	56	85	88	86
text	71	34	46	79	83	81

The performance on this task is comparable to the Enamex task. Without ambiguity resolution (in the "Generated list" columns), the precision is low, typically under 50%. This is the impact of frequent and ambiguous words like "will" (Toyota Will) and noise in our list (e.g., new, car, fuel). The ambiguity resolution algorithms (in the "H1, H2, and H3" columns) raise the precision above 80%. The remaining recall errors are due to rare car brands (e.g., "BMW X5 4.8is" or "Ford Edge"). The remaining precision errors are due to organization-car ambiguity (e.g., "National" as in "National Post" versus "Chevrolet National") and noise in the list (e.g., Other, SUV). We believe that the good performance of gazetteer generation combined with ambiguity resolution on an entirely new domain emphasizes their domain-independent character and shows the strength of the unsupervised approach.

5 Supervised Versus Unsupervised

We describe our system as unsupervised, but the distinction between supervised and unsupervised systems is not always clear. In some systems that are apparently unsupervised, it could be argued that the human labour of generating labeled training data has merely been shifted to embedding clever rules and heuristics in the system.

In our gazetteer generator (Section 2.1), the supervision is limited to a seed of four entities per list Less than four examples results in lower precision and more than four examples results in lower recall [4]. In our ambiguity resolver (Section 2.2), we attempt to minimize the use of domain knowledge of specific entity types. Our system exploits human-generated HTML markup in Web pages to generate gazetteers. However, because Web pages are available in such a quantity and because the creation of Web pages is now intrinsic to the workflow of most organization and individuals, we believe this annotated data comes at a negligible cost. For these reasons, we believe it is reasonable to describe our system as unsupervised.

6   Conclusion

In this paper, we presented a named-entity recognition system that advances the state-of-the-art of NER by avoiding the need for supervision and by handling novel types of named-entities. In a comparison on the MUC corpus, our system outperforms a baseline supervised system but it is still not competitive with more complex supervised systems. There are (fortunately) many ways to improve our model. One interesting way would be to generate gazetteers for a multitude of named-entity types (e.g., all 200 of Sekine's types) and use list intersection as an indicator of ambiguity. This idea would not resolve the ambiguity itself but would clearly identify where to invest further efforts.

Acknowledgements

We would like to thank Caroline Barrière, who provided us with helpful comments on an earlier version of this work. Support of the Natural Sciences and Engineering Research Council and of the Communications and Information Technology division of the Ontario Centres of Excellence is gratefully acknowledged.

References

1. Chinchor, N. (1998) MUC-7 Named Entity Task Definition, version 3.5. *Proc. of the Seventh Message Understanding Conference.*
2. Cohen, W. and Fan, W. (1999) Learning Page-Independent Heuristics for Extracting Data from Web Page, *Proc. of the International World Wide Web Conference.*
3. Collins M. and Singer, Y. (1999) Unsupervised Models for Named Entity Classification. *Proc. of the Joint SIGDAT Conference on Empirical Methods in Natural Language Processing and Very Large Corpora.*
4. Etzioni, O., Cafarella, M., Downey, D., Popescu, A.-M., Shaked, T., Soderland, S., Weld, D. S. and Yates, A. (2005) Unsupervised Named-Entity Extraction from the Web: An Experimental Study. *Artificial Intelligence*, 165, pp. 91-134.
5. Evans, R. (2003) A Framework for Named Entity Recognition in the Open Domain. *Proc. Recent Advances in Natural Language Processing.*
6. Hearst, M. (1992) Automatic Acquisition of Hyponyms from Large Text Corpora. *Proc. of International Conference on Computational Linguistics.*
7. Lin, D. and Pantel, P. (2001) Induction of Semantic Classes from Natural Language Text. *Proc. of ACM SIGKDD Conference on Knowledge Discovery and Data Mining.*
8. Ling, C., and Li, C. (1998). Data Mining for Direct Marketing: Problems and Solutions. *Proc. International Conference on Knowledge Discovery and Data Mining.*

9. Mikheev, A. (1999) A Knowledge-free Method for Capitalized Word Disambiguation. *Proc. Conference of Association for Computational Linguistics.*
10. Mikheev, A., Moens, M. and Grover, C. (1999) Named Entity Recognition without Gazetteers. *Proc. Conference of European Chapter of the Association for Computational Linguistics.*
11. Nadeau, D. (2005) Création de surcouche de documents hypertextes et traitement du langage naturel, Proc. *Computational Linguistics in the North-East.*
12. Palmer, D. D. and Day, D. S. (1997) A Statistical Profile of the Named Entity Task. *Proc. ACL Conference for Applied Natural Language Processing.*
13. Petasis, G., Vichot, F., Wolinski, F., Paliouras, G., Karkaletsis, V. and Spyropoulos, C. D. (2001) Using Machine Learning to Maintain Rule-based Named-Entity Recognition and Classification Systems. *Proc. Conference of Association for Computational Linguistics.*
14. Riloff, E. and Jones, R (1999) Learning Dictionaries for Information Extraction using Multi-level Bootstrapping. *Proc. of National Conference on Artificial Intelligence.*
15. Sekine, S., Sudo, K., Nobata, C. (2002) Extended Named Entity Hierarchy, *Proc. of the Language Resource and Evaluation Conference.*
16. Zhu, X., Wu, X. and Chen Q. (2003) Eliminating Class Noise in Large Data-Sets, *Proc. of the International Conference on Machine Learning.*

Unsupervised Labeling of Noun Clusters

Theresa Jickels and Grzegorz Kondrak

Department of Computing Science,
University of Alberta,
Edmonton, AB, T6G 2E8, Canada
{theresa, kondrak}@cs.ualberta.ca
http://www.cs.ualberta.ca/~kondrak

Abstract. Semantic knowledge is important in many areas of natural language processing. We propose a new unsupervised learning algorithm to annotate groups of nouns with hypernym labels. Several variations of the algorithm are presented, including a method that utilizes semantic information from WordNet. The algorithm's results are compared against an independently-developed labeling method. The evaluation is performed using labels assigned to noun clusters by several participants of a specially designed human study.

1 Introduction

Ontologies, also known as semantic networks and lexical databases, are important resources in natural language processing. These resources all encode a specific type of semantic knowledge. Constructing them manually is expensive and time-consuming. In this paper, we focus on the task of automatic construction of ontologies from large corpora of texts.

A well-known example of a hand-built ontology is WordNet [8]. Lexical entries in WordNet are organized into comprehensive networks of synonym sets (*synsets*). Words that have more than one meaning (polysemous words) may participate in several different synsets. The synsets are linked by various *lexical relations*. The principal lexical relation in WordNet is *hypernymy*, the *is-a* relation between nouns. For example, *bird* is a hypernym of *robin*. Hyponymy is the inverse of hypernymy. The hypernymy/hyponymy links form the backbone of the noun hierarchy. They link each synset to its immediately more general and more specific synsets. A chain of hypernymy links can be traversed from each synset to one of the eleven abstract concepts that are at the top of the hierarchy.

The labeling of groups of nouns can be seen as automatic identification of hyponymy relations. We do not differentiate between instances and hyponyms. For example, the set of terms (*table, chair, desk, sofa, dresser, bookcase*) can be labeled with the term *furniture*. For a group of movie titles such as (*Deep Impact, Armageddon, Godzilla, Titanic, Truman Show*), possible labels include *movie*, or *film*. By providing a label for a set of terms, we implicitly define a number of hypernymy relations between the label and the terms in the set.

L. Lamontagne and M. Marchand (Eds.): Canadian AI 2006, LNAI 4013, pp. 278–287, 2006.
© Springer-Verlag Berlin Heidelberg 2006

We propose an unsupervised algorithm for the purpose of labeling groups of nouns. It addresses a specific subset of the problem of automatic gathering of semantic relations. Since the algorithm is unsupervised, it can produce labels quickly, and without the prohibitive cost of human involvement in annotating training data.

The principal features that we use for labeling noun clusters are dependency relations, which are syntactic relationships between words in a sentence. For example, from the sentence *"Smith, the chairman, is a workaholic"*, we can extract the nominal *subject* relation (*N:subj:N*) between *Smith* and *workaholic*, and the *appositive* relation (*N:appo:N*) between *Smith* and *chairman*. The presence or lack of a minus sign indicates whether the head of the relationship is the right or left noun. For example, the above appositive relation is denoted as a *N:appo:N* relation in the context of the word *Smith*, and a *-N:appo:N* relation in the context of the word *chairman*. We use dependency relations extracted from a corpus by a dependency parser Minipar [6] to build clusters of nouns.

The noun clusters that are labeled by our algorithm are constructed using the *Clustering by Committee* method [10]. The basic idea behind the method is to select a small number of representative terms (a *committee*) that form the core of each cluster. This approach prevents polysemous concepts from interfering with the cluster creation. The algorithm can be summarized as follows. For each element, a small number of its closest neighbors are identified. Next, the algorithm defines as many cluster *committees* as possible, but discards those that are too similar to other committees. Finally, each element in the data is assigned to its most similar cluster.

The applications of noun labeling include question answering and named entity classification. In generating an answer to a question such as "Who was the first prime minister of Canada?", it may be very helpful to know that there exist a hypernymy relationship between *Sir John A. Macdonald* and *prime minister*. Given the named entity *Carnegie Mellon*, it is more useful to classify it specifically as a *university* than as an *organization*.

The organization of this paper is as follows. Section 2 is devoted to the related work. Section 3 introduces our approach to unsupervised labeling of noun clusters. Section 4 contains description of the experiments and their results. Section 5 concludes the paper.

2   Related Work

In this section, we discuss several techniques that have been used in the automatic gathering of semantic relations, including the method of Pantel and Ravichandran [9] which addresses virtually the same task as this paper.

Chodorow et al. [4] extract hypernyms from the definitions of nouns in machine readable dictionaries with the goal of producing a semantic network. Typically, the head of the definition phrase is taken to be the hypernym of the noun. For example, if a definition of *golden retriever* is *a golden-haired dog*, then *dog* would be identified as the hypernym of *golden retriever*. Heuristic rules are used to extract the head of the definition, and then the information is worked into a hierarchical structure, with substantial human involvement.

A later paper by Ide and Veronis [5], examines the progress made with these methods, with the conclusion that a dictionary by itself is not enough to automatically produce the correct results. This conclusion is attributed to the varied structure in the dictionary definitions, missing information, and the fact that different dictionaries produce markedly different hierarchies.

Hearst [3] extracts hypernymy relations directly from text by the means of syntactic patterns. For instance, a phrase such as *dolls, tops and other toys* yields *toy* as a hypernym of *doll*. She proposed six different patterns, but used only one of them for the evaluation against WordNet. Out of 152 hypernymy relations extracted from an encyclopedia using the pattern, 106 had both terms present in WordNet, including 61 in existing hypernymy relations.

Fleischman and Hovy [2] propose a feature-based system for classifying names into a few categories, such as *politician, businessman* and *entertainer*. Features like previous and following n-grams, topic features, and WordNet features were used to train several classifiers on a semi-automatically produced training set. The classifiers included decision trees, neural networks, SVM, and a Naive Bayes classifier. The best results were obtained with the decision tree method, which achieved 70.4% accuracy.

Caraballo [1] aims at automatically creating a hierarchical semantic lexicon from a body of text. The hierarchy consists of noun clusters grouped under their hypernyms. First, groups of similar nouns are extracted from a few syntactic relationships, such as conjunctions and appositives. The hypernyms are added during the latter part of the construction. Clustering the nouns with a bottom-up method produces the general hierarchy, as similar nouns are placed under the same parent in a binary tree. The percentage of correct hypernyms ranged from 33% under a strict evaluation, to 60% under a lenient evaluation.

Independently of our work, Pantel and Ravichandran [9] proposed a method for automatically labeling the clusters produced by the *Clustering by Committee* method. Their method involves three stages. Stage 1 requires calculating two vectors for each word in the clusters: a frequency count vector, and a mutual information vector, which is discounted to reduce the effect of data sparseness. Stage 2 produces a committee for each cluster, with the goal of isolating the most representative members of the cluster. Stage 3 forms a signature for each cluster, derived from the feature vectors of the committee members. The candidate labels are selected by considering a set of four dependency relations, which the authors identified as the most important. The relative scores for possible labels are calculated using the pointwise mutual information values between the labels and the dependency relations.

Pantel and Ravichandran tested their method on 1432 noun clusters extracted from the Aquaint corpus. The results of automatic labeling were evaluated by human judges. The top answer was judged correct 72% of the time. Among the top five answers, a correct label was present in 85.6% of the cases. No name was produced for 21 (1.5%) of the clusters.

3   Cluster Labeling

Our new algorithm for cluster labeling is an unsupervised learning method, which removes the need for the time-consuming manual annotation of the data. The idea is to utilize the labels that are frequently present in the aggregate data.

Consider Table 1, which shows a cluster containing horse-race names taken from the dependency data. We refer to terms that occur in the dependency relations as *feature words*. A term is said to be a feature word of a feature if it is listed as an instance of that feature. It turns out that good labels for clusters, such as *race* in this case, are often present among feature words in their dependency data. However, most of the feature words are not appropriate as labels, leaving the problem of how to identify the good labels.

Table 1. Sample dependency data for a noun group

Cluster	Features	Feature words
Preakness Stakes	**-N:before:N** 23	
Preakness		day 19
Belmont Stakes		start 2
Travers		race 2
Santa Anita Derby	**-N:subj:N** 80	
Kentucky Derby		race 51
Florida Derby		run 7
		goal 7
		event 8
		victory 3
		start 2
		history 2
	⋮	⋮

Our algorithm learns weights for each feature in order to pick out the good labels from the rest of the data. It is not merely a case of choosing the most common feature or the most frequently occurring feature word. Our solution is to assign variable weights to features, which reflect their relative importance with respect to the likelihood of containing appropriate cluster labels. We refer to these weights as *feature scores*. Each iteration of the algorithm redistributes the feature scores to better represent their values in relation to possible labels. As a feature score increases (or decreases) through iterations, so do the label scores of the feature words associated with that feature. As a result, the feature scores of important features are amplified by the presence of good labels in that feature, while unimportant features are given low scores. Consequently, the good labels are more likely to be present in features with high scores than in features with low scores.

3.1   The Algorithm

The input to our unsupervised labeling algorithm is the dependency data of the clusters, and the list of features. The dependency data are extracted with the LaTaT package [7]. The output of the training process is a feature score for each feature f in the feature set F. The labeling is performed on the basis of the feature scores computed by the algorithm. The final output is a ranked list of possible labels for each cluster.

---

1) **For** each f in F **do**
2) $FS(f):=1$
    end for
3) **Repeat**
4)   **For** each f in F **do**
5) $FS'(f):=0$
            end for
6)   **For** each Cluster in the training set **do**
7)   **For** each feature word a in the cluster **do**
8) $LS(a):=\sum_{\substack{f\in F \\ C(f,a)}} FS(f)$

            end for
9)   **For** each f in F **do**
10) $FS'(f):=FS'(f)+\sum_{C(f,a)}LS(a)$

            end for
    end for
11) $\delta:=\sum_{f\in F}|FS'(f)b-FS(f)|$
12)   **For** each f in F **do**
13) $FS(f):=\dfrac{|F|}{\sum_{f\in F}FS'(f)}FS'(f)$

    end for
14) **Until** $\delta=0$
15) **For** each Cluster in the testing set **do**
16)   Label:= $Max_{a}\{LS(a):=\sum_{\substack{f\in F \\ C(f,a)}}FS(f)\}$

17)   **Print** Label
    end for

Fig. 1. The cluster labeling algorithm

The algorithm is shown in Figure 1. First, the feature scores $FS(f)$ are initialized (lines 1–2). The main loop (lines 3–14) encompasses the learning process. During an iteration, the label scores $LS(a)$ for each feature word are calculated by summing the scores of the features in which the feature word occurs (lines 7–8). (The predicate $C(f,a)$ is true if and only if the feature f has a as a feature word.) For each feature, a temporary score ($FS'(f)$) accumulates the label scores of each feature word in that feature (lines 9–10). After each cluster has had the values calculated, the feature scores of each feature are replaced with the normalized temporary score (lines 12–13). The iterative learning process continues until the feature scores converge. In principle, a threshold might be set for convergence, but in practice the values for the feature scores have always converged, so the algorithm stops when the values of the feature scores stop changing. The feature word with the maximum sum of feature scores is selected as the final cluster label (lines 15-17).

3.2   Variations on the Basic Method

The algorithm described in the previous section to automatically assigns weights to all features for the purpose of selecting labels. We also experimented with methods that use fixed subsets of features with equal weights. The baseline approach is to use all the available features. The second set, referred to as Answer Distribution Features (ADF), contains four features and their complements that we identified as the most important on the basis of the analysis of our development set. The final set, referred to as PRF, is composed of the four features selected by Pantel and Ravichandran [9] in their labeling method. The ADF and PRF feature sets are shown in Table 2.

Table 2. The feature subsets used in the experiments

The ADF subset:	-N:appo:N, -N:subj:N, -N:conj:N, -N:nn:N,
	N:appo:N, N:subj:N, N:conj:N, N:nn:N
The PRF subset:	N:appo:N, -N:subj:N, -N:like:N, -N:such as:N

WordNet is a useful source of hypernymy relations.[1] For all terms in a given cluster, we recursively collected all WordNet hypernyms up to the top of the hierarchy. Then, we intersected the set of hypernyms with the output of our learning algorithm. We refer to this combined approach as the intersection method.

We also experimented with two other methods of improving the accuracy of the algorithm: filtering out low-frequency feature words, and considering only clusters containing mostly names. However, in both cases, the accuracy gains on the development set did not translate into substantial improvements on the test set.

4   Experimental Setup and Results

The entire data consisted of 1088 clusters. We used the first one hundred clusters as the development set. The test set was constructed by randomly selecting one hundred clusters form the remaining data. The training set consisted of all available clusters, except the ones included in the test set.

---

[1] For accessing WordNet, version 2.0, we used the QueryData interface [11].

4.1   Evaluation

We conducted a study in order to produce the answer key to our test set, and to examine human performance on the task of classifying clusters. Eight participants were asked to come up with one or more labels for all clusters in the test set. without accessing any external resources nor conferring with other participants.

For example, for the set of terms {*din, noise, roar, sound, rumble, sonic boom, explosion, buzz, hum, noise level, cacophony, echo, drone, clatter, flash, loud noise, thunder, gunfire, whir*}, the participants of the study provided the following labels: *sound* (4 times), *noise* (2), *audio* (1), *decibel* (1), *level of noise* (1), *noise pollution* (1), and *can hear these* (1). For comparison, the algorithm described in Section 3 produces the following labels and scores: *sound* 113.4, *noise* 106.5, *light* 74.9, *rework* 70.6, *echo* 68.7, *all* 64.8, *scream* 63.4, *hiss* 63.4, *smoke* 63.4, *band* 63.4.

Several of the participants indicated that the labeling was quite difficult. The average number of labels given by a participant was .96 per cluster. Agreement between labels from different testers was at 42.8%. This was calculated as the average number of participants who agree on a label that is the result for the highest number of participants. In some instances the most common response was "no label". There were no instances where all the participants assigned the same label to a cluster, but there were several where no two participants gave the same label.[2]

The performance of various methods was measured by computing precision and recall against the labels provided by the participants of the study. A cluster label was considered correct if it was proposed by at least one of the participants. Precision was the percentage of generated labels that were correct. Recall was calculated as the percentage of clusters that were assigned at least one correct label. The maximum possible recall was 86%, because none of the human-proposed labels occurs in the dependency data for 14% of the clusters.

Our evaluation method is different from the one adopted by Pantel and Ravichandran [9]. They presented human evaluators with a list of possible labels that included the top five labels generated by their algorithm, one label proposed by an independent annotator, and up to five names extracted from WordNet. The evaluators were asked to judge the labels as correct, partially correct, or incorrect. In contrast, our evaluation approach did not restrict the choice of labels to a fixed list. In order to perform a fair comparison, we asked the authors of the other labeling algorithm to run it on our test set. The results are discussed in the following section.

4.2   The Test Set Results

Figure 2 shows the results of various methods on the test set. In most cases. the graph has data points corresponding to recall and precision for the following

---

[2] The complete cluster data and detailed results of the study are publicly available at http://www.cs.ualberta.ca/~kondrak

numbers of possible labels returned: 1, 2, 4, 8, 10, 14, 18, 20. The intersection between WordNet and our iterative training method is represented by data points for 1 and 5 labels returned, reflecting a small size of the majority of intersection sets. The results of Pantel and Ravichandran have data points for 1, 2, and 3 labels returned. The pure WordNet method, which produces an unordered set of hypernyms, is represented by a single data point.

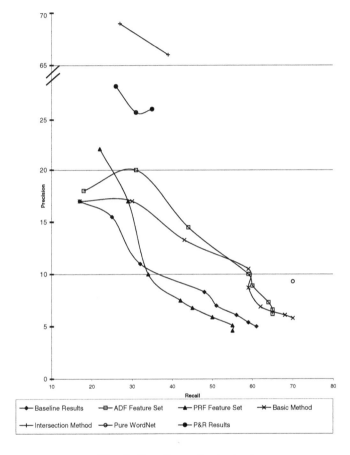

Fig. 2. Results on the test set

The algorithm presented in Section 3 performs substantially better than the baseline and the PRF feature set, except when only one label is returned. However, it does not do better than the ADF Feature Set. The pure WordNet method yields a high recall rate of 70%, combined with a low precision rate of 9.3%. Compared to our results, the algorithm of Pantel and Ravichandran, which makes extensive use of word mutual information vectors, appears to achieve similar recall, but with higher precision. However, our intersection method yields much higher precision at a comparable recall level.

4.3 Discussion

The overall accuracy of most of the approaches tested on the Test Set is quite low. The labels assigned by humans were often compound phrases, while the automated methods generate mostly single word labels. In addition, many of the human labels are too general, and some are plain wrong. While most names are easily labeled as referring to people by the human participants, the specific professions or roles that those people have in common are not so easily identified. There were frequent cases of an algorithmic method identifying more specific labels than the human participants. For example, in the case of a cluster including names *Tim Couch, Peyton Manning* and *Doug Pederson*, only one person gave a relatively specific label: *sportsman*. The remaining participants provided general labels such as *people*, an inaccurate one (*football*), or no label at all. In contrast, the top label generated by our algorithm was *quarterback*.

5 Conclusion

We proposed a new unsupervised learning algorithm for labeling clusters of nouns with hypernyms. The algorithm uses only the dependency information for the clusters, and does not require annotated data. We investigated several variations of the algorithm, including an intersection method that combined the results of the algorithm with information obtained by WordNet. For the purpose of an unbiased evaluation of various methods and a comparison with an independently proposed alternative approach, we conducted a human study that included several participants. The results of the experiments indicate that our algorithm does substantially better than the baseline, and that the combination of the algorithm with WordNet achieves over 65% precision.

Acknowledgments

Thanks to Dekang Lin for sharing the dependency data and the LaTaT package, to Patrick Pantel for running his system on our test set, and to the participants of the human study for devoting their valuable time to labeling the noun clusters. This research was supported by the Natural Sciences and Engineering Research Council of Canada.

References

1. Sharon A. Caraballo. 1999. Automatic construction of a hypernym-labeled noun hierarchy from text. In *Proceeding of the 37th annual meeting of the Association for Computational Linguistics (ACL-99)*, pages 120–126.
2. M. Fleischman and E. Hovy. 2002. Fine grained classification of named entities. In *19th International Conference on Computational Linguistics (COLING)*.
3. Marti A. Hearst. 1992. Automatic acquisition of hyponyms from large text corpora. In *14th International Conference on Computational Linguistics*.

4. Martin S. Chodorow; Roy J. Byrd; George E. Heidorn. 1985. Extracting semantic hierarchies from a large on-line dictionary. In *Proceeding of the 23rd annual meeting of the Association for Computational Linguistics (ACL-85)*, pages 299–304.
5. Nancy Ide and Jean Veronis. 1994. *Knowledge Extraction from Machine-Readable Dicitionaries: An Evaluation.*
6. Dekang Lin. 1998. Dependency-based evaluation of MINIPAR. In *Workshop on the Evaluation of Parsing Systems.*
7. Dekang Lin. 2001. Latat: Language and text analysis tools. In *Proceedings of Human Language Technology Conference*, pages 222–227.
8. George A. Miller, Richard Beckwith, Christiane Fellbaum, Derek Gross, and Katherine J. Miller. 1993. Introduction to wordnet: An on-line lexical database.
9. Patrick Pantel and Deepak Ravichandran. 2004. Automatically labeling semantic classes. In *Proceedings of Human Language Technology / North American chapter of the Association for Computational Linguistics (HLT/NAACL-04)*, pages 321–328.
10. Patrick Pantel. 2003. *Clustering by Committee.* Department of Computing Science, University of Alberta.
11. Jason Rennie. 2000. Wordnet::querydata: a Perl module for accessing the WordNet database. http://www.ai.mit.edu/people/jrennie/WordNet.

Language Patterns in the Learning of Strategies from Negotiation Texts

Marina Sokolova[1] and Stan Szpakowicz[1,2]

[1] School of Information Technology and Engineering,
University of Ottawa, Ottawa, Canada
[2] Institute of Computer Science,
Polish Academy of Sciences, Warsaw, Poland
{sokolova, szpak}@site.uottawa.ca

Abstract. The paper shows how to construct language patterns that signal influence strategies and tactical moves corresponding to such strategies. We apply corpus analysis methods to the extraction of certain multi-word patterns from the text data of electronic negotiations. The patterns thus acquired become features in the task of classifying those texts. A series of machine learning experiments predicts the negotiation outcome from the texts associated with first halves of negotiations. We compare the results with the classification of complete negotiations.

1 Introduction

Communication between people, in which participants pursue their goals in order to reach an agreement, can be described as negotiation. The negotiators' language exposes their strategies which serve to achieve their goals [22]. Negotiations conducted by electronic means (e-negotiations) exhibit the characteristics of the negotiation process; the characteristics are reflected in texts exchanged in negotiations. At the syntactic level, personal pronouns, modal verbs, volition verbs, mental verbs and temporal adjectives are the language signals of such influence strategies as logical necessity, appeal or intention to continue negotiations; [18] proposes them as a data representation for electronic negotiations.

This work investigates how a strategy can be implemented in language by means of multi-word expressions. To this end, we look at syntactic representations of the negotiator's influence. The communicative grammar of English [11] supplies a structure for such representations, which we will call *language patterns*. Corpus analysis techniques help find the types of patterns common in real data. A similar framework is used in extraction pattern acquisition; for an overview see [20].

The work we present here has focussed on the construction of the knowledge-based data features, which pertains to knowledge-based feature generation [6]. In a series of experiments we use the words in language patterns for early prediction of the negotiation outcomes. In these experiments, the outcomes of the whole negotiations are classified from the text of the first half of a negotiation. The obtained results are compared with the classification of complete negotiations.

L. Lamontagne and M. Marchand (Eds.): Canadian AI 2006, LNAI 4013, pp. 288–299, 2006.
© Springer-Verlag Berlin Heidelberg 2006

We run our experiments on the texts gathered in e-negotiations. The data come from the Web-based negotiation support system *Inspire* [7].

Our findings tie into active research topics outside the negotiation studies. Language expressions of strategies and tactics can show attitudes and emotional involvement of negotiators, thus they directly relate to subjectivity and sentiment analysis [14]. Language patterns can be a valuable resource for the prediction of strategies in many forms of electronic communication. Extending patterns to include expressions of threats and intimidation may help detect a possibility of breakdown of interpersonal electronic communication [23].

2 Negotiation Strategies and Communication

Negotiation is a process in which two or more parties aim to settle what each shall give and take in a transaction between them. This section surveys strategies and tactics which negotiators employ in order to reach their goals. Strategies depend on many factors, including the negotiation protocols, criteria of success, or the roles of negotiators (such as buyer or facilitator). Negotiation strategies and their verbal communication are intensively studied for face-to-face negotiations [15, 22]. In e-negotiations participants employ strategies just like participants in more traditional face-to-face and phone negotiations. The use of electronic means, however, tends to influence the negotiators' conduct. Researchers have yet to agree how deep this influence is.

The behaviour of e-negotiators involves more risk and aggression than in face-to-face negotiations [3]. There is a tendency to adopt an aversive emotional style to achieve negotiation goals. There are suggestions that e-negotiators behave differently if they negotiate within their social group [22]. On the other hand, personal power (it includes emotions and adverse behaviour) diminishes when negotiations are conducted electronically [19]. The researchers cited here agree on the "weak get strong" effect of e-negotiations. Due to relaxed social norms, the effect allows some e-negotiators perform better than they would in face-to-face negotiations.

Electronic negotiations give us only written communication between negotiators. As a result, negotiation strategies affect, and are affected by, the interpersonal nature of communication, depend on the negotiation type (e-negotiations are an example) and influence it. At the same time, the scope of written communication affects interpersonal exchange and negotiation; the converse holds as well. Figure 1 summarizes our points.

Negotiators apply strategies to the big picture of negotiations. In interpersonal communications this is done through the influence strategies which employ argumentation, substantiation, appeal and so on. The language signals of influence – strategic words – form a feature set that allows machine learning methods to link e-negotiation outcomes with the negotiators' strategies [18]. A more detailed strategy implementations are given by tactics in negotiations [15, 22]. Tactics are applications of both influence and affective, or emotion-based, strategies. A negotiator delivers tactics using either such moves as commands, requested

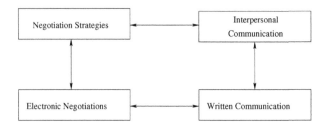

Fig. 1. Strategies and communication

actions, questions, or responses to those moves. The negotiator's tactics aim
to bring the negotiator closer to a goal. They work on a smaller time scale than
strategies and are multi-dimensional. Tactics depend on one's role in negotiation
(buyer, facilitator and so on) and in communication (such as speaker or hearer).
There may be various initiative or response. With respect to interpersonal communication, tactics correspond to propositions, questions, and demands.

Research on negotiations usually describes qualitatively the language representations of propositions, questions, and demands. See [2, 15] for further refer-
ences. Such descriptions tend to be hard to quantify and turn into an algorithm
or procedure. We study the language patterns and look for ways of detecting
the outcome of negotiations from pattern-based representations. This work continues research on the language signals of strategies in e-negotiations and on
features for electronic negotiation texts [17, 18].

3   Language and Strategies

Language discloses information about the e-negotiator's feelings and evaluation
of issues (exposing affects) and allows inference about their abilities and intentions (forming impressions). Such disclosure is characterized by five parameters:
polarization, immediacy, intensity, lexical diversity, and powerful or powerless
style [15]. We focus on *immediacy* and on *powerful* and *powerless* language. Immediacy signals a negotiator's desire to move closer to the opponent [1] who is
positively evaluated and to move away from the disliked one. It shows positive
or negative directions of the negotiator's affect. High immediacy is more explicit
than low immediacy. Powerful language is consistent and direct, but its specific
characteristics usually are not defined. In research, powerful language is defined
as the one that does not have characteristics of powerless language: hesitation,
hedges, tag questions, disclaimers and so on. Powerful language positively corre-
lates with the use of influence strategies. For an overview of these issues, see [2].

The main purpose of tactical moves is to influence the opponent. The negotiator wants to argue the necessity of the next action or prevent an undesirable

---

[1] We refer like this to the other party in bilateral negotiation, though in general
negotiation need not be adversarial.

step. It is done via logical necessity and appeal and the use of modal verbs, personal pronouns and volition and mental verbs [18]. Here we extend the study by considering various implementations of influence and building their language patterns. Leech and Svartvik's approach to language in communication [11] gives the necessary systematic background for our study. It combines pragmatics, the communicative grammar, and the meaning of English verbs. Propositions, questions, and demands – the strategy implementations at the level of pragmatics – are conveyed by declarative, interrogative and imperative sentences respectively. Depending on the situation, various grammatical structures and the choice of words allow the implementation of different types of instances: commands, suggestions, prohibitions and so on [10, 11]. Figure 2 illustrates these relations.

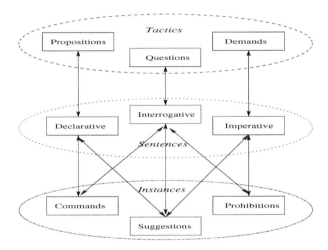

Fig. 2. Tactics and language

4   Building Language Patterns for Influence

When the goal is to convince the opponent to perform an action, logical necessity and appeal can be further sub-categorized as *command, request, advice, suggestion, tentative suggestion* (positive actions). The categories are listed in the order of decreasing strength with which the negotiators impose their will. When the goal is to prevent the opponent from performing an action, the following categories appear: *prohibition* and *negative advice* (negative actions) [9]. All the categories for positive actions may involve the speaker. The categories for the speaker's negative actions become *refusal* and *denial*, depending on the main verb.

We build language patterns from personal pronouns and content nouns (for example those denoting negotiation issues), modal verbs and their negations, main verbs and optional modifiers. They have the forms

– *I/we* μ *ModalVerb* μ *MainVerb* (when the speaker signals involvement by using a first-person pronoun),
– *You* μ *ModalVerb* μ *MainVerb*,
– *ContentNoun* μ *ModalVerb* μ *MainVerb*,

where *ContentNoun* can be a noun phrase and μ denotes an optional modifier. We will concentrate on how the use of pronouns and content nouns, modal verbs and main verbs is connected with influence strategies, their directness and power of delivery.

The choice between a personal pronoun and a content noun (or noun phrase) is the choice between high and low immediacy [15]. The use of personal pronouns signals higher immediacy. In that case the negotiator explicitly says what he wants the opponent to do. The use of nouns shows a more subtle strategy. The negotiator states what he wants to have but avoids asking the opponent explicitly.

The directness of speech and the intensity of influence can be studied through the use of the modal auxiliary verbs, or modals. The primary modals are more direct; they deliver the strongest influence. The secondary modals are moderate; they deliver a weaker influence. See Table 1.

Table 1. Primary and secondary modals

Primary modals	can, may, must (need), will, shall, have (got) to
Secondary modals	could, might, ought to, would, should

Modals have both logical and pragmatic meanings. They express permission, possibility, and necessity as the representatives of logic, and condescension, politeness, tact, and irony as the representatives of practice. In Table 2 we list the most common meanings of the primary modals in positive statements.

Table 2. The meaning of the primary modals

Modals	Meaning
can	possibility, ability, permission
may	possibility, permission, exclamatory wish
must (need)	obligation or requirement (speaker's authority), logical necessity
will	prediction, willinness, insistence, intention
shall	prediction, intention
have (got) to	obligation or requirement, logical necessity

The secondary modals tend to be more hypothetical, polite, tentative, formal, and indirect than the primary modals. The secondary modals refer to the past, while the primary modals refer to the present. In general, the difference between the primary and the secondary modals can be stated thus: the secondary modals are more conditional than the primary modals. The presence of secondary modals also makes the statement less powerful than the presence of primary modals. Table 3 lists the patterns.

Table 3. Tactics and the language patterns

Tactic	Pattern
Command, Requests, involv. a speaker	*You should/must/will/have to/need to* MainVerb ContentNoun *should/must/will/has to/needs to* MainVerb *I/we should/must/will/have to/need to* MainVerb
Advise, Suggestion, Tentative Suggestion involv. a speaker	*You can/could/would/might/may* MainVerb ContentNoun *can/could/would/might/may* MainVerb *I/we can/could/might/may* Verb
Prohibition,	*You cannot/do not/have not* MainVerb ContentNoun *cannot/does not/has not* MainVerb
Negative Advice	*You could not/would not/should not* MainVerb ContentNoun *could not/should not/does not* MainVerb
Refusal, denial	*I/we cannot/could not/should not/do not* Verb *I/we cannot/could not/should not/do not* Verb

One of indicators of directness and influence is the category of the main verb in a pattern. We employ a set of categories from [10] where the main verbs are categorized by the meaning of the actions they describe. The mental activity verbs such as cognition or perception verbs have a special place in communication. They are common as a face-saving technique and signal influence by politeness [2]. Event verbs denote actions that have a beginning and an end, whereas state verbs correspond to actions without defined limits and strong differentiation between them. Activity and process verbs are those that show a goal-oriented action and a series of steps towards a defined end. The verbs of perception and cognition, as well as attitude, are necessarily subjective and more personal than the verbs denoting activity, process, event and state of having or being. The use of perception, cognition and attitude verbs signals the openness to feedback from the opponent. The examples of verbs in all these categories are: read, work, negotiate (activity); tell, say, explain (communication); hope, know, suppose, understand (cognition); become, reply, agree, pay (event); feel, see, hear (perception); like, love, hate (attitude); change, increase, continue (process); consist, cost, depend, be (state of having or being)[10].

5   Extraction of Language Patterns from E-Negotiation Texts

We conduct an empirical study of e-negotiation textual data. E-negotiations take place in various domains (for example, in a legal or business setting), and involve various users (such as buyers, sellers, mediators, facilitators). As in traditional negotiations, participants in e-negotiations have established goals and exhibit strategic behaviour [1]. The negotiation outcome – success or failure – is the result of those strategic choices. E-negotiations held by humans, however, share the uncertainty intrinsic to any human behaviour.

The case study data come from the *Inspire* negotiations [7]. They contain the records of 2557 negotiations, 1461 of them successful. The *Inspire* text data is the largest text collection gathered through e-negotiations. It is a training negotiation between a buyer and a seller who may exchange free-form messages. Negotiation is successful if the virtual purchase has occurred within the designated time, and is unsuccessful otherwise. The system registers the outcome. We consider a transcript as a single example, with all messages concatenated chronologically, preserving the original punctuation and spelling. A successful negotiations is a positive example, an unsuccessful negotiation – a negative example. The *Inspire* data contain 1,514,623 word tokens and 27,055 word types. The types constitute the initial feature set. Figure 3 presents a sample of negotiations; patterns in *italic* appear in the *Inspire* data 3 or more times.

... This should help you propose a deal that is mutually beneficial. *This could also* be determined by a matrix that adds your package ratings to mine to find the maximum joint points...*I put it* back to the 60 days we discussed earlier. *I think it's* a little early to be making positional commitments on single issues. *You should seriously* re-consider this tactic.

Fig. 3. A sample of e-negotiation

To acquire language patterns from the data, we use a bootstrapping procedure with increasing window [18]. The procedure starts with a trigram model of *Inspire* data. The three-word patterns from Table 3 are extracted for all the *MainVerb* categories [10]. Next, a 4-gram model provides the four-word patterns with one modifier, either before or after *ModalVerb*. Finally, a 5-gram model gives the patterns with two modifiers. Tables 4 and 5 present the number of patterns and their diversity for each of tactical moves, verb categories, personal pronouns (Pron) and content nouns (ContN). We found few five-word patterns, because the data contain surprisingly few modifiers.

Table 4. Tactics and verbs, the number of instances of the patterns

Main Verb Categories	Command, Request		Suggestion		Prohibition, Refusal Negative Advice	
	Pron	ContN	Pron	ContN	Pron	ContN
Activity, Communication	43	11	501	49	50	11
Cognition	203	15	804	87	80	10
Event	307	36	3800	491	1700	123
Perception	27	6	909	286	36	7
Process	65	17	818	80	194	32
State of Having, Being	213	335	1279	966	113	173

Table 5. Tactics and verbs, the number of different patterns

Main Verb Categories	Command, Request		Suggestion		Prohibition, Refusal Negative Advice	
	Pron	ContN	Pron	ContN	Pron	ContN
Activity, Communication	24	9	126	45	23	5
Cognition	56	11	258	71	36	7
Event	105	36	635	318	187	66
Perception	14	5	171	74	8	4
Process	37	15	168	70	48	21
State of Having, Being	41	108	171	345	21	36

The distribution of the patterns corresponds to the relations presented by the scheme in Figure 1. The patterns cover several well-known types of communication. We found that the most frequently used tactical move is suggestion. This move is typical of business communication, including e-negotiations. The prevalence of patterns with personal pronouns is the hallmark of interpersonal communication. The dominance of the event verbs among other verb categories is due to the fact that we are dealing with negotiation processes. Finally, the high number and diversity of the cognition and perception verbs typify written communication.

Here are examples of the most frequent patterns (in parentheses, the number of occurrences in the *Inspire* data): you can accept (293), i would be (272), you can see (271), we can make (243), i cannot accept (230).

6   Early Classification of the Negotiation Outcomes

Early prediction of upcoming events is an important learning task in many domains. So far only the outcomes of the complete negotiations have been classified using either non-textual data [8, 13] or textual data [17]. In this section we aim to find the empirical setting that gives a reliable prediction of the negotiation outcomes from the first part of negotiations. Prediction is *reliable* if the classification results are statistically close to those achieved on complete negotiations. When we classify the *Inspire* data, the accuracy on the binary attributes of the complete negotiations is 71.2%±2.6 and the equally-weighted F-score – 74.1%±4.8 [17]. Mean and standard deviation are calculated for the results of Naive Bayes[2] [5], Support Vector Machine [4] and Decision Trees [16] on four features sets, including the strategic words and the most frequent features.

In the machine learning experiments we present here, the learning data consist of the texts of the first half of negotiations. This segment is labelled by the outcome of the whole negotiation. We employ the language patterns and their variations to investigate the effect on the classification results. First, the acquired patterns are used as data features. Next, the data features are all word types

---

[2] High standard deviation is due to the poorer performance of Naive Bayes compared with other classifiers.

that appear in the patterns. Next, we add the condition words that often appear before the patterns. Attributes have binary values: 1 if a word or a pattern appears in the first part of a negotiation, and 0 otherwise.

According to the Information Gain estimation [24], in the first part of negotiations the use of the following patterns influences the negotiation outcome: you should not be, we must be, I cannot accept, I should do, you cannot/can't accept, we cannot/can't agree, I cannot/can't make (in the order from the most to the least important). The patterns, however, are very sparse. In further experiments we use these:

Tact I, the word types that constitute the language patterns;

Tact II, the pattern word types and condition words, for example, *as, if, whatever;*

Top 500, 500 most frequent unigrams of the *Inspire* data; their total occurrences equal to 1,255,445, thus making 81% of the data.

Tact I and Tact II are two knowledge-based representations, and Top 500 is a baseline.

We use Support Vector Machines (SVM), Decision Trees (DT) and Naive Bayes (NB). Kernel methods, especially SVM, have been successfully used for text classification. The accuracy and running time of SVM greatly depend on the polynomial which the algorithm builds. We performed an exhaustive accuracy search for the polynomial's defining parameters: the degree and the upper bound on coefficients. We apply Decision Tree induction mainly because people can analyze its results (in contrast with the results of kernel methods). We showed in previous work that Decision Trees give high accuracy on successful negotiations. We apply the Naive Bayes classifier (NB) because it is fast and because it gave us high accuracy on unsuccessful negotiations [17]. In the present experiments with NB, we have used the normal distribution and the kernel density estimators.

To estimate how the classification algorithms work, we calculate the accuracy (Acc) and equally-weighted F-score (F) on the test data.[3] The results are estimated by tenfold cross-validation. To ensure that all data splits are the same, we use the Weka 3 toolkit [24]. Table 6 reports the results. Columns Acc and F list the best accuracy and corresponding F-score. For the best accuracy the tuned parameter values are: c=0.1 for DT, C=0.01 on Tact I and Tact II, C=0.005 on Top 500 for SVM, kernel estimation for NB. Column Gap reports the gap between the best and the worst accuracy across the adjustable parameters. The highest accuracy and F-score are in *italic.*

Our results show that the knowledge-based representations provide reliable prediction, *more steady* when contrasted with the classification accuracy and F-score on the complete negotiations (70.8%±1.6 versus 71.2%±2.6 and 75.4%±2.0 versus 74.1%±4.8, respectively).

Compared with the performance on the most frequent features, all three classifiers marginally improve the prediction accuracy and narrow the gap between

---

[3] Acc equals 55.8%, when all negotiations are classified as positives. Corresponding F is equal to 71.6.

Table 6. F-score, accuracy, and the accuracy gap; first half of negotiations

Representations	Attr	NB			SVM			DT		
		F	Acc	Gap	F	Acc	Gap	F	Acc	Gap
Tact I	124	73.9	70.5	0.1	*77.9*	*72.8*	1.2	74.5	69.3	1.9
Tact II	137	73.2	69.7	0.1	77.8	72.7	1.5	74.9	69.8	1.5
Top 500	500	71.3	68.9	0.4	75.1	70.6	7.1	73.1	68.4	2.6

the best and the worst accuracy. Parallel increase of F-score indicates that this is due to the increase of true positive rates. The higher accuracy and F-score of SVM can be attributed to its overall ability to perform well on the binary data. True positive (*Pos*) and true negative (*Neg*) rates show how the classifiers work on different data classes; see Table 7 for the rates contributing to the best accuracy.

Table 7. True positive and true negative rates, first half of negotiations

Representations	Attr	NB		SVM		DT	
		Pos	Neg	Pos	Neg	Pos	Neg
Tact I	124	75.1	64.7	*85.9*	56.2	80.2	55.6
Tact II	137	74.1	64.2	85.5	56.3	80.7	55.9
Top 500	500	69.4	*68.2*	81.8	57.4	77.1	57.3

The results in Table 7 demonstrate that the language signals of influence tactics assist in the correct prediction of successful negotiations. For all three classifiers, true positive rates have been improved compared with the baseline results. The correct prediction of unsuccessful negotiations, however, diminishes when knowledge-based representations are used. We conclude that the language implementations of strategies are more easily detected in successful negotiations than in unsuccessful negotiations.

True positive and true negative rates underline that Naive Bayes always outperforms other classifiers in the correct classification of negative examples. Its classification of positive examples, however, is substantially better on the knowledge-based representations than on the most frequent unigrams. The performance of Naive Bayes is more balanced on the most frequent words than on the words learned by the patterns. The latter applies to Decision Trees and SVM, but on the lesser extent. Decision Trees and SVM are consistently correct in classifying positive examples. SVM's true positives being > 85% on the knowledge-based representations, and DT's – more than 80%.

7   Conclusions and Future Work

We have presented a method of building language patterns for the tactical moves of influence strategies. A pattern consist of a modal verb, a main verb, and a personal pronoun or a content noun. The modal defines which move corresponds to the pattern and the power of language. The main verb contributes to the power of language, and the pronoun or noun – to the immediacy of disclosure.

In our empirical study, we acquired the patterns from the data of electronic negotiations. The patterns and words used in them have been employed to learn the negotiation outcomes in machine learning experiments. We have considered their influence on the correct early prediction of the negotiation outcome. The obtained results have shown that the language signals of influence strategies and their tactics give a reliable prediction of the negotiation outcome from the first half of the negotiation.

One of the most natural extensions of the present study is the application of the method to communication other than electronic negotiations. From a machine learning point of view, future analysis of the NB's strong performance on unsuccessful negotiations and somehow weak performance on successful negotiations will contribute to an investigation of its learning bias. We also suggest another interesting direction for future work. Language implementation of strategies conveys opinions, emotions and personal viewpoints of the negotiator [15]. They deliver information, express the negotiator's attitude towards the given information and the reality he deals with. A study of the language signals relates to *sentiment analysis*, a field that recently has attracted much attention of Natural Language Processing and Machine Learning researchers [12]. Our research is especially close to sentiment analysis in dialogues [25] because they both study language in interpersonal communication. The next direction is to incorporate semantic knowledge from lexical resources such as Longman Dictionary of Contemporary English [21]. This will broaden the application area of the study we have presented here.

Acknowledgment

This work has been supported by the Natural Sciences and Engineering Research Council of Canada and by the Social Sciences and Humanities Research Council of Canada. The authors thank Stan Matwin for comments on the preliminary machine learning results and the anonymous reviewers for useful suggestions.

References

1. J. Brett. *Negotiating Globally*, Jossey-Bass, San Francisco, 2001.
2. N. Burrell, R. Koper, "The efficacy of powerful/powerless language on attitudes and source credibility", *Persuasion: advances through meta-analysis*, M. Allen and R. Preiss (ed.), p.p. 203 – 215, Hampton Press, 1998.
3. C. Cellich, S. Jain. *Global Business Negotiations : A Practical Guide*, Thomson, South-Western, 2004.
4. N. Cristianini, J. Shawe-Taylor. *An Introduction to Support Vector Machines and other kernel-based learning methods*, Cambridge University Press, 2000.
5. R. Duda, P. Hart, and D. Stork. *Pattern Classification*, Wiley, 2000.

6. E. Gabrilovich, S. Markovitch. "Feature Generation for Text Categorization Using World Knowledge", in *Proceedings of the 19th IJCAI*, p.p. 1048 - 1053, 2005.

7. G. Kersten and others. *Electronic negotiations, media and transactions for socio-economic interactions*, http://interneg.org/enegotiation/index.html, 2002–2006.

8. G. Kersten, G. Zhang, "Mining Inspire Data for the Determinants of Successful Internet Negotiations", *Central European Journal of Operational Research*, 11(3), p.p. 297 – 316, 2003.

9. G. Leech. *Principles of Pragmatics*, Longman, 1983.

10. G. Leech. *Meaning and the English Verb*, Longman, 2004.

11. G. Leech, J. Svartvik. *A Communicative Grammar of English*, Longman, 2002.

12. T. Mullen, N. Collier. "Sentiment Analysis Using Support Vector Machines with Diverse Information Sources", in *Proceedings of EMNLP*, p.p. 412 – 418, 2004.

13. V. Nastase. "Concession Curve for Inspire Data", *Group Decision and Negotiations*, 15(2), 2006.

14. B. Pang, L. Lee. "A Sentimental Education: Sentiment Analysis Using Subjectivity Summarization Based on Minimum Cuts", in *Proceedings of the 42nd ACL*, pp. 271 – 278, 2004.

15. L. Putnam, M. Roloff (ed.). *Communication and Negotiation*, London: Sage, 1992.

16. J. R. Quinlan. *C4.5: Programs for Machine Learning*, Morgan Kaufmann Publishers, San Mateo, California, 1993.

17. M. Sokolova, V. Nastase, M. Shah, and S. Szpakowicz, "Feature Selection for Electronic Negotiation Texts", *Proceedings of Recent Advances in Natural Language Processing (RANLP'2005)*, p.p. 518 – 524 , 2005.

18. M. Sokolova, S. Szpakowicz."Analysis and Classification of Strategies in Electronic Negotiations", in *Proceedings of the 18th Canadian AI*, p.p. 145 – 157, Springer, 2005.

19. M. Ströbel. Effects of Electronic Markets on Negotiation Processes, in *Proceedings of European Conference on Information Systems (ECIS'2000)*, p.p. 445 – 452, 2000.

20. K. Sudo, S. Sekine, and R. Grishman. "An Improved Extraction Pattern Representation Model for Automatic IE Pattern Acquisition", in *Proceedings of the 41st ACL*, p.p. 224 – 231, 2003.

21. D. Summers(ed.),*Longman Dictionary of Contemporary English*. Longman, 2003.

22. L. Thompson. *The Mind and Heart of the Negotiator*, Pearson Prentice Hall, 2005.

23. Y. Tohkura. "Future of Communication Science and Technologies in Information Society", Pleanary Lecture at *the 18th International Congress on Acoustics*, Kyoto, Japan, 2004 http://www.stanford-jc.or.jp/research-project/scti/summary/materials

24. I. Witten, E. Frank. *Data Mining*, Morgan Kaufmann, 2005. http://www.cs.waikato.ac.nz/ml/weka/

25. L. Vidrascu, L. Devillers. "Detection of Real-Life Emotions in Call Centers", in *Proceedings of the 9th European Conference on Speech Communication and Technology*, 2005.

Using Natural Language Processing to Assist the Visually Handicapped in Writing Compositions

Jacques Chelin, Leila Kosseim, and T. Radhakrishnan

Department of Computer Science and Software Engineering,
Concordia University, Montreal, Canada
{jj_chel, kosseim, krishnan}@cse.concordia.ca

Abstract. Over the last decades, more and more visually handicapped students have attempted post-secondary studies. This situation has created many new challenges. One of them is the need to study text and electronic documents in depth and in a reasonable time. Blind students cannot flip through the pages of a book, skim through the text or use a highlighter. In this paper, we propose a solution in the form of an experimental prototype and show how natural language processing techniques can profitably assist blind students in meeting their academic objectives. The techniques used include the automatic creation of indices, passage retrieval and the use of WordNet for query rewriting. The paper presents a technology application of a practically usable software.

The system was evaluated quantitatively and qualitatively. The evaluation is very encouraging and supports further investigation.

1 Introduction

The visually handicapped have consistently progressed over the last decades in their efforts towards inclusion in the mainstream[7]. Integration in education and professional life in particular was possible due to the deployment of computers in every day life, without which it would not have been possible, or at least not to the same degree. In the wake of this integration, more and more blind students are attempting post-secondary studies.

This situation has created many new challenges and new needs specifically related to the in depth study of documents in a reasonable time so as to produce assignment submissions and research papers. In this paper, we discuss how Natural Language Processing (NLP) techniques can assist blind students in meeting their academic objectives. We present a prototype system built as an information probing and gathering environment. Its goal is to reduce the time it takes a student to do research on a specific topic and ultimately produce a paper in a time frame close to their sighted friends.

1.1 The Problem

On a regular basis, post-secondary students, especially those in Liberal Arts, have to do research on specific topics. Their task consists in consulting a wide

L. Lamontagne and M. Marchand (Eds.): Canadian AI 2006, LNAI 4013, pp. 300–311, 2006.
© Springer-Verlag Berlin Heidelberg 2006

variety of books, documents and Web sites and producing an essay, anything from a few pages to a full-fledged thesis. To be able to better understand the difficulties that visually handicapped students face when trying to write a paper, we need to give a quick description of the tools they use to read and write.

The visual handicap can be divided into two broad categories, the partially sighted and the totally blind. We only address the latter here. One way to make up for the absence of sight is the use of speech. The way computer technology is used in this case is to provide spoken output as screen readers that use an internal speech synthesizer. Words appearing on the screen are read aloud. The major problem with using speech as a medium is that it provides a very small working window due to the constraints of short term memory and linearity of speech. [6] provided evidence that people can remember about 7 chunks (in our case, terms) in short-term memory. [3] goes even further and suggested as little as 3 to 5 terms.

The other way to compensate for the loss of visual ability is through the sense of touch. For two centuries now, the blind have been able to read by moving their fingers across raised dots on thick paper. The appearance of computer based 'Braille displays' in which each dot can be raised or lowered through electromechanical devices has caused a huge leap in the accessibility to electronic documents. The major constraint here is that the user can only 'see' a 40-character window.

1.2   A Comparison

To write a paper, a student normally scans a substantial amount of documents quickly and easily using fast reading techniques; develops an outline while reading one or more of these documents more systematically, highlighting and taking notes; reviews and rearranges his notes and uses them to create a draft of his document; refines the document iteratively until it is complete; at all times, refers back to previous readings and versions.

At first sight, all these steps may seem easy, even mundane. However, for the visually handicapped, several problems exist. To name only a few:

- The amount of material to be read is, by itself, often a challenge – even for a sighted student.
- Reading difficulties go from very mild to very severe for handicapped students. This can be due to many factors such as a lack of reading and summarization skills, visual handicaps, dyslexia, . . .
- Note taking is an art in itself. The classic index card method facilitates sorting of notes but is tedious and can hardly be used by students with visual handicaps.
- Contrary to sighted users who can see a full screen of information, the blind have no overview of documents. Everything is always seen through a 40 character window for Braille users, or a window of less than 8 spoken words for speech users.

What is more, the above problems are encountered while performing all major steps in writing compositions: Research, Analysis, Outlining and Composition.

2   Previous Work

As witnessed by the CSUN series of conferences (e.g. [1, 2]), the topic of hardware and software applications to help the visually disabled has received a lot of attention. However, the resulting software applications are either geared at reading or writing, but not both. In addition, most of the features provided are text annotation tools and very little NLP techniques are used. As many of these systems are commercially available, no paper describing their inner working seems to be available.

WYNN[1], Kurzweil 1000[2] and textHELP[3] are all tools to read and create documents mainly targeted for learning disabled students or users with learning difficulties like dyslexia, attention deficit disorder (ADD) and other literacy difficulties. These products typically provide text annotation tools such as bookmarking, note taking or outlining facilities. However, these facilities are often crude. For example, the user often cannot directly go to the position of a bookmark in the original document (through a hyperlink for example), or integrate bookmarks into existing outlines; thus limiting his access.

To our knowledge, NLP techniques used to improve the reading and writing tasks of the visually handicapped include only word prediction (in textHELP and WYNN) and homonym checking (in textHELP). Homonym support provides auditory and visual reinforcement of commonly confused like-sounding words. To avoid the confusion between homophones, the program color codes confusable words and lists possible alternatives with audible definitions and sample sentences. Word prediction allows the application to predict the most likely word to be typed given the previous context. The user types a letter and the program offers a list of the most likely words beginning with that letter. If the required word is on the list, it can be quickly selected. If the word is not on the list, typing the next letter will bring up a different choice and so on. Again, as these systems are commercial, it is not clear if a language model is used, or if a simple dictionary look-up is performed.

A related research project is that of [9], who developed an authoring environment to assist users in writing hypermedia documents. The system, based on a cognitive model of writing, offers features such as an outliner to help organise ideas and for creating and manipulating view areas. However, as this tool was not designed for the visually impaired, these features do not specifically address their needs. In addition, it provides no feature for skimming documents or other features to help find the content to be presented in the final document.

3   Proposed Solution

In order to assist the visually handicapped, a prototype system called ESCAS[4] was developed. The system can be seen as an information probing and gathering

---

[1] http://www.freedomscientific.com/LSG/products/wynn.asp
[2] http://www.kurzweiledu.com
[3] http://www.texthelp.com
[4] ©Jacques Chelin, 2006

environment or more practically as a text editor with features to assist in reading and writing documents. Its goal is to reduce the time it takes a student to do research on a specific topic and ultimately produce a paper in a time frame close to their sighted friends. To achieve this, the system assists the user in:

- Determining the relevance of documents without having to read them entirely.
- Accessing information related to a user specific theme or subject much faster than traditional methods.
- Freeing the user from tedious searches and reading chores for more productive and creative work.

The purpose here is to investigate where and how far NLP techniques can facilitate the access of students to information pertinent to their research. These techniques will convey additional information about the content of a document and faster access to relevant positions within the document.

Text annotation tools, such as the facility to create and annotate outlines, bookmarks, notes ... are the typical tools offered to help the visually handicapped (see section 2). These tools facilitate the access and the composition of documents, but cannot help in manipulating their *content*. We therefore looked at various NLP techniques to zoom in on material within an input document that is particularly relevant to the subject being developed by the user. In the case of sighted users, this can be achieved by skimming or fast reading through the material. Our intent here is not only to replace skimming with what NLP can offer but also go beyond skimming and implement such functionality that could be of help even to those who have no handicaps.

3.1 Indexing

When skimming literature, the user is looking for specific information quickly. To achieve this, a useful support is an index. In a standard index at the end of a paper book, important terms (words or phrases) are arranged alphabetically and are associated with the page numbers where they can be found. Blind students generally use scanned versions of paper documents. As the books were designed for paper medium, they do not contain hyperlinks to help users navigate quickly. The scanned version of an paper-book index is therefore of no help to blind users. They need direct access to the actual segment of text (be it a paragraph, a sentence ...).

Many approaches to index generation have been proposed to find terms that are representative of the document and to relate them to each other semantically (e.g. [4], [10]). In ESCAS, our goal is to generate many automatic pointers to text excerpts and to perform this task on the fly whenever a new document is loaded in the system. A syntactic analysis or chunking of the document is therefore not an option as it may not be fast enough and may not be able to parse all sentences. As we are more interested in recall than in precision, we opted for a non-linguistic approach.

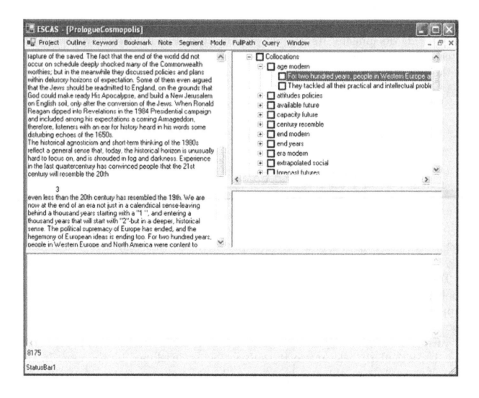

Fig. 1. Collocation-based index in ESCAS

In ESCAS, each index term is considered as a text node. Visually, under that node, instead of a page number, the user can see the actual text excerpt which contains the entry. By just pressing a key (*Enter* in our case) on an occurrence, the user is taken to its exact location in the text. For the user, the index is handy because, in addition to giving access to the original text segment, the index can be used to scan through a list of sentences rather than to have to keep switching to the text from a list of page numbers. The index includes both single-word terms and two-word terms. First, the text is tokenised, stopwords are removed and the remaining words are stemmed using the Porter stemmer [8]. For each stem, we then keep a list of pointers to the paragraphs in which they occur and to the position of the stem in the text. We also keep one of the original words from which the stem was derived such that the user is presented with a word and not a stem.

Single words are often not enough to convey the full meaning that the user wishes to explore. Most of the time, the user is looking for material that is characterized by a combination of two or more words rather than just one. For example, no one would contend that *Supreme Being* together is more semantically rich than *Supreme* and *Being* taken separately. The idea here is to establish the set of word combinations that reflect the meaning of the document.

In ESCAS, we thus extract collocations of 2 consecutive words. Collocations are of interest to us for two reasons. First, they are important for computational lexicography. Being a multi-word term combined together in a significant way, they are used to create a more useful index. Second, since the process of generating collocations uses a ranking scheme which integrates the importance of specific words within a document, this process produces a set of terms that characterize the documents. These terms can then be selected by the user to perform query rewriting (see section 3.3) with a single touch of a function key.

To identify collocations, we used the standard technique of Hypothesis testing with the Pearsons chi-square test described in [5]. Essentially, Pearsons chi-square test compares the observed frequency of pairs of words with the frequency expected if the two words were independent. For more technical details, the interested reader is referred to [5].

Figure 1 shows a screen shot of the system with a collocation-based index. The index term *age modern* is found twice in the text. By clicking on either excerpts *For two hundred years, people . . .* or *They tackled all their practical and . . .* , the user is taken directly in the right position in the document.

3.2   Paragraph Retrieval

As discussed in section 1.1, blind students have a difficult time skimming documents because they do not have an overall view of the text. They currently must read each document to determine their relevance, then select only a few and read them back again to analyze their content. The idea behind paragraph retrieval is to suggest to the user places where he would start reading that would be the most relevant to the subject being treated. If he could do a structured reading of the material, he would save time by having less to read or not having to read the material more than once. This problem can be reformulated as an Information Retrieval (IR) task where the query is the subject of the thesis or paper being written. We wish to provide a student with search facilities when reading a document and cater at the same time for the different levels of understanding of that student.

In ESCAS, the document being studied is divided into a set of paragraph vectors using the data accumulated during the parsing of the document for index terms (see previous section). We implemented the standard vector-space IR model with a tf-idf weighting scheme, where partial matching allows the ranking of the degree of similarity measured by the cosine of the angle between a paragraph vector and the query vector. Initially, the query is taken to be the topic of the composition. Only the paragraphs relevant to the topic (or those having the highest cosines) are retrieved.

3.3   Query Rewriting and Reformulation

The problem with IR is that often very pertinent paragraphs containing terms semantically close to the query (such as synonyms) are not retrieved while noise is introduced in the retrieval set with paragraphs that are not pertinent. As

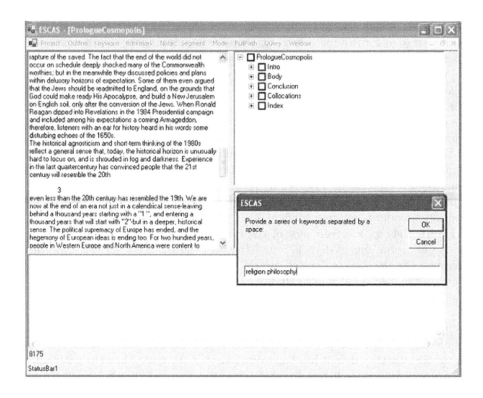

Fig. 2. Paragraph retrieval in ESCAS

an example, let's assume that a Philosophy term paper has to be written on *Potentiality and Actuality: Aristotle's reintroduction of unrealized possibilities and reaffirmation of becoming.* A query based on this subject would not include the word *Being* since that word is not among the words in the query. So the student has to somehow add this word to the query to improve the retrieval. Based on the new retrieval results, new words or phrases will suggest themselves (through the index for example) and the user will start exploring the material with different queries.

Figure 2 shows a screen shot of the system with paragraph retrieval. The benefit that can be derived from this feature is faster access to pertinent material within the text or exploring the material in unexpected but interesting directions. One must remember here that we are trying to find a substitute for skimming. Furthermore, this iterative reformulation exercise suggests that the problem can be viewed as having three dimensions or can be positioned within a three-dimensional space, the type of retrieval, the expansion of the query and the level of understanding of the user.

WordNet. Query Reformulation can quickly turn short if the user does not have some help in getting more ideas on the subject. WordNet was thus incorporated into the system. The idea was to make available to the user synonyms,

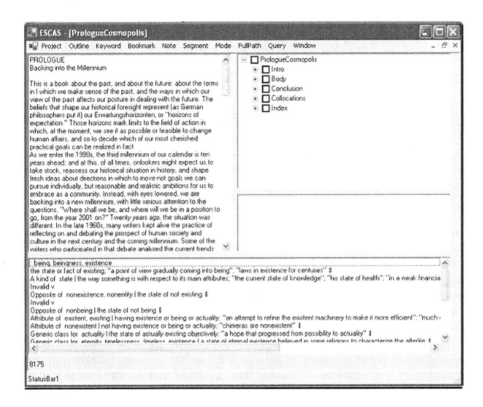

Fig. 3. Example of using WordNet in ESCAS

hypernyms, hyponyms, and other lexically and semantically related terms. Their respective links allow the user to explore a certain domain and thus structure and enrich his query reformulation process. With a function key, ESCAS allows the user to expand his query from where the cursor is in the Wordnet data so he can resubmit that query within his exploration process. Figure 3 shows a small excerpt of the links available when a search is done on hyponyms of the word *Being* in WordNet.

4   Evaluation

To evaluate the system, both a quantitative and a qualitative evaluation were performed, but with only one blind university student. We also showed the system to the coordinator of Concordia University's Office for Students with Disabilities - himself blind, and gathered his opinion. One of the major difficulties in performing the evaluation, is to find blind students who are willing and have the time to evaluate the system. Remember that blind students require more time to do their course work. Asking them to spend time on the evaluation of a proto-type adds a load to their already busy schedule. Nevertheless, as discussed later, a more complete evaluation with several blind and non-blind post-secondary students is planned for.

4.1   Qualitative Evaluation

From the beginning, a blind student was involved in the project. Didier is now a 2nd year Concordia University student enrolled in Philosophy and Religion. Since CECEP (Québec's pre-university level), he had to write compositions for his course work. He was involved in the project since 2001, helping us determine the requirements of blind students, and since 2002, Didier had been given various prototypes to try out and evaluate.

Through Didier's use of the system, we interviewed him and asked him to describe his experience. After some training period where he had some good and some bad experiences, Didier characterizes his experience as follows: *If you know where you are going, ESCAS is a fantastic and indispensable tool. If you don't, it is a bad tool. More concretely, you must first have a good idea of your topic and your material first before creating an outline and fleshing it out into a paper.* In the beginning he retrieved many documents and paragraphs, then spend a lot of time reviewing it all. He was falling into the familiar trap of beginning students who would highlight the whole book.

Today, Didier claims that it takes him about half the time to write a composition when using the system. He can skim literature more quickly and can concentrate on more creative thinking than he could without the system. All in all, Didier has been using the system every semester since we offered it to him and he considers it a necessary tool for reading and writing.

We also showed the system to the coordinator of Concordia University's Office for Students with Disabilities - himself blind. Although he did not use the system for an actual essay writing exercise, he was very enthusiastic about it and will recommend it to his peers at various local colleges (Dawson, Vanier, Marianopolis and Cégep du Vieux-Montréal).

4.2   Quantitative Evaluation

From the beginning, the goal of the system was to reduce the time gap between blind and regular students in writing compositions. To measure the utility of the NLP tools, we therefore needed to compare the time it took a typical user to write a composition with and without the system. Dider feels that it now takes him about half the time to write an essay; but we wanted *hard* data to support this claim. The difficulty here, is that any person (hopefully students, too) get better at a task each time they perform it. We cannot ask the same person to write a composition on the same topic twice; the second time will surely be faster and better. We cannot compare different compositions written by the same person, as they may be of different levels of difficulty, different level of research will be involved ... Since Didier had kept record of all his course work since 2001, we then compared the time it took him to write compositions for his courses compared to the professors' requirements for regular students. In

2001, Didier did not have the software, in 2002 and 2003, he was given various prototypes that did not include NLP tools, and since 2004, he was given ESCAS. Table 1 shows the data for years 2001, 2004 and 2005.

Table 1. Time to write a composition with/without the system compared to professors' requirements

Year	Regular Students			Didier's Actual Time			Time	
	Given	Due	Time	Given	Handed-in	Time	Ratio	Diff.
2001 - w/o ESCAS	01-Mar	15-Apr	45 days	01-Mar	30-May	90 days	2.00	45
2001 - w/o ESCAS	09-Feb	30-Apr	81 days	09-Feb	27-Jun	138 days	1.70	57
2004 - w/ ESCAS	08-Sep	02-Dec	84 days	08-Sep	06-Dec	88 days	1.05	4
2004 - w/ ESCAS	08-Sep	13-Dec	95 days	08-Sep	19-Dec	101 days	1.06	6
2005 - w/ ESCAS	07-Feb	07-Mar	30 days	07-Feb	30-Mar	53 days	1.77	23
2005 - w/ ESCAS	16-Nov	09-Dec	23 days	02-Nov	12-Dec	40 days	1.74	17
2005 - w/ ESCAS	09-Nov	23-Nov	14 days	16-Nov	15-Dec	29 days	2.07	15

In 2001, it took Didier about twice as long to write a composition than regular students. If the professor gave 45 days to regular students, it would take him 90 days to achieve the same task. In 2004, the data seems to show a net reduction in time - he handed in his work about the same time as regular students. However, for 2005, it takes him twice as long again ... The data was inconclusive.

However, when looking at the difference between the time of a regular student and that of the evaluator, we see three clusters of data corresponding to each of the three years. ESCAS does show an improvement. The higher differences in 2005 compared to 2004, can be explained by more material having to be read and more courses taken simultaneously. Why would differences reflect reality better than ratios? Given the evaluator is adamant that he takes less time when using the application, we would like to suggest an explanation. The student doing the evaluation has a physical deficiency, not an intellectual one. Using a ratio would assume that every task takes more time affecting the overall proportion uniformly on all the variables. This would correspond more to an intellectual deficiency. In the case of a physical deficiency, accessing the material takes more time. But once the material is available, the creative and intellectual skills come into play. ESCAS does not help at all at the intellectual level. Considering the differences instead of the ratios amounts to looking at the extensions in time required to finish the paper. Let us apply this rule to the first and last entries. We can safely assume that the time to access the material for a sighted person is marginal when compared to the problems met by a blind person. Giving this access time a value of 1, we have 44 days and 13 days of intellectual work respectively. We also assume parity at the intellectual level. We have a resulting 46 days (90-44) and 16 days (29-13) of access time. This gives us a true ratio difference of 46.0 to 16.0 which is a huge difference when compared with the 2.0 and 2.07 pair.

To conclude, with the small amount of data analysed, we have not scientifically demonstrated that ESCAS helps. Future work definitely includes a formal evaluation of the system with several students, and compare their use of the system. The goal here is to make sure that we have not developed a system geared towards the personal preferences of one person, but that it is actually useful for most blind students. For this, we plan on asking the participation several blind and non-blind subjects from a post-secondary school. However, we doubt that a truly quantitative evaluation can be performed. As with any software, the perceived benefits may not correspond to the actual benefits. Overall, if the user freely chooses to use the system, it may be enough to declare it useful.

5 Conclusion and Future Work

In this paper, we presented ESCAS[5], a prototype system to assist the visually handicapped in writing compositions. The system can be seen as an information probing and gathering environment that offers features based on NLP techniques. The purpose here is to investigate where and how far existing NLP techniques can facilitate the access of students to information pertinent to their research. These techniques convey additional information about the content of a document and faster access to relevant positions within the document.

Currently, the evaluation of the system is more qualitative, than formal. Future work definitely includes a formal evaluation of the system with several students, and compare their use of the system. The goal here is to make sure that we have not developed a system geared towards the personal preferences of one person, but that it is actually useful for most blind students. For this, we plan on asking the participation several blind and non-blind subjects from a post-secondary school. However, we doubt that a truly quantitative evaluation can be performed. As with any software, the perceived benefits may not correspond to the actual benefits. Overall, if the user freely chooses to use the system, it may be enough to declare it useful.

Acknowledgment. The authors would like to thank Didier and Leo for their time evaluating the system and for their constant feedback and encouragement. Many thanks also to the anonymous referees for their valuable comments on a previous version of this paper.

References

1. *CSUN's 19th Annual International Conference "Technology and Persons with Disabilities"*, Los Angeles, March 2004.
2. *CSUN's 20th Annual International Conference "Technology and Persons with Disabilities"*, Los Angeles, March 2005.
3. N. Cowan. The magical number 4 in short-term memory: A reconsideration of mental storage capacity. *Behavioral and Brain Sciences*, 24:87–185, 2001.
4. Julia Hodges, Shiyun Yie, Ray Reighart, and Lois Boggess. An automated system that assits in the generation of document indexes. *Natural Language Engineering*, 2:137–160, 1996.

---

[5] ©Jacques Chelin, 2006

5. Christopher D. Manning and Hinrich Schütze. *Foundations of Statistical Natural Language Processing*. MIT Press, 1999.

6. G. A. Miller. The magical number seven, plus or minus two: Some limits on our capacity for processing information. *Psychological Review*, 63:81–97, 1956.

7. Fred Orelove and Lissa Power-deFur. *Inclusive Education: Practical Implementation of the Least Restrictive Environment*. Jones and Bartlett Publishers, 1997.

8. M.F. Porter. An algorithm for suffix stripping. *Program*, 14(3):130–137, 1980.

9. T. Shimizu, S. Smoliar, and J. Boreczky. AESOP: An Outline-Oriented Authoring System. In *Proceedings of the Thirty-first Annual Hawaii International Conference on System Sciences*, pages 207–215, Hawaii, January 1998.

10. N. Wacholder, D. K. Evans, and J. L. Klavans. Automatic identification and organization of index terms for interactive browsing. In *International Conference on Digital Libraries. Proceedings of the 1st ACM/IEEE-CS joint conference on Digital libraries*, pages 126–134, 2001.

Text Compression by Syntactic Pruning

Michel Gagnon[1] and Lyne Da Sylva[2]

[1] Département de génie informatique,
École Polytechnique de Montréal
Michel.Gagnon@polymtl.ca
[2] École de bibliothéconomie et des sciences de l'information,
Université de Montréal
Lyne.Da.Sylva@UMontreal.CA

Abstract. We present a method for text compression, which relies on pruning of a syntactic tree. The syntactic pruning applies to a complete analysis of sentences, performed by a French dependency grammar. Sub-trees in the syntactic analysis are pruned when they are labelled with targeted relations. Evaluation is performed on a corpus of sentences which have been manually compressed. The reduction ratio of extracted sentences averages around 70%, while retaining grammaticality or readability in a proportion of over 74%. Given these results on a limited set of syntactic relations, this shows promise for any application which requires compression of texts, including text summarization.

1 Introduction

This paper is a contribution to work in text summarization, whose goal is to produce a shorter version of a source text, while still retaining its main semantic content. Research in this field is flourishing (see namely [14, 15, 16]); it is motivated by the increasing size and availability of digital documents, and the necessity for more efficient methods of information retrieval and assimilation.

Methods of automatic summarization include extracting (summarizing by using a limited number of sentences extracted from the original text) and abstracting (producing a new, shorter text). Extraction algorithms have a strong tendency to select long sentences from the text (since word frequency and distribution are often crucial, and are higher in long sentences even when sentence length is factored in). Shortening the extracted sentences can be a way to further reduce the resulting summary, provided that the (essential) meaning of the sentence is preserved. Such summaries can presumably allow for shorter reading time. We have thus developed a method for sentence reduction.

After presenting our objectives and previous related work, this article details the methodology, and then presents and discusses experimental results. The conclusion outlines future work.

2 Objectives

Three objectives are sought in this paper. First, we present the method for text compression based on syntactic pruning of sentences after a dependency-analysis tree has been

L. Lamontagne and M. Marchand (Eds.): Canadian AI 2006, LNAI 4013, pp. 312–323, 2006.
© Springer-Verlag Berlin Heidelberg 2006

computed. Secondly, although we recognize the existence of numerous resources for the syntactic analysis of English texts (and the evaluation thereof), equivalent systems for French are scarce. Given resources at our disposal, namely a broad-coverage grammar for French, we present a system for compression of French sentences. Finally, we give evaluation results for the sentence reduction approach on a corpus of manually-reduced sentences; this aims to determine whether, after compression, the resulting reduced sentences preserve the grammaticality and essential semantics of the original sentences. Success would suggest this approach has potential as a summarization method.

3 Related Work

3.1 Text Compression in Abstracting

An abstract is "a summary at least some of whose material is not present in the input" ([14], page 129). An abstract may reduce sentences from the source text, join sentence fragments, generalize, etc. Work under this banner has occasionally involved sentence reduction, for instance by identifying linguistic reduction techniques which preserve meaning [11, 17]. Also related is work on information selection and fusion: Barzilay et al. [2] focus on fusing information from different sentences into a single representation, and Thione et al [18] apply reduction and fusion techniques to a representation of text structure based on discourse parsing. Sentence reduction techniques vary considerably and some are much harder to implement than others; however, all require a fairly good syntactic analysis of the source text. This implies having a wide-coverage grammar, a robust parser, and generation techniques which defy most existing systems.

3.2 Text Reduction Based on Syntactic Analysis

We hypothesize that a robust syntactic analysis can be valuable as a basis for text reduction. Grefenstette [8] experiments with sentence reduction based on a syntactic analysis provided by a robust phrase structure parser [9]. Only some of his reductions guarantee keeping grammatical sentences. Mani et al. [10] compress sentences (extracted from a text) based on a phrase-structure syntax analysis indirectly based on Penn Treebank data; pruning is performed (among other operations) on certain types of phrases in specific configurations, including parentheticals, sentence-initial PPs and adverbial phrases such as "In particular,", "Accordingly," "In conclusion," etc. Knight and Marcu [12] compare a noisy-channel and a decision-tree approach applied to a phrase-structure analysis; they conclude that retaining grammaticality and information content can be two conflicting goals. [13] studies the effectiveness of applying the syntactic-based compression developed by [12] to sentences extracted for a summary.

3.3 Potential for Dependency Analyses

With the exception of [12], previous work on summarization based on a syntactic analysis mostly reports disappointing evaluation results. Significantly, no system involves dependency-based grammars. We are interested in exploring the potential of pruning a dependency-syntax analysis; the latter is based on a representation which directly encodes grammatical relations and not merely phrase structure. We believe that this allows a better characterization of the sub-parts of the tree that can safely be pruned while retaining essential meaning. Indeed, grammatical relations such as subject and direct object should correlate with central parts of the sentence, whereas subordinate clauses and temporal or locative adjuncts should correlate with peripheral information. Phrase structure tags such as "PP" (prepositional phrase) or "AdvP" (adverbial phrase) are ambiguous as to the grammatical contribution of the phrase to the sentence. Pruning decisions based on syntactic function criteria appear to us better motivated than those based on phrase structure. (Note that this is still different from pruning a semantic representation (e.g. [5]).

We are aware of no similar work on French. An equivalent of the Penn TreeBank for French is available [1], but is based on phrase structure. For our part, we were granted access to the source code for a robust, wide-coverage grammar of French, developed within a commercial grammar-checking product (Le Correcteur 101[TM], by Machina Sapiens and now Lingua Technologies[1]). The grammar is dependency-based: syntactic trees consist of nodes corresponding to the words of the sentence, and links between nodes are labelled with grammatical relations (of the type "subject", "direct object", "subordinate clause", "noun complement", etc.).

Les médias sont-ils responsables de l'efficacité des publicités qu'ils véhiculent ?
Arbre **sont**/verbe
   Sujet **les médias**/nom
   RepriseSujet **ils**/pronPers
   Attrib **responsables**/adj
     ComplAdj **de l'efficacité**/nom
       ComplNom **des publicités**/nom
         Relat **véhiculent**/verbe
           ObjetDirect **qu'**/pronRelat
           Sujet **ils**/pronPers
   FinProp **?**/ponctFinale

Fig. 1. Sample dependency tree: main verb is labelled as "Arbre". Some sub-trees are simplified.

The grammar aims to perform a complete syntactic analysis of the sentence (see Figure 1 for an indented presentation). In case of failure (due to severe writer error or to limits of the grammar), it provides a series of partial analyses of fragments of the sentence. In all cases, the parser ranks analyses using a weighting mechanism which is a function of weights of individual sub-trees and their combination. The detailed analysis produced by the grammar can be the basis of syntactic pruning for text reduction (this is illustrated in Figure 1).

This grammar has many advantages. In addition to its large coverage, it is able to provide a full analysis even with erroneous input (given its embedding within a grammar checking software product). It is indeed wide-coverage: its 80,000 lines of C++ code represent many person-years of development; the grammar consists of over 2500

---

[1] www.LinguaTechnologies.com

grammar rules and a dictionary containing over 88,000 entries. Note that other recent work [4] also uses this grammar in a non-correcting context, pertaining to controlled languages. The grammar does, however, have peculiarities which we discuss below. In brief, certain linguistic phenomena are ignored when they have no effect on correction.

> [Dans le monde en pleine effervescence d'Internet,]**locAdj** l'arrivée de HotWired marque le début de la cybermédiatisation [, le premier véritable média sur Internet]**app**.
> →
> L'arrivée de HotWired marque le début de la cybermédiatisation.

Fig. 2. Sample reduction: locative adjunct (locAdj) and apposition (app)

4 Methodology

We developed an algorithm which performs sentence reduction using syntactic pruning of the sentences. It proceeds by analyzing the sentence, then filtering the targeted relations, while applying anti-filters which prevent certain unwanted pruning by the filter. We should be able to maintain the sentence's grammaticality, insofar as we prune only subordinate material, and never the main verb of the sentence.

4.1 Analysis

The grammar of Le Correcteur 101 is used in its entirety. Extracted sentences are submitted one by one and a complete syntactic analysis of each is performed. Although the parser usually supplies all plausible analyses (more than one, in the case of ambiguous syntactic structures), our algorithm uses only the top-ranking one. This has some limitations: sometimes the correct analysis (as determined by a human judge) is not the highest-ranking one; in other instances, it shares the top rank with another analysis which appears first in the list, given the arbitrary ranking of equal-weight analyses. Our algorithm systematically chooses the first one, regardless. The impact of incorrect analyses is great, as it radically changes results: complements may be related by a different relation in the different analyses, and thus the reduction performed may not be the one intended. This fact (which has no bearing on the appropriateness of the syntactic pruning) has an impact on the evaluation of results.

4.2 Filtering

A filtering operation follows, which removes all sub-trees in the dependency graph that are labelled with relations from a predefined list. The entire sub-tree is removed, thus reducing the sentence (for example giving the result in Figure 1). The list of syntactic relations that trigger reduction is kept in an external file, allowing for easy testing of various sets of relations. We adapted the output of Le Correcteur 101 to produce parses corresponding to the full tree and to the pruned tree. The simplest version of a filter consists of a single mother-daughter pair related by relation R, where either node may be specified with a part-of-speech tag or by a lexical item. A more complex version involves multi-daughter structures, or grandmother-granddaughter pairs.

A preliminary test was performed using a wide number of relations. Only obligatory complements and phrasal specifiers (such as determiners) were kept. This resulted in a large reduction, producing much shorter sentences which however tended to be ungrammatical. It was determined that a much more focused approach would have a better chance of reducing the text while still preserving important elements and grammaticality. A second run, reported in [6], involved only the following relations: optional prepositional complements of the verb, subordinate clauses, noun appositions and interpolated clauses ("incises", in French). These are encoded with 6 relations, out of the 246 relations used by 101. For the current experiment, we used evaluation results from the previous one to fine tune our filtering algorithm. The present system targets 33 different relations (out of a possible 246), including the 6 mentioned above, and whose dsitribution is given in Table 1.

Table 1. Distribution of pruned relations

Relation category	Number of relations
Relative clauses	9
Subordinate clauses	5
Appositions and interpolated clauses	7
Noun modifiers	2
Emphasis markers	4
Adverbial modifiers	6
Total	33

The list was determined through introspection, on the grounds that these relations typically introduce peripheral syntactic information (see the conclusion for planned work on this aspect).

4.3   Anti-filters

The purpose of anti-filters is to prevent the removal of a sub-tree despite the relation it is labelled with. Two aspects of the anti-filters must be described. First, anti-filters can be lexically-based. For example, special processing must be applied to verb complements, to avoid incomplete and ungrammatical verb phrases. The grammar attaches all (obligatory) prepositional complements of the verb (for example, the obligatory locative "à Montréal" in "Il habite à Montréal") with the same relation as optional adjuncts such as time, place, manner, etc. This was done during the development of the grammar to reduce the number of possible analyses of sentences with prepositional phrases (given that this type of ambiguity is rampant, yet never relevant for correction purposes). To circumvent this problem, lexically-specified anti-filters were added for obligatory complements of the verb (e.g. the pair "habiter" and "à"). Since this is not encoded in the lexical entries used by the grammar, it had to be added; for our tests, we hand-coded only a number of such prepositional complements, for the verbs identified in our corpus (while pursuing a related research project of automatically identifying most interesting verb-preposition pairs through corpus analysis).

Secondly, anti-filters may examine more than a local sub-tree (i.e. one level). Indeed, anti-filters are expressed using the same "syntax" as the filter and may involve

Fig. 3. Sample pattern for 3-level anti-filters

three-level trees. This is useful for sentences containing specific types of complement clauses. Verbs which require an if-clause ("complétive en si"), such as "se demander" ("to wonder if/whether"), have their complement labelled with a subordinate clause relation (again, to reduce the number of unnecessary ambiguous analyses by the grammar) and the complementizer "si" is a dependent of the embedded verb. Yet this clause is an obligatory complement and should not be pruned (just as direct objects and predicative adjectives are not), but would be subject to pruning due to the "subordinate clause" label it receives and the distance between the main verb and the complementizer "si", which allows its identification as an obligatory clause. This requires a more complex pattern, since two relations are involved (see Figure 3).

5 Evaluation

In order to evaluate the performance of the pruning algorithm, we first built a corpus of sentences which were compressed by a human judge and then compared the automatically-reduced sentences to the manually reduced ones.

The test corpus consisted of 219 sentences of various lengths, extracted from the Corfrans corpus[2] which contains approximately 3000 sentences. We extracted random sentences, equally distributed among the different lengths of the sentences. We wished to have different lengths, so that we could evaluate how the reduction performance correlated with sentence length. Intuitively, short sentences should be hard to reduce, since the information they contain tends to be minimal. Longer sentences are expected to contain more unessential information, which makes them easier to reduce, but are also difficult to analyse, which may cause errors in the reduction.

For our tests, sentences of 5 or fewer words were discarded altogether. Among the rest, about 25% of sentences have between 6 and 15 words, about 25% have between 16 and 24 words, about 25% have between 25 and 35 words, and the remaining 25% have between 36 and 131 words (with a large spread in sentence length for that last interval). The final distribution is shown in Table 2.

The manual reduction was done using the following guidelines: the only operation allowed is the removal of words (no addition, rewording nor reordering); truth values and logical inferences must be preserved; only optional complements can be removed; resulting sentences are not syntactically nor semantically ill-formed; the only "errors"

---

[2] http://www.u-grenoble3.fr/idl/cursus/enseignants/tutin/corpus.htm

Table 2. Details of the evaluation corpus

Sentence length	# sentences	Total
6-15	5 sentences each	50
16-24	6 sentences each	54
25-35	5 sentences each	55
36-80, 82-86, 88, 89, 91, 94, 95, 99, 100, 104, 113, 131	1 sentence each	60

tolerated are unadjusted punctuation, affixation (agreement) or capitalization. An example is that shown in Figure 2 above.

The methodology used explains the small size of the corpus: evaluation necessitated a careful, manual reduction of all sentences. No evaluation corpus was at our disposal for this collection of dependency analyses of French texts and their reduced equivalent. According to [3], there is only one genuine annotated corpus for French, developed by Abeillé and her team [1]. The same lack of resources in French is remarked in [7].

6   Results

Each sentence was examined to determine (i) if it had been pruned, (ii) whether the result preserved essential content and (iii) how it compared to a manual reduction by a human expert. Of 219 sentences, 181 were reduced by our algorithm (82.6%). We partitioned the corpus into two halves, containing the shorter and longer sentences, respectively. In the short sentence partition (sentences with at most 28 words), 82 of 110 (74.5%) have been reduced, and in the second partition (sentences with more than 28 words), 99 of 109 (90.8%). This gives more evidence that short sentences are harder to reduce than long sentences.

Good (slightly ungrammatical)
Je désire que la vérité éclate et que si vraiment, comme tout semble le faire croire, c'est cet épicier qui était le diable, il est convenablement châtié.   *I want the truth to shine and the grocer to be apropriately punished, if really, as everything make us believe it, he was the devil* → Je désire que la vérité éclate et que si vraiment, c'est cet épicier qui était le diable, il est convenablement châtié.   *I want the truth to shine and the grocer to be apropriately punished, if really, he was the devil*
Acceptable
Le Soleil lui-même a de nombreuses répliques dans le ciel ;   *The Sun itself has many replicas in the sky ;* → Le Soleil lui-même a de nombreuses répliques ; *The Sun itself has many replicas;*
Bad
Je n'entretiens aucun doute sur le caractère national qui doit être donné au Bas-Canada ;   *I have no doubt about the national character that must be given to Low-Canada ;* → Je n'entretiens aucun doute ;   *I have no doubt ;*

Fig. 4. Sample of good, acceptable and bad reductions

Table 3. Quality of reductions

Sentences	Good	Acceptable	Bad	Total
Overall	106 (58.6%)	29 (16.0%)	46 (25.4%)	181
Short sentences	56 (68.3%)	13 (15.9%)	13 (15.9%)	82
Long sentences	50 (50.5%)	16 (16.2%)	33 (33.3%)	99

6.1   Semantic Content and Grammaticality

Correct reductions are those which are either good (i.e. the main semantic content of the original sentence is retained in the reduction - as in Figure 2) or acceptable (i.e. a part of the semantic content is lost, but the meaning of the reduced sentence is compatible with that of the original). Bad reductions are those where crucial semantic content was lost, or which are strongly ungrammatical. Some cases were ungrammatical but still considered acceptable (e.g. punctuation errors). See Figure 4 for sample reductions.

Table 3 shows that about 58% of the reductions were judged, by a human judge, to be "good"; 16% were "acceptable" and 25% "bad". If we consider separately the short sentences of the test corpus (with sentence length not exceeding 28 words), we see that the number of good reductions is greater in the short sentence partition (68% compared to 50%); there are more bad reductions among long sentences (33% compared to about 16%). The system thus appears weaker in the task of reducing longer sentences.

Table 4 shows the proportion of correctly reduced sentences (good or acceptable), among the 181 sentences that have been pruned. We see that most of the reduced sentences are correctly reduced and, as expected, the proportion of long sentences that are correctly reduced is significantly low, compared to short sentences.

Table 4. Ratio of reduced sentences

Sentences	Proportion of correctly reduced sentences (out of 181)
Overall	74.6%
Short sentences	84.2%
Long sentences	66.7%

6.2   Compression

We calculated the compression rate for each reduced sentence (i.e. the size of the pruned sentence, in words, compared to the number of words of the original sentence). We compared this to the "ideal" compression rate, corresponding to the manual reduction (which we refer to as the "Gold standard"). To estimate the performance of the reduction for different length sentences, results are shown for the corpus overall, and for both long and short sentence partitions. The first two columns give the average reduction rate for the reduction realized by the human judge (the Gold standard) and our system, respectively. The next three columns give some evaluation of the reduction. Classic precision and recall are calculated in terms of the number of words retained by the system, based on the Gold standard. Finally, agreement is a measure of the number of shared words between reduced sentence and Gold standard (divided by the total number of words in both). These simple measures (based on an ordered "bag of words") appear warranted, since word order had been preserved by the reduction method.

We note that, considering the overall reduction rate, 70.4% of words have been retained by the system. This shows potential for useful reduction of an extract. This result is not far from the ideal reduction rate (65.9%), but looking at the figures in Table 2, we see that 25.4% of the reduced sentences are incorrectly reduced. Correct pruning in some sentences is offset by incorrect pruning in others. Also, agreement is not very high, but precision and recall show that much of the content is preserved in our reductions, and that these reduced sentences do not contain too much noise. The reason for low agreement values is that a reduced sentence usually differs from its Gold standard by the presence or absence of a whole phrase, which usually contains many words.

Table 5. Reduction rate in terms of words (%)

Sentences	Gold standard vs Original sentence (%)	System reduction vs Original sentence (%)	Precision	Recall	Agreement (%)
Overall	65.9	70.4	79.1	83.8	67.6
Short sentences	78.4	80.7	86.9	89.2	77.4
Long sentences	53.6	60.3	71.3	78.4	57.9
Among "correct" reductions	67.3	73.9	80.5	87.9	71.4
Among "bad" reductions	60.0	57.1	73.4	68.1	52.8

The reduction rate in the last two lines of Table 5 separates correct (good or acceptable) reductions from bad ones. Thus, if only the correctly reduced sentences are considered, our system achieved 73.9% compression, while the human expert compressed by a ratio of 67.3% for the same sentences. Hence our correct reductions were still not reduced enough by human standards. Considering only the bad reductions, our compression rate is lower (57.1%) than that of the human judge (60%), but only slightly.

Where the reduction rate is smaller, reductions are typically worse (57.1% compression for bad reductions compared to 73.9% for correct ones). We can make the same observation for the sentence length (60.3% compression for long sentence compared to 80.7% for short ones). By analyzing the bad sentences, we see that most of them are long sentences that are incorrectly analyzed by the parser. Thus, long sentences, which would usually benefit more from the reduction process, unfortunately suffer from their difficulty to be correctly analyzed.

6.3   Some Problems with the Grammar or the Corpus

As expected, some incorrectly reduced sentences (28, or 12.8%) are due to the fact that no correct analysis has been returned by the parser. And when the grammar had trouble finding the right analysis among several, it sometimes suggested corrections that were inappropriate (in 2 cases). In 6 cases, severe errors in the original sentence prevented the parser from finding a good analysis (for example, the sentence contained both a short title and the actual sentence, not separated by a dash or other punctuation; or it lacked the proper punctuation). In 6 cases, the parser was unable to give a complete analysis, but provided analyses of fragments instead. Finally, in 14 cases (6.4%), adjuncts were removed but were actually obligatory and should not have been.

7   Discussion

7.1   Shortcomings of the System

By a closer inspection of sentences that are incorrectly reduced, we found that in some cases, a good reduction would necessitate major changes in our model, or some semantic information that is beyond the scope of the parser. In the example in Figure 5, the prepositional modifier "dans une opposition rigide et unilatérale" (in a rigid and unilateral opposition) cannot be argued to be required (syntactically) by either "peuvent" (can), nor "être" (to be) nor "pensés" (thought). Yet, semantically, removing the phrase produces an ungrammatical or semantically incoherent sentence. Although our goal is to test the hypothesis that syntactic pruning can yield useful sentence compression, we must recognize that the system suffers from its lack of semantics. Indeed, for each relation, the semantics of the pruned element should actually be taken into account before deciding whether pruning is appropriate.

> L'histoire des sciences est venue quant à elle montrer que le vrai et le faux ne peuvent être pensés dans une opposition rigide et unilatérale.   *History of science showed, as far as it is concerned, that the true and the false cannot be thought in a rigid and unilateral opposition.* →
> L'histoire des sciences est venue montrer que le vrai et le faux ne peuvent être pensés.   *History of science showed that the true and the false cannot be thought.*

Fig. 5. Sample unrecoverable reduction

The system is limited by the fact that it only takes the first analysis from the parser. It also does not adapt its processing according to sentence length, yet we have observed that this is not independent of the correctness of the pruning. We suspect that certain relations have a greater impact (a systematic comparison of relations pruned by the human judge and by the system has yet to be performed).

7.2   Possible Improvements

Two methods could be explored to control the pruning. Since sentences judged to be incorrectly reduced are those which undergo more reduction, it suggests that a compression threshold could be determined, below which pruning should not be applied (this could take the relation name into account). Also, we could use the fact that the system uses a grammar which can detect errors in sentences: submitting reduced sentences to parsing and correction could provide a way of refusing reduction when the result is ungrammatical.

We can also suggest a way of circumventing the problem of our system only using the first analysis (and hence sometimes going astray): the first N analyses could be used and pruned, comparing output; this output could be ranked according to compression ratio, rank of the original tree and frequency (as two original trees may be pruned to the same one)[3]. Finally, an experiment could be devised to compare the efficiency of different sets of pruning rules.

8   Conclusion and Future Work

We have proposed a method for text reduction which uses pruning of syntactic relations. The reduction rate achieved by our system (about 70% reduction of sentences) shows great promise for inclusion in a text reduction system such as summarization. Compared to previous work [6], we got a higher number of reduced sentences (82.6% vs 70.0%) and a better reduction rate (70.4% vs 74%). At the same time, the ratio of correctly reduced sentences has been significantly increased (74.6% vs 64%). Precision and recall values are about 80%, which is not bad, but should be improved to make our system suitable to be used in a real application. The loss of performance is due principally to the lack of semantic analysis and the limitations of the parser, which are beyond the scope of our model.

Future work will mainly focus on comparing our results with similar syntactic pruning based on phrase structure and other corpora and parsers (for French texts, initially). The Corfrans corpus at our disposal is tagged with phrase-structure analyses, so a comparison of both approaches should prove interesting. We also have access to a similar dependency grammar for English (developed as part of a grammar checker as well), in addition to other well-known freely-available English parsers. Its coverage is not as wide as that of Le Correcteur 101, but has a lexicon of verbs completely specified as to obligatory prepositional complements. For this reason, we intend to pursue experiments on English texts. The limits of the parser seem to strongly influence the results, so more experiments should be realized with very good parsers.

Acknowledgements

This researched was funded by a grant from the National Science and Engineering Research Council awarded to Lyne Da Sylva. Many thanks to Claude Coulombe, president of Lingua Technologies, for use of the source code for Le Correcteur 101. We also wish to thank our research assistants, Frédéric Doll and Myriam Beauchemin.

References

1. A. Abeillé, L. Clément, and F. Toussenel. Building a treebank for french. In Abeillé A., editor, *Treebanks: Building and Using Parsed Corpora*, pages 165–188. Kluwer Academic Publishers, 2003.
2. R. Barzilay, K. McKeown, and M Elhadad. Information fusion in the context of multi-document summarization. In *Proceedings of the 37th Annual Meeting of the Association for Computational Linguistics*, pages 550–557, New Brunswick, NJ, 1999. Association for Computational Linguistics.

---

[3] We thank an anonymous reviewer of this paper for this idea.

3. P. Blache and J.-Y. Morin. Une grille d'évaluation pour les analyseurs syntaxiques. In *TALN 2003*, pages 77–86, Batz-sur-mer, 11-14 juin 2003.
4. C. Coulombe, F. Doll, and P. Drouin. Intégration d'un analyseur syntaxique à large couverture dans un outil de langage contrôlé en français. *Lingvisticae Investigationes (Machine Translation, Controlled Languages and Specialised Languages)*, 28(1), 2005.
5. M. Fiszman, T.C. Rindflesch, and H. Kilicoglu. Abstraction summarization for managing the biomedical research literature. In *Proceedings of the Computational Lexical Semantics Workshop, HLT-NAACL 2004*, pages 76–83, Boston, Massachussetts, USA, May 2-7, 2004.
6. M. Gagnon and L. Da Sylva. Text summarization by sentence extraction and syntactic pruning. In *Computational Linguistics in the North-East (CLiNE)*, Gatineau, 2005.
7. M.-J. Goulet and J. Bourgeoys. Le projet gÉraf : guide pour l'évaluation des résumés automatiques français. In *TALN 2004,*, Fès, 19-21 avril 2004.
8. G. Grefenstette. Producing intelligent telegraphic text reduction to provide an audio scanning service for the blind. In *Working Notes of the Workshop on Intelligent Text Summarization*, pages 111–117, Menlo Park, CA, 1998. American Association for Artificial Intelligence Spring Symposium Series.
9. G. Grefenstette. Light parsing as finite-state filtering. In *Proceedings ECAI '96 Workshop on Extended Finite State Models of Language*, Budapest, August 11-12, 1996.
10. M. Inderjeet and M.T. Maybury. *Advances in Automatic Text Summarization*. MIT Press, 1999.
11. H. Jing and K McKeown. The decomposition of human-written summary sentences. In *Proceedings of the 22nd International Conference on Research and Development in Information Retrieval (SIGIR'99)*, pages 129–136, New York, 1999. Association for Computing Machinery.
12. K. Knight and D. Marcu. Summarization beyond sentence extraction: A probabilistic approach to sentence compression. *Artificial Intelligence*, 139:91–107, 2002.
13. C.-Y. Lin. Improving summarization performance by sentence compression - a pilot study. In *Proceedings of the Sixth International Workshop on Information Retrieval with Asian Languages (IRAL 2003)*, Sapporo, Japan, July 7, 2003.
14. I. Mani. *Automatic Summarization*. John Benjamins, Amsterdam; Philadelphia, 2001.
15. J.-L. Minel. Résumé automatique de textes. *Traitement automatique des langues*, 45(1), 2004.
16. NIST. Document understanding conference - introduction. Technical report, [http://www-nlpir.nist.gov/projects/duc/intro. html].
17. H. Saggion and G. Lapalme. Selective analysis for the automatic generation of summaries. In C. Beghtol, L. Howarth, and N. Williamson, editors, *Dynamism and Stability in Knowledge Organization – Proceedings of the Sixth International ISKO Conference*, pages 176–181, Toronto, jul 2000. International Society of Knowledge Organization, Ergon Verlag.
18. G.L. Thione, M.H. van den Berg, L. Polanyi, and C. Culy. Hybrid text summarization: Combining external relevance measures with structural analysis. In *Proceedings of the ACL2004 Workshop Text Summarization Branches Out*, Barcelona, Spain, July 25-26, 2004.

Beyond the Bag of Words:
A Text Representation for Sentence Selection

Maria Fernanda Caropreso[1] and Stan Matwin[1,2]

[1] School of Information Technology and Engineering. University of Ottawa
Ottawa, Ontario K1N 6N5
{caropres, stan}@site.uottawa.ca
[2] Institute for Computer Science, Polish Academy of Science, Wavsaw

Abstract. Sentence selection shares some but not all the characteristics of Automatic Text Categorization. Therefore some but not all the same techniques should be used. In this paper we study a syntactic and semantic enriched text representation for the sentence selection task in a genomics corpus. We show that using technical dictionaries and syntactic relations is beneficial for our problem when using state of the art machine learning algorithms. Furthermore, the syntactic relations can be used by a first order rule learner to obtain even better performance.

1 Introduction

Sentence selection (SS) consists in identifying the relevant sentences for a particular purpose. This is a necessary step in many document-processing tasks, such as Text Summarization (TS) and Information Extraction (IE). The proportion of sentences considered relevant for the above tasks in a given document is usually low, making some pre-filtering a prerequisite.

Sentence selection can be considered a particular case of Automatic Text Categorization (ATC), which consists in automatically building programs capable of labeling natural language texts with categories from a predefined set. ATC is performed using standard Machine Learning methods in a supervised learning task. The standard text representation used in ATC is the Bag of Words (BOW), which consists of representing each document by the words that occur in it. This representation is also used in related tasks such as Information Retrieval (IR) and IE. Different ways of expanding this representation have been tried on these areas of research, some of the expansions aiming to add some semantic or syntactic knowledge. For example, on the semantic side, stemming words[1], clustering similar terms together [10], and using background knowledge [25] have been tried. Less work has been done on the syntactic side. The latest include using noun phrases [11] [14] and statistical phrases [13] [1] in the representation, defining position related predicates in an Inductive Logic Programming (ILP) system [2], and incorporating the order of noun phrases in the representation [8].

---

[1] Even when stemming requires only morphological processing, we consider it to semantically expand the representation since several words will represent the same sense once stemmed.

L. Lamontagne and M. Marchand (Eds.): Canadian AI 2006, LNAI 4013, pp. 324–335, 2006.
© Springer-Verlag Berlin Heidelberg 2006

Even when SS and ATC are related, not all their characteristics are the same. One of the differences is that the sentences are short in length, with few words from the vocabulary happening in each of them. That would result in an even more sparse representation than in the ATC case. Another difference is that ATC is usually used to recognize the general topic of a document, while SS concentrates on more specific details. Because of these differences, some variations to the standard representations and techniques usually used for ATC might be beneficial for SS.

We address the task of sentence selection working on a corpus of texts on genetics. The sentences are short in length and the vocabulary of this corpus is highly specific. We believe that, because of these characteristics, the use of syntactic and semantic knowledge could be even more beneficial than in a collection of a more general nature. The extensions that we propose in this paper have, to our best knowledge, been tried neither for document classification nor for sentence selection.

Our work is devoted to identification of relevant sentences in scientific abstracts on genetics. Those abstracts are written in natural language and can be searched via the Internet using keyword queries. However, the queries would retrieve a large superset of relevant papers [17] from which we would like to identify the sentences that express an interaction between genes and/or proteins. Due to the continuous submission of new abstracts, this task becomes repetitive and time consuming. Because of that, automatic sentence selection is considered of interest to the scientific community. We automatically learn classifiers that categorize the sentences from the abstracts into two classes: those that describe an interaction between genes and/or proteins and those that do not. In those classifiers we study the usefulness of including syntactic and semantic knowledge in the text representation. We accomplish this by adding into the representation pairs of related words (to which we will refer as syntactic bi-grams) obtained from a syntactic parser together with technically related dictionaries. Our experiments include the state of the art machine learning algorithms Naïve Bayes and Support Vector Machine, as well as a relational learner for which a particular relational representation was created.

In the remainder of this paper we first introduce some related work and we present the details of our approach and our dataset. Afterwards we present the representations that we used and the experiments we performed together with their results and their analysis. We finish the paper presenting our conclusions and future work.

2   Related Work

The usefulness of syntactic and statistical phrases compared to the BOW was first studied by Fagan [4] in the IR context. In these experiments it was shown that statistical phrases were not only easier to obtain but they also improved performance more than syntactic phrases.

In [11] and [12] Lewis compared different representations using either words or syntactic phrases (but not a combination of both) for IR and ATC. The results with the phrases representation showed no significant improvement with respect to the representation using the BOW. Mitra et al. [14] study the usefulness of linguistic knowledge for an IR system. The results indicate that the noun phrases are useful for lowly ranked answers but not so much for the highly ranked answers where the words alone perform well. Similar results were obtained in ATC by Furnkranz et al. [6]

when building syntactic phrases following some particular syntactic patterns learned from the data by an extraction system. Dumais et al. [3] studied the use of syntactic phrases with a variety of text classifiers on the Reuters-21578 collection showing no benefit at all from the use of this representation. Scott and Matwin [19] also noted no significant improvement of the performance by adding noun phrases to the representation of the same corpus but using a different Machine Learning algorithm.

Furnkranz et al. [5], Mladenic and Grobelnik [13] and Caropreso et al. [1] studied the usefulness of statistical phrases in ATC. The more discriminating phrases were added to the BOW. The experiments showed that the use of these phrases could in some cases improve the classification.

Maarek's system GURU [27] used lexical affinities for indexing purposes in an IR task. Linguistically, lexical affinities are words that are involved in a modifier-modified relationship and that appear often together in the language. This work, however, only takes into consideration the closeness of the chosen words.

Cohen and Singer [2] study the importance of introducing the order of the words in the text representation by defining position related predicates in an ILP system. This has been extended by Goadrich et al. [8] in recent research in the IE area, incorporating the order of noun phrases into the representation. In other work in IE, Ray and Craven [18] incorporate syntactic phrases to a Hidden Markov Model (HMM) that recognizes the grammatical structure of sentences expressing biomedical relations. The results show that this approach learns more accurate models than simpler HMMs that do not use phrases in the representation. One more approach to IE that uses syntactic information is Temkin and Gilder work [23]. In this work a Context Free Grammar (CFG) was defined to recognize protein, gene and small molecule interactions. The results show that efficient parsers can be constructed for extracting these relations.

Several studies have introduced semantic knowledge in ATC. Siolas [20] does that by building a kernel that take into account the semantic distance: first between the different words based on WordNet, and then using Fisher metrics in a way similar to Latent Semantic Indexing (LSI). Zelikovitz and Hirsh [25] show that the ATC accuracy can be improved by adding extra semantic knowledge into the LSI representation coming from unclassified documents.

3 Our Approach and Dataset

We study the usefulness of including syntactic and semantic knowledge in the text representation for the selection of sentences from technical genomic texts. In this specific context, the occurrence (or not) of specialized terms is expected to discriminate between sentences that contain information about genes and/or proteins interaction, and those that do not contain that information. We expect syntactic bi-grams formed by words that are syntactically linked to provide detailed information on whether two genes and/or proteins are interacting with each other. Such phrases could be formed for example by an adjective modifying a noun, the main noun in the subject or object role of a sentence together with its verb, or the main noun in a prepositional phrase together with either the noun or verb it modifies. Using the syntactic bi-grams together with their single words, we represented the sentences and we evaluated the classification performance of this representation compared to the

BOW. Our experiments include state of the art machine learning algorithms Naïve Bayes and Support Vector Machine, and they were performed using Weka [24]. A relational representation was also obtained using the links information, and its performance evaluated using the relational learner Aleph [21].

It is understood by linguistics that syntactically related words express semantic concepts [26]. By using syntactic bi-grams we are then already incorporating into the representation some basic semantics. We further enrich the representation by introducing some more semantic knowledge to help with the specific vocabulary. A list of proteins and genes was extracted from the SwissProt Protein Knowledgebase[2]. The words found in this list were replaced in our representation by a lexical marker (the word geneprot). A list of words commonly used in the genetic bibliography to denote interactions was borrowed from Temkin and Gilder work [23] and included as facts in one of the experiments with the relational representation.

Our experiments were done on a corpus created by, the CADERIGE project[3]. The examples consist of only one sentence, which were automatically selected from Med-Line abstracts with a query *Bacillus subtilis transcription*. The sentences were then pre-filtered to keep only those 932 that contain at least two names of either genes or proteins. The remaining sentences were manually categorized as positive or negative according to whether they describe or they do not describe a genomic interaction. The resulted was a balanced dataset with 470 positive and 462 negative examples.

Some earlier work done on this corpus is presented in [15]. It reports the recall and precision result obtained by the C4.5 algorithm and a variation of Naïve Bayes (NB) algorithm (that specializes it for the case of short documents). The attributes were all words after stemming, stop word removal and some filtering using Information Gain. The best results were 84.12% recall and 87.89% precision with the variation of NB.

While modifying the representation of the corpus for our experiments, around 5% of the examples were lost due to failure of the parser on those sentences. Our final dataset contains 885 examples, being 440 positive and 445 negative.

4   Syntactic Representation and Experiments

In this section we present an example of the analysis performed by the Link Parser [22], the links it recognized in our collection and how they are used in the text representation. We then present the experiments that we performed and the results that we obtained when using that representation to learn a classifier for the positive examples of our dataset.

The Link Parser was selected for specifically providing the relation between words in the sentence by establishing a link between them In order to create a syntactic representation we ran the parser on each sentence of the data collection, identified some syntactic links, such as the object of a verb, and we built syntactic bi-grams with the linked words. Out of the many links identified by the parser, we only took into consideration those ones that we believe could help enrich our representation:

---

[2] Swiss-Prot is an annotated protein sequence database available on-line at http://ca.expasy.org/sprot/. Among all the information provided is a "Short description of entries in Swiss-Prot" from which we extracted the names of proteins and genes.

[3] CADERIGE Project, http://caderige.imag.fr/

- A and AN: link an adjective or a noun (respectively) to the noun it modifies.
- Ss: links the head of a noun phrase to the verb to which the phrase is the subject.
- Os: links the head of a noun phrase to the verb to which the phrase is the object.
- Pa: links forms of the verb "have" to a participle verb.
- Mg: links nouns with present participles
- MVp and J (or Jp): MVp links the verb to a preposition at the beginning of a prepositional phrase, and J (or Jp) links that preposition to the noun that is head of the noun phrase inside the prepositional phrase. We established the M relation, which links the verb in a MVp to the noun in a corresponding Js.

Figure 1 shows all the links we identified among the set of links returned by the Link Parser for the first sentence of our collection.[4] From this analysis, the following syntactic bi-grams could be built: spo0a_mutant, s210a_mutant, spoiie_activation, promoter_activation, mutant_exhibited, it_was, exhibited_change, exhibited_wild-type, defective_activation, wild-type_binding, was_defective.

The previous are all the syntactic bi-grams we built. In the following experiments only some of them were used at a time, according to the kind of link we were permitting (e.g. when representing noun phrases only the A and AN links were permitted). The type of the link and the morphological information (i.e. which words are nouns, adjectives and verbs, which is also provided by the Link Parser) were not included in the representation. We are planning to include this information in our future work. Some of the previous syntactic bi-grams were modified because they contained a gene or protein name from the SwissProt list. Thus s210a_mutant was replaced by gene-prot_mutant. Unfortunately spo0a and spoiie were not found in the list and therefore were not replaced by our lexical marker.

The s210a.a spo0a.a mutant.n exhibited.v no.d change.n from wild-type binding.v

although it was.v defective.a in spoiia.n and spoiie.a promoter.n activation.n

Fig. 1. Links identified for the first sentence of our collection

It must be noticed that the extra effort of parsing is reduced in our experiments since the abstracts were pre-filtered and only few sentences possibly containing an interaction between genes/proteins were kept. In larger datasets a more efficient parsing approach could be taken, as for example the partial parsing within a fixed size window presented by Jacquemin [28].

---

[4] The Link parser returns for each sentence several different links sets, and a cost vector value associated to each of them. Only the highest ranked links set was used in these experiments.

After learning and evaluating classifiers for the different representations, the results were compared using Accuracy, Precision, Recall and F1-measure. Given a contingency table containing TP (True Positives), FP (False Positives), FN (False Negatives) and TN (True Negatives), the previous measures are defined as:

- Accuracy = (TP + TN) / (TP + TN+ FP +FN)
- Precision (Pr) = TP / (TP + FP)
- Recall (Re) = TP / (TP + FN)
- F1 = 2*Pr*Re / (Pr + Re)

As a baseline we use the BOW representation (all the words that appear in any of the links.) We compare its performance with the one obtained when using it together with some or all of the recognized syntactic bi-grams. We differentiate the Noun Phrases representation, the Subject and Object representation, the Prepositional Phrases representation and the representation using all the links together.

Previous to the classification, a subset of the total set of features was selected using the information gain metric. This filter kept some of the syntactic bi-grams among the most discriminating features, giving a first confirmation of their usefulness for the classification task [1]. Among the selected syntactic bi-grams, several include our lexical marker, even when by itself it was not selected as discriminant when using the BOW representation. Some examples of these syntactic bi-grams are `geneprot-protein`, `mutant-geneprot`, `encodes-geneprot`. Some examples of other syntactic bi-grams also kept after filtering are `bacillus-subtilis`, `indicated-analysis`, `protein-encodes`.

Table 1 shows the Accuracy, Precision, Recall and F1-measure obtained by the Naïve Bayes Simple and the Support Vector Machine learners of the Weka Package. The experiments were performed using the default parameters for each learner and the number of features that resulted in the best accuracy in preliminary experiments.

Table 1. Averaged Accuracy, Precision, Recall and F1-measure in 10 runs of 10-fold cross-validation. The results in bold denote a statistically significant increase over the BOW (first column). The use of italic denotes a statistically significant decrease with respect to the BOW.

Learning Algorithm	Performance measure	Words in links	Noun Phrases Bi-grams	Subject and Object Bi-grams	Prep. Phrases Bi-grams	All the syntactic Bi-grams
Naïve Bayes 500 features	Accuracy	0.81	0.81	0.81	*0.80*	**0.83**
	Precision	0.81	*0.80*	0.81	**0.82**	**0.83**
	Recall	0.82	0.83	*0.81*	*0.78*	**0.85**
	F1-measure	0.82	0.81	*0.81*	*0.80*	**0.84**
SVM 500 features	Accuracy	0.77	0.77	0.77	**0.78**	**0.81**
	Precision	0.78	**0.79**	0.78	**0.80**	**0.84**
	Recall	0.76	0.76	**0.77**	0.75	**0.79**
	F1-measure	0.77	0.77	0.77	0.77	**0.81**

In most cases, the results do not show statistically significant difference with respect to the BOW when using noun phrase bi-grams and subject/object bi-grams to enrich the BOW representation. When using prepositional phrase bi-grams the results are mixed depending on the measure of choice. However, when using all the syntactic bi-grams together, the results show a consistent statistically significant increase for the four considered measures. That indicates that at least two kinds of the used syntactic bi-grams are relevant to the classification when combined.

We also performed preliminary experiments using the Decision Tree Learner from the Weka Package. Although the pattern of increased accuracy when using all the syntactic bi-grams holds, the values were only in the 70% range. This low performance was already noticed by Ould [16] who argued that it might be due to the sparseness of the representation.

5 Relational Representation and Experiments

As noted in the previous experiments, the syntactic relation between some words in a sentence seems to be relevant to the sentence selection task we are performing. It is natural then to think of a relational representation that can capture these relations. This new representation can then be used by a relational learner system, exploiting the advantages of this kind of systems [7]. Among others, predicates to help the classification can be easily defined, and relations among three words could be discovered (as two bi-grams with a transitive relation).

In order to obtain this relational representation, the same links obtained for the syntactic representation were used and relations were built between the linked words. The predicate "link(s,w1,w2)" used in our representation expresses that in the sentence s1 there is a relation between the two words w1 and w2 as indicated by the presence of a link found by the parser.

Given the same sentence from figure 1, the following relations could be built:

```
link(s1,mutant,s210a),          link(s1,was,it),
link(s1,mutant,geneprot),       link(s1,defective,was),
link(s1,exhibited,mutant),      link(s1,activation,defective),
link(s1,change,exhibited),      link(s1,activation,spoiie),
link(s1,wildtype,exhibited),    link(s1,activation,promoter)
link(s1,binding,wildtype),
```

This relational representation introduces the syntactic relations of the words in the sentences. This representation was compared in our experiments with a baseline using propositional logic denoting whether a word occurs or not in a sentence but missing the information of the relations between words, which is equivalent to the BOW. Instead of physically creating the propositional representation, we simulated it by defining the predicate *lexexist* that represents the presence of a word in a particular sentence and the fact that the word is involved in a link (some words, as for example the articles, were not included in any of the considered links). For this, we use the unbounded variable "_" that will take any value. The predicate definition is:

```
lexexist(S,W)  :- link(S,W,_).
lexexist(S,W)  :- link(S,_,W).
```

We also compared the previous relational representation performance with the one obtained when adding extra background knowledge. For this purpose, we added to the representation the list of words denoting interactions presented in [23]. Each of the words in the list was given as a parameter of the fact *interaction*. The predicate *interacts* was defined representing the fact that a particular word in a sentence is linked to an interaction word.

```
interaction(initiate).
interaction(stimulate).    interacts(S,W):-link(S,W,I),interaction(I).
interaction(regulate).     interacts(S,W):-link(S,I,W),interaction(I).
. . . .
```

In this way we performed three different experiments by providing Aleph with only one file containing the genomic information in a relational representation and by instructing it on what kind of rules could be learned. Figure 2 shows some of the rules learned when allowing words, syntactic links and interactions. In the following we analyze those rules.

Our first observation is that few training examples are covered by each rule, the first one covering 29 positive examples and 1 negative example, and thereafter dropping to 16 examples (approximately 2% of the training examples.) The second observation is that geneprot is already chosen in the third rule, marking the usefulness of having replaced the technical vocabulary by this lexical marker. However, the gene/protein *sigmak,* which was not found in the Swissprot list and therefore was not replaced, seems to be very discriminating in this dataset. This gives us the hint that we might want to consider different levels in a hierarchy of genes/proteins instead of a single-level list. We will consider this in our future work.

```
[Rule1]pos(S):-lexexist(S,sigmak).[29;1]
[Rule2]pos(S):-lexexist(S,_expression),lexexist(S,fusion).[16;0]
[Rule3]pos(S):-lexexist(S,geneprot),lexexist(S,vivo).[15;1]
[Rule4]pos(S):-link(S,processing,B).[14;1]
[Rule5]pos(S):-link(S,B,geneprot),link(S,B,bdependent).[14;1]
[Rule6]pos(S):-link(S,geneprot,transcription),link(S,is,B).[13;0]
[Rule7]pos(S):-link(S,show,B),interacts(S,C).[12;1]
. . . .
[Rule12]pos(S):-link(S,geneprot,protein).[11;1]
[Rule13]pos(S):-link(S,geneprot,gene).[10;1]
. . . .
[Rule17]pos(S):-interacts(S,transcription),interacts(S,geneprot).[11;0]
. . . .
```

Fig. 2. Some rules learned when allowing words, syntactic links and interactions

Starting with rule 4 the links help to discover discriminating rules. In rule 4 we notice that it is not always a pair of words that is important, but as in this case, the fact that the word *processing* is linked to another one makes it discriminating of the class. In rule 5 there is a word linked to both *geneprot* and *bdependent*, being the double link relevant for the discriminating rule. In rules 6, 12 and 13 we find the pairs *geneprot_transcription, geneprot_protein* and *geneprot_gene* being the most discriminating after various other rules have been applied.

Finally, we observe the use of the predicate *interacts* in rule 7 where it establishes that there is a word linked to an interaction term. In rule 17 it establishes that both *transcription* and *geneprot* are linked to an interaction word.

When running the experiments, around 80 rules were learned. They were used without any pruning on the test sets. The average Accuracy, Precision, Recall and F1-measure obtained after 10 runs of 10-fold cross-validation for the 3 experiments are shown in table 2.

We observe a higher accuracy with respect to the results obtained by Naïve Bayes and Support Vector Machine, even when the representation equivalent to the BOW is used. We explain this as the result of two main characteristics:

1. the flexibility of the relations: letting the learner choose what are the important parts of a relation, as if only one or both words were fixed, makes them more flexible than the pre-fixed phrases used in the syntactic representation. The relational representation also gives the opportunity of bridging two non-linked words by the mean of a third one linked to both (see rule 5 in the examples).
2. the sparseness of the collection: having many rules, each one adjusted to the few examples it covers, seems to be beneficial for this short sentences collection with very sparse vocabulary.

Table 2. Averaged Accuracy, Precision, Recall and F1-measure in 10 runs of 10-fold cross-validation running Aleph. The results in bold denote a statistically significant increase over the basic relational representation (Words and Links, in the central column). The use of italic denotes a statistically significant decrease with respect to the basic relational representation.

Learning Algorithm	Performance measure	Only Words	Words and Links	Words, Links and Interactions
Aleph	Accuracy	*0.90*	0.93	**0.94**
	Precision	*0.94*	0.95	0.96
	Recall	*0.87*	0.92	**0.93**
	F1-measure	*0.90*	0.94	**0.94**

Similar to the previous results, we observe a statistically significant increase in the performance (according to the four considered measures) when the links are used in the representation. That marks once again the importance of a syntactic representation.

Finally we also observe a statistically significant increase in accuracy and recall when adding some semantic background knowledge to the representation, i.e. the interactions list (the last column in table 3). This increase in the recall was not at the expense of the precision.

6 Conclusions and Future Work

In this paper we have presented the problem of sentence selection from a genetic corpus and how we envisioned the contribution of semantic and syntactic knowledge in this task. We directly introduced semantic knowledge in the representation by replacing the words found in a list of genes/proteins. Basic semantic knowledge was also incorporated in the representation by mean of syntactic relations. This was accomplished extending the set of features with bi-grams obtained from a syntactic parser. We have empirically showed that this knowledge is useful for sentence selection from this genetic corpus when using several different machine learning methods. We have also shown that the relational learner Aleph performs better than the other algorithms tried, even when an analogous to the BOW was used. The use of the syntactic information in the relational representation highly significantly improved the performance (e.g. an increase of 0.04 for the F1 measure with respect to the representation using only words). This confirmed the results previously obtained with other algorithms using the syntactic bi-grams. Adding extra semantic knowledge to this representation by identifying the interaction words further helped with the classification by improving the recall with no decrement of the precision.

In the future we plan to extend the use of semantic background knowledge to include hierarchies of genes/proteins. One possible source for that could be the publicly available Gene Ontology. We also plan to extend the use of syntactic knowledge by differentiating the links according to the kind of relation they denote (noun phrases, subject, etc.) and introducing morphological information (whether a word is a noun, an adjective, a verb, etc.) We would also like to use the relational representation in state of the art classification methods by transforming the predicates into features in a vector space or probabilistic model. We plan to do this by applying propositionalization as presented by Kramer [9]. Finally, we plan to try this approach on a similar but larger dataset in the genetic abstracts context, as well as on a different domain on Legal documents, the HOLJ Corpus created by Hachey and Grover [29].

Acknowledgements

This work is supported by the Natural Sciences and Engineering Council of Canada and the Ontario Centres of Excellence.

References

1. Caropreso, M.F., Matwin, S, and Sebastiani, F. "A learner-independent evaluation of the usefulness of statistical phrases for automated text categorization". In Amita G. Chin (ed.), *Text Databases and Document Management: Theory and Practice*, Idea Group Publishing, Hershey, US, 2001, pp. 78-102.
2. W. W. Cohen and Y. Singer (1999): Context-sensitive learning methods for text categorization in ACM Trans. Inf. Syst. 17(2): 141-173 (1999).
3. S. T. Dumais, J. Platt, D. Heckerman, and M. Sahami. Inductive learning algorithms and representations for text categorization. In G. Gardarin, J. C. French, N. Pissinou, K. Makki, and L. Bouganim, editors, Proceedings of CIKM-98, 7th ACM International Conference on Information and Knowledge Management, pages 148{155, Bethesda, US, 1998. ACM Press, New York, US.
4. J. L. Fagan. Experiments in automatic phrase indexing for document retrieval: a comparison of syntactic and non-syntactic methods. PhD thesis, Department of Computer Science, Cornell University, Ithaca, US, 1987.

5. J. Furnkranz. A study using n-gram features for text categorization. Technical Report TR-98-30, Oesterreichisches Forschungsinstitut Artificial Intelligence, Wien, AT, 1998.
6. J. Furnkranz, T. M. Mitchell, and E. Rilo®. A case study in using linguistic phrases for text categorization on the WWW. In Proceedings of the 1st AAAI Workshop on Learning for Text Categorization, pages 5{12, Madison, US, 1998.
7. J. Furnkranz. Inductive Logic Programming (a short introduction and a thesis abstract).
8. M. Goadrich, L. Oliphant and J. Shavlik (2004). Learning Ensembles of First-Order Clauses for Recall-Precision Curves: A Case Study in Biomedical Information Extraction. *Proceedings of the Fourteenth International Conference on Inductive Logic Programming*, Porto, Portugal.
9. S. Kramer. Relational Learning vs. Propositionalization. PhD. Thesis, Vienna University of Technology, Vienna, Austria, 1999.
10. D. D. Lewis and W. B. Croft. Term clustering of syntactic phrases. In Proceedings of SIGIR-90, 13th ACM International Conference on Research and Development in Information Retrieval, pages 385{404, Bruxelles, BE, 1990.
11. Lewis D D, "Representation and Learning in Information Retrieval", Ph.D. dissertation, University of Massachusetts, 1992.
12. D. D. Lewis. An evaluation of phrasal and clustered representations on a text categorization task. In N. J. Belkin, P. Ingwersen, and A. M. Pejtersen, editors, Proceedings of SIGIR-92, 15th ACM International Conference on Research and Development in Information Retrieval, pages 37-50, Kobenhavn, DK, 1992. ACM Press, New York, US.
13. Mladenic, D. and Grobelnik, M. Word sequences as features in text learning. Proceedings of *ERK-98, the seventh Electrotecnical and Computer Science Conference* (pp. 145-148). Ljubljana, Slovenia. 1998
14. M. Mitra, C. Buckley, A. Singhal, and C. Cardie, "An Analysis of Statistical and Syntactic Phrases". *5TH RIAO Conference, Computer-Assisted Information Searching On the Internet*, 200-214, 1997.
15. Nédellec C., Ould Abdel Vetah M., and Bessières P., "Sentence Filtering for Information Extraction in Genomics: A Classification Problem," *Proceedings of the International Conference on Practical Knowledge Discovery in Databases* (PKDD'2001), pp. 326–338, Springer Verlag, LNAI 2167, Freiburg, September, 2001.
16. Ould, M. Apprentissage Automatique Applique a l'Extraction d'Information a Partir de Textes Biologiques. PhD Thesis. L'Universite Paris-Sud. France. 2005
17. Ould, M., Caropreso, F., Manine, P., Nedellec, C., Matwin, S., "Sentence Categorization in Genomics Bibliography: a Naïve Bayes Approach", Informatique pour lèanalyse du transcriptome, Paris, 2003.
18. Soumya Ray, Mark Craven. Representing Sentence Structure in Hidden Markov Models for Information Extraction. Proceedings of the 17th International Joint Conference on Artificial Intelligence (IJCAI-2001)
19. Sam Scott, Stan Matwin. Feature Engineering for Text Classification. Proceedings of ICML-99, 16th International Conference on Machine Learning, 1999.
20. Siolas, G. Modèles probabilistes et noyaux pour l'extraction d'informations à partir de documents. Thèse de doctorat de l'Université Paris 6. July 2003.
21. Srinivasan, A. The Aleph Manual. 1993.
   http://web.comlab.ox.ac.uk/oucl/research/areas/machlearn/Aleph/aleph_toc.html
22. D. Sleator and D. Temperley. 1991. Parsing English with a Link Grammar. Carnegie Mellon University Computer Science technical report CMU-CS-91-196, October 1991.
23. Temkin JM, Gilder MR. Extraction of protein interaction information from unstructured text using a context-free grammar. Bioinformatics. 19(16):2046-53, 2003.

24. Ian H. Witten and Eibe Frank. Data Mining: Practical machine learning tools and techniques, 2nd Edition, Morgan Kaufmann, San Francisco, 2005.
25. Sarah Zelikovitz and Haym Hirsh. Improving Text Classification with LSI Using Background Knowledge. Proceedings of CIKM-01, 10th ACM International Conference on Information and Knowledge Management. 2001
26. Fillmore, Charles J. The Case for Case. In Bach and Harms (Ed.): Universals in Linguistic Theory. New York: Holt, Rinehart, and Winston, 1-88. 1968.
27. Maarek, Y., Berry, D.M. & Kaiser, G.E.: GURU: Information Retrieval for Reuse, in P.Hall (ed.), Landmark Contributions in Software Reuse and Reverse Engineering, 1994
28. Christian Jacquemin. *What is the tree that we see through the window: A linguistic approach to windowing and term variation.* Information Processing and Management, 32(4):445--458, 1996.
29. Ben Hachey and Claire Grover. Sequence Modelling for Sentence Classification in a Legal Summarisation System. In: *Proceedings of the 2005 ACM Symposium on Applied Computing*, 2005.

Sentiment Tagging of Adjectives
at the Meaning Level

Alina Andreevskaia and Sabine Bergler

Department of Computer Science and Software Engineering, Concordia University
1455 De Maisonneuve Blvd. West H3G 1M8 Montreal, Quebec
{andreev, bergler}@cs.concordia.ca

Abstract. We present a sentiment tagging system which is based on multiple bootstrapping runs on WordNet synsets and glosses using different non-intersecting seed lists of manually annotated words. The system is further enhanced by the addition of a module for partial sense disambiguation of sentiment-bearing adjectives using combinatorial patterns. This (1) enables sentiment annotation at the sense, rather than whole word level, and (2) provides an effective tool for the automatic cleaning of the lists of sentiment-annotated words. The resulting cleaned list of 2907 English sentiment-bearing adjectives achieved a performance comparable to that of human annotation, as evaluated by the agreement rate between two manually annotated lists of sentiment-marked adjectives. The issues of sentiment tag extraction, evaluation and precision/recall tradeoffs are discussed.

1 Introduction

In recent years, the task of *sentiment tagging*, or tagging language elements — usually phrases or texts — as positive, negative or other (neutral or mixed) according to the sentiment they express, has attracted considerable attention of researchers (e.g., [1, 2, 3, 4, 5]). Multiple-perspective question answering, summarization, information extraction, and other applications can benefit substantially from systems that are able to identify the sentiment of a text or phrase.

The existing approaches to sentiment tagging of texts or phrases use information about the sentiment conveyed by the words that make up the text. This information can be acquired either at run time, as done by [1], or in advance by creating a lexicon of sentiment-tagged words (e.g., [4, 6, 7, 8, 9]). A number of systems use automatic or, more often, semi-automatic or custom-made manual lists as input for sentiment tagging of texts. One of the common features of such lists of words is that they are annotated with sentiment at the word, rather than at the individual meaning level. Since some meanings of a word can be sentiment-laden, while others are not, word-level annotations of sentiment markers in such lists substantially limit the performance of sentiment tagging systems. For example, there is a considerable number of adjectives that have both neutral and sentiment-laden meanings, and the neutral meaning is often the most frequent one. Table 1 shows frequency scores assigned to some of such

L. Lamontagne and M. Marchand (Eds.): Canadian AI 2006, LNAI 4013, pp. 336–346, 2006.
© Springer-Verlag Berlin Heidelberg 2006

adjectives in WordNet [10]. These scores reflect the number of occurrences of a given sense in semantic concordances created by WordNet editors.

Table 1. Frequencies of sentiment-marked and neutral meanings (based on WordNet)

Word	Total frequency of neutral senses	Total frequency of sentiment senses	Total occurrences[1]
great	141 (75%)	46 (25%)	187
dark	90 (90%)	10 (10%)	100
cold	41 (76%)	13 (24%)	54
right	20 (28%)	50 (71%)	70

The Table 1 shows that in the corpus used by WordNet authors, on every occurrence of the word *great*, which manual lists classify as positive [11, 12], there is a 75% chance that this word is used in one of its neutral, non-sentiment-bearing meanings. This would lead to sentiment annotation system error in up to 75% of cases where *great* is found in a text. While 75% error rate attributable to the presence of neutral senses represents an extreme case, the error rate of 20% to 50%, according to our manual analysis, appears to be very common for polysemous words with at least one sentiment-laden meaning. Since the sentiment of each meaning for every English word has not been identified yet, this problem cannot be addressed by sentiment aggregation to the word level using probabilities of the occurrence of a given sense in a text: to date, the only way to arrive at the conclusion that a word appears in texts in neutral meanings at a certain rate is through manual annotation at the sense level. An additional problem with such aggregation is that it would still lead to a substantial number of errors where words used in sentiment-bearing meanings are deemed neutral.

Thus, the inclusion of such adjectives at the word level into the lists of sentiment-bearing words that are then used as sentiment markers in sentiment tagging of phrases and texts introduces errors and has a detrimental effect on the overall system performance. This problem is often further exacerbated by the high frequency of such words in natural language. The analysis of this example suggests that sense-level annotation of sentiment markers can substantially improve the accuracy of sentiment tagging of texts and phrases.[2]

The first step in the development of such fine-grained sentiment tagging systems is the development of the lists of words annotated with sentiment at the sense level. To date, no lists manually annotated with sentiment at the meaning level have been created. In this paper we first describe the system used to

---

[1] The number in this column is the sum of all WordNet frequency scores for all the senses of the given word. If there was no frequency assigned to the sense in WordNet it was considered to be equal to 0.

[2] Kennedy and Inkpen (2006) use more fine-grained annotations for rare cases where the same word can have positive and negative meanings, but they are not considering words that can be both neutral and sentiment-bearing.

produce a list of sentiment-bearing words with sense-level annotations for the use in sentiment tagging systems and then evaluate the performance of this list vs. the manually annotated General Inquirer Harvard IV list (GI, [12]), which is used here as the gold standard.

2   Sentiment Tag Extraction at the Meaning Level

The algorithm developed to produce a list of sentiment-bearing words with sense-level annotations is based on a two-phase process that uses a manually annotated seed list compiled by Hatzivassiloglou and McKeown [11] (HM), as well as the information contained in WordNet [10] and in the eXtended WordNet [14] to assign sentiment tags to words and their senses. The general architecture of the system is presented in Fig. 1.

2.1   Sentiment Tag Extraction from WordNet Glosses

The system starts with multiple runs of the **Semantic Tag Extraction Program (STEP)** algorithm, developed by the authors for word sentiment tag extraction at the word level [15]. The STEP algorithm represents a three-pass bootstrapping system that makes use of WordNet entries as a special kind of structured text, which is built to establish semantic equivalence between the left-hand and the right-hand parts of the dictionary entry, and therefore are designed to match as close as possible the components of meaning of the word. The STEP algorithm starts with a small set of seed words of known sentiment (positive or negative) drawn from HM [11]. This list is augmented during the first pass by adding synonyms, antonyms and hyponyms of the seed words provided in WordNet.[3] This step yields an average 5-fold increase in the size of the original list; the average accuracy of the resulting lists is comparable to manual annotations (78%, which is similar to the agreement on sentiment tags between HM and GI). On the second pass, the system goes through all WordNet glosses and identifies the entries that contain in their definitions the sentiment-bearing words from the seed list produced in pass 1. These words are added to the corresponding category — positive, negative or neutral (the remainder). The third, clean-up pass is then performed to partially disambiguate the identified Word-Net glosses with Brill's part-of-speech tagger [17]. The tagger performs with up to 95% accuracy and eliminates errors introduced into the list by part-of-speech ambiguity of some words acquired during the first pass and from the seed list. At this step, we also filter out all words that have been assigned contradicting, that is positive <u>and</u> negative, sentiment values within the same run.

In order to increase the reliability of the assigned tags and expand the list of sentiment-tagged adjectives, we performed multiple runs of the system with non-intersecting seed lists of 22 words each, extracted at random from HM. The results of these 58 independent runs were then collapsed, producing a union of all adjectives considered positive or negative in at least one run. For each word we

---

[3] WordNet is queried using the WordNet:QueryData interface [16].

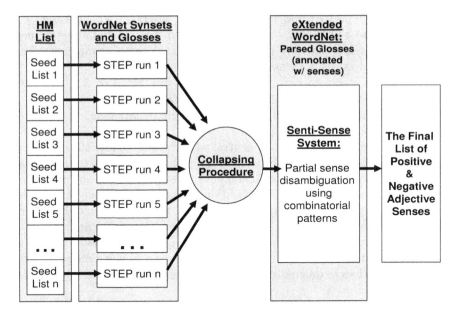

Fig. 1. System architecture

computed a Net Overlap Score by subtracting the total number of runs assigning this word a negative sentiment from the total of the runs that consider it positive. Words that were not tagged as sentiment-bearing by STEP were deemed neutral by default. Since many of the clearly sentiment-laden adjectives that form the core of the category of sentiment were identified by STEP in multiple runs and had, therefore, multiple duplicates in the combined list, the collapsing procedure resulted in a lower accuracy (66.5% — when GI neutrals were included[4]) but produced a much larger list of English adjectives marked as positive (n = 3, 908) or negative (n = 3, 905). The remainder of WordNet's 22, 141 adjectives was not selected by any STEP run and hence was deemed neutral (n = 14, 328).

2.2   NP-Based Filtering: Senti-Sense System

The analysis of STEP's output showed that most errors made by the system occur at the boundary between neutral and sentiment-marked adjectives, while the

---

[4] Overall, the system's 66.5% accuracy on the collapsed runs is comparable to the accuracy reported in the literature. Esuli and Sebastiani (2006) achieved 67.6% accuracy in their experiments with classification into three categories: positive, negative and objective. Kamps et al. (2004) achieved 67.3% accuracy on 663 adjectives reachable through WordNet relationships from *good* and *bad*. In order to make a meaningful comparison with the results reported in [18], we also did an evaluation of STEP's results on positives and negatives only (i.e., the neutral adjectives from GI were excluded) and compared our labels to the remaining 1266 GI adjectives. The accuracy on this subset was 73.4%, which is comparable to the numbers reported by Turney and Littman (2002) for experiments with a very large corpus.

confusion between positive and negative sentiment was rare. In many cases, seed adjectives fed into STEP (e.g., *great*, *cold*, etc.) had both neutral and sentiment marked meanings and, therefore, could appear in the glosses of sentiment-bearing as well as neutral words, for example:

> *readheaded* — having red hair and unusually **fair** skin.
> *sporty* — exhibiting or calling for sportsmanship or **fair** play.

This led to erroneous inclusion of neutral adjectives into either the positive or negative categories. Therefore, the two critical tasks that the system had to address were (1) the improvement of differentiation between neutral and sentiment-bearing adjectives, and (2) the identification of occurrences of sentiment-laden meaning(s) of a given polysemous adjective from the occurrences of its neutral meaning(s). In order to address these tasks, we developed a filtering procedure that builds upon the observation that nouns are good indicators of the senses of adjectives that modify them [19, 20]. Thus, we used co-occurrence patterns of nouns and adjectives to differentiate neutral and sentiment-bearing adjectives at the meaning level.

A number of approaches successfully use syntactic patterns to assign semantic tags, such as 'subjectivity', 'humans', 'locations', 'buildings', etc., to words [21, 22]. Riloff et al. (2003) describe a machine learning approach used in the Meta-bootstrapping and Basilisk systems for learning subjective nouns based on an extraction pattern bootstrapping algorithm. In both systems, the algorithm starts with a seed list of subjective nouns and an unannotated corpus to create a pool of patterns which, in turn, is used to classify other nouns as 'subjective' or 'objective'. Hatzivassiloglou and McKeown (1997) developed a system that was looking for a specific co-occurrence pattern — a conjunction linking two adjectives — to draw conclusions about the sentiment value of one member of the pair based on the known sentiment of the other member. Automated pattern learning and matching has also been employed in general word-sense disambiguation systems (e.g., [23]).

Our approach uses machine learning to generate and generalize the patterns that permit differentiation between sentiment-laden and neutral adjectives based on the semantic category of the noun they modify. The system that we developed for partial word sense disambiguation in sentiment-bearing words using combinatorial patterns (thereafter Senti-Sense system) proceeded as follows. First, the list of all non-ambiguous, monosemous sentiment-bearing adjectives has been extracted from HM. The resulting list of 363 positive or negative adjectives was then used as a seed list for the pattern extraction algorithm. As was the case in STEP, this seed list was then augmented by all the synonyms of these words found in their WordNet synsets, which resulted in 1019 word-senses. All entries in this extended list have a WordNet sense number assigned to them.[5] The

---

[5] It is also possible to use synset offset to identify the sense by the synset it belongs to, but we chose to record the sense numbers instead, because eXtended WordNet uses this notation.

system then searched the eXtended WordNet[6] for glosses that contain adjectives from this sense-tagged list. If an adjective was found, the parses and sense-tags provided in eXtended WordNet (XWN) were used to identify the noun that this adjective modified as well as the sense in which this noun was used. Then the full hypernym ancestry of that noun was extracted from WordNet's hypernym hierarchy.

When all adjective-noun pairs have been extracted from XWN, the Senti-Sense system performed pattern induction and matching. It grouped the nouns that can take on sentiment-bearing modifiers, identified common hypernyms of these nouns, and then generalized the pattern to the level of that hypernym. The example below illustrates the generalization algorithm on the example of several adjective-noun pairs.

selfish$_{a1}$ actor$_{n1}$
$actor_{n1} \rightarrow performer_{n1} \rightarrow entertainer_{n1} \rightarrow person_{n1} \rightarrow organism_{n1} \rightarrow living\_thing_{n1} \rightarrow object_{n1}$
high-ranking$_{n1}$ administrator$_{n1}$
$administrator_{n1} \rightarrow head_{n4} \rightarrow leader_{n1} \rightarrow person_{n1} \rightarrow organism_{n1} \rightarrow living\_thing_{n1} \rightarrow object_{n1}$
skillful$_{a1}$ opponent$_{n2}$
$opponent_{n2} \rightarrow person_{n1} \rightarrow organism_{n1} \rightarrow living\_thing_{n1} \rightarrow object_{n1}$

The three adjective-noun pairs presented above were returned by the search for occurrences of the unambiguous sentiment-marked adjectives *selfish, high-ranking*, and *skillful*. For every occurrence of these adjectives in WordNet glosses, the system pulled out the adjective, the noun it modified, and the complete list of hypernyms in the WordNet hierarchy for this noun. The hypernym trees leading to each of the three nouns — *actor, administrator*, and *opponent* — converged at the hypernym *person* and reached the highest level hypernym *object*.[7] Thus, the system derived the pattern that all of the nouns found under the hypernym *person* could take sentiment-bearing modifiers.

Based on the 1006 adjective-noun pairs found in XWN, the system produced 48 such patterns that were then used to evaluate the positive and negative adjectives retrieved by the multiple STEP runs. For example, the adjective *bright* identified as positive by STEP when fed into the Senti-Sense system, returned a candidate pair $bright_{a3}\ person_{n1}$, where $person_{n1} \rightarrow organism_{n1} \rightarrow$

---

[6] The eXtended WordNet provides parses for most WordNet glosses as well as part-of-speech and sense assignments for words in them. The project is currently under development (the current version is XWN 2.0-1) and the quality of the tags varies and may be based on manual annotations ("gold" quality), on the results of multiple automatic disambiguation systems ("silver" quality) or on single system output ("normal" quality). Nevertheless, it still provides useful information that can be used to discover and apply syntactic patterns for sentiment tagging.

[7] In order to avoid overgeneralization and to maintain the discriminating ability of the patterns, the top of the hypernym tree is not included in matching. Thus, in this case, no generalization to the highest hypernym level *object* was made.

living_thing$_{n1}$ → *object*$_{n1}$. Given the pattern rule formulated in the example above, the Senti-Sense system concluded that the adjective *bright* in the sense 3 is sentiment-bearing. The WordNet gloss for *bright* in sense 3 is *characterized by quickness and ease in learning*. At the same time, another pair with the same adjective — *bright*$_{a2}$ *plumage*$_{n1}$, where *plumage*$_{n1}$ → *body_covering*$_{n1}$ → *covering*$_{n1}$ → *natural_object*$_{n1}$ → *object*$_{n1}$, was not matched to any pattern characteristic of sentiment bearing words, and the adjective *bright* in sense 2 was deemed neutral.

Since positive and negative adjectives usually modify nouns from the same semantic classes, the Senti-Sense system can be effective in differentiating neutral and sentiment-laden adjectives. However it would not be particularly suitable for differentiation of the sentiment-bearing words into positives and negatives. Nevertheless, since the boundary between neutral and sentiment-bearing words represents the greatest source of errors in word sentiment determination, Senti-Sense can be a valuable extension for sentiment tag extraction systems, such as STEP. Moreover, given that Senti-Sense operates at the word meaning level, it can be used to identify which senses of a given adjective actually bear the sentiment value, and, by bringing sentiment tagging to a more refined sense level, it can further contribute to the accuracy of sentiment tagging systems.

In the section that follows, we describe the experiment that applied Senti-Sense to the list of positive and negative words generated by the multiple STEP runs. The performance gain associated with the use of Senti-Sense is evaluated relative to the GI, which is used here as a gold standard.

3   Results and Evaluation

The 58 STEP runs on non-overlapping seed lists drawn from HM produced, after collapsing the results of all runs, a list of 3,908 English adjectives marked as positive and a list of 3,905 negative adjectives. The remainder of WordNet's 22,141 adjectives was either not found in any STEP run or was assigned a zero Net Overlap Score and hence was deemed neutral (n = 14,328).

Table 2 summarizes the results produced by these STEP runs before and after cleaning with Senti-Sense. We evaluated the tags produced by the multiple STEP runs against the General Inquirer Harvard IV list of 1904 adjectives. The GI list also contains adjectives that were not classified as "Positiv" or "Negativ", and, by default were considered in our evaluation as neutrals. The system performance was evaluated only on the words that are present both in our results and in GI. Since Senti-Sense assigns the sentiment tags at the sense level and the GI list is annotated with sentiment at the word level, for the purposes of this evaluation only, the sense-level positive or negative tags were reassigned to the whole word: if at least one sense of an adjective was classified by Senti-Sense as sentiment-laden, the whole word was deemed to have that sentiment value. The words that were left in the neutral category, thus, had only neutral senses.

Since there is a substantial inter-annotator disagreement in word sentiment annotation, the evaluation of machine-made annotations should take into account the baseline level of inter-annotator agreement that can be achieved in this task by independent teams of human annotators. The agreement statistics between the manually annotated lists of adjectives created by Hatzivassiloglou and McKeown and the General Inquirer team of annotators is presented in the table below for comparison.

Table 2. System results

	STEP 22-58 vs. GI	Senti-Sense vs. GI	HM vs. GI
Total tagged words	1904	1415	774
Agreement on tags	1267	1081	609
% of same tags	66.5%	76.6%	78.7%

Overall, the accuracy of the adjective list increased considerably after it was cleaned using Senti-Sense: differentiating between sentiment-marked and neutral senses of seed words added another 10% to the accuracy on the intersection between the system results and the gold standard (Table 2). Since Senti-Sense was based on NP patterns that identify only sentiment-laden senses, filtering was done only on those adjectives that were classified by STEP as positive or negative, while the composition of the category of neutrals was left intact.[8] Table 3 provides detailed statistics for each of these three categories.

Table 3. Precision (P), recall (R) and F-scores (F) on three sentiment categories

Sentiment	STEP 22-58 vs. GI			Senti-Sense vs. GI			HM vs. GI		
	P	R	F	P	R	F	P	R	F
Positive	0.68	0.77	0.72	0.95	0.61	0.74	0.90	0.51	0.67
Negative	0.75	0.70	0.72	0.91	0.54	0.68	0.98	0.46	0.63
Neutral	0.57	0.53	0.55	0.57	0.53	0.55	-	-	-

The absence of an exhaustive list of sentiment-tagged words (which makes the task of machine-made annotation meaningful) does not allow the reliable assessment of the recall measure on STEP and Senti-Sense outputs. The closest available proxy is the GI list itself: the proportion of GI adjectives correctly identified by the system as positive, negative or neutral and the total number of GI adjectives that were not found can give an idea of system performance on this measure. The tradeoffs between system precision and recall before and after Senti-Sense filtering are presented in Table 3. Table 3 shows that the gain associated with Senti-Sense filtering of positive and negative adjectives was substantial: the precision on positive adjectives increased from 68% to 95%, while

---

[8] The adjectives that were marked as sentiment-bearing by STEP but for which no occurrences in NP-patterns were found were not included in any of the three groups, since no definite conclusion about their sentiment could be made on this data.

on negatives it went up from 75% to 91%. These results are comparable to the precision of human annotation (Table 3). This gain, however, came with a considerable reduction in the size of the filtered list: Senti-Sense filtering reduced the list of sentiment-laden adjectives found by multiple STEP runs from 7813 to 2907. The gain in precision accompanied by the drop in recall has left the F-scores practically unchanged.

4   Conclusions and Future Work

This paper presented a sentiment tagging system which is based on multiple runs of the Semantic Tag Extraction Program (STEP) on non-intersecting seed lists drawn from manually annotated HM list. We demonstrated how the addition of a module for partial word sense disambiguation of sentiment-bearing adjectives using combinatorial patterns (Senti-Sense system) (1) enables sentiment annotation at the sense, rather than the whole word level, and (2) provides an effective tool for the automatic cleaning of the lists of sentiment-annotated words. In our experiment, the cleaned list of 2907 adjectives achieved an accuracy comparable to that of human annotation, as evaluated by the agreement rate between two manually annotated lists: HM and GI.

The availability of a list of words annotated with sentiment tags at the sense, rather than word level, and the ability to use Senti-Sense system to partially disambiguate adjectives in texts based on the semantic category of the noun they modify, opens up the possibility to develop more accurate sentiment tagging systems. Moreover, sentiment tagging systems that make use of sense-level sentiment information would be able to perform accurate tagging of small snippets of text (such as e-mails), where scarcity of lexical markers would hinder the effectiveness of sentiment tagging systems that rely on probabilistic assessment of multiple low-accuracy textual markers.

One of the promising directions for future research is the application of the Senti-Sense algorithm to sense-level annotation of other semantic categories. One of the first candidate categories on the list is that of increase/decrease in magnitude, intensity or quality (e.g., *reduce, add, improve*); such words are known to interact with the category of sentiment by escalating the intensity of the sentiment conveyed by sentiment-marked words (the words with "increase" semantics) or by reversing the sentiment expressed by these words to the opposite (the words with "decrease" semantics) [24]. This property makes the study of the increase/decrease category particularly relevant for sentiment tagging research.

The improvement of Senti-Sense recall represents another important direction for future research. To date, the system has been trained only on 1003 adjective-noun pairs extracted from the eXtended WordNet glosses, which are annotated with word senses. Training Senti-Sense on a larger corpora annotated with WordNet senses is likely to reveal additional combinatorial patterns that can be used for partial sense disambiguation in suspected sentiment-laden words. This would result in a more comprehensive set of combinatorial patterns that would further improve the Senti-Sense recall.

Finally, most of the current NLP research on sentiment annotation of words for use in sentiment tagging of texts and phrases is focused on annotation of adjectives. While adjectives are one of the most important sentiment markers in texts [25], other parts of speech, such as nouns and verbs, also play an important role in producing the overall sentiment of phrases and texts. The development of the lists of sentiment-laden nouns and verbs can contribute to further improvement of the accuracy of sentiment tagging systems.

References

1. Turney, P., Littman, M.: Measuring Praise and Criticism: Inference of Semantic Orientation from Association. ACM Transactions on Information Systems **21** (2003)
2. Pang, B., Lee, L.: A sentiment Education: Sentiment Analysis using Subjectivity Summarization based on Minimum Cuts. In: Proceedings of ACL-04, 42nd Meeting of the Association for Computational Linguistics, Philadelphia (2004)
3. Kamps, J., Marx, M., Mokken, R.J., de Rijke, M.: Using WordNet to Measure Semantic Orientation of Adjectives. In: Proceedings of LREC 2004, the 4th International Conference on Language Resources and Evaluation. Volume IV., Lisbon, Portugal (2004)
4. Hu, M., Liu, B.: Mining and Summarizing Customer Reviews. In: Proceedings of KDD'04, the ACM SIGKDD International Conference on Knowledge Discovery and Data Mining, Seattle, WA (2004)
5. Yu, H., Hatzivassiloglou, V.: Towards Answering Opinion Questions: Separating Facts from Opinions and Identifying the Polarity of Opinion Sentences. In: Proceedings of EMNLP-03, the 8th Conference on Empirical Methods in Natural Language Processing. (2003)
6. Subasic, P., Huettner, A.: Affect Analysis of Text Using Fuzzy Typing. IEEE-FS **9** (2001)
7. Das, S.R., Chen, M.Y.: Yahoo! For Amazon: Sentiment Extraction from Small Talk on the Web. In: Proceedings of APFA-01, the Asia Pacific Finance Association Annual Conference. (2001)
8. Hurst, M., Nigam, K.: Retrieving Topical Sentiments from Online Document Collection. In Shanahan, J.G., Qu, Y., Wiebe, J., eds.: Computing Attitude and Affect in Text: Theory and Application., Springer Verlag (2006)
9. Whitelaw, C., Garg, N., Argamon, S.: Using Appraisal Taxonomies for Sentiment Analysis. In: Proceedings of CIKM-05, the ACM SIGIR Conference on Information and Knowledge Management, Bremen, Germany (2005)
10. Fellbaum, C., ed.: WordNet: An Electronic Lexical Database. MIT Press, Cambridge, MA (1998)
11. Hatzivassiloglou, V., McKeown, K.B.: Predicting the Semantic Orientation of Adjectives. In: Proceedings of ACL-97, the 35th Annual Meeting of the Association for Computational Linguistics, Madrid, Spain (1997)
12. Stone, P., Dumphy, D., Smith, M., Ogilvie, D.: The General Inquirer: a Computer Approach to Content Analysis. M.I.T. Studies in Comparative Politics. M.I.T. Press, Cambridge, MA (1966)
13. Kennedy, A., Inkpen, D.: Sentiment Classification of Movie and Product Reviews using Contextual Valence Shifters. In: FINEXIN 2005, Workshop on the Analysis of Informal and Formal Information Exchange during Negotiations, Ottawa, Canada (2005)

14. Harabagiu, S., Miller, G., Moldovan, D.: WordNet2 - a Morphologically and Semantically Enhanced Resource. In: Proceedings of SigLex-99: Standardizing Lexical Resources, Univ. of Mariland (1999)
15. Andreevskaia, A., Bergler, S.: Semantic Tagging using WordNet Glosses. In: Proceedings of LREC-06, the 5th Language Resources and Evaluation Conference, Genoa, Italy (2006)
16. Rennie, J.: WordNet::QueryData: a Perl Module for Accessing the WordNet Database. http://people.csail.mit.edu/~jrennie/WordNet (2000)
17. Brill, E.: Transformation-Based Error-Driven Learning and Natural Language Processing: A Case Study in Part-of-Speech Tagging. Computational Linguistics **21** (1995)
18. Turney, P., Littman, M.: Unsupervised Learning of Semantic Orientation from a Hundred-Billion-Word Corpus. Technical Report ERC-1094 (NRC 44929), National Research Council of Canada (2002)
19. Audibert, L.: Word Sense Disambiguation Criteria: a Systematic Study. In: Proceedings of COLING-04, the 20th Conference on Computational Linguistics, Geneva, Switzerland (2004)
20. Yarowsky, D.: One Sense per Collocation. In: ARPA Workshop on Human Language Technology. (1993)
21. Riloff, E., Wiebe, J., Wilson, T.: Learning Subjective Nouns using Extraction Pattern Bootstrapping. In: Proceedings of CoNLL-03, the 7th Conference on Natural Language Learning. (2003)
22. Thelen, M., Riloff, E.: A Bootstrapping Method for Learning Semantic Lexicons using Extraction Pattern Contexts. In: Proceedings of EMNLP 2002, the 7th Conference on Empirical Methods in Natural Language Processing. (2002)
23. Mihalcea, R.: Word Sense Disambiguation using Pattern Learning and Automatic Feature Selection. Natural Language Engineering **1** (2002)
24. Polanyi, L., Zaenen, A.: Contextual Valence Shifters. In Shanahan, J.G., Qu, Y., Wiebe, J., eds.: Computing Attitude and Affect in Text: Theory and Application. Springer Verlag (2006)
25. Hatzivassiloglou, V., Wiebe, J.: Effects of Adjective Orientation and Gradability on Sentence Subjectivity. In: Proceedings of COLING-2000, the 18th International Conference on Computational Linguistics, Morgan Kaufman (2000)

Adaptive Fraud Detection Using Benford's Law

Fletcher Lu[1], J. Efrim Boritz[2], and Dominic Covvey[2]

[1] Canadian Institute of Chartered Accountants,
66 Grace Street, Scarborough, Ontario, M1J 3K9
f2lu@ai.uwaterloo.ca
[2] University of Waterloo, 200 University Avenue West,
Waterloo, Ontario, Canada, N2L 3G1
jeboritz@watarts.uwaterloo.ca,
dcovvey@csg.uwaterloo.ca

Abstract. Adaptive Benford's Law [1] is a digital analysis technique that specifies the probabilistic distribution of digits for many commonly occurring phenomena, even for incomplete data records. We combine this digital analysis technique with a reinforcement learning technique to create a new fraud discovery approach. When applied to records of naturally occurring phenomena, our adaptive fraud detection method uses deviations from the expected Benford's Law distributions as an indicators of anomalous behaviour that are strong indicators of fraud. Through the exploration component of our reinforcement learning method we search for the underlying attributes producing the anomalous behaviour. In a blind test of our approach, using real health and auto insurance data, our Adaptive Fraud Detection method successfully identified actual fraudsters among the test data.

1 Introduction

In this paper we illustrate the implementation of a fraud discovery system which uses a new approach for discovering fraud that combines a reinforcement learning (RL) technique with a digital analysis method. The idea behind this approach is to use the digital analysis to uncover data anomalies and then utilize the reinforcement learning component to reveal the attributes contributing to the anomaly, thereby uncovering underlying fraudulent behaviour.

As Bolton and Hand [2] noted, fraud detection methods may be divided into both supervised and unsupervised methods. For supervised methods, both fraudulent and non-fraudulent records are used to train a system, which then searches and classifies new records according to the trained patterns. The limitation to supervised methods is that one must have both classes of records identified for the system to train on. Thus, this approach is limited to only previously known methods of committing fraud.

Unsupervised methods, in contrast, typically identify records that do not fit expected norms. The advantage of this approach is that one may identify new instances of fraud. The common approach to this method is to use forms of outlier detection. The main limit to this approach is that we are essentially identifying anomalies that may or may not be fraudulent behaviour. Just because a behaviour is anomalous does not necessarily mean that the behaviour is fraudulent. Instead they can be used as indicators of

L. Lamontagne and M. Marchand (Eds.): Canadian AI 2006, LNAI 4013, pp. 347–358, 2006.
© Springer-Verlag Berlin Heidelberg 2006

possible fraud, whereby the strength of the anomalous behaviour (how much it deviates from expected norms), may be used as a measure of ones confidence in how likely the behaviour may be fraudulent. Investigators may then be employed to analyze these anomalies. However, given the often enormous numbers of records involved in typical fraud application areas such as credit card, cellular phone and healthcare records, even with identified anomalies, investigating the anomalies can be a considerable burden to resources. The novelty of our approach is that we extend the typical outlier detection methods with a reinforcement learning component.

The reinforcement learning component of our algorithm builds on identified outliers by associating with our outliers, underlying attributes that may be linked together to build a case for fraud. Reinforcement learning has typically been used in the past to find the best choice of actions when trying to perform some physical task requiring a sequence of actions to accomplish a desirable goal such as navigating through a maze. The core idea which makes reinforcement learning useful to fraud discovery is its ability to link together states through a pattern of state-action pairs in a policy. In our algorithm we will link together anomalies according to their underlying attributes using the magnitude of the anomalous behaviour as a measure of its desireablity within the reinforcement learning context (in other words anomalies are equivalent to the rewards in an RL environment).

To identify our outliers, we use a digital analysis technique known as adaptive Benford's Law [1]. Benford's Law specifies the distribution of the digits for *naturally* occurring phenomena. For a long time this technique, commonly used in areas of taxation and accounting, was considered mostly a mathematical curiosity as it described the frequency with which individual and sets of digits for naturally growing phenomena such as population measures should appear [3]. Such naturally growing phenomena, however, has been shown to include practical areas such as spending records and stock market values [4]. One of the limits to the use of classic Benford's Law in fraud detection has been its requirement that analyzed records have no artificial cutoffs. In other words, records must be complete. However, in many practical application areas, one only has information for a subset, such as a single year, of financial records. Recent work by Lu and Boritz [1] has removed this limitation with an *adaptive* Benford's Law, making it more practically useful.

In our paper we will explain the algorithm for our technique and test our new fraud discovery technique against outlier detection methods using real healthcare and auto insurance records, demonstrating improvements in classifying fraudsters.

1.1 Complications in Practical Fraud Detection Research

Two major complications for fraud detection researchers are:

1. Secrecy with regards to details on fraud detection techniques.
2. Limits on available real fraud records.

Both of these complications stem from the nature of the application area. It is quite natural that in order to stay ahead of fraudsters, those employing fraud detection methods tend to keep secret their algorithm details in order to avoid fraudsters from knowing these details and developing methods to circumnavigate them. This secrecy makes it difficult to compare new fraud detection techniques with previous methods. The second complication is due to the fact that companies do not generally like to reveal the amounts of fraud within their field as it tends to have a detrimental impact on shareholder confidence as well as consumer confidence. In addition, laws in Canada as well as many other countries do not require the explicit reporting of fraud losses. Without available real fraud records, many researchers use artificially created synthetic fraud records to test their methods. However, synthetic records for testing are only as useful as they are truly representative of actual fraudulent and non-fraudulent records.

We deal with the first complication by developing a general technique that is not meant to be application area specific but is meant as an improvement over the general Benford's Law outlier detection approach. Many fraud detection techniques are *ad hoc* and use specific details about their application area for detection. For instance, cellular phone detection uses the fact that one can uncover phone usage stealing by identifying that the same phone is calling from two different locations at the same time, which would imply at least one of the calls is from an illegitimate user. Since our fraud discovery technique is meant as an improvement over previous Benford's Law outlier detection methods, we compare our method specifically with that outlier detection approach.

We deal with the second complication by testing our method on real auto insurance records that have been audited and classified for actual fraud. In order to demonstrate robustness, we also apply our method to real healthcare insurance records. However, these records have yet to be audited for fraud and thus we use it only to demonstrate the technique's operation on a differing application area and to illustrate the adaptive Benford's Law component of our fraud detection method on a real fraud application.

2 Background

2.1 Benford's Law

Benford's Law is a probability distribution with strong relevance to accounting fraud. Much of the research on Benford's Law has been in areas of statistics [5, 6] as well as auditing [7, 8].

Benford's Law is a mathematical formula that specifies the probability of leading digit sequences appearing in a set of data. What we mean by *leading digit sequences* is best illustrated through an example. Consider the set of data

$$S = \{231, 432, 1, 23, 634, 23, 1, 634, 2, 23, 34, 1232\}.$$

There are twelve data entries in set S. The digit sequence '23' appears as a leading digit sequence (i.e. in the first and second position) 4 times. Therefore, the probability of the first two digits being '23' is $\frac{4}{9} \approx 0.44$. The probability is computed out of 9 because only 9 entries have at least 2 digit positions. Entries with less than the number of digits being analyzed are not included in the probability computation.

The actual mathematical formula of Benford's law is:

$$P(D = d) = \log_{10}(1 + \frac{1}{d}), \tag{1}$$

where $P(D = d)$ is the probability of observing the digit sequence d in the first 'y' digits and where d is a sequence of 'y' digits. For instance, Benford's Law would state that the probability that the first digit in a data set is '3' would be $\log_{10}(1+\frac{1}{3})$. Similarly, the probability that the first 3 digits of the data set are '238', would be $\log_{10}(1 + \frac{1}{238})$. The numbers '238' and '23885' would be instances of the first three digits being '238'. However this probability would not include the occurrence '3238', as '238' is not the *first* three digits in this instance.

2.2   Benford's Law Requirements

In order to apply equation 1 as a test for a data set's digit frequencies, Benford's Law requires that:

1. The entries in a data set should record values of similar phenomena. In other words, the recorded data cannot include entries from two different phenomena such as both census population records and dental measurements.
2. There should be no built-in minimum or maximum values in the data set. In other words, the records for the phenomena must be complete, with no artificial start value or ending cutoff value.
3. The data set should not be made up of assigned numbers, such as phone numbers.
4. The data set should have more small value entries than large value entries.

Further details on these rules may be found in [3]. Under these conditions, Benford noted that the data for such sets, when placed in ascending order, often follows a geometric growth pattern.[1] Under such a situation, equation 1 specifies the probability of observing specific leading digit sequences for such a data set.

The intuitive reasoning behind the geometric growth of Benford's Law is based on the notion that for low values it takes more time for some event to increase by 100% from '1' to '2' than it does to increase by 50% from '2' to '3'. Thus, when recording numerical information at regular intervals, one often observes low digits much more frequently than higher digits, usually decreasing geometrically.

Adaptive Benford's Law modifies classic Benford's Law by removing the second requirement of 'no built-in minimum or maximum values', thus allowing for the technique to be more generally applicable to a wider array of real records which often are incomplete. For more details on the Adaptive Benford method see [1].

2.3   Reinforcement Learning

In reinforcement learning, an environment is modelled as a network of states, $\{s \in S\}$. Each state is associated with a set of possible actions, $a_s \in A_s$ and a reward for entering that state $\{r_s \in R_s\}$. We can transition from one state s(i) to another s(j) by choosing an action a_s and with a certain probability $P(s_j|s_i, a_{s_i})$ we transition to another state. A policy is a mapping of states to action. The objective is to find an optimal policy that maximizies the long-term rewards one may obtain as one navigates through the network. In order to find an optimal policy, we perform a task known as policy evaluation

---

[1] Note: The actual data does *not* have to be recorded in ascending order. This ordering is merely an illustrative tool to understand the intuitive reasoning for Benford's law.

which determines value estimates for states given a fixed policy, π. The value estimate for a state represents the sum of the discounted future rewards for a state following a policy π. A variety of methods for policy evaluation have developed over time such as the maximum likelihood approach[9], the temporal differencing method [10] and the monte carlo matrix inversion method [11].

One property of the reinforcement learning approach is that it is designed to handle intractably large state spaces. This trait makes it well suited to an environment such as fraud detection where there are usually extremely large numbers of records to process in order to find the relatively small number of occurences of fraud among the total amount of data available. Reinforcement learning also incorporates an exploration component that allows it to search for better actions leading to higher long-term reward values. Such an exploration component is key also for finding *new* instances of previously unknown fraud cases as we wish our fraud discovery method to be able to do. These two traits are the main components motivating our use of a reinforcement learning approach for fraud detection.

3   Algorithm

As we noted in the introduction, our fraud detection method's objective is to improve over outlier detection methods for finding instances of fraud. Outlier detection methods, as we stated previously, actually only indicate anomalous instances. In order to determine whether an anomalous instance is actually a result of a fraudulent occurence typically requires the careful analysis of an auditor. Therefore, we need to consider how an auditor actually determines fraud. Without domain specific knowledge, such as the cell phone example we gave in the introduction, one typically builds a case for fraud by linking together suspicious occurences. Even with domain specific knowledge, such as our cellular phone example, one may still need to link suspicious (anomalous) cases together. For example, even in the cellular phone example where we know that the same cell phone cannot be calling from two different locations at the same time, we do not necessarily know which of the two calls is the fraudulent one and indeed both may be from illegal users. Thus, what is needed is to build a case of fraud by linking together anomalous instances that are related by some set of traits.

Reinforcement learning is well suited to linking together states through its state-action policy mapping. For reinforcement learning to be used as a fraud detection method, we need to be able to relate rewards with anomalies. We do so by setting the reward values as the magnitude that our anomalous instances deviate from expected values. In turn, the states of our RL environment relate to individual records of our application environment and the actions are the attributes of a record. In such a way, two records, with the same attributes are linked together by a common attribute just as an action can relate two states of a classic reinforcement learning environment network.

The best way to illustrate our fraud detection algorithm is through an example. Figure 1 is an example of purchase records for some consumer. Included in the record are the purchased item, the store it was purchased in, the location of the store, the form of payment used to buy the item and the amount of the purchase under 'Digit Sequences'. We apply our fraud detection algorithm by first determining if there are

| States | Actions/Attributes | | | | Digit |
	Purchase Item	Store	Location	Form of Payment	Sequences
1	shoes	storeA	street15	credit	$52
2	hat	storeB	street12	cash	$38
3	hat	storeC	street17	debit	$22
4	TV	storeB	street11	cheque	$640

Fig. 1. Sample Application: Purchase Records

| States | Actions/Attributes | | | | Digit | Rewards/Magnitude |
	Purchase Item	Store	Location	Form of Payment	Sequences	of Anomalies
1	shoes	storeA	street15	credit	$52	1.6
2	hat	storeB	street12	cash	(38)	3.2
3	hat	storeC	street17	debit	$22	6.2
4	TV	storeB	street11	cheque	$640	1.1

Fig. 2. Sample Application: Analysing Digits with Rewards

any sets of digit sequences that conform to a Benford distribution. In our example there is only one set of numbers, the purchase values that can be compared with a Benford distribution. We compute the frequency with which each digit sequence from 1 to 999 appears in our purchase value records.[2] We then compare these actual digit frequencies with Benford's Law's expected frequencies. If they fall within a certain confidence interval, we will accept that the numerical data follows a Benford's Law distribution.

Assuming the purchase records are a Benford distribution, then we compute a measure of how much any given purchase value deviates from expected Benford value by:

$$Reward(i) = \frac{f_{1i}}{b_{1i}} + \frac{f_{2i}}{b_{2i}} + \frac{f_{3i}}{b_{3i}}, \qquad (2)$$

where f_{ji} is the frequency that a digit sequence of length j for state i appears in the dataset and b_{ji} is the expected Benford's Law distribution frequency that the digit sequence of length j for state i should appear.

As an example, consider figure 2 where state 2 has a purchase value of $38. In our algorithm we consider only leading digit sequences.[3] Therefore there are two leading digit sequences, the sequence of just '3' as well as '38'. If 3 appears 22 times in our record, while 38 appears 5 times, then $f_{12} = 22$ and $f_{22} = 5$. Assuming that Benford's Law states that the sequence '3' should appear 10 times and '38' should appear 5 times, then $b_{12} = 10$ and $b_{22} = 5$. Note since there are not three digits in our purchase value $f_{33} = 0$ and does not contribute to the reward function of equation 2. We thus produce a Reward value for state 2 of $Reward(2) = \frac{22}{10} + \frac{5}{5} = 3.2$. We thus can compute reward values associated with each state. Figure 2 illustrates our records with their associated computed rewards.

---

[2] Benford's Law works with digit sequences of any length. For most practical purposes, the frequencies of sequences of three digits or less are evaluated. For longer digit lengths, the probabilities become so small that they are of little practical value.

[3] See [1] for a justification for this choice.

| States | Actions/Attributes | | | | Digit | Rewards/Magnitude |
	Purchase Item	Store	Location	Form of Payment	Sequences	of Anomalies
1	shoes	storeA	street15	credit	$52	1.6
2	hat	storeB	street12	cash	$38	3.2
3	hat	storeC	street17	debit	$22	6.2
4	TV	storeB	street11	cheque	$640	1.1

Fig. 3. Sample Application: Choosing a Record/State

Once the reward values have been computed, we can now explore our environment as a reinforcement learning network. We do so by first choosing a start state. In figure 3 we chose state 2. This results in a reward value of 3.2. We then need to choose an action. Our actions are any unused attributes of our record. In this case we have four possible actions. There are numerous methods for choosing an action. See [9] for various techniques.

| States | Actions/Attributes | | | | Digit | Rewards/Magnitude |
	Purchase Item	Store	Location	Form of Payment	Sequences	of Anomalies
1	shoes	storeA	street15	credit	$52	1.6
2	hat	storeB	street12	cash	$38	3.2
3	hat	storeC	street17	debit	$22	6.2
4	TV	storeB	street11	cheque	$640	1.1

Fig. 4. Sample Application: State to Action to Next State Transition

If we choose action/attribute 'Store'. The specific instance of this action in state 2 is 'storeB'. We therefore search the store column for any other states/records with 'storeB' as an entry. Every possible record with such an entry is a possible next state. In our example state 4 is a possible next state which, as figure 4 illustrates will be our next state. We use a uniform random distribution to choose which of our possible next state candidates will be selected.

Now that we have a method of exploring our environment, we can apply a reinforcement learning algorithm such as temporal differencing or maximum likelihood to find an optimal policy to our system. Any such policy will link together records with the greatest anomalies forming a pattern that builds a case of fraudulent activity just as an auditor may do.

Once you have an optimal policy, the states/records that the auditor wishes to build a case for fraud for, may be used as the start state and then the auditor simply executes the optimal policy choices to find all states that are most strongly linked to that given start state. In this way, the auditor finds all underlying attributes/actions that are in common with the high reward returning states. This requires only a single trace through the system since the optimal policy has already done the exploration that an auditor would have traditionally had to do saving time and man-hours.

A few details which we have not gone into due to space constraints include how to choose when to stop your explorations, handling records that contain multiple columns with digits conforming to a Benford distribution as well as dealing with exploring non-optimal policies. An important reason to obtain less than optimal policies is that less than optimal policies may still also contain fraudulent patterns. One method to obtain such less than optimal policies is by iteratively removing the optimal policy and then rerunning the algorithm.

In addition, two points for those unfamiliar with Benford's Law and auditing in general may question are that the reward structure of equation 2 does not give higher rewards for digits that appear less frequently than the Benford's Law predicts and that numbers with more digits will possibly have a bias to higher rewards since there are more digits that can contribute to the reward value. Regarding the first point, one could use an alternative formula to equation 2 such as:

$$Reward(i) = q_{1i} + q_{2i} + q_{3i}, \tag{3}$$

where

$$q_{ji} = \begin{cases} \frac{f_{ji}}{b_{ji}} & \text{for } f_{ji} > b_{ji} \\ \frac{b_{ji}}{f_{ji}} & \text{otherwise} \end{cases}. \tag{4}$$

We use equation 2 in our implementation due to our application area of insurance where generally, auditors are most interested in over-charges rather than under-charges. Naturally, this may not be the case in other application areas such as tax filings where one may be concerned with under reporting of figures. In regards to the second point about numbers with more digits having higher rewards, this situation is a Benford's Law phenomenon. Certainly more digits provide more information to the auditor, but this bias is generally not of concern in practical auditing terms as successive digits have geometrically (10 times less for ever digit position to the left you move) less influence on the over all reward relative to the higher leading digits. Further discussions on the influence of successive significant digits may be found in [3]. The authors will gladly provide further details on any of these points on request.

4   Experiments

As stated in section 3 our application analyzes the first, the first two and the first three digit sequences of a dataset, comparing them to expect Benford frequencies. Therefore, for each data set analyzed, we are comparing it to three different Benford's Law digit frequency distributions, one of only length 1 digit, another of length 2 digits and a third of length 3 digits. For conciseness we have reported our digit frequency analyzes through graphs whereby we include the first digit frequencies 1 to 9 on the x-axis values from 1 to 9, the first two digit sequences composed of 10, 11,...,99 on the x-axis from 10 to 99 and the first three digit sequences on the x-axis from 100,...999. When looking at the numerical results, one should keep in mind a single graph is actually three sets of different distributions. The expected Benford curve will contain disjunction points at the points between 9 to 10, and 99 to 100 because they are the points at which a new Benford probability distribution starts and ends.

As stated in section 1.1, we have two databases with which to test our fraud detection method on, a record of healthcare insurance claims provided by Manulife Financial as well as records of auto insurance claims. However, the healthcare insurance claims have yet to be audited and therefore we use it only to illustrate both the robustness of how

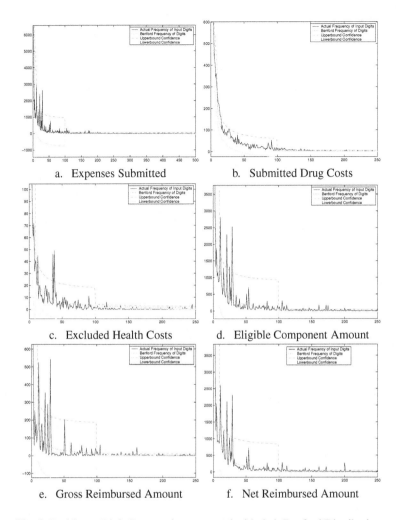

a. Expenses Submitted

b. Submitted Drug Costs

c. Excluded Health Costs

d. Eligible Component Amount

e. Gross Reimbursed Amount

f. Net Reimbursed Amount

Fig. 5. Healthcare Digit Frequencies compared with their Benford Distributions

our system is generalized enough to operate on differing application areas as well as the operation of identifying anomalous data in conjunction with the attributes related to those anomalies. The second database composed of auto insurance has been audited with identified fraudulent and non-fraudulent records with associated attributes. We therefore use the second database as a test of the utility of our system for identifying real fraud cases.

The healthcare data consisted of 94 columns/attributes with 31,804 rows/records. We therefore had 94 candidate data sets to test to see if they conform to a Benford distribution. 83 of the columns were eliminated due to one of the three Adaptive Benford's Law requirements not being satisfied. Of the remaining 11 data sets, 5 were eliminated using a 90% confidence interval based on training data provided by Manulife. Figure 5 illustrates the frequencies of the digit sequences for the remaining six data sets

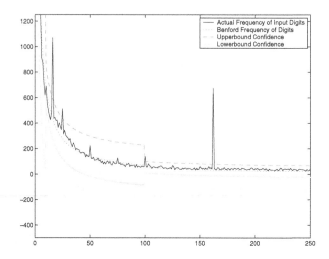

Fig. 6. Auto Insurance Digit Frequencies

that do conform to the Benford distributions. Included on the graphs are the 90% lower and upper bound confidence intervals as well as the the expected Benford frequencies.[4] The six graphs from a to e of figure 5 resulted in 23, 31, 8,21, 14 and 18 respectively of total suspicious attributes, which are currently being investigated for by auditors for fraud.

For our auto insurance database, Ernst and Young provided data which was already audited for fraud. The researchers conducted a test of the system as a blind test where we were unaware of which, if any, of the records and attributes were fraudulent. In this case, only one column of the database conformed to a Benford distribution satisfying the three requirements of Adaptive Benford. Figure 6 illustrates the digit frequencies of the auto insurance data. There were 30 remaining non-Benford attribute columns which may be used as actions to match on in our Reinforcement Learning environment. The database consisted of 17,640 records.

Figure 7 illustrates corresponding rewards resulting from our most optimal policy to our fourth most optimal policy. We obtained the most optimal, second most optimal, etc. polices by successively eliminating the optimal policy currently found and rerunning the optimal policy search. The thirty columns of our graphs represent the thirty attributes that are possible to be chosen from. The height of the bars is the sum of the reward values that would be obtained following the respective policy for each type of attribute the policy chooses. As one can see, the heights for the successively worsening policies result in, not surprisingly, worsening reward values.

Our optimal policy successfully identified the one company that was producing several fraudulent insurance claims. This single fraud generating company corresponds to two of the large spikes appearing in figure 6. However, an important note on our

---

[4] Confidence intervals were computed based on variance values of training data provided by Manulife and used 2 standard deviations from the expected Benford frequencies for the upper and lower bounds.

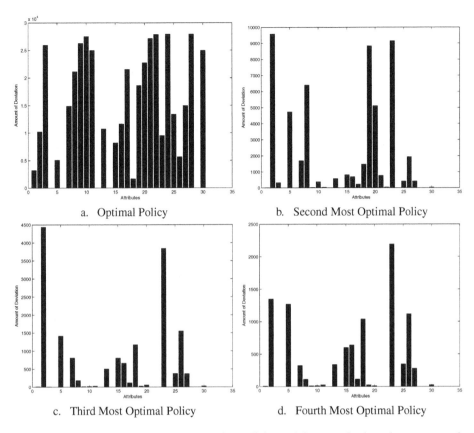

a. Optimal Policy

b. Second Most Optimal Policy

c. Third Most Optimal Policy

d. Fourth Most Optimal Policy

Fig. 7. The attributes of successively worsening policies and the reward values they correspond to across all records

method is that standard Benford outlier methods would have not identified this company because although there was a 'company name' attribute field, this company was not listed consistently in the same way in that field. Instead, they used variations on the name such as abbreviations and reorderings of the words that the name consisted of. Our policy was able to identify the company instead by linking together agents who submitted fraudulent claims on behalf of the company with their locations and in turn to the company. This linking is exactly the kind of fraud case building that the reinforcement learning component is designed to build.

5 Conclusions

In this paper we have presented a new fraud detection method which expands on the current simpler outlier detection approaches. We specifically used a Benford distribution as a benchmark for our unsupervised learning method to discover new fraud cases. We enhanced the method with a reinforcement learning model of our environment in order to link together anomalous outliers to build a case for fraud. In so doing, we are essentially simulating the behaviour of human auditors. We tested our system with a blind test on auto insurance data successfully identifying instances of fraud perpetrated by several people but linked to one underlying company.

In terms of future research, we plan to incorporate other outlier detection methods with our current Benford method as well as apply our method to greater amounts of audited data from a variety of different application areas.

Acknowledgements. The authors wish to thank Manulife Financial as well as Ernst and Young for providing the insurance data. We would also like to thank the Natural Sciences and Engineering Research Council (NSERC) for providing funding.

References

1. F. Lu and J. E. Boritz. Detecting Fraud in Health Insurance Data: Learning to Model Incomplete Benford's Law Distributions. In *16th European Conference on Machine Learning*, pages 633–640, Porto, Portugal, 2005. Springer.
2. Richard J. Bolton and David J. Hand. Statistical Fraud Detection: A Review. *Statistical Science*, 17(3):235–255, 1999.
3. Mark J. Nigrini. *Digital Analysis Using Benford's Law*. Global Audit Publications, Vancouver, B.C., Canada, 2000.
4. Mark J. Nigrini. Can Benford's Law Be Used In Forensic Accounting? *The Balance Sheet*, June:7–8, 1993.
5. Roger S. Pinkham. On the Distribution of First Significant Digits. *Annals of Mathematical Statistics*, 32:1223–1230, 1961.
6. Theodore P. Hill. A Statistical Derivation of the Significant-Digit Law. *Statistical Science*, 4:354–363, 1996.
7. Charles A.P.N. Carslaw. Anomalies in Income Numbers: Evidence of Goal Oriented Behaviour. *The Accounting Review*, 63:321–327, 1988.
8. Nita Crowder. Fraud Detection Techniques. *Internal Auditor*, April:17–20, 1997.
9. R. S. Sutton and A. G. Barto. *Reinforcement Learning: An Introduction*. MIT Press, Cambridge, Massachusetts, 1998.
10. R. S. Sutton. Learning to predict by the method of Temporal Differences. In *Machine Learning*, volume 3, pages 9–44, 1988.
11. F. Lu and D. Schuurmans. Monte Carlo Matrix Inversion Policy Evaluation. In *UAI: Proceedings of the 19th Conference*, pages 386–393, San Francisco, 2003. Morgan Kaufmann.
12. Mark J. Nigrini and Linda J. Mittermaier. The Use of Benford's Law as an Aid in Analytical Procedures. In *Auditing: A Journal of Practice and Theory*, volume 16(2), pages 52–67, 1997.

Partial Local FriendQ Multiagent Learning: Application to Team Automobile Coordination Problem

Julien Laumonier and Brahim Chaib-draa

DAMAS Laboratory, Department of Computer Science
and Software Engineering, Laval University, Canada
{jlaumoni, chaib}@damas.ift.ulaval.ca

Abstract. Real world multiagent coordination problems are important issues for reinforcement learning techniques. In general, these problems are partially observable and this characteristic makes the solution computation intractable. Most of the existing approaches calculate exact or approximate solutions using the world model for only one agent. To handle a special case of partial observability, this article presents an approach to approximate the policy measuring a degree of observability for pure cooperative vehicle coordination problem. We compare empirically the performance of the learned policy for totally observable problems and performances of policies for different degrees of observability. If each degree of observability is associated with communication costs, multiagent system designers are able to choose a compromise between the performance of the policy and the cost to obtain the associated degree of observability of the problem. Finally, we show how the available space, surrounding an agent, influence the required degree of observability for near-optimal solution.

1 Introduction

In real world cooperative multiagent problem, each agent has often a partial view of the environment. If communication is possible without cost, the multiagent problem becomes totally observable and can be solved optimally using reinforcement learning techniques. However, if the communication has a cost, the multiagent system designer has to find a compromise between increasing the observability and consequently the performance of the learned policy and the total cost of the multiagent system. Some works present formal models to take into account the communication decision into the multiagent decision problem [1], [2]. For the non-cooperative multiagent problem, some works introduce also explicitly communication into general sum games [3] [4].

To allow the multiagent system designer to choose a compromise between performance and partial observability, we propose, in this article, to take into account the degree of observability for a cooperative multiagent system by measuring the performance of the associated learned policy. In this article, the degree of observability is defined as the agent's vision distance. Obviously, decreasing

L. Lamontagne and M. Marchand (Eds.): Canadian AI 2006, LNAI 4013, pp. 359–370, 2006.
© Springer-Verlag Berlin Heidelberg 2006

the observability reduces the number of accessible states for agents and therefore decrease the performance of the policy. A subclass of coordination problems is purely cooperative multiagent problems where all agents have the same utility function. This kind of problems is known as team games [5]. In this kind of games, if we consider problems where agents' designer neither has the transition function nor the reward function, we can use learning algorithms. Many of these algorithms have been proven to converge to Pareto-optimal equilibrium such as Friend Q-learning [6] and OAL [7]. Consequently, one can take an optimal algorithm to find the policy for the observable problem.

As we restrict our problem to team problems, the following assumptions are defined: (1) Mutually exclusive observations, each agent sees a partial view of the real state but all agents together see the real state. (2) Possible communication between agents but not considered as an explicit part of the decision making. (3) The problem involves only negative interactions between agents. One problem which meets these assumptions is the choosing lane decision problem [8] related to Intelligent Transportation Systems [9]. In this problem, some vehicles, which have to share a part of the road, decide to change lane or not, in order to increase traffic flow and reduce collisions. In this article, we show empirically that the performance of the learning algorithm is closely related to the degree of observability. Moreover, we show that there exists a relation between the available space for each agent and a "correct" degree of observability that allow a good policy approximation.

This paper is organized as follows. Section 2 describes the formal model and algorithms used in our approach. Section 3 describes the vehicle coordination problem with more details. Section 4 explains our approach by introducing a partial local state. Section 5 provides the results and a discussion about them. Section 6 presents the related works and Section 7 concludes.

2   Formal Model and Algorithms

Reinforcement learning allows an agent to learn by interacting with its environment. For a mono agent system, the basic formal model for reinforcement learning is Markov Decision Process [10]. Using this model, Q-Learning algorithm calculates the optimal values of the expected reward for the agent in a state s if the action a is executed. To do this, the following update function is used:

$$Q(s,a) = (1 - \alpha)Q(s,a) + \alpha[r + \gamma \max_{a \in A} Q(s',a)]$$

where r is the immediate reward, s' is the next state and α is the learning rate. An *episode* is defined as a sub-sequence of interaction between the agent and its environment.

On the other hand, game theory studies formally the interaction of rational agents. In a one-stage game, each agent i has to choose an action to maximize its own utility $U^i(a^i, a^{-i})$ which depends on the others' actions a^{-i}. An action can be *mixed* if the agent chooses it with a given probability and can be *pure* if it is chosen with probability 1. In game theory, the solution concept is the notion of equilibrium. For an agent, the equilibria are mainly based on the best response to other's actions. Formally, an action a_{br}^i is a best response to actions a^{-i} of the others agents if

$$U^i(a_{br}^i, a^{-i}) \geq U^i(a'^i, a^{-i}), \; \forall a'^i.$$

The set of best responses to a^{-i} is noted $BR^i(a^{-i})$.

The Nash equilibrium is the best response for all agents. Formally, a joint action a_N, which regroups the actions for all agents, is a Nash equilibrium if

$$\forall i, \; a_N^i \in BR^i(a^{-i})$$

where a_N^i is the action of the ith agent in the Nash equilibrium and a_N^{-i} is the actions of other agents at Nash equilibrium. A solution is Pareto optimal if there does not exist any other solution such that one agent can improve its reward without decreasing the reward of another.

The model which combines reinforcement learning and game theory, is *stochastic games* [11]. This model is a tuple $< Ag, S, A^i, \mathcal{P}, \mathcal{R}^i >$ where

- Ag is the set of agents where $\text{card}(Ag) = N$,
- $S = \{s_0, \cdots, s_M\}$ is the finite set of states where $|S| = M$,
- $A^i = \{a_0^i, \cdots, a_p^i\}$ is the finite set of actions for the agent i,
- $\mathcal{P} : S \times A^1 \times \cdots \times A^N \times S \to \Delta(S)$ is the transition function from current state, agents actions and new state to probability distribution over state,
- $\mathcal{R}^i : S \times A^1 \times \cdots \times A^N \to \mathbb{R}$ is the immediate reward function of agent i. In team Markov games, $\mathcal{R}^i = \mathcal{R}$ for all agents i.

Among the algorithms which calculate a policy for team Markov games, Friend Q-Learning algorithm, introduced by Littman [6], allows to build a policy which is a Nash Pareto optimal equilibrium in team games. More specifically, this algorithm, based on Q-Learning, uses the following function for updating the Q-values:

$$Q(s, \boldsymbol{a}) = (1 - \alpha)Q(s, \boldsymbol{a}) + \alpha[r + \gamma \max_{\boldsymbol{a} \in \boldsymbol{A}} Q(s', \boldsymbol{a})]$$

with $\boldsymbol{a}$, the joint action for all agents $(\boldsymbol{a} = (a^1, \cdots, a^N))$.

3   Problem Description

Vehicle coordination is a sub-problem of Intelligent Transportation Systems which aims to reduce congestion, pollution, stress and increase safety of the traffic. Coordination of vehicles is a real world problem with all the difficulties that can be encountered: partially observable, multi-criteria, complex dynamic, and continuous. Consequently, we establish many assumptions to apply the multiagent reinforcement learning algorithm to this problem.

The vehicle coordination problem presented here is adapted from Moriarty and Langley [8]. More precisely, three vehicles, each of them represented by an agent, have to coordinate to maintain velocity and to avoid collisions. Each vehicle is represented by a position and a velocity and can change lane to the left, to the right or stay on the same lane. The objective for a learning algorithm is to find the best policy for each agent in order to maximize the common reward which is the average velocity at each turn and to avoid collision.

Figure 1 represents the initial state. The dynamic, the state and the actions are sampled in the easiest way. The vehicles' dynamic are simplified to the following first order equation with only velocity $y(t) = v \times t + y_0$. For this example, we simulate the road as a ring meaning that a vehicle is placed on the left side when it quits through the right side. The state of the environment is described by the position x^i, y^i and the velocity v^i of each agent i. Collisions occur when two agents are in the same tile. The agents do not know the transitions between states which is calculated according to the velocities of the agents and their actions. At every step, each vehicle tries to accelerate until a maximum of 5 m/s is reached. If another vehicle is in front of him, the agent in charge of the vehicle, sets its velocity to the front vehicle's velocity. At each step, a vehicle can choose three actions: stay on the same lane, change to the right lane and change to the left lane. Each episode has a maximum of 10 steps. The reward at each step is set to the average velocity among all vehicles. If a collision occurs, the episode stops. The size of the set of states is in $O((X \times Y \times |V|)^N)$ with X the number of lane, Y the length of the road, V the set of possible velocity and N the number of agents. We assume, in this problem, that each agent is able to see only its own local state (position, velocity). To obtain the states of other agents, we assume that communication is needed.

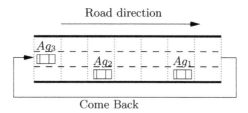

Fig. 1. Initial state for problem

4   Partial Observability

In this section, we introduce our approach describing Friend Q-learning algorithm with a local view for the agents. Then, we introduce the same algorithm that use the partial local view for a distance d. This partial local view can reduce the set of state and/or the set of joint actions. If no reduction is done, the exact algorithm associated is Friend Q-learning. When only the set of states is reduced, we propose Total Joint Actions Q-learning (TJA). From this algorithm, we reduce the set of joint actions and we propose another algorithm: Partial Joint Actions Q-learning (PJA). In this article, we do not consider the reduction of joint actions alone, because this reduction is lower than the reduction of the set of states.

4.1   FriendQ with a Local View

To introduce partial observability, we use the notion of local Q-Value and local state. Each agent uses the same algorithm but on different state. A local state is defined from the real state of the multiagent system for a center agent. All other agents positions are defined relatively to this central agent. This means that the same real state belongs to the set S will give different local states. For an agent i, the set possible local state is S^i. We introduce a function f^i which transforms the real state s to a local state s^i for agent i. Formally, $\forall s \in S, \exists s^i \in S^i$ such that $f^i(s) = s^i$ for all agents i. In this version of the algorithm, each agent uses Friend Q-learning algorithm as described in section 2 but by updating its Q-values for the local states and not for the real state.

4.2   FriendQ with a Partial Local View

To measure the effect of partial observability on the performance we define the partial state centered on one agent by introducing a distance of observalibity d. Consequently, the initial problem becomes a d-partial problem. The distance d can be viewed as an influence area for the agent. Increasing this distance increases the degree of observability. We define d_{total} as the maximal possible distance of observability for a given problem. Moreover, from a communication point of view, in real world problems, the communication cost between two agents depends on the distance between them. Communicating with a remote agent is costlier than with a close agent.

   In d-partial problem, the new state is defined as the observation of the center agent for a range d. More precisely, an agent j is in the partial state of a central agent i if its distance is lower or equal than d from the central agent i. Formally, the function f_d^i uses the parameter d to calculate the new local state. Figure 2 provides an example of the application of f_d^i on a state s and get the result partial states for each agent with a distance $d = 2$. Agent 1 sees only Agent 3 but Agent 3 sees both other agents. The new size of the set of state is $O(((2d+1)^2 \times V)^N)$. The number of state is divided by around $(Y/(2d+1))^N$, if we neglect the number of lanes which is often small compared to the length of the road.

TJA Q-Learning. In a first step, as in classical Friend Q-learning, we consider an algorithm that takes into account the complete joint actions. This assumption implies that all agents are able to communicate their actions to others at each step without cost. The Q-value update function is now :

$$Q(f_d^i(s), \boldsymbol{a}) = (1 - \alpha)Q(f_d^i(s), \boldsymbol{a}) + \alpha[r + \gamma \max_{\boldsymbol{a} \in \boldsymbol{A}} Q(f_d^i(s'), \boldsymbol{a})]$$

for agent i. When $d = d_{total}$, we have a small reduction factor on the state set of XY, because we do not take into account, in our specific problem, the absolute position of the center agent.

PJA Q-learning. In a second step, the algorithm takes into account only the actions where agents are in the partial local view as specified by d. This reduce

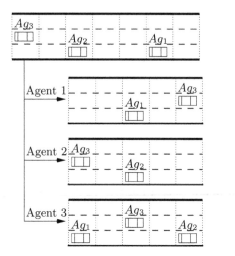

Fig. 2. State and Partial States for $d = 2$

dramatically the number of joint actions which have to be tested during the learning. This partial local observability allows us to consider a variable number of agents in the multiagent system.

Formally, we define a function g^i which transforms the joint action $\boldsymbol{a}$ into a partial joint action $g_d^i(\boldsymbol{a}, s)$. This partial joint action contains all actions of agent which are in the distance d of agent i. The Q-value update function is now :

$$Q(f_d^i(s), g_d^i(\boldsymbol{a}, s)) = (1 - \alpha)Q(f_d^i(s), g_d^i(\boldsymbol{a}, s)) + \alpha[r + \gamma \max_{\boldsymbol{a_d} \in G_d^i(\boldsymbol{A}, S)} Q(f_d^i(s'), \boldsymbol{a_d})]$$

for agent i where $G_d^i(\boldsymbol{A}, S)$ returns the set of joint actions with a central agent i and a distance d. We can see that the result of the partial joint action depends on the current state.

5   Results

In this section, we compare empirically the performance of the totally observable problem (FriendQ) and the performance of approximated policy (TJA and PJA). We present three kind of results: first of all, we compare the algorithms on a small problem P_1 defined by size $X = 3$, $Y = 7$, the set of velocities $V = 0, \cdots, 5$ and the number of agents $N = 3$. Consequently, in this problem, the maximal distance that we can use to approximate the total problem is $d_{total} = 3$. The 3-partial state is a local representation of the totally observable state because we are sure that all agents are visible from others in this representation. In the initial state (Figure 1), velocities of the agents are $v^1 = 1$, $v^2 = 2$ and $v^3 = 3$. We present, for all results, the average total sum reward over 25 learnings with each episode lasts 10 steps.

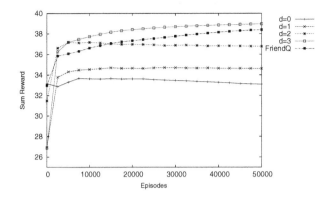

Fig. 3. Rewards for Total Joint Action Q-learning for problem P_1

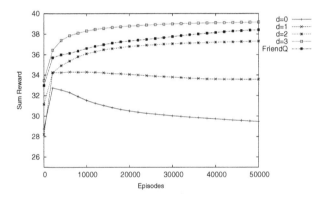

Fig. 4. Rewards for Partial Joint Action Q-learning for problem P_1

Figure 3 shows the result of TJA Q-learning with distance from $d = 0$ to $d = 3$. This algorithm is compared to the total observation problem resolved by Friend Q-Learning. For $d = 0$, $d = 1$ and $d = 2$, TJA converges to a local maximum, which increases with d. In these cases, the approximated values are respectively about 86%, 89% and 94% of the optimal value. When $d = 3$, that is, when the local view is equivalent to the totally observable view, the average sum rewards converges to the total sum rewards of Friend Q-learning. However, since we do not take into account the absolute position of the center agent, TJA converges quickly than Friend Q-learning. Figure 4 shows the results of PJA Q-Learning on the same problem. As previously, for $d = 0$, $d = 1$ and $d = 2$, PJA converges to local maxima respectively about 76%, 86% and 97% of the optimal value. These values are lower than TJA's values but, for $d = 2$, the value is still close to the optimal.

For the second result, we compare PJA Q-learning for two different problems. We define a correct approximation distance d_{app} for each problem, where the associated policy is closed to the optimal value. The first problem is the same as previously (Figure 4) and we can show that $d_{app} = 3$ for this problem. In the second problem P_2, we enlarge the number of lanes and the length of the road ($X = 5, Y = 20, V = 0, \cdots, 5$ and $N = 3$). This problem increases the number of states but decreases the possible interactions between vehicles because they have more space. For the second problem P_2, Figure 5 shows the comparison between Friend Q-learning and PJA Q-learning from $d = 0$ to $d = 7$. We can see that from $d = 4$, there is only small differences between PJA and Friend Q-learning. Consequently, for this problem, we can see that $d_{app} = 4$. The problem of this approach is the need of calculating the optimal policy, which can be intractable, to get d_{app}.

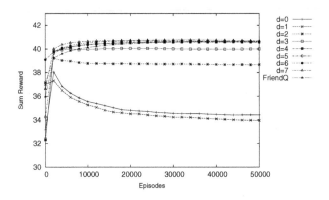

Fig. 5. Rewards for Partial Joint Action Q-learning for problem P_2

As we can see, we need to generalize this result to know the d_{app} parameter without calculating the optimal policy, which can be absolutely intractable for big problems. To present the third result, we calculate the ratio $DS = XY/N$ which represents the degree of space for each agent. Obviously, if the space (X or Y) increases, then each agent has more space for itself. As we study a problem where the team of agent has to handle only negative interaction, the higher the ratio, the more space agents have. We compare the performance of our PJA algorithm for different ratios. The ratio for the two first problems is respectively $DS_{P_1} = 7$ and $DS_{P_2} = 33$. We add two new problems P_3 ($X = 5$, $Y = 20, V = 0, \cdots, 5$ and $N = 5$) and P_4 ($X = 6, Y = 28, V = 0, \cdots, 5$ and $N = 4$) where the ratio are respectively 20 and 42. Table 1 presents the results for each problem after 50000 episodes. For each problem, we define the correct approximation distance d_{app} such as $1 - (\frac{R_{d_{app}}}{R_{friendQ}}) < \epsilon$. When $\epsilon = 0.01$, $d_{app}^{P_1} = 3$, $d_{app}^{P_2} = 4$, $d_{app}^{P_3} = 2$ and $d_{app}^{P_4} = 2$.

To discover a relation between the ratio DS and the value of d_{app}, we compare in Figure 6, the link between DS and the degree of observability defined as $\frac{d_{app}}{d_{total}}$ where d_{total} is the maximal distance for a given problem. For example, d_{total} for the problem P_1 is 3. We can see that the degree of observability decreases with the degree of space for each agent. We calculate an interpolated curve assuming

Table 1. Average Rewards and standard deviation after 50000 episodes

Algorithms	P_1	ϵ_{P_1}	P_2	ϵ_{P_2}	P_3	ϵ_{P_3}	P_4	ϵ_{P_4}
FriendQ	38.4 ± 1.1	-	40.6 ± 0.3	-	37.0 ± 1.2	-	37.6 ± 0.3	-
PJA $d = 7$	-	-	40.6 ± 0.2	∼ 0%	37.2 ± 0.7	∼ 0%	38.4 ± 0.2	∼ 0%
PJA $d = 6$	-	-	40.5 ± 0.2	∼ 0%	37.9 ± 0.7	∼ 0%	38.8 ± 0.4	∼ 0%
PJA $d = 5$	-	-	40.6 ± 0.2	∼ 0%	37.8 ± 0.9	∼ 0%	38.7 ± 0.4	∼ 0%
PJA $d = 4$	-	-	40.5 ± 0.2	∼ 0%	38.3 ± 0.8	∼ 0%	38.7 ± 0.2	∼ 0%
PJA $d = 3$	39.1 ±0.2	∼ 0%	40.0 ± 0.2	∼ 2%	38.7 ± 0.6	∼ 0%	38.9 ± 0.2	∼ 0%
PJA $d = 2$	37.3 ±0.2	∼ 3%	38.6 ± 0.2	∼ 5%	37.7 ± 0.5	∼ 0%	38.5 ± 0.1	∼ 0%
PJA $d = 1$	33.5 ±0.2	∼ 14%	33.9 ± 0.3	∼ 15%	35.2 ± 0.3	∼ 5%	35.1 ± 0.4	∼ 8%
PJA $d = 0$	29.4 ±0.3	∼ 24%	34.4 ± 0.4	∼ 15%	33.5 ± 0.4	∼ 10%	34.3 ± 0.3	∼ 11%

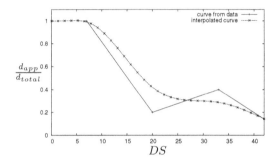

Fig. 6. Link between observability and degree of space

that the degree of observability cannot be higher than 1 when $DS < 7$. We can see that the needed observability decreases and tends to 0 when DS increases. With this relation between both parameters, observability and degree of space, we can evaluate, for other problems how would be the d_{app} value.

Thus, introducing the locality of the view allows us to limit the observability of the state. More precisely, this approach allows us to use partial version of Friend Q-learning in real world problems where the state is always partially observable. We obtain an approximation of the optimal policy without knowing the transition function. This approximation can be very close to the optimal policy.

In our approach, we do not take into account communication explicitly for many reasons. First of all, in real world problem, choosing the right communication cost is not an easy task. Furthermore, as we said previously, the communication cost depends not only on the sent message but also on the distance between sender and receivers. This problem complicates design of communication cost. Consequently, knowing the value of the approximated policy and the associated communication policy (and consequently, the cost of this policy) to obtain the n-partial state, the multiagent system designer can find a good approximation for the real world problem.

6   Related Work

The most general model which is related to our work is Partially Observable Stochastic Games (POSG). This model formalizes theoretically the observations for each agent. The resolution of this kind of games has been studied by Emery-Montermerlo [12]. This resolution is an approximation using Bayesian games. However, this resolution is still based on the model of the environment unlike our approach which do not take into account this information explicitly since we assume that the environment is unknown.

Concerning the space search reduction, Sparse Cooperative Q-Learning [13] allows agents to coordinate their actions only on predefined set of states. In the other states, agents learn without knowing the existence of the other agents. However, the states where the agents have to coordinate themselves are selected statically before the learning process, unlike in our approach. The joint actions set reduction has been studied by Fulda and Ventura who propose Dynamic Joint Action Perception (DJAP) [14]. DJAP allows a multiagent Q-learning algorithm to select dynamically the useful joint actions for each agent during the learning. However, they concentrated only on joint actions and they tested only their approach on problems with few states.

Introducing communication into decision has been studied by Xuan, Lesser, and Zilberstein [1] who proposed a formal extension to Markov Decision Process with communication when each agent observes a part of the environment but all agents observe the entire state. Their approach proposes to alternate communication and action in the decentralized decision process. As the optimal policy computation is intractable, the authors proposed some heuristics to compute approximation solutions. The main differences with our approach is the implicit communication and the model-free learning in our approach. More generally, Pynadath and Tambe [2] has proposed an extension to distributed POMDP with communication called COM-MTDP, which take into account the cost of communication during the decision process. They presented some complexity results for some classes for team problems. As Xuan, Lesser, and Zilberstein [1], this approach is mainly theoretical and does not present model-free learning.

The locality of interactions in an MDP has been theoretically developed by Dolgov and Durfee [15]. They presented a graphical approach to represent the compact representation of an MDP. However, their approach has been developed to solve an MDP and not to solve directly a multiagent reinforcement learning problem where the transition function is unknown.

Regarding the reinforcement learning in a vehicle coordination problem, Ünsal, Kachroo and Bay [16] have used multiple stochastic learning automata to control longitudinal and lateral path of one vehicle. However, the authors did not extend their approach to multiagent problem. In his work, Pendrith [17] presented a distributed variant of Q-Learning (DQL) applied to lane change advisory system, that is closed to our problem described in this paper. His approach uses a local perspective representation state which represents the relative velocities of the vehicles around. Consequently, this representation state is closely related to our 1-partial state representation. Contrary to our algorithms,

DQL does not take into account the actions of the vehicles around and update Q-Values by an average backup value over all agents at each time step. The problem of this algorithm is the lack of learning stability.

7   Conclusion

In this article, we proposed an approach to evaluate a good approximation of a multiagent decision process, introducing a degree of observability for each agents. Without taking into account explicit communication to obtain a degree of observability, we proposed Friend Q-learning algorithms extension which uses only observable state and observable actions from the other agents. We show that only partial view is needed to obtain a good policy approximation for some team problems, especially the changing lane problem between vehicles. We show a relation between a good degree of observability and the space allowed for each agent. However, this relation is only empirical and our approach is only restricted to negative interaction management problems. It is possible that in other problems, this relation could be different.

Adapting multiagent learning algorithm for real world problems is really challenging and many works need to be done to achieve this goal. For future work, we plan to evaluate more theoretically the relation between the degree of observability, the performance of the learned policy and the speed of learning. To define some formal bounds, we will certainly need to use complex communication cost. Finally, introducing the distance for a measure of observability is basic. We plan to discover others kind of distance between observability to generalize our approach to positive and negative interaction management problems in teams. Also, it will be very interesting to study the effect of partial local view to non cooperative cases.

References

1. Xuan, P., Lesser, V., Zilberstein, S.: Communication decisions in multi-agent cooperation: Model and experiments. In Müller, J.P., Andre, E., Sen, S., Frasson, C., eds.: the Fifth International Conference on Autonomous Agents, Montreal, Canada, ACM Press (2001) 616–623
2. Pynadath, D.V., Tambe, M.: The communicative multiagent team decision problem: Analyzing teamwork theories and models. Journal of AI Research **16** (2002) 389–423
3. Aras, R., Dutech, A., Charpillet, F.: Cooperation in Stochastic Games through Communication. In: fourth Internantional Conference on Autonomous Agents and Multi-Agent Systems (AAMAS'05) (poster), Utrecht, Nederlands (2005)
4. Verbeeck, K.: Exploring Selfish Reinforcement Learning in Stochastic Non-Zero Sum Games. PhD thesis, Vrije Universiteit Brussel (2004)
5. Bui, H.H.: An Approach to Coordinating Team of Agents under Incomplete Information. PhD thesis, Curtin University of Technology (1998)
6. Littman, M.: Friend-or-Foe Q-learning in General-Sum Games. In Kaufmann, M., ed.: Eighteenth International Conference on Machine Learning. (2001) 322–328

7. Wang, X., Sandholm, T.W.: Reinforcement Learning to Play An Optimal Nash Equilibrium in Team Markov Games. In: 16th Neural Information Processing Systems: Natural and Synthetic conference. (2002)
8. Moriarty, D.E., Langley, P.: Distributed learning of lane-selection strategies for traffic management. Technical report, Palo Alto, CA. (1998) 98-2.
9. Varaiya, P.: Smart cars on smart roads : Problems of control. IEEE Transactions on Automatic Control **38**(2) (1993) 195–207
10. Sutton, R.S., Barto, A.G.: Reinforcement Learning: An Introduction. MIT Press, Cambridge, MA (1998)
11. Basar, T., Olsder, G.J.: Dynamic Noncooperative Game Theory. 2nd edn. Classics In Applied Mathematics (1999)
12. Emery-Montermerlo, R.: Game-theoretic control for robot teams. Technical Report CMU-RI-TR-05-36, Robotics Institute, Carnegie Mellon University (2005)
13. Kok, J.R., Vlassis, N.: Sparse Cooperative Q-learning. In Greiner, R., Schuurmans, D., eds.: Proc. of the 21st Int. Conf. on Machine Learning, Banff, Canada, ACM (2004) 481–488
14. Fulda, N., Ventura, D.: Dynamic Joint Action Perception for Q-Learning Agents. In: 2003 International Conference on Machine Learning and Applications. (2003)
15. Dolgov, D., Durfee, E.H.: Graphical models in local, asymmetric multi-agent Markov decision processes. In: Proceedings of the Third International Joint Conference on Autonomous Agents and Multiagent Systems (AAMAS-04). (2004)
16. Ünsal, C., Kachroo, P., Bay, J.S.: Simulation study of multiple intelligent vehicle control using stochastic learning automata. IEEE Transactions on Systems, Man and Cybernetics - Part A : Systems and Humans **29**(1) (1999) 120–128
17. Pendrith, M.D.: Distributed reinforcement learning for a traffic engineering application. In: the Fourth International Conference on Autonomous Agents. (2000) 404 – 411

Trace Equivalence Characterization Through Reinforcement Learning

Josée Desharnais, François Laviolette,
Krishna Priya Darsini Moturu, and Sami Zhioua

IFT-GLO, Université Laval, Québec (QC) Canada, G1K-7P4
{first_name.last_name}@ift.ulaval.ca

Abstract. In the context of probabilistic verification, we provide a new notion of trace-equivalence divergence between pairs of Labelled Markov processes. This divergence corresponds to the optimal value of a particular derived Markov Decision Process. It can therefore be estimated by Reinforcement Learning methods. Moreover, we provide some PAC-guarantees on this estimation.

1 Introduction

The general field of this research is program verification. Typically, the goal is to check automatically whether a system (program, physical device, protocol, etc.) conforms to its pre-established specification. Both the specification and the implementation are represented using a formal model (generally a transition system) and then a verification algorithm checks for conformance between the two models. This is usually done with the knowledge of the models of the two processes. Our work fits in a more realistic setting where we want to check the conformance between a specification and an implementation (physical device, piece of code, etc.) for which only the model of the specification is available.

The model we work with is called a *Labelled Markov Process* (LMP) [2]; it is a labelled transition systems where transitions are labelled by an action and weighted by a probability (see Figure 1). The action is meant to be synchronized

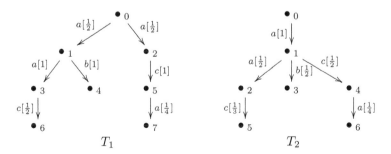

T_1 $\qquad$ T_2

Fig. 1. Labelled Markov Processes

through interaction with the environment. Apart from the modelling of intrinsically probabilistic systems like randomized protocols, probabilities are also used

L. Lamontagne and M. Marchand (Eds.): Canadian AI 2006, LNAI 4013, pp. 371–382, 2006.
© Springer-Verlag Berlin Heidelberg 2006

as an abstraction mechanism, for example to hide complex details in suitably chosen probability distributions. The state space of an LMP can be infinite; finite LMPs are also called Probabilistic labelled transition systems or Markov decision processes without rewards. In this paper we will always suppose that it has a tree like representation which, up to bisimulation [2], is always possible. In recent years, a lot of work has been done on pseudo-metrics between probabilistic systems. The reason is that when one wants to compare systems, an equivalence like bisimulation is quite limited: systems are equivalent or they are not. In the presence of probabilities this is even worse because, for one thing, a slight change in the probabilities of equivalent processes will result in non equivalent processes. A pseudometric is an indication of how far systems are. Few pseudometrics have been defined but none of them come with an efficient way to compute it. Moreover, these metrics can only deal with processes whose models are known.

This paper is a first step towards the computation of a suitable measure of non equivalence between processes in the presence of unknown models. We have observed that while verification techniques can deal with processes of about 10^{12} states, Reinforcement Learning (RL) algorithms do a lot better; for example, the *TD-Gammon* program deals with more than 10^{40} possible states [13]. Thus we define a *divergence* notion between LMPs, noted $\text{div}_{\text{trace}}(\,.\,\|\,.\,)$, that can be computed with RL algorithms. We call it a divergence rather than a distance because it is not symmetric and does not satisfy the triangle inequality. However, it does have the important property that it is always positive or zero and it is equal to zero if and only if the processes are *probabilistic trace-equivalent* [9]. Two processes are *probabilistic trace-equivalent* (we will simply say trace-equivalent) if they accept the same sequences of actions with the same probabilities. For example, T_1 and T_2 in Figure 1 accept the same traces: $\varepsilon, a, aa, ab, ac, aac, aca$ but they are not trace-equivalent since $P^{T_1}(aac) = \frac{1}{4}$ whereas $P^{T_2}(aac) = \frac{1}{6}$.

2   The Approach

We first informally expose our approach through a one-player stochastic game. Then, we will define a divergence between a specification model (denoted "Spec") and a real system (denoted "Impl") for which the model is not available but on which we can interact (exactly as a black-box). This divergence will be the value of the maximal expected reward obtained when playing this game. The formalization and proofs will follow.

2.1   Defining a Game Using Traces

A *trace* is a sequence of actions (possibly empty) that is meant to be executed on a process. Its execution results in the observation of success or failure of each action[1]. For example, if trace aca is executed, then four observations are possible:

---

[1] Note that the execution is sometimes called the trace itself whereas the sequence of actions is called a test.

$a^\times$, $a^\checkmark c^\times$, $a^\checkmark c^\checkmark a^\times$ and $a^\checkmark c^\checkmark a^\checkmark$, where $a^\checkmark$ means that a is accepted whereas $a^\times$ means that it is refused. To each trace is associated a probability distribution on observations. For example, in T_2 of Figure 1, the observations related to trace aca have the distribution $p_{a^\times} = 0$, $p_{a^\checkmark c^\times} = \frac{1}{1}\,\frac{1}{2} = \frac{1}{2}$, $p_{a^\checkmark c^\checkmark a^\times} = \frac{1}{1}\,\frac{1}{2}\,\frac{3}{4} = \frac{3}{8}$, $p_{a^\checkmark c^\checkmark a^\checkmark} = \frac{1}{8}$. Based on this setting, we have the straightforward result [12]:

Proposition 1. *Two processes are trace-equivalent iff they yield the same probability distribution on observations for every trace.*

In the light of this result, a suitable choice to define our divergence could simply be the maximum value, over all traces τ, of the Kullback-Leibler divergence between the probability distributions on observations when running each trace τ on "Spec" and "Impl". The Kullback-Leibler divergence between two distributions Q and P is defined as $\mathrm{KL}(Q\|P) := \mathrm{E}_{h\sim Q} \ln \frac{1}{P(h)} - \mathrm{E}_{h\sim Q} \ln \frac{1}{Q(h)}$ [4]. Unfortunately, because of the high number of possible traces (on huge systems), the maximum value over all Kullback-Leibler divergences is not tractable.

However, $\mathrm{E}_{h\sim Q} \ln \frac{1}{Q(h)}$, the entropy of Q, can be seen as as a quantification over the likeliness to obtain different observations when interacting with "Spec" and a perfect clone of it (which we call "Clone"). "Clone" is simply a copy of the specification but given in the form of a black-box (exactly as "Impl"). In some sense, $\mathrm{E}_{h\sim Q} \ln \frac{1}{P(h)}$ can also be seen as how likely we can obtain different observations when interacting (via some τ) with both "Spec" and "Impl". Hence, the maximum possible Kullback Leibler divergence should be obtained when executing a suitable trade-off reflecting the fact that the probability of seeing different observations between "Spec" and "Impl" should be as large as possible, and as small as possible between "Spec" and "Clone". Here is a one-player stochastic game on which a similar tradeoff underlies the optimal solution (see Figure 2).

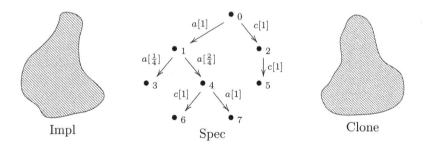

Fig. 2. Implementation, Specification, and Clone

Game₀: The player plays on "Spec", starting in the initial state; then

Step 1 : The player chooses an action a.

Step 2 : Action a is run on "Spec", "Impl" and on a clone of "Spec".

Step 3 : If a succeeds on the three processes, the new player's state is the reached state in "Spec"; go to Step 1. Else the game ends and the player gets a $(+1)$ reward for different observations between "Spec" and "Impl" added up with a (-1) reward for different observations between "Spec" and "Clone". That is, writing I for "Impl", C for "Clone" and Obs for observation,

$$R := (Obs.I \neq Obs(Spec)) - (Obs(Spec) \neq Obs.C)$$

where 0 and 1 are used as both truth values and numbers.

For example, if action a is executed on the three LMPs and observation FSS is obtained (i.e., Failure in "Impl", Successes in "Spec" and "Clone"), then an immediate reward of $(+1)$ is given. Notice that once an action fails in one of the three processes the game is stopped. Hence the only scenario allowing to move ahead is: SSS. It is easy to see that if "Spec" and "Impl" are trace-equivalent, the optimal strategy will have expected reward zero, as wanted. Unfortunately the converse is not true: there are trace-inequivalent LMPs for which every strategy has expected reward zero. Here is a counterexample: consider three systems with one a-transition from one state to another one. The probability of this transition is $\frac{1}{2}$ for the "Spec" (and "Clone") and 1 for the implementation.

Thus, the maximal possible expected reward of $Game_0$ will not lead to a notion of trace-equivalence divergence, but we will show that the following slight modification of $Game_0$ does lead to a suitable notion of divergence.

Definition 1. $Game_1$ is $Game_0$ with *Step 1* replaced by

Step 1' : The player chooses an action and makes a prediction on its success or failure on "Spec"

and the reward function is replaced by

$$R := \big(Obs(Spec) = \texttt{Pred}\big)\big((Obs.I \neq Obs(Spec)) - (Obs(Spec) \neq Obs.C)\big) \quad (1)$$

For example, if $a^\checkmark$ is selected and the observation is FSS we obtain a reward of $1((F \neq S) - (S \neq S)) = 1\,(1 - 0) = 1$, but for FFS, we obtain $0\,(0 - 1) = 0$.

Observe that because the player has a full knowledge of what is going on in "Spec", the prediction in Step 1' together with this new reward signal gives (implicitly) more control to the player. Indeed, the latter has the possibility to reduce or augment the probability to receive a non zero reward if he expects this reward to be negative or positive. Next section will formalize these ideas in a more Reinforcement Learning setting.

2.2   Constructing the MDP $\mathcal{M}$

In artificial intelligence, Markov Decision Processes (MDPs) offer a popular mathematical tool for planning and learning in the presence of uncertainty [10]. MDPs are a standard formalism for describing multi-stage decision making in probabilistic environments (what we called a one-player stochastic games in the preceding section). The objective of the decision making is to maximize a cumulative measure of long-term performance, called the reward.

In an MDP, an agent interacts with an environment at a discrete, low-level time scale. On each time step, the agent observes its current state $s_t \in S$ and chooses an action a_t from an action set A. One time step later, the agent transits to a new state s_{t+1}, and receives a reward r_{t+1}. For a given state s and action a, the expected value of the immediate reward is denoted by $R^a_{s\,s'}$ and the transition to a new state s' has probability $Pr^{\mathcal{M}}_{s\,s'}(a)$, regardless of the path taken by the agent before state s (this is the *Markov property*). The goal in solving MDPs is to find a *way of behaving*, or policy, which yields a maximal reward. Formally, a policy is defined as a probability distribution for picking actions in each state. For any policy $\pi : S \times A \to [0, 1]$ and any state $s \in S$, the *value function* of π for state s is defined as the expected infinite-horizon discounted return from s, given that the agent behaves according to π: $V^\pi(s) := E_\pi\{r_{t+1} + \gamma r_{t+2} + \gamma^2 r_{t+3} + \cdots | s_t = s\}$ where s_0 is the initial state and γ is a factor between 0 and 1 used to discount future rewards. The objective is to find an optimal policy, π^* which maximizes the value $V^\pi(s)$ of each state s. The *optimal value function*, V^*, is the unique value function corresponding to any optimal policy.

If the MDP has finite state and action spaces, and if a model of the environment is known (i.e., immediate rewards $R^a_{s\,s'}$ and transition probabilities $Pr^{\mathcal{M}}_{s\,s'}(a)$), then DP algorithms (namely policy evaluation) can compute V^π for any policy π. Similar algorithms can be used to compute V^*. RL methods, in contrast, compute approximations to V^π and V^* directly based on the interaction with the environment, without requiring a complete model, which is exactly what we are looking for in our setting.

We now define the MDP on which the divergence between two LMPs will be computed. The model of the first LMP, (called "Spec") is needed and must be in a tree-like representation. It is a tuple $(States, s_0, Actions, Pr^{Spec})$ where s_0 is the initial state and $Pr^{Spec}_{s\,s'}(a)$ is the transition probability from state s to state s' when action a has been chosen (for example, in Figure 2, $Pr^{Spec}_{1\,4}(a) = \frac{2}{4}$). Since it has a tree-like structure, for any state $s \in States$, there is a unique sequence of actions (or trace, denoted $tr.s$) from s_0 to s. For the second LMP (called "Impl"), only the knowledge of all possible conditional probabilities $P^I(a^\checkmark|\tau)$ and $P^I(a^\times|\tau)$ of observing the success or failure of an action a given any successfully executed trace τ is required. For example, in Figure 2, $P^C(c^\checkmark|aa) = \frac{2}{4} \div (\frac{2}{4} + \frac{1}{4}) = \frac{2}{3}$. Finally, we write $P^C(a^\checkmark|\tau)$ and $P^C(a^\times|\tau)$ for the conditional probabilities of a copy of the first LMP (called "Clone"): this is for readability and is no additional information since $P^C(a^\checkmark|\tau) = P^S(a^\checkmark|\tau)^2$.

Definition 2. Given "Impl", "Spec", and "Clone", the set of states of the MDP $\mathcal{M}$ is $S := States \cup \{Dead\}$, with initial state s_0; its set of actions is $Act := Actions \times \{\,\checkmark, \times\}$. The next-state probability distribution is the same for $a^\checkmark$ and $a^\times$ (which we represent generically with $a^\cdot$); it is defined below, followed with the definition of the reward function.

---

[2] Note that the complete knowledge of $P^I(.|.)$ and $P^C(.|.)$ is needed to construct the MDP, but if one only wants to run a Q-learning algorithm on it, only a possibility of interaction with "Clone" and "Impl" is required.

$$Pr^{\mathcal{M}}_{s\,s'}(a^{\text{-}}) := \begin{cases} Pr^{Spec}_{s\,s'}(a)\,P^I(a^{\checkmark}|tr.s)\,P^C(a^{\checkmark}|tr.s) & \text{if } s' \neq Dead \\ 1 - P^S(a^{\checkmark}|s)\,P^I(a^{\checkmark}|tr.s)\,P^C(a^{\checkmark}|tr.s) & \text{if } s' = Dead \end{cases}$$

$$R^{a^{\text{-}}}_{s\,s'} := \begin{cases} 0 & \text{if } s' \neq Dead \\ \dfrac{1}{Pr^{\mathcal{M}}_{s\,s'}(a^{\text{-}})}\,P^S(a^{\text{-}}|s)\,\Delta^{a^{\text{-}}}_{tr.s} & \text{if } s' = Dead \end{cases}$$

where • $P^S(a^{\checkmark}|s) := \sum_{s' \in States} Pr^{Spec}_{s\,s'}(a)$, and $P^S(a^{\times}|s) := 1 - P^S(a^{\checkmark}|s)$,

• $\Delta^{a^{\checkmark}}_{\tau} := P^I(a^{\times}|\tau)\,P^C(a^{\checkmark}|\tau) - P^I(a^{\checkmark}|\tau)\,P^C(a^{\times}|\tau)$ and $\Delta^{a^{\times}}_{\tau} := -\Delta^{a^{\checkmark}}_{\tau}$.

The additional *Dead* state in the MDP indicates the end of an episode and is reached if at least one of the three systems refuses the action. This is witnessed by the next state probability distribution.

Let us now see how the reward function $R^{a^{\text{-}}}_{s\,s'}$ accords with Game$_1$ presented in the previous section. The simplest case is if the reached state is not *Dead*: it means that the action succeeded in the three systems (SSS) which indicates a similarity between them. Consequently the reward is zero for both $a^{\checkmark}$ and $a^{\times}$, as indicated by Step 3 of the game. Let us now consider the case $s' = Dead$. We want the following relation between $R^{a^{\text{-}}}_{s\,s'}$ and $R^{a^{\text{-}}}_{s\,S}$, precisely because the latter represents the average reward of running action $a^{\text{-}}$ on a state s:

$$R^{a^{\text{-}}}_{s\,S} = Pr^{\mathcal{M}}_{s\,Dead}(a^{\text{-}})\,R^{a^{\text{-}}}_{s\,Dead} + \sum_{s' \in S \backslash \{Dead\}} Pr^{\mathcal{M}}_{s\,s'}(a^{\text{-}})\,\underbrace{R^{a^{\text{-}}}_{s\,s'}}_{0} = Pr^{\mathcal{M}}_{s\,Dead}(a^{\text{-}})\,R^{a^{\text{-}}}_{s\,Dead} \quad (2)$$

However Game$_1$ and Equation (1) give us another computation for $R^{a^{\text{-}}}_{s\,S}$. In the case where $a^{\text{-}} = a^{\checkmark}$ is chosen, then the reward is computed only if a succeeds in "Spec", that is, we get a $(+1)$ reward on observation FSS, a (-1) on SSF, and $(+0)$ on observations SSS or FSF. If a fails, the reward is $(+0)$. Thus,

$$R^{a^{\checkmark}}_{s\,S} = \underbrace{P^I(a^{\times}|tr.s)\,P^S(a^{\checkmark}|s)\,P^C(a^{\checkmark}|tr.s)}_{FSS \,\mapsto\, (+1)} - \underbrace{P^I(a^{\checkmark}|tr.s)\,P^S(a^{\checkmark}|s)\,P^C(a^{\times}|tr.s)}_{SSF \,\mapsto\, (-1)}$$

$$= P^S(a^{\checkmark}|s)\,\Delta^{a^{\checkmark}}_{tr.s}.$$

In the case where $a^{\times}$ is chosen, the opposite mechanism is adopted, that is, the reward is computed only if a fails in "Spec" and hence only the situations SFF $(+1)$ and FFS (-1) are relevant. We therefore obtain the following equation:

$$R^{a^{\text{-}}}_{s\,S} := P^S(a^{\text{-}}|s)\,\Delta^{a^{\text{-}}}_{tr.s}. \quad (3)$$

The reward $R^{a^{\text{-}}}_{s\,Dead}$ in Definition 2 is obtained by combining Equations (2) and (3).

2.3 Value of a Policy in $\mathcal{M}$

In order to define a formula for policy evaluations on any state s in our setting, we start from the Bellman Equation [13].

$$V^\pi(s) = \sum_{a^- \in Act} \pi(s, a^-) \sum_{s' \in S} Pr^{\mathcal{M}}_{s\,s'}(a^-) \, (R^{a^-}_{s\,s'} + \gamma \, V^\pi(s'))$$

$$= \sum_{a^- \in Act} \pi(s, a^-) \, (Pr^{\mathcal{M}}_{s\,Dead}(a^-) R^{a^-}_{s\,Dead} + \sum_{s' \in S \setminus \{Dead\}} Pr^{\mathcal{M}}_{s\,s'}(a^-)(0 + \gamma \, V^\pi(s')))$$

$$= \sum_{a^- \in Act} \pi(s, a^-) \, (R^{a^-}_{s\,S} + \sum_{s' \in S \setminus \{Dead\}} Pr^{\mathcal{M}}_{s\,s'}(a^-) \, \gamma \, V^\pi(s')) \tag{4}$$

where the second equality follows from Equation (2).

Now, let us denote by S_i the set of states of $S \setminus \{Dead\}$ at depth i (i.e., that can be reached from s_0 in exactly i steps[3]). We call *trace-policy* a deterministic (not stochastic) policy for which the same action is selected for states at the same depth. A trace-policy can thus be represented by a trace of the MDP (e.g.: $\pi = a_1^\checkmark a_2^\times a_3^\times a_4^\checkmark a_5^\times$). Let $P_j^{\mathcal{M}+\pi}(s)$ be the probability to be in s, j steps away from the initial state when following trace-policy π. For example, starting from the LMPs of Figure 2 with trace-policy $\pi := a^\checkmark a^\checkmark b^\checkmark$, $P_2^{\mathcal{M}+\pi}(4) = Pr^{Spec}_{0\,1}(a) \, Pr^{Spec}_{1\,4}(a) = \frac{2}{4}$, but $P_3^{\mathcal{M}+\pi}(7) = 0$. The value of the trace-policy $\pi = a_1^- a_2^- \ldots a_n^-$ on s_0 is thus determined as follows from Equation (4):

$$V^\pi(s_0) = \sum_{a^- \in Act} \pi(s_0, a^-) \, (R^{a^-}_{s_0\,S} + \sum_{s' \in S \setminus \{Dead\}} Pr^{\mathcal{M}}_{s_0\,s'}(a^-) \, \gamma \, V^\pi(s'))$$

$$= R^{a_1^-}_{s_0\,S} + \sum_{s' \in S \setminus \{Dead\}} Pr^{\mathcal{M}}_{s_0\,s'}(a_1^-) \, \gamma \, \left(R^{a_2^-}_{s'\,S} + \sum_{s'' \in S} Pr^{\mathcal{M}}_{s'\,s''}(a_2^-) \, \gamma \, V^\pi(s'') \right)$$

$$\vdots$$

$$= \sum_{i=0}^{n-1} \sum_{s \in S_i} P_{i+1}^{\mathcal{M}+\pi}(s) \, \gamma^i \, R^{a_{i+1}^-}_{s\,S} \tag{5}$$

$$= \sum_{i=0}^{n-1} \gamma^i \sum_{s \in S_i} P_{i+1}^{\mathcal{M}+\pi}(s) \, P^S(a_{i+1}^-|s) \, \Delta^{a_{i+1}^-}_{tr.s}$$

$$= \sum_{i=0}^{n-1} \gamma^i \, P^S(a_{i+1}^-|a_1 \ldots a_i) \, \Delta^{a_{i+1}^-}_{a_1 \ldots a_i} \tag{6}$$

Note that there is an abuse of language when we say that a trace-policy is a policy of the MDP, because we assume that after the last action of the sequence, the episode ends even if the *Dead* state is not reached.

3 Theorems and Definition of $\mathrm{div}_{\mathrm{trace}}(\,\cdot\,\|\,\cdot\,)$

We prove in this section that solving the MDP induced by a specification and an implementation yields a trace equivalence divergence between them which is positive and has value 0 if and only if the two processes are trace-equivalent.

Let us first state three easy lemmas which will be useful in this section.

---

[3] Since "Spec" is assumed tree-like, the S_i's are pairwise disjoint.

Lemma 1. *The following are equivalent.*

1. $P^I(a^\times|\tau) = P^C(a^\times|\tau)$.
2. $P^I(a^\checkmark|\tau) = P^C(a^\checkmark|\tau)$.
3. $\Delta_\tau^{a^\cdot} = 0$.

Lemma 2. *Let* $\pi = a_1^\cdot a_2^\cdot \ldots a_n^\cdot$ *be a trace-policy, and* $\tau_\pi = a_1 a_2 \ldots a_n$ *its corresponding trace. Then for any* $a^\cdot \in Act$, *writing* $\pi a^\cdot$ *for* $a_1^\cdot a_2^\cdot \ldots a_n^\cdot a^\cdot$, *we have*

$$\left(V^{\pi a^\cdot}(s_0) = V^\pi(s_0)\right) \quad \text{iff} \quad \left(P^I(a^\cdot|\tau_\pi) = P^C(a^\cdot|\tau_\pi) \quad \text{or} \quad P^S(a^\cdot|\tau_\pi) = 0\right).$$

Proof. By Equation (6), we have $V^{\pi a^\cdot}(s_0) - V^\pi(s_0) = \gamma^n \, \Delta_{\tau_\pi}^{a^\cdot} \, P^S(a^\cdot|\tau_\pi)$; this implies the result because by Lemma 1, $\Delta_{\tau_\pi}^{a^\cdot} = 0 \Leftrightarrow P^I(a^\cdot|\tau_\pi) = P^C(a^\cdot|\tau_\pi)$. □

Lemma 3. $\forall a^\cdot \in Act, s \in S\backslash\{Dead\} \quad P^S(a^\cdot|tr.s) = 0 \Rightarrow P^S(a^\cdot|s) = 0$

Proof. Because "Spec" is tree-like, the probability of reaching s by following $tr.s$ is strictly positive. By contraposition, assume that the probability of observing $a^\cdot$ from s is strictly positive, then so is the probability of observing $a^\cdot$ after $tr.s$. □

From now on, we will use the notation $\overline{a^\cdot}$ to mean the opposite of $a^\cdot$, that is, if $a^\cdot = a^\checkmark$ then $\overline{a^\cdot} = a^\times$ and if $a^\cdot = a^\times$ then $\overline{a^\cdot} = a^\checkmark$.

Theorem 1. *The following are equivalent:*

(i) *The specification and implementation processes are trace-equivalent.*
(ii) $\forall a^\cdot \in Act, s \in S\backslash\{Dead\} \quad R_{s\,S}^{a^\cdot} = 0$
(iii) $\forall$ *trace-policy* $\pi \quad V^\pi(s_0) = 0$

Proof. $(i) \Rightarrow (ii)$. Since $tr.s$ is a trace $\forall s \neq Dead$, and since $P^S(.|.) = P^C(.|.)$,

$$P^S(.|.) = P^I(.|.) \Rightarrow \forall a^\cdot \in Act, s \in S\backslash\{Dead\} \quad P^C(a^\cdot|tr.s) = P^I(a^\cdot|tr.s)$$
$$\Leftrightarrow \forall a^\cdot \in Act, s \in S\backslash\{Dead\} \quad \Delta_{tr.s}^{a^\cdot} = 0 \quad \text{(by Lemma 1)}$$
$$\Rightarrow \forall a^\cdot \in Act, s \in S\backslash\{Dead\} \quad R_{s\,S}^{a^\cdot} = 0 \quad \text{(by Equation (3))}$$

$(ii) \Rightarrow (i)$. Let τ be a trace and $a^\cdot \in Act$. Case 1: there exists an $s \in S\backslash\{Dead\}$ such that $\tau = tr.s$. Then by (ii) and Equation (3), we have $\Delta_{tr.s}^{a^\cdot} P^S(a^\cdot|s) = 0$. This implies either $\Delta_{tr.s}^{a^\cdot} = 0$ or $P^S(a^\cdot|s) = 0$. By Lemma 1, we know that the first case implies the result. The second case requires to see the opposite action. Indeed, $P^S(a^\cdot|s) = 0$ implies that $P^S(\overline{a^\cdot}|s) = 1$. By (ii), $R_{s\,S}^{\overline{a^\cdot}} = 0$. By the same argument, we can deduce that either $\Delta_{tr.s}^{\overline{a^\cdot}} = 0$ or $P^S(\overline{a^\cdot}|s) = 0$, and therefore that $\Delta_{tr.s}^{\overline{a^\cdot}} = 0$. Since $\overline{\overline{a^\cdot}} = a^\cdot$, by Lemma 1(replacing $a^\cdot$ by $\overline{a^\cdot}$), we have $P^I(a^\cdot|tr.s) = P^C(a^\cdot|tr.s)$, as wanted. Case 2: if no such s exists, then τ has probability zero in "Spec" and trivially $P^S(a^\cdot|\tau) = 1 = P^I(a^\cdot|\tau)$ as wanted.

$(ii) \Rightarrow (iii)$ follows from Equation (5).

$(iii) \Rightarrow (ii)$. Fix $a^\cdot \in Act$ and $s \in S\backslash\{Dead\}$, and let $n \geq 0$ such that $s \in S_n$, and let $a_1 \ldots a_n = tr.s$. Now, define $\pi = a_1^\checkmark \ldots a_n^\checkmark$. By (iii) and Equation (6), we have $0 = 0 - 0 = V^{a_1^\cdot \ldots a_n^\cdot a^\cdot}(s_0) - V^\pi(s_0) = \gamma^n \, \Delta_{tr.s}^{a^\cdot} \, P^S(a^\cdot|tr.s)$. By Lemma 3, $\Delta_{tr.s}^{a^\cdot} P^S(a^\cdot|s) = 0$, which, by Equation 3, implies the result. □

Theorem 2. *Two LMPs are not trace-equivalent if and only if $V^\pi(s_0) > 0$ for some trace-policy π.*

Proof. ($\Rightarrow$): by Theorem 1, we have that $V^\pi(s_0) \neq 0$ for some trace-policy $\pi = a_1^- a_2^- \dots a_n^-$. Define $J := \{j \in \{1, \dots n\} \mid P^C(a_j^- | a_1 \dots a_{j-1}) \, \Delta^{a_j^-}_{a_1 \dots a_{j-1}} < 0\}$, and note that $P^C(a_j^- | a_1 \dots a_{j-1}) > 0$ and $\Delta^{a_j^-}_{a_1 \dots a_{j-1}} < 0$ for any $j \in J$. Thus, for any such j, $\Delta^{\overline{a_j^-}}_{a_1 \dots a_{j-1}} > 0$ (see Definition 2). Let π_1 be the policy obtained from π by replacing each action $a_j^- \in J$ by its opposite. Then, by Equation (6), $V^{\pi_1}(s_0) > 0$, as desired. ($\Leftarrow$): follows from Theorem 1. $\qquad\square$

Lemma 4. *For every trace-policy π and every $a^- \in Act$,*

$$V^\pi(s_0) \leq V^{\pi a^-}(s_0) \quad or \quad V^\pi(s_0) \leq V^{\pi \overline{a^-}}(s_0).$$

Proof. As for Theorem 2, the result follows from Equation (6) and the fact that $\Delta^{a^-}_{\tau_\pi} = -\Delta^{\overline{a^-}}_{\tau_\pi}$ where τ_π is the trace corresponding to π. $\qquad\square$

Theorem 3. *Let $\mathcal{M}$ be the MDP induced by "Spec", "Impl", and "Clone". If $\gamma < 1$ or $|\mathcal{M}| < \infty$ then $V^\star(s_0) \geq V^\pi(s_0)$ for any trace-policy π.*

Proof. As explained in the preceding section, a trace policy $a_1^- \dots a_n^-$ is not a policy of $\mathcal{M}$ but of the sub-MDP whose state space is $S \setminus \cup_{i=n+1}^\infty S_i$. If $|\mathcal{M}| < \infty$, the result is a direct consequence of Lemma 4. Otherwise, it is sufficient to show

$$\forall \epsilon > 0 \; \forall \text{ trace-policy } \pi \; \exists \text{ policy } \pi' \text{ such that } |V^{\pi'}(s_0) - V^\pi(s_0)| < \epsilon.$$

Let $\epsilon > 0$ and $\pi = a_1^- \dots a_n^-$ be a trace-policy. Because of Lemma 4, w.l.o.g., we may suppose n to be large enough to satisfy $\sum_{i=n+1}^\infty \gamma^i < \epsilon$. Since on each episode, the reward signal is (-1), (0) or $(+1)$, it is easy to see that any policy π' of $\mathcal{M}$ that coincides with π on $\mathcal{M}_\pi$ will have the desired property. $\qquad\square$

We can now give the definition of the central notion of this paper.

Definition 3. Let "Spec" and "Impl" be two LMPs and $\mathcal{M}$ their induced MDP. We define their *trace-equivalence divergence* as

$$\text{div}_{\text{trace}}(\text{"Spec"} \| \text{"Impl"}) := V^\star(s_0).$$

Clearly, $\text{div}_{\text{trace}}(\text{"Spec"} \| \text{"Impl"}) \geq 0$, and $= 0$ iff "Spec" and "Impl" are trace-equivalent.

4   Implementation and PAC Guarantees

As mentioned in Section 2, the full model of the MDP might not be available. Therefore, it is not appropriate to use a Dynamic Programming [1] algorithm such as value iteration [13] to solve the MDP. Instead, we use a Q-Learning algorithm [15]. Q-Learning is an off-policy Temporal Difference (TD) control algorithm which directly approximates $V^\star(s_0)$. The algorithm has been proven to converge to the optimal value [8, 14, 16]. Moreover, some results about its convergence rates have been proposed [5]. However, in the field of verification, the main goals are (∗) to find the difference between the implementation of a system and its specification and also (∗∗) to have a guarantee on the fact that this difference is very small in the case where we do not find any such difference during the investigation. Hence, from that perspective, a PAC-guarantee for the Q-Learning algorithm is the most appropriate tool.

Definition 4. We say that we have a *PAC (Probably Approximately Correct) guarantee* for a learning algorithm on an MDP $\mathcal{M}$ if, given an a priori precision $\epsilon > 0$ and a maximal probability error δ, there exists a function $f(\mathcal{M}, \epsilon, \delta)$ such that if the number of episodes is greater than $f(\mathcal{M}, \epsilon, \delta)$, then

$$Prob\{|\overline{V^{\hat{\pi}}(s_0)} - V^\star(s_0)| \leq \epsilon\} \geq 1 - \delta \tag{7}$$

where $\hat{\pi}$ is the policy returned by the Q-learning algorithm and $\overline{V^{\hat{\pi}}(s_0)}$ is the estimation of $V^\star(s_0)$ given by this algorithm.

The Q-learning algorithm does have a PAC guarantee [11], but the function $f(\mathcal{M}, \epsilon, \delta)$ is very difficult to compute, which makes this guarantee unusable in practice. The Fiechter RL algorithm [6] comes with a simpler PAC guarantee and hence one can use it in the current setting. The main drawback of the Fiechter algorithm remains its inefficiency compared to Q-Learning.

However we can still reach goal (∗) using any RL learning algorithm. Indeed, in the case where the two processes are not trace-equivalent, we can guarantee a bottom bound for the optimal value using Hoeffding inequality [7] based on the following idea. Let $\hat{\pi}$ be the policy returned by the RL algorithm. Let $\overline{V^{\hat{\pi}}(s_0)}$ be the estimation of $V^{\hat{\pi}}(s_0)$ using a Monte Carlo [13] algorithm with m episodes. Given $\epsilon, \delta \in]0, 1[$, according to the Hoeffding inequality, if $m \geq \frac{1}{\epsilon^2} \ln(\frac{2}{\delta})$, we have Equation (7) with $V^\star(s_0)$ replaced by $\overline{V^{\hat{\pi}}(s_0)}$. Since $V^{\hat{\pi}}(s_0)$ never exceeds the optimal value $V^\star(s_0)$, we have the following PAC guarantee: $Prob\{\overline{V^{\hat{\pi}}(s_0)} - V^\star(s_0) \leq \epsilon\} \geq 1 - \delta$. Note that, in addition, the algorithm returns the policy $\hat{\pi}$ that proves the result. A specific difference between the implementation and its specification is therefore identified, orienting the debugging phase that would follow. This is a major difference with the traditional testing approach consisting of simply running an a priori defined test during the debugging phase.

Finally, observe that if $\overline{V^{\hat{\pi}}(s_0)}$ is too close to zero, or exactly zero, then the Hoeffding inequality gives no guarantee on the trace equivalence or inequivalence. Recall that this difficulty occurs only if we use an algorithm without a tractable PAC guarantee: the problem does not happen with the Fiechter RL algorithm. Nevertheless, even with Q-Learning, we think that our approach is better than traditional testing because, as explained above, it can find new tests by its own.

4.1   Experimental Results

The approach described so far has been implemented using Java. Two action selection algorithms have been experimented: ϵ-greedy and SoftMax. For both methods, we tried several functions to decrease the ϵ (resp. the τ) values. The combination that produced the best results is SoftMax such that the temperature τ is decreasing from 0.8 to 0.01 according to the function : $\tau = \frac{k}{\text{currentEpisod}+l}$ (variables k and l are constants). The learning rate α (also called step size) must decrease in order to assure convergence of the Q-Learning algorithm. We tried several decreasing functions and the best convergence results are with $\frac{1}{x}$ where x is the number of times the state-action has been visited. The discount factor γ is fixed to 0.8 in our algorithm. The two following graphics show how the

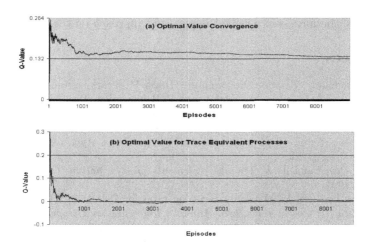

Q-Learning algorithm converges to the optimal value. This value is, in our setting, the trace-equivalence divergence between the specification and the implementation processes. In the above graphics, we tracked the optimal value in one execution of 10000 episodes. In graphic (a), it is easy to see that the estimated value gets close to the real optimal value (0.132 represented by the line) as the number of episodes increases. Graphic (b), however, is obtained by running the algorithm on trace-equivalent processes. It shows how the estimated value for that case converges to zero.

5   Conclusion

The main contribution of this paper is a completely new approach to estimate how far two LMPs are from being trace-equivalent. Indeed, we introduce a notion of trace-equivalence divergence $\text{div}_{\text{trace}}(. \| .)$ that can be estimated via some Monte-Carlo estimation using Reinforcement Learning algorithms. Traditional approaches, on the other hand, are based on costly complete calculations on the models. The advantage of using an RL approach therefore opens a way for analyzing very huge systems and even infinite ones.

In this paper, we showed that $\text{div}_{\text{trace}}(. \| .)$ is a real divergence operator and gave some related PAC-guarantees. However, we did not have enough room to show how $\text{div}_{\text{trace}}(. \| .)$ is increasing as the LMPs are farther from being trace-equivalent. This is intuitively clear. The proof, however, is related to the fact that, as for Kullback-Leibler divergence, the divergence D_π induced by any fixed trace-policy π is of Bregman [3] (here the Bregman function related to D_π is $\sum_{i \in I} x_i \left(1 - \frac{1}{2}x_i\right)$).

For future work, we want to improve our PAC-guarantees, and even obtain a PAC-guarantee that will not depend on the state space S of the MDP $\mathcal{M}$. We also want to modify the construction of $\mathcal{M}$, in order to speed up the calculation. For example, we could generalize our notion of divergence in a setting where the FFF observation does not stop the episode anymore. Finally, since the LMP formalism is mathematically quite similar to the MDP and HMM (Hidden Markov Model) formalisms, the next step will be to apply our approach on these formalisms.

References

1. R. E. Bellman. *Dynamic Programming*. Dover Publications, Incorporated, 2003.
2. R. Blute, J. Desharnais, A. Edalat, and P. Panangaden. Bisimulation for labelled Markov processes. In *Proc. of the Twelfth IEEE Symposium On Logic In Computer Science, Warsaw, Poland*, 1997.
3. Y. Censor. *Parallel Optimization: Theory, Algorithms, Applications*. Oxford University Press, 1997.
4. T. M. Cover and J. A. Thomas. *Elements of Information Theory*, chapter 12. Wiley, 1991.
5. E. Even-Dar and Y. Mansour. Learning rates for Q-learning. In *COLT '01/EuroCOLT '01: Proc. of the 14th Annual Conference on Computational Learning Theory*, pages 589–604, London, UK, 2001. Springer-Verlag.
6. C. N. Fiechter. *Design and Analysis of Efficient Reinforcement Learning Algorithms*. PhD thesis, Univ. of Pittsburgh, 1997.
7. W. Hoeffding. Probability inequalities for sums of bounded random variables. *American Statistical Association Journal*, 58:13–30, 1963.
8. T. Jaakkola, M. I. Jordan, and S. P. Singh. Convergence of stochastic iterative dynamic programming algorithms. In J. D. Cowan, G. Tesauro, and J. Alspector, editors, *Advances in Neural Information Processing Systems*, volume 6, pages 703–710. Morgan Kaufmann Publishers, 1994.
9. C.-C. Jou and S. A. Smolka. Equivalences, congruences, and complete axiomatizations for probabilistic processes. In J.C.M. Baeten and J.W. Klop, editors, *CONCUR 90 First International Conference on Concurrency Theory*, number 458 in Lecture Notes In Computer Science. Springer-Verlag, 1990.
10. Leslie Pack Kaelbling, Michael L. Littman, and Andrew P. Moore. Reinforcement learning: A survey. *Journal of Artificial Intelligence Research*, 4:237–285, 1996.
11. M. Kearns and S. Singh. Finite-sample convergence rates for q-learning and indirect algorithms. In *Proc. of the 1998 conference on Advances in neural information processing systems II*, pages 996–1002, Cambridge, MA, USA, 1999. MIT Press.
12. K. G. Larsen and A. Skou. Bisimulation through probabilistic testing. *Inf. Comput.*, 94(1):1–28, 1991.
13. R. S. Sutton and A. G. Barto. *Introduction to Reinforcement Learning*. MIT Press, Cambridge, MA, USA, 1998.
14. J. N. Tsitsiklis. Asynchronous stochastic approximation and Q-learning. *Machine Learning*, 16(3):185–202, 1994.
15. C. Watkins. *Learning from Delayed Rewards*. PhD thesis, Univ. of Cambridge, 1989.
16. C. Watkins and P. Dayan. Q-learning. *Machine Learning*, 8:279–292, 1992.

Belief Selection in Point-Based Planning Algorithms for POMDPs

Masoumeh T. Izadi[1], Doina Precup[1], and Danielle Azar[2]

[1] McGill University
[2] American Lebanese University Byblos

Abstract. Current point-based planning algorithms for solving partially observable Markov decision processes (POMDPs) have demonstrated that a good approximation of the value function can be derived by interpolation from the values of a specially selected set of points. The performance of these algorithms can be improved by eliminating unnecessary backups or concentrating on more important points in the belief simplex. We study three methods designed to improve point-based value iteration algorithms. The first two methods are based on reachability analysis on the POMDP belief space. This approach relies on prioritizing the beliefs based on how they are reached from the given initial belief state. The third approach is motivated by the observation that beliefs which are the most overestimated or underestimated have greater influence on the precision of value function than other beliefs. We present an empirical evaluation illustrating how the performance of point-based value iteration (Pineau et al., 2003) varies with these approaches.

1 Introduction

Partially Observable Markov Decision Processes (POMDPs) are a standard framework for studying decision making under uncertainty. In POMDPs, the state of the system in which the decisions take place is never fully observed. Only observations that depend probabilistically on the hidden state are available. The best exact algorithms for POMDPs can be very inefficient in both space and time. Therefore a huge research effort has been devoted to developing approximation techniques in this field. Most planning algorithms attempt to estimate values for belief states, i.e. probability distributions over the hidden states of the system.

Recent research has been devoted to algorithms that take advantage of the fact that for most POMDP problems, a large part of the belief space is never experienced by the agent. Such approaches, which are known as point-based methods, consider only a finite set of belief points and compute values for the different actions only for these points. The plan generalization over the entire simplex is done based on the assumption that nearby points will have nearby values. Point-based value iteration methods (Pineau et al., 2003) have been very successful in solving problems which are orders of magnitude larger than classical POMDP problems. This algorithm performs point-based updates on a small set B of reachable points. The error of the approximation is proved to be bounded and it can be decreased by expanding the set of beliefs. However, value improvement depends to a large extent on which belief points are added to this set. Hence,

L. Lamontagne and M. Marchand (Eds.): Canadian AI 2006, LNAI 4013, pp. 383–394, 2006.
© Springer-Verlag Berlin Heidelberg 2006

the choice of belief points is a crucial problem in point-based value iteration, especially when dealing with large problems, and has been discussed by several authors. Spaan and Vlassis (2004) explored the use of a large set of randomly generated reachable points. Pineau et al. (2003) discussed several heuristics for sampling reachable belief states. Smith and Simmons (2004) designed a heuristic search value iteration algorithm which maintains an upper and lower bound on the value function to guide the search for more beneficial beliefs to consider for backups.

In this paper we address the issue of dynamically generating a good ordering of beliefs in an efficient way. We explore the point-based value iteration algorithm in combination with several belief point selection heuristics. First, we make some corrections to the reachability metric proposed by Smith and Simmons (2005). This metric is designed to give more priority of being selected to points that are reachable in the near future. The intuition is that in discounted reward problems, belief points that are only reachable in many time steps do not play an important part in the computation of the value function approximation and we can ignore them. We compare this metric to the 1-norm distance metric previously suggested by Pineau et.al (2003) and study the applicability of this metric to the point-based value iteration algorithm. We also propose and investigate new methods for point selection in belief space for PBVI based on reachability analysis and belief value estimation error. Empirical results comparing these approaches is provided.

2   Background on Partially Observable Markov Decision Processes

Formally, a POMDP is defined by the following components: a finite set of hidden states S; a finite set of actions A; a finite set of observations Z; a transition function $T : S \times A \times S \rightarrow [0, 1]$, such that $T(s, a, s')$ is the probability that the agent will end up in state s' after taking action a in state s; an observation function $O : A \times S \times Z \rightarrow [0, 1]$, such that $O(a, s', z)$ gives the probability that the agent receives observation z after taking action a and getting to state s'; an initial belief state b_0, which is a probability distribution over the set of hidden states S; and a reward function $R : S \times A \times S \rightarrow \mathfrak{R}$, such that $R(s, a, s')$ is the immediate reward received when the agent takes action a in hidden state s and ends up in state s'. Additionally, there can be a discount factor, $\gamma \in (0, 1)$, which is used to weigh less rewards received farther into the future.

The goal of planning in a POMDP environment is to find a way of choosing actions, or policy π, which maximizes the expected sum of future rewards

$$V^\pi(b) = E\left[\sum_{t=0}^{T} \gamma^t r_{t+1} | b, \pi\right] \tag{1}$$

where T is the number of time steps in an episode (typically assumed finite) and r_{t+1} denotes the reward received at time step $t + 1$. The agent in a POMDP does not have knowledge of the hidden states, it only perceives the world through noisy observations as defined by the observation function O. Hence, the agent must keep a complete history of its actions and observations, or a sufficient statistic of this history, in order to act optimally. The sufficient statistic in a POMDP is the belief state b, which is a vector of length $|S|$ specifying a probability distribution over hidden states. The elements of this vector, $b(i)$, specify the conditional probability of the agent being in state s_i, given the initial belief b_0 and the history (sequence of actions and observations) experienced so far.

After taking action a and receiving observation z, the agent updates its belief state using Bayes' Rule:

$$b'_{baz}(s') = P(s'|b,a,z) = \frac{O(a,s',z)\sum_{s\in S}b(s)T(s,a,s')}{P(z|a,b)} \tag{2}$$

where denominator is a normalizing constant and is given by the sum of the numerator over all values of $s' \in S$:

$$P(z|a,b) = \sum_{s\in S}b(s)\sum_{s'\in S}T(s,a,s')O(a,s',z)$$

We can transform a POMDP into a "belief state MDP" (Cassandra et al, 1997). Under this transformation, the belief state b becomes the (continuous) state of the MDP. The actions of the belief MDP are the same as in the original POMDP, but the transition and reward functions are transformed appropriately, yielding the following form of Bellman optimality equation for computing the optimal value function, V^*:

$$V^*(b) = \max_{a\in A}\sum_{z\in Z}P(z|a,b)\left[\sum_{s\in S}b(s)\left(\sum_{s'}b'_{baz}(s')R(s,a,s')\right) + \gamma V^*(b'_{baz})\right] \tag{3}$$

where b'_{baz} is the unique belief state computed based on b, a and z, as in equation (2). As in MDPs, the optimal policy that the agent is trying to learn is greedy with respect to this optimal value function. The problem here is that there is an infinite number of belief states b, so solving this equation exactly is very difficult.

Exact solution methods for POMDPs take advantage of the fact that value functions for belief MDPs are piecewise-linear and convex, and thus can be represented using a finite number of hyperplanes in the space of beliefs YSondik1971. Value iteration updates can be performed directly on these hyperplanes. Unfortunately, exact value iteration is intractable for most POMDP problems with more than a few states, because the size of the set of hyperplanes defining the value function can grow exponentially with each step. For any fixed horizon n, the value function can be represented using a set of α-vectors. The value function is the upper bound over all the α-vectors: $V_n(b) = \max_\alpha \sum_s \alpha(s)b(s)$. Given V_{n-1}, V_n can be obtained using the following backup operator:

$$V_n(b) \leftarrow \max_{a\in A}\left[\sum_{z\in Z}P(z|a,b)\left(\sum_{s\in S}\sum_{s'\in S}b(s)b'_{baz}(s')R(s,a,s') + \gamma\max_{\alpha_{n-1}}\sum_{s'\in S}b'_{baz}(s')\alpha_{n-1}(s')\right)\right]$$

where α_{n-1} are the α-vectors used to represent V_{n-1}.

Exact value iteration algorithms (e.g. Sondik, 1971; Cassandra et al, 1997; Zhang & Zhang, 2001) perform this backup by manipulating directly the α-vectors, using set projection and pruning operations. Although many α-vectors can usually be pruned without affecting the values, this approach is still prohibitive for large tasks. Approximate methods attempt instead to approximate the value function in some way. These solution methods usually rely on maintaining hyperplanes only for a subset of the belief simplex. Different methods use different heuristics in order to define which belief points are of interest (e.g. Hauskrecht, 2000; Pineau et al, 2003; Smith and Simmons, 2004).

3 Point Based Value Iteration

The computational inefficiency of exact value updates leads to the exploration of various approximation methods that can provide good control solutions with less computational effort. Point-based value iteration (PBVI) is based on the idea of maintaining values, and α-vectors for a selected set of belief points. This approach is designed based on the intuition that much of the belief simplex will not be reachable in general.

The algorithm starts with a set of beliefs, and computes α-vectors only for these beliefs. The belief set B can then be expanded, in order to cover more of the belief space. New α-vectors can then be computed for the new belief set, and the algorithm continues.

The update function with a fixed set of belief points B can be expressed as an operator H on the space of value functions, such that $V_{i+1} = H V_i$, where H is defined in (3). In order to show the convergence of such algorithms, we need to show that H is a contraction mapping, and that each estimate V_i is an upper bound on the optimal value function. If both of these conditions hold, the algorithm will converge to a fixed point solution, $\bar{V}^* \geq V^*$.

4 Belief Point Selection

In the PBVI algorithm, the selection of the belief points that will be used to represent the value function is done in an anytime fashion, with the goal of covering as densely as possible the set of reachable beliefs. The belief set B is initialized with just the initial belief state, b_0. Then, the space of reachable beliefs is sampled by a forward simulation, taking one action and receiving one observation. Different heuristics for sampling points have been proposed in (Pineau et al, 2003), but the Stochastic Simulation by Explorative Action heuristic (SSEA) is considered to perform best in general. In this approach, all possible actions at a given belief state in B are considered. One observation is sampled for each action and the new belief states are computed using (2). Then, the algorithm greedily picks the belief state that is farthest away from B, in the sense of the L_1 distance (also called 1-norm). Hence, the number of points in B at most doubles at each iteration, because at most one extra belief point is added for each existing belief. This heuristic is motivated by an analytical upper bound on the approximation error, which depends on the maximum L_1 distance from any reachable belief to B:

$$\varepsilon_B = \max_{b' \in \bar{\Delta}} \min_{b \in B} ||b - b'||_1 \qquad (4)$$

where $\bar{\Delta}$ is the set of all reachable beliefs. This heuristic attempts to greedily reduce ε_B as quickly as possible. The authors also discuss other approaches for picking belief states, such as picking beliefs randomly (similarly to grid-based methods), or sampling reachable beliefs by using either random or greedy actions. In all of these cases (with the exception of random sampling), the space of reachable beliefs is covered gradually, as the algorithm progresses. This is due to the fact that at each point, the candidate beliefs that are considered are reachable in one time step from the current beliefs. Moreover, because PBVI is greedy in picking the next belief state to add, it can potentially overlook, at least for a few iterations, belief states that are important from the point of view of estimating the value function. Spaan and Vlassis (2004) propose a different way of choosing belief points in the PERSEUS algorithm, which is aimed at addressing this problem. They sample a large set of reachable beliefs B during a random walk, but then only update a subset of of B, which is sufficient to improve the value function estimate overall. The core belief selection heuristic proposed by Izadi et al. (2005) tries to start a point-based value iteration with a set of beliefs which span the whole simplex of reachable beliefs. Although this will help the algorithm converge to a good approximation in only a few iterations, finding this set of desired beliefs is computationally demanding, and the approach is problematic for large problems. Heuristic search value iteration (HSVI) (Smith & Simmons, 2004) keeps the value function bounded between an upper bound and a lower bound, an approach aimed at ensuring good performance for the candidate control policies. The algorithm was improved in (Smith & Simmons, 2005), by designing a tighter bound and much smaller size controllers, which makes HSVI better in terms of planning time and achieved values. However, the derivation contained in their paper has some problems, which we correct below.

4.1 Selecting Belief States Based on Reachability

In order to reason about the space of reachable beliefs, one can consider the initial belief vector, b_0, and all possible one-step sequences of actions and observations following it. Equation (2) then defines the set of all beliefs reachable in one step. By considering all one-step action-observation sequences that can occur from these beliefs, we can obtain all beliefs reachable from b_0 in two steps, and so on. This will produce a tree rooted at the initial belief state b_0. The space of reachable beliefs consists of all the nodes of this tree (which is infinite in general, but cut to a finite depth in finite-horizon tasks). The discounted reachability ρ is a mapping from the space of reachable beliefs Δ to the real numbers, defined as: $\rho(b) = \gamma^L$ where L is the length of the shortest sequence of transitions from the initial belief state b_0 to b. This definition implies that

$$\rho(b'_{baz}) \geq \gamma\rho(b) \tag{5}$$

because either b'_{baz} is obtained in one step from b (in which case we have equality), or if not, it may be obtained along a shorter path. Based on the definition of discounted reachability, Smith and Simmons (2005) define a generalized sample spacing measure δ_P ($0 \leq p < 1$). Their argument is that they want to give more weight to beliefs that are reachable in the near future, because their values influence the value function estimates more. To do this, they divide the L_1 norm of the beliefs by $(\rho(b))^p$. However, this division actually has an opposite effect, emphasizing more beliefs that are in the distant future. To correct this problem, we redefine the sample spacing measure from (Smith and Simmons, 2005) as:

$$\delta_p(b) = \max_{b \in \Delta} \min_{b' \in \beta} \|b - b'\|_1 [\rho(b)]^p \tag{6}$$

where p is a parameter in $[0, 1)$. Note that if $p = 1$, we obtain exactly the heuristic described in (Pineau et al, 2003), and given here in equation (4). However, the theoretical development for that case has to be different than the one we will give here. In this case, an equal weight is given to beliefs that are at equal distance to the current set of belief points, regardless how easy or hard they are to reach. We now show that the results in (Smith & Simmons, 2005) hold with this new definition of $\delta_p(b)$.

First we need to show that the update operator on the selected set of points by the above metric is a contraction mapping. To do this, consider the following weighted norm:

$$\|V - \bar{V}\|_\xi = \max_b |V(b) - \bar{V}(b)|\xi(b) \tag{7}$$

In other words, this is like a max norm but the elements are weighted by weights ξ.

Theorem 1. *The exact Bellman update is a contraction mapping under the norm (7) with contraction factor γ^{1-p}.*

Proof. For the proof, it is easier to consider action-value functions. We will use the same notation as (Smith and simmons, 2005) in order to facilitate the comparison with their results. Let $Q_a^V(b)$ be the value of executing action a in belief state b, given that the value function estimate for states is v:

$$Q_a^V(b) = R(b,a) + \gamma \sum_{b'} Pr(b'|b,a)V(b')$$

For any action $a \in A$, and for any value function estimators V and $\bar{V}$ we have:

$$
\begin{aligned}
\|Q_a^V - Q_a^{\bar{V}}\|_{\rho^p} &= \max_b |Q_a^V(b) - Q_a^{\bar{V}}| \times [\rho(b)]^p \\
&= \max_b \gamma \sum_{b'} Pr(b'|b,a)|V(b') - \bar{V}(b')|[\rho(b)]^p \\
&= \max_b \gamma \sum_{b'} Pr(b'|b,a)|V(b') - \bar{V}(b')| \left[\frac{\gamma\rho(b)}{\gamma}\right]^p \\
&\leq \max_b \gamma \sum_{b'} Pr(b'|b,a)|V(b') - \bar{V}(b')| \left[\gamma^{-1}\rho(b')\right]^p \quad \text{(using (5))} \\
&\leq \max_b \gamma^{1-p} \sum_{b'} Pr(b'|b,a) \max_{b''} |V(b'') - \bar{V}(b'')| \left[\rho(b'')\right]^p \\
&= \gamma^{1-p} \sum_{b'} Pr(b'|b,a)\|V - \bar{V}\|_{\rho^p} \\
&= \gamma^{1-p} \|V - \bar{V}\|_{\rho^p}
\end{aligned}
$$

As a side note we need to mention that equation (10) in (Smith & Simmons, 2005) will be violated by their definition of $\delta_p(b)$ and the contraction factor as stated there is not correct.

Let HV be a "greedification" operator on the value function, defined as: $HV(b) = \max_a Q_a^V(b), \forall b$. Then, for any belief state b in the reachable belief space Δ we have:

$$|HV(b) - H\bar{V}(b)| \leq \max_a |Q_a^V(b) - Q_a^{\bar{V}}(b)|$$

Multiplying both sides by $[\rho(b)]^p$ we obtain:

$$|HV(b) - H\bar{V}(b)|[\rho(b)]^p \leq \max_a |Q_a^V(b) - Q_a^{\bar{V}}(b)|[\rho(b)]^p$$

Maximizing over b, we obtain:

$$\|HV - H\bar{V}\|_{\rho^p} \leq \max_a \|Q_a^V - Q_a^{\bar{V}}\|_{\rho^p} \leq \gamma^{1-p}\|V - \bar{V}\|_{\rho^p}$$

which completes the proof. $\diamond$.

The next theorem bounds the error of a policy based on an approximate value function $\hat{V}$.

Theorem 2. *The expected error introduced by a policy $\hat{\pi}$ induced by an approximate value function $\hat{V}$, starting at the initial belief b_0 is bounded by:*

$$\frac{2\gamma^{1-p}}{1-\gamma^{1-p}}\|V^* - \hat{V}\|_{\rho^p}$$

Proof. Let $b \in \Delta$ be an arbitrary belief state and π^* be the optimal policy. Let $V^{\hat{\pi}}$ be the value function of policy $\hat{\pi}$. Note that $Q_{\hat{\pi}(b)}^{V^{\hat{\pi}}}(b) = V^{\hat{\pi}}(b)$. Note that by the definition of the H operator, $Q_{\hat{\pi}(b)}^{\hat{V}}(b) = H\hat{V}(b)$. Note also that or the optimal value function, by its definition, $V^* = HV^*$. We have:

$$|V^{\pi^*}(b) - V^{\hat{\pi}}(b)| = |V^*(b) - Q_{\hat{\pi}(b)}^{V^{\hat{\pi}}}(b)|$$
$$= |V^*(b) - Q_{\hat{\pi}(b)}^{V^{\hat{\pi}}}(b) + Q_{\hat{\pi}(b)}^{\hat{V}}(b) - Q_{\hat{\pi}(b)}^{\hat{V}}(b)|$$
$$\leq |V^*(b) - H\hat{V}| + |Q_{\hat{\pi}(b)}^{\hat{V}}(b) - Q_{\hat{\pi}(b)}^{V^{\hat{\pi}}}(b)| \text{ (by grouping terms)}$$
$$\leq |HV^*(b) - H\hat{V}(b)| + \gamma\sum_{b'} Pr(b'|b,\hat{\pi}(b))|\hat{V}(b') - V^{\hat{\pi}}(b')|$$

Multiplying both sides by $[\rho(b)]^p$ we get:

$$|V^*(b) - V^{\hat{\pi}}(b)|[\rho(b)]^p \leq |HV^*(b) - H\hat{V}(b)|[\rho(b)]^p$$
$$+ \gamma\sum_{b'} Pr(b'|b,\hat{\pi}(b))|\hat{V}(b') - V^{\hat{\pi}}(b')| \left[\frac{\rho(b)\gamma}{\gamma}\right]^p$$
$$\leq |HV^*(b) - H\hat{V}(b)|[\rho(b)]^p$$
$$+ \gamma^{1-p}\sum_{b'} Pr(b'|b,\hat{\pi}(b))|\hat{V}(b') - V^{\hat{\pi}}(b')|[\rho(b')]^p$$
$$\leq |HV^*(b) - H\hat{V}(b)|[\rho(b)]^p + \gamma^{1-p}\|\hat{V} - V^{\hat{\pi}}\|_{\rho^p}$$

By taking a max wrt b we obtain:

$$\|V^{\pi^*} - V^{\hat{\pi}}\|_{\rho^p} \leq \|HV^* - H\hat{V}\|_{\rho^p} + \gamma^{1-p}\|\hat{V} - V^{\hat{\pi}}\|_{\rho^p}$$
$$\leq \gamma^{1-p}\left(\|V^* - \hat{V}\|_{\rho^p} + \|\hat{V} - V^{\hat{\pi}}\|_{\rho^p}\right)$$
$$\leq \gamma^{1-p}\left(\|V^* - \hat{V}\|_{\rho^p} + \|\hat{V} - V^*\|_{\rho^p} + \|V^* - V^{\hat{\pi}}\|_{\rho^p}\right)$$
$$\leq \gamma^{1-p}\left(2\|V^* - \hat{V}\|_{\rho^p} + \|V^* - V^{\hat{\pi}}\|_{\rho^p}\right)$$

Solving this we obtain:

$$\|V^* - V^{\hat{\pi}}\|_{\rho^p} \le \frac{2\gamma^{1-p}}{1-\gamma^{1-p}}\|V^* - \hat{V}\|_{\rho^p}$$

Hence, the regret at b_0 will be bounded as follows:

$$V^*(b_0) - V^{\hat{\pi}}(b_0) \le \frac{2\gamma^{1-p}}{1-\gamma^{1-p}}\|V^* - \hat{V}\|_{\rho^p} \qquad \diamond$$

Theorem 3. *Let H_B be the update operator applied using only beliefs from set B. Then the error induced by a single application of H_B instead of the true operator H is bounded in ρ^p norm as:*

$$\|HV - H_BV\|_{\rho^p} \le \frac{(R_{max} - R_{min})\delta_p(B)}{1-\gamma^{1-p}}$$

Proof. We follow a similar argument to the one in (Pineau et al, 2003). Let b' be the reachable belief that is currently not included in the set B with the worst error in ρ^p norm. Let $b \in B$ be the belief on the current simples that is closest to b', in the sense of the ρ^p norm. The true optimal α-vector at b' would be α', but instead we use the estimate α that comes from b. Then, we have:

$$\begin{aligned}
\|HV - H_BV\|_{\rho^p} &= (\alpha'b' - \alpha b')\rho(b') = (\alpha'b' - \alpha'b + \alpha'b - \alpha b')\rho(b') \\
&\le [\alpha'(b' - b) + \alpha(b - b')][\rho(b)]^p \text{ (because α is the optimal belief at b)} \\
&= (\alpha' - \alpha)(b' - b)[\rho(b')]^p \\
&\le \|\alpha' - \alpha\|_\infty \max_{b'} \min_b \|b' - b\|_\infty [\rho(b')]^p = \|\alpha' - \alpha\|_\infty \delta_p(B) \\
&\le \frac{R_{max} - R_{min}}{1-\gamma^{1-p}}\delta_p(B)
\end{aligned}$$

where R_{max} and $Rmin$ are the maximum and minimum rewards that can be achieved, and we used the result from Theorem 1 for the contraction factor in the denominator. $\diamond$

Theorem 4. *The error $\|V_t - V_t^B\|$ at any update step t is at most:*

$$\frac{(R_{max} - R_{min})\delta_p(\beta)}{(1-\gamma^{1-p})^2}$$

Proof. The proof is identical to the one in (Pineau et al., 2003) but with the results from Theorem 1 and Theorem 3 plugged in. $\diamond$

Algorithm 1 presents an approach for expanding the belief set using the reachability heuristic. Note that instead of looking at all reachable beliefs, we just sample, for each belief in the current set, one possible successor. Of course, this algorithm could be changed to take more samples, or to look farther into the future. However, farther lookahead is less likely to matter, because of the weighting used in the heuristic. The drawback of this approach is that after a few cycles the strategy will sample points from

Algorithm 1. Average-norm Belief Expansion (Initial belief set B)

for all $b \in B$ **do**
   for all $a \in A$ **do**
      Sample the current state s from b
      Sample the next state s' from $T(s,a,\cdot)$
      Sample the next observation z from $O(a,s',\cdot)$
      Compute the next belief b'_{baz} reachable from b
   end for
   $b^* = \arg\max_{b'_{baz}} \delta(b'_{baz})$
   $B = B \cup \{b^*\}$
end for
return B

a rather restricted set of points and that could lead to smaller and smaller improvements. It must be noted that for instance for domains with deterministic observations and transitions this approach gives very similar results to the stochastic simulation with explorative actions (SSEA) heuristic, because of the narrow distribution of reachable beliefs. Considering that PBVI converges to a good approximation in just a few expansions, and that the factor γ is usually between 0.75 to 0.99, the effect of $\delta_P(B)$ is not much different, in Algorithm 1, compared to the effect of $\varepsilon(B)$ in SSEA-PBVI.

4.2 Breath First Selection

A more extreme alternative to the reachability heuristics is to include *all* the beliefs that are reachable in the near future in the set of belief points. Theoretically, this should provide the best approximation in terms of the weighted norm that we are considering. But in many problems this is not feasible, because the size of the fringe of the belief tree grows exponentially. But, in order to get an estimate of how well we could do in this case, we consider adding one belief point for every possible action from every belief in the current set. The observations are still sampled. The main idea is that we typically expect the number of actions to be small, but the number of possible observations to be quite large. Obviously, this could be extended to sample k observations for each action. the algorithm using this idea is presented in Algorithm 2. In this case the size of B for the next set of point-based backups will be increased at most by a factor of $|A|$. Because this approach adds significantly more beliefs at each step, we would expect it to obtain a good approximation in a smaller number of expansions. But we want to ensure that the number of beliefs is also small enough to enable efficient value function backups.

4.3 Value-Based Selection

One interesting feature of point-based methods is that they can use the current estimate of the value function itself to decide which belief points to select next. So far, though, only one point-based algorithm, Stochastic Simulation with Greedy Action, PBVI-SSGA introduced in (Pineau et al, 2005), exploits this feature. Value-based methods attempt to include critical points in the set of selected beliefs, based on the current value approximation. We build upon the fact that the reachable states with highest and

Algorithm 2. Breadth First Belief Expansion (Initial belief set B)

> **for all** $b \in B$ **do**
>> **for all** $a \in A$ **do**
>>> Sample current state s from b
>>> Sample next state s' from $T(s, a, \cdot)$
>>> Sample next observation z from $O(a, s', \cdot)$
>>> Compute the next belief b'_{baz} reachable from b
>>> **if** $b'_{baz} \notin B$ **then** $B = B \bigcup \{b'_{baz}\}$
>> **end for**
> **end for**
> **return** B

lowest expected rewards (as predicted by the current value function approximation) are the more desirable points for improving the precision of the value function. This method is presented in Algorithm 3. As seen here, the set of beliefs B at most triples in size with each expansion.

Algorithm 3. Value-based belief expansion (Initial belief space B)

> **for all** $b \in B$ **do**
>> **for all** $a \in A$ **do**
>>> Sample s from b
>>> Sample s' from $T(s, a, \cdot)$
>>> Sample z from $O(a, s', \cdot)$
>>> Compute the next belief b'_{baz} reachable from b
>> **end for**
>> $max_b = \arg\max_{b'_{baz}} b'_{baz}\alpha$ and $min_b = \arg\min_{b'_{baz}} b'_{baz}\alpha$ where α is the best belief vector at the respective beliefs
>> $B = B \bigcup \{max_b, min_b\}$
> **end for**
> **return** B

5   Empirical Evaluation

In order to compare the performance of the belief selection methods discussed in the previous sections, we selected a few standard domains previously used in the literature. Table 1 lists these problems with information about the problem size.

In each domain, we ran 250 trajectories starting from a fixed given initial belief following the approximately optimal policy generated by each method. We measure the the discounted sum of the rewards obtained on these trajectories. Table 2 shows this measure averaged over 10 independent runs, for the hallway, hallway2 and RockSample problems, and five runs for the tag domain (due to time restrictions). We present average performance and standard deviation over these runs. The first column in this table shows the standard PBVI algorithm in which Stochastic Simulation with Explorative Action has been used for belief set expansion. For the second algorithm, the parameter p is

Table 1. Domains used in the experiments

Domain	$|S|$	$|\mathcal{A}|$	$|O|$	$\mathcal{R}$
hallway	60	5	21	[0,1]
hallway2	90	5	17	[0,1]
tag	870	5	30	[-10,10]
RockSample[4,4]	257	9	2	[-100,10]

Table 2. Comparison of solution quality between different belief point selection strategies

Domain	PBVI (1-norm)	Average-norm	Breadth-First	Value-based
hallway	0.51 ± 0.03	0.52 ± 0.03	0.52 ± 0.03	0.51 ± 0.03
hallway2	0.35 ± 0.03	0.37 ± 0.04	0.38 ± 0.03	0.30 ± 0.04
tag	-9.12 ± 0.59	-8.16 ± 0.8	-9.27 ± .68	-8.18 ± 1.27
RockSample[4,4]	17.78 ± 1.08	19.36 ± 2.5	15.05 ± 3.13	8.57 ± 0.21

chosen such that the resulting value function fits best the true value function according to the average-norm heuristic. The second column reports these results with $p = 0.99$; however, we experimented with many different settings of p and all results are very similar. The third and fourth columns contain results for the breadth-first and value-based heuristics.

We used 5 expansions of the set of beliefs B to reach an optimal solution. for all of the algorithms except for breadth-first. For the latter, we performed 3 expansions for the hallways and RockSample problems and 2 expansions for the tag domain. This is because the set B grows much faster for this algorithm. The complexity of the optimal value function can be measured by the number of α-vectors used to represent it. PBVI keeps at most one α-vector for each belief state in the set B. In the domains hallway, hallway2, and tag, there are 5 choices of actions and a high level of stochasticity. In the RockSample domain, actions are deterministic, and there is significantly less noise in the observations.

In the experiments, the set B almost always contains 32 points for the 1-norm and average-norm heuristics. The average size of B is 66 for the value-based method, but in the RockSample domain, only 15 belief points are selected on average by this heuristic. This is mainly due to the fact that the deterministic transitions make it difficult to explore a large enough part of the belief simplex using this method. The small size of the belief set results in poor performance on this domain, compared to the other approaches. We conjecture that a different way of facilitating exploration, perhaps by starting from different initial beliefs, would help. The breadth-first heuristic is much more aggressive in expanding the belief set, averaging 150 belief points for the hallway problems and 294 beliefs for the RockSample domain.

Overall, neither the breadth-first nor the value-based heuristic seem to help much. The average-norm heuristic is preferable to the 1-norm, as it uses roughly the same number of belief points but provides a better quality solution. In general the effect of these methods is difficult to narrow down, and further experimentation with different domains is required. We believe the exploration-exploitation trade-off should also be considered in future experimentation, since it impacts significantly the quality of the solutions we obtain.

6 Conclusions and Future Work

The set of points selected for value iteration in point-based methods is very important for the quality of the computed approximate plan. In this paper, we introduced and evaluated several point selection criteria for point-based POMDP approximation methods. First, we studied the reachability metric as an alternative to 1-norm distance between belief states. This approach gives a higher priority beliefs in the immediate future. We also tried considering all beliefs which are only one step away from our current set. The number of backed up belief points is considerably larger in this case, so in principle this can allow a better approximation, although in the examples we studied the control quality does not improve much. We also tested the idea of using the value as a guide to select points. The empirical results do not show a clear winner among all these methods; the exploration-exploitation trade-off seems to play an important role, and should be taken into consideration in future studies.

The methods discussed in this paper focus on belief selection for the expansion phase of the PBVI. However, different methods can be adopted for choosing only belief points to perform backups in the value iteration phase of this algorithm as well. We expect such methods to have a greater influence on the speed of point-based methods in general, which is also suggested by the results of Spaan and Vlassis. We intend to study this further in the future.

References

A. R. Cassandra, M. L. Littman, and L. P. Kaelbling. A simple, fast, exact methods for partially observable Markov decisi on processes. In *Proceedings of UAI*, pages 54-61, 1997

Masoumeh T. Izadi, Ajit Rajwade, and Doina Precup. Using core beliefs for point-based value iteration. In *Proceedings of IJCAI*, pages 1751-1753, 2005.

M. Hauskrecht. Value-function approximations for Partially Observable Markov Decision Processes. In *Journal of Artificial Intelligence Research*, vol.13, pages 33 -94, 2000.

Joelle Pineau, Geoff Gordon, and Sebastian Thrun. Point-based value iteration: An anytime algorithms for POMDPs. In *Proceedings of IJCAI*, pages 1025–1032, 2003.

Trey Smith, an d Ried Simmons Heuristic search value iteration for POMDPs. In *Proceedings of UAI* pages 520-527, 2004.

Trey Smith, an d Ried Simmons Point-based POMDP Algorithm: Improved Analysis and Implementation. In *Proceedings of ICML*,2005.

E.J. Sondik The optimal control of Partially Observable Markov Process. *Ph.D. thesis, Stanford University*, 1971.

M.T.J. Spaan, and N. Vlassis Perseus: Randomized point-base value iteration for POMDPs. In *Journal of Artificial Intelligencce Research*, pages 195-220, 2005.

N.L. Zhang, and W. Zhang Speeding up the convergence of value iteration in partially observable Markov decision processes. In *Journal of Artificial Intelligience Research*, vol.14, pages 2 9-51, 2001.

Learning and Evaluation in the Presence of Class Hierarchies: Application to Text Categorization

Svetlana Kiritchenko[1,4], Stan Matwin[1,2], Richard Nock[3], and A. Fazel Famili[4]

[1] University of Ottawa, Canada
{svkir, stan}@site.uottawa.ca
[2] Institute of Computer Science, Polish Academy of Sciences, Warsaw, Poland
[3] Université Antilles-Guyane, Martinique, France
rnock@martinique.univ-ag.fr
[4] Institute for Information Technology, National Research Council Canada
Fazel.Famili@nrc-cnrc.gc.ca

Abstract. This paper deals with categorization tasks where categories are partially ordered to form a hierarchy. First, it introduces the notion of consistent classification which takes into account the semantics of a class hierarchy. Then, it presents a novel global hierarchical approach that produces consistent classification. This algorithm with AdaBoost as the underlying learning procedure significantly outperforms the corresponding "flat" approach, i.e. the approach that does not take into account the hierarchical information. In addition, the proposed algorithm surpasses the hierarchical local top-down approach on many synthetic and real tasks. For evaluation purposes, we use a novel hierarchical evaluation measure that has some attractive properties: it is simple, requires no parameter tuning, gives credit to partially correct classification and discriminates errors by both distance and depth in a class hierarchy.

1 Introduction

Hierarchical categorization deals with categorization problems where categories (aka classes) are organized in hierarchies. More formally, categories are partially ordered, usually from more generic to more specific. The hierarchical way of organization of entities or notions is very helpful for humans to retain, find and analyze things. Therefore, it is not surprising that people maintain large collections of articles, images or emails in hierarchies of topics or systematize a large body of biological knowledge in hierarchies of concepts (aka ontologies). Such organization allows to focus on a specific level of details ignoring specialization of lower levels and generalization of upper levels.

Hierarchical categorization is an automatic approach of placing new items into a collection with a predefined hierarchical structure. In this work we focus mainly on one application area, hierarchical text categorization. However, the proposed techniques can be applied to automatic hierarchical categorization of entities of any kind. Hierarchical text categorization has many important real-world applications. In fact, most of the large textual collections are organized hierarchically, e.g. web repositories, digital libraries, patent libraries, email folders, etc. Dealing

L. Lamontagne and M. Marchand (Eds.): Canadian AI 2006, LNAI 4013, pp. 395–406, 2006.
© Springer-Verlag Berlin Heidelberg 2006

with hierarchies effectively and efficiently is becoming a necessity in many text categorization applications.

Theoretically, hierarchical categorization can be easily substituted with "flat" categorization if we ignore the class structure and replace a hierarchy with a set of categories. However, by doing this we would disregard relevant information. For most text categorization tasks the category hierarchies have been carefully composed by humans and represent our knowledge on the subject matter. This additional information can boost the performance of a classification system if we find the way to incorporate it in the learning process.

In this work we explore two main aspects of hierarchical text categorization: learning algorithms and performance evaluation. First, we introduce the notion of consistent hierarchical classification that makes classification results even more comprehensible. In consistent classification any category label is assigned together with all its ancestor labels to any instance. Among the previously introduced hierarchical learning algorithms, only a local top-down approach produces consistent classification. We propose a new global hierarchical approach that is aimed to perform consistent classification. This is a general framework of converting a conventional "flat" learning algorithm into a hierarchical one. In our experiments we used AdaBoost as the underlying learning approach. However, any conventional method capable of performing multi-label classification can be used within this framework. Our experiments on real and synthetic data indicate that the proposed approach significantly outperforms the corresponding "flat" approach as well as the local top-down method. In addition, we design a new hierarchical evaluation measure. We argue that conventional "flat" measures as well as the existing hierarchical measures cannot discriminate between different types of errors a hierarchical classification system can make. Therefore, we propose a new hierarchical evaluation measure that is simple and straight-forward to compute, gives credit to partially correct classification and has much discriminating power.

2   Related Work

Until the mid-1990s machine learning researchers mostly ignored the hierarchical category structure present in some text categorization applications by turning a hierarchy into a flat set of categories. In 1997 Koller and Sahami carried out the first proper study of a hierarchical text categorization problem [1]. They presented a divide-and-conquer (aka local) principle, the most intuitive for hierarchical text categorization. After this work a number of approaches to hierarchical text categorization have been proposed [2, 3, 4].

Hierarchical categorization methods can be divided in two types [3]: *global* (or big-bang) and *local* (or top-down level-based). In a *global* approach only one classifier is built to discriminate all categories in a hierarchy simultaneously. It is similar to the "flat" approach except it somehow takes into account the relationships between the categories in a hierarchy. Hierarchical modifications to association rule learning [5], decision tree learning [6], SVM [7] and probabilistic learning [8] are considered global approaches.

A *local* approach builds separate classifiers for each internal node of a hierarchy. A local classifier usually proceeds in a top-down fashion first picking the most relevant categories of the top level and then recursively making the choice among the low-level categories, children of the relevant top-level categories. The local approach has been widely used with different learning algorithms: probabilistic learning [1], neural networks [4], and SVM [2].

Unlike previous work, we focus on hierarchical learning methods that build classifiers consistent with a given class hierarchy. The local approach naturally produces consistent labeling since we classify an instance into a category only if we have already classified it into the parent category in the previous classification step. However, a local classifier works only with limited (local) information at each classification node. Moreover, it is highly sensitive to the decisions made at the top of a hierarchy: once an error is committed near the top, it cannot be recovered regardless of how good the classifiers are at lower levels. A global approach, on the other hand, uses all available information at the same time and, therefore, has a better chance for correct classification. Finally, in many real-life situations, one classifier produced by a global approach is easier to maintain and to interpret by end users than a bunch of classifiers built by a local method. For these reasons, we propose a new global approach specifically designed to produce consistent classification.

3   Hierarchical Categorization Task

In this section we formally define a hierarchical classification task. We start with a definition for partial ordering, a relation present in a hierarchical structure.

Definition 1 (Poset). *A finite partially ordered set (poset) is a structure $\mathcal{H} = \langle C, \leq \rangle$, where C is a finite set and $\leq \subseteq C \times C$ is a reflexive, anti-symmetric, transitive binary relation on C.*

Given a relation $\leq$, we define a relation $<$ as $q < p$ if $q \leq p$ and $q \neq p$. For any two categories $p, q \in C$ such that $q < p$ and $\nexists r \in C : q < r < p$, we call p a parent category of q and q a child category of p. For any category $p \in C$, its ancestor set is $Ancestors(p) = \{q \in C : q \geq p\}$, and its offspring set is $Offspring(p) = \{q \in C : q \leq p\}$ (note that both sets include category p). We call categories that have no children leaves and categories that have both parents and children intermediate (or internal) classes.

Definition 2 (Hierarchical Categorization). *Hierarchical categorization task is the task of assigning a Boolean value to each pair $\langle d_j, c_i \rangle \in D \times C$, where D is a domain of instances and $C = \{c_1, \ldots, c_{|C|}\}$ is a set of predefined categories with a given poset structure $\mathcal{H} = \langle C, \leq \rangle$.*

In a hierarchical categorization task the category hierarchy $\mathcal{H} = \langle C, \leq \rangle$ describes the relations between the categories and comes from the application task at hand. The hierarchy is assumed to represent the domain knowledge and is not modified in any way.

In general, a hierarchical categorization task is *multi-label* which means that an instance can be assigned to any number of categories from 0 to $|C|$.

For any poset $\mathcal{H} = \langle C, \leq \rangle$ that represents a hierarchy we assume the existence of the root (or top) class $Root(\mathcal{H})$ that is the ancestor of all other categories in the hierarchy: $\{Root(\mathcal{H})\} = \bigcap_{p \in C} Ancestors(p)$. The root class itself has no parents.

Generally, category hierarchies are of a broader-narrower type where a subcategory represents a subtype or a part of the parent category. Category hierarchies are usually represented in the form of a directed acyclic graph (DAG). DAGs are more general than trees in that nodes in a DAG can have multiple parents.

4   Hierarchical Consistency

The notion of hierarchical consistency is intended to make the results of hierarchical classification more comprehensible for users. Since hierarchies are mostly designed in the way that lower level categories are specialization of higher level categories, which is represented by transitive relations, such as "is-a" and "part-of", we can assume that an instance belonging to a category also belongs to all ancestor nodes of that category. Therefore, we would like a classifier explicitly assign all the relevant labels, including the ancestor labels, to a given instance. In this way, the assigned labels would clearly indicate the position of an instance in a category hierarchy.

Definition 3 (Hierarchical Consistency). *A label set $C_i \subseteq C$ assigned to an instance $d_i \in D$ is called consistent with a given hierarchy if C_i includes complete ancestor sets for every label $c_k \in C_i$, i.e. if $c_k \in C_i$ and $c_j \in Ancestors(c_k)$, then $c_j \in C_i$.*

We assume that every instance belongs to the root of a class hierarchy; therefore, from now on we will always exclude the root node from any ancestor set since including it does not provide any additional information on the instance.

Definition 4 (Hierarchical Consistency Requirement). *Any label assignments produced by a hierarchical classification system on a given hierarchical categorization task should be consistent with a corresponding class hierarchy.*

5   Hierarchical Global Learning Algorithm

We propose a new hierarchical global approach to learn a classifier that produces consistent labeling on unseen instances. The method is simple and effective and can be applied to any categorization task with a class hierarchy represented as a DAG. The main idea of the algorithm is to transform an initial (possibly single-label) task into a multi-label task by expanding the label set of each training example with the corresponding ancestor labels or, in other words, by expanding intermediate classes with examples from their offspring nodes. As a result, in the modified dataset each intermediate category would contain training examples originally assigned to this category and examples originally assigned to descendant nodes of the category in a hierarchical graph. This data modification forces a learning algorithm to focus on high level categories by providing a large number of training examples for those categories. The correct classification of unseen instances into high level categories is very important in hierarchical categorization since high level categories define the most general topics for documents. For example, if we classify a news article about an art exhibition into category "sports" (if "arts" and "sports" are among the top level categories), it would be completely wrong. On the other hand, a mistake made for lower levels, e.g. classification of a document on minor hockey into category "professional hockey", would not be so drastic.

We expect the presented strategy to be successful in the hierarchical settings because a hierarchical structure is typically designed to reflect the semantic closeness of categories. Therefore, we anticipate that related categories share some attributes. In the text categorization context, that means shared vocabulary. For example, categories "hockey" and "American football" have their own specific vocabulary, such as "goalkeeper" or "NHL" for "hockey" and "Super Bowl" or "touchdown" for "football". At the same time, these two categories likely share some common terms, such as "team" or "game", that also appear in their parent category "sports". Our method allows a learning algorithm to explore such common attributes in order to improve classification, especially for high level categories.

Overall, the algorithm consists of three steps:

1. Transformation of training data making them consistent with a given class hierarchy;
2. Application of a regular learning algorithm on a multi-label dataset;
3. Re-labeling of inconsistently classified test instances.

On the first step, we replace each example (d_i, C_i), $d_i \in D$, $C_i \subseteq C$, with $(d_i, \hat{C}_i)$, where $\hat{C}_i = \{\bigcup_{c_k \in C_i} Ancestors(c_k)\}$. Then, we apply a regular learning algorithm, e.g. AdaBoost, on the modified multi-label dataset. Since we train a classifier on the consistent data, we expect that most test instances would be classified consistently as well. However, it is not guaranteed. Some of the test instances can end up with inconsistent labels. This happens if the confidence score of some class A passes a given threshold while the confidence score of one of its ancestor classes does not. For such instances we need to do the third post-processing step. At this step we re-label the instances in a consistent manner by considering the confidence in the predictions for class A and all its ancestor classes. One possible procedure here is to calculate the average of these confidences. If the average is greater than a threshold, we label the instance with class A and all its ancestor classes; if the average is lower than the threshold, we do not assign class A to the instance. This procedure acts as a kind of weighted voting. Each ancestor class votes with its own confidence score. Large positive scores would indicate some certainty in the assigning the class, while negative values would vote against this class assignment.

5.1   Hierarchical AdaBoost

In this work we use the new hierarchical global approach with a state-of-the-art learning algorithm AdaBoost.MH [9],[1] a boosting method designed for multi-class multi-label problems.

AdaBoost.MH works iteratively at each iteration t learning a new "weak" hypothesis h_t on a current distribution P_t over the training examples. After each step, the distribution P_t is modified to increase the weight of the incorrectly classified training examples and decrease the weight of the correctly classified examples. As a result, on the next round $t + 1$ a "weak" learner h_{t+1} is forced to focus on examples that are hardest to classify. After a specified number of iterations T, the learning process is stopped, and a weighted voting of the "weak" predictions is used as a final hypothesis: $H(d, \ell) = \sum_{t=1}^{T} \alpha_t h_t(d, \ell)$, $d \in D$, $\ell \in C$, where D is a domain of documents and C is a set of categories. In other words, for each test instance and each class the final hypothesis outputs a real value, called a confidence score. For single-label classification, the classification decision is simply the top-ranked class, the class with the highest confidence score. In a multi-label case, however, we have to select a threshold to cut off class labels for a given instance. One such possible threshold is zero: any positive confidence score indicates that the class should be assigned to an instance, any negative score indicates that the class should not be assigned to an instance. However, we can optimize this threshold value with a simple procedure defined as follows. We train AdaBoost.MH on an available training set S, get the confidence predictions on the same set S, and sort the confidence scores in the decreasing order (t_1, t_2, ..., t_n). Then, we try the confidence scores one by one as possible thresholds and find t_k that results in the best F-measure on the training set S. The final threshold to use on test data is calculated as $\frac{t_k + t_{k+1}}{2}$. This threshold smoothing helps us avoid overfitting when the boosting progresses and gains high confidence in prediction.

6   Hierarchical Evaluation Measure

Most researchers evaluate hierarchical classification systems based on standard "flat" measures: accuracy/error and precision/recall. However, these measures are not suitable for hierarchical categorization since they do not differentiate among different kinds of misclassification errors. Intuitively, misclassification to a sibling or a parent node of the correct category is much better than misclassification to a distant node. To overcome this problem, a hierarchical measure based on the notion of distance has been proposed. The distance between a correct and assigned category, $distance(x, y)$, is the length of the (unique) undirected path from node x to node y in a hierarchical tree. This distance measure gives different

---

[1] In our experiments we used software BoosTexter (http://www.cs.princeton.edu/~schapire/BoosTexter/), an implementation of AdaBoost.MH specifically designed for text categorization. BoosTexter uses decision stumps (one-level decision trees) as its "weak" learners.

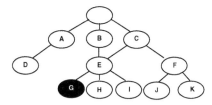

Fig. 1. A sample DAG class hierarchy. The solid ellipse G represents the real category of an instance.

penalties to misclassification into a neighboring or a distant category. However, it has some drawbacks. First, it is not easily extendable to DAG hierarchies (where multiple paths between two categories can exist) and multi-label tasks. Second, it does not change with depth. Misclassification into a sibling category of a top level node and misclassification into a sibling of a node 10-level deep are considered the same type of error (distance of 2). However, an error at the 10th level seems a lot less harmful than an error at the top level.

To express the desired properties of a hierarchical evaluation measure, we formulate the following requirements:

1. The measure gives credit to partially correct classification, e.g. misclassification into node I when the correct category is G (Figure 1) should be penalized less than misclassification into node D since I is in the same subgraph as G and D is not.

2. The measure punishes distant errors more heavily:

a) the measure gives higher evaluation for correctly classifying one level down comparing to staying at the parent node, e.g. classification into node E is better than classification into its parent C since E is closer to the correct category G;

b) the measure gives lower evaluation for incorrectly classifying one level down comparing to staying at the parent node, e.g. classification into node F is worse than classification into its parent C since F is farther away from G.

3. The measure punishes errors at higher levels of a hierarchy more heavily, e.g. misclassification into node I when the correct category is its sibling G is less severe than misclassification into node C when the correct category is its sibling A.

Formally, if we denote $HM(c_1|c_2)$ the hierarchical evaluation of classifying an instance $d \in D$ into class $c_1 \in C$ when the correct class is $c_2 \in C$ in a given tree hierarchy $\mathcal{H} = \langle C, \leq \rangle$, then

1. for any instance $(d, c_0) \in D \times C$, if $Ancestors(c_1) \cap Ancestors(c_0) \neq \oslash$ and $Ancestors(c_2) \cap Ancestors(c_0) = \oslash$, then $HM(c_1|c_0) > HM(c_2|c_0)$;

2. a) for any instance $(d, c_0) \in D \times C$, if $c_1 = Parent(c_2)$ and $distance(c_1, c_0) > distance(c_2, c_0)$, then $HM(c_1|c_0) < HM(c_2|c_0)$;

b) for any instance $(d, c_0) \in D \times C$, if $c_1 = Parent(c_2)$ and $distance(c_1, c_0) < distance(c_2, c_0)$, then $HM(c_1|c_0) > HM(c_2|c_0)$;

3. for any instances $(d_1, c_1) \in D \times C$ and $(d_2, c_2) \in D \times C$, if $distance(c_1, c_1') = distance(c_2, c_2')$, $level(c_1) = level(c_2) + \Delta$, $level(c_1') = level(c_2') + \Delta$, $\Delta > 0$,

$c_1 \neq c'_1$, $c_2 \neq c'_2$, and $level(x)$ is the length of the unique path from the root to node x, then $HM(c'_1|c_1) > HM(c'_2|c_2)$.

Clearly, conventional "flat" measures do not satisfy any of the three requirements. Distance-based hierarchical measures satisfy the second principle, but not always the first and not the third. Thus, we propose a new hierarchical evaluation measure that satisfies all three principles. The new measure is the pair precision and recall with the following addition: each example belongs not only to its class, but also to all ancestors of the class in a hierarchical graph, except the root (we exclude the root of a class hierarchy, since all examples belong to the root by default). We call the new measures hP (hierarchical precision) and hR (hierarchical recall).

Formally, in the multi-label settings, for any instance (d_i, C_i), $d \in D$, $C_i \subseteq C$ classified into subset $C'_i \subseteq C$ we extend sets C_i and C'_i with the corresponding ancestor labels: $\hat{C}_i = \{\bigcup_{c_k \in C_i} Ancestors(c_k)\}$, $\hat{C}'_i = \{\bigcup_{c_l \in C'_i} Ancestors(c_l)\}$. Then, we calculate (micro-averaged) hP and hR as follows:

$$hP = \frac{\sum_i |\hat{C}_i \cap \hat{C}'_i|}{\sum_i |\hat{C}'_i|} \qquad hR = \frac{\sum_i |\hat{C}_i \cap \hat{C}'_i|}{\sum_i |\hat{C}_i|}$$

For example, suppose an instance is classified into class F while it really belongs to class G (Figure 1). To calculate our hierarchical measure, we extend the set of real classes $C_i = \{G\}$ with all ancestors of class G: $\hat{C}_i = \{B, C, E, G\}$. We also extend the set of predicted classes $C'_i = \{F\}$ with all ancestors of class F: $\hat{C}'_i = \{C, F\}$. So, class C is the only correctly assigned label from the extended set: $|\hat{C}_i \cap \hat{C}'_i| = 1$. There are $|\hat{C}'_i| = 2$ assigned labels and $|\hat{C}_i| = 4$ real classes. Therefore, we get $hP = \frac{|\hat{C}_i \cap \hat{C}'_i|}{|\hat{C}'_i|} = \frac{1}{2}$ and $hR = \frac{|\hat{C}_i \cap \hat{C}'_i|}{|\hat{C}_i|} = \frac{1}{4}$.

Following the common practice in conventional text categorization, we can combine the two values hP and hR into one hF-measure:

$$hF_\beta = \frac{(\beta^2 + 1) \cdot hP \cdot hR}{(\beta^2 \cdot hP + hR)}, \beta \in [0, +\infty)$$

In our experiments we used $\beta = 1$, giving precision and recall equal weights.

Theorem 1. *The new hierarchical measure hF satisfies all three requirements for hierarchical evaluation measures listed above[2].*

The new measure is easy to compute: it is based solely on a given hierarchy, so no parameter tuning is required. It is formulated for a general case of multi-label classification with a DAG class hierarchy. Furthermore, we have experimentally proved (results not shown here) that the new measure is superior to standard "flat" measures in terms of statistical consistency and discriminancy - the two criteria Huang and Ling propose to compare classification performance measures [10]. The consistency property means that if we have two classifiers A and B

---

[2] The proof of the theorem is straight-forward and is available at http://www. site.uottawa.ca/~svkir/papers/thesis.zip.

and A is more accurate in terms of non-hierarchical measures, it is most likely that our hierarchical measure agrees, and A is better than B in terms of hF as well. The discriminancy property implies that if non-hierarchical measures cannot tell apart the performances of classifiers A and B, our measure is more discriminating and prefers one over the other in most situations.

7   Experiments

We report the results of the experiments on real and synthetic data to compare the proposed hierarchical global approach with "flat" and hierarchical local methods.

7.1   Datasets

Synthetic. We make use of synthetic data to be able to control the size of a class hierarchy and the presence or absence of attribute inheritance between an ancestor class and its descendant classes. The data are designed as follows. For a specified number of levels and for a specified out-degree, i.e. the number of children classes for each intermediate category, we build a balanced tree hierarchy. For each class, including the internal ones, we allocate 3 binary attributes and generate 10 training and 5 test instances per class. Each instance is assigned to exactly one class. The instances are generated randomly according to the following distribution: attributes associated with the class of an instance are set to 1 with 70% probability, all other attributes are set to 1 with 20% probability. We test synthetic data for two extreme situations. The first one is when each class inherits the distribution of attributes from its parent class on top of its own distribution. In other words, the attributes for a class and all its ancestor classes have the high probability (70%) of 1; all other attributes have the small probability (20%). The second situation is when there is no inheritance of attribute distribution: only the attributes associated with the class of an instance have 70% probability of 1, all others have 20% probability. We ran experiments for hierarchies with the number of levels and out-degree each ranging from 2 to 5. Experiments are repeated 100 times for every configuration.

20 newsgroups. This is a widely used dataset of Usenet postings. Following [8], we use a two-level tree hierarchy grouping 15 categories in 5 parent nodes.

RCV1_V2. This is a cleaned version of a new benchmark collection of Reuters news articles. The dataset consists of over 800,000 documents labeled with 103 topics comprising a 4-level hierarchy. Due to the large size of the corpus, we are able to split the data in training and testing subsets in a time-sensitive manner. Articles from 10 full months (September, 1996 - June, 1997) form 10 splits: the first half of a month is used for training, while the second half is used for testing.

Medline. We have also composed 3 large-scale biological datasets for a task of predicting gene functions from biomedical literature. We chose Gene Ontology (GO) to be our category hierarchy. GO provides a hierarchically organized set of all possible functions that a gene can have in a living organism. It consists of 3 parts: biological process (P), molecular function (F), and cellular component (C). Each part can be seen as an independent DAG hierarchy. We use the Saccharomyces Genome Database (SGD) to obtain manually assigned pairs of a biomedical article describing a yeast gene and the gene's function in GO terms. Overall, we collect 3 datasets, one for each GO hierarchy.

For real datasets, the conventional "bag-of-words" representation is used. All documents are pre-processed: stop words are removed, remaining words are stemmed and converted into binary attributes (a stem is present or not). A simple feature selection technique based on document frequencies is applied. Experiments are run on 10 random training/test splits (in proportion 2:1) for each dataset, except for RCV1_V2 where splits are time-sensitive.

7.2   Comparison with "Flat" AdaBoost

The first set of experiments compares the performance of hierarchical global AdaBoost with the corresponding "flat" approach, i.e. standard AdaBoost that does not take into account any hierarchical information. Both algorithms are run for equal numbers of iterations. The results are presented in Table 1 (columns 5, 7). Evidently, hierarchical AdaBoost significantly outperforms its "flat" version. The differences are more pronounced for larger hierarchies with attribute distribution inheritance as expected. The main difference between the two algorithms is the initial re-labeling that makes training data consistent with a class hierarchy. In really hard tasks, e.g. on the biological data, where the number of classes is very large and the number of training instances per class is very small, the "flat" algorithm suffers a lot producing very poor results. At the same time, this additional step allows the hierarchical method to assemble more training data and learn more accurate classifiers for high level categories, which are favored by the hierarchical evaluation measure.

7.3   Comparison with Hierarchical Local Approach

In the second set of experiments we compare the performances of the hierarchical global and hierarchical local approaches using AdaBoost as the underlying learning algorithm. In the hierarchical local approach we run AdaBoost at each internal node of a hierarchy for the same number of iterations as the global hierarchical AdaBoost. Table 1 (columns 6, 7) shows the results. For most synthetic and real tasks the global approach outperforms the local method. Both algorithms take advantage of extended training data. However, the global approach explores all the categories simultaneously (in a global fashion) assigning only labels with high confidence scores. The local method, on the other hand, uses only local information and, therefore, is forced to make classification decisions at each internal node of a hierarchy, in general, pushing most instances deep down. As a result, the global algorithm is always superior to the local one in terms of precision while slightly yielding in recall. This reflects the conservative nature of the global approach comparing to the local one. Therefore, it should be the method of choice for tasks where precision is the key measure of success. We

Table 1. Comparison of "flat", hierarchical local, and hierarchical global AdaBoost. Numbers in bold are significantly better with 99% confidence.

dataset	# of categories	depth	out-degree	boost. iter.	hF_1 measure		
					"flat"	local	global
newsgroups	20	2	3	500	75.51	**80.01**	79.26
RCV1_V2	103	4	4.68	500	73.10	74.03	**75.86**
medline_P	1025	12	5.41	500	15.32	**59.27**	59.25
medline_F	1078	10	10.29	500	8.78	**43.36**	38.17
medline_C	331	8	6.45	500	42.81	72.07	**73.35**
synthetic	6	2	2	200	68.30	73.42	**76.22**
(with attr.	14	3	2	500	58.35	69.40	**74.21**
inheritance)	30	4	2	1000	44.90	68.18	**73.22**
	62	5	2	2000	20.88	68.44	**72.70**
	12	2	3	400	53.47	61.99	**63.45**
	39	3	3	1000	29.51	58.81	**60.69**
	120	4	3	3500	2.67	57.40	**58.22**
	20	2	4	600	41.35	54.26	**55.25**
	84	3	4	2500	6.98	**50.66**	50.70
	30	2	5	900	29.99	47.26	**47.87**
synthetic	6	2	2	200	61.69	59.83	**65.95**
(no attr.	14	3	2	500	42.47	44.00	**51.53**
inheritance)	30	4	2	1000	24.49	33.44	**40.18**
	62	5	2	2000	8.45	26.03	**32.61**
	12	2	3	400	41.53	43.87	**48.02**
	39	3	3	1000	14.50	26.33	**29.97**
	120	4	3	3500	0.79	17.97	**21.91**
	20	2	4	600	26.72	32.51	**35.01**
	84	3	4	2500	2.46	17.96	**19.70**
	30	2	5	900	17.14	26.04	**27.12**

can also notice that an increase in out-degree (k) adds a significant number of categories ($\sim k^{depth-1}$) to the global method while only slightly (linearly) complicating the task for the local method. This results in the smaller advantage of global AdaBoost on synthetic hierarchies with large out-degrees and its loss on the highly "bushy" "medline_F" data.

8   Conclusion

In this paper we study a hierarchical categorization problem. We show that hierarchical classification should be consistent with a class hierarchy to fully reproduce the semantics of hierarchical relations. We discuss performance measures for hierarchical classification and introduce natural, desired properties that these measures ought to satisfy. We define a novel hierarchical evaluation measure and show that, unlike the conventional "flat" as well as the existing hierarchical measures, the new measure satisfies the desired properties. It is also simple, requires no parameter tuning, and has much discriminating power. We present a novel hierarchical global algorithm that produces consistent classification. This algorithm with AdaBoost as the underlying learning procedure significantly outperforms the corresponding "flat" approach, i.e. the approach that does not take into account the hierarchical information. The proposed algorithm also outperforms the hierarchical local top-down approach on many synthetic and real tasks.

In future work, we plan to perform similar experiments with other multi-label classification algorithms as underlying learning components. Unlike AdaBoost.MH, some algorithms may be found behaving consistently in the hierarchical framework even without the post-processing step.

Acknowledgments

This research has been supported by Natural Sciences and Engineering Research Council of Canada (NSERC), National Research Council of Canada (NRC), and the Ontario Centres of Excellence (OCE).

References

1. Koller, D., Sahami, M.: Hierarchically Classifying Documents Using Very Few Words. In: Proceedings of the International Conference on Machine Learning (ICML). (1997) 170–178
2. Dumais, S., Chen, H.: Hierarchical Classification of Web Content. In: Proceedings of the ACM International Conference on Research and Development in Information Retrieval (SIGIR). (2000) 256–263
3. Sun, A., Lim, E.P.: Hierarchical Text Classification and Evaluation. In: Proceedings of the IEEE International Conference on Data Mining (ICDM). (2001) 521–528
4. Ruiz, M., Srinivasan, P.: Hierarchical Text Categorization Using Neural Networks. Information Retrieval **5** (2002) 87–118
5. Wang, K., Zhou, S., He, Y.: Hierarchical Classification of Real Life Documents. In: Proceedings of the SIAM International Conference on Data Mining. (2001)
6. Blockeel, H., Bruynooghe, M., Dzeroski, S., Ramon, J., Struyf, J.: Hierarchical Multi-Classification. In: Proceedings of the SIGKDD Workshop on Multi-Relational Data Mining (MRDM). (2002) 21–35
7. Tsochantaridis, I., Hofmann, T., Joachims, T., Altun, Y.: Support Vector Machine Learning for Interdependent and Structured Output Spaces. In: Proceedings of the International Conference on Machine Learning (ICML). (2004)
8. McCallum, A., Rosenfeld, R., Mitchell, T., Ng, A.: Improving Text Classification by Shrinkage in a Hierarchy of Classes. In: Proceedings of the International Conference on Machine Learning (ICML). (1998) 359–367
9. Schapire, R., Singer, Y.: Improved Boosting Algorithms Using Confidence-rated Predictions. Machine Learning **37** (1999) 297–336
10. Huang, J., Ling, C.: Using AUC and Accuracy in Evaluating Learning Algorithms. IEEE Trans. on Data and Knowledge Engineering **17(3)** (2005) 299–310

Adaptive Clustering Algorithms

Alina Câmpan and Gabriela Şerban

Department of Computer Science
"Babeş-Bolyai" University
1, M. Kogalniceanu Street,
Cluj-Napoca, Romania
Tel.: +40.264.405327; Fax: +40.264.591.960
{alina, gabis}@cs.ubbcluj.ro

Abstract. This paper proposes an adaptive clustering approach. We focus on re-clustering an object set, previously clustered, when the feature set characterizing the objects increases. We have developed adaptive extensions for two traditional clustering algorithms (*k-means* and *Hierarchical Agglomerative Clustering*). These extensions can be used for adjusting a clustering, that was established by applying the corresponding non-adaptive clustering algorithm before the feature set changed. We aim to reach the result more efficiently than applying the corresponding non-adaptive algorithm starting from the current clustering or from scratch. Experiments testing the method's efficiency are also reported.

1 Introduction

A large collection of clustering algorithms is available in the literature. The papers [9], [10] and [11] contain comprehensive overviews of the existing clustering techniques. Generally, these methods apply on a set of objects measured against a known set of features (attributes). But there are applications where the attribute set characterizing the objects evolves. For obtaining in these conditions a partition of the object set, the clustering algorithm can be, obviously, applied over and over again, beginning from scratch or from the current partition, each time when the attribute set changes. But this can be inefficient. We agree to call a clustering method *adaptive*, if it produces a clustering by adjusting an existing partition to attribute set extension.

We propose two adaptive clustering algorithms, named *Core Based Adaptive k-means (CBAk)* and *Hierarchical Core Based Adaptive Clustering (HCBAC)*. They follow a common approach, based on detecting stable structures (cores) inside the existing clusters and resuming the clustering process from these structures, when the attribute set increases. We aim to reach the result more efficiently than applying the corresponding non-adaptive algorithm starting from the current partition or from scratch.

L. Lamontagne and M. Marchand (Eds.): Canadian AI 2006, LNAI 4013, pp. 407–418, 2006.
© Springer-Verlag Berlin Heidelberg 2006

2   Adaptive Core Based Clustering

2.1   Related Work

There are few approaches reported in the literature that refer to the problem of adapting the result of a clustering when the object feature set is extended. Early works treat the sequential use of features in the clustering process, one by one. An example of such a monothetic approach is mentioned in [11]. A more recent paper [16] analyzes the problem of adapting a clustering produced by the *DBSCAN* algorithm, using some additional structures and distance approximations in an Euclidian space. However, adapting a clustering resulted from a partitioning by relocation algorithm, or from a hierarchical agglomerative one has not been reported, to our knowledge.

2.2   Theoretical Model

Let $X = \{O_1, O_2, \ldots, O_n\}$ be the set of objects to be clustered. Each object is measured with respect to a set of m initial attributes and is therefore described by an m-dimensional vector $O_i = (O_{i1}, \ldots, O_{im}), O_{ik} \in \Re^+, 1 \leq i \leq n, 1 \leq k \leq m$. Usually, the attributes associated to objects are standardized, in order to ensure an equal weight to all of them [9].

In the following, we agree to denote by $\mathcal{A}$ one of the two non-adaptive traditional clustering algorithms, whom adaptive extensions we are studying in this paper: *k-means* and *Hierarchical Agglomerative Clustering Algorithm (HACA)*.

Let $\mathcal{K} = \{K_1, K_2, \ldots, K_p\}$ be the set of clusters discovered in data by applying $\mathcal{A}$. We mention that, in the case of *HACA*, the clustering process stops when p clusters are reached, and $\mathcal{K}$ represents the last attained partition. Each cluster is a set of objects, $K_j = \{O_1^j, O_2^j, \ldots, O_{n_j}^j\}, 1 \leq j \leq p$. The centroid (cluster mean) of the cluster K_j is denoted by f_j, where $f_j = \left(\dfrac{\sum\limits_{k=1}^{n_j} O_{k1}^j}{n_j}, \ldots, \dfrac{\sum\limits_{k=1}^{n_j} O_{km}^j}{n_j} \right)$.

Even if it is not a typical concept of hierarchical clustering, we will make use in our approach of the centroid notion for *HACA*, also.

The measure used for discriminating objects can be any *metric* or *semi-metric* function d. We used the *Euclidian distance*:

$$d(O_i, O_j) = d_E(O_i, O_j) = \sqrt{\sum_{l=1}^{m} (O_{il} - O_{jl})^2}.$$

The measured set of attributes is afterwards extended with s ($s \geq 1$) new attributes, numbered as $(m+1), (m+2), \ldots, (m+s)$. After the extension, the objects' vectors become $O_i' = (O_{i1}, \ldots, O_{im}, O_{i,m+1}, \ldots, O_{i,m+s}), 1 \leq i \leq n$.

We want to analyze the problem of recalculating the objects' grouping into clusters, after the attribute set extension. The new clusters can be, obviously, obtained by applying $\mathcal{A}$ on the set of extended objects starting:

- from scratch if $\mathcal{A}$ is *HACA*;
- from scratch or from the current partition $\mathcal{K}$ if $\mathcal{A}$ is *k-means*.

We try to avoid this process by replacing it with one less expensive but not less accurate. Therefore, we will try to efficiently adapt the current partition ($\mathcal{K}$), produced by $\mathcal{A}$.

We denote by $K'_j, 1 \leq j \leq p$, the set containing the same objects as K_j, after the extension. By $f'_j, 1 \leq j \leq p$, we denote the mean (center) of the set of K'_j. These sets $K'_j, 1 \leq j \leq p$, will not necessarily represent clusters after the attribute set extension. The newly arrived attributes can change the objects arrangement into clusters. But there is a chance, when adding one or few attributes to objects, that the old arrangement in clusters to be close to the actual one. With these being said, we agree, however, to continue to refer the sets K'_j as clusters.

We take as starting point the previous partition into clusters and study in which conditions an extended object $O_i^{j'}$ is still "correctly" placed into its cluster K'_j. We intuitively started from the fact that, at the end of the initial *k-means* clustering process, all objects are closer to the centroid of their cluster than to any other centroid. So, for any cluster j and any object $O_i^j \in K_j$, inequality (1) below holds.

$$d_E(O_i^j, f_j) \leq d_E(O_i^j, f_r), \forall j, r, \ 1 \leq j, r \leq p, \ r \neq j. \tag{1}$$

This inequality will not hold for every object in respect to the clusters produced by *HACA*. But as we used as linkage-metric in *HACA* average-link, it is likely, that a lot of objects will satisfy inequality (1) for this algorithm as well.

When attribute set extension happens, we will detect in each cluster a subset of objects (core) that could reach together in a cluster, if we would cluster the extended object set. We will use inequality (1), of objects closeness to the centers, as the stability condition for delimiting cores inside clusters. So, a core of cluster K_j will consist of those objects in K_j that have a considerable chance to remain stable in a cluster, and not to divide between more clusters as a result of the attribute set extension.

Definition 1.

a) We denote by $StrongCore_j = \{O_i^{j'} | O_i^{j'} \in K'_j, O_i^j$ satisfies inequality (1) **before and after** attribute set extension} i.e. the set of all objects in K'_j closer, **before and after** extension, to the center of their cluster than to the center of any other cluster.

b) Let $sat(O_i^{j'})$ be the set of all clusters $K'_r, \forall r, 1 \leq r \leq p, r \neq j$ not containing $O_i^{j'}$ and for which object $O_i^{j'}$ satisfies inequality (1) **after** attribute set extension. We denote by $WeakCore_j = \{O_i^{j'} | O_i^{j'} \in K'_j, O_i^j$ satisfies inequality

(1) **before** extension and $|sat(O_i^{j'})| \geq \dfrac{\sum\limits_{k=1}^{n_j} |sat(O_k^{j'})|}{n_j}\}$

c) $Core_j = StrongCore_j$ iif $StrongCore_j \neq \emptyset$; otherwise, $Core_j = WeakCore_j$.
$OCore_j = K'_j \setminus Core_j$ is the set of out-of-core objects in cluster K'_j.

d) We denote by $CORE$ the set $\{Core_j, 1 \leq j \leq p\}$ of all cluster cores and by $OCORE$ the set $\{OCore_j, 1 \leq j \leq p\}$.

As we have already mentioned, for a partition produced by k-means, the inequality (1) holds, before the attribute set extension, for every object and its cluster.

We have chosen the above cluster cores definition because of the following reason. In our algorithms, $Core_j$ will be the seed for cluster j in the adaptive process. But it is possible, especially in the case of $HACA$, that the $StrongCore$ of clusters to be empty. For managing this situation, when the $StrongCore$ of a cluster is detected to be empty, we weaken the core forming conditions. Correspondingly, we defined the $WeakCore$ of a cluster, which consists of the most stable objects in K'_j.

The cluster cores, chosen as we described, will serve as seed in the adaptive clustering process. All objects in $Core_j$ will surely remain together in the same group if clusters do not change. This will not be the case for all core objects, but for most of them, as we will see in the results section.

3   The *Core Based Adaptive k-Means* Algorithm

We give next the *Core Based Adaptive k-means* algorithm. The algorithm starts by calculating the old clusters cores. The cores will be the new initial clusters from which the iterative processing begins. Next, the algorithm proceeds in the same manner as the classical k-means method does. We mention that the algorithm stops when the clusters from two consecutive iterations remain unchanged or the number of steps performed exceeds the maximum allowed number of iterations.

```
Algorithm Core Based Adaptive k-means is
Input: - the set X = {O₁,...,Oₙ} of m-dimensional previously clustered
            objects,
        - the set X' = {O'₁,...,O'ₙ} of (m+s)-dimensional extended objects
          to be clustered; O'ᵢ has the same first m components as Oᵢ,
        - the metric dₑ between objects in a multi-dimensional space,
        - p, the number of desired clusters,
        - K = {K₁,...,Kₚ} the previous partition of objects in X,
        - noMaxIter the maximum number of iterations allowed.
Output: - the new partition K' = {K'₁,...,K'ₚ} for the objects in X'.
Begin
    For all clusters Kⱼ ∈ K
        Calculate Coreⱼ = (StrongCoreⱼ ≠ ∅)?StrongCoreⱼ : WeakCoreⱼ
        K'ⱼ = Coreⱼ
        Calculate f'ⱼ as the mean of objects in K'ⱼ
    EndFor
    While (K' changes between two consecutive steps) and
          (there were not performed noMaxIter iterations) do
```

```
        For all clusters K'_j do
          K'_j = {O'_i | d_E(O'_i, f'_j) ≤ d_E(O'_i, f'_r), ∀r, 1 ≤ r ≤ p, 1 ≤ i ≤ n}
        EndFor
        For all clusters K'_j do
          f'_j = the mean of objects in K'_j
        EndFor
    EndWhile
End.
```

4 The *Hierarchical Core Based Adaptive* Algorithm

We give next the *Hierarchical Core Based Adaptive* algorithm. The algorithm
starts by calculating the old clusters cores. For each cluster j, the objects in
$OCore_j$ will be extracted and distributed each one in its singleton. This is a
divisive step. Clearly, from this cluster adjustment process will result a number p'
of clusters, $p \leq p' \leq n$. In order to reach again the targeted number p of clusters,
we proceed next to merge clusters in the same manner as the classical *HACA*
does. But, as we do not generally start again from singletons, the number of
steps will be significantly reduced. Also, as we will demonstrate by experiments,
we do not significantly lose quality of clusters obtained by *HCBAC* compared to
the quality of clusters provided by *HACA*. We mention that the algorithm stops
when p clusters are obtained.

```
Algorithm Hierarchical Core Based Incremental Clustering is
Input: - the set X = {O_1,...,O_n} of m-dimensional previously clustered
         objects,
       - the set X' = {O'_1,...,O'_n} of (m+s)-dimensional extended objects
         to be clustered, O'_i has the same first m components as O_i,
       - the metric d_E between objects in a multi-dimensional space,
       - p, the number of desired clusters,
       - K = {K_1,...,K_p} the previous partition of objects in X.
Output: - the re-partition K' = {K'_1,...,K'_p} for the objects in X'.
Begin
    For all clusters K_j ∈ K do
       Calculate Core_j = (StrongCore_j ≠ ∅)?
                     StrongCore_j : WeakCore_j
       Calculate OCore_j = K_j \ Core_j
    EndFor
    C = ∅ // the current cluster set
    For i = 1 to p do
       If Core_i ≠ ∅
          C = C ∪ {Core_i}
       EndIf
       For all O ∈ OCore_i do
          C = C ∪ {O} //add a singleton to C
       EndFor
    EndFor
```

```
While | C |> p do
    (C_u*, C_v*) := argmin_(C_u,C_v) d_E(C_u, C_v)
    C_new = C_u* ∪ C_v*
    C = C \ {C_u*, C_v*} ∪ {C_new}
EndWhile
K' = C
```
End.

As distance between two clusters $d_E(C_u, C_v)$ we considered the average-link metric:

$$d_E(C_u, C_v) = \frac{\sum_{a_i \in C_u} \sum_{b_j \in C_v} d_E(a_i, b_j)}{| C_u | \times | C_v |}.$$

This linkage metric leads to higher probability of well formed and stable cores than would lead the single-link metric, for example.

5 Experimental Evaluation

In this section we present some experimental results obtained by applying the *CBAk* and *HCBAC* algorithms described in section 3 and 4. We will compare each of two algorithms with its corresponding non-adaptive version (*CBAk* vs *k-means, HCBAC* vs *HACA*).

5.1 Quality Measures

Number of iterations. It determines the global calculus complexity and it is used for evaluating the performances of both *CBAk* and *HCBAC*.

The movement degree of the core objects and of the extra-core objects. quantifies how the objects in either $Core_j \in CORE$, or $OCore_j \in OCORE$, remain together in clusters after the algorithm ends. It is measured for *CBAk*. It is not used for evaluating *HCBAC* because, once placed into a cluster, any set of objects will not be splitted anymore between clusters, in the agglomerative process.

As expected, more stable the core objects are and more they remain together in respect to the initial sets $Core_j$, better was the decision to choose them as seed for the adaptive clustering process.

We denote by $S = \{S_1, S_2, \ldots, S_p\}, S_i \subseteq K_i$, a set of clusters' subsets (as *CORE* and *OCORE* are). We express the *stability factor* of S as:

$$SF(S) = \frac{\sum_{j=1}^{p} \frac{|S_j|}{\text{no of clusters where the objects in } S_j \text{ ended}}}{\sum_{j=1}^{p} |S_j|} \tag{2}$$

The worst case is when each object in S_j ends in a different final cluster, and this happens for every set in S. The best case is when every S_j remains compact and it is found in a single final cluster. So, the limits between which $SF(CORE)$ varies are given below, where the higher the value of $SF(CORE)$ is, the better was the cores choice:

$$\frac{p}{\sum\limits_{j=1}^{p} |Core_j|} \leq SF(CORE) \leq 1 \tag{3}$$

Squared sum error (SSE) is used for comparing the quality of the partitions produced by *CBAk* and by *k-means*. SSE of a partition K is defined as:

$$SSE(K) = \sum_{K_j \in K} \sum_{O_i \in K_j} (d(O_i, f_j))^2 \tag{4}$$

When comparing two partitions $\mathcal{K}_1$ and $\mathcal{K}_2$ for the same data set, we will say that $\mathcal{K}_1$ is better than $\mathcal{K}_2$ iff $SSE(\mathcal{K}_1) < SSE(\mathcal{K}_2)$.

The degree of compactness of a partition is the measure equivalent to *SSE* for *HCBAC*. The degree of compactness, or the *dispersion* (*DISP*) of a partition K is defined as follows:

$$DISP(K) = \frac{\sum\limits_{k=1}^{p} \dfrac{\sum\limits_{O_i, O_j \in K_k, i>j} d(O_i, O_j)}{C_{|K_k|}^2}}{p} \tag{5}$$

where $K = \{K_1, \ldots, K_p\}$ is the cluster set obtained after applying a clustering algorithm. *DISP* expresses the average distance between objects in a cluster, for all clusters and $C_{|K_k|}^2$ represents the number of combinations of 2 elements from the set K_k.

As expected, the smaller the dispersion is, more compact clusters we have obtained and better was the cores choice at the beginning of the adaptive clustering process.

Clustering tendency. For measuring the clustering tendency of a data set, we use the Hopkins statistics, H [14], an approach that uses statistical tests for spatial randomness. H takes values between 0 and 1, and a value near 1 indicates that the data is highly clustered. Usually, for a data set with clustering tendency, we expect for H values greater than 0.5.

Information gain. For comparing the informational relevance of the attributes we used the *information gain (IG)* measure ([12]).

As case studies, for experimenting our theoretical results and for evaluating the performance of the algorithms, we consider some experiments that are briefly described in the following subsections.

We have to mention that the data were taken from the website "http://www.cormactech.com/neunet".

5.2 Experiment 1. Cancer

The breast cancer database was obtained from the University of Wisconsin Hospitals, Madison, Dr. William H. Wolberg.

The objects to be clusterized in this experiment are patients: each patient is identified by 9 attributes ([15]). The attributes have been used to represent instances and each one takes integer values between 1 and 10. Each instance has one of 2 possible classes: benign or malignant. In this experiment there are 457 patients (objects).

5.3 Experiment 2. Dermatology

The objects to be clusterized in this experiment are also patients: each patient is identified by 34 attributes, 33 of which are linear valued and one of them is nominal. There are 1617 objects (patients).

The aim of the clustering process is to determine the type of Eryhemato-Squamous Disease ([8]).

In the dataset constructed for this domain, the family history feature has the value 1 if any of these diseases has been observed in the family, and 0 otherwise. The age feature simply represents the age of the patient. Every other feature (clinical and histopathological) was given a degree in the range of 0 to 3. Here, 0 indicates that the feature was not present, 3 indicates the largest amount possible, and 1, 2 indicate the relative intermediate values.

5.4 Experiment 3. Wine

These data are the results of a chemical analysis of wines grown in the same region in Italy but derived from three different cultivars. The analysis determined the quantities of 13 constituents found in each of the three types of wines ([1]).

The objects to be clusterized in this experiment are wine instances: each is identified by 13 attributes. There are 178 objects (wine instances).

We have to mention that all attributes in this experiment are continuous.

5.5 *CBAk* Results

In this section we comparatively present the results obtained by applying the *CBAk* algorithm and *k-means*, for the experimental data. We mention that the results are calculated in average, for several executions. We considered two variants for *k-means*: resuming from the current partition (denoted by v1) and starting from scratch (denoted by v2).

From Table 1 we observe that using the *CBAk* algorithm the number of iterations for finding the solution is less than or at most equal to the number of *k-means* iterations, for both variants (v1 and v2). The cores' stability factor, $SF(CORE)$, is high, taking into account that most of the objects are contained

Table 1. The comparative results for *k-means* and *CBAk*

Experiment	Cancer	Dermatology	Wine
No of objects	457	366	178
No of attributes (m+s)	9	34	13
No of new attributes (s)	4	3	4
No of clusters	2	6	3
No of k-means iterations for m attributes	5.66	10.43	9.26
No of k-means (v1) iterations for (m+s) attributes	4	1	4.94
No of k-means (v2) iterations for (m+s) attributes	7	10.33	6.85
No of CBAk iterations for (m+s) attributes	4	1	4.66
No of objects StrongCore/WeakCore (% from no of objects) - CBAk	96.4/0	100/0	91.66/0
No of objects Core/OutOfCore (% from no of objects) - CBAk	96.4/3.6	100/0	91.66/8.34
SF(CORE) - CBAk	0.67	1	0.587
SF(OCORE) - CBAk	0.84	-	0.77
k-means (v1) SSE for (m+s) attributes	13808.78	12740.23	49.73
k-means (v2) SSE for (m+s) attributes	13808.78	13049.22	49.021
CBAk SSE for (m+s) attributes	13808.78	12796.65	50.17
H for s attributes	0.666	0.68122	0.7018
H for m+s attributes	0.7148	0.6865	0.7094

in cores. We mention that for every run of each experiment, SSE(CBAk) has been roughly equal to SSE(k-means), both for v1 and v2.

In Table 2 we present, for each experiment, the attributes in decreasing order of their information gain (IG) - the new attributes are emphasized.

Table 2. The decreasing order of attributes in respect to the information gain measure

Experiment	Order of attributes	IG of new attributes / IG of old attributes (%)
Cancer	2 3 **6** 7 5 4 **8** 1 **9**	64,7%
Dermatology	22 21 23 1 **34** 30 28 13 26 7 17 9 29 10 16 11 25 15 6 27 4 20 **32** 8 5 24 3 31 12 2 19 18 14 **33**	7,6%
Wine	7 **10 12 13** 6 1 2 **11** 9 4 5 3 8	57%

From Table 2 it results that the importance of the added attributes influences the number of iterations performed by the *CBAk* algorithm for finding the solution.

A problem with the *k-means* algorithm is that it is sensitive to the selection of the initial partition (centroids) and may converge to a local minimum of the squared error value if the initial partition is not properly chosen. In order to evaluate properly our algorithm, we considered the same initial centroids when running *k-means* for the initial and feature-extended object set (m and $m + s$ number of attributes). It would be interesting to analyze how a good initial centroids choice affects the results.

5.6 *HCBAC* Results

In this section we comparatively present the results obtained by applying the *HCBAC* and *HACA* algorithms, for the experimental data.

Table 3. The comparative results for *HACA* and *HCBAC*

Experiment	Cancer	Dermatology	Wine
No of objects	457	366	178
No of attributes (m+s)	9	34	13
No of new attributes (s)	4	3	4
No of clusters	2	6	3
No of HACA iterations for m attributes	455	360	175
No of HACA iterations for (m+s) attributes (N1)	455	360	175
No of HCBAC iterations for (m+s) attributes (N2)	22	27	2
Reduction of the no of iterations (N1-N2)/N1(%)	95.16 %	92.5 %	98.8 %
DISP(HACA) for m attributes	5.3507	8.0207	0.83
DISP(HACA) for (m+s) attributes	7.6505	7.9284	0.9871
DISP(HCBAC) for (m+s) attributes	7.702	8.1697	0.8337
No of objects StrongCore/WeakCore (% from no of objects) HCBAC	95/0	92.6/0	98.8/0

From Table 3 we observe that using the *HCBAC* the number of iterations for finding the solution is smaller than in the case of *HACA*. Also, the clusters obtained by *HCBAC* are roughly equally dispersed as those given by *HACA*. So, the clusters quality remains at about the same level, but the clustering process is more efficient.

5.7 Adaptive Horizontal Fragmentation in Object Oriented Databases

A practical problem, where the proposed methods can be efficiently used, is the adaptive horizontal fragmentation of object oriented databases.

A horizontal fragmentation approach that uses data mining clustering methods for partitioning object instances into fragments has been presented in [4], [5], [6], [7]. Essentially, that approach takes full advantage of existing data, where statistics are already present, and develops fragmentation around user applications (queries) that are to be optimized by the obtained fragmentation. But real databases applications evolve in time, and consequently they require re-fragmentation in order to deal with new applications entering the system and others leaving. Obviously, for obtaining the fragmentation that fits the new user applications set, the original fragmentation scheme can be applied from scratch. However, this process can be inefficient.

We have applied the *CBAk* method in the case when new user applications arrive in the system and the current fragments must be accordingly adapted ([2]). The obtained results were good. The adaptive fragmentation keeps the fragmentation quality around the non-adaptive one and the processing time is improved, as the incremental method performs, generally, in less time than the full fragmentation process.

6 Conclusions and Future Work

In this paper we proposed a new approach for adapting the result of a clustering when the attribute set describing the objects increases. Two traditional algorithms, *k-means* and *HACA*, were adapted to follow this approach. The experiments on different data sets prove that, in most cases, the results are reached more efficiently using the proposed adaptive methods than running the corresponding classical algorithms, on the feature-extended object set. But there are some situations when it is better to resort to a non-adaptive clustering of the feature-extended object set, than using the proposed algorithms. Intuitively, such situations can be: the addition of a large number of features or the addition of new features with large information gain and contradictory information with respect to the old feature set.

Further work could be done in the following directions:

- to make experiments that would cover a range of additional cases like: varied number of added features, discrete or continuous features and to consider a more substantial number of features and objects;
- to isolate conditions to decide when it is more effective to adapt the result of a clustering of the feature-extended object set than to resume or restart the clustering using *k-means* or *HACA*;
- to study how the information brought into the system by the newly added attributes, their correlation with the initial ones, influences the performance of the adaptive algorithms;
- to apply the adaptive algorithms on precise problems, from where the need of such algorithms originated.

References

1. Aeberhard, S., Coomans, D., de Vel, O.: THE CLASSIFICATION PERFOR-MANCE OF RDA. Tech. Rep. **92–01**, Dept. of Computer Science and Dept. of Mathematics and Statistics, James Cook University of North Queensland (1992)
2. Campan, A., Darabant, A.S., Serban, G., Clustering Techniques for Adaptive Horizontal Fragmentation in Object Oriented Databases. In Proceedings of the International Conference on Theory and Applications of Mathematics and Informatics ICTAMI 2005, Alba-Iulia, Romania, (2005) (to appear).

3. CorMac Technologies Inc, Canada: Discover the Patterns in Your Data. http://www.cormactech.com/neunet (2006)
4. Darabant, A.S., Campan, A., Semi-supervised learning techniques: k-means clustering in OODB Fragmentation. In pRoceedings of IEEE International Conference on Computational Cybernetics ICCC 2004, Vienna University of Technology, Austria, August 30 - September 1, (2004) 333–338
5. Darabant, A.S., Campan, A., Hierarchical AI Clustering for Horizontal Object Fragmentation. In Proceedings of Int. Conf. of Computers and Communications, Oradea, May, (2004) 117–122
6. Darabant, A.S., Campan, A., AI Clustering Techniques: a New Approach to Object Oriented Database Fragmentation. In Proceedings of the 8th IEEE International Conference on Intelligent Engineering Systems, Cluj Napoca, (2004) 73–78
7. Darabant, A.S., Campan, A., Cret, O., Hierarchical Clustering in Object Oriented Data Models with Complex Class Relationships. In Proceedings of the 8th IEEE International Conference on Intelligent Engineering Systems, Cluj Napoca, (2004) 307–312
8. Demiroz, G., Govenir, H. A., Ilter, N.: Learning Differential Diagnosis of Eryhemato-Squamous Diseases using Voting Feature Intervals. Artificial Intelligence in Medicine
9. Han, J., Kamber, M.: Data Mining: Concepts and Techniques. Morgan Kaufmann Publishers (2001)
10. Jain, A., Dubes, R.: Algorithms for Clustering Data. Prentice Hall, Englewood Cliffs, New Jersey (1998)
11. Jain, A., Murty, M. N., Flynn, P.: Data clustering: A review. ACM Computing Surveys, **31(3)** (1999) 264-323
12. Quinlan, J. R.: C4.5: Programs for Machine Learning, Morgan Kaufmann. San Mateo, California (1993)
13. Şerban, G., Câmpan, A.: Core Based Incremental Clustering, Studia Universitatis "Babeş-Bolyai", Informatica, **L(1)** (2005) 89–96
14. Tan, P.-N., Steinbach, M., Kumar, V., Introduction to Data Mining. Addison Wesley, chapters 8,9, (2005)
15. Wolberg, W., Mangasarian, O. L.: Multisurface method of pattern separation for medical diagnosis applied to breast cytology. Proceedings of the National Academy of Sciences, U.S.A., Volume **87**, December (1990) 9193–9196
16. Wu, F., Gardarin, G., Gradual Clustering Algorithms. Proceedings of the 7th International Conference on Database Systems for Advanced Applications (DASFAA'01), (2001) 48–57

Classification Based on Logical Concept Analysis

Yan Zhao and Yiyu Yao

Department of Computer Science, University of Regina,
Regina, Saskatchewan, Canada S4S 0A2
{yanzhao, yyao}@cs.uregina.ca

Abstract. This paper studies the problem of classification by using a concept lattice as a search space of classification rules. The left hand side of a classification rule is composed by a concept, including its extension and its intension, and the right hand side is the class label that the concept implies. Particularly, we show that logical concepts of the given universe are naturally associated with any consistent classification rules generated by any partition-based or covering-based algorithm, and can be characterized as a special set of consistent classification rules. An algorithm is proposed to find a set of the most general consistent concepts.

1 Introduction

The objectives of classification tasks can be divided into description and prediction. Description focuses on the discovery of rules that describe data, and prediction involves the use of discovered rules to make prediction. A classification rule is normally expressed in the form of "if ϕ then ψ", or symbolically, $\phi \Rightarrow \psi$. The left hand side is a formula that characterizes a subset of the objects, and the right hand side is a label that indicates the class of this set of objects.

Generally, a classification task can be understood as a search in a particular search space of possible solutions. The features of a search space determine the properties of the rules to be constructed; the structure and the complexity of the search space are primary measures of the difficulty of a classification problem. Given a particular search space, different search strategies, such as depth-first, breath-first and best-first methods, together with some heuristics can be used to explore the normally very large space [6, 14].

Many search spaces for classification tasks have been intensively studied. For example, a *version space* [6] has the most specific bound and the most general bound, such that the most specific bound contains the set of maximally specific formulas with respect to some training data, and the most general bound contains the set of maximally general formulas with respect to some other training data. It allows the general-to-specific and the specific-to-general breadth-first search at the same time. The left hand side of classification rules are all possible generalizations that could be created from these two bounding sets.

As another example, a *granule network* [14] systematically organizes all the granules and formulas with respect to the given universe. Each node consists of

L. Lamontagne and M. Marchand (Eds.): Canadian AI 2006, LNAI 4013, pp. 419–430, 2006.
© Springer-Verlag Berlin Heidelberg 2006

a granule which is a subset of objects in the universe, and each arc leading from a granule to its child is labelled by an atomic formula. A path from a coarse granule to a fine granule indicates a conjunctive relation. The left hand side of a classification rule is a disjunction of a conjunctive set of atomic formulas.

A clustering-based classifier presents another search space. For example, for a k-NN classifier [5], based on some pre-selected distance metric, k clusters are constructed. Each is assigned a particular class. The left hand side of a classification rule is a disjunction of a set of clusters. The problem of this search space is that using a relatively large k may include some not so similar pixels. On the other hand, using a very small k may exclude some potential accurate rules. The optimal value of k depends on the size and the nature of the data.

This paper intends to introduce another search space, a concept lattice, for classification tasks. As a result, the left hand side of a classification rule is a concept, including a set of objects (an extension) and a set of properties (an intension).

There are several advantages of using concept analysis for classification. Concepts are extremely precise in the sense that an intention and an extension are two-way definable. This ensures that the constructed concept-based rules are most descriptive and accurate. All the concepts are naturally organized into a concept hierarchy. Once concepts are constructed and described, one can study relationships between concepts in terms of their intensions and extensions, such as sub-concepts and super-concepts, disjoint and overlap concepts, and partial sub-concepts. These relationships can be conveniently expressed in the form of rules and associated with quantitative measures indicating the strength of rules. Knowledge discovery and data mining, especially rule mining, can be viewed as a process of forming concepts and finding relationships between concepts in terms of intensions and extensions [12, 13].

The rest of the paper is organized as follows. Section 2 formalizes the basic settings of information tables and a decision logic language. After that, the notion of formal concepts and one of its logical transformations are discussed in Section 3. Section 4 studies the relationship between consistent classification rules and consistent concepts, and proposes a heuristic method to explore the most general consistent concepts. Conclusions are made in Section 5.

2   Information Tables and a Decision Logic Language

An information table provides a convenient way to describe a finite set of objects by a finite set of attributes.

Definition 1. *An information table S is the tuple:*

$$S = (U, At, \{V_a \mid a \in At\}, \{I_a \mid a \in At\}),$$

where U is a finite nonempty set of objects, At is a finite nonempty set of attributes, V_a is a nonempty set of values for attribute $a \in At$, and $I_a : U \to V_a$ is an information function.

To describe the information in an information table, we adopt the decision logic language L that was discussed in [7].

Definition 2. *A decision logic language L consists of a set of formulas, which are defined by the following two rules:*

(i) An atomic formula of L is a descriptor $a = v$, where $a \in At$ and $v \in V_a$;
(ii) The well-formed formulas (wffs) of L is the smallest set, containing the atomic formulas and closed under $\neg$ and $\wedge$.

In an information table S, the satisfiability of a formula $\phi \in L$ by an object is written as $x \models_S \phi$, or in short $x \models \phi$ if S is understood.

With the notion of satisfiability, one may obtain a set-theoretic interpretation of formulas of L. That is, if ϕ is a formula, the set $m_S(\phi)$, defined by $m_S(\phi) = \{x \in U | x \models \phi\}$, is called the meaning of the formula ϕ in S. If S is understood, we simply write $m(\phi)$. The meaning of a formula ϕ is the set of all objects having the properties expressed by the formula ϕ. If $m_S(\phi) \neq \emptyset$, then ϕ is meaningful in S. With ϕ and $m(\phi)$, a connection between formulas of L and subsets of U is thus established.

A subset $X \subseteq U$ is called a definable granule in an information table S if there exists at least one formula ϕ such that $m_S(\phi) = X$. The notion of definability of subsets in an information table is essential to data analysis. In fact, definable subsets are the basic units that can be described and discussed, upon which other notions can be developed.

A formula ϕ_i is a refinement of another formula ϕ_j, or equivalently, ϕ_j is a coarsening of ϕ_i. The refinement relation can be denoted by logical implication, written as $\phi_i \rightarrow \phi_j$. In the context of an information table S, $\phi_i \rightarrow_S \phi_j$, if and only if $m(\phi_i) \subseteq m(\phi_j)$. Given two formulas ϕ_i and ϕ_j, the meet $\phi_i \wedge \phi_j$ defines the largest intersection of the granules $m(\phi_i)$ and $m(\phi_j)$, and the join $\phi_i \vee \phi_j$ defines the smallest union of the granules $m(\phi_i)$ and $m(\phi_j)$.

3   Formal Concept Analysis and Logical Concept Analysis

Formal concept analysis (FCA) deals with the characterization of a concept consisting of its intension and extension [3, 11]. By considering the decision logic language, we can transform formal concepts to a logical setting, and perform logical concept analysis (LCA) [4]. LCA extends an intension from a set of properties to a logical formula defined by these properties. By extending FCA to LCA, we enhance the flexibility for description, management, updating, querying, or navigation in the concepts.

3.1   Formal Concept Analysis

Denote $\mathcal{F}$ as the set of all atomic formulas in the decision logic language L, i.e., $\mathcal{F} = \{a = v | a \in At, v \in V_a\}$. For $O \subseteq U$ and $F \subseteq \mathcal{F}$, define

$$O' = \{f \in \mathcal{F} \mid \forall x \in O : \ x \models_S f\}, \tag{1}$$
$$F' = \{x \in U \mid \forall f \in F : \ x \models_S f\}. \tag{2}$$

So O' is the set of atomic formulas common to all the objects in O, and F' is the set of objects possessing all the atomic formulas in F.

Lemma 1. *[11] Let an information table S be a formal context, $O_i, O_j \subseteq U$ and $F_i, F_j \subseteq \mathcal{F}$. Then*

$$\begin{array}{ll}
(1) \quad O_i \subseteq O_j \Rightarrow O_i' \supseteq O_j', & (1') \quad F_i \subseteq F_j \Rightarrow F_i' \supseteq F_j'; \\
(2) \quad O \subseteq O'', & (2') \quad F \subseteq F''; \\
(3) \quad O' = O''', & (3') \quad F' = F'''; \\
(4) \quad (O_i \cup O_j)' = O_i' \cap O_j', & (4') \quad (F_i \cup F_j)' = F_i' \cap F_j'.
\end{array}$$

Definition 3. *[11] A formal concept of an information table S is defined as a pair (O, F), where $O \subseteq U, F \subseteq \mathcal{F}, O' = F$ and $F' = O$. The extension of the concept (O, F) is O, and the intension is F.*

3.2   Logical Concept Analysis Limited to Conjunction

FCA, discussed above, deals with both intensions and extensions in the set-theoretic setting, and does not consider the relationships between the elements of intensions. By involving the decision logic language L, we move to a logical setting for LCA.

Intuitively, the set-based intensions imply a conjunctive relation on the included atomic formulas. In this paper, we only focus our attention on logical conjunction. Thus, we can define two logically conjunctive dual functions as follows:

$$O^* = \bigwedge O' = \bigwedge \{ f \in \mathcal{F} \mid \forall x \in O : x \models_S f \}, \tag{3}$$

$$= \dot{\bigvee}_{t \in T} \bigwedge O_t', \text{ where } \bigcup_{t \in T} O_t = O; \tag{4}$$

$$\phi^* = m_S(\phi) = \{ x \in U \mid x \models_S \phi \}, \tag{5}$$

$$= \bigcap_{t \in T} \phi_t^*, \text{ where } \bigcup (\phi_t^*)' = (\phi^*)'. \tag{6}$$

Here, we use two different notations for O^*. Equation 3 intersects the common properties of all the objects in O by using the logic-based conjunctor; Equation 4 computes the least upper bound of all the conjunctively definable formulas of subsets of objects by using the context-based disjunctor.

Note that the context-based conjunctive operator $\dot{\wedge}$ and disjunctive operator $\dot{\vee}$ are different from the logic-based conjunctor $\wedge$ and disjunctor $\vee$. For two formulas $\phi, \psi \in L$ in the context of an information table, $\phi \dot{\wedge} \psi$ returns the greatest lower bound of ϕ and ψ (more specific), and $\phi \dot{\vee} \psi$ returns the least upper bound of ϕ and ψ (more general), with respect to the given universe.

Transposition from a set $F \subseteq \mathcal{F}$ to a conjunctive formula needs to replace $\supseteq, \cap$ and $\cup$ by $\rightarrow, \dot{\wedge}$ and $\dot{\vee}$, respectively. Thus, Lemma 1 can be transformed as:

Lemma 2. *Let an information table S be a context, $O_i, O_j \subseteq U$ and $\phi_i, \phi_j \in L$. Then*

(1) $O_i \subseteq O_j \Rightarrow O_i^* \to O_j^*,$ (1') $\phi_i \to \phi_j \Rightarrow \phi_i^* \subseteq \phi_j^*;$

(2) $O \subseteq O^{**},$ (2') $\phi^{**} \to \phi;$

(3) $O^* \equiv O^{***},$ (3') $\phi^* = \phi^{***};$

(4) $(O_i \cup O_j)^* \equiv \phi_i^* \dot\vee \phi_j^*,$ (4') $(\phi_i \dot\wedge \phi_j)^* = \phi_i^* \cap \phi_j^*.$

Definition 4. *A conjunctive concept of an information table S is defined as a pair (O, ϕ), where $O \subseteq U$, ϕ is a conjunctive formula, $O^* \equiv \phi$ and $\phi^* = O$. The extension of the conjunctive concept (O, ϕ) is O, and the intension is ϕ.*

All the conjunctive concepts form a complete concept lattice, which possesses the following two properties:

$$\bigwedge_{t \in T} (O_t, \phi_t) = \left(\bigcap_{t \in T} O_t, \left(\dot\bigwedge_{t \in T} \phi_t \right)^{**} \right),$$

$$\bigvee_{t \in T} (O_t, \phi_t) = \left(\left(\bigcup_{t \in T} O_t \right)^{**}, \dot\bigvee_{t \in T} \phi_t \right).$$

For concepts (O_i, ϕ_i) and (O_j, ϕ_j) in the concept lattice, we write $(O_i, \phi_i) \leq (O_j, \phi_j)$, and say (O_i, ϕ_i) is a sub-concept of (O_j, ϕ_j), or (O_j, ϕ_j) is a super-concept of (O_i, ϕ_i), if $O_i \subseteq O_j$, or $\phi_i \to \phi_j$.

4 Classification Based on Conjunctive Concept Analysis

Without loss of generality, we assume that there is a unique attribute *class* taking class labels as its values. The set of attributes in an information table is expressed as $At = D \cup \{class\}$, where D is the set of attributes used to describe the objects, also called the set of descriptive attributes. An information table for classification is also called a decision table.

4.1 Classification Rules

Each classification rule, in the form of $\phi \Rightarrow class = c_i$, or simply, $\phi \Rightarrow c_i$, is derived from, and associated with a definable granule X, such that ϕ describes X, and c_i labels X. Therefore, each classification rule $\phi \Rightarrow c_i$ can be expressed by a decision relation between a definable pair including a granule X and its formula ϕ, and a class label, i.e., $(X, \phi) \Rightarrow c_i$. It is clear that all the objects that satisfy the formula ϕ are in the granule X. However, ϕ might not contain all the properties X processes. It only defines X, and distinguishes X from the other granules. In this case, a definable pair (X, ϕ) possesses only the one-way definability, and is not a concept, which is two-way definable.

Two well-studied rule measures, confidence and generality, are defined as:

$$\text{Confidence}: \quad conf(\phi \Rightarrow c_i) = \frac{|m(\phi \cap c_i)|}{|m(\phi)|}; \tag{7}$$

$$\text{Generality}: \quad generality(\phi \Rightarrow c_i) = \frac{|m(\phi)|}{|U|}. \tag{8}$$

The higher the confidence value is, the more accurate the rule is. When the confidence of a rule is 100%, we say the rule is consistent, or certain. Otherwise, it is approximate, or probabilistic. The higher the generality value is, the more applicable the rule is.

Suppose a set $\mathcal{R}$ of consistent classification rules are discovered from an information table. Partition the universe U into a training set $U_{training}$ and a testing set $U_{testing}$, then the descriptive accuracy can be defined as:

$$description\_accu(U_{training}) = \frac{|\bigcup_{\forall \phi \in \mathcal{R}} m(\phi)|}{|U_{training}|}. \tag{9}$$

When the description accuracy reaches 1, we say that the rule set $\mathcal{R}$ covers the entire training set.

We say an object $x \in U_{testing}$ is accurately classified, if there exists one learned rule $\phi \Rightarrow c_i$ in the set $\mathcal{R}$, such that $x \models \phi$ and $I_{class}(x) = c_i$. We simply denote $x \models \mathcal{R}$. The prediction accuracy is defined as:

$$prediction\_accu(U_{testing}) = \frac{|\{x \in U_{testing} | x \models \mathcal{R}\}|}{|U_{testing}|}. \tag{10}$$

Classification rule mining does not find all possible rules that exist in the information table, but only a subset to form an accurate classifier [2]. Different classification algorithms discover different subsets based on different heuristics.

4.2   Consistent Classification Rules and Consistent Concepts

Definition 5. *Let an information table S be a context, a conjunctive concept (X, ϕ) is called a consistent concept of S if it implies a unique label $c_i \in V_{class}$, and $conf(\phi \Rightarrow c_i) = 100\%$.*

Suppose (X, ϕ) is a conjunctively definable pair (CDP), i.e., ϕ is defined by a conjunction of a set of atomic formulas. We can obtain the following inductions:

For a CDP (X, ϕ), if $conf(\phi \Rightarrow c_i) = 100\%$,
  then the conjunctively consistent concept $(X, X^*) \Rightarrow c_i$, and $X^* \to \phi$,
    the conjunctively consistent concept $(\phi^*, \phi^{**}) \Rightarrow c_i$, and $\phi^{**} \to \phi$,
    there might exist a subset $Y \subseteq X$, such that the conjunctively consistent concept $(Y, Y^*) \Rightarrow c_i$.

Suppose (X, ϕ) is a conjunctive concept.

If (X, ϕ) consistently implies class c_i,
  then for any $\psi \to \phi$, the CDP (ψ^*, ψ) has $conf(\psi \Rightarrow c_i) = 100\%$,
    the conjunctively consistent concept $(\psi^*, \psi^{**}) \Rightarrow c_i$,
    there might exist a subset $Y \subseteq X$, such that the conjunctively consistent concept $(Y, Y^*) \Rightarrow c_i$.

Definition 6. *A most general consistent concept is a consistent concept in the information table, and its super-concepts are not consistent concepts.*

If a super-concept of the concept (X, ϕ) is a most general consistent concept, it is denoted as $\overline{(X, \phi)}$.

Each consistent classification rule is associated with a granule, and is defined by some conditional attributes in the information table. If the conditions can be conjuncted, the formula and the granule form a CDP. Further, each CDP is associated with a conjunctively consistent concept. If the concept is not a general consistent concept, then there must exist a super concept corresponding to it. We can use the following flow to illustrate the underlining logic:

1. Given $conf(\phi \Rightarrow c_i) = 100\%$, where $c_i \in V_{class}$;
2. if ϕ is a conjunctor, then the CDP $(\phi^*, \phi) \Rightarrow c_i$;
3. then the conjunctively consistent concept $\underline{(\phi^*, \phi^{**})} \Rightarrow c_i$;
4. then the most general consistent concept $\overline{(\phi^*, \phi^{**})} \Rightarrow c_i$.

As a result, instead of finding all the consistent classification rules, we can find the set of all the most general consistent concepts that characterizes the complete consistent rule set.

All the most general consistent concepts in an information table compose a covering of the universe, i.e., there may be an overlap between every two most general consistent concepts, and all the most general consistent concepts cover the entire universe. This can be easily proved by making the given decision table satisfy the first normal form, that requires all attribute-values in the table are atomic. In this case, for any object $x \in U$, the conjunctive formula

$$\bigwedge (a = I_a(x)), \text{ for all } a \in At$$

forms an intension ϕ, and the pair (ϕ^*, ϕ) forms a concept. Clearly, the family of all concepts as such (ϕ^*, ϕ) cover the universe. Due to the fact that a most general consistent concept can cover one or more than one concepts, all the most general consistent concepts is a covering of the universe.

A covering-based algorithm tends to generate a set of rules that cover the objects of the given information table. For some covering-based algorithms, a granule that is covered by a rule is biased to be as big as possible. Suppose $\mathcal{R}$ is a set of conjunctively consistent rules that are generated by a covering-based classification algorithm, and B is the set of rules defined by the most general consistent concepts. Then

(1) $|\mathcal{R}| \geq |B|$,
(2) For $\phi \in \mathcal{R}, b \in B$, and $lhs(\phi)^{**} = lhs(b)$,
     $lhs(b) \rightarrow lhs(\phi)$ and $|lhs(\phi)^*| \leq |lhs(b)^*|$,
     where lhs stands for the left hand side of a rule.

A partition-based algorithm is normally biased to generate a shorter tree. Each CDP that maps to a rule is often not a most general consistent concept. Suppose $\mathcal{R}$ is the set of consistent rules that are generated by any partition-based algorithm, then the second property still holds, and $|\mathcal{R}| \leq |B|$. Limited by the bias of partition-based algorithms, finding the most general consistent concept from a corresponding CDP is not easy.

4.3   A Simple Example

The decision Table 1 has four descriptive attributes A, B, C and D, and a decision attribute *class*. The entire search space, the concept lattice includes 45 conjunctive concepts. For the purpose of classification, we are only interested in the consistent concepts defined by subsets of descriptive attributes, such that concept $(X, \phi) \Rightarrow c_i$. Based on these consistent concepts, we further need to find out the most general consistent concepts, such that for each concept, there does not exist a more general concept implies the same class. As we listed, there are six the most general consistent concepts. The conjunctive concepts, the consistent concepts and the most general consistent concepts are summarized in Table 2.

The ID3 algorithm [8] produces a set of six consistent rules that partition the universe. The PRISM algorithm [1], (shown in Figure 1), generates another set of consistent rules that cover the universe. Each rule can map to one of the most general consistent concepts. For example,

- The left hand side of an ID3 rule "$a_3 \wedge b_1 \wedge c_2 \Rightarrow -$" can be described by a CDP $(\{10\}, a_3 \wedge b_1 \wedge c_2)$, which maps to a concept $(\{10\}, a_3 \wedge b_1 \wedge c_2 \wedge d_1)$, which is more specific than a most general consistent concept $(\{2, 6, 10\}, b_1 \wedge c_2)$.
- The left hand side of a PRISM rule "$a_1 \wedge b_2 \Rightarrow +$" can be described by a CDP $(\{3, 4\}, a_1 \wedge b_2)$, which maps to a concept $(\{3, 4\}, a_1 \wedge b_2 \wedge d_1)$, which is more specific than a most general consistent concept $(\{3, 4, 8, 11, 12\}, b_2 \wedge d_1)$.

The comparisons among the ID3 CDPs, the PRISM CDPs and the most general consistent concepts are illustrated in Table 3.

4.4   An Algorithm for Finding the Most General Consistent Concepts

There are two approaches for finding the most general consistent concepts. One approach is to find them in the concept lattice by brute force. First, construct the concept lattice of the given information table. Then, find the consistent concepts. Thirdly, eliminate all the non-most general concepts. This approach encounters a complexity problem for the first step. If we search the universe U for definable granules, then the search space is $2^{|U|}$. If we search the set $\mathcal{F}$ of all atomic formulas for a subset of atomic formulas, then the search space of is $\prod_{a \in D}(|V_a| + 1)$. In most cases, $\prod(|V_a| + 1) \leq 2^{|U|}$. This means we need to test at least $\prod(|V_a| + 1)$ conjunctively definable formulas, and their conjunctive definable granules, in order to verify if each CDP is a conjunctive concept or not.

The other approach is to generate the most general consistent concept by heuristic. First, apply a heuristic covering algorithm to produce a set of consistent classification rules. Then, find the corresponding concepts to each rule. Finally, eliminate those non-most general concepts. If the set of classification rules cover the universe, the corresponding set of conjunctive concepts and the most general consistent concepts also does. Since the number of classification rules is limited, this approach must be much more efficient than the first one. The PRISM algorithm [1], illustrated in Figure 1, is a good candidate for generating the most general consistent concepts.

Table 1. A decision table

	A	B	C	D	class
o_1	a_1	b_1	c_1	d_2	−
o_2	a_1	b_1	c_2	d_2	−
o_3	a_1	b_2	c_1	d_1	+
o_4	a_1	b_2	c_2	d_1	+
o_5	a_2	b_1	c_1	d_2	−
o_6	a_2	b_1	c_2	d_1	−
o_7	a_2	b_2	c_1	d_2	−
o_8	a_2	b_2	c_2	d_1	+
o_9	a_3	b_1	c_1	d_2	+
o_{10}	a_3	b_1	c_2	d_1	−
o_{11}	a_3	b_2	c_1	d_1	+
o_{12}	a_3	b_2	c_2	d_1	+

Table 2. The conjunctive concepts, the consistent concepts and the most general consistent concepts of Table 1

Conjunctive concepts

Extension	Intension
$\{1,2,3,4,5,6,7,8,9,10,11,12\}$	$\emptyset$
$\{1,2,3,4\}$	a_1
$\{5,6,7,8\}$	a_2
$\{9,10,11,12\}$	a_3
$\{1,2,5,6,9,10\}$	b_1
$\{1,2\}$	$a_1 \wedge b_1 \wedge d_2$
$\{5,6\}$	$a_2 \wedge b_1$
$\{9,10\}$	$a_3 \wedge b_1$
$\{3,4,7,8,11,12\}$	b_2
$\{3,4\}$	$a_1 \wedge b_2 \wedge d_1$
$\{7,8\}$	$a_2 \wedge b_2$
$\{11,12\}$	$a_3 \wedge b_2 \wedge d_1$
$\{1,3,5,7,9,11\}$	c_1
$\{1,3\}$	$a_1 \wedge c_1$
$\{5,7\}$	$a_2 \wedge c_1 \wedge d_2$
$\{9,11\}$	$a_3 \wedge c_1$
$\{1,5,9\}$	$b_1 \wedge c_1 \wedge d_2$
$\{1\}$	$a_1 \wedge b_1 \wedge c_1 \wedge d_2$
$\{5\}$	$a_2 \wedge b_1 \wedge c_1 \wedge d_2$
$\{9\}$	$a_3 \wedge b_1 \wedge c_1 \wedge d_2$
$\{3,7,11\}$	$b_2 \wedge c_1$
$\{3\}$	$a_1 \wedge b_2 \wedge c_1 \wedge d_1$
$\{7\}$	$a_2 \wedge b_2 \wedge c_1 \wedge d_2$
$\{11\}$	$a_3 \wedge b_2 \wedge c_1 \wedge d_1$
$\{2,4,6,8,10,12\}$	c_2
$\{2,4\}$	$a_1 \wedge c_2$
$\{6,8\}$	$a_2 \wedge c_2 \wedge d_1$
$\{10,12\}$	$a_3 \wedge c_2 \wedge d_1$
$\{2,6,10\}$	$b_1 \wedge c_2$
$\{2\}$	$a_1 \wedge b_1 \wedge c_2 \wedge d_2$
$\{6\}$	$a_2 \wedge b_1 \wedge c_2 \wedge d_1$
$\{10\}$	$a_3 \wedge b_1 \wedge c_2 \wedge d_1$
$\{4,8,12\}$	$b_2 \wedge c_2 \wedge d_1$
$\{4\}$	$a_1 \wedge b_2 \wedge c_2 \wedge d_1$
$\{8\}$	$a_2 \wedge b_2 \wedge c_2 \wedge d_1$
$\{12\}$	$a_3 \wedge b_2 \wedge c_2 \wedge d_1$
$\{3,4,6,8,10,11,12\}$	d_1
$\{10,11,12\}$	$a_3 \wedge d_1$
$\{6,10\}$	$b_1 \wedge c_2 \wedge d_1$
$\{3,4,8,11,12\}$	$b_2 \wedge d_1$
$\{3,11\}$	$b_2 \wedge c_1 \wedge d_1$
$\{4,6,8,10,12\}$	$c_2 \wedge d_1$
$\{1,2,5,7,9\}$	d_2
$\{1,2,5,9\}$	$b_1 \wedge d_2$
$\{1,5,7,9\}$	$c_1 \wedge d_2$

Consistent concepts

Extension	Intension	$c_i \in V_{Class}$
$\{1,2\}$	$a_1 \wedge b_1 \wedge d_2$	−
$\{5,6\}$	$a_2 \wedge b_1$	−
$\{3,4\}$	$a_1 \wedge b_2 \wedge d_1$	+
$\{11,12\}$	$a_3 \wedge b_2 \wedge d_1$	+
$\{5,7\}$	$a_2 \wedge c_1 \wedge d_2$	−
$\{9,11\}$	$a_3 \wedge c_1$	+
$\{1\}$	$a_1 \wedge b_1 \wedge c_1 \wedge d_2$	−
$\{5\}$	$a_2 \wedge b_1 \wedge c_1 \wedge d_2$	−
$\{9\}$	$a_3 \wedge b_1 \wedge c_1 \wedge d_2$	+
$\{3\}$	$a_1 \wedge b_2 \wedge c_1 \wedge d_1$	+
$\{7\}$	$a_2 \wedge b_2 \wedge c_1 \wedge d_2$	−
$\{11\}$	$a_3 \wedge b_2 \wedge c_1 \wedge d_1$	+
$\{2,6,10\}$	$b_1 \wedge c_2$	−
$\{2\}$	$a_1 \wedge b_1 \wedge c_2 \wedge d_2$	−
$\{6\}$	$a_2 \wedge b_1 \wedge c_2 \wedge d_1$	−
$\{10\}$	$a_3 \wedge b_1 \wedge c_2 \wedge d_1$	−
$\{4,8,12\}$	$b_2 \wedge c_2 \wedge d_1$	+
$\{4\}$	$a_1 \wedge b_2 \wedge c_2 \wedge d_1$	+
$\{8\}$	$a_2 \wedge b_2 \wedge c_2 \wedge d_1$	+
$\{12\}$	$a_3 \wedge b_2 \wedge c_2 \wedge d_1$	+
$\{6,10\}$	$b_1 \wedge c_2 \wedge d_1$	−
$\{3,4,8,11,12\}$	$b_2 \wedge d_1$	+
$\{3,11\}$	$b_2 \wedge c_1 \wedge d_1$	+

Most general consistent concepts

Extension	Intention	$c_i \in V_{Class}$
$\{1,2\}$	$a_1 \wedge b_1 \wedge d_2$	−
$\{5,6\}$	$a_2 \wedge b_1$	−
$\{5,7\}$	$a_2 \wedge c_1 \wedge d_2$	−
$\{2,6,10\}$	$b_1 \wedge c_2$	−
$\{9,11\}$	$a_3 \wedge c_1$	+
$\{3,4,8,11,12\}$	$b_2 \wedge d_1$	+

Table 3. Compare the ID3, PRISM CDPs with the most general consistent concepts of Table 1

ID3 CDPs	PRISM CDPs	Most general consistent concepts	$c_i \in V_{class}$
$(\{1,2\}, a_1 \wedge b_1)$	$(\{1,2\}, a_1 \wedge b_1)$	$(\{1,2\}, a_1 \wedge b_1 \wedge d_2)$	−
$(\{5,6\}, a_2 \wedge b_1)$	$(\{5,6\}, a_2 \wedge b_1)$	$(\{5,6\}, a_2 \wedge b_1)$	
$(\{10\}, a_3 \wedge b_1 \wedge c_2)$	$(\{6,10\}, b_1 \wedge d_1)$	$(\{2,6,10\}, b_1 \wedge c_2)$	
	$(\{2,6,10\}, b_1 \wedge c_2)$		
$(\{7\}, b_2 \wedge d_2)$	$(\{5,7\}, a_2 \wedge c_1)$	$(\{5,7\}, a_2 \wedge c_1 \wedge d_2)$	
	$(\{5,7\}, a_2 \wedge d_2)$		
$(\{9\}, a_3 \wedge b_1 \wedge c_1)$	$(\{9\}, a_3 \wedge d_2)$	$(\{9,11\}, a_3 \wedge c_1)$	+
	$(\{9,11\}, a_3 \wedge c_1)$		
$(\{3,4,8,11,12\}, b_2 \wedge d_1)$	$(\{3,4\}, a_1 \wedge b_2)$	$(\{3,4,8,11,12\}, b_2 \wedge d_1)$	
	$(\{11,12\}, a_3 \wedge b_2)$		
	$(\{4,8,12\}, b_2 \wedge c_2)$		
	$(\{3,4,8,11,12\}, b_2 \wedge d_1)$		

Input: a decision table
Output: a set of consistent classification rules
For each $c_i \in V_{\text{class}}$, do the following:
1. Calculate the probability of $p(c_i|\phi)$ of the class c_i given each atomic formula $\phi \in \mathcal{F}$.
2. Select the first ϕ_t for which $p(c_i|\phi_t)$ is the maximum. Create a subset of the training set comprising all the instances which contain the selected ϕ_t.
3. Repeat Steps 1 and 2 until the local $p(c_i|\phi_t)$ reaches 1 or stop if no more subsets can be extracted. At this time, check if there is any other condition ϕ_s such that the local $p(c_i|\phi_s)$ also reaches 1.
4. Remove all the objects covered by the rule(s) from the table.
5. Repeat Step 1-4 until all the objects of class c_i have been removed.

Fig. 1. The PRISM algorithm

Input: a decision table
Output: a set of the most general consistent concepts
1. Apply the PRISM algorithm to generate a set of consistent classification rules: $\{\phi \Rightarrow c_i | c_i \in V_{class}\}$.
2. Construct a CDP for each consistent rule: $\{(\phi^*, \phi) \Rightarrow c_i\}$.
3. Construct a conjunctively consistent concept for each CDP: $\{(\phi^*, \phi^{**}) \Rightarrow c_i\}$.
4. For each conjunctively consistent concept (ϕ^*, ϕ^{**}), if there exists another conjunctively consistent concept (ϕ_t^*, ϕ_t^{**}) such that $\phi^* \subset \phi_t^*$, then (ϕ^*, ϕ^{**}) is not a most general consistent concepts, and is eliminated.

Fig. 2. PRISM-concept: An algorithm for finding the most general consistent concepts

Figure 2 describes the procedure of finding a set of the most general consistent concepts based on the PRISM algorithm. This algorithm is thus called the PRISM-concept algorithm. PRISM-concept has a higher computational complexity than PRISM because of the concept construction process. It prunes the rule set to the most kernel by considering the subset relation of concept extensions. The set of the most general consistent concepts cannot be more simplified, as a result of its extension cannot be bigger, and its intension cannot be coarser.

4.5   Experiments

In order to evaluate the proposed PRISM-concept algorithm, we choose three sample datasets from UCI machine learning repository [10], and use SGI's MLC++ utilities 2.0 to generate categorical data [9]. We use 5-cross validation to divide training sets and testing sets, upon which the partition-based ID3, the covering-based PRISM, and the LCA-based PRISM-concept are tested for comparison. We keep track the number of rules, accuracy of both description and prediction for three datasets. The experimental results are reported in Figure 3.

The number of PRISM-concept rules is between which of ID3 and PRISM, due to the difference between the partition-based and the covering-based algorithms, and the nature of generalization capability of the concept-based rules. Since the

Cleve	1st			2nd			3rd			4th			5th		
303 records (training/testing: 243/60) 13 conditional attributes 2 decision classes	ID3	PRISM	PRISM-concept	ID3	PRISM	PRISM-concept	ID3	PRISM	PRISM-concept	ID3	PRISM	PRISM-concept	ID3	PRISM	PRISM-concept
# of rules	69	192	117	78	171	104	71	184	96	68	172	93	73	169	111
Acc. of description. (%)	98.35	98.35		97.94	98.35		98.77	99.18		98.35	98.77		97.94	98.35	
Acc. of prediction (%)	80.00	91.67	81.67	81.67	91.67	81.67	74.69	90.00	81.67	68.33	88.33	78.03	73.33	95.00	86.67

Vote	1st			2nd			3rd			4th			5th		
435 records (training/testing: 348/87) 16 conditional attributes 2 decision class	ID3	PRISM	PRISM-concept	ID3	PRISM	PRISM-concept	ID3	PRISM	PRISM-concept	ID3	PRISM	PRISM-concept	ID3	PRISM	PRISM-concept
# of rules	31	167	107	28	152	89	28	167	110	28	141	82	34	154	97
Acc. of description (%)	100	100		100	100		100	100		100	100		100	100	
Acc. of prediction (%)	94.25	97.70	97.70	88.51	96.55	95.40	90.80	96.55	96.55	89.66	97.70	97.70	91.95	100	98.85

Iris	1st			2nd			3rd			4th			5th		
150 records (training/testing: 120/30) 4 conditional attributes 3 decision class	ID3	PRISM	PRISM-concept	ID3	PRISM	PRISM-concept	ID3	PRISM	PRISM-concept	ID3	PRISM	PRISM-concept	ID3	PRISM	PRISM-concept
# of rules	5	14	9	6	13	9	6	13	9	6	12	9	6	13	9
Acc. of description (%)	96.67	96.67		97.50	97.50		97.50	97.50		98.33	98.33		97.50	97.50	
Acc. of prediction (%)	76.67	90.00	90.00	73.33	86.67	86.67	73.33	86.67	86.67	70.00	83.33	83.33	73.33	86.67	86.67

Fig. 3. Compare ID3, PRISM and PRISM-concept on three sample datasets

PRISM-concepts are generated from a set of PRISM rules, PRISM and PRISM-concept have the same description accuracy, and it is normally higher than what ID3 can reach. This indicates that for the purpose of keeping a higher description accuracy, we can greatly simplify the set of covering-based consistent rules by using a set of the most general consistent concept-rules.

The prediction accuracy of PRISM-concept rules is also between which of ID3 and PRISM. That is because PRISM has the greatest number of rules. That makes it more flexible to do testing, especially when error or missing records happen in testing datasets. As a fact that the intension of a most general consistent concept is the conjunction of all properties possessed by the extension, thus, it precisely describes the given training set, even might overfit the training set. Overfitting rules are good for description, but not good for testing.

Although we use the consistent classification tasks (i.e., $\phi \Rightarrow c_i$) as an example going through the paper, it does not mean that conjunctive concepts cannot cope with approximation classification tasks in general (i.e., $conf(\phi \Rightarrow c_i) \leq 1$).

Suppose $conf(\phi \Rightarrow c_i) = \alpha < 1$, where $c_i \in V_{class}$ is the class label satisfying the majority of the object set ϕ^*. If ϕ is a conjunctor, then the CDP (ϕ^*, ϕ) has $conf((\phi^*, \phi) \Rightarrow c_i) = \alpha$; and the conjunctive concept (ϕ^*, ϕ^{**}) has $conf((\phi^*, \phi^{**}) \Rightarrow c_i) = \alpha$, which is not a consistent concept. However, a super concept of (ϕ^*, ϕ^{**}), denoted as $(\widetilde{\phi^*, \phi^{**}})$, might or might not indicate the same class label c_i. If $conf((\widetilde{\phi^*, \phi^{**}}) \Rightarrow c_i)$ is satisfiable to the user, then the sub-concept (ϕ^*, ϕ^{**}) can be pruned.

5   Conclusion

Logical concept analysis provides an alternative way to study classification tasks. For consistent classification problems, a consistent classification rule corresponds to a conjunctively definable pair, each conjunctively definable pair corresponds to a conjunctively consistent concept, and each conjunctively consistent concept corresponds to a most general consistent concept. All the most general consistent concepts form a special set of consistent classification rules, which can describe the given universe precisely and concisely by its nature.

There are two approaches to find the set of the most general consistent concepts. One is from the concept lattice. The other is from a set of heuristic covering-based rules. The study shows that these two approaches can find a unique and complete set of the most general consistent concepts.

Logical concept analysis can also be applied for probabilistic classification problems. Though, to generalize a (inconsistent) concept to its super concept, in order to simplify the concept rule set, one needs to use more heuristics and thresholds. That is a research topic we set up for the next stage.

References

1. Cendrowska, J., PRISM: an algorithm for inducing modular rules, *International Journal of Man-Machine Studies*, 27, 349-370, 1987.
2. Clark, P. and Matwin, S., Using qualitative models to guide induction learning, *Proceedings of International Conference on Machine Learning*, 49-56, 1993.
3. Demri, S. and Orlowska, E., Logical analysis of indiscernibility, in: *Incomplete Information: Rough Set Analysis*, Orlowska, E. (Ed.), Physica-Verlag, Heidelberg, 347-380, 1998.
4. Ferré, S. and Ridoux, O., A logical generalization of formal concept analysis, *Proceedings of International Conference on Conceptual Structures*, 371-384, 2000.
5. Khan, M., Ding, Q., and Perrizo, W., K-nearest neighbor classification on spatial data streams using P-trees, *Proceedings of PAKDD'02*, 517-528, 2002.
6. Mitchell, T., *Version Spaces: An Approach to Concept Learning*, PhD thesis, Computer Science Department, Stanford University, Stanford, California, 1978.
7. Pawlak, Z., *Rough Sets: Theoretical Aspects of Reasoning about Data*, Kluwer Academic Publishers, Dordrecht, 1991.
8. Quinlan, J.R., Learning efficient classification procedures and their application to chess end-games, in: *Machine Learning: An Artificial Intelligence Approach*, 1, 463-482, 1983.
9. SGI's MLC++ utilities 2.0: the discretize utility. http://www.sgi.com/tech/mlc
10. UCI Machine Learning Repository.
    http://www1.ics.uci.edu/~mlearn/MLRepository.html
11. Wille, R., Concept lattices and conceptual knowledge systems, *Computers Mathematics with Applications*, 23, 493-515, 1992.
12. Yao, Y.Y., On Modeling data mining with granular computing, *Proceedings of COMPSAC'01*, 638-643, 2001.
13. Yao, Y.Y. and Yao, J.T., Granular computing as a basis for consistent classification problems, *Special Issue of PAKDD'02 Workshop on Toward the Foundation of Data Mining*, 5(2), 101-106, 2002.
14. Zhao, Y. and Yao, Y.Y., Interactive user-driven classification using a granule network, *Proceedings of the Fifth International Conference of Cognitive Informatics (ICCI05)*, 250-259, 2005.

Machine Learning in a Quantum World

Esma Aïmeur, Gilles Brassard, and Sébastien Gambs

Université de Montréal
Département d'informatique et de recherche opérationnelle
C.P. 6128, Succ. Centre-Ville, Montréal (Québec), H3C 3J7 Canada
{aimeur, brassard, gambsseb}@iro.umontreal.ca
http://www.iro.umontreal.ca/∼{aimeur, brassard, gambsseb}

Abstract. Quantum Information Processing (QIP) performs wonders in a world that obeys the laws of quantum mechanics, whereas Machine Learning (ML) is generally assumed to be done in a classical world. We initiate an investigation of the encounter of ML with QIP by defining and studying novel learning tasks that correspond to Machine Learning in a world in which the information is fundamentally quantum mechanical. We shall see that this paradigm shift has a profound impact on the learning process and that our classical intuition is often challenged.

1   Introduction

Quantum Information Processing (QIP) is the field that studies *the implication of quantum mechanics for information processing purposes.* Quantum information is very different from its classical counterpart: it cannot be measured reliably and it is disturbed by observation, but it can exist in a superposition of classical states. Classical and quantum information can be used together to realize wonders that are out of reach of classical information processing, such as being able to factorize efficiently large integers [21], search in an unstructured database with a quadratic speedup compared to the best classical algorithms [8] and allow two people to communicate in perfect secrecy under the nose of an eavesdropper having at her disposal unlimited computing power and technology [3].

Machine Learning (ML) is the field that studies techniques to *give to machines the ability to learn from past experience.* Typical tasks in ML include the ability to predict the class (*classification*) or some unobserved characteristic (*regression*) of an object based on some observations in *supervised learning*, or the ability to find some structure hidden within data (*clustering* or *density estimation*) in *unsupervised learning*. In general in ML, a machine is trained using a learning algorithm that takes as input a training dataset. This training dataset is implicitly assumed to be fundamentally classical, meaning that it contains "classical" observations about "classical" objects.

In this paper, we address the following question: What if the training dataset contains *quantum objects*? In particular what are the consequences for the learning process if we want to find analogues or develop new ML algorithms in this setting? The outline of the paper is as follows. In Section 2, we review some

L. Lamontagne and M. Marchand (Eds.): Canadian AI 2006, LNAI 4013, pp. 431–442, 2006.
© Springer-Verlag Berlin Heidelberg 2006

basic notions of QIP. In Section 3, we describe some previous encounters of ML and QIP before defining in Section 4 what learning could mean in the quantum context. We then illustrate our model in Section 5 by giving specific examples of clustering algorithms adapted to this new paradigm, including a simulated experiment. We conclude and state open problems in Section 6.

2   Review of Quantum Information Processing Concepts

In this section, we briefly review some essential notions of QIP [14]. A *qubit* (or *quantum bit*) is the quantum analogue of the classical bit. In contrast with its classical counterpart, a qubit can exist in a *superposition* of states. For instance, an electron can be *simultaneously* on two different orbits in some atom. Formally, using the Dirac notation, a qubit is described as $|\psi\rangle = \alpha|0\rangle + \beta|1\rangle$ where α and β are complex numbers called the *amplitudes* of classical states $|0\rangle$ and $|1\rangle$, respectively, subject to the *normalization* condition that $|\alpha|^2 + |\beta|^2 = 1$. When state $|\psi\rangle$ is *measured*, either $|0\rangle$ or $|1\rangle$ is observed, with probability $|\alpha|^2$ or $|\beta|^2$, respectively. Furthermore, measurements are *irreversible* because the state of the system *collapses* to whichever value ($|0\rangle$ or $|1\rangle$) has been observed, thus losing all memory of former amplitudes α and β.

All other operations allowed by quantum mechanics are *reversible* (and even *unitary*). They are represented by *gates*, much as in a classical circuit. For instance, the *Walsh–Hadamard* gate H maps $|0\rangle$ to $\frac{1}{\sqrt{2}}|0\rangle + \frac{1}{\sqrt{2}}|1\rangle$ and $|1\rangle$ to $\frac{1}{\sqrt{2}}|0\rangle - \frac{1}{\sqrt{2}}|1\rangle$. Figure 1 illustrates the notions seen so far, where time flows from left to right. Note that a *single line* carries quantum information, whereas a *double line* carries classical information; $\mathcal{M}$ denotes a measurement.

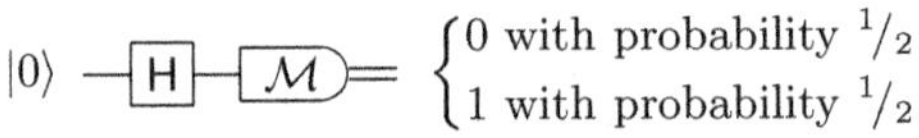

$$|0\rangle \;-\boxed{H}-\boxed{\mathcal{M}}= \begin{cases} 0 \text{ with probability } {}^1\!/_2 \\ 1 \text{ with probability } {}^1\!/_2 \end{cases}$$

Fig. 1. Example of a simple quantum circuit

In this very simple example, we apply a Walsh–Hadamard gate to state $|0\rangle$, which yields $\frac{1}{\sqrt{2}}|0\rangle + \frac{1}{\sqrt{2}}|1\rangle$. The measurement produces either 0 or 1, each with probability $|\frac{1}{\sqrt{2}}|^2 = {}^1\!/_2$, and the state collapses to the observed classical value.

The notion of qubit has a natural extension, which is the *quantum register*. A quantum register $|\psi\rangle$, composed of n qubits, lives in a 2^n-dimensional Hilbert space $\mathcal{H}$. Register $|\psi\rangle = \sum_{i=0}^{2^n-1} \alpha_i|i\rangle$ is specified by complex numbers $\alpha_0, \alpha_1, \ldots, \alpha_{2^n-1}$ subject to normalization condition $\sum |\alpha_i|^2 = 1$. Here, basis state $|i\rangle$ denotes the binary encoding of integer i. The *tensor product* $\otimes$ is used to represent the *composition* of two quantum systems. For instance, if we have two quantum states $|\psi\rangle = \alpha|0\rangle + \beta|1\rangle$ and $|\phi\rangle = \gamma|0\rangle + \delta|1\rangle$ and we put them next to each other, we can describe the composite system as $|\Gamma\rangle = |\psi\rangle \otimes |\phi\rangle = \alpha\gamma|00\rangle + \alpha\delta|01\rangle + \beta\gamma|10\rangle + \beta\delta|11\rangle$. As a shorthand notation, we write $|\psi\rangle^{\otimes k}$ for a quantum register composed of k identical copies of state $|\psi\rangle$.

Fig. 2. SWAP gate   **Fig. 3.** Control-U gate

Unitary operations can also be applied to two or more qubits. For example, Fig. 2 illustrates a SWAP gate, which exchanges the qubits on its wires. Another kind of unitary gate frequently encountered in QIP is the *Control*-U gate, illustrated in Fig. 3: operation U is performed on the bottom wire, known as the *target*, if and only if the top wire, known as the *source*, is set to $|1\rangle$.

The *density matrix* is a formalism used to represent *one's knowledge about a particular quantum system*. It is a *complete* description of what can be observed about it. If we know that a quantum system is in a specific state $|\psi\rangle$, then its density matrix ρ is equal to $|\psi\rangle\langle\psi|$, where $\langle\psi|$ is the *conjugate transpose* of $|\psi\rangle$, the latter being considered as a column vector in the Hilbert space. In this case, ρ is said to be *pure*. A *mixed* state is a probability distribution over an ensemble $\{(p_1, |\psi_1\rangle), \ldots, (p_k, |\psi_k\rangle)\}$ of pure states, subject to $\sum_{i=1}^{k} p_i = 1$, where p_i is the probability associated with pure state $|\psi_i\rangle$. The density matrix ρ corresponding to this mixture is defined as $\sum_{i=1}^{k} p_i|\psi_i\rangle\langle\psi_i|$.

Two fundamental theorems set limits on what can be done with a quantum state. The *no-cloning theorem* [23] prevents us from cloning perfectly an unknown (or partially known) quantum state unless it is known to belong to a set of pairwise orthogonal states. A consequence of *Holevo's Theorem* [12] states that it is impossible to extract more than n bits of classical information from n qubits. Therefore, although n qubits need an exponential number 2^n of amplitudes to be described, only a linear amount of information can be extracted from them. Quantum information features many additional intriguing non-classical properties, such as *entanglement* and *interference*. See [14].

3   Previous Encounters of Machine Learning with Quantum Information Processing

In any field of computer science, it is natural to ask whether or not it is possible, using the QIP paradigm, to obtain more efficient and more powerful information processing capabilities. For example, we can seek faster algorithms, or savings on the communication cost in distributed contexts, or security upgrading in cryptographic settings, etc. When looking specifically at ML and QIP, there are several ways one could imagine to try mixing them. From a theoretical point of view, some work has already been done in computational learning theory that compares learnability in the classical and the quantum settings. Two models have been generalized to the quantum world: the Probably Approximately Correct (PAC) learning model of Valiant [22] and the model of exact learning from membership queries of Angluin [1].

According to the quantum analogues of these models, the goal is to infer properties of a function f, whose access is provided through a quantum *oracle* that can be queried in a superposition of questions. Servedio and Gortler have studied both Valiant's and Anguluin's models and proved interesting results [20]. One of their discoveries is that the quantum paradigm does *not* provide any advantage in exact learning from membership queries or in PAC learning, if we care only about the number of queries: every function (concept) that can be "learned" (in the specific sense given in each of these models) with a polynomial number of quantum queries can also be learned with a polynomial number of classical queries. However, this equivalence does not hold for *computing time*: Servedio [19] has constructed an explicit class of concepts that are *polynomial-time learnable from quantum membership queries but not from classical queries*, based on the cryptographic assumption that one-way functions exist.

Other previous encounters of ML with QIP include the definition of quantum analogues for ML approaches such as neural networks [6], the design of classical clustering algorithms inspired from quantum mechanics [13], the application of the maximum likelihood principle to quantum channel modelling [24], etc.

4   Learning in a Quantum World

4.1   Training with a Quantum Dataset

Machine learning algorithms learn from a training dataset, which is given as input to the algorithm. The dataset contains observations about objects, which were obtained empirically or acquired from experts. In the *classical* setting, the observations and the objects are implicitly considered to be classical. In the case of *supervised* learning, the training dataset can be described as $D_n = \{(\mathbf{x}_1, y_1), \ldots, (\mathbf{x}_n, y_n)\}$, where $\mathbf{x}_i$ would be some *observations* on the *characteristics* of the ith object (or data point) and y_i is the corresponding *class* of that object. As a typical example, each object can be described using d real-valued attributes and we are dealing with binary classification. In this case $\mathbf{x}_i \in \mathbb{R}^d$ and $y_i \in \{-1, +1\}$. The main difference between supervised and *unsupervised* learning is that in the latter case the y_i values are unknown. This could mean that we know the possible labels in general but not the *specific* label of each data point, or that even the number of classes and their labels are unknown to us.

In a quantum world, a ML algorithm still needs a training dataset from which to perform learning, but this dataset now contains *quantum* objects. This forces us to rethink the entire learning process because quantum information obeys different physical laws, compared to classical information. Quantum mechanically, a training dataset containing n quantum states can be described as $D_n = \{(|\psi_1\rangle, y_1), \ldots, (|\psi_n\rangle, y_n)\}$, where $|\psi_i\rangle$ is the ith quantum state of the training set and y_i is the corresponding class of that quantum state. A typical example occurs when a quantum state lives in a Hilbert space formed by d qubits: $|\psi_i\rangle \in \mathbb{C}^{2^d}$ and $y_i \in \{-1, +1\}$ for binary classification. Even though we restrict ourselves to classical classes in this work, further generalization would be possible in which objects can be in a quantum superposition of classes.

Imagine a scenario in which a space probe has been sent away from Earth. In its exploration process, the probe encounters various quantum phenomena, from which it samples to constitute a training dataset. The samples could be labelled by the origin of the quantum phenomenon (*supervised learning*), or left unlabelled if their source is unknown (*unsupervised learning*). Afterwards, the probe would search for an intrinsic hidden structure within the quantum data.

4.2   Learning Classes

There are many ways in which quantum states can be specified in the training dataset. To this end, we introduce several learning classes that differ in the form of the training dataset, the learner's technological sophistication and his learning goal. For learning class $L_{goal}^{context}$, subscript *goal* refers to the learning goal and superscript *context* to the training dataset and/or the learner's abilities. Possible values for *goal* are c, which stands for doing ML with a classical purpose, and q for ML with a quantum purpose. The superscript *context* can be c for "classical" if everything is classical (with a possible exception for the goal) or q if something "quantum" is going on. Other values for *context* can be used when we need to be more specific. For example, L_c^c corresponds to ML in the usual sense, in which we want to use classical means to learn from classical observations about classical objects. Another example is L_c^q, in which we have access to a quantum computer for help but the goal remains to perform a classical ML task: the quantum computer could serve to speed up the ML process.

We are more concerned with the case of "*goal* $= q$". The simplest instance corresponds to L_q^c, which is defined as the quantum learning class in which all the training set quantum state descriptions are given classically (i.e. $D_n = \{(\psi_1, y_1), \dots, (\psi_n, y_n)\}$, where ψ_i is the classical description of quantum state $|\psi_i\rangle$). Learning becomes more challenging when the dataset is available only in its quantum form, in which case more copies make life easier. Class $L_q^{\otimes k}$ is defined as the learning class in which we are given k copies of each training quantum state (i.e. $D_n = \{(|\psi_1\rangle^{\otimes k}, y_1), \dots, (|\psi_n\rangle^{\otimes k}, y_n)\}$; recall that $|\psi_i\rangle^{\otimes k}$ symbolizes k copies of state $|\psi_i\rangle$). Contrast these classes with ML in a classical world (such as L_c^c), in which additional copies of an object are obviously useless.

4.3   Possible Learning Strategies

Several types of strategies can be imagined, depending on the learning class and the task we wish to realize. Here, we study the case of *binary* classification for the purpose of illustrating the strategies with a "concrete" example. Consider the quantum classification task of predicting the class of an unknown quantum state $|\psi_?\rangle$ given a *single copy of this state* (This constraint can be relaxed by considering the case of multiple copies of the state to be classified—see the *quantum template matching* problem of [17]). The easiest situation occurs when $D_n \in L_q^c$ since we have complete classical knowledge of the *training* states. Despite this advantage, it is not possible in general to devise a process that would always classify correctly unknown quantum states even should they be known to be identical to one of the training states (see last paragraph in Section 4.5). Nevertheless, when $D_n \in L_q^c$, it is possible to analytically devise the optimal measurement that minimizes the training error. It remains to be seen how well such an approach would fare when faced with a new quantum state. Alternatively, in some cases, we can devise an *unambiguous discrimination* measurement, which would never give the wrong classification for objects in the training set, but would sometimes refuse to answer at all. This is analogous to the classical case in which a classifier has to either predict class "−1" or "+1" with the highest possible confidence, but is allowed to abstain (by answering "0") when it has low confidence in its best prediction.

If $D_n \in L_q^{\otimes k}$ then possible strategies include: (1) estimate the training set quantum states by making measurements (joint or not) on some copies; (2) devise a classification mechanism that uses copies of the training set quantum states only at the time of demand (i.e. when the time to classify $|\psi_?\rangle$ comes); or (3) compose a hybrid strategy based on (1) and (2).

Note that strategy (1) corresponds to the concept of *quantum tomography*, in which one tries to reconstruct as faithfully as possible the classical description of a quantum state from a finite number of copies of this state. Strategy (2) is unique to the quantum world and we call a classifier resulting from this strategy a *one-time classifier* because we sacrifice some parts of the training set when the classification need arises. Using this strategy, once the classification is done, the information contained in the sacrificed part of the training set is lost forever. This has no classical counterpart because nothing in principle prevents a classical classifier from being used an unbounded number of times. A hybrid strategy (3) could be built on the advantages of both previous strategies, for instance by acquiring some classical knowledge about the training set by performing state estimation and then using this knowledge in the design of a one-time classifier.

We have considered in this paper only the case of binary classification. Moving to the multiclass setting has to be done with care [18], even more so if we consider quantum classes that can be in a superposition.

4.4 Hierarchy of Quantum Learning Classes

The different quantum learning classes form a hierarchy in an information-theoretic sense, meaning that the higher a class is located in the hierarchy, the potentially better classification of an unknown state it allows. The class L_q^c is at the top of the hierarchy since it corresponds to *complete knowledge* about the quantum states in the training set. Let $\equiv_\ell$, $\leq_\ell$ and $<_\ell$ denote the *equivalence*, the *weaker or equal* and the *strictly weaker* relationships within the hierarchy, respectively. The following statements are obvious.

- $L_q^{\otimes k} \equiv_\ell L_q^c$ as $k \to \infty$.
- $L_q^{\otimes 1} \leq_\ell \ldots \leq_\ell L_q^{\otimes k} \leq_\ell L_q^{\otimes k+1} \leq_\ell \ldots \leq_\ell L_q^c$.
- $L_q^{\otimes k} + L_q^{\otimes 1} \leq_\ell L_q^{\otimes k+1}$, where "+" denotes a restriction that the first k copies must be measured separately from the the last.

The interesting question is whether or not this hierarchy is strict: can all these $\leq_\ell$ be replaced by $<_\ell$? There are good reasons to believe that the answer is positive since it is usually the case that more information can be obtained about a quantum state when more copies are available, and it has been proven in some cases that joint measurements are more informative than individual measurements [15, 5]. But it does not *necessarily* follow that this additional classical information provides for a better quantum classifier when the time comes to identify unknown state $|\psi_?\rangle$.

4.5 Bounds on the Training Error

Let m_- be the number of quantum states in D_n for which $y_i = -1$ (negative class) and its complement m_+ be the number of states in D_n for which $y_i = +1$ (positive class), with $m_- + m_+ = n$, the total number of data points in D_n. The mixture ρ_- is defined as $\frac{1}{m_-} \sum_{i=1}^{n} \frac{1-y_i}{2} |\psi_i\rangle\langle\psi_i|$ and the mixture ρ_+ as $\frac{1}{m_+} \sum_{i=1}^{n} \frac{1+y_i}{2} |\psi_i\rangle\langle\psi_i|$. If $D_n \in L_q^c$, the problem of classifying an unknown state $|\psi_?\rangle$ taken from the training set is equivalent to distinguishing between ρ_- and ρ_+. The success probability of this classification process is linked to the *statistical overlap* of these distributions. In fact, this kind of problem has already been studied in *quantum detection and estimation theory* [10], a field that predates QIP itself. Some results from this field can be used to *give bounds on the best training error* we could hope for from a ML algorithm. For instance, the probability of distinguishing between the two classes with the optimal quantum process is bounded above by $(1 + D(\rho_-, \rho_+))/2$, where $D(\rho_-, \rho_+) = \mathrm{Tr}|p_-\rho_- - p_+\rho_+|$ is a distance measure between ρ_- and ρ_+ due to Helstrom [10] (here, p_- and p_+ represent the *a priori* probabilities of ρ_- and ρ_+, respectively). For unambiguous discrimination, bounds have been developed much more recently [11]. The goal of a ML algorithm in the quantum setting is to give a constructive way to come close to (or to achieve) these bounds.

Note that, contrary to classical ML, where it is always possible—albeit not always advisable—to bring the training error down to zero (for instance using a memory-based classifier such as 1-nearest neighbour), it is *impossible to do so in the quantum case* unless the states of the training set are pairwise orthogonal.

5   Illustration: Clustering with a Quantum Dataset

5.1   Measure of Distance Between Quantum States

The quantity $Fid(|\psi\rangle, |\phi\rangle) = |\langle\phi|\psi\rangle|^2$ is an important notion in QIP, which is called the *fidelity*. Note that the fidelity is similar to a measure commonly used in *classical* information retrieval, namely the *cosine similarity*. The fidelity is a *similarity measure* between two quantum states, which ranges from 0 if they are orthogonal (meaning perfectly distinguishable) to 1 if the states are identical. Properties of the fidelity [14, §9.2.2] include *symmetry*, $Fid(|\psi\rangle, |\phi\rangle) = Fid(|\phi\rangle, |\psi\rangle)$, and *invariance under unitary operations*, meaning that applying the same unitary operation U on two different quantum states does not change their fidelity: $Fid(|\mathsf{U}\psi\rangle, |\mathsf{U}\phi\rangle) = Fid(|\psi\rangle, |\phi\rangle)$. In its standard form, the fidelity is not really a metric because it does not obey the triangle inequality, but it can be made to do so if we use $Dist(|\psi\rangle, |\phi\rangle) = \arccos Fid(|\psi\rangle, |\phi\rangle)$.

The value of $Dist(|\psi\rangle, |\phi\rangle)$ ranges from 0 if the states are identical to $\frac{\pi}{2}$ if they are orthogonal. This *distance* now respects the triangle inequality $Dist(|\psi\rangle, |\phi\rangle) \leq Dist(|\psi\rangle, |\varphi\rangle) + Dist(|\varphi\rangle, |\phi\rangle)$.

5.2 Control-Swap as a Fidelity Estimator

The Control-Swap test (C-Swap test) [2, 4] makes it possible to estimate the similarity between two unknown quantum states $|\psi\rangle$ and $|\phi\rangle$, as measured by their fidelity $Fid(|\psi\rangle, |\phi\rangle)$. Figure 4 illustrates this concept.

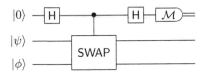

Fig. 4. Circuit of the Control-SWAP test

The input to the circuit is $|0\rangle|\psi\rangle|\phi\rangle$. After applying the first Walsh–Hadamard gate H, the state evolves to the superposition $\frac{1}{\sqrt{2}}|0\rangle|\psi\rangle|\phi\rangle + \frac{1}{\sqrt{2}}|1\rangle|\psi\rangle|\phi\rangle$. Application of the C-Swap gate, exchanges $|\psi\rangle$ and $|\phi\rangle$ if the state of the upper wire is $|1\rangle$. Therefore, the state evolves to $\frac{1}{\sqrt{2}}|0\rangle|\psi\rangle|\phi\rangle + \frac{1}{\sqrt{2}}|1\rangle|\phi\rangle|\psi\rangle$. Afterwards, the second Walsh–Hadamard gate H transforms the state to $\frac{1}{2}|0\rangle(|\psi\rangle|\phi\rangle + |\phi\rangle|\psi\rangle) + \frac{1}{2}|1\rangle(|\psi\rangle|\phi\rangle - |\phi\rangle|\psi\rangle)$. Finally, measurement of the top qubit yields classical outcome 0 with probability 1 if $|\psi\rangle$ and $|\phi\rangle$ are identical. In general, the measurement outcome is 1 with probability $\frac{1}{2} - \frac{1}{2}|\langle\phi|\psi\rangle|^2$. It follows that the C-Swap test provides an *estimator* for the *fidelity* between $|\psi\rangle$ and $|\phi\rangle$. With k copies of these states, we can estimate $Fid(|\psi\rangle, |\phi\rangle)$ as $1 - 2 \times \#|1\rangle/k$. Note that a side effect of the C-Swap test is to irreversibly disturb the input states, unless they happened to be identical.

5.3 Examples of Possible Quantum Clustering Algorithms

If $D_n \in L_q^{\otimes k}$, the most obvious strategy for clustering the training set of quantum states would follow the "type (1)" approach outlined in Section 4.3: By way of quantum tomography, use all the available copies in order to reconstruct a classical description of each training state. A classical clustering algorithm could then be applied on the resulting approximate descriptions. Obviously, the accuracy of this approach is limited by that of the classically estimated quantum states. Fortunately, this is a well-studied problem.

The optimal mean fidelity achievable for the reconstructed state $|\psi_{guess}\rangle$, compared to the true state $|\psi_{true}\rangle$, is a function of the dimension of the state and of the number of copies. The exact formula is $Fid(|\psi_{guess}\rangle, |\psi_{true}\rangle) = \frac{k+1}{k+d}$, where k is the number of available copies and d the dimension of the Hilbert space (see [9] for an interesting discussion on the subject). This means that in order to achieve good fidelity in the reconstruction, an exponential number of copies in the number of qubits is required. In the case when d is small and k is large, this tomographic approach can generate a reasonably faithful classical description of the state. From this classical description, it is possible to compute directly (i.e. using a classical computer), the fidelity between two quantum states. From there, classical clustering algorithms can be used.

Recall that the main goal of clustering is to *group similar objects together* while *putting objects that are dissimilar into different clusters*. Thus, it should be intuitively clear that the approach to clustering outlined above is wasteful of the precious quantum resources. Indeed, there is no need to determine a classical approximation of two quantum states if the genuine purpose of the operation is merely to estimate the distance between them according to some metric. A more promising approach to quantum clustering is to estimate that distance directly through a joint measurement of the two quantum states. The simplest way to do this (but not necessarily the best) is to use the C-Swap test of Section 5.2 to estimate fidelity as a measure of distance.

For example, if we are in $L_q^{\otimes(n-1)e}$, we can estimate the fidelity between each pair of states in the training dataset by applying the C-Swap test e times independently for each pair. We could then use a classical algorithm, such as *k-medians*, to perform clustering. In the next section, we report on a simulated experiment along these lines.

Other strategies can be devised, which are even more quantum. For instance, we could adapt a classical algorithm to the quantum setting, such as an *agglomerative algorithm* that would grow clusters around *quantum seeds* in an adaptive manner. This algorithm first sacrifices some parts of the training set during the seeding phase to identify states whose pairwise dissimilarity is high, which will be used as seeds. During the second phase, each state is compared to the seeds using the C-Swap test estimation and agglomerated around the most similar one.

5.4 Experimentation

In this section, we present some preliminary results on a very simple clustering experiment. As a proof of concept, we chose to test on synthetic data an algorithm based on the C-Swap test outlined in the previous section. The data is composed of five clusters. Each cluster is centred on a 13-qubit pure state generated randomly and uniformly according to the Haar measure in a 8192-dimensional Hilbert space. For each cluster, twenty pure states were obtained by applying a random perturbation to the cluster centre so that the fidelity of the resulting states with the cluster centre were never below some threshold, henceforth called the *fidelity threshold*. Note that we can make the clustering problem more difficult by lowering this threshold since this results in less dense clusters, which can even overlap when the fidelity threshold is too low.

We used the C-Swap test to estimate the fidelity between each pair of states in the training set. The greater the number of samples are available for the C-Swap test, the more accurate is the resulting estimate. However, there is no need to estimate those fidelities with exceedingly high precision (which would be too expensive in the required number of copies) because a rough estimate of the

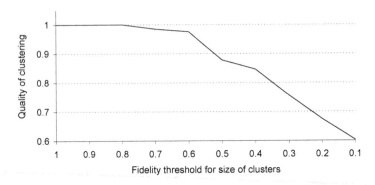

Fig. 5. Evolution of the clustering quality (averaged over 5 trials) as the fidelity threshold decreases. A quality value of 1 indicates perfect clustering. Random "clustering" would correspond to a quality of approximately 0.37, below this curve.

similarity between states is generally sufficient in order to group similar objects in the same cluster and to put dissimilar objects in different clusters.

After generating the 100 pure states as described above, we permuted them randomly and we removed all information as to which was their initial cluster. The first clustering phase consisted in building a *similarity matrix* in which each entry (x, y) represented the estimated fidelity between states x and y. The fidelity between each pair of states was estimated using the C-Swap test with 20 samples, which corresponds roughly to an absolute error of 0.15 in the fidelity estimates. During the second clustering phase, the similarity matrix was given as input to a classical clustering algorithm inspired by k-medians. This algorithm selected five states at random as cluster centres (we told the algorithm the original number of clusters) and then performed iteratively two steps until stabilization (or quasi-stabilization). In the first step, states were assigned to their most similar centre; in the second step, the centre of each cluster was recomputed by selecting the point that maximized its similarity with the other points of the cluster.

The *quality* of this clustering process was measured by determining how well points that were originally in the same cluster were still together and conversely how well points that were originally in different clusters remained separated. For this purpose, we used a metric ranging from 1 if all the points are perfectly placed after clustering to -1 if they are completely messed up. According to this metric, a completely random "clustering", in which each state would be assigned to a random cluster, exhibits an average "quality" of approximately 37%.

Figure 5 summarizes the results obtained for different values of the fidelity threshold. As expected, the quality of the clustering process is at its best when the fidelity threshold is high, because in this case the original clusters form tightly packed balls that are far from each other. This quality remains above 97% even for a fidelity threshold as low as 0.6. The quality continues to decrease with the fidelity threshold, reaching a level of roughly 60% for a fidelity threshold of 0.1. Note that this is not very good compared to the worthless quality of 37% obtained by random "clustering". This phenomenon is due partly to the fact that clusters start to overlap as the fidelity threshold decreases, and also to the imperfect quality of the estimates obtained using the C-Swap test. Naturally, if one is not satisfied with those C-Swap estimates, there is always the option of sacrificing more copies of the training states to refine the estimates.

6   Conclusions and Open Problems

In this paper, we have described a novel task and a new learning model that corresponds to performing ML in a world in which information behaves according to the laws of quantum mechanics—which is, of course, *the* real world. Using quantum information has a great impact on the learning process and many of our classical ML intuitions are being challenged in this world. On the other hand, this model offers many interesting questions and perspectives, and studying it could lead to insights both in ML and QIP. For practical purposes, quantum ML algorithms have the potential to give a constructive answer to some detection scenarios. From a theoretical viewpoint, studying this model could lead to discoveries about the notion of learning from a generic perspective and how it is linked to the underlying physical theory on which it is based.

We have illustrated our model by showing some examples of clustering algorithms, but algorithms for other ML tasks can also been designed. Currently, we are developing quantum versions of ID3 [16] and AdaBoost [7] for classification by exploiting, respectively, the relationship between Shannon and von Neumann entropy, and the resemblance between the notions of weak classifier and weak measurement. We conclude this paper by mentioning but a few of our many open problems: define analogues of classical notions of ML to the quantum setting such as the *test* and the *generalization errors* or the *margin*, study the different models of classical and quantum *noise* (see [14, §8.3] for different forms of quantum noise) and how they affect the robustness of the quantum ML algorithms, improve classical ML algorithms with quantum computation or devise brand new algorithms adapted to this setting, study and define other classes of learning such as when the training set is composed of mixed states, etc.

Acknowledgements

The authors are supported in parts by the Natural Sciences and Engineering Research Council of Canada. Gilles Brassard is also supported by the Canadian Institute for Advanced Research and the Canada Research Chair Programme.

References

1. Angluin, D., "Queries and concept learning", *Machine Learning* **2**, pp. 319–342, 1988.
2. Barenco, A., Berthiaume, A., Deutsch, D., Ekert, A., Jozsa, R. and Macchiavello, C., "Stabilisation of quantum computations by symmetrisation", *SIAM Journal of Computing* **26**(5), pp. 1541–1557, 1997.

3. Bennett, C. H. and Brassard, G., "Quantum cryptography: Public key distribution and coin tossing", *Proceedings of IEEE International Conference on Computers, Systems and Signal Processing*, Bangalore, pp. 175–179, 1984.
4. Buhrman, H., Cleve, R., Watrous, J. and de Wolf, R., "Quantum fingerprinting", *Physical Reviews Letters* **87**(16), article 167902, 2001.
5. Chiribella, G., Mauro D'Ariano, G., Perinotti, P. and Sacchi, M., "Covariant quantum measurements which maximize the likelihood", *Physical Reviews A* **70**, article 061205, 2004.
6. Ezhov, A. A. and Berman, G. P., *Introduction to Quantum Neural Technologies*, Rinton Press, 2003.
7. Freund, Y. and Shapire, R., "A decision-theoretic generalization of on-line learning and an application to boosting", *Journal of Computer and System Sciences* **55**(1), pp. 119–139, 1997.
8. Grover, L. K., "Quantum mechanics helps in searching for a needle in a haystack", *Physical Review Letters* **79**, pp. 325–328, 1997.
9. Hayashi, A., Hashimoto, T. and Horibe, M., "Reexamination of optimal quantum state estimation of pure states", *Physical Reviews A* **72**, article 032325, 2005.
10. Helstrom, C. W., *Quantum Detection and Estimation Theory*, Academic Press, 1976.
11. Herzog, U. and Bergou, J. A., "Optimal unambiguous discrimination of two mixed quantum states", *Physical Reviews A* **71**, article 050301, 2005.
12. Holevo, A. S., "Bounds for the quantity of information transmitted by a quantum mechanical channel", *Problems of Information Transmissions* **9**, pp. 177–183, 1973.
13. Horn, D. and Gottlieb, A., "The method of quantum clustering", *Proceedings of the Conference Neural Information Processing Systems (NIPS)*, pp. 769–776, 2001.
14. Nielsen, M. A. and Chuang, I. L., *Quantum Computation and Quantum Information*, Cambridge University Press, 2000.
15. Peres, A. and Wootters, W. K., "Optimal detection of quantum information", *Physical Reviews Letters* **66**(9), pp. 1119–1122, 1991.
16. Quinlan, J. R., "Induction of decision trees", *Machine Learning* **1**, pp. 81–106, 1986.
17. Sasaki, M. and Carlini, A., "Quantum learning and universal quantum matching machine", *Physical Reviews A* **66**(2), article 022303, 2002.
18. Sen, P., "Random measurement bases, quantum state distinction and applications to the hidden subgroup problem", *Proceedings of 21st Annual IEEE Conference on Computational Complexity (CCC)*, to appear, 2006.
19. Servedio, R., "Separating quantum and classical learning", *Proceedings of the International Conference on Automata, Languages and Programming (ICALP)*, pp. 1065–1080, 2001.
20. Servedio, R. and Gortler, A., "Equivalences and separations between quantum and classical learnability", *SIAM Journal of Computing* **33**(5), pp. 1067–1092, 2004.
21. Shor, P. W., "Polynomial-time algorithms for prime factorization and discrete logarithms on a quantum computer", *SIAM Journal of Computing* **26**, pp. 1484–1509, 1997.
22. Valiant, L. G., "A theory of the learnable", *Communications of the ACM* **27**, pp. 1134–1142, 1984.
23. Wootters, W. K. and Žurek, W. C., "A single quantum cannot be cloned", *Nature* **66**, pp. 802–803, 1982.
24. Ziman, M., Plesch, M., Bužek, V. and Štelmachovič, P., "Process reconstruction: From unphysical to physical maps via maximum likelihood", *Physical Reviews A* **71**, article 022106, 2005.

A New Attempt to Silhouette-Based Gait Recognition for Human Identification

Murat Ekinci

Computer Vision Lab.,
Department of Computer Engineering,
Karadeniz Technical University, Trabzon, Turkey
ekinci@ktu.edu.tr

Abstract. Human identification at distance by analysis of gait patterns extracted from video has recently become very popular research in biometrics. This paper presents multi-projections based approach to extract gait patterns for human recognition. Binarized silhouette of a motion object is represented by 1-D signals which are the basic image features called the distance vectors. The distance vectors are differences between the bounding box and silhouette, and extracted using four projections to silhouette. Eigenspace transformation is applied to time-varying distance vectors and the statistical distance based supervised pattern classification is then performed in the lower-dimensional eigenspace for human identification. A fusion strategy developed is finally executed to produce final decision. Based on normalized correlation on the distance vectors, gait cycle estimation is also performed to extract the gait cycle. Experimental results on four databases demonstrate that the right person in top two matches 100% of the times for the cases where training and testing sets corresponds to the same walking styles, and in top three-four matches 100% of the times for training and testing sets corresponds to the different walking styles.

1 Introduction

Gait recognition is the term typically used in the computer community to refer to the automatic extraction of visual cues that characterize the motion of a walking person in video and is used for identification purpose in surveillance [1][2][3][4][7]. Often in surveillance applications, it is difficult to get face information at the resolution required for recognition. As for gait is one of the few biometrics and a behavioral biometric source that can be measured at a distance.

Gait recognition methods can be broadly divided into two groups, model based and silhouette based approaches. Model based approaches [3][16] recover explicit features describing gait dynamics, such as stride dimensions and the kinematics of joint angles. The silhouette approach [7] [8][9][2], characterizes body movement by the statistics of the patterns produced by walking. These patterns capture both the static and dynamic properties of body shape.

In this paper, it is attempted to develop a simple but effective representation of silhouette for gait-based human identification using silhouette analysis. Similar

L. Lamontagne and M. Marchand (Eds.): Canadian AI 2006, LNAI 4013, pp. 443–454, 2006.
© Springer-Verlag Berlin Heidelberg 2006

observations have been made in [8][9][2], but the idea presented here implicitly captures both structural (appearances) and transitional (dynamics) characteristics of gait. A more robust approach for gait cycle estimation which is very important step in gait recognition is also presented. Instead of width/length time signal of bounding box of moving silhouette usually used in existing gait period analysis [3][10][11][2], here we analyze four projections extracted directly from differences between silhouette and the bounding box, and further convert them into associated four 1D signals. The novel approach presented is basically to produce the distance vectors, which are four 1-D signals are extracted for each projections, they are top-, bottom-, left-, and right-projections. Then normalized correlation-based a similarity function is executed to estimate gait cycle of moving silhouette. As following main purpose, depending on four distance vectors, PCA based gait recognition algorithm is first performed. A statistical distance based similarity is then achieved to obtain similarity measures on training and testing data. Next, fusion strategies on that similarities are calculated to produce final decision. Robust results for human identification have been obtained at the experiments on four different databases.

2   Gait Feature Extraction and Classification

Given a sequence of images obtained from a static camera, the moving person is first detected and tracked to compute the corresponding sequence of motion regions in each frame. Motion segmentation is achieved via background modeling/subtraction using a dynamic background frame estimated and updated in time, more details are given in [6]. Then a morphological filter operator is applied to the resulting images to suppress spurious pixel values. Once a silhouette generated, a bounding box is placed around silhouette. Silhouette across a motion sequence are automatically aligned by scaling and cropping based on the bounding box.

2.1   Gait Signature Extraction

Silhouette representation is based on the projections to silhouette which is generated from a sequence of binary silhouette images $bs(t) = bs(x,y,t)$, indexed spatially by pixel location (x,y) and temporally by time t. There are four different image features called the distance vectors. They are top-, bottom-, left- and right-distance vectors. The distance vectors are the differences between the bounding box and the outer contour of silhouette. An example silhouette and the distance vectors corresponding to four projections are shown in the middle of figure 1. The distance vectors are separately represented by four 1D signals. The size of 1D signals for left-right projections is equal to the height of the bounding box. For the top-bottom projections, it is equal to the width of the bounding box. The data in that signals are the number of columns at each row and the number of the rows at each column in which between bounding box and silhouette for left-right-projections, and for top-bottom projections, respectively.

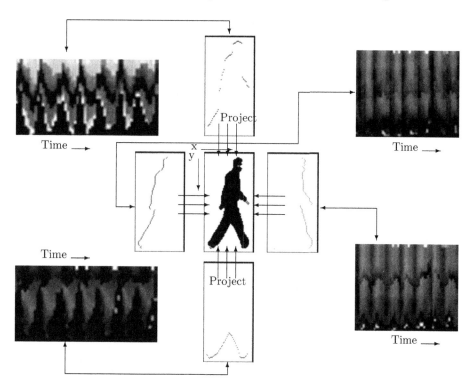

Fig. 1. Silhouette representation. (**Middle**) Silhouette and four projections, (**Left**) temporal plot of the distance vectors for top and bottom projections, (**Right**) temporal plot of the distance vectors for left and right projections.

Form a new 2D image $F_T(x,t) = \sum_y \overline{bs}(x,y,t)$, where each column (indexed by time t) is the top-projections (row sum) of silhouette image $bs(t)$, as shown in figure 1.top-left. The meaning of $\overline{bs}(x,y,t)$ is complement of silhouette shape, that is empty pixels in the bounding box. Each value $F_T(x,t)$ is then a count of the number of rows empty pixels between the top side of the bounding box and the outer contours in that columns x of silhouette image $bs(t)$. The result is a 2D pattern, formed by stacking row projections (from top of the bounding box to silhouette) together to form a spatio-temporal pattern. A second pattern which represents the bottom-projection $F_B(x,t) = \sum_{-y} \overline{bs}(x,y,t)$ can be constructed by stacking row projections (from bottom to silhouette), as shown in figure 1.bottom-left. The third pattern $F_L(y,t) = \sum_x \overline{bs}(x,y,t)$ is then constructed by stacking columns projections (from left of the bounding box to silhouette) and the last pattern $F_R(y,t) = \sum_{-x} \overline{bs}(x,y,t)$ is also finally constructed by stacking columns projections (from right to silhouette), as shown in figure 1.top-right and bottom-right 2D patterns, respectively. The variation of each component of the each distance vectors can be regarded as gait signature of that object. From the temporal distance vector plots, it is clear that the distance vector is roughly periodic and gives the extent of movement of different part of the subject. The brighter a pixel in 2D patterns in figure 1, the larger value is the value of the distance vector in that position.

2.2   Training

The representation of 2D silhouette shape by four 1D signals, called distance vectors, significantly reduces the subsequent computational cost. To eliminate the influence of spatial scale and signal length of the distance vectors, the algorithm scales these distance vector signals with respect to magnitude and size through the sizes of the bounding boxes. Next, eigenspace transformation based on Principal Component Analysis (PCA) is applied to time varying distance vectors derived from a sequence of silhouette images to reduce the dimensionality of the input feature space. The training process similar to [2][5] is illustrated as follows:

Given k class for training, and each class represents a sequence of the distance vector signals of a person in one gait cycle. Multiple sequences of each person can be separately added for training. Let $V_{i,j}^w$ be the jth distance vector signal in the ith class for w projection to silhouette and N_i the number of such distance vector signals in the ith class. The total number of training samples is $N_t^w = N_1^w + N_2^w + ... + N_k^w$, as the whole training set can be represented by $[V_{1,1}^w, V_{1,2}^w, .., V_{1,N_1}^w, V_{2,1}^w, ..., V_{k,N_k}^w]$. The mean m_v^w and the global covariance matrix $\sum^w$ of w projection training set can easily be obtained by

$$m_v^w = \frac{1}{N_t^w} \sum_{i=1}^{k} \sum_{j=1}^{N_i^w} V_{i,j}^w \tag{1}$$

$$\sum^w = \frac{1}{N_t^w} \sum_{i=1}^{k} \sum_{j=1}^{N_i^w} (V_{i,j}^w - m_v^w)(V_{i,j}^w - m_v^w)^T \tag{2}$$

Here each V^w represents the distance vectors, F_w, for w projection (Top-Bottom-Left-Right) as explained in section 2.1. If the rank of matrix $\sum$ is N, then the N nonzero eigenvalues of $\sum$, $\lambda_1, \lambda_2, .., \lambda_N$, and associated eigenvectors $e_1, e_2, .., e_N$ can be computed based on theory of *singular value decomposition* [5]. The first few eigenvectors correspond to large changes in training patterns, and higher-order eigenvectors represent smaller changes [2]. As a result, for computing efficiency in practical applications, those small eigenvalues and their corresponding eigenvectors are ignored. Then a transform matrix $T^w = [e_1^w, e_2^w, .., e_s^w]$ to project an original distance vector signal $V_{i,j}^w$ into a point $P_{i,j}^w$ in the eigenspace is constructed by taking only $s < N$ largest eigenvalues and their associated eigenvectors for each projections to silhouette. Therefore, s values are usually much smaller than the original data dimension N. Then the projection average A_i^w of each training sequence in the eigenspace is calculated by averaging of $P_{i,j}^w$.

2.3   Pattern Classification

Statistical distance measuring has initially been selected for classification. The accumulated distance between the associated centroids A^w (obtained in the process of training) and B^w (obtained in the process of testing) can be easily computed by

$$d_S(A, B) = \sqrt{(\frac{A_1 - B_1}{s_1})^2 + ... + (\frac{A_p - B_p}{s_p})^2} = \sqrt{(A - B)^t S^{-1}(A - B)} \quad (3)$$

Where $S = diag(s_1^2, ..., s_p^2)$. In the distance measure, the classification result for each projection is then accomplished by choosing the minimum of d. The classification process is carried out via the nearest neighbor classifier. The classification is performed by classifying the test sequence into class c that can minimize the similarity distance between the test sequence and all training sequences by

$$c = arg_i \ min \ d_i(T, R_i) \quad (4)$$

where T represents a test sequence, R_i represents the ith training sequence, d is the similarity measures described in above.

A fusion task includes two different strategies is finally developed. In **the strategy 1**, each projection is separately treated. Then the strategy 1 is combining the distances of each projections at the end by assigning equal weight. The final similarity using strategy 1 is calculated as follows:

$$D_i = \sum_{j=1}^{4} \alpha_j * d_{ji} \quad (5)$$

where D_i is the fused distance similarity value, j is the algorithm's index for projection, α its normalized weight, d_i its single projection distance similarity value and 4 is the number of projections (left, right, top, bottom). As conclusion, if any two distance similarity vectors in four projections give maximum similarities for same person, then the identification is determined as positive. This fusion strategy has rapidly increased the recognition performance in the experiments.

At the experiments, it has been seen that some projection has given more robust results than others. For example, while human moves in lateral view with respect to image plane, the back side of human can give more individual characteristics in gait. So, the projection corresponding to that side can give more reliable results. We called dominant feature to this case. As a result, **the strategy 2** has also been developed to further increase the recognition performance. In the strategy 2, if the projection selected as dominant feature gives positive or at least two projections of others give positive for an individual, then identification by fusion process is to be positive. The dominant feature in this work is automatically assigned by estimating the direction of motion objects under tracking. At the next section, the dominant features determined by experimentally for different view points with respect to image plane are also given.

3 Gait Cycle Estimation

Gait cycle estimation is especially very important at the gait identification. Several vision methods have exploited this fact to compute the period of human gait from image features [10][11][2]. Most works using silhouette-based

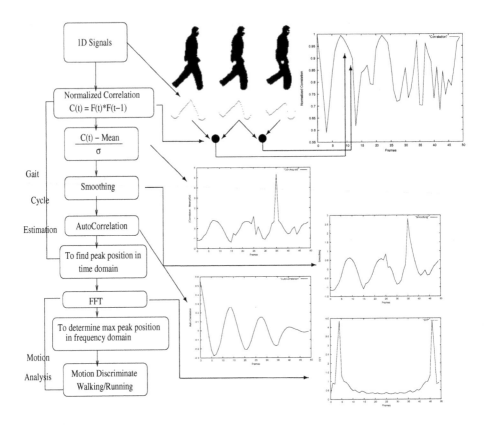

Fig. 2. Gait cycle estimation, and motion analysis

gait recognition in literature estimate gait cycle depending on the variation of bounding box over time. Sarkar et.al [7] estimate gait periodicity by counting the number of foreground pixels in silhouette in each frame over time. These approaches can work for near frontoparallel views, would not work for frontal views. The algorithm present in this work uses silhouette data itself only, not depending to bounding box, and is also view-invariant technique to estimate gait cycle.

The algorithm steps are shown in figure 2 and as follows. The output of the detecting/tracking module gives a sequence of bounding boxes for every object [6]. First step in the algorithm is to take projections, and to calculate the normalized correlation between consecutive frames. The elimination of the influence of spatial scale and signal length are inherently achieved by selecting consecutive frames. At the cycle estimation, to quantify the signals of the correlation results, we may first remove their background component by subtracting their mean and dividing by their standard deviation, and then smooth them with a symmetric average filter. Further, we compute their autocorrelation to find peaks, as shown in figure 2.

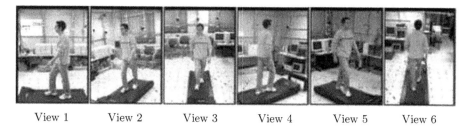

View 1   View 2   View 3   View 4   View 5   View 6

Fig. 3. The six CMU database viewpoints

Some of the experimental results on the algorithm proposed and variations of the bounding box which were used in [10][11][2], were compared in the work [15]. Test sequence includes two main different actions, ones contains 17 people (2 child, 15 adults) walking and running, the other sequence also contains 22 persons (2 females, 20 males) walking only, frame rate is 25 frame per second, and the original resolution is 352x 240. All subjects walk/run along a straight-line path at free cadences in different views (laterally, frontally, obliquely). At the experiments for the subjects move frontally with respect to the image plane, although the periodical characteristics of moving silhouettes are correctly detected by left- and right-projections based the distance vectors, but there has not been able to achieved any periodical characteristics by the results of the signals depending on the bounding box. The gait cycle estimation presented here has achieved more robust experimental results than the variation of the bounding box based gait cycle estimation for frontal views. For lateral and oblique views, both algorithms can easily detect the gait cycles. Additionally, the gait cycle estimation algorithm was also used to discriminate the human motions, such as walking and running, by re-implementing cycle period in time, and by moving to Fourier domain, as shown in Fig. 2. In that domain, the main frequency of motion is estimated by determining the peak which has largest impulse from the significant peaks in the frequency power spectrum. The more details were not given here because it not main purpose in this paper, but they can be found in the work [15].

4   Experiments and Results

The performance of the proposed algorithm has been evaluated on CMU's MoBo database[13], NLPR gait database [2], KTU database, and USF database [7]. The Viterbi algorithm was used to identify the test sequence, since it is efficient and can operate in the logarithmic domain using only additions [12]. The performance of the algorithm presented is evaluated on four different databases of varying of difficulty.

4.1   CMU Database

This database has 25 subjects (23 males, 2 females) walking on a treadmill. Each subject is recorded performing four different types of walking: slow walk, fast walk, inclined walk, and slow walk holding ball. There are about 8 cycles in each sequence, and each sequences is recorded at 30 frames per second. It also contains six simultaneous motion sequence of 25 subjects, as shown in figure 3.

One of the cycle in each sequence was used for testing, others for training. First, we did the following experiments on this database: 1) train on slow walk and test on slow walk, 2) train on fast walk and test on fast walk, 3) train on walk carrying a ball and test on walk carrying a ball, 4) train on slow walk and test on fast walk, 5) train on slow walk and test on walk carrying a ball, 6) train on fast walk and test on slow walk, 7) train on fast walk and test on walk carrying a ball, 8) train on walk carrying a ball and test on slow walk, 9) train on walk carrying a ball and test on fast walk.

The results obtained using the proposed method are summarized on the all cases 1)-9) in Table 1. It can be seen that the right person in the top two matches 100% of times for the cases where testing and training sets correspond to the same walk styles. When the strategy developed in the fusion as dominant feature (projections) is used, the recognition performance is increased, as seen in Table 1. For the case of training with fast walk and testing on slow walk, and vice versa, the dip in performance is caused due to the fact that for some individual as biometrics suggests, there is a considerable change in body dynamics and stride length as a person changes his speed. Nevertheless, the right person in the top three matches 100% of the times for that cases, and dominant projection strategy has also increased the recognition performance for Ranks 1 and 2. For the case of training with walk carrying ball and testing on slow and fast walks, and vice versa, encouraging results have also been produced by using the proposed method, and the dominant feature property has still increased the recognition performance, as given in Table 1.

For the other view points, the experimental results are also summarized on the cases 1)-4) in Table 2. When the all experimental results for the different view points are considered, it can be seen that, the right person in the top two matches 100% and in the top four matches 100% of the times for the cases 1)-2) and for the cases 3)-4), respectively. It is also seen that, when the dominant

Table 1. Classification performance on the CMU data set for viewpoint 1

Test/Train	All projections: equal				Dominant: Right projection		
	Rank 1	Rank 2	Rank 3	Rank 4	Rank 1	Rank 2	Rank 3
Slow/Slow	72	100	100	100	84	100	100
Fast/Fast	76	100	100	100	92	100	100
Ball/Ball	84	100	100	100	84	100	100
Slow/Fast	36	92	100	100	52	100	100
Fast/Slow	20	60	100	100	32	88	100
Slow/Ball	8	17	33	58	42	96	100
Fast/Ball	4	13	33	67	17	50	88
Ball/Slow	8	17	38	67	33	88	100
Ball/Fast	13	29	58	92	29	63	100

Table 2. Classification performance on the CMU data set for all views. Eight gait cycles were used, seven cycles for training, one cycle for testing.

View	Test/Train	All projections equal			Dominant: Right projection		
		Rank 1	Rank 2	Rank 3	Rank 1	Rank 2	Rank 3
4	Slow/Slow	76	100	100	84	100	100
	Fast/Fast	84	100	100	96	100	100
	Slow/Fast	12	44	80	24	64	100
	Fast/Slow	20	64	100	32	76	100
					Dominant: Left projection		
5	Slow/Slow	80	100	100	80	100	100
	Fast/Fast	88	100	100	88	100	100
	Slow/Fast	16	44	80	24	64	100
	Fast/Slow	24	56	96	32	68	100
					Dominant: Right projection		
3	Slow/Slow	80	100	100	88	100	100
	Fast/Fast	72	100	100	76	100	100
	Slow/Fast	20	64	100	28	76	100
	Fast/Slow	24	56	92	28	68	100
					Dominant: Right projection		
6	Slow/Slow	72	100	100	84	100	100
	Fast/Fast	76	100	100	80	100	100
	Slow/Fast	16	44	88	36	76	100
	Fast/Slow	16	40	72	24	56	100

feature is used, gait recognition performance is also increased. Consequently, the proposed method for gait recognition can easily be seen that, it is view-invariant.

4.2 NLPR Database

The *NLPR* database [2] includes 20 subjects and four sequences for each viewing angle per subject, two sequences for one direction of walking, the other two sequences for reverse direction of walking. For instance, when the subject is walking laterally to the camera, the direction of walking is from right to left for two of four sequences, and from right to left for the remaining. Those all gait sequences were captured as twice (we called two experiments) on two different days in an outdoor environment. All subjects walk along a straight-line path at

Lateral view   Oblique view   Frontal view

Fig. 4. Some images in the NLPR database

Table 3. Performance on the NLPR data set for three views

Walking Direction	View	Training	Test	Rank1	Rank2	Rank3
One Way Walking	Lateral	Exp. 1	Exp. 1	65	100	100
		Exp. 1	Exp. 2	55	100	100
	Frontal	Exp. 1	Exp. 1	60	100	100
		Exp. 1	Exp. 2	35	100	100
	Oblique	Exp. 1	Exp. 1	40	90	100
		Exp. 1	Exp. 2	30	60	100
Reverse Way Walking	Lateral	Exp. 1	Exp. 1	60	100	100
		Exp. 1	Exp. 2	50	100	100
	Frontal	Exp. 1	Exp. 1	60	100	100
		Exp. 1	Exp. 2	40	100	100
	Oblique	Exp. 1	Exp. 1	45	100	100
		Exp. 1	Exp. 2	35	75	100

free cadences in three different views with respect to the image plane, as shown in figure 4, where the white line with arrow represents one direction path, the other walking path is reverse direction.

We did the following experiments on this database: 1) train on one image sequence and test on the remainder, all sequences were produced from first experiment, 2) train on two sequences obtained from first experiment and test on two sequences obtained from second experiment. This is repeated for each viewing angle, and for each direction of walking. The results for the experiments along with cumulative match scores in three viewing angle are summarized in Table 3. When the experimental results are considered, the right person in the top two matches 100% of times for lateral and frontal viewing angles, and in the top three matches 100% of times for oblique view.

4.3   KTU Database

The database established for gait recognition has 22 people (2 females, 20 males), and subjects are walking laterally to the camera, the directions of walking is from left to right, and from right to left. The database includes two sequences for each subject. One sequence includes 3 gait cycle for each direction, and the length of each gait cycle varies with the pace of the walker, but the average is about 26 frames. The subjects walk along a straight-line path at free cadences, and 15 subjects were walking outside, seven subjects were walking inside. The results for the experiments along with cumulative match scores in lateral view are also summarized in Table 4. Three gait cycles were used, two cycles for training, one cycle for testing. Walking from left to right and the other direction are separately tested to achieve initial experimental results. When the results of each projection based distance vectors are re-implemented by using dominant feature strategy as explained in section 2.3, significantly improvements on the gait recognition has also been achieved. This is the robust implementation and is one of the novelty presented by this paper.

Table 4. Performance on KTU data set: (The abbreviation used :L⇒ R : From Left to Right)

Direction	Outdoor(15 person)		Indoor(7 person)		All(22 person)		
	Rank 1	Rank 2	Rank 1	Rank 2	Rank 1	Rank 2	Rank 3
L⇒ R	67	100	86	100	68	95	100
R⇒ L	67	100	71	100	68	100	100

4.4 USF Database

Finally, the USF database [7] is considered. The database has variations as regards viewing direction, shoe type, and surface type. At the experiments, one of the cycle in each sequence was used for testing, others (3-4 cycles) for training. Different probe sequences for the experiments along with the cumulative match scores are given in Table 5 for the algorithm presented in this paper and three different algorithms [17][2][8]. The same silhouette data from USF were directly used. These data are noisy, e.g., missing of body parts, small holes inside the objects, severe shadow around feet, and missing and adding some parts around the border of silhouettes due to background characteristics. In Table 5, G and C indicate grass and concrete surfaces, A and B indicate shoe types, and L and R indicate left and right cameras, respectively. The number of subjects in each subset is also given in square bracket. It is observed that, the proposed method has given the right person in top three matches 100% of the times for training and testing sets corresponding to the same camera.

Table 5. Performance on the USF database for four algorithm

Exp.	The method			Baseline[17]		NLPR[2]		UMD[8]	
	Rnk 1	Rnk 2	Rnk 3	Rnk 1	Rnk 5	Rnk 1	Rnk 5	Rnk 1	Rnk 5
GAL[68]	35	80	100	79	96	70	92	91	100
GBR[44]	34	82	100	66	81	58	82	76	81
GBL[44]	25	55	91	56	76	51	70	65	76
CAL[69]	39	90	100	30	46	27	38	24	46
CBL[41]	30	78	100	10	33	14	26	15	33
CBR[41]	29	66	100	24	55	21	45	29	39
GAR[68]	34	60	90	–	-	-	-	-	-

5 Conclusion

This paper has described a novel gait recognition approach that uses multi projections of silhouettes as the basic feature for classification. The approach on gait cycle estimation and on gait recognition is view-invariant and is fully automatic for real time applications. The performance of the gait recognition method proposed was also illustrated using different gait databases. The more details on the comparison of the performance of the proposed algorithm with those of a few recent silhouette-based methods described in literature can also be found in previous work in [14].

References

1. M. S. Nixon, J. N. Carter, Advances in Automatic Gait Recognition, Proc. of IEEE Int. Conf. on Automatic Face and Gesture Recognition, 2004.
2. L. Wang, T. Tan, H. Ning, W. Hu, Silhouette Analysis-Based Gait Recognition for Human Identification, IEEE Trans. on PAMI Vol.25, No. 12, Dec.,2003.
3. C. BenAbdelkader, R. G. Cutler, L. S. Davis, Gait Recognition Using Image Self-Similarity, EURASIP Journal of Applied Signal Processing, April, 2004.
4. G. V. Veres,*et.al.*What image information is important in silhouette-based gait recognition?, Proc. IEEE Conf. on Computer Vision and Pattern Recognition, 2004.
5. P. Huang, C. Harris, M. Nixon, Human Gait Recognition in Canonical Space Using Temporal Templates, IEE Proc. Vision Image and Signal Proc. Conf., 1999.
6. M. Ekinci, E. Gedikli, Background Estimation Based People Detection and Tracking for Video Surveillance, Lecture Notes in Comp. Sci., LNCS 2869, pp.421-429, 2003.
7. S. Sarkar, *et.al.* The HumanID Gait Challenge Problem: Data Sets, Performance, and Analysis. IEEE Trans. on Pat. Anal. and Mach. Intell., Vol.27, No. 2, 2005.
8. A. Kale, *et. al.*, Identification of Humans Using Gait. IEEE Trans. on Image Processing, Vol.13, No.9, September 2004.
9. Yanxi Liu, R. T. Collins, T. Tsin, Gait Sequence Analysis using Frieze Patterns, Proc. of European Conf. on Computer Vision, 2002.
10. C. BenAbdelkader, *et.al.*Stride and Cadence as a Biometric in Automatic Person Identification and Verification, Proc. Int. Conf. Aut. Face and Gesture Recog.,2002.
11. R. Collins, R. Gross, and J. Shi, Silhouette-Based Human Identification from Body Shape and Gait, Proc. Int. Conf. Automatic Face and Gesture Recognition, 2002.
12. J. Phillips *et.al*, The FERET Evaluation Methodology for Face recognition Algorithm, IEEE Trans. Pattern Analysis and Machine Intell., vol.22, no.10, Oct.2000.
13. R. Gross, J. Shi, The CMU motion of body (MOBO) database, Tech. Rep. CMU-RI-TR-01-18, Robotics Institute, Carnegie Mellon University, June 2001.
14. Murat Ekinci, A New Approach for Human Identification Using Gait Recognition, The IEE Proc. of ICCSA 2006, Lecture Notes in Computer Science, May, 2006.
15. M. Ekinci, E. Gedikli A Novel Approach on Silhouette Based Human Motion Analysis for Gait Recognition, Springer-Verlag, Lecture Notes in Computer Science, LNCS 3804, pp.219-226, December 2005.
16. A. I. Bazin, M. S. Nixon, Verification Using Probabilistic Methods, IEEE Workshop on Applications of Computer Vision, 2005.
17. P. Phillips, et.al., Baseline Results for Challenge Problem of Human ID using Gait Analysis, Proc. Int. Conf. Automatic Face and Gesture Recognition, 2002.

Learning Naïve Bayes Tree for Conditional Probability Estimation

Han Liang[1,*] and Yuhong Yan[2,**]

[1] Faculty of Computer Science, University of New Brunswick
Fredericton, NB, Canada E3B 5A3
[2] National Research Council of Canada
Fredericton, NB, Canada E3B 5X9
yuhong.yan@nrc.gc.ca

Abstract. Naïve Bayes Tree uses decision tree as the general structure and deploys naïve Bayesian classifiers at leaves. The intuition is that naïve Bayesian classifiers work better than decision trees when the sample data set is small. Therefore, after several attribute splits when constructing a decision tree, it is better to use naïve Bayesian classifiers at the leaves than to continue splitting the attributes. In this paper, we propose a learning algorithm to improve the conditional probability estimation in the diagram of Naïve Bayes Tree. The motivation for this work is that, for cost-sensitive learning where costs are associated with conditional probabilities, the score function is optimized when the estimates of conditional probabilities are accurate. The additional benefit is that both the classification accuracy and Area Under the Curve (AUC) could be improved. On a large suite of benchmark sample sets, our experiments show that the CLL tree outperforms the state-of-art learning algorithms, such as Naïve Bayes Tree and naïve Bayes significantly in yielding accurate conditional probability estimation and improving classification accuracy and AUC.

1 Introduction

Classification is a fundamental issue of machine learning in which a classifier is induced from a set of labeled training samples represented by a vector of attribute values and a class label. We denote attribute set $\mathbf{A} = \{A_1, A_2, \ldots, A_n\}$, and an assignment of value to each attribute in $\mathbf{A}$ by a corresponding bold-face lower-case letter $\mathbf{a}$. We use C to denote the class variable and c to denote its value. Thus, a training sample is represented as $E = (\mathbf{a}, c)$, where $\mathbf{a} = (a_1, a_2, \ldots, a_n)$, and a_i is the value of attribute A_i. A classifier is a function f that maps a sample E to a class label c, i.e. $f(\mathbf{a}) = c$. The inductive learning algorithm returns a function h that approximates f. The function h is called a hypothesis.

---

* The author is a visiting worker at NRC-IIT.
** The authors thank Dr. Harry Zhang and Jiang Su from University of New Brunswick for their discussions on this paper.

L. Lamontagne and M. Marchand (Eds.): Canadian AI 2006, LNAI 4013, pp. 455–466, 2006.
© Springer-Verlag Berlin Heidelberg 2006

The classifier can predict the assignment of C for an unlabeled testing sample $E_t = (\mathbf{b})$, i.e. $h(\mathbf{b}) = c_t$.

Various inductive learning algorithms, such as decision trees, Bayesian networks, and neural networks, can be categorized into two major approaches: probability-based approach and decision boundary-based approach. In a generative probability learning algorithm, a probability distribution $p(A, C)$ is learned from the training samples as a hypothesis. Then we can theoretically compute the probability of any E in the probability space. A testing sample $E_t = (\mathbf{b})$ is classified into the class c with the maximum posterior class probability $p(c|\mathbf{b})$ (or simply class probability), as shown below.

$$h(\mathbf{b}) = \arg\max_{c \in C} p(c|\mathbf{b}) = \arg\max_{c \in C} p(c, \mathbf{b})/p(\mathbf{b}) \tag{1}$$

Decision tree learning algorithms are well known as decision boundary-based. Though their probability estimates are poor, the algorithms can make good decisions on which side of the boundary a sample data falls. Decision trees work better when the sample data set is large. It is because, after several splits of attributes, the number of samples at the subspaces is too few on which to base the decision, while naïve Bayesian classifier works better in this case. Therefore, instead of continuing to split the attributes, naïve Bayesian classifiers are deployed at the leaves. [5] proposed this hybrid model called Naïve Bayes Tree (NBTree). It is reported that NBTree outperforms C4.5 and naïve Bayes in classification accuracy and AUC.

In this paper, we propose to use NBTree to improve the conditional probability estimation given the support attributes, i.e. $p(C|\mathbf{A})$. Accurate conditional probability is important in many aspects. First, in cost-sensitive classification, knowing the accurate conditional probability is crucial in making a decision. Determining only the decision boundary is not enough. Second, improving conditional probability can possibly improve classification accuracy, though it is not a necessary condition. Third, improving conditional probability can improve AUC which is a metric used for ranking.

Our proposed learning algorithm is a greedy and recursive procedure similar to NBTree. In each step of expanding the decision tree, the Conditional Log Likelihood (CLL) is used as the score function to select the best attribute to split, where let the CLL of a classifier B, given a (sub) sample set S be

$$CLL(\mathbf{B}|\mathbf{S}) = \sum_{s=1}^{n} \log P_B(C|\mathbf{A}) \tag{2}$$

The splitting process ends when some conditions are met. Then for the samples at leaves, naïve Bayesian classifiers are generated. We call the generated tree CLL Tree (CLLTree). We present that on a large suite of benchmark sample sets, our empirical results show that CLLTree significantly outperforms the state-of-art learning algorithms, such as NBTree and naïve Bayes in yielding accurate probability estimation, classification accuracy and AUC.

2   Related Work in Decision Tree Probability Estimation

The probability generated from decision tree is calculated from the sub sample sets at leaves corresponding to the conjunction of the conditions along the paths back to the root [8]. Assume a leaf node defines a subset of 100 samples, 90 of which are in the positive class and others are in the negative class, then each sample is assigned the same probability of 0.9 (90/100) that it belongs to the positive class, i.e. $\hat{p}(+|\mathbf{A_p} = \mathbf{a_p}) = 90\%$, where $\mathbf{A_p}$ is the set of attributes on the path. Viewed as probability estimators, decision trees consist of piecewise uniform approximations within regions defined by axis-paralleled boundaries. Aiming at this fact, [8] presented two methods to improve the probability estimation of decision tree. First, by using Laplace estimation, probability estimates can be smoothed from small sample data at the tree leaves. Second, by turning off pruning and "collapsing" in C4.5, decision trees can generate finer trees to give more precise probability estimation. The final version is called C4.4.

Another improvement to tackle the "uniform probability distribution" problem of decision trees is to stop splitting at a certain level and put another probability density estimator at each leaf. [5] proposed an NBTree that uses decision tree as the general structure and deploys naïve Bayes classifiers at the leaves. This learning algorithm first uses classification accuracy as the score function to do univariate splits and when splitting does not increase the score function, a naïve Bayesian classifier is created at the leaf. Thus, sample attributes are divided into two sets: $\mathbf{A} = \mathbf{A_p} \cup \mathbf{A_l}$, where $\mathbf{A_p}$ is the set of path attributes and $\mathbf{A_l}$ is the set of leaf attributes. [10] proposed one encode of $p(C, \mathbf{A})$ for NBTree. The proposed Conditional Independent Tree (CITree) denotes $p(\mathbf{A}, C)$ as below:

$$p(\mathbf{A}, C) = \alpha p(C|\mathbf{A_p}(L))p(\mathbf{A_l}(L)|\mathbf{A_p}(L), C) \tag{3}$$

where α is a normalization factor. The term $p(C|\mathbf{A_p}(L))$ is the joint conditional distribution of path attributes and the term $p(\mathbf{A_l}(L)|\mathbf{A_p}(L), C)$ is the leaf attributes presented by naïve Bayes $p(\mathbf{A_l}|\mathbf{A_p}(L), C) = \prod_{i=1}^{n} p(A_{li}|\mathbf{A_p}(L), C)$. CITree explicitly defines conditional dependence among the path attributes and independence among the leaf attributes. The local conditional independence assumption of CITree is a relaxation of the (global) conditional independence assumption of naïve Bayes.

Building decision trees with accurate probability estimation, called Probability Estimation Trees (PETs), has received a great deal of attention recently [8]. The difference of PET and CITree is that PET represents the conditional probability distribution of the path attributes, while a CITree represents a joint distribution over all attributes.

Another related work involves *Bayesian networks* [7] which are directed acyclic graphs that encode conditional independence among a set of random variables. Each variable is independent of its non-descendants in the graph given the state of its parents. Tree Augmented Naïve Bayes (TAN) [3] approximates the interaction between attributes by using a tree structure imposed on the naïve Bayesian framework. We point out that, although TAN takes advantage of tree structure, it is not a decision tree. Indeed, decision trees divide a sample space into multiple subspaces and local conditional probabilities are independent among those subspaces. Therefore, attributes in decision trees can repeatedly appear, while TAN describes the joint probabilities among attributes, so each attribute appears only once. In decision trees, $p(C|\mathbf{A})$ is decomposable when a (sub) sample set is split into subspaces, but it is non-decomposable in TAN.

3   Learning Naïve Bayes Tree for Conditional Probability Estimation

In this section, we present our work on improving conditional probability estimation of naïve Bayes Tree. First, we select the evaluation metrics. Second, we present the principles of representing CLL in CLL Tree. Last, we present a new algorithm for learning the naïve Bayes tree.

3.1   The Performance Evaluation Metrics

Accurate conditional probability $p(C|\mathbf{A})$ is important for many applications. Since it is justified that $\log p$ is a monotonic function of p and we use conditional log likelihood (CLL) for calculation, we mix the usage of CLL and conditional probability hereafter. In cost-sensitive classification, the optimal prediction for a sample $\mathbf{b}$ is the class c_i that minimize [2]

$$h(\mathbf{b}) = \arg \min_{c_i \in C} \sum_{c_j \in C - c_i} p(c_j|\mathbf{b})C(c_i, c_j) \qquad (4)$$

One can see that the score function in cost-sensitive learning directly relies on the conditional probability. It is not like the classification problem where only the decision boundary is important. Accurate estimation of conditional probability is necessary for cost-sensitive learning.

Better conditional probability estimation means better classification accuracy (ACC) (c.f. Equation 1). ACC is calculated as the percentage of the correctly classified samples over all the samples: $ACC = \frac{1}{N} \sum I(h(\mathbf{a}) = c)$, here N is the number of samples. However, improving conditional probability estimation is not a necessary condition for improving ACC. ACC can be scaled up through other ways, e.g. boundary-based approaches. On the other side, even if conditional probability is greatly improved, it may still lead to wrong classification.

Ranking is different from both classification and probability estimation. For example, assume that $E+$ and $E-$ are a positive and a negative sample respectively, and that the actual class probabilities are $p(+|E+) = 0.9$ and $p(-|E-) = 0.1$. An algorithm that gives class probability estimates $\hat{p}(+|E+) = 0.55$ and $\hat{p}(+|E-) = 0.54$, gives a correct order of $E+$ and $E-$ in the ranking. Notice that the probability estimates are poor and the classification for $E-$ is incorrect. However, if a learning algorithm produces accurate class probability estimates, it certainly produces a precise ranking. Thus, aiming at learning a model to yield accurate conditional probability estimation will usually lead to a model yielding precise probability-based ranking.

In this paper, we use three different metrics CLL, ACC and AUC to evaluate learning algorithms.

3.2   The Representation of CLL in CLLTree

The representation of conditional probability in the diagram of CLLTree is as follows:

$$\log(p(C|\mathbf{A})) = \log(p(C|\mathbf{A_1}, \mathbf{A_p}) = \log(p(C|\mathbf{A_p})) + \log(p(\mathbf{A_1}|C, \mathbf{A_p})) - \log(p(\mathbf{A_1}|\mathbf{A_p}))$$

(5)

$\mathbf{A_p}$ divides a (sub) sample set into several subsets. All decomposed terms are the conditional probability of $\mathbf{A_p}$. $p(C|\mathbf{A_p})$ is the conditional probability on the path attributes; $p(\mathbf{A_1}|C, \mathbf{A_p})$ is the naïve Bayesian classifier at a leaf; and $p(\mathbf{A_1}|\mathbf{A_p})$ is the joint probability of $\mathbf{A_1}$ under condition of $\mathbf{A_p}$.

In each step of generating the decision tree, CLL is calculated based on Equation 5. Assuming A_{li} denotes a leaf attribute, here, $p(C|\mathbf{A_p})$ is calculated by the ratio of the number of samples that have the same class value to all the samples at a leaf; $p(\mathbf{A_1}|C, \mathbf{A_p})$ can be represented by $\prod_{i=1}^{m} p(A_{li}|C, \mathbf{A_p})$ (m is the number of attributes at a leaf node), and each $p(A_{li}|C, \mathbf{A_p})$ can be calculated by the ratio of the number of samples that have the same attribute value of A_{li} and the same class value to the number of samples that have the same class value; likewise, $p(\mathbf{A_1}|\mathbf{A_p})$ can also be represented by $\prod_{i=1}^{m} p(A_{li}|\mathbf{A_p})$, and each $p(A_{li}|\mathbf{A_p})$ can be calculated by the ratio of the number of samples that have the same attribute value of A_{li} to the number of samples at that leaf. The attribute to optimize CLL is selected as the next level node to extend the tree. We exhaustively build all possible trees in each step and keep only the best on for the next level expansion. Supposing finite k attributes are available. When expanding the tree at level q, there are $k - q + 1$ attributes to be chosen. This is a greedy way. CLLTree makes an assumption on probability, i.e. the probability dependency on the path attributes and the probability independency on the leaf attributes. Besides, it also has another assumption on the structure that each node has only one parent.

3.3   A New Algorithm for Learning CLLTree

From the discussion in the previous sections, CLLTree can represent any joint distribution. Therefore, the probability estimation based on CLLTree is accurate. But the structure learning of a CLLTree could theoretically be as time-consuming as learning an optimal decision tree. A good approximation of a CLLTree, which gives relatively accurate estimates of class probabilities, is desirable in many applications. Similar to a decision tree, building a CLLTree could be a greedy and recursive process. On each iteration, choose the "best" attribute as the root of the (sub) tree, split the associated data into disjoint subsets corresponding to the values of that attribute, and recur this process for each subset until certain criteria are satisfied. If the structure of a CLLTree is determined, a leaf naïve Bayes is a perfect model to represent the local conditional distribution at leaves. The algorithm is described below.

Algorithm 1. Learning Algorithm $CLLTree(T, S, A)$

T: CLLTree
S: a set of labeled samples
A: a set of attributes

    for each attribute $a \in A$ **do**
        Partition S into $S_1, S_2, ..., S_k$, where k is the number of possible values of attribute a. Each sub set is corresponding to a value of a. For continuous attributes, a threshold is set up in this step.
        Create a naïve Bayes for each S_i.
        Evaluate the split on the attribute a in terms of CLL.
    Choose the attribute A_t with the highest split CLL.
    if the split CLL is not improved greatly than the CLL of attribute A_t **then**
        create a leaf naïve Bayes for this attribute.
    else
        for all values S_a of A_t **do**
            $CLLTree(T_a, S_a, A - A_t)$.
        add T_a as a child of T
    Return T

In our algorithm, we adopt a heuristic search process in which we choose an attribute with the greatest improvement on the performance of the resulting tree. Precisely speaking, on each iteration, each candidate attribute is chosen as the root of the (sub) tree, the resulting tree is evaluated, and we choose the attribute that achieves the highest CLL value. We consider two criteria for halting the search process. For one, we could stop splitting when none of the alternative attributes significantly improve probability estimation, in the form of CLL. Or, to make a leaf naïve Bayes work accurately, there are at least 30 samples at the current leaf. We define a split to be significant if the relative increase in CLL is greater than 5%. Note that we train a leaf naïve Bayes by adopting an inner 5-fold cross-validation on the sub sample set S which fall into the current leaf. For example, if an attribute has 3 attribute values which will result in three leaf naïve Bayes, the inner 5-fold cross-validations will be run in three leaves. Furthermore, we compute CLL by putting the samples from all the leaves together rather than computing the CLL for each leaf separately.

It is also worth noting, however, the different biases between learning a CLL-Tree and learning a traditional decision tree. In decision tree, the building process is directed by the purity of the (sub) sample set measured by information gain, and the crucial point in selecting an attribute is whether the resulting split of the samples is "pure" or not. However, such a selection strategy does not necessarily lead to the truth of improving the probability estimation of a new sample. In building a CLLTree, we intend to choose the attributes that maximize the posterior class probabilities $p(C|\mathbf{A})$ among the samples at the current leaf as much as possible. That means, even though there possibly exists the high impurity of its leaves, it could still be a good CLLTree.

4 Experimental Methodology and Results

For the purpose of our study, we used 33 well-recognized sample sets from many domains recommended by Weka [9]. There is a brief description of these sample sets in Table 1. All sample sets came from the UCI repository[1]. The preprocessing stages of sample sets were carried out within the Weka platform, mainly including the following three steps:

1. Applying the filter of ReplaceMissingValues in Weka to replace the missing values of attributes.
2. Applying the filter of Discretize in Weka to discretize numeric attributes. Therefore, all the attributes are treated as nominal.
3. It is well known that, if the number of values of an attribute is almost equal to the number of samples in a sample set, this attribute does not contribute

Table 1. Description of sample sets used by the experiments

Sample Set	Size	Attr.	Classes	Missing	Numeric
anneal	898	39	6	Y	Y
anneal.ORIG	898	39	6	Y	Y
audiology	226	70	24	Y	N
balance	625	5	3	N	Y
breast	286	10	2	Y	N
breast-w	699	10	2	Y	N
colic	368	23	2	Y	Y
colic.ORIG	368	28	2	Y	Y
credit-a	690	16	2	Y	Y
credit-g	1000	21	2	N	Y
diabetes	768	9	2	N	Y
glass	214	10	7	N	Y
heart-c	303	14	5	Y	Y
heart-h	294	14	5	Y	Y
heart-s	270	14	2	N	Y
hepatitis	155	20	2	Y	Y
hypoth.	3772	30	4	Y	Y
iris	150	5	3	N	Y
kr-vs-kp	3196	37	2	N	N
labor	57	17	2	Y	Y
letter	20000	17	26	N	Y
lymph	148	19	4	N	Y
mushroom	8124	23	2	Y	N
p.-tumor	339	18	21	Y	N
segment	2310	20	7	N	Y
sick	3772	30	2	Y	Y
soybean	683	36	19	Y	N
splice	3190	62	3	N	N
vehicle	846	19	4	N	Y
vote	435	17	2	Y	N
vowel	990	14	11	N	Y
waveform	5000	41	3	N	Y
zoo	101	18	7	N	Y

Table 2. Experimental results for CLLTree versus Naïve Bayes Tree (NBTree), naïve Bayes (NB) and Tree Augmented Naïve Bayes (TAN); C4.4, C4.4 with bagging (C4.4-B) and C4.5 with Laplace estimation (C4.5-L): Conditional Log Likelihood (CLL) & standard deviation

Sample Set	CLLTree	NBTree	NB	TAN	C4.4	C4.4-B
anneal	-10.78	-18.46	-14.22	-6.29	-7.84	-13.74
anneal.ORIG	-22.28	-33.33 ●	-23.58	-19.55	-22.17	-40.13 ●
audiology	-75.58	-95.28	-65.91	-67.19	-15.37 ○	-35.95 ○
balance-scale	-29.81	-31.75 ●	-31.75 ●	-34.78 ●	-52.78 ●	-46.71 ●
breast-cancer	-18.88	-20.47	-18.37	-18.17	-18.56	-17.07
breast-w	-11.43	-17.47	-18.28	-12.14	-11.17	-10.13
colic	-30.82	-34.42	-30.63	-26.22	-17.80 ○	-15.18 ○
colic.ORIG	-24.96	-38.50 ●	-21.24	-22.36	-17.66 ○	-16.09 ○
credit-a	-26.98	-34.52 ●	-28.79	-28.07	-28.06	-26.58
credit-g	-52.61	-62.44	-52.79	-56.16	-61.03 ●	-53.68
diabetes	-40.30	-42.70	-40.78 ●	-42.51	-43.05	-40.19
glass	-26.06	-31.06	-24.08	-26.15	-21.02	-29.77
heart-c	-17.92	-15.70	-13.91	-14.01	-15.85	-25.93 ●
heart-h	-15.93	-14.73	-13.49	-12.96	-14.78	-24.12 ●
heart-statlog	-12.01	-16.31	-12.25	-14.60 ●	-14.00	-12.61
hepatitis	-9.38	-9.18	-8.53	-8.16	-6.81	-6.20
hypothyroid	-95.50	-98.23	-97.14	-93.72	-90.14	-104.87 ●
iris	-2.73	-2.69	-2.56	-3.12	-3.63	-4.01 ●
kr-vs-kp	-18.39	-28.01	-93.48 ●	-60.27 ●	-8.65 ○	-7.92 ○
labor	-1.50	-1.03	-0.71	-2.23	-2.22	-2.13
letter	-1853.63	-2193.71 ●	-2505.15 ●	-1272.27 ○	-1048.56 ○	-2927.76 ●
lymph	-9.16	-8.48	-6.22	-7.15	-7.75	-9.85
mushroom	0.00	-0.14 ●	-105.77 ●	-0.19	-2.10 ●	-2.18 ●
primary-tumor	-74.57	-74.19	-65.56 ○	-69.75	-50.98 ○	-82.41
segment	-61.82	-111.94 ●	-124.32 ●	-40.15 ○	-48.76	-97.61 ●
sick	-24.51	-45.55 ●	-46.05 ●	-28.91 ●	-21.10 ○	-19.66 ○
soybean	-17.39	-28.63	-26.25	-8.06 ○	-18.39	-61.37 ●
splice	-46.58	-47.11	-46.53	-46.89	-66.48 ●	-78.71 ●
vehicle	-98.66	-137.97 ●	-172.12 ●	-57.52 ○	-55.24 ○	-70.21 ○
vote	-7.78	-7.35	-27.25 ●	-7.91	-6.90	-6.10
vowel	-38.23	-45.93	-89.80 ●	-21.87 ○	-71.55 ●	-152.25 ●
waveform-5000	-228.39	-309.13 ●	-378.00 ●	-254.80 ●	-318.55 ●	-351.30 ●
zoo	-2.14	-1.29	-1.22	-1.07	-2.74	-4.59 ●

●, ○ statistically significant degradation or improvement compared with CLLTree

any information to classification. So we used the filter of Remove in Weka to delete these attributes. Three occurred within the 33 sample sets, namely Hospital Number in sample set horse-colic.ORIG, Instance Name in sample set Splice and Animal in sample set zoo.

To avoid the zero-frequency problem, we used the Laplace estimation. More precisely, assuming that there are n_c samples that have the class label as c, t total samples, and k class values in a sample set. The frequency-based probability estimation calculates the estimated probability by $p(c) = \frac{n_c}{t}$. The Laplace estimation calculates it as $p(c) = \frac{n_c+1}{t+k}$. In the Laplace estimation, $p(a_i|c)$ is calculated by $p(a_i|c) = \frac{n_{ic}+1}{n_c+v_i}$, where v_i is the number of values of attribute A_i and n_{ic} is the number of samples in class c with $A_i = a_i$.

In our experiments, two groups of comparisons have been performed. We compared CLLTree with naïve Bayesian related algorithms, such as NBTree, NB, TAN; and with PETs variant algorithms, such as C4.4 ,C4.4-B(C4.4 with bagging), C4.5-L(C4.5 with Laplace estimation) and C4.5-B(C4.5 with bagging). We

Table 3. Summary on t-test of experimental results: CLL comparisons on CLLTree, NBTree, NB, TAN, C4.4 and C4.4-B. An entry $w/t/l$ means that the algorithm at the corresponding row wins in w sample sets, ties in t sample sets, and loses in l sample sets, compared to the algorithm at the corresponding column.

	C4.4-B	C4.4	TAN	NB	NBTree
C4.4	19/7/7				
TAN	16/12/5	8/17/8			
NB	14/9/10	5/14/14	3/18/12		
NBTree	10/15/8	5/16/12	2/20/11	7/22/4	
CLLTree	14/13/6	6/19/8	5/23/5	11/21/1	10/23/0

implemented CLLTree within the Weka framework [9], and used the implementation of other learning algorithms in Weka. In all experiments, the experimental result for each algorithm was measured via a ten-fold cross validation. Runs with various algorithms were carried out on the same training sets and evaluated on the same test sets. In particular, the cross-validation folds were the same for all the experiments on each sample set. Finally, we conducted two-tailed t-test with a significantly different probability of 0.95 to compare our algorithm with others. That is, we speak of two results for a sample set as being "significantly different" only if the difference is statistically significant at the 0.05 level according to the corrected two-tailed t-test [6].

Table 2 and 4 show the experimental results in terms of CLL and AUC. The corresponding summaries of t-test results are demonstrated in Table 3 and 5. Multi-class AUC has been calculated by M-measure[4] in our experiments. Table 6 and 7 display the ACC comparison and t-test results respectively. In all t-test tables, entry $w/t/l$ means that the algorithm in the corresponding row wins in w sample sets, ties in t sample sets, and loses in l sample sets. Our observations are summarized as follows.

1. CLLTree outperforms NBTree in terms of CLL and AUC significantly, and slightly better in ACC. The results in CLL (Table 3) show that CLLTree wins in 10 sample sets, ties in 23 sample sets and loses in 0 sample sets. In AUC (Table 5), CLLTree wins in 5 sample sets, ties in 27 sample sets and loses only in one. Additionally, CLLTree surpasses NBTree in the ACC performance as well. It wins in 3 sample sets and loses in 1 sample set.

2. CLLTree is the best among the rest of learning algorithms in AUC. Compared with C4.4, it wins in 19 sample sets, ties in 14 sample sets and loses in 0 sample sets. Since C4.4 is the state-of-art decision tree algorithm designed specifically for yielding accurate ranking, this comparison also provides evidence to support CLLTree. Compared with naïve Bayes, our algorithm also wins in 9 sample sets, ties in 21 sample sets and loses in 3 sample sets.

3. In terms of the average classification accuracy (Table 6), CLLTree achieves the highest ACC among all algorithms. Compared with naïve Bayes, it wins in 11 sample sets, ties in 21 sample sets and loses in 1 sample set. The average ACC for naïve Bayes is 82.82%, lower than that of CLLTree. Furthermore,

Table 4. Experimental results for CLLTree versus Naïve Bayes Tree (NBTree), naïve Bayes (NB) and Tree Augmented Naïve Bayes (TAN); C4.4 and C4.4 with bagging (C4.4-B): Area Under the Curve (AUC) & standard deviation

Sample Set	CLLTree	NBTree	NB	TAN	C4.4	C4.4-B
anneal	95.97	96.31	96.18	96.59	93.67	94.48
anneal.ORIG	93.73	93.55	94.50	95.26	91.01 ●	93.21
audiology	70.36	70.17	70.02	70.25	64.04 ●	69.05 ●
balance-scale	84.69	84.64	84.64	78.34 ●	61.40 ●	66.55 ●
breast-cancer	68.00	67.98	70.18	66.18	60.53 ●	64.55 ●
breast-w	98.64	99.25○	99.25 ○	98.72	98.22	98.83
colic	82.08	86.78	84.36	85.04	83.96	88.20 ○
colic.ORIG	81.95	79.83	81.18	81.93	83.00	85.98
credit-a	92.06	91.34	91.86	91.35	89.59 ●	90.53 ●
credit-g	79.14	77.53	79.10	77.92	70.07 ●	74.21 ●
diabetes	82.57	82.11	82.61	81.33	76.20 ●	79.10 ●
glass	82.17	79.13	78.42 ●	78.32 ●	80.11	80.30
heart-c	83.89	84.00	84.11	84.03	83.27 ●	83.65
heart-h	83.87	83.90	84.00	83.88	83.30 ●	83.64
heart-statlog	91.34	89.83	91.34	88.19 ●	82.81 ●	86.51 ●
hepatitis	83.48	85.69	89.36	86.06	79.50	82.43
hypothyroid	88.23	87.66	88.10	87.84	80.62 ●	81.44 ●
iris	98.72	98.85	98.99	98.49	98.67	98.77
kr-vs-kp	99.82	99.44	95.19 ●	98.06 ●	99.93	99.97 ○
labor	95.29	96.63	98.67	93.75	87.17	90.79
letter	99.36	98.51●	96.91 ●	99.12 ●	95.52 ●	98.41 ●
lymph	89.12	88.94	90.25	89.16	86.30	88.17
mushroom	100.00	100.00	99.80 ●	100.00	100.00	100.00
primary-tumor	75.33	74.71	75.58	75.43	68.53 ●	73.05 ●
segment	99.40	99.11●	98.35 ●	99.63 ○	99.08 ●	99.49
sick	98.44	94.46●	95.87 ●	98.31	99.03	99.23
soybean	99.81	99.72	99.79	99.87	98.02 ●	98.95 ●
splice	99.45	99.44	99.46 ●	99.40	98.06 ●	98.74 ●
vehicle	86.68	85.86	80.58 ●	91.14 ○	85.96	89.02 ○
vote	98.50	98.61	97.15 ●	98.78	97.43	98.31
vowel	99.35	98.59●	95.98 ●	99.64	91.574 ●	96.44 ●
waveform-5000	94.74	93.71●	95.32 ○	93.87 ●	81.36 ●	90.04 ●
zoo	88.64	89.02	88.88	88.93	80.26 ●	80.88 ●
average	89.83	89.55	89.58	89.54	85.70	87.97

●, ○ statistically significant degradation or improvement compared with CLLTree

Table 5. Summary on *t*-test of experimental results: AUC comparisons on CLLTree, NBTree, NB, TAN, C4.4 and C4.4-B

	C4.4-B	C4.4	TAN	NB	NBTree
C4.4	0/15/18				
TAN	12/19/2	18/13/2			
NB	14/12/7	21/7/5	4/20/9		
NBTree	8/20/5	19/12/2	3/25/5	7/25/1	
CLLTree	14/16/3	19/14/0	6/25/2	9/21/3	5/27/1

CLLTree also outperforms TAN significantly. It wins 6 sample sets, ties in 24 sample sets and loses in 3 sample sets. The average ACC for TAN is 84.64%, which is lower than our algorithm as well. And last, CLLTree is also better than C4.5, the implementation of traditional decision trees, in 8 sample sets.

4. Although C4.4 outperforms CLLTree in CLL, our algorithm is definitely better than C4.4 in the overall performance. C4.4 sacrifices its tree size

Table 6. Experimental results for CLLTree versus Naïve Bayes Tree (NBTree), naïve Bayes (NB) and Tree Augmented Naïve Bayes (TAN); C4.5, C4.5 with Laplace estimation (C4.5-L), and C4.5 with bagging (C4.5-B): Classification Accuracy (ACC) & standard deviation

Sample Set	CLLTree	NBTree	NB	TAN	C4.5	C4.5-L	C4.5-B
anneal	99.06	98.40	94.32●	98.34	98.65	98.76	98.76
anneal.ORIG	89.94	91.27	88.16	90.88	90.36	90.23	91.78
audiology	78.40	76.66	71.40●	72.68●	77.22	76.69	80.67
balance-scale	91.44	91.44	91.44	86.22●	64.14●	64.14●	73.30●
breast-cancer	72.14	71.66	72.94	70.09	75.26	75.26	73.09
breast-w	95.08	97.23○	97.30○	94.91	94.01	93.81	95.34
colic	78.08	82.50	78.86	80.57	84.31○	84.50○	84.56○
colic.ORIG	75.57	74.83	74.21	76.11	80.79○	80.08○	82.64○
credit-a	85.13	84.86	84.74	84.43	85.06	84.97	85.83
credit-g	76.01	75.54	75.93	75.86	72.61●	72.25●	73.89
diabetes	75.63	75.28	75.68	75.09	73.89	73.88	73.91
glass	58.69	58.00	57.69	58.43	58.14	58.28	57.98
heart-c	80.54	81.10	83.44	82.85	79.14	79.41	79.48
heart-h	81.41	82.46	83.64	82.14	80.10	80.03	80.90
heart-statlog	83.59	82.26	83.78	79.37●	79.78	79.85	79.44
hepatitis	81.20	82.90	84.06	82.40	81.12	81.12	81.38
hypothyroid	92.90	93.05	92.79	93.23	93.24	93.24	93.25
iris	93.73	95.27	94.33	91.67	96.00	96.00	95.53
kr-vs-kp	98.93	97.81	87.79●	92.05●	99.44●	99.44○	99.42○
labor	93.93	95.60	96.70	90.33	84.97	84.97	85.23
letter	86.24	83.49●	70.09●	83.11●	81.31●	80.51●	83.69●
lymph	82.79	82.21	85.97	84.07	78.21	78.21	78.97
mushroom	100.00	100.00	95.52●	99.99	100.00	100.00	100.00
primary-tumor	46.17	45.84	47.20	46.76	41.01●	41.01●	43.42
segment	93.13	92.64	89.03●	94.54○	93.42	93.19	93.97
sick	97.80	97.86	96.78●	97.61	98.16	98.18	98.17
soybean	93.07	92.30	92.20	95.24○	92.63	92.55	93.66
splice	95.39	95.42	95.42	95.39	94.17●	94.08●	94.51
vehicle	68.83	68.91	61.03●	73.71○	70.74	70.38	71.93
vote	94.65	94.78	90.21●	94.57	96.27	96.27	96.32
vowel	91.59	88.01●	66.09●	93.10	75.57●	73.29●	79.44●
waveform-5000	84.40	81.62●	79.97●	80.72●	72.64●	72.21●	75.54●
zoo	93.86	94.55	94.37	96.73	92.61	92.61	93.51
average	85.13	85.02	82.82	84.64	82.87	82.70	83.92

●, ○ statistically significant degradation or improvement compared with CLLTree

Table 7. Summary on t-test of experimental results: ACC comparisons on CLLTree, NBTree,NB, TAN, C4.5, C4.5-L and C4.5-B

	C4.5	C4.5-L	C4.5-B	TAN	NB	NBTree
C4.5-L	3/30/0					
C4.5-B	6/27/0	7/26/0				
TAN	8/22/3	10/19/4	3/25/5			
NB	8/13/12	8/14/11	5/15/13	3/19/11		
NBTree	7/24/2	8/24/1	5/25/3	3/26/4	11/22/0	
CLLTree	8/23/2	7/23/3	4/26/3	6/24/3	11/21/1	3/29/1

to improve probability estimation, which could produce the "overfitting" problem and will be noise sensitive. Therefore, in a practical perspective, CLLTree is more suitable for many real applications.

5   Conclusion

In this paper, we have proposed a novel algorithm CLLTree to improve probability estimation in NBTree. The empirical results prove our expectation that CLL and AUC are significantly improved and ACC is slightly better compared to other classic learning algorithms. There is still room to improve probability estimation. For example, after the structure is learned, we can use parameter learning algorithms to tune the conditional probability estimates on the path attributes. And we can find the right tree size for our model, i.e. possibly using model-selection criteria to decide when to stop the splitting.

References

1. C. Blake and C.J. Merz. Uci repository of machine learning database.
2. Charles Elkan. The foundations of cost-sensitive learning. In *Proceedings of the Seventeenth International Joint Conference on Artificial Intelligence*, 1991.
3. N. Friedman, D. Geiger, and M. Goldszmidt. Bayesian network classifiers. *Machine Learning*, 29, 1997.
4. D. J. Hand and R. J. Till. A simple generalisation of the area under the roc curve for multiple class classification problems. *Machine Learning*, 45, 2001.
5. Ron Kohavi. Scaling up the accuracy of naive-bayes classifiers: a decision-tree hybrid. In *Proceedings of the Second International Conference on Knowledge Discovery and Data Mining*, 1996.
6. C. Nadeau and Y. Bengio. Inference for the generalization error. *Machine Learning*, 52(40), 2003.
7. J. Pearl. *Probabilistic Reasoning in Intelligent Systems*. Morgan Kaufmann, 1988.
8. F. J. Provost and P. Domingos. Tree induction for probability-based ranking. *Machine Learning*, 52(30), 2003.
9. I. H. Witten and E. Frank. *Data Mining –Practical Machine Learning Tools and Techniques with Java Implementation*. Morgan Kaufmann, 2000.
10. H. Zhang and J. Su. Conditional independence trees. In *Proceedings of the 15th European Conference on Machine Learning (ECML2004)*. Springer, 2004.

On the Performance of Chernoff-Distance-Based Linear Dimensionality Reduction Techniques

Mohammed Liakat Ali[1], Luis Rueda[2], and Myriam Herrera[3]

[1] School of Computer Science, University of Windsor
401 Sunset Avenue, Windsor, ON, N9B 3P4, Canada
ali1p@uwindsor.ca
[2] Department of Computer Science, University of Concepción
Edmundo Larenas 215, Concepción, Chile
lrueda@inf.udec.cl
[3] Institute of Informatics, National University of San Juan
Cereceto y Meglioli, San Juan, 5400, Argentina
mherrera@iinfo.unsj.edu.ar

Abstract. We present a performance analysis of three linear dimensionality reduction techniques: Fisher's discriminant analysis (FDA), and two methods introduced recently based on the Chernoff distance between two distributions, the Loog and Duin (LD) method, which aims to maximize a criterion derived from the Chernoff distance in the original space, and the one introduced by Rueda and Herrera (RH), which aims to maximize the Chernoff distance in the transformed space. A comprehensive performance analysis of these methods combined with two well-known classifiers, linear and quadratic, on synthetic and real-life data shows that LD and RH outperform FDA, specially in the quadratic classifier, which is strongly related to the Chernoff distance in the transformed space. In the case of the linear classifier, the superiority of RH over the other two methods is also demonstrated.

1 Introduction

Linear dimensionality reduction (LDR) techniques have been studied for a long time in the field of machine learning. They are typically the preferred ones due to their efficiency – they perform in linear time complexity, and are simpler to implement and understand. Various schemes that yield LDR have been reported in the literature for reducing to dimension one, including *Fisher's classifier* [4, 18], the *perceptron algorithm* (the basis of the back propagation *neural network* learning algorithms) [5, 9, 13, 14], *piecewise recognition models* [11], *random search optimization* [12], *removal classification structures* [1], *adaptive linear dimensionality reduction* [8] (which outperforms Fisher's classifier for some data sets), *linear constrained distance-based classifier analysis* [3] (an improvement to Fisher's approach designed for hyperspectral image classification), and *recursive Fisher's discriminant* [2]. All of these approaches suffer from the lack of optimality, and thus, although they find linear discriminant (or dimensionality reduction) functions, the classifier is *not optimal*. Rueda et al. [17] have shown that the optimal classifier between two normally distributed classes can be linear even when the

L. Lamontagne and M. Marchand (Eds.): Canadian AI 2006, LNAI 4013, pp. 467–478, 2006.
© Springer-Verlag Berlin Heidelberg 2006

covariance matrices *are not equal*. In [15], a new approach to selecting the *best hyperplane classifier* (BHC), which is obtained from the optimal pairwise linear classifier, has been introduced.

Loog et al. have recently proposed a new LDR technique for normally distributed classes [6], namely LD, which takes the Chernoff distance in the original space into consideration to minimize the error rate in the transformed space. They consider the concept of *directed distance matrices*, and a linear transformation in the original space, to finally generalize Fisher's criterion in the transformed space by substituting the within-class scatter matrix for the corresponding directed distance matrix. Observing the fact that the LD criterion does not maximize the Chernoff distance in the *transformed* space, even though it considers that distance in the *original* space, Rueda et al. proposed a new criterion for linear discriminant analysis [16], namely RH. They observed that the Chernoff distance, which provides a bound and approximation for the true probability of classification error, has to be maximized in the reduced space, as opposed to considering that distance in the original space.

On the other hand, assessing the performance of LDR techniques combined with other classifiers is a quite important problem in pattern recognition, and in this paper we present a performance analysis based on empirical simulations on synthetic and real-life data, which shows the performance of existing LDR techniques when coupled with traditional classifiers. We shall compare the performance of the following methods: Fisher's discriminant analysis (FDA) [4], Loog and Duin dimensionality reduction (LD) [6, 7], and Rueda and Herrera dimensionality reduction (RH) [16]. We show the superiority of RH when dealing with both the quadratic and linear classifiers, and the relationship between these two classifiers and the Chernoff distance between distributions in the transformed space.

2 Linear Dimensionality Reduction Schemes

In this section, we briefly discuss the three LDR schemes involved in our performance analysis. We discuss the two-class problem first, and then the multi-class scenario. We assume we are dealing with two normally distributed classes ω_1 and ω_2 whose a priori probabilities are given by p_1 and p_2, and which are represented by two normally distributed n-dimensional random vectors $x_1 \sim N(m_1; S_1)$ and $x_2 \sim N(m_2; S_2)$. The aim is to find a linear transformation matrix A of dimensions $d \times n$ in such a way that the classification error in the transformed space is minimized.

Let $S_W = p_1 S_1 + p_2 S_2$ and $S_E = (m_1 - m_2)(m_1 - m_2)^t$. The FDA criterion consists of maximizing the distance between the transformed distributions by finding A that maximizes the following function [4]:

$$J_F(A) = tr\left\{(A S_W A^t)^{-1}(A S_E A^t)\right\}. \tag{1}$$

The matrix A that maximizes (1) is obtained by finding the eigenvalue decomposition of the matrix:

$$S_F = S_W^{-1} S_E, \tag{2}$$

and taking the d eigenvectors whose eigenvalues are the largest ones. Since the eigenvalue decomposition of the matrix (2) leads to only one non-zero eigenvalue, $(\mathbf{m}_1 - \mathbf{m}_2)^t(\mathbf{m}_1 - \mathbf{m}_2)$, whose eigenvector is given by $(\mathbf{m}_1 - \mathbf{m}_2)$, we can only reduce to dimension $d = 1$.

On the other hand, the LD criterion consists of minimizing the classification error in the transformed space by obtaining the matrix $\mathbf{A}$ that maximizes the function [7]:

$$
J_{LD_2}(\mathbf{A}) = tr\left\{(\mathbf{A}\mathbf{S}_W\mathbf{A}^t)^{-1} \left[\mathbf{A}\mathbf{S}_E\mathbf{A}^t - \mathbf{A}\mathbf{S}_W^{\frac{1}{2}}\frac{p_1\log(\mathbf{S}_W^{-\frac{1}{2}}\mathbf{S}_1\mathbf{S}_W^{-\frac{1}{2}}) + p_2\log(\mathbf{S}_W^{-\frac{1}{2}}\mathbf{S}_2\mathbf{S}_W^{-\frac{1}{2}})}{p_1p_2}\mathbf{S}_W^{\frac{1}{2}}\mathbf{A}^t\right]\right\} \quad (3)
$$

The solution to this criterion is given by the matrix $\mathbf{A}$ that is composed of the d eigenvectors (whose eigenvalues are maximum) of the following matrix:

$$
\mathbf{S}_{LD_2} = \mathbf{S}_W^{-1}\left[\mathbf{S}_E - \mathbf{S}_W^{\frac{1}{2}}\frac{p_1\log(\mathbf{S}_W^{-\frac{1}{2}}\mathbf{S}_1\mathbf{S}_W^{-\frac{1}{2}}) + p_2\log(\mathbf{S}_W^{-\frac{1}{2}}\mathbf{S}_2\mathbf{S}_W^{-\frac{1}{2}})}{p_1p_2}\mathbf{S}_W^{\frac{1}{2}}\right]. \quad (4)
$$

Another LDR criterion that has been recently proposed is the RH criterion, which aims to find the linear transformation that maximizes the Chernoff distance in the transformed space. Let $p(\mathbf{y}|\omega_i)$ be the class-conditional probability that a vector $\mathbf{y} = \mathbf{A}\mathbf{x}$ in the transformed space belongs to class ω_i. The Chernoff distance between two distributions, $p(\mathbf{y}|\omega_1)$ and $p(\mathbf{y}|\omega_2)$, is given as follows [4]:

$$
\int p^\beta(\mathbf{y}|\omega_1)p^{1-\beta}(\mathbf{y}|\omega_2)d\mathbf{y} = e^{-k(\beta)}, \quad (5)
$$

where

$$
k(\beta) = \frac{\beta(1-\beta)}{2}(\mathbf{A}\mathbf{m}_1 - \mathbf{A}\mathbf{m}_2)^t[\beta\mathbf{A}\mathbf{S}_1\mathbf{A} + (1-\beta)\mathbf{A}\mathbf{S}_2\mathbf{A}]^{-1}(\mathbf{A}\mathbf{m}_1 - \mathbf{A}\mathbf{m}_2)
$$
$$
+ \frac{1}{2}\log\frac{|\beta\mathbf{A}\mathbf{S}_1\mathbf{A} + (1-\beta)\mathbf{A}\mathbf{S}_2\mathbf{A}|}{|\mathbf{A}\mathbf{S}_1\mathbf{A}|^\beta|\mathbf{A}\mathbf{S}_2\mathbf{A}|^{1-\beta}}. \quad (6)
$$

The RH approach, assuming that $p_1 = \beta$ and $p_2 = 1 - \beta$ (note that $\beta \in [0, 1]$), aims to find $\mathbf{A}$ that maximizes the following function [16]:

$$
J_{c_{12}}^*(\mathbf{A}) = tr\{(\mathbf{A}\mathbf{S}_W\mathbf{A}^t)^{-1}\mathbf{A}\mathbf{S}_E\mathbf{A}^t
$$
$$
+ \frac{\log(\mathbf{A}\mathbf{S}_W\mathbf{A}^t) - p_1\log(\mathbf{A}\mathbf{S}_1\mathbf{A}^t) - p_2\log(\mathbf{A}\mathbf{S}_2\mathbf{A}^t)}{p_1p_2}\} \quad (7)
$$

This criterion has no direct solution, and so a gradient-based solution has been proposed in [16].

For the multi-class problem we assume that we are dealing with k classes, $\omega_1, \ldots, \omega_k$, whose *a priori* probabilities are given by $p_1, \ldots, p_k$, and which are represented by k n-dimensional normally distributed random vectors, $\mathbf{x}_1 \sim N(\mathbf{m}_1; \mathbf{S}_1), \ldots, \mathbf{x}_k \sim N(\mathbf{m}_k; \mathbf{S}_k)$. For the FDA criterion, we define $\mathbf{S}_E = \sum_{i=1}^k p_i(\mathbf{m}_i - \mathbf{m})(\mathbf{m}_i - \mathbf{m})^t$, where $\mathbf{m} = \sum_{i=1}^{k} p_i \mathbf{m}_i$, and $\mathbf{S}_W = \sum_{i=1}^{k} p_i \mathbf{S}_i$. Then the FDA criterion aims to find a matrix $\mathbf{A}$ that maximizes the criterion function given in (1), and which is obtained by finding the d eigenvalues (whose eigenvectors are the largest ones) of the matrix given in (2).

The LD criterion for the multi-class problem aims to find the transformation $d \times n$ matrix $\mathbf{A}$ that maximizes the following function [6]:

$$
J_{LD}(\mathbf{A}) = \sum_{i=1}^{k-1} \sum_{j=i+1}^{k} p_i p_j tr \left\{ (\mathbf{A}\mathbf{S}_W \mathbf{A}^t)^{-1} \mathbf{A}\mathbf{S}_W^{\frac{1}{2}} \right.
$$

$$
\left[(\mathbf{S}_W^{-\frac{1}{2}} \mathbf{S}_{ij} \mathbf{S}_W^{-\frac{1}{2}})^{-\frac{1}{2}} \mathbf{S}_W^{-\frac{1}{2}} \mathbf{S}_{E_{ij}} \mathbf{S}_W^{-\frac{1}{2}} (\mathbf{S}_W^{-\frac{1}{2}} \mathbf{S}_{ij} \mathbf{S}_W^{-\frac{1}{2}})^{-\frac{1}{2}} + \frac{1}{\pi_i \pi_j} \left(\log(\mathbf{S}_W^{-\frac{1}{2}} \mathbf{S}_{ij} \mathbf{S}_W^{-\frac{1}{2}}) \right. \right.
$$

$$
\left. \left. - \pi_i \log(\mathbf{S}_W^{-\frac{1}{2}} \mathbf{S}_i \mathbf{S}_W^{-\frac{1}{2}}) - \pi_j \log(\mathbf{S}_W^{-\frac{1}{2}} \mathbf{S}_j \mathbf{S}_W^{-\frac{1}{2}}) \right) \right] \mathbf{S}_W^{\frac{1}{2}} \mathbf{A}^t \right\} , \tag{8}
$$

where $\mathbf{S}_{E_{ij}} = (\mathbf{m}_i - \mathbf{m}_j)(\mathbf{m}_i - \mathbf{m}_j)^t$, $\pi_i = \frac{p_i}{p_i + p_j}$, $\pi_j = \frac{p_j}{p_i + p_j}$, and $\mathbf{S}_{ij} = \pi_i \mathbf{S}_i + \pi_j \mathbf{S}_j$. The multi-class LD criterion is maximized as it is done for the two-dimensional case, by finding the matrix $\mathbf{A}$ composed of the d eigenvectors (whose eigenvalues are the largest) of the following matrix:

$$
\mathbf{S}_{LD} = \sum_{i=1}^{k-1} \sum_{j=i+1}^{k} p_i p_j \mathbf{S}_W^{-1} \mathbf{S}_W^{\frac{1}{2}} \left[(\mathbf{S}_W^{-\frac{1}{2}} \mathbf{S}_{ij} \mathbf{S}_W^{-\frac{1}{2}})^{-\frac{1}{2}} \mathbf{S}_W^{-\frac{1}{2}} \mathbf{S}_{E_{ij}} \mathbf{S}_W^{-\frac{1}{2}} (\mathbf{S}_W^{-\frac{1}{2}} \mathbf{S}_{ij} \mathbf{S}_W^{-\frac{1}{2}})^{-\frac{1}{2}} \right.
$$

$$
\left. + \frac{1}{\pi_i \pi_j} \left(\log(\mathbf{S}_W^{-\frac{1}{2}} \mathbf{S}_{ij} \mathbf{S}_W^{-\frac{1}{2}}) - \pi_i \log(\mathbf{S}_W^{-\frac{1}{2}} \mathbf{S}_i \mathbf{S}_W^{-\frac{1}{2}}) - \pi_j \log(\mathbf{S}_W^{-\frac{1}{2}} \mathbf{S}_j \mathbf{S}_W^{-\frac{1}{2}}) \right) \right] \mathbf{S}_W^{\frac{1}{2}} , \tag{9}
$$

The RH criterion for the multi-class problem aims to maximize the weighted sum of Chernoff pairwise distances in the transformed space by finding the matrix $\mathbf{A}$ that maximizes [16]:

$$
J_c^*(\mathbf{A}) = \sum_{i=1}^{k-1} \sum_{j=i+1}^{k} J_{c_{ij}}^*(\mathbf{A}) . \tag{10}
$$

where

$$
J_{c_{ij}}^*(\mathbf{A}) = tr\{ (\mathbf{A}\mathbf{S}_{W_{ij}} \mathbf{A}^t)^{-1} \mathbf{A}\mathbf{S}_{E_{ij}} \mathbf{A}^t
$$

$$
+ \frac{\log(\mathbf{A}\mathbf{S}_{W_{ij}} \mathbf{A}^t) - p_i \log(\mathbf{A}\mathbf{S}_i \mathbf{A}^t) - p_j \log(\mathbf{A}\mathbf{S}_j \mathbf{A}^t)}{p_i p_j} \} \tag{11}
$$

Again, the maximum for this criterion does not have a direct solution, and hence a gradient-based search method has been proposed in [16]; $\mathbf{S}_{E_{ij}}$ and $\mathbf{S}_{W_{ij}}$ correspond to the between-class and within-class matrices respectively. Since the gradient solution for the RH criterion needs to initialize $\mathbf{A}$, we have used either the result of FDA or LD, depending upon the one that gives the largest Chernoff distance in the transformed space.

3 Performance on Synthetic Data

In order to compare the classification performance of the three above-discussed methods, we present an empirical analysis of the classification accuracy and Chernoff distance in the transformed space on synthetic and real life data. In this section, we discuss the former results, while the latter results are presented in a subsequent section.

To obtain the error rates and Chernoff distances discussed in this paper, we performed a few simulations on synthetic data, which involve ten different datasets of dimensions $n = 10, 20, \ldots, 100$ each with two randomly generated normally distributed classes. The two classes of each dataset, ω_1 and ω_2, are then fully specified by their parameters, μ_1, μ_2, Σ_1 and Σ_2. We also randomly generated p_1 in the range [0.3,0.7], and assigned $p_2 = 1 - p_1$. We trained the three classifiers, FDA, LD and RH using these parameters, and for each dataset we generated 100,000 samples for testing purposes. For each dataset, we found the corresponding transformation matrix $\mathbf{A}$ for each dimension $d = 1, \ldots, n - 1$. After the linear transformation is performed we apply one of two classifiers: the linear classifier, which is obtained by averaging the covariances matrices in the transformed space, and the quadratic classifier which is the one that minimizes the error rate assuming that the parameters of the transformed data are given by $\mathbf{A}m_i$ and $\mathbf{A}S_i\mathbf{A}^t$.

The minimum error rates obtained for each individual classifier for synthetic data are shown in Table 1. The first column represents the dimension of each datset. The next columns correspond to the error rate and the *best* dimension d^* for the three dimensionality reduction methods and for each classifier, quadratic and linear. The '*' symbol beside the error rate indicates that the lowest among the three methods, FDA, LD and RH, was obtained. Note that for FDA, $d^* = 1$, since, as pointed out earlier, the objective matrix contains only one non-zero eigenvalue. We observe that for the quadratic classifier LD and RH outperformed FDA for all the datasets. Also, LD and RH jointly achieved minimum error rate for seven datasets, while RH obtained the best error rate in

Table 1. Error rates for the three classifiers, FDA, LD and RH, where the samples are projected onto the d^*-dimensional space with d^* gives the lowest error rate for $d = 1, \ldots, n - 1$

	Quadratic classifier						Linear classifier					
	FDA		LD		RH		FDA		LD		RH	
n	error	d^*	error	d^*	error	d^*	error	d^*	error	d^*	error	d^*
10	0.286530	1	0.053140*	9	0.053230	9	0.289790	1	0.288820*	6	0.288830	9
20	0.222550	1	0.019680	18	0.019580*	18	0.227000	1	0.220180	3	0.218780*	4
30	0.151190	1	0.002690*	24	0.002690*	24	0.182180*	1	0.182480	27	0.182480	27
40	0.287250	1	0.006600	36	0.006570*	36	0.297840	1	0.295370	8	0.294660*	6
50	0.370450	1	0.005490*	49	0.005490*	49	0.396160*	1	0.397450	1	0.397450	1
60	0.320760	1	0.000680*	56	0.000680*	56	0.322920	1	0.316030	21	0.315250*	23
70	0.381870	1	0.000010*	28	0.000010*	28	0.381960	1	0.381910*	30	0.381910*	30
80	0.323140	1	0.000000*	37	0.000000*	37	0.342980	1	0.334170	23	0.334080*	25
90	0.324740	1	0.000000*	30	0.000000*	30	0.326360	1	0.324740*	1	0.324740*	1
100	0.198610	1	0.000000*	31	0.000000*	31	0.278590*	1	0.278730	78	0.278720	72

nine out of ten datasets. For the linear classifier, again, LD and RH outperformed FDA, and also RH achieved the lowest error rate in six out of ten datasets, outperforming LD.

In Table 2, the results for the dimensionality reduction and classification for dimension $d = 1$ are shown. For the quadratic classifier, we observe that as in the previous case, LD and RH outperformed FDA, and that the latter did not obtained the lowest error rate in any of the datasets. On the other hand, RH yields the lowest error rate in nine out of ten datasets, outperforming LD. FDA, however, did perform very well for the linear classifier, achieving the lowest error rate in eight out of ten datasets. RH, though not the best, outperformed LD yielding the lowest error rate in two out of ten datasets. Note also that the good performance of FDA and the linear classifier is due to the fact that the optimal Bayes classifier for normal distributions is linear when the covariances are coincident.

Table 2. Error rates for the quadratic and linear classifiers in the one-dimensional space, where the transformed data has been obtained using the FDA, LD and RH methods

n	Quadratic classifier error rates			Linear classifier error rates		
	FDA	LD	RH	FDA	LD	RH
10	0.286530	0.169750	0.154790*	0.289790*	0.320460	0.385010
20	0.222550	0.218260	0.204680*	0.227000	0.229260	0.222490*
30	0.151190	0.022950*	0.022950*	0.182180*	0.277120	0.277120
40	0.287250	0.219680	0.219590*	0.297840*	0.458030	0.458030
50	0.370450	0.237150	0.237080*	0.396160*	0.397450	0.397450
60	0.320760	0.122350*	0.122440	0.322920*	0.440710	0.440710
70	0.381870	0.061530*	0.061530*	0.381960*	0.402320	0.402320
80	0.323140	0.060320*	0.060320*	0.342980*	0.444530	0.444530
90	0.324740	0.087150*	0.087150*	0.326360	0.324740*	0.324740*
100	0.198610	0.093410*	0.093410*	0.278590*	0.332370	0.332370

In order to perform a finer comparison of the classifiers for a specific dataset, we picked $n = 10$, and plotted the error rates for all the reduced spaces, where $d = 1, 2, \ldots, 9$. These plots are depicted in Figs. 1 and 2 for the quadratic and linear classifiers respectively. FDA is not shown in the figures, since it only reduces to dimension $d = 1$. We observe how RH outperforms LD in most of the cases, and how in both techniques, the error rate decreases as the dimension d of the transformed space increases.

To analyze the relationship between the Chernoff distance, which is a bound and an approximation of the error rate for Bayesian quadratic classifiers (when the underlying distributions are normal), we depict, in Table 3, the Cherfnoff distance for FDA, LD and RH, for the reduced space of dimension $d = 1$. As expected, for LD and RH, the Chernoff distance is much higher than for FDA. Also, we observe that in all cases (except for $n = 100$) the Chernoff distance in the transformed space obtained by RH is higher than that of LD. This denotes that RH maximizes that distance in the transformed space, and hence it is more likely to obtain a lower error rate in the actual classification, as observed in Tables 1 and 2. In order to observe the relation between the Chernoff distance and the error rate from a different perspective, we graphically show that distance for two cases, $n = 10$ and $n = 20$, for the different reduced spaces corresponding to

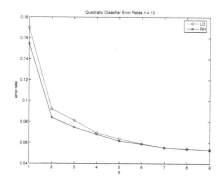
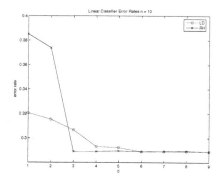

Fig. 1. Error rates, $n = 10$, quadratic classifier   **Fig. 2.** Error rates, $n = 10$, linear classifier

Table 3. Chernoff distance in the transformed space, whose dimension is $d = 1$

n	FDA	LD	RH
10	1.356689	3.990860	4.431230*
20	2.440234	2.608052	2.975204*
30	3.583576	18.412905	18.412905*
40	1.339673	2.664509	2.665077*
50	0.595728	2.508774	2.508884*
60	0.769184	5.636596	5.636756*
70	0.268591	8.032135	8.032135*
80	0.855710	8.510208	8.510208*
90	0.182060	7.904976	7.904976*
100	2.394710	7.469918*	7.469918*

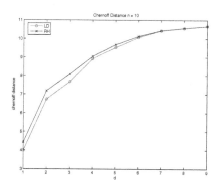
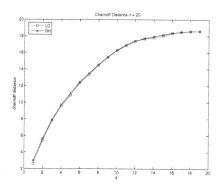

Fig. 3. Chernoff distance for $n = 10$ **Fig. 4.** Chernoff distance for $n = 20$

$d = 1, \ldots, n - 1$. We, again, observe that the Chernoff distance effectively increases as the dimension of the reduced space increases, and hence corroborates the tendency in the classification error rate, as shown previously for the quadratic classifier.

4 Performance on Real-Life Data

As in the experiments on synthetic data, to obtain the error rates and Chernoff distances discussed in this paper, we also performed a few simulations on real life data which involve 44 two-class, d-dimensional datasets drawn from the UCI machine learning repository [10]. Originally, seven datasets were of two classes, and the others were multi-class, from which we extracted pairs of classes. We have assumed the classes are normally distributed, and so the mean and covariance was obtained for each class, and the prior probabilities were estimated as $p_i = n_i/(n_i + n_j)$, where n_i and n_j are the number of samples for class ω_i and ω_j respectively. We have trained the classifiers using the three methods in discussion, namely FDA, LD, and RH, and obtained the mean of the error rate for a ten-fold cross-validation experiment. The results for the best value of d, where $d = 1, \ldots, n - 1$ with n the dimension of the original space, are shown in Table 4. The first column indicates the name of the dataset and the pair of classes separated by ";" (when classes are not given, it means the problem itself is two-class), where the name of the dataset is as follows: W = Wisconsin breast cancer, B = Bupa liver, P = Pima, D = Wisconsin diagnostic breast cancer, C = Cleveland heart-disease, S = SPECTF heart, I = Iris, T = Thyroid, G = Glass, N = Wine, J = Japanese vowels, L = Letter and E = Pendigits. The other columns represent the error rates as in Table 1. For the quadratic classifier, RH outperformed both FDA and LD, since the former obtained the lowest error rate in 34 out of 44 cases, while FDA and LD obtained the lowest error rate in 17 and 16 cases respectively. In the case of the linear classifier, RH also outperformed FDA and LD – the former was the best in 31 cases, while the latter two in 15 and 26 cases respectively. In this case, although RH is coupled with a linear classifier, while it optimizes the Chernoff distance and is expected to work well with a quadratic classifier, RH obtained the lowest error rate in more cases than LD.

To show the results from a different perspective, and to analyze the classifiers on different dimensions $d = 1, \ldots, n - 1$, we plotted the error rate of the SPECTF dataset for all values of d, and for two methods, LD and RH. FDA was excluded, since as pointed out earlier, the data can only be transformed to dimension 1. The corresponding plots for the quadratic classifier and the linear classifier are depicted in Figs. 5 and 6 respectively. For the quadratic classifier, the error rate (in general) decreases as the dimension d of the new space increases. Also, in this case, the RH clearly leads to a lower error rate than LD, while both converge to similar error rates for values of d close to n. This reflects the fact that as the Chernoff distance in the transformed space increases, the error rate of the quadratic classifier decreases. For the linear classifier, the behavior is different, in the sense that the the error rate starts decreasing to a certain point, to increase again after $d = 20$, while in most of the cases, RH leads to a lower error rate than LD.

The plots of the Chernoff distance for different values of $d = 1, \ldots, n-1$, for RH and LD, and for the SPECTF and the Ionosphere datasets are depicted in Figs. 7 and 8 respectively. It is quite clear that in both cases, the Chernoff distance in the transformed space (y-axis), which is computed as in (7), increases as the dimension d of the transformed space increases. While for the SPECTF dataset RH leads to a much higher Chernoff distance than LD, the difference is marginal for the Ionosphere dataset. This, again, shows that since RH seeks for maximizing the Chernoff distance

Table 4. Error rates for the two-class datasets drawn from the UCI machine learning repository

Dataset	Quadratic classifier						Linear classifier					
	FDA	d^*	LD	d^*	RH	d^*	FDA	d^*	LD	d^*	RH	d^*
W	0.030754	1	0.027835*	1	0.030754	1	0.039621	1	0.038150*	6	0.039621	1
B	0.362017	1	0.388571	4	0.353613*	1	0.309916	1	0.330168	5	0.301261*	5
P	0.226435*	1	0.251265	2	0.226435*	1	0.229033*	1	0.230383	7	0.229033*	1
D	0.031522*	1	0.040266	27	0.031522*	1	0.042079	1	0.029889*	20	0.036785	28
C	0.164943	1	0.168276	11	0.161379*	11	0.161609	1	0.158391	8	0.144828*	5
S	0.247773	1	0.045588	41	0.042810*	36	0.233646	1	0.176373*	19	0.180378	15
I,1,2	0.000000*	1	0.000000*	1	0.000000*	1	0.000000*	1	0.000000*	1	0.000000*	1
I,1,3	0.000000*	1	0.000000*	1	0.000000*	1	0.000000*	1	0.000000*	1	0.000000*	1
I,2,3	0.050000	1	0.030000*	1	0.040000	2	0.030000*	1	0.040000	1	0.030000*	1
T,1,2	0.021637	1	0.010819	4	0.005263*	3	0.059357	1	0.032749	4	0.027193*	4
T,1,3	0.022222*	1	0.027778	2	0.027778	2	0.038889	1	0.027778*	4	0.027778*	4
T,2,3	0.000000*	1	0.000000*	2	0.000000*	1	0.000000*	1	0.000000*	1	0.000000*	1
G,1,2	0.310000*	1	0.397619	7	0.397619	8	0.281905*	1	0.295714	8	0.289048	7
G,1,3	0.223611	1	0.204167	1	0.112500*	8	0.223611	1	0.204167	1	0.161111*	8
G,1,5	0.000000*	1	0.000000*	5	0.000000*	1	0.000000*	1	0.000000*	5	0.000000*	1
G,1,7	0.020000*	1	0.040000	8	0.020000*	1	0.040000	1	0.030000*	1	0.040000	1
G,2,3	0.158611	1	0.213333	8	0.153611*	8	0.158611*	1	0.167222	4	0.166111	8
G,2,5	0.109722	1	0.098333*	7	0.098333*	6	0.099722	1	0.088333*	7	0.088333*	6
G,2,7	0.027273*	1	0.063636	7	0.027273*	1	0.046364	1	0.037273	8	0.018182*	8
G,3,5	0.000000*	1	0.000000*	1	0.000000*	1	0.025000	1	0.000000*	6	0.000000*	7
G,3,7	0.060000	1	0.020000*	2	0.040000	4	0.060000*	1	0.060000*	1	0.060000*	1
G,5,7	0.050000*	1	0.070000	4	0.050000*	1	0.050000	1	0.050000	8	0.025000*	2
N,1,2	0.007143	1	0.007692	6	0.000000*	6	0.007692	1	0.007143*	11	0.007692	1
N,1,3	0.000000*	1	0.000000*	3	0.000000*	1	0.000000*	1	0.000000*	3	0.000000*	1
N,2,3	0.016667	1	0.016667	3	0.008333*	7	0.016667	1	0.008333*	12	0.016667	1
J,1,2	0.001435*	1	0.005263	3	0.001435*	1	0.001435*	1	0.001435*	11	0.001435*	1
J,1,3	0.000370*	1	0.001108	7	0.000370*	1	0.001108*	1	0.001108*	11	0.001108*	1
J,4,5	0.007512	1	0.001778*	7	0.004865	3	0.004417	1	0.000881*	9	0.004861	1
J,6,7	0.000000*	1	0.000000*	1	0.000000*	1	0.000000*	1	0.000000*	1	0.000000*	1
J,8,9	0.066800	1	0.051309*	11	0.052896	6	0.069473	1	0.071601	11	0.068404*	8
L,C,G	0.083547	1	0.051096	15	0.047083*	10	0.083547	1	0.084903	12	0.081574*	6
L,D,O	0.033400	1	0.015402	15	0.014777*	10	0.032784	1	0.030216*	14	0.032776	12
L,J,T	0.009741	1	0.004520	10	0.003875*	8	0.009741	1	0.009741	15	0.009087*	10
L,K,R	0.098878	1	0.041405*	12	0.042081	10	0.096207	1	0.095522	13	0.094207*	1
L,M,N	0.031751	1	0.015847	13	0.014590*	13	0.034936	1	0.033033*	13	0.034936	1
L,O,Q	0.045591*	1	0.057280	11	0.046253	1	0.046237	1	0.050133	11	0.045583*	9
L,P,R	0.020505	1	0.012176	9	0.010248*	9	0.022432	1	0.021787*	7	0.022428	6
L,U,V	0.010748	1	0.007595	15	0.006966*	9	0.012018	1	0.011381*	10	0.011381*	9
L,V,W	0.027057	1	0.027048	15	0.022438*	10	0.029706	1	0.031035	13	0.028381*	5
E,1,2	0.003051	1	0.001312	10	0.000873*	10	0.006556*	1	0.006556*	10	0.006556*	1
E,3,4	0.002277	1	0.002277	1	0.002273*	8	0.002277*	1	0.002277*	1	0.002277*	1
E,5,6	0.001370	1	0.000457	6	0.000000*	8	0.001826	1	0.002283	11	0.001822*	13
E,7,8	0.000911	1	0.000455*	3	0.000455*	3	0.000911	1	0.000455*	1	0.000911	1
E,9,10	0.011357	1	0.000472*	12	0.000943	12	0.012300	1	0.009933	11	0.008518*	6

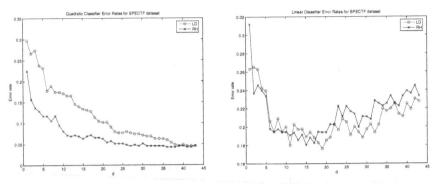

Fig. 5. Quadratic classifier error rates, SPECTF   **Fig. 6.** Linear classifier error rates, SPECTF

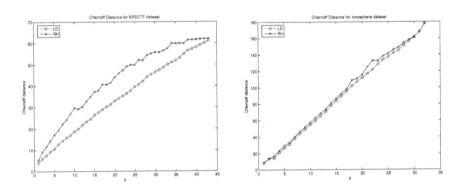

Fig. 7. Chernoff distance for SPECTF   **Fig. 8.** Chernoff distance for Ionosphere

Table 5. Error rates for the multi-class classification on the Iris dataset, where $d = 1, 2, 3$

	Quadratic Classifier			Linear Classifier		
d	FC	LD	RH	FC	LD	RH
1	0.026667	0.020000*	0.020000*	0.020000*	0.020000*	0.020000*
2	0.026667	0.020000*	0.026667	0.020000*	0.020000*	0.020000*
3	0.026667*	0.026667*	0.026667*	0.020000*	0.020000*	0.020000*

in the transformed space, it is more likely to lead to the lowest error rate in the transformed space. This has been observed and corroborates the superiority of RH over LD and FDA, as shown in Table 4.

To conclude the paper, we show some results obtained by testing the three LDR techniques for the multi-class case on real-life data. The dataset involved in the experiments is, again, drawn from the UCI machine learning repository [10], namely the Iris dataset whose original space is of dimension four, and whose number of classes is three. The error rates for reducing the dimension to $d = 1, \ldots, n - 1$, where $n = 4$, are shown in Table 5. Note that for the quadratic classifier, LD and RH are superior to FDA. For the linear classifier, the three dimensionality reduction methods produce similar results.

5   Conclusions

We have presented a comprehensive performance analysis of three linear dimensionality reduction techniques, namely FDA, LD and RH. Our analysis has been carried out by combining these dimensionality reduction methods with well-known, linear and quadratic, on synthetic and real-life data. We have shown that on the synthetic data, LD and RH clearly outperform FDA, as it is expected since the latter does not take the Chernoff distance into consideration. We observed, also, that RH outperformed LD, and that this is due to the fact that the former optimizes the Chernoff distance in the transformed space, and hence the quadratic classifier is more likely to lead to a lower error rate. Although this would not be the case for the linear classifier, we observed that RH, in general, outperforms LD when coupled with the linear classifier.

We have also presented a comprehensive empirical analysis on real-life data drawn from standard repositories, and encountered that RH outperformed by a large margin both LD and FDA when using the quadratic classifier. For the linear classifier, RH performed the best of the three dimensionality reduction techniques. By analyzing the Chernoff distance in the transformed space, we noticed that the latter is highly related to the success of the quadratic classifier after the data is transformed.

Acknowledgments. This research work has been partially supported by NSERC, the Natural Sciences and Engineering Research Council of Canada, CFI, the Canadian Foundation for Innovation, OIT, the Ontario Innovation Trust, and the Institute of Informatics, National University of San Juan, Argentina.

References

1. M. Aladjem. Linear Discriminant Analysis for Two Classes Via Removal of Classification Structure. *IEEE Trans. on Pattern Analysis and Machine Intelligence*, 19(2):187–192, 1997.
2. T. Cooke. Two Variations on Fisher's Linear Discriminant for Pattern Recognition. *IEEE Transations on Pattern Analysis and Machine Intelligence*, 24(2):268–273, 2002.
3. Q. Du and C. Chang. A Linear Constrained Distance-based Discriminant Analysis for Hyperspectral Image Classification. *Pattern Recognition*, 34(2):361–373, 2001.
4. R. Duda, P. Hart, and D. Stork. *Pattern Classification*. John Wiley and Sons, Inc., New York, NY, 2nd edition, 2000.
5. R. Lippman. An Introduction to Computing with Neural Nets. In *Neural Networks: Theoretical Foundations and Analsyis*, pages 5–24. IEEE Press, 1992.
6. M. Loog and P.W. Duin. Linear Dimensionality Reduction via a Heteroscedastic Extension of LDA: The Chernoff Criterion. *IEEE Transactions on Pattern Analysis and Machine Intelligence*, 26(6):732–739, 2004.
7. M. Loog and R. Duin. Non-iterative Heteroscedastic Linear Dimension Reduction for Two-Class Data. In *Proceedings of the Joint IAPR International Workshops SSPR 2002 and SPR 2002*, volume LNCS 2396, pages 508–517. Springer, 2002.
8. R. Lotlikar and R. Kothari. Adaptive Linear Dimensionality Reduction for Classification. *Pattern Recognition*, 33(2):185–194, 2000.
9. O. Murphy. Nearest Neighbor Pattern Classification Perceptrons. In *Neural Networks: Theoretical Foundations and Analysis*, pages 263–266. IEEE Press, 1992.
10. D. Newman, S. Hettich, C. Blake, and C. Merz. UCI repository of machine learning databases, 1998. University of California, Irvine, Dept. of Computer Science.

11. A. Rao, D. Miller, K. Rose, , and A. Gersho. A Deterministic Annealing Approach for Parsimonious Design of Piecewise Regression Models. *IEEE Transactions on Pattern Analysis and Machine Intelligence*, 21(2):159–173, 1999.

12. S. Raudys. On Dimensionality, Sample Size, and Classification Error of Nonparametric Linear Classification. *IEEE Transactions on Pattern Analysis and Machine Intelligence*, 19(6):667–671, 1997.

13. S. Raudys. Evolution and Generalization of a Single Neurone: I. Single-layer Perception as Seven Statistical Classifiers. *Neural Networks*, 11(2):283–296, 1998.

14. S. Raudys. Evolution and Generalization of a Single Neurone: II. Complexity of Statistical Classifiers and Sample Size Considerations. *Neural Networks*, 11(2):297–313, 1998.

15. L. Rueda. Selecting the Best Hyperplane in the Framework of Optimal Pairwise Linear Classifiers. *Pattern Recognition Letters*, 25(2):49–62, 2004.

16. L. Rueda and M. Herrera. Linear Discriminant Analysis by Maximizing the Chernoff Distance in the Transformed Space. *Submitted for Publication*, 2006.

17. L. Rueda and B. J. Oommen. On Optimal Pairwise Linear Classifiers for Normal Distributions: The Two-Dimensional Case. *IEEE Transations on Pattern Analysis and Machine Intelligence*, 24(2):274–280, February 2002.

18. A. Webb. *Statistical Pattern Recognition*. John Wiley & Sons, N.York, second edition, 2002.

Discriminative vs. Generative Classifiers for Cost Sensitive Learning

Chris Drummond

Institute for Information Technology,
National Research Council Canada,
Ottawa, Ontario, Canada, K1A 0R6
Chris.Drummond@nrc-cnrc.gc.ca

Abstract. This paper experimentally compares the performance of discriminative and generative classifiers for cost sensitive learning. There is some evidence that learning a discriminative classifier is more effective for a traditional classification task. This paper explores the advantages, and disadvantages, of using a generative classifier when the misclassification costs, and class frequencies, are not fixed. The paper details experiments built around commonly used algorithms modified to be cost sensitive. This allows a clear comparison to the same algorithm used to produce a discriminative classifier. The paper compares the performance of these different variants over multiple data sets and for the full range of misclassification costs and class frequencies. It concludes that although some of these variants are better than a single discriminative classifier, the right choice of training set distribution plus careful calibration are needed to make them competitive with multiple discriminative classifiers.

1 Introduction

This paper compares the performance of discriminative and generative classifiers. It focuses on cost sensitive learning when the misclassification costs, and class frequencies, may change, or are simply unknown ahead of time. The distinction between these two types of classifier has only recently been made clear within the data mining and machine learning communities [1], although both have a long history. For a traditional classification task, it seems intuitive that directly learning the decision boundary, as discriminative classifiers do, is likely to be the more effective option. Indeed, many experiments have shown that such classifiers often have better performance than generative ones [1, 2]. There is also some theory suggesting why this holds true, at least asymptotically [2].

Nevertheless the debate continues, with some research showing that the conclusion is not as simple as the discriminative classifier being always better. Some restrictions on the sort of distributions the generative model learns have been shown to improve the accuracy of classification [3] over and above that of discriminatory classifiers. In addition, although theory suggests that the asymptotic performance of the discriminative classifier maybe better, a generative one may

L. Lamontagne and M. Marchand (Eds.): Canadian AI 2006, LNAI 4013, pp. 479–490, 2006.
© Springer-Verlag Berlin Heidelberg 2006

outperform it for realistic training set sizes [4]. Further, generative classifiers are a natural way to include domain knowledge, leading some researchers to propose a hybrid of the two [5].

This paper explores the advantages, and disadvantages, of using a generative classifier for cost sensitive learning. Cost sensitive learning is a research area which has grown considerably in recent years. This type of learning seems a much more natural fit with generative classifiers. Without clear knowledge of the class frequencies and misclassifications costs, a discrimination boundary cannot be constructed whereas class likelihood functions can still be learned.

Researchers have proposed simple ways of modifying popular algorithms for probability estimation [6, 7], experimentally comparing these new variants with the original discriminative forms. This paper presents a much more comprehensive set of experiments comparing the generative and discriminative versions of the algorithms. It displays the results graphically, for multiple data sets, using cost curves [8]. This provides a clear picture of the difference in performance of these algorithms for all possible class distributions and misclassification costs. It concludes that although all the generative forms improve considerably on a single discriminative classifier, the right choice of training set distribution plus careful calibration are needed to make them competitive with multiple discriminative classifiers.

2   Discriminative vs. Generative Classifiers

The difference between a discriminative and a generative classifier is the difference in being able to recognize something and being able to reproduce it. A discriminative classifier learns a border; one side it labels one class, the other side it labels another. The border is chosen to minimize error rate, or some correlated measure, effectively discriminating between classes. When misclassification costs are included, a discriminative classifier chooses a border such as to minimize expected cost. A generative classifier learns the full joint distribution of class and attribute values and could generate labeled instances according to this distribution. To classify an unlabeled instance, it applies decision theory. For classification, we want to reliably recognize something as belonging to a particular class. Learning the full distribution is unnecessary and, as discussed in the introduction, often results in lower performance.

One situation where the generative classifier should dominate is when these misclassification costs change independent of the joint distribution. Then the boundary will need to change, necessitating re-learning the discriminative classifier. But the distribution learned by the generative classifier will still be valid. All that is required is that decision theory be used to relabel the instances. A closely related situation, where the generative classifier should also dominate, is when changes in distribution affect only a few marginals. A common way to factor the joint distribution is by using Bayes rule:

$$P(Cl, D) = P(D|Cl)P(Cl) \tag{1}$$

The distribution is the product of the likelihood function $P(D|Cl)$ (the probability of data D given class Cl) and the prior probability of the class $P(Cl)$. If only the prior probabilities change, the joint probability can be reconstructed using the new values of these marginals. The priors may be known for different applications in the same domain or they may need estimating. But even in the latter case, it is a multinomial distribution and easy to reliably estimate.

The close relationship between prior probabilities, or class frequencies, and costs is clarified in the decision theoretic equation:

$$Best(L) = \min_i C(L_{\bar{i}}|Cl_i)P(Cl_i|D) = P(D) \min_i C(L_{\bar{i}}|Cl_i)P(D|Cl_i)P(Cl_i) \quad (2)$$

Here $C(L_{\bar{i}}|Cl_i)$ is the cost of misclassifying an instance, which is assumed to be independent of how it is misclassified (As this paper is only concerned with two class problems, this assumption is trivially true). The best class label to choose is the one with the lowest expected cost. Using Bayes rule, we can covert this to the likelihood multiplied by the prior and the misclassification cost. Thus if the likelihood is constant, changes in class frequencies and misclassification costs have the same influence on the choice of best label.

3   Cost Curves

This section gives a brief introduction to cost curves [8], a way to visualize classifier performance over different misclassification costs and class distributions.

The error rate of a binary classifier is a convex combination of the likelihood functions $P(-|+)$, $P(+|-)$, where $P(L|Cl)$ is the probability that an instance of class Cl is labeled L and the coefficients $P(+)$, $P(-)$ are the class priors:

$$E[Error] = \underbrace{P(-|+)}_{FN} P(+) + \underbrace{P(+|-)}_{FP} P(-)$$

Estimates of the likelihoods are the false positive (FP) and false negative (FN) rates. A straight line, such as the one in bold in Figure 1, gives the error rate on the y-axis (ignore the axis labels in parentheses for the moment), for each possible prior probability of an instance belonging to the positive class on the x-axis. If this line is completely below another line, representing a second classifier, it has a lower error rate for every probability. If they cross, each classifier is better for some range of priors. Of particular note are the two trivial classifiers, the dashed lines in the figure. One always predicts that instances are negative, the other that instances are positive. Together they form the majority classifier, the shaded triangle in Figure 1, which predicts the most common class. The figure shows that any single classifier with a non-zero error rate will always be outperformed by the majority classifier if the priors are sufficiently skewed. It will therefore be of little use in this situation.

If misclassification costs are taken into account, expected error rate is replaced by expected cost, defined by Equation 3. The expected cost is also a convex combination of the priors, but plotting it against them would produce a y-axis

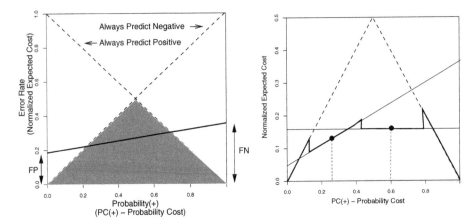

Fig. 1. Majority Classifier   **Fig. 2.** The Cost Curve

that no longer ranges from zero to one. The expected cost is normalized by dividing by the maximum value, given by Equation 4. The costs and priors are combined into the $PC(+)$ the Probability Cost on the x-axis, as in Equation 5. Applying the same normalization factor results in an x-axis that ranges from zero to one, as in Equation 6. The positive and negative Probability Costs now sum to one, as was the case with the probabilities.

$$E[Cost] = FN * C(-|+)P(+) + FP * C(+|-)P(-) \tag{3}$$
$$max(E[Cost]) = C(-|+)P(+) + C(+|-)P(-) \tag{4}$$
$$PC(+) = C(-|+)P(+) \tag{5}$$
$$Norm(E[Cost]) = FN * PC(+) + FP * PC(-) \tag{6}$$

With this representation, the axes in Figure 1 are simply relabeled, using the text in parentheses, to account for costs. Misclassification costs and class frequencies are more imbalanced the further away from 0.5, the center of the diagram. The lines are still straight. There is still a triangular shaded region, but now representing the classifier predicting the class with the smaller expected cost. For simplicity, we shall continue to refer to it as the majority classifier.

In Figure 2 the straight continuous lines are the expected cost for discriminative classifiers for two different class frequencies, or costs, indicated by the vertical dashed lines. To build a curve requires many different classifiers, each associated with the $PC(+)$ value used to generate it. Let's assume each classifier is used in the range from half way between its $PC(+)$ value and that of its left neighbor to half way between this value and that of its right neighbor. The resulting black curve, which includes the trivial classifiers, is shown in Figure 2. It has discontinuities where the change over between classifiers occurs.

To produce a curve for a generative classifier, each instance is associated with the $PC(+)$ value at which the classifier changes the way it is labeled.

If the instances are sorted according to this value, increasing $PC(+)$ values generate unique FP and TP pairs. A curve is constructed in the same way as that for the discriminative classifiers. But now there are many more points, one for each instance in the test set, typically producing a much smoother looking curve.

4   Experiments

This section discusses experiments comparing the performance of various popular algorithms, as implemented in the machine learning system called Weka [9]. The main set of experiments compares the expected cost of a single generative classifier to that of a single discriminative classifier and to a series of such classifiers trained on data sets with different class frequencies. The question it addresses is to what extent the existing variants of standard algorithms are effective for cost sensitive learning. Further experiments look at how these probability estimators might be improved, firstly by calibration and secondly by using more balanced training sets.

To produce different $PC(+)$ values, the training set is under-sampled, the number of instances of one class being reduced to produce the appropriate class distribution. This is done for 16 $PC(+)$ values, roughly uniformly covering the range 0 to 1. The FP and TP values are estimated using ten-fold stratified cross validation. Experimental results, drawn from a larger experimental study [10], are given for 8 data sets from the UCI collection [11].

4.1   Decision Trees

We begin with the decision tree algorithm J48, Weka's version of C4.5 [12]. Figure 3 shows cost curves for the 8 data sets (the name is just above the x-axis). The gray solid curves give the expected cost for the generative classifier. This is calculated from probability estimates based on the class frequency at the leaves of the tree, adjusted for the class distribution in the training set.

To interpret these graphs, let us note that, in these experiments at least, there is little or no difference between discriminative and generative classifiers for the particular $PC(+)$ value at which they were trained. The main advantage of a generative classifier is that it will operate effectively at a quite different $PC(+)$ values. The solid black curve is for 14 discriminative classifiers generated by under-sampling. It acts, essentially, as a lower bound on the expected cost of using the generative classifier. The bold black straight line is the standard classifier trained (with default settings) at the original data set frequency, indicated by the vertical line. At this frequency, the black line, the gray solid curve, and the black curve have a similar expected cost (being essentially the same classifier). The cost sensitivity of the generative classifier is seen by comparing the distance of the gray curve to the straight black line and the distance to the black curve, as one moves away from the original frequency. Closer to the black curve is better.

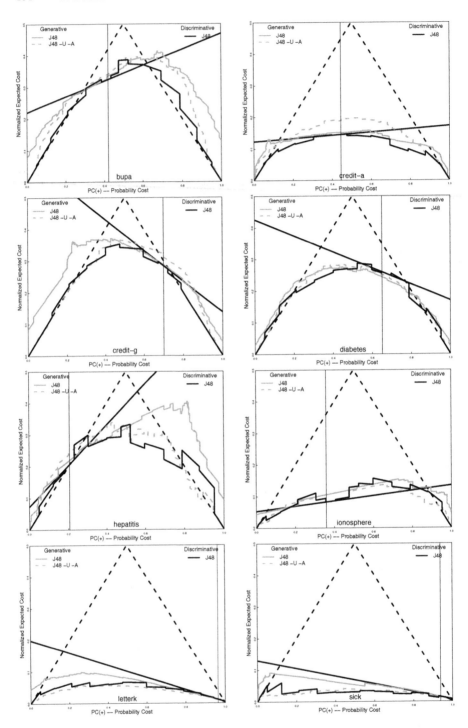

Fig. 3. Cost Curves: Decision Tree Generative Classifier

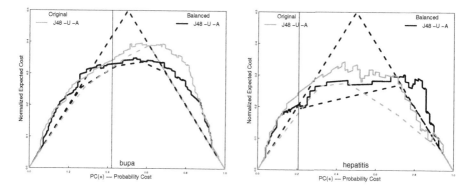

Fig. 4. Improving the Decision Tree Generative Classifier

Although close to the original frequency there is little to separate the curves, the difference grows as the distance increases. For $PC(+)$ values closer to zero and one, the solid gray curves are much better than the single discriminative classifiers and quite close to the multiple ones. Unfortunately, here the performance is worse than the majority classifier, making any gain over the discriminative classifier of dubious merit. One way to improve the probability estimates is to use Laplace correction at the leaves of an unpruned tree [6]. In Figure 3 this variant is indicated by the dashed gray curve. Generally, this improves on the standard algorithm, again it is most clear far away from the original frequency. For some data sets, e.g. letterK and Sick, it is indistinguishable from the black solid curve. But for other data sets, e.g. credit-a and hepatitis, without pruning means it is worse than the standard classifier around the original frequency.

There are two commonly methods to improve cost sensitivity: calibration and changing the training set distribution. Calibration refines the existing probability estimates to better reflect the true distribution using the training, or a hold-out, data. Figure 4 compares the cost curves to their lower envelopes, the dashed curves. The envelopes represent perfect calibration. The figure also shows results for using a balanced set for training the generative classifier. For many data sets, like Bupa and Hepatitis, balancing the training set makes the cost curve more symmetric. Calibration has greater potential impact, although often the best one might expect to do as well as the majority classifier far away from the original frequency.

4.2   Support Vector Machines

The original Support Vector Machine [2] had no means of producing probability estimates and only acted as a discriminative classifier. Platt [7] showed that a sigmoid could be applied to the normal output, the distance to the optimal hyperplane (the sign deciding the class), to represent the posterior probability. This sigmoid is learned from the training set (or by cross validation)

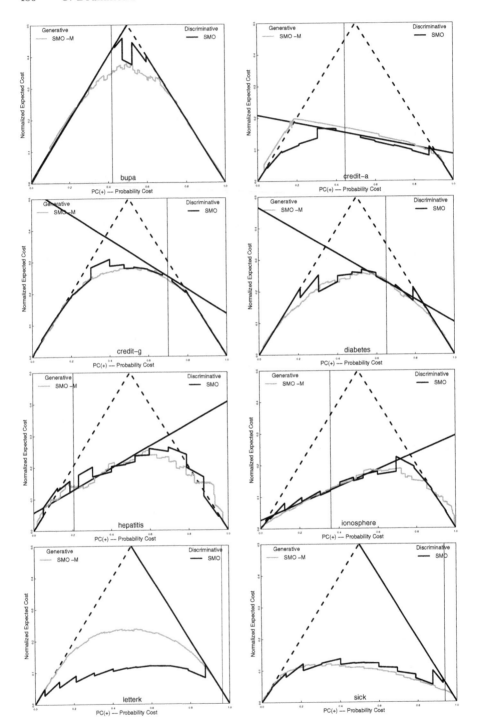

Fig. 5. Cost Curves: Support Vector Machine Generative Classifier

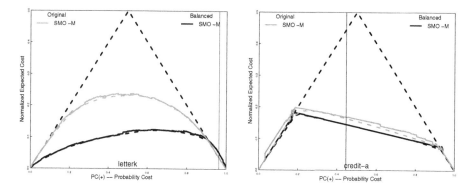

Fig. 6. Improving the Support Vector Machine Generative Classifier

using cross entropy as the error measure. Figure 5 shows that this variant, the gray curve, is extremely competitive with the multiple discriminative classifiers. For only a couple of data sets, letterK and credit-a, are the two discernibly different.

Figure 6 shows, there is typically little difference between the cost curves (solid lines) and their lower envelopes (dashed lines), so calibrating the classifier should have little effect. This is not surprising as fitting a sigmoid is, itself, a form of calibration. Although the sigmoid only has two degrees of freedom, one can see more flexible schemes are unlikely to improve calibration much. This may be why no real benefit was seen using isotonic regression [13]. There is one data set, LetterK, that shows a large difference in expected cost. This is an extremely imbalanced domain and by training the classifier on a balanced data set, the black curves in Figure 6, considerable improvement is gained. For, credit-a the difference is smaller and largely on the left hand side of the original frequency. But here neither better balance nor calibration reduce the problem.

4.3   Neural Networks

Weka implements the traditional PDP algorithm [14] which is trained using back propagation and minimizes the squared error of the network output. This can be used as a discrimination classifier or, by using the standard sigmoid output of the network, as a probability estimator. As Figure 7 shows, much like the standard decision tree, it improves on a single discriminative classifier but mainly where the majority classifier is best. It certainly falls way short of the performance of the multiple discriminative classifiers. Figure 8 shows that balancing the training set offers some improvement but much of the error is due to poor calibration. It is noteworthy that the Weka algorithm minimizes squared error. Minimizing cross entropy, like the generative version of the Support Vector Machine, should produce better probability estimates [15].

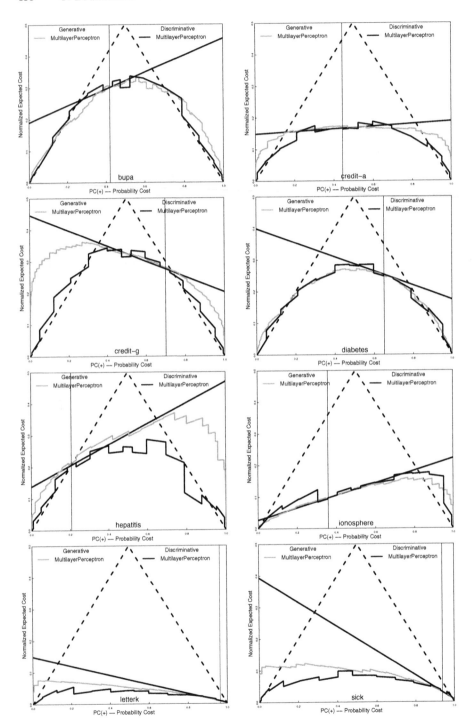

Fig. 7. Cost Curves: Multilayer Perceptron Generative Classifier

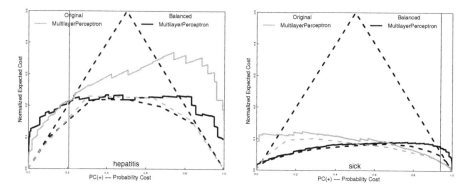

Fig. 8. Improving the Multilayer Perceptron Generative Classifier

5   Discussion

In summary, the sigmoid variant for the Support Vector Machine, with a balanced training set, was extremely effective as a generative classifier. Decision trees with Laplace correction and, to lesser extent, the Multilayer Perceptron faired reasonably and both showed potential for improvement. Although balancing is useful, calibration offers the most potential benefit and is notably inherent in the Support Vector Machine sigmoid fitting procedure.

In this paper, a curve made up of 16 discriminative classifiers has been used as a "gold standard". A good generative classifier is assumed to be one whose performance is close to this "gold standard". But to get good cost sensitive performance, one could simply use the 16 classifiers. The main advantage of the generative classifier is that it is a single classifier, reducing learning time and storage considerably. Another advantage is that a single classifier may be more understandable. Yet neither the Support Vector Machine nor the Multilayer Perceptron is easily understandable without extra processing. Even for the decision tree algorithm, as the generative version is unpruned, the classifier is more complex than any single discriminative classifier. It may be possible that a few, a lot less than the 16, judiciously chosen, discriminative classifiers would be very competitive. A tree with a stable splitting criterion but variable cost sensitive pruning [16] would have identical lower branches for all $PC(+)$ values, making a collection of trees more easily understandable.

6   Conclusions

This paper experimentally compared the performance of discriminative and generative classifiers for cost sensitive leaning. It showed that variants of commonly used algorithms produced reasonably effective generative classifiers. Where the classifiers were less effective, simple techniques like choosing the right training set distribution and calibration would improve their performance considerably.

References

1. Rubinstein, Y.D., Hastie, T.: Discriminative vs informative learning. In: Knowledge Discovery and Data Mining. (1997) 49–53
2. Vapnik, V.: Statistical Learning Theory. Wiley (1998)
3. Tong, S., Koller, D.: Restricted Bayes optimal classifiers. In: Proceedings of the 17th National Conference on Artificial Intelligence. (2000) 658–664
4. Ng, A.Y., Jordan, M.: On discriminative vs. generative classifiers: A comparison of logistic regression and naive Bayes. In: Advances in Neural Information Processing Systems 14. MIT Press (2002)
5. Jaakkola, T.S., Haussler, D.: Exploiting generative models in discriminative classiers. In: Advances in Neural Information Processing Systems. MIT Press (1999) 487–493
6. Provost, F., Domingos, P.: Tree induction for probability-based ranking. Machine Learning **52** (2003)
7. Platt, J.: Probabilistic outputs for support vector machines and comparison to regularized likelihood methods. In: Advances in Large-Margin Classifiers. MIT Press (2000) 61–74
8. Drummond, C., Holte, R.C.: Cost curves: An improved method for visualizing classifier performance. Machine Learning (In Press)
9. Witten, I.H., Frank, E.: Data Mining: Practical machine learning tools and techniques. Morgan Kaufmann (2005)
10. Drummond, C.: Discriminative vs. generative classifiers: An in-depth experimental comparison using cost curves. http://iit-iti.nrc-cnrc.gc.ca/personnel/drummond_christopher_e.html (2006)
11. Blake, C.L., Merz, C.J.: UCI repository of machine learning databases. http://www.ics.uci.edu/~mlearn/MLRepository.html (1998)
12. Quinlan, J.R.: C4.5 Programs for Machine Learning. Morgan Kaufmann (1993)
13. Zadrozny, B., Elkan, C.: Transforming classifier scores into accurate multiclass probability estimates. In: Proceedings of the Eighth International Conference on Knowledge Discovery & Data Mining. (2002)
14. Rumelhart, D.E., McClelland, J.L.: Parallel distributed processing: explorations in the microstructure of cognition. MIT Press (1986)
15. Bishop, C.M.: Neural networks for pattern recognition. OUP (1996)
16. Drummond, C., Holte, R.C.: Exploiting the cost (in)sensitivity of decision tree splitting criteria. In: Proceedings of the 17th International Conference on Machine Learning. (2000) 239–246

The K Best-Paths Approach to Approximate Dynamic Programming with Application to Portfolio Optimization

Nicolas Chapados and Yoshua Bengio

Université de Montréal, Dept. IRO, P.O. Box 6128
Montréal, Québec, H3C 3J7, Canada
{chapados, bengioy}@iro.umontreal.ca
http://www.iro.umontreal.ca/~{chapados, bengioy}

Abstract. We describe a general method to transform a non-markovian sequential decision problem into a supervised learning problem using a K-best-paths algorithm. We consider an application in financial portfolio management where we can train a controller to directly optimize a Sharpe Ratio (or other risk-averse non-additive) utility function. We illustrate the approach by demonstrating experimental results using a kernel-based controller architecture that would not normally be considered in traditional reinforcement learning or approximate dynamic programming.

1 Introduction

Dynamic programming is a general computational technique for solving sequential optimization problems that can be expressed in terms of an additive cost function [1,5]. However, it suffers from the so-called *curse of dimensionality*, wherein the computational cost of a solution grows exponentially with the problem dimension (size of the state, action and disturbance spaces). In recent years, many approximation algorithms—notably under the names *reinforcement learning* (RL) or *neurodynamic programming* (NDP)—have been proposed for tackling large-scale problems, in particular by making use of simulation and function approximation methods [6, 22, 20]

Most of these methods remain within the confines of traditional dynamic programming, which assumes that the function to be optimized can be separated as a sum of individual cost-per-time-step terms and, for finite-horizon problems, a terminal cost. Unfortunately, for more complex utility functions, which may *depend on the trajectory of visited states*, dynamic programming does not provide ready solutions.

In finance, it has long been known that the problem of optimal portfolio construction can be expressed as a stochastic optimal control problem, which can be solved by dynamic programming [14, 16, 12]. Still, such formulations assume that the investor is governed by additive utility functions. In practice, this is far from being the case: many risk averse investors care as much about portfolio trajectory as they care about abstract higher moments of a conditional return distribution.

L. Lamontagne and M. Marchand (Eds.): Canadian AI 2006, LNAI 4013, pp. 491–502, 2006.
© Springer-Verlag Berlin Heidelberg 2006

This explains the popularity of performance measures used by practitioners and professional fund managers, such as the Sharpe Ratio [17,18], Information Ratio [9], Sortino Ratio [21] and Calmar Ratio. A common theme among these utility functions is that they depend on the entire sequence of returns (or statistics of the sequence); they cannot conveniently separated into a form amenable to solution by dynamic programming.

One might argue that dynamic programming should be abandoned altogether, and one ought instead to revert to general nonlinear programming algorithms [4] to attempt optimizing under such utilities. This is the approach followed, in a certain sense, by Bengio's direct optimization of a financial training criterion [2], Moody's direct reinforcement algorithm [13] and Chapados and Bengio's direct maximization of expected returns under a value-at-risk constraint [7]. However, these methods are found lacking in two respects: (i) they still rely on, either time-separable utilities (such as the quadratic utility), or on approximations of trajectory-dependent utilities that enable time-separability, (ii) they fundamentally rely on stochastic gradient descent optimization, and as such can be particularly sensitive to local minima.

This paper investigates a different avenue for portfolio optimization under general utility functions. It relies on formulating portfolio optimization on historical data as a deterministic shortest path problem, where we extract not only the single best path, but the K best paths, yielding, after some transformations, a training set to train a supervised learning algorithm to act as a controller. This controller can directly be used in a portfolio management task.

The paper is organized as follows: first, we introduce the overall approach (section 2); next we investigate in more detail the K best paths algorithm that we used (section 3); we then summarize some experimental portfolio optimization results (sections 4 and 5); and conclude.

2   Problem Formulation

We consider a discrete-time system in an observable state $x_t \in R^N$ at time t, and which must take an action $u_t \in R^M$ at every time step. The system evolves according to a state-transition equation $x_{t+1} = f_t(x_t, u_t, w_t)$, where w_t is a random disturbance. At each time-step, the system experiences a random reward $g_t(x_t, u_t, w_t)$. Our objective is to maximize an expected utility of the sequence of received rewards over a finite horizon $t = 0, \ldots, T$),

$$J_0^*(x_0) = \max_{u_1,\ldots,u_{T-1}} \mathop{\mathrm{E}}_{w_1,\ldots,w_{T-1}} [U(g_0, g_1, \ldots, g_T)| x_0] . \tag{1}$$

Obviously, if $U(g_0, g_1, \ldots, g_T)$ can be written as $\sum_t g_t$, the finite-horizon problem is solved by writing the *value function* $J_t(x_t)$ in terms of Bellman's recursion,

$$J_T^*(x_T) = g_T(x_T) \tag{2}$$
$$J_t^*(x_t) = \max_{u_t} \mathop{\mathrm{E}}_{w_t} \left[g_t(x_t, u_t, w_t) + J_{t+1}^*(f_t(x_t, u_t, w_t)) \right] . \tag{3}$$

From the value function, the optimal action u_t^* at time t is obtained as that reaching the maximum in the equation above.

2.1 Solving for a General Utility

Our objective is to devise an effective algorithm to obtain optimal actions in the case of a general utility function. Although no recursion such as Bellman's can readily be written in the general case, a key insight lies in the simple observation that, given a **realized trajectory** of rewards, most utility functions (at least those of interest, for instance, in finance) can be computed quickly, in time $O(T)$. Hence, if we are given K such trajectories, we can find the best one under a *general utility function* U in time $O(K(T + \log K))$.

A second observation is that given this sequence of actions, we have obtained what amounts to a set of $\langle \text{state}_t, \text{action}_t \rangle$ pairs at each time-step within the trajectory. We can make use of these as a *training set for a supervised learning algorithm*. In other words, we can bypass completely the step of estimating a value function under the desired utility function, and instead directly train a controller (also called an *actor* in reinforcement learning [22]) to make decisions.

The two preceding observations can be combined into the following algorithm for solving eq. (1):

1. **Generate** a large number of candidate trajectories;
2. **Rescore** (sort) the trajectories under the desired utility function U;
3. Use the best rescored trajectory to **construct a dataset** of $\langle \text{state}, \text{action} \rangle$ pairs; carry out steps 1–3 until the dataset is large enough.
4. Using the dataset from steps 1–3, **train a supervised learning algorithm** to output the action label given the input state.

As is common practice in reinforcement learning [6], this algorithm estimates the expectation in eq. (1) with a sample average over a large number of trajectories. Furthermore, as we shall see below, we can dispense with a generative model of trajectories by using historical data.

2.2 Generating Good Trajectories

It remains the question of *generating good trajectories* in the first place. This is where a K best paths algorithm is involved: under an "easier" (i.e. additive) utility function and a large historical time period (which will become the training set), we use the K best paths algorithm to generate the candidate trajectories of step (1) above. Obviously, both the "easier" and desired utility functions, henceforth respectively called the *source* and *target* utilities, must be correlated, so that searching for good solutions under one function has a high likelihood of yielding good solutions under the other. We discuss this point more fully below. Figure 1 (left part) illustrates schematically the complete algorithm.

2.3 Known Uses

This algorithm is certainly not the first one to make use of a K best paths algorithm: they have been used extensively in speech recognition and natural language processing (e.g. [15]). However, in these contexts, the rescored action

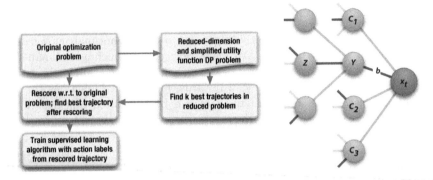

Fig. 1. (Left) Summary of the proposed algorithm for finding good trajectories under a non-additive utility function. **(Right)** Intuition behind the recursive relationship underlying the REA K-best-paths algorithm; see text for details.

labels found by the K best paths are either discarded (speech) or not used beyond proposing alternative hypotheses (NLP). In particular, no use is made of the rescored trajectories for training a controller.

Recent publications in the reinforcement learning literature have explored the idea of converting a RL problem into a supervised learning problem [11]. However, all of the proposed approaches so far have focused on staying within an additive utility function framework and assume the presence of a generative model to construct trajectory histories.

3   Enumerating the K Best Paths

We rely on a very time- and memory-efficient implementation of the Recursive Enumeration Algorithm (REA) of Jiménez and Marzal [10]. This algorithm can be made very effective by implicitly constructing a path from its *differences* with a previous path. It builds upon a generalization of Bellman's recursion of eq.(3) to a statement of optimality of higher-order paths in terms of lower-order ones. Although the precise algorithm statement is not repeated for space reasons, an intuition into the algorithm's working can be obtained from Figure 1 (right part):

- Suppose that the best path to a vertex x_t ends with $\cdots - Z - Y - x_t$.
- According to the REA recursion, the **second best path** up to x_t is given by the best of:
  1. Either the **first best path** up to the immediate predecessors of x_t, namely the *candidate vertices* $\{C_1, C_2, C_3\}$, followed by a transition to x_t.
  2. Or the **second best path** up to Y, followed by the transition b to x_t. The second best path to Y is found by applying the algorithm recursively.

4   Application: Portfolio Optimization

The portfolio optimization setting that we consider is a multi-period, multi-asset problem with transaction costs. We assume that the assets (e.g. stocks, futures) are sufficiently liquid that market impacts can be neglected. We invest in a universe of M asset, and the state x_t at time t is given by

$$x_t = (n_{t,1}, \ldots, n_{t,M}, p_{t,1}, \ldots, p_{t,M}),$$

where $n_{t,i} \in \mathbf{Z}$ is the number of shares of asset i held, and $p_{t,i} \in \mathbf{R}_+$ is the price of asset i at time t. We can only hold an integral number of shares and short (negative) positions are allowed. The possible actions are $u_t \in \mathbf{Z}^M$ which are interpreted as buying or selling the number $u_{t,i}$ of shares asset i. To limit the search space, both $n_{t,i}$ and $u_{t,i}$ may be restricted to a small integer.

The cost function $g_t(x_t, u_t)$ at time t is the \$ amount required to carry out u_t (i.e. establish the desired position), accounting for transaction costs. The source utility function U over all time steps is defined simply as the sum of negative individual costs,[1]

$$U(g_0, \ldots, g_{T-1}) = -\sum_{t=0}^{T-1} g_t.$$

Moreover, we impose the constraints that both the initial and final portfolios be empty (i.e. they cannot hold any shares of any asset). With those constraints in place, maximizing U over a time horizon $t = 0, \ldots, T$ is equivalent to finding a strategy that *maximizes the terminal wealth* of the investor over the horizon. We call this source utility function the "terminal wealth" utility.

Note that with this utility function, we never need to explicitly represent the cash amount on hand (i.e. it is not part of the state variables) since we use the **value function itself** (*viz.* $J_t^*(x_t)$ in eq. (3)) to stand for the cash currently on hand. This formulation has the advantage that we never need to discretize the cash currently being held, which allows minute price variations and small transaction costs to be handled without loss of precision.

4.1   Target Utilities

Denote by $v_t = n_t' p_t$ the *portfolio value* at time t, and by

$$\rho_t = \frac{v_t - v_{t-1}}{v_{t-1}}$$

the *portfolio relative return* between time-steps $t-1$ and t.

In the experiments below, we consider two target utility functions:

1. **Average Return Per Time-Step:**

$$\bar{\rho}_T = \frac{1}{T} \rho_t.$$

---

[1] This function would incorporate a discounting factor if the horizon was very long; we assume that this is not the case.

2. **Sharpe Ratio:**

$$SR_T = \frac{\bar{\rho}_T - r_f}{\hat{\sigma}_T},$$

where r_f is an average *government risk-free rate* over the horizon, and $\hat{\sigma}_T$ is the sample standard deviation of returns

$$\hat{\sigma}_T = \frac{1}{T-1} \sum_{t=1}^{T} (\rho_t - \bar{\rho}_T)^2.$$

The Sharpe Ratio is one of the most widely-used risk-corrected performance measures used by portfolio managers.

4.2   Choosing a Good K

It remains to answer the question of choosing an appropriate value of K for a particular problem. To give an indication as to how one might proceed, Figure 2 shows various utility functions as a function of the index of the K-th best path, when extracting 2.5×10^6 paths from a historical price sample.[2] We clearly observe that, beyond a certain point, the quality of the rescored trajectories stops increasing. We investigate when one should stop extracting further trajectories.

Assume that, given a random trajectory i, a source utility function U and a target utility function V, the utility values of the trajectory follow a joint probability distribution $p(u, v)$, where $u = U(i)$ and $v = V(i)$. This is illustrated in Figure 3 (left part). Assume further that we are interested in sampling trajectories that have at least an unconditional target utility of α or better, namely $v \geq \alpha$. Given an observed value of the source utility u, the probability that the target utility be greater than this level is given by

$$P(v \geq \alpha | u) = \frac{1}{\eta(u)} \int_{\alpha}^{\infty} p(u, \tilde{v}) \, d\tilde{v},$$

where $\eta(u) = \int_{-\infty}^{\infty} p(u, \tilde{v}) \, d\tilde{v}$ is a normalization factor. For each trajectory i, call this probability p_i^{α}. For K trajectories, the probability that *at least one* exceeds α under V can sometimes be computed analytically and is upper-bounded by $\sum_{k=1}^{K} p_k^{\alpha}$. Hence, assuming an estimator of the joint distribution $p(u, v)$, we can compute the number K that would yield a desired confidence of exceeding the target utility threshold α.

The right part of Figure 3 illustrates this idea. It shows a kernel density estimate [23] of the joint distribution between U (terminal wealth utility) and V (Sharpe Ratio utility), along with the regression line between the two (dashed red line), for the same sample path history as reported in Figure 2. Even though the

---

[2] Four-asset problem (futures on BritishPound, Sugar, Silver, HeatingOil), allow from -3 to $+3$ shares of each asset in the portfolio; maximum variation of $+1$ or -1 share per time-step; proportional transaction costs of 0.5%, trajectory length = 30 time-steps).

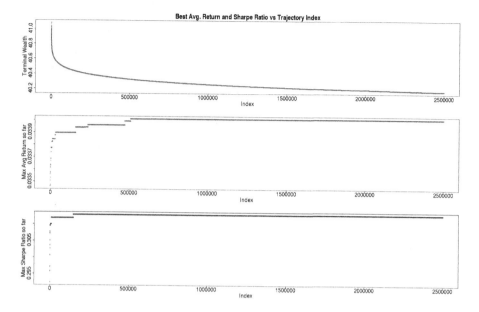

Fig. 2. Utility as a function of the extracted path index (up to 2.5×10^6 extracted paths). **(Top)** The source utility function (terminal wealth), which decreases monotonically by virtue of being extracted in that order by the K-best-paths algorithm. **(Middle)** First target utility: average return per time-step (running maximum value). **(Bottom)** Second target utility: Sharpe Ratio (running maximum value).

slope of the regression line appears small, it is highly statistically significant (t-statistic greater than 200 yielding a p-value of zero-slope null hypothesis smaller than 10^{-16}.) Here is the complete correlation structure between the "terminal wealth" source utility, and both the "average return per time-step" and "Sharpe Ratio" target utilities:

	Terminal Wealth	Avg. Return	Sharpe Ratio
Terminal Wealth	1.00	0.36	0.13
Avg. Return	0.36	1.00	0.45
Sharpe Ratio	0.13	0.45	1.00

5 Experimental Results

We conclude by presenting results on a real-world portfolio management problem. We consider a four-asset problem on commodity futures (feeder cattle, cotton, corn, silver). Since individual commodity futures contracts expire at specific dates, we construct, for each commodity, a *continuous return series* by considering the return series of the contract closest to expiry, and *rolling over* to the next contract at the beginning of the contract expiration month. This return series is converted back into a price series.

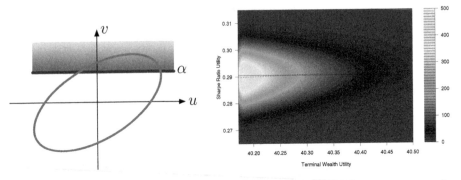

Fig. 3. (Left) Exploiting the correlation between the source and target utility functions: we want the number K of extracted paths to be large enough to sample "good target utility" region (shaded) well enough. **(Right)** Kernel density estimate of the relationship between the terminal wealth (source utility) and the Sharpe Ratio (target utility); even though the dashed red regression line has a small positive slope, it is extremely statistically significant.

Instead of a single train–test split, the simulation is run in the context of *sequential validation* [3]. In essence, this procedure uses data up to t to train, then tests on the single point $t + 1$ (and produces a single out-of-sample performance result), then adds $t + 1$ to the training set, tests on $t + 2$, and so forth, until the end of the data. An initial training set of 1008 points (four years of daily trading data) was used.

From a methodology standpoint, we proceeded in two steps: (i) computing a controller training set with the targets being the "optimal" action under the Sharpe Ratio utility, (ii) running a simulation of a controller trained with that training set, and comparing against a naïve controller. We describe each in turn.

5.1   Constructing the Training Set

The construction of the training set follows the outline set forth in Figure 1 (left part). To run the K-best-paths algorithm, we allow from -1 to $+1$ shares of each asset in portfolio, maximum variation in each asset of -1 to $+1$ shares per time-step, and proportional transaction costs of 0.5%.

We use, as targets in the training set, the "optimal" action under the Sharpe Ratio utility function, obtained after rescoring on 1.0^6 paths. Since extracting trajectories spanning several thousands time-steps is rather memory intensive, we reverted to a slightly suboptimal local-trajectory solution:

- We split the initial asset price history (spanning approximately 1500 days) into overlapping 30-day windows. The overlap between consecutive windows is 22 days.
- We solve the Sharpe Ratio optimization problem independently within each 30-day window.

- To account for boundary effects, we drop the seven first and last actions within each window.
- We concatenate the remaining actions across windows.

We thus obtain the sequence of target actions across a long horizon.[3]
For the input part of the training set, we used:

- The current portfolio state (4 elements);
- The asset returns at horizons of length $h \in \{1, 22, 252, 378\}$ days (16 elements).

5.2 Controller Architecture

Given the relatively small size of the training set, we could afford to use *kernel ridge regression* (KRR) as the controller architecture [19]. Any (preferably non-linear) regression algorithm, including neural networks, can be brought to bear. For an input vector $\mathbf{x}$, the forecast given by the KRR estimator has a particularly simple form,

$$f(\mathbf{x}) = k(\mathbf{x}, \mathbf{x}_i)(M + \lambda I)^{-1}\mathbf{y}$$

where $k(\mathbf{x}, \mathbf{x}_i)$ is the vector of kernel evaluations of the test vector $\mathbf{x}$ against all elements of the training set $\mathbf{x}_i$, M is the Gram matrix on the training set, and $\mathbf{y}$ is the matrix of targets (in this case, the optimal actions under the Sharpe Ratio utility, found in the previous section). We made use of a standard Gaussian kernel, with $\sigma = 3.0$ and fixed $\lambda = 10.0$ (both found by cross-validation on a non-overlapping time period).

5.3 Results

For validation purposes, we compared against two benchmarks models:

- The same KRR controller architecture, but with the targets replaced by the 10-day ahead 22-day asset returns, followed by a $\mathrm{sign}(\cdot)$ operation. Hence, this controller takes a long position if it believes that an asset will experience a positive return over the short-term, and symmetrically takes a short position if it believes otherwise. For this controller, the current portfolio state is not included within the inputs, since it cannot be established at training time, yielding a total of 16 inputs instead of 20.
- The same targets as previously, but with a linear forecasting model (estimated by ordinary least squares) instead of KRR.

Performance results over the out-of-sample period 2003–2004 (inclusive) appear in Figure 4. Further performance statistics appear in Table 1. We observe that, at constant annual volatility (around 10%), the KRR model trained with the proposed methodology (Sharpe Ratio utility function) outperforms the two benchmarks.

---

[3] It is obvious that this approach will not capture long-range dependencies between actions (more than 30 days in this case). However, for the specific case of the Sharpe Ratio, the impact of an action is not usually felt at a long distance, and thus this approach was found to work well in practice. Needless to say, it will have to be adjusted to other more complex utility functions.

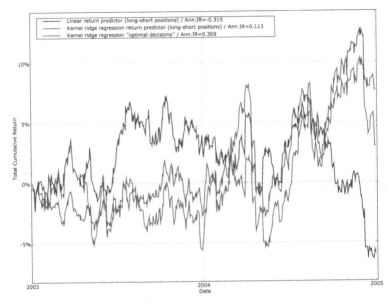

Fig. 4. Out-of-sample financial simulation results for the 2003–2004 period, comparing a controller trained with the proposed algorithm (red; Information Ratio = 0.369) against two benchmark models (resp. IR=−0.315 for linear controller (blue) and IR=0.113 for KRR controller (green))

Table 1. Financial performance statistics for the out-of-sample simulation results on the 2003–2004 period

	Benchmark Linear Model	Benchmark KRR Model	Sharpe Ratio "Optimal" Targets; KRR Model
Average monthly relative return	-0.14%	0.20%	0.43%
Monthly return standard deviation	2.68%	2.89%	3.07%
Worst monthly return	-5.80%	-6.21%	-7.14%
Best monthly return	5.15%	6.80%	6.73%
Annual Information Ratio[†]	-0.31	0.11	0.37
Average daily net exposure	-5.3%	10.8%	28.3%
Average portfolio effective leverage	74.7%	73.4%	59.6%
Average monthly portfolio turnover	499%	175%	80%
Average daily hit ratio	48.1%	50.6%	51.6%

[†] with respect to U.S. 3-month T-Bill.

6   Discussion and Future Work

The current results, although demonstrating the value of the proposed algorithm, probably raise more questions than they answer. In particular, we did not consider the impact on rescoring performance of the choice of source utility function. Moreover, we so far ignored the major efficiency gains that can be achieved by an intelligent pruning of the search graph, either in the form of beam searching or action enumeration heuristics.

Another question that future work should investigate is that with the methodology proposed here, the supervised learning algorithm optimizes the controller with respect to a regression (or classification) criterion which can disagree with the target utility when the target training set trajectory is not perfectly reproduced. In order to achieve good generalization, because of unpredictability in the data and because of the finite sample size, the trained controller will most likely not reach the supervised learning targets corresponding to the selected trajectory. However, among all the controllers that do not reach these targets and that are reachable by the learning algorithm, we will choose one that minimizes an ordinary regression or classification criterion, rather than one that maximizes our financial utility. Ideally, we would like to find a compromise between finding a "simple" controller (from a low-capacity class) and finding a controller which yields high empirical utility. One possible way to achieve such a trade-off in our context would be to consider the use of a *weighted training criterion* (e.g. similar to ones used to train boosted weak learners in Adaboost [?]) that penalizes regression or classification errors more or less according to how much the target utility would decrease by taking the corresponding "wrong" decisions, different from the target decision.

References

1. R.E. Bellman. *Dynamic Programming*. Princeton University Press, NJ, 1957.
2. Yoshua Bengio. Using a financial training criterion rather than a prediction criterion. *International Journal of Neural Systems*, 8(4):433–443, 1997.
3. Yoshua Bengio and Nicolas Chapados. Extensions to metric based model selection. *Journal of Machine Learning Research*, 3(7–8):1209–1228, October–November 2003.
4. Dimitri P. Bertsekas. *Nonlinear Programming*. Athena Scientific, Belmont, MA, second edition, 2000.
5. Dimitri P. Bertsekas. *Dynamic Programming and Optimal Control*, volume I. Athena Scientific, Belmont, MA, second edition, 2001.
6. Dimitri P. Bertsekas and John N. Tsitsiklis. *Neuro-Dynamic Programming*. Athena Scientific, Belmont, MA, 1996.
7. Nicolas Chapados and Yoshua Bengio. Cost functions and model combination for VaR-based asset allocation using neural networks. *IEEE Transactions on Neural Networks*, 12:890–906, Juillet 2001.
8. Yoav Freund and Robert E. Schapire. Experiments with a new boosting algorithm. In *Machine Learning: Proceedings of Thirteenth International Conference*, pages 148–156, 1996.
9. Richard C. Grinold and Ronald N. Kahn. *Active Portfolio Management*. McGraw Hill, 2000.
10. Víctor Manuel Jiménez Pelayo and Andrés Marzal Varó. Computing the K shortest paths: a new algorithm and an experimental comparison. In *Proc. 3rd Worksh. Algorithm Engineering*, July 1999.
11. John Langford and Bianca Zadrozny. Relating reinforcement learning performance to classification performance. In *22nd International Conference on Machine Learning (ICML 2005)*, Bonn, Germany, August 2005.

12. Robert C. Merton. Lifetime portfolio selection under uncertainty: The continuous-time case. *The Review of Economics and Statistics*, 51(3):247–257, 1969.

13. John Moody and Matthew Saffel. Learning to trade via direct reinforcement. *IEEE Transactions on Neural Networks*, 12(4):875–889, 2001.

14. Jan Mossin. Optimal multiperiod portfolio policies. *The Journal of Business*, 41(2):215–229, 1968.

15. L. Rabiner and B.H. Juang. *Fundamentals of Speech Recognition*. Prentice Hall, 1993.

16. Paul A. Samuelson. Lifetime portfolio selection by dynamic stochastic programming. *The Review of Economics and Statistics*, 51(3):239–246, 1969.

17. W. F. Sharpe. Mutual fund performance. *Journal of Business*, pages 119–138, January 1966.

18. W. F. Sharpe. The sharpe ratio. *The Journal of Portfolio Management*, 21(1):49–58, 1994.

19. John Shawe-Taylor and Nello Cristianini. *Kernel Methods for Pattern Analysis*. Cambridge University Press, 2004.

20. Jennie Si, Andrew G. Barto, Warren B. Powell, and Don Wunsch, editors. *Handbook of Learning and Approximate Dynamic Programming*. IEEE Press Series on Computational Intelligence) (Hardcover. Wiley–IEEE Press, 2004.

21. F. Sortino and L. Price. Performance measurement in a downside risk framework. *The Journal of Investing*, pages 59–65, Fall 1994.

22. R. S. Sutton and A. G. Barto. *Reinforcement Learning: An Introduction*. MIT Press, Cambridge, MA, 1998.

23. M.P. Wand and M.C. Jones. *Kernel Smoothing*. Chapman and Hall, London, 1995.

Learning Naive Bayes for Probability Estimation by Feature Selection

Liangxiao Jiang[1,*] and Harry Zhang[2]

[1] Faculty of Computer Science, China University of Geosciences
Wuhan, Hubei, P.R. China 430074
ljiang@cug.edu.cn
[2] Faculty of Computer Science, University of New Brunswick
P.O. Box 4400, Fredericton, NB, Canada E3B 5A3
hzhang@unb.ca

Abstract. Naive Bayes is a well-known effective and efficient classification algorithm. But its probability estimation is poor. In many applications, however, accurate probability estimation is often required in order to make optimal decisions. Usually, probability estimation is measured by conditional log likelihood (CLL). There have been some learning algorithms proposed recently to extend naive Bayes for high CLL, such as ERL [8, 9] and BNC-2P [10]. Unfortunately, their computational complexity is relatively high. Is there a simple but effective and efficient approach to improve the probability estimation of naive Bayes? In this paper, we propose to use feature selection for this purpose. More precisely, a search process is conducted to select a subset of attributes, and then a naive Bayes is deployed on the selected attribute set. In fact, feature selection has been successfully applied to naive Bayes and achieves significant improvement in classification accuracy. Among the feature selection algorithms for naive Bayes, selective Bayesian classifiers (SBC) by Langley et al. [13] demonstrates good performance. In this paper, we first study the performance of SBC in terms of probability estimation, and then propose an improved SBC algorithm SBC-CLL, in which the CLL score is directly used for attribute selection, instead of using classification accuracy. Our experiments show that both SBC and SBC-CLL achieve significant improvement over naive Bayes, and that SBC-CLL outperforms SBC substantially, in probability estimation measured by CLL. Our work provides an efficient and surprisingly effective approach to improve the probability estimation of naive Bayes.

1 Introduction

Classification is one of the fundamental problems in machine learning and data mining. In classification, the goal is to learn a classifier from a given set of instances with class labels, which correctly assigns a class label to an instance.

---

* This work was done when the author was a visiting scholar at University of New Brunswick.

L. Lamontagne and M. Marchand (Eds.): Canadian AI 2006, LNAI 4013, pp. 503–514, 2006.
© Springer-Verlag Berlin Heidelberg 2006

Typically, an instance e is represented by a vector of attributes $(A_1, \cdots, A_n)$. The performance of a classifier is usually measured by its classification accuracy (the percentage of instances correctly classified). Classification has been extensively studied and various learning algorithms have be developed, such as decision trees, artificial neural networks, Bayesian networks, et al.

In classification, a tacit assumption is that the costs incurred by different types of misclassifications are equal, which is often not true in many real-world applications. For example, in direct marketing, the cost incurred by predicting a customer who is going to buy your products as one not to buy, is significantly greater than the converse. To take the misclassification costs into account, the optimal decision (Bayes optimal prediction) for a given instance e is to assign e to the class i that minimizes the conditional risk [5]:

$$R(i|e) = \sum_j P(j|e)C(i,j), \tag{1}$$

where $C(i,j)$ is the cost of classifying an instance of class i into class j and $P(j|e)$ is the probability that e belongs to class j (class probability). Apparently, to accomplish Bayes optimal prediction, we need accurate estimates of the probability $P(j|e)$. Thus, accurate probability estimation is required, instead of just a classification.

If our target is accurate probability estimation and we are given only a set of training instances with class labels, conditional log likelihood (CLL) is often used as the performance measure [7, 10, 11]. Given a classifier G and a set of instances $D = \{e_1, e_2, \ldots, e_i \ldots, e_N\}$, where $e_i = (a_{i1}, a_{i2} \ldots, a_{in}, c_i)$, N is the number of instances, n is the number of attributes, and c_i the class label of e_i. The conditional log likelihood $CLL(G|D)$ of a classifier G on D is defined as:

$$CLL(G|D) = \sum_{i=1}^{N} log P_G(c_i|a_{i1}, a_{i2} \ldots, a_{in}). \tag{2}$$

Most current classification algorithms, however, are designed for maximizing classification accuracy. Although many classification learning algorithms, such as naive Bayes and decision trees, also produce probability estimates as a by-product, their probability estimates are often poor [18, 1]. This fact raises a natural question: how to learn a classifier with accurate probability estimation? In this paper, we focus on naive Bayes, an effective and efficient classification algorithm [12, 4]. Naive Bayes is defined as follows.

$$g(e) = \arg\max_{c \in C} P(c) \prod_{i=1}^{n} P(a_i|c), \tag{3}$$

where $e = (a_1, \cdots, a_n)$ is an instance and $g(e)$ is the class assigned to e by naive Bayes. Essentially naive Bayes assumes that all attributes are independent given the class (conditional independence assumption). That is:

$$P(a_1, a_2, \ldots, a_n|c) = \prod_{i=1}^{n} P(a_i|c). \tag{4}$$

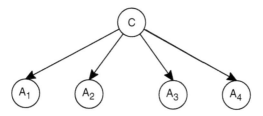

Fig. 1. An example of naive Bayes

Figure 1 shows graphically the structure of naive Bayes. In naive Bayes, each attribute node has the class node as its parent, but does not have any parent from attribute nodes.

Because of the simplicity and effectiveness of naive Bayes in classification, we might expect that its probability estimation could be also accurate. Unfortunately, naive Bayes has been found to work poorly for regression problems [6], and produces poor probability estimation [1]. An obvious reason is that the conditional independence assumption is rarely true in reality. In fact, there has been a substantial amount of research work in relaxing the conditional independence assumption of naive Bayes to improve its classification performance. Only in very recent years, some researchers have begun to study the learning algorithms for improving the probability estimation of naive Bayes or Bayesian networks, such as ERL [9] and BNC-2P [10]. But their computational complexity is often high.

Is there a simple, efficient but effective way to improve the probability estimation of naive Bayes, such that it can be scaled up to handle large data sets? This is the main motivation of this paper. Actually, we find out that feature selection, which has been used successfully in improving the classification accuracy of naive Bayes [13], is also an effective and efficient way to accomplish this task.

The rest of the paper is organized as follows. In Section 2, we introduce the related work in extending naive Bayes. In Section 3, we study empirically the probability estimation performance of one existing feature selection algorithm for naive Bayes and propose a new algorithm. In Section 4, we make a conclusion and outline our main directions for future research.

2 Related Work

There has been a substantial amount of research on extending naive Bayes for classification, which can be broadly divided into two categories: (1) structure extension: extending the structure of naive Bayes to represent the dependencies among attributes, (2) feature selection: selecting a subset of attributes, in which the conditional independence assumption is (approximately) true.

Extending the structure of naive Bayes to explicitly represent attribute dependencies is a direct way to relax the conditional independence assumption. The resulting model is essentially a Bayesian network. Thus, learning the structure is unavoidable. However, learning the optimal structure is a NP-hard problem [2]. In practice, imposing restrictions on the structures of Bayesian networks is necessary. For example, learning tree augmented naive Bayes (TAN) [7] leads to a more acceptable computational complexity. TAN is an extended tree-like naive Bayes, in which the class node directly points to all attribute nodes and an attribute node can have only one parent from another attribute node. However, even in a TAN learning algorithm, structure learning is still unavoidable and takes a significant amount of time.

Feature selection is simpler than structure extension. Among the feature selection algorithms for naive Bayes, selective Bayesian classifiers(SBC) by Langley et al. [13] demonstrates significant improvement over naive Bayes in terms of classification accuracy. The feature selection process of SBC consists of a forward search through the space of attribute subsets. SBC starts from an empty set, and adds the attribute that achieves the highest improvement in accuracy to the set in each iteration until the adding of the attribute does not lead to the improvement of accuracy.

All the research work mentioned before is for classification. In very recent years, researchers have started to pay attention to extending naive Bayes for accurate probability estimation, measured by the CLL score in Equation 2. Note that traditional probability-base learning attempts to optimize likelihood, instead of conditional likelihood. One major advantage for optimizing likelihood is that maximum likelihood parameters (the probabilities in a Bayesian network or naive Bayes) can be efficiently estimated in closed form, while computing maximum conditional likelihood parameters seems intractable[7].

Greiner, et al. propose an algorithm ERL to compute the maximum conditional likelihood parameters by gradient decent [8, 9]. For naive Bayes, the parameters are the probabilities $P(c)$ and $P(a_i|c)$ in Equation 3, which can be easily estimated by computing the related frequencies from the training data, if the goal is to maximize likelihood. For conditional likelihood, however, a search process is needed. A search process based on gradient decent is computationally feasible, although it is still time-consuming.

Grossman and Domingos [10] present an algorithm BNC-2P for learning TAN for probability estimation. The basic idea for BNC-2P is, using conditional likelihood in structure learning while setting parameters by maximum likelihood. Their experiments show that this approach yields better probability estimation. Due to the structure learning, however, the scalability of BNC-2P is limited. In fact, the time complexity of BNC-2P is roughly $O(n^3)$, where n is the number of attributes.

Lowd and Domingos [14] propose an approach based on EM, called NBE, to learning naive Bayes models for probability estimation. Their goal is to learn an accurate representation of the joint distribution for fast inference, not merely for classification. So, their work is essentially about learning naive Bayes to maximize likelihood. Nevertheless, NBE is not faster than the typical Bayesian network learning algorithm WinMine [3], because of the EM method that takes substantial time to converge [14].

The learning algorithms for probability estimation previously described are sophisticated and with high computational complexity. Is there a simple and efficient way to improve naive Bayes for probability estimation? We find out that feature selection is actually an effective and efficient method for this purpose, just as it does in classification. In this paper, we first investigate the traditional SBC algorithm for probability estimation. Then, we propose a revised SBC algorithm SBC-CLL that adopts conditional log likelihood as the scoring function in the search process. We conduct experiments to test SBC and SBC-CLL on all the 36 benchmark data sets from Weka[19]. The experimental results show that SBC achieves significant improvement over naive Bayes and SBC-CLL also outperforms SBC substantially.

3   Feature Selection for Probability Estimation of Naive Bayes

Feature selection has been successfully applied to naive Bayes to improve its classification accuracy. For example, SBC outperforms naive Bayes significantly in classification accuracy [13]. Can we apply feature selection to naive Bayes for probability estimation? Let us see the following example.

Assume that the attribute set $\mathbf{A} = \{A_1, A_2, A_3, A_4\}$, in which A_2 and A_4 are completely dependent on A_1 and A_3 respectively (that is, $A_1 = A_2$, $A_3 = A_4$), and A_1 and A_2 are completely independent from A_3 and A_4. Then the true probability distribution is :

$$P(A_1, A_2, A_3, A_4, C) = P(C)P(A_1|C)P(A_3|C).$$

However, the probability estimate produced by naive Bayes is :

$$P_{nb}(A_1, A_2, A_3, A_4, C) = P(C)P^2(A_1|C)P^2(A_3|C).$$

Obviously, the probability estimate of naive Bayes is inaccurate. However, if we do feature selection and deploy naive Bayes on the subset $\{A_1, A_3\}$, the resulting naive Bayes represents exactly the true distribution.

From the preceding example, we can see that feature selection could work well for probability estimation. Then the key is how to find a subset of attribute that achieves good probability estimation. Do the classification accuracy based feature selection methods, such as SBC, also result in significant improvement on probability estimation? We will conduct an empirical study to answer this question.

Note that we are aiming at accurate probability estimation. It is more natural using a scoring function based on probability estimation, such as the CLL score defined in Equation 2, instead of using accuracy. We propose an improved SBC algorithm, which is similar to SBC, except that the CLL score is used to select attributes. The algorithm is called selective Bayesian classifiers based on CLL, or simply SBC-CLL, illustrated below.

Algorithm. SBC-CLL(**D**, **A**)
Input: A set **D** of training instances and a set **A** of attributes.
Output: An naive Bayes classifier.
Let $\mathbf{A_s}$ be the selected subset of attributes.
Let the naive Bayes on $\mathbf{A_s}$ be $NB(\mathbf{A_s})$.
$\mathbf{A_s}$ = empty
cll = the CLL score of $NB(\mathbf{A_s})$
While A is not empty
       $currentCLL = -\infty$
       $bestAttribute$ = empty
       for each attribute $A \in \mathbf{A}$
           if the CLL score of $NB(\mathbf{A_s} \bigcup \{A\}) > currentCLL$
               $currentCLL$ =the CLL score of $NB(\mathbf{A_s} \bigcup \{A\})$
               $bestAttribute = A$
       if $currentCLL > cll$
         $cll = currentCLL$
         $\mathbf{A_s} = \mathbf{A_s} \bigcup \{A\}$
         remove $bestAttribute$ from **A**
       else return $\mathbf{A_s}$

We conduct experiments to study the performance of SBC and SBC-CLL in terms of probability estimation. In our experiments, the CLL score of a classifier is computed using Equation 2.

We implemented SBC and SBC-CLL in Weka framework [20], and ran our experiments on 36 UCI data sets recommended by Weka, which are described in Table 1. We downloaded these data sets in format of *arff* from main web of Weka [19]. In our experiments, we adopted the following three preprocessing steps on each data set.

1. Missing values: We used the unsupervised filter *ReplaceMissingValues* in Weka to replace the missing values in each data set.
2. Discretization of numeric attributes: We used the unsupervised filter *Discretize* in Weka to discretize the numeric values of attributes in each data set.
3. Removal of useless attributes: Apparently, if the number of values of an attribute is almost equal to the number of instances in a data set, it does not contribute useful information to future prediction. For example, the student ID numbers are useless for prediction. Thus, we removed this type of attributes using the unsupervised filter *Remove* in Weka. In fact, only the three attributes named "Hospital Number" in data set *colic.ORIG*, "instance name" in data set *splice*, and "animal" in data set *zoo*, were deleted.

In all experiments, the CLL score of a classifier on a data set was obtained via 10 runs of ten-fold cross validation. Runs with the various classifiers were carried out on the same training sets and evaluated on the same test sets. Finally, we conducted two-tailed t-test with a 95% confidence level to compare two classifiers. In our experiments, we also observed classification accuracy.

Table 1. Description of data sets used in the experiments

No.	Dataset	Instances	Attributes	Classes	Missing	Numeric
1	anneal	898	39	6	Y	Y
2	anneal.ORIG	898	39	6	Y	Y
3	audiology	226	70	24	Y	N
4	autos	205	26	7	Y	Y
5	balance-scale	625	5	3	N	Y
6	breast-cancer	286	10	2	Y	N
7	breast-w	699	10	2	Y	N
8	colic	368	23	2	Y	Y
9	colic.ORIG	368	28	2	Y	Y
10	credit-a	690	16	2	Y	Y
11	credit-g	1000	21	2	N	Y
12	diabetes	768	9	2	N	Y
13	Glass	214	10	7	N	Y
14	heart-c	303	14	5	Y	Y
15	heart-h	294	14	5	Y	Y
16	heart-statlog	270	14	2	N	Y
17	hepatitis	155	20	2	Y	Y
18	hypothyroid	3772	30	4	Y	Y
19	ionosphere	351	35	2	N	Y
20	iris	150	5	3	N	Y
21	kr-vs-kp	3196	37	2	N	N
22	labor	57	17	2	Y	Y
23	letter	20000	17	26	N	Y
24	lymphography	148	19	4	N	Y
25	mushroom	8124	23	2	Y	N
26	primary-tumor	339	18	21	Y	N
27	segment	2310	20	7	N	Y
28	sick	3772	30	2	Y	Y
29	sonar	208	61	2	N	Y
30	soybean	683	36	19	Y	N
31	splice	3190	62	3	N	N
32	vehicle	846	19	4	N	Y
33	vote	435	17	2	Y	N
34	vowel	990	14	11	N	Y
35	waveform-5000	5000	41	3	N	Y
36	zoo	101	18	7	N	Y

We compared SBC with naive Bayes in terms of CLL and accuracy. The detailed results are shown in Table 2.

From Table 2, we have the following observations:

1. SBC achieves significant improvement over naive Bayes in CLL. Compared to naive Bayes, SBC wins in **15** data sets, loses in **2** data sets, and ties in all the others. This shows that feature selection is an effective approach to improving the probability estimation of naive Bayes.

2. In terms of accuracy, SBC also achieves significant improvement over naive Bayes. Compared to naive Bayes, SBC wins in **11** data sets, loses in **2** data sets, and ties in all the others. Our experimental results repeated the experimental results in [13].

Table 2. Experimental results for comparing *naive Bayes* and *selective Bayesian classifiers* in term of CLL and accuracy. NB: *naive Bayes*; SBC: *selective Bayesian classifiers*. The symbols v and * respectively denotes statistically significant improvement and degradation over *naive Bayes* using two-tailed t-test with a 95% confidence level.

Datasets	CLL comparisons		accuracy comparisons	
	NB	SBC	NB	SBC
anneal	-14.22±6.16	-12.4±6.53	94.32±2.23	96.94±2.03 v
anneal.ORIG	-23.58±5.6	-22.9±5.66	88.16±3.06	89.68±2.92
audiology	-65.91±24.28	-23.33±6.96 v	71.4±6.37	74.06±7.07
autos	-45.57±18.12	-19.91±5.94 v	63.97±11.35	68.69±11.27
balance-scale	-31.75±1.51	-31.75±1.51	91.44±1.3	91.44±1.3
breast-cancer	-18.37±4.49	-16.64±2.79	72.94±7.71	72.53±7.52
breast-w	-18.28±14.16	-13.07±9.54 v	97.3±1.75	96.58±2.19
colic	-30.63±11.38	-16.78±4.33 v	78.86±6.05	83.37±5.56 v
colic.ORIG	-21.24±5.74	-18.58±3.58	74.21±7.09	74.83±6.17
credit-a	-28.79±8.1	-27.26±5.39	84.74±3.83	85.36±3.99
credit-g	-52.79±6.35	-51.99±5.62	75.93±3.87	74.76±3.85
diabetes	-40.78±7.49	-38.57±6.34	75.68±4.85	76±5.24
glass	-24.08±5.42	-23.75±4.76	57.69±10.07	56.37±10.04
heart-c	-13.91±6.71	-13.91±4.57	83.44±6.27	81.12±7.15
heart-h	-13.49±5.37	-14.86±4.61	83.64±5.85	80.19±7.03
heart-statlog	-12.25±4.96	-12.18±3.91	83.78±5.41	80.85±7.61
hepatitis	-8.53±5.98	-6.73±2.98	84.06±9.91	82.51±8.48
hypothyroid	-97.14±13.29	-93.89±9.11	92.79±0.73	93.46±0.5 v
ionosphere	-34.79±19.94	-10.31±4.79 v	90.86±4.33	91.25±4.14
iris	-2.56±2.35	-2.01±1.73	94.33±6.79	96.67±4.59
kr-vs-kp	-93.48±7.65	-97.93±4.58	87.79±1.91	94.34±1.3 v
labor	-0.71±0.99	-2.75±1.5 *	96.7±7.27	82.63±12.69 *
letter	-2505.15±98.42	-2386.21±92.62 v	70.09±0.93	70.71±0.9 v
lymph	-6.22±3.96	-7.52±2.98	85.97±8.88	80.24±9.58 *
mushroom	-105.77±23.25	-21.43±3.57 v	95.52±0.78	99.7±0.22 v
primary-tumor	-65.56±8.27	-65.07±8.18	47.2±6.02	44.49±6.76
segment	-124.32±33.74	-64.22±14.01 v	89.03±1.66	90.65±1.77 v
sick	-46.05±11.99	-34.08±9.14 v	96.78±0.91	97.51±0.72 v
sonar	-22.67±11.47	-13.71±4.28 v	76.35±9.94	69.78±9.74
soybean	-26.25±11.03	-18.58±5.5 v	92.2±3.23	91.99±3.16
splice	-46.53±12.85	-49.11±12.23	95.42±1.14	94.95±1.29
vehicle	-172.12±27.55	-84.56±11.55 v	61.03±3.48	60.98±3.62
vote	-27.25±13.85	-7.55±3.52 v	90.21±3.95	95.59±2.76 v
vowel	-89.8±11.38	-83.78±10.66 v	66.09±4.78	68.59±4.5 v
waveform-5000	-378±32.64	-242.07±22.97 v	79.97±1.46	81.17±1.45 v
zoo	-1.22±1.06	-3.22±1.66 *	94.37±6.79	94.04±7.34

Table 3. Experimental results for comparing *naive Bayes* and *selective Bayesian classifiers based on CLL* in term of CLL and accuracy. NB: *naive Bayes*; SBC-CLL: *selective Bayesian classifiers based on CLL*. The symbols v and * respectively denotes statistically significant improvement and degradation over *naive Bayes* using two-tailed t-test with a 95% confidence level.

Datasets	CLL comparisons		accuracy comparisons	
	NB	SBC-CLL	NB	SBC-CLL
anneal	-14.22±6.16	-8.97±5.08 v	94.32±2.23	97.02±1.97 v
anneal.ORIG	-23.58±5.6	-21.63±5.45 v	88.16±3.06	90.27±2.91 v
audiology	-65.91±24.28	-25.78±9.51 v	71.4±6.37	73.64±6.62
autos	-45.57±18.12	-17.73±6.41 v	63.97±11.35	70.36±9.79 v
balance-scale	-31.75±1.51	-31.75±1.51	91.44±1.3	91.44±1.3
breast-cancer	-18.37±4.49	-17.29±3.12	72.94±7.71	71.8±7.35
breast-w	-18.28±14.16	-8.78±6.09 v	97.3±1.75	95.9±2.38
colic	-30.63±11.38	-18.56±4.98 v	78.86±6.05	81.12±6
colic.ORIG	-21.24±5.74	-18.9±4.23 v	74.21±7.09	75.54±6.83
credit-a	-28.79±8.1	-25.62±6.03 v	84.74±3.83	85.41±3.8
credit-g	-52.79±6.35	-51.29±6.17	75.93±3.87	75.83±3.93
diabetes	-40.78±7.49	-36.4±5.66 v	75.68±4.85	77.58±4.82
glass	-24.08±5.42	-24.3±5.43	57.69±10.07	56.79±9.74
heart-c	-13.91±6.71	-13.46±4.82	83.44±6.27	81.39±6.93
heart-h	-13.49±5.37	-12.98±4.1	83.64±5.85	80.07±6.63
heart-statlog	-12.25±4.96	-11.36±3.85	83.78±5.41	81.96±6.24
hepatitis	-8.53±5.98	-6.8±3.83	84.06±9.91	83.45±8.93
hypothyroid	-97.14±13.29	-86.64±9.86 v	92.79±0.73	93.47±0.54 v
ionosphere	-34.79±19.94	-11.77±6.12 v	90.86±4.33	91.34±4.21
iris	-2.56±2.35	-1.9±1.68	94.33±6.79	96.67±4.69
kr-vs-kp	-93.48±7.65	-83.41±5.04 v	87.79±1.91	92.46±1.81 v
labor	-0.71±0.99	-0.94±1.27	96.7±7.27	94.93±8.68
letter	-2505.15±98.42	-2313.32±79.85 v	70.09±0.93	69.47±0.84 *
lymph	-6.22±3.96	-5.73±3.33	85.97±8.88	85.02±8.8
mushroom	-105.77±23.25	-18.56±4.04 v	95.52±0.78	99.39±0.29 v
primary-tumor	-65.56±8.27	-64.91±8.19 v	47.2±6.02	47.14±6.09
segment	-124.32±33.74	-56.32±10.2 v	89.03±1.66	90.97±1.72 v
sick	-46.05±11.99	-32.17±8.76 v	96.78±0.91	97.38±0.78 v
sonar	-22.67±11.47	-14.1±6.96 v	76.35±9.94	76.32±9.47
soybean	-26.25±11.03	-14.03±5.62 v	92.2±3.23	93.19±2.61
splice	-46.53±12.85	-42.45±11.18 v	95.42±1.14	95.51±1.14
vehicle	-172.12±27.55	-73.44±8.2 v	61.03±3.48	62.62±4.35
vote	-27.25±13.85	-7.07±3.77 v	90.21±3.95	95.40±2.73 v
vowel	-89.8±11.38	-83.49±9.96 v	66.09±4.78	68.71±4.43 v
waveform-5000	-378±32.64	-235.79±18.18 v	79.97±1.46	79.61±1.65
zoo	-1.22±1.06	-1.1±1.07	94.37±6.79	96.25±5.56

The detailed results for comparing SBC-CLL with naive Bayes are shown in Table 3. From Table 3, we can see substantial improvement of SBC-CLL over naive Bayes. We summarize the highlights briefly as follows:

1. SBC-CLL achieves surprisingly significant improvement in probability estimation. Compared to *naive Bayes*, SBC-CLL wins in **24** data sets, loses in **0** data set, and ties in all the others.
2. SBC-CLL also outperforms naive Bayes significantly in accuracy. Compared to naive Bayes, it wins in **10** data sets, loses in **1** data set, and ties in all the others.

We actually conducted a two-tailed t-test with a 95% confidence level to compare each pair of naive Bayes, SBC, and SBC-CLL. The results are summarized in Table 4 and Table 5, corresponding to accuracy and CLL respectively. The key observation from Table 4 is that SBC-CLL outperforms SBC significantly in probability estimation. SBC-CLL wins in **15** data sets, loses in **0** data set. In addition, from Table 5, we can see that the classification performance of SBC-CLL is still competitive with SBC (**1** win and **4** losses).

Table 4. The comparison results of two-tailed t-test on CLL with the 95% confidence level. An entry $w/t/l$ in the table means that the algorithm at the corresponding row wins in w data sets, ties in t data sets, and loses in l data sets, compared to the algorithm at the corresponding column.

	NB	SBC
SBC	15/19/2	
SBC-CLL	24/12/0	15/21/0

Table 5. The comparison results of two-tailed t-test on classification accuracy with the 95% confidence level. An entry $w/t/l$ in the table means that the algorithm at the corresponding row wins in w data sets, ties in t data sets, and loses in l data sets, compared to the algorithm at the corresponding column.

	NB	SBC
SBC	11/23/2	
SBC-CLL	10/25/1	1/31/4

In summary, we observed from our experiments that feature selection is an effective approach to improving the probability estimation of naive Bayes, and that CLL-based feature selection is even more effective than accuracy-based feature selection. Note that the time complexity of both SBC and SBC-CLL is $O(n^2)$, where n is the number of attributes. Thus, both are significantly more efficient than ERL[9, 11], NBE [14], and BNC-2P[10].

4   Conclusions and Future Work

In this paper, we investigated the feature selection approach to improving the probability estimation of naive Bayes. We empirically studied SBC in terms of probability estimation, and then proposed an improved SBC algorithm SBC-CLL, which uses the CLL score as the criterion for selecting attributes. Our experiments show that SBC outperforms naive Bayes significantly and SBC-CLL performs significantly better than either SBC or naive Bayes in probability estimation. This paper has two major contributions: find out that feature selection is an efficient and effective approach to improving the probability estimation of naive Bayes, and propose a new algorithm SBC-CLL that performs surprisingly well for probability estimation. Our work provides a simple but effective and efficient approach to extending naive Bayes for probability estimation.

Our work shows that SBC-CLL is surprisingly effective in probability estimation compared with naive Bayes. SBC-CLL is also simpler and significantly more efficient than other sophisticated methods, such as ERL and BNC-2P. However, it is not clear whether SBC-CLL is competitive with ERL or BNC-2P in probability estimation. In our future work, we will compare SBC-CLL with ERL and BNC-2P.

It seems that using a CLL-based scoring function can help probability estimation. In principle, the CLL-based scoring function could be used to improve the probability estimation of other classification algorithms, such as NBTree[15]. It is another direction for our future research.

References

1. Bennett, P. N.: Assessing the calibration of Naive Bayes' posterior estimates. Technical Report No. CMU-CS00-155 (2000)
2. Chickering, D. M. (1996). Learning Bayesian networks is NP-Complete. In Fisher, D. and Lenz, H., editors, Learning from Data: Artificial Intelligence and Statistics V, pages 121-130. Springer-Verlag.
3. Chickering, D. M.: The WinMine Toolkit. Technical Report MSR-TR-2002-103 (2002)
4. Domingos, P., Pazzani M.: Beyond Independence: Conditions for the Optimality of the Simple Bayesian Classifier. Machine Learning **29** (1997) 103-130
5. Duda, R. O., Hart, P. E.: Pattern Classification and Scene Analysis. A Wiley-Interscience Publication (1973)
6. Frank, E., Trigg, L., Holmes, G., Witten, I. H.: Naive Bayes for Regression. Machine Learning **41(1)** (2000) 5-15
7. Friedman, Geiger, and Goldszmidt. "Bayesian Network Classifiers", Machine Learning, Vol. 29, 131-163, 1997.
8. R. Greiner, W. Zhou: Structural Extension to Logistic Regression: Discriminative Parameter Learning of Belief Net Classifiers. Proceedings of the Eighteenth National Conference on Artificial Intelligence (pp. 167-173), 2002. AAAI Press.
9. R. Greiner, X. Su, B. Shen, and W. Zhou: Structural extension to logistic regression: Discriminative parameter learning of belief net classifiers. Machine Learning, 59(3), 2005.
10. D. Grossman, P. Domingos: Learning Bayesian Network Classifiers by Maximizing Conditional Likelihood. Proceedings of the Twenty-First International Conference on Machine Learning (pp. 361-368), 2004. Banff, Canada: ACM Press.

11. Y. Guo, R. Greiner: Discriminative Model Selection for Belief Net Structures. Proceedings of the Twentieth National Conference on Artificial Intelligence (pp. 770-776), 2005. AAAI Press.
12. P. Langley, W. Iba, and K. Thomas: An analysis of Bayesian classifiers. in Proceedings of the Tenth National Conference of Artificial Intelligence, pages 223C228. AAAI Press, 1992.
13. P. Langley, S. Sage: Induction of selective Bayesian classifiers. in Proceedings of the Tenth Conference on Uncertainty in Artificial Intelligence, 1994, pp. 339-406.
14. Lowd, D., Domingos, P.: Naive Bayes Models for Probability Estimation. Proceedings of the Twenty-Second International Conference on Machine Learning. ACM Press(2005) 529-536
15. Kohavi, R.: Scaling Up the Accuracy of Naive-Bayes Classifiers: A Decision-Tree Hybrid. Proceedings of the Second International Conference on Knowledge Discovery and Data Mining (KDD-96). AAAI Press (1996) 202-207
16. Merz,C., Murphy,P. and Aha,D., UCI repository of machine learning databases. In Dept of ICS, University of California, Irvine. http://www.ics.uci.edu/mlearn/MLRepository.html, 1997.
17. Pearl, J. (1988). Probabilistic Reasoning in Intelligent Systems. San Francisco, CA: Morgan Kaufmann.
18. Provost, F. J., Domingos, P.: Tree Induction for Probability-Based Ranking. Machine Learning **52(3)** (2003) 199-215
19. http://prdownloads.sourceforge.net/weka/datasets-UCI.jar
20. Witten, I. H., Frank, E.: data mining-Practical Machine Learning Tools and Techniques with Java Implementation. Morgan Kaufmann (2000)

Lazy Averaged One-Dependence Estimators

Liangxiao Jiang[1,*] and Harry Zhang[2]

[1] Faculty of Computer Science, China University of Geosciences
Wuhan, Hubei, P.R.China, 430074
ljiang@cug.edu.cn
[2] Faculty of Computer Science, University of New Brunswick
P.O.Box 4400, Fredericton, NB, Canada E3B 5A3
hzhang@unb.ca

Abstract. Naive Bayes is a probability-based classification model based on the conditional independence assumption. In many real-world applications, however, this assumption is often violated. Responding to this fact, researchers have made a substantial amount of effort to improve the accuracy of naive Bayes by weakening the conditional independence assumption. The most recent work is the *Averaged One-Dependence Estimators* (AODE) [15] that demonstrates good classification performance. In this paper, we propose a novel lazy learning algorithm *Lazy Averaged One-Dependence Estimators*, simply LAODE, by extending AODE. For a given test instance, LAODE firstly expands the training data by adding some copies (clones) of each training instance according to its similarity to the test instance, and then uses the expanded training data to build an AODE classifier to classify the test instance. We experimentally test our algorithm in Weka system [16], using the whole 36 UCI data sets [11] recommended by Weka [17], and compare it to naive Bayes [3], AODE [15], and LBR [19]. The experimental results show that LAODE significantly outperforms all the other algorithms used to compare.

1 Introduction

Classification is one of the most important tasks in machine learning and data mining. In classification, a classifier is learned from a set of training instances with class labels. An instance is represented by a tuple of attributes $(A_1, \ldots, A_n)$, which are used collectively to predict the value c of the class variable C. The Bayesian classifier assigns the class with the maximum posterior probability to an instance, defined as follows.

$$\arg \max_{c \in C} P(c) P(a_1, a_2, \ldots, a_n | c). \tag{1}$$

Assume that all attributes are independent given the class (conditional independence assumption). That is:

$$P(a_1, a_2, \ldots, a_n | c) = \prod_{i=1}^{n} P(a_i | c). \tag{2}$$

---

* This work was done when the author was a visiting scholar at University of New Brunswick.

L. Lamontagne and M. Marchand (Eds.): Canadian AI 2006, LNAI 4013, pp. 515–525, 2006.
© Springer-Verlag Berlin Heidelberg 2006

The resulting classifier is called *the naive Bayesian classifier*, or simply *naive Bayes*:

$$\arg\max_{c \in C} P(c) \prod_{i=1}^{n} P(a_i|c). \tag{3}$$

Figure 1 shows graphically the structure of naive Bayes. In naive Bayes, each attribute node has the class node as its parent, but does not have any parent from attribute nodes. Naive Bayes is based on the conditional independence assumption that is violated in many applications.

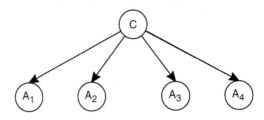

Fig. 1. An example of naive Bayes

In order to relax this assumption effectively, we need to represent and manipulate independence assertions. *Bayesian networks* [12] provide an appropriate language for this. Unfortunately, it has been proved that learning an optimal Bayesian network is NP-hard [2]. To avoid the computational complexity for learning a Bayesian network, learning improved naive Bayes has attracted much attention from researchers. Related work can be broadly divided into two categories: eager learning and lazy learning, depending on when the major computation occurs. Eager learning does major computation at training time. There are a variety of eager learning algorithms for extending naive Bayes, such as SBC [9], TAN [6], NBTree [8], and AODE [15]. AODE (*Averaged One-Dependence Estimators*) is the most recent work on improving naive Bayes, which weakens the attribute independence assumption by averaging all models from a restricted class of one-dependence classifiers.

Different from eager learning, lazy learning spends little or no effort during training and delays computation until classification time. There are some lazy learning algorithms for extending naive Bayes, such as LBR (lazy Bayesian rule) [19], SNNB (selective neighborhood naive Bayes) [18], and LWNB (locally weighted naive Bayes) [4].

Since AODE demonstrates good performance in classification, we could expect that an extension of AODE from the lazy approach could be more accurate, if we can overcome the issues in developing lazy AODE. In this paper, we propose a novel lazy algorithm called *Lazy Averaged One-Dependence Estimators*, or simply LAODE, which is essentially an extension of AODE from lazy learning approach.

The rest of the paper is organized as follows. In Section 2, we introduce the related work on improving naive Bayes. In Section 3, we present our lazy algorithm LAODE. In Section 4, we describe the experimental setup and results in detail. In Section 5, we make a conclusion and outline our main directions for future research.

2   Related Work

Naive Bayes has been extensively studied, and there is a large amount of research work on extending naive Bayes. From the approach of eager learning, extending the structure of naive Bayes to represent attribute dependencies is a straightforward way to overcome the conditional independence assumption. The resulting model is called augmented naive Bayes(ANB) [6]. Learning an optimal augmented naive Bayes, however, is equivalent to learning an optimal Bayesian network, which is computationally infeasible. Thus, learning restricted augmented naive Bayes is more practical. *Tree augmented naive Bayes* (TAN) [6] is tree-like structure, in which the class node directly points to all attribute nodes and each attribute node is allowed to have at most one parent from another attribute node. Figure 2 shows an example of TAN. TAN achieves significant improvement over naive Bayes in classification accuracy.

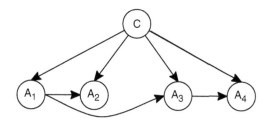

Fig. 2. An example of tree augmented naive Bayes

TAN can be further extended by building an ensemble of TANs that are used collectively to perform classification. This is the basic idea of AODE [15]. In AODE, an aggregate of one-dependence classifiers are learned and the prediction is produced by averaging the predictions of all these qualified classifiers. The notion of x-dependence is introduced by Sahami [14]. An x-dependence estimator means that the probability of an attribute is conditioned by the class variable and at most x other attributes, which corresponds to an augmented naive Bayes with at most x attribute parents. In AODE, a one-dependence classifier is built for each attribute, in which the attribute is set to be the parent of all other attributes. That means, the structure of the TAN for each attribute is fixed. Thus, AODE avoids structure learning. For simplicity, AODE directly averages the aggregate consisting of many special tree augmented naive Bayes. Figure 3 shows an example of the aggregate of AODE.

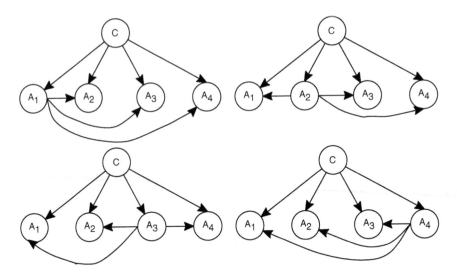

Fig. 3. An example of the aggregate of AODE

AODE classifies a test instance using Equation 4.

$$\arg\max_{c \in C}\left(\frac{\sum_{i=1 \wedge F(a_i) \geq m}^{n} P(a_i, c) \prod_{j=1, j \neq i}^{n} P(a_j | a_i, c)}{numParent}\right) \qquad (4)$$

where $F(a_i)$ is a count of the number of training instances having attribute-value a_i and is used to enforce the limit m that they place on the support needed in order to accept a conditional probability estimate, n is the number of attributes, and $numParent$ is the number of the root attributes, which satisfy the condition that the training instances contain more than m examples with the value a_i for the parent attribute A_i. In the current AODE, $m = 30$. The experimental results in [15] show that AODE achieves substantial improvement over TAN.

There is also some research work to extend naive Bayes from the lazy approach. Zheng and Webb [19] propose a lazy learning approach called *lazy Bayesian rule* (LBR). LBR generates a rule most appropriate to the test instance before classifying it. The training instances that satisfy the antecedent of the rule are chosen as the training data for the local naive Bayes, and this local naive Bayes only uses the attributes that do not appear in the antecedent of the rule. Their experiments show that LBR obtains lower error rates significantly than naive Bayes, C4.5 [13], and lazy decision tree [5] etc.

Xie et al. [18] propose a lazy model called *selective neighborhood naive Bayes* (SNNB). At first, SNNB constructs multiple naive Bayes on multiple neighborhoods by using different radius values for the test instance. Then, it selects the most accurate one to classify the test instance. Their experimental results show that SNNB outperforms naive Bayes, and the state-of-the-art classification algorithms NBTree [8] and C4.5 [13] in terms of classification accuracy. Note that the computational complexity of SNNB is high.

Frank et al. [4] present a lazy algorithm to combine instance-based k-nearest neighbor with naive Bayes, called *locally weighted naive Bayes* (LWNB). In LWNB, each of k nearest neighbors is weighted in terms of its distance to the test instance. Then a local naive Bayes is built from the weighted training instances. Their experimental results show that LWNB outperforms naive Bayes significantly. Although their experiments show that LWNB is not particularly sensitive to the choice of the k value as long as it is not too small, its performance is certainly affected by the value of k to some extent.

3 Lazy Averaged One-Dependence Estimators

Generally speaking, lazy learning is often expected to have some advantages over eager learning in performance, since it generates a hypothesis for each instance, instead of generating one hypothesis for all instances. Thus, the hypotheses yielded from a lazy learning approach, generally speaking, are expected to be more accurate than the ones produced by the corresponding eager approach. Since AODE performs well, it is natural to create a lazy extension of AODE, which would be expected to performs better than AODE. This is the main motivation of this paper.

From the preceding section, we can see that, in addition to the good classification performance, AODE [15] is efficient, since it avoids structure learning. In fact, even though AODE learns an ensemble of TANs, its training time complexity is $O(Nn^2)$ and classification time complexity is $O(kn^2)$, where N is the number of training instances, n is the number of attributes, and k is the number of classes. It is at least as efficient as many TAN learning algorithms, such as the ChowLiu TAN learning algorithm [6] with the training complexity of $O(Nn^2)$ and the Superparent TAN learning algorithm [7] with the training complexity of $O(Nn^3)$. Therefore, because of the simplicity and efficiency of AODE, developing its lazy extension is practical.

There are two possible ways to develop the lazy AODE. One is, find the instances in the training set which are similar to the test instance (the nearest neighbors) and then learn an AODE from the nearest neighbors. One issue to do this is the lack of training instances in learning AODE. Note that AODE is a probability-based model in which accurate and reliable probability estimation is essential. The second approach is to use the whole training data set but assign different weights to the training instances. That is, the closer is an instance to the test instance, the higher weight is assigned to it. Then we have an expanded data set that is biased to the test instance. Thus, the model learned from it would be also more suitable to the test instance than the one learned from the original training data. In addition, since all the probability estimates are computed from the expanded data, the issue of lack of data would not be as serious as the first approach.

We adopt the second approach and propose a lazy AODE learning algorithm called *Lazy Averaged One-Dependence Estimators*, or simply LAODE. As discussed previously, our basic idea is to build an AODE for the test instance on expanded training data. LAODE uses a simple method called instance cloning [10] to expand the training data. More precisely, a number of clones (duplicates) of each training instance are added to the training data based on how similar it is to the test instance. This method has been successfully used in learning local naive Bayes [10]. To clone a training instance based on its similarity to the test instance, we need a function to measure the similarity. LAODE uses a similarity function that simply counts the number of identical attributes. More precisely, the similarity between two instances x and y is defined as:

$$s(x, y) = \sum_{i=1}^{n} \delta(a_i(x), a_i(y)), \tag{5}$$

where

$$\delta(a_i(x), a_i(y)) = \begin{cases} 1 & a_i(x) = a_i(y) \\ 0 & a_i(x) \neq a_i(y) \end{cases} \tag{6}$$

$a_i(x)$ and $a_i(y)$ are the values of attribute A_i for x and y respectively. This function very roughly measures the similarity between two instances.

Given a training data set $\mathbf{T}$ and a test instance x, LAODE firstly applies Equation 5 to calculate the similarity $s(x, y)$ for each training instance y in $\mathbf{T}$, and adds $s(x, y)$ clones of y into $\mathbf{T}$. Then, LAODE learns an AODE on the expanded $\mathbf{T}$, which is used to calculate the class label of x. The LAODE learning algorithm is depicted in detail as follows.

Algorithm. LAODE($\mathbf{T}$, x)
Input: a set $\mathbf{T}$ of training instances and a test instance x
Output: the class label of x
    1. For each training instance y in $\mathbf{T}$.
    2.   Compute $s(x, y)$ using the similarity function in Equation 5.
    3.   Add $s(x, y)$ clones of y into $\mathbf{T}$.
    4. Deploy an AODE classifier on $\mathbf{T}$.
    5. Use the AODE classifier to classify x.
    6. Return the class label of x.

In LAODE, the base probabilities $P(a_i, c)$ and $P(a_j|a_i, c)$ are estimated using the same Laplace estimation in AODE as follows:

$$P(a_i, c) = \frac{F(a_i, c) + 1}{N + v_i * k} \tag{7}$$

$$P(a_j|a_i, c) = \frac{F(a_j, a_i, c) + 1}{F(a_i, c) + v_j} \tag{8}$$

where $F(\bullet)$ is the frequency with which a combination of terms appears in the training data, N is the number of training instances, v_i is the number of values of the root attribute A_i, v_j is the number of values of the leaf attribute A_j, and k is the number of classes.

As a lazy learning algorithm, LAODE spends no effort during training time and delays all computation until classification time. Given a test instance, in addition to compute an ensemble of TANs as in AODE, LAODE needs to expand the training data set using the similarity function in Equation 5. The time complexity for the expansion step is $O(N(n+s))$, where N is the number of training instances, n is the number of attributes, s is the average similarity value between the test instance and each training instance. After the data expansion, the size of the resulting training data is roughly sN. The time complexity for building a TAN is $O(snN)$, and there are totally n TANs to build in AODE. Then the time complexity for building an AODE is $O(sn^2N)$. As mentioned before, the time complexity of AODE for classification is $O(kn^2)$, where k is the number of classes. Since $k << N$ in practice, the time complexity of LAODE is thus $O(sn^2N)$.

4   Experimental Methodology and Results

We run our experiments on 36 UCI data sets [11] recommended by Weka [17], which are listed in Table 1. We downloaded these data sets in the format of *arff* from the main web of Weka [16]. In our experiments, we adopted the following four steps to preprocess data sets.

1. Missing values in each data set are filled in using the unsupervised filter *ReplaceMissingValues* in Weka.
2. Numeric attributes are discretized using the unsupervised filter *Discretize* in Weka.
3. The attributes useless for prediction are removed. It is obvious that, if the number of values of an attribute is almost equal to the number of instances in the data set, this attribute is useless for prediction purpose. Thus, we removed this type of attributes using the unsupervised filter *Remove* in Weka. In fact, only the three attributes named "Hospital Number" in data set *colic.ORIG*, "instance name" in data set *splice* and "animal" in data set *zoo*, were deleted.
4. For the sake of computational complexity, each large data set (containing more than 20000 instances) is replaced by a subset of 25% instances randomly sampled from the original data set. We used the unsupervised filter *Resample* in Weka to do it.

We conduct experiments to compare LAODE with NB [3], AODE [15], and LBR [19], in terms of classification accuracy. In our experiments, the classification accuracy of each classifier on a data set was obtained via ten-fold cross validation. Runs with the various classifiers were carried out on the same training sets and evaluated on the same test sets. Finally, we conducted a two-tailed t-test with a 95% confidence level to compare each pair of algorithms.

Table 2 shows the detailed experimental results on classification accuracy and standard deviation of each classifier on each data set, and the average values are summarized at the bottom of the table. The symbols v and * in the table

Table 1. Description of data sets used in the experiments

No.	Data set	Instances	Attributes	Classes	Missing	Numeric
1	anneal	898	39	6	Y	Y
2	anneal.ORIG	898	39	6	Y	Y
3	audiology	226	70	24	Y	N
4	autos	205	26	7	Y	Y
5	balance-scale	625	5	3	N	Y
6	breast-cancer	286	10	2	Y	N
7	breast-w	699	10	2	Y	N
8	colic	368	23	2	Y	Y
9	colic.ORIG	368	28	2	Y	Y
10	credit-a	690	16	2	Y	Y
11	credit-g	1000	21	2	N	Y
12	diabetes	768	9	2	N	Y
13	Glass	214	10	7	N	Y
14	heart-c	303	14	5	Y	Y
15	heart-h	294	14	5	Y	Y
16	heart-statlog	270	14	2	N	Y
17	hepatitis	155	20	2	Y	Y
18	hypothyroid	3772	30	4	Y	Y
19	ionosphere	351	35	2	N	Y
20	iris	150	5	3	N	Y
21	kr-vs-kp	3196	37	2	N	N
22	labor	57	17	2	Y	Y
23	letter	20000	17	26	N	Y
24	lymphography	148	19	4	N	Y
25	mushroom	8124	23	2	Y	N
26	primary-tumor	339	18	21	Y	N
27	segment	2310	20	7	N	Y
28	sick	3772	30	2	Y	Y
29	sonar	208	61	2	N	Y
30	soybean	683	36	19	Y	N
31	splice	3190	62	3	N	N
32	vehicle	846	19	4	N	Y
33	vote	435	17	2	Y	N
34	vowel	990	14	11	N	Y
35	waveform-5000	5000	41	3	N	Y
36	zoo	101	18	7	N	Y

respectively denotes statistically significant improvement and degradation over LAODE. Table 3 shows the comparison results of two-tailed t-test with a 95% confidence level between each pair of algorithms, in which each entry $w/t/l$ means that the classifier at the corresponding row wins in w data sets, ties in t data sets, and loses in l data sets, compared to the classifier at the corresponding column.

From Table 2 and Table 3, we can see that LAODE significantly outperforms NB [3], AODE [15], and LBR [19]. Now, we summarize the highlights as follows:

Table 2. The detailed experimental results on classification accuracy and standard deviation. LAODE: lazy averaged one-dependence estimators; NB: naive Bayes; AODE: averaged one-dependence estimators; LBR: lazy Bayesian rule. The symbols v and * in the table respectively denotes statistically significant improvement and degradation over LAODE with a 95% confidence level.

Data set	LAODE	NB	AODE	LBR
anneal	98.77±1.23	94.32±2.38 *	96.66±2.10 *	97.10±1.30 *
anneal.ORIG	89.43±2.91	87.53±4.69	88.64±4.19	90.87±2.81
audiology	79.62±5.72	71.23±7.03 *	71.66±7.34 *	71.23±7.03 *
autos	83.33±5	64.83±11.2 *	76.02±7.61 *	72.67±10.7 *
balance-scale	88.96±2.42	91.36±1.38	89.76±1.84	91.36±1.38
breast-cancer	69.62±6.96	72.06±7.97	72.04±7.13	71.7±7.54
breast-w	97.14±1.91	97.28±1.84	96.85±2.77	97.28±1.84
colic	81±4.71	78.81±5.05	80.45±3.92	81.53±6.31
colic.ORIG	76.1±5.33	75.26±5.26	75.81±5.78	74.71±5.38
credit-a	84.78±3.07	84.78±4.28	85.36±4.85	84.93±4.54
credit-g	76.2±3.33	76.3±4.76	76.9±3.41	75.7±4.62
diabetes	75.92±4.65	75.4±5.85	76.31±4.79	75.27±5.83
glass	59.85±8.24	60.32±9.69	62.23±10.4	59.39±10.0
heart-c	82.81±4.76	84.14±4.16	82.46±6	84.47±3.58
heart-h	83.03±6.22	84.05±6.69	84.72±6.1	84.05±6.69
heart-statlog	80.74±6.72	83.7±5	82.59±5.8	83.7±5
hepatitis	85.08±6.95	83.79±8.79	83.79±8.21	83.79±8.79
hypothyroid	93.21±0.82	92.79±1.02	93.53±1.12	93.11±0.75
ionosphere	92.31±2.7	90.89±3.49	92.3±3.83	90.89±3.49
iris	93.33±5.44	94.67±8.2	93.33±8.31	94.67±8.2
kr-vs-kp	91.86±0.83	87.89±1.81 *	91.18±0.83 *	96.72±0.90 v
labor	88.33±13.72	93.33±11.7	91.67±11.8	93.33±11.7
letter-5000	86.4±1.75	67.28±2.03 *	79.36±2.23 *	76.78±2.12 *
lymph	84.33±8.16	85.67±9.55	87±10.58	85±9.18
mushroom	99.96±0.06	95.57±0.45 *	99.95±0.06	99.93±0.12
primary-tumor	47.5±5.89	46.89±4.32	47.19±2.99	46.6±4.62
segment	95.37±1.08	88.92±1.95 *	92.60±1.57 *	92.90±1.28 *
sick	97.91±0.48	96.74±0.53 *	97.45±0.55 *	97.93±0.68
sonar	79.38±8.6	77.5±11.99	78.45±11.4	76.95±7.65
soybean	94.58±2.21	92.08±2.34 *	93.4±2.72	92.67±1.98 *
splice	96.68±0.99	95.36±1.00 *	96.21±1.07 *	95.64±1.34 *
vehicle	74±5.54	61.82±3.54 *	72.22±4.16	71.15±4.31
vote	94.5±3.26	90.14±4.17 *	94.5±3.26	94.49±3.29
vowel	93.94±1.58	67.07±4.21 *	90.20±1.85 *	86.46±4.07 *
waveform-5000	83.68±1.3	79.96±1.92 *	84.16±1.1	83.1±1.58
zoo	96.18±6.54	94.18±6.6	95.09±5.18	94.18±6.6
Mean	85.44±4.20	82.33±4.91	84.78±4.63	84.51±4.65

1. LAODE achieves significant improvement over naive Bayes. LAODE performs significantly better than naive Bayes in 14 data sets, loses in 0 data set, ties in all others. In addition, the average accuracy of LAODE is 85.44%, higher than that of naive Bayes (82.33%).

Table 3. The compared results of two-tailed t-test on accuracy with the 95% confidence level. An entry $w/t/l$ in the table means that the algorithm at the corresponding row wins in w data sets, ties in t data sets, and loses in l data sets, compared to the algorithm at the corresponding column.

	NB	AODE	LBR
AODE	13/23/0		
LBR	10/26/0	1/33/2	
LAODE	14/22/0	9/27/0	8/27/1

2. LAODE achieves significant improvement over AODE. LAODE outperforms AODE in 9 data sets, ties in 27 data sets, and loses in 0 data set. In addition, the average accuracy of LAODE is higher than that of AODE (84.78%).
3. LAODE outperforms LBR. The average accuracy of LAODE is higher than that of LBR (84.51%). More importantly, LAODE outperforms LBR in 8 data sets, loses in 1 data set, and ties in all others.
4. LAODE has better robustness and stability than all the other algorithms. The average standard deviation of LAODE is 4.20, which is the lowest in all the algorithms.

5   Conclusions

In this paper, we proposed a novel lazy learning algorithm LAODE, by modifying the corresponding eager learning algorithm AODE [15]. LAODE first creates a expanded training data set by cloning training instances according to the similarity to the test instance, then uses the expanded training data set to build an AODE classifier to classify the test instance. We experimentally tested LAODE in Weka [16], using the whole 36 UCI data sets [11] recommended by Weka [17], and compared it to NB [3], AODE [15], and LBR [19]. The experimental results show that LAODE significantly outperforms all the other algorithms. Thus, LAODE could be a good choice when high classification accuracy is desired.

In principle, the method presented in this paper can be applied to some other Bayesian network algorithms, such as the ChowLiu TAN learning algorithm and the Superparent TAN learning. This is one direction for our future research.

References

1. Aha, D.W. Lazy Learning. Dordrecht: Kluwer Academic, 1997
2. Chickering, D. M. (1996). Learning Bayesian networks is NP-Complete. In Fisher, D. and Lenz, H., editors, Learning from Data: Artificial Intelligence and Statistics V, pages 121-130. Springer-Verlag.
3. Duda, R.O., Hart, P.E. Pattern Classification and Scene Analysis. New Yaork: John Wiley, 1973

4. Frank, E., Hall, M., Pfahringer, B.: Locally Weighted Naive Bayes. Proceedings of the Conference on Uncertainty in Artificial Intelligence (2003). Morgan Kaufmann(2003), 249-256.
5. Friedman, J., Kohavi, R., Yun, Y.: Lazy decision trees. Proceedings of the Thirteenth National Conference on Artificial Intelligence (pp. 717-724). Menlo Park, CA: AAAI Press (1996).
6. Friedman, Geiger, and Goldszmidt. "Bayesian Network Classifiers", Machine Learning, Vol. 29, 131-163, 1997.
7. E. J. Keogh and M. J. Pazzani. Learning augmented Naive Bayes classifiers. In Proceedings of the Seventh International Workshop on AI and Statistics. 1999.
8. Kohavi, R.: Scaling Up the Accuracy of Naive-Bayes Classifiers: A Decision-Tree Hybrid. Proceedings of the Second International Conference on Knowledge Discovery and Data Mining (KDD-96). AAAI Press (1996) 202-207
9. Langley, P., Sage, S. Induction of selective Bayesian classifiers. in Proceedings of the Tenth Conference on Uncertainty in Artificial Intelligence, 1994, pp. 339-406.
10. Jiang, L., Zhang, H., Su, J.: Instance Cloning Local Naive Bayes. Proceedings of the Canadian Conference on AI 2005. Springer (2005) 280-291
11. Merz,C., Murphy,P. and Aha,D., UCI repository of machine learning databases. In Dept of ICS, University of California, Irvine. http://www.ics.uci.edu/mlearn/MLRepository.html, 1997.
12. Pearl, J. (1988). Probabilistic Reasoning in Intelligent Systems. San Francisco, CA: Morgan Kaufmann.
13. Quinlan, J. R.: C4.5: Programs for Machine Learning. Morgan Kaufmann: San Mateo, CA (1993)
14. M. Sahami. Learning Limited Dependence Bayesian Classifiers. In Proceedings of the Second International Conference on Knowledge Discovery and Data Mining, pages 335-338. AAAI Press, 1996.
15. G. I. Webb, J. Boughton, and Z. Wang. Not so naive Bayes: Aggregating one-dependence estimators. Machine Learning, Vol. 58, 5-24, 2005.
16. Witten, I. H., Frank, E.: data mining-Practical Machine Learning Tools and Techniques with Java Implementation. Morgan Kaufmann (2000)
17. http://prdownloads.sourceforge.net/weka/datasets-UCI.jar
18. Xie, Z., Hsu, W., Liu, Z., Lee, M.: SNNB: A Selective Neighborhood Based Naive Bayes for Lazy Learning. Proceedings of the Sixth Pacific-Asia Conference on KDD. Springer (2002) 104-114
19. Zheng, Z., Webb, G. I.,: Lazy Learning of Bayesian Rules. Machine Learning, Vol. 41, 53-84, 2000.

Probabilistic Inference Trees for Classification and Ranking

Jiang Su and Harry Zhang

Faculty of Computer Science, University of New Brunswick
P.O. Box 4400, Fredericton, NB, Canada E3B 5A3
hzhang@unb.ca
http://www.cs.unb.ca/profs/hzhang/

Abstract. In many applications, an accurate ranking of instances is as important as accurate classification. However, it has been observed that traditional decision trees perform well in classification, but poor in ranking. In this paper, we point out that there is an inherent obstacle for traditional decision trees to achieving both accurate classification and ranking. We propose to understand decision trees from probabilistic perspective, and use probability theory to compute probability estimates and perform classification and ranking. The new model is called probabilistic inference trees (PITs). Our experiments show that the PIT learning algorithm performs well in both ranking and classification. More precisely, it significantly outperforms the state-of-the-art decision tree learning algorithms designed for ranking, such as C4.4 [10] and Ling and Yan's algorithm [6], and performs competitively with the traditional decision tree learning algorithms, such as C4.5, in classification. Our research provides a novel algorithm for the applications in which both accurate classification and ranking are desired.

1 Introduction

Classification is one of the primary tasks in machine learning and data mining. However, an accurate ranking of instances based on the class membership probability $p(c|E)$ (the probability of instance E in class c) is also desired in many applications. For example, in direct marketing, we often need to promote the top X% of potential buyers during gradual roll-out and deploy different promotion strategies to potential buyers with different likelihood of buying some products. To accomplish this task, a ranking of customers, as well as a classification of *buyer* and *non-buyer*, is desirable.

Decision trees have been widely used in many applications, due to their attractive properties, such as efficiency and comprehensibility. Certainly, the classification performance of decision trees, measured by accuracy (the percentage of instances correctly classified), is among the most competitive classification algorithms. It has been observed, however, that decision trees yield poor probability estimates [7, 9] and rankings [10]. Thus, learning a decision tree with accurate probability estimation , called probability estimation trees (PETs), has received

L. Lamontagne and M. Marchand (Eds.): Canadian AI 2006, LNAI 4013, pp. 526–537, 2006.
© Springer-Verlag Berlin Heidelberg 2006

a great deal of attention recently [10, 6]. Note that ranking discussed in this paper is based on the class probability. So, if a decision tree produces accurate probability estimation, its ranking is also accurate.

Some researchers ascribe the poor probability estimation of decision trees to decision tree learning algorithms [10]. To our observation, however, the representation also plays an important role. A traditional decision tree essentially represents an explicit decision boundary, and an instance E is classified into class c if E falls into the decision area (a leaf in the decision tree) corresponding to c. The class probability $p(c|E)$ is typically estimated by the fraction of instances of class c in the leaf into which E falls. Thus, all the instances falling into the same leaf have the same class probability.

Certainly, the representation of decision trees is fully expressive theoretically. In practice, however, there is an intrinsic obstacle to building an accurate PET under the paradigm of traditional decision trees, because two contradictory factors are in play at the same time. On one hand, traditional decision tree algorithms, such as C4.5, prefer a small tree to avoid the overfitting problem for high accuracy. A small tree, however, has a small number of leaves, and then there are more instances in a leaf. That also means more instances have the same class probability, which prevents accurate probability estimation. On the other hand, if the tree is large, there is very little data with each leaf node, due to the well-known fragmentation problem [5]. Thus, the probability estimation would be inaccurate and unreliable. In addition, a large tree has a high risk to overfit the training data and would have poor classification accuracy. This is a contradiction existing in traditional decision trees.

In fact, our observation has been verified by the recent research work. Traditional decision tree learning algorithms, such as C4.5[11], are biased to small trees, and use post-pruning to further reduce the tree size. The resulting trees tend to have good accuracy, but poor probability estimation [7, 9]. Recent research suggests that a large tree tends to produce accurate probability estimation. For example, it has been observed that no pruning in a decision tree learning algorithm helps probability estimation [1]. Provost and Domingos [10] showed that the probability estimation of C4.5 can be improved significantly by turning off the post pruning mechanism. Ferri, *et al.* [3] evaluated the expected error pruning and pessimistic error pruning, and observed that even slight pruning decreases the quality of probability estimation. However, it is well-known that a large tree tends to have poor classification accuracy.

It seems difficult to overcome the contradiction under the paradigm of traditional decision trees. Our motivation is to extend the representation of traditional decision trees from probabilistic perspective. More precisely, we treat a decision tree as a probabilistic model, apply probability theory to compute probabilities, and perform both classification and ranking based on probability.

The notations used in this paper are as follows. We denote a set of attributes by a bold-face upper-case letter, for example, $\mathbf{X} = (X_1, X_2, \cdots, X_n)$, and an assignment of values to each attribute in an attribute set by a corresponding bold-face lower-case letter, for example, $\mathbf{x}$. We use C to denote the class variable and c to denote its value. Thus, a training instance $E = (\mathbf{x}, c)$, where $\mathbf{x} = (x_1, x_2, \cdots, x_n)$, and x_i is the value of attribute X_i.

The rest of the paper is organized as follows. Section 2 introduces the related work in learning decision trees with accurate probability estimation and ranking. In Section 3, we propose to perform classification and ranking in a decision tree from probabilistic perspective. In Section 4, we describe in detail the experimental setup and results. We conclude in Section 5.

2   Related Work

Since traditional decision tree algorithms, such as C4.5, have been observed to produce poor probability estimation [9], a substantial amount of work has been done recently on accurate PETs [10]. Provost and Domingos [10] pointed out that the reason behind the poor estimation of decision trees is not the decision tree representation, but the inductive algorithm. They proposed a few techniques to modify C4.5 for accurate probability estimation: (1)turning off the pruning and collapsing; (2)using Laplace correction to smooth probability estimates. The resulting algorithm is called C4.4. They also found out that bagging, an ensemble method, improves the probability estimation of decision trees significantly.

Ling and Yan proposed a method to improve the probability estimation of decision trees [6]. In their method, the class probability of an instance is estimated using an average of the probability estimates from all leaves of the tree, instead of only using the leaf into which it falls. Thus, each leaf contributes to the class probability estimate of an instance in different degree.

Although decision trees are not generally treated as a probabilistic model, they can be used to represent probability, called probabilistic trees [2]. Figure 1 shows an example of a probabilistic tree, in which each leaf L represents a conditional

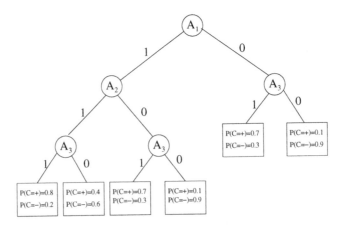

Fig. 1. An example of an probabilistic tree

probability distribution $p(C|\mathbf{x_p}(L))$, where $\mathbf{x_p}(L)$ are the values of attributes that occur in the path from the root to L, called the path attributes of L.

Kohavi proposed to deploy a naive Bayes in each leaf to represent $P(C|\mathbf{x_p}(L))$, and the resulting decision tree is called NBTree [5]. The algorithm for learning an NBTree is similar to C4.5. Actually, deploying a model at each leaf to calibrate the probability estimates of a decision tree has been proposed by Symth, Gray and Fayyad [12]. They also noticed that every instance from a particular leaf has the same probability estimate, and thus suggested to place a kernel-based probability density estimator at each leaf.

In our previous work [15, 13], we proposed to use a decision tree to represent conditional independence, called conditional independence tree (CITrees). The basic idea for CITrees is to iteratively explore and represent conditional attribute independencies at each step in constructing a decision tree, and thus decompose a traditional decision tree into smaller trees. CITrees demonstrate good performance in both classification and ranking. However, learning a CITree tends to have relatively higher computational complexity compared with learning a traditional decision tree.

In this paper, we propose a simple approach to apply probability theory to a traditional decision tree to perform both classification and ranking. Our idea is that, we use C4.5 without pruning to learn a decision tree, but treat the tree as a probabilistic tree, and use probability theory to compute probabilities that are used to perform classification and ranking.

3 Probabilistic Inference Trees

3.1 An Example

Example. Consider to use a decision tree to represent a conference paper review procedure, in which there are two reviewers: the primary reviewer (Pri) and the second reviewer (Sec). When the primary reviewer recommends to reject a paper, it will be rejected certainly. Otherwise, the recommendation from the second reviewer will be taken into account. Let a and r denote "accept" and "reject" respectively. The decision tree is shown in Figure 2.

In a traditional decision tree learning algorithm, such as C4.5, some pruning techniques, such as *expected error pruning* and *pessimistic error pruning*, are used to overcome the overfitting problem. A node (attribute) is removed if it does not lead to statistically significant improvement in classification. In Figure 2, node Sec will be removed, since it only discriminates one more instance and the sample size is small. In the pruned tree, instances $E_1 = (Pri = a, Sec = r)$ and $E_2 = (Pri = a, Sec = a)$ will be classified into "accept", which is reasonable in classification. However, in terms of ranking, intuitively, we want to give instance E_2 a higher rank than instance E_1, since two reviewers are consistent on E_2. Note that the pruned tree cannot do it, but the original tree can. This example shows that node (attribute) Sec does not significantly contribute to classification, but it does to ranking. Therefore, a decision tree for accurate ranking tends to be large.

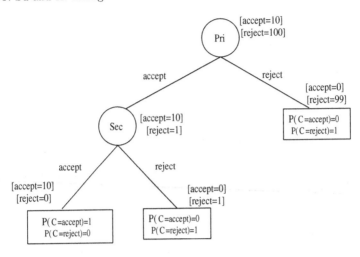

Fig. 2. The decision tree for the review procedure, in which the number of training instances in each class on a node are attached to it

3.2   Performing Classification and Ranking Based on Probability

A traditional decision tree can be viewed as a probabilistic model, if each leaf L represents not only a classification but also the corresponding probability distribution $p(c|\mathbf{x_p}(L))$, shown in Figure 1. Certainly, $p(c|\mathbf{x_p}(L))$ can be used to do classification as follows.

$$C_{dt}(E) = \arg\max_c p(c|\mathbf{x_p}(L)),\tag{1}$$

where L is the leaf into which E falls, $\mathbf{x_p}(L)$ is the value of the path attributes of L, and $C_{dt}(E)$ is the classification assigned to E by the decision tree.

For probability estimation, the class probability $P(c|E)$ can be also approximated by $p(c|\mathbf{x_p}(L))$:

$$P(c|E) \approx p(c|\mathbf{x_p}(L)).\tag{2}$$

Equation 1 and 2 can be used to do classification and ranking respectively. Then, the probability estimate for $p(c|\mathbf{x_p}(L))$ is critical. $p(c|\mathbf{x_p}(L))$ is often estimated by using the fraction of instances of class c in L. But it is problematic, since the contradiction discussed in Section 1 seems unavoidable.

We notice that probability theory provides a more suitable way to estimate $p(c|\mathbf{x_p}(L))$. In a decision tree, an internal node (attribute) X can represent the conditional probability distribution $p(C, X|\mathbf{x_p}(X))$, where $\mathbf{x_p}(X)$ is the value of the path attributes of X. Since for internal nodes (especially the ones close to the root), the fragmentation problem is not as serious as leaf nodes, their probability estimates would be more accurate than leaf nodes. More importantly, they can be used to compute probabilities for leaf nodes. According to the product rule in probability theory, we know

$$p(c|\mathbf{x_p}(L)) = \alpha p(c) \prod_{X_i \in \mathbf{X_p}(L)} p(x_i|c, \mathbf{x_p}(X_i)),\tag{3}$$

where $p(c)$ is prior probability, $p(x_i|c, \mathbf{x_p}(X_i))$ are the conditional probability of $X_i = x_i$ given c and the path attributes $\mathbf{x_p}(X_i)$, and α is a normalization factor. For example, in Figure 2, we have

$$p(C = a|Pri = a, Sec = r) = \alpha p(C = a)P(Pri = a|C = a)p(Sec = r|C = a, Pri = a).$$

In Equation 3, we need to estimate $p(x_i|c, \mathbf{x_p}(X_i))$ for each path attribute X_i. In principle, we can learn the conditional probability distribution $p(C, X|\mathbf{x_p}(X_i))$ from the data associated with X_i. But the learning process would be complex. In our implementation, we adopt frequency-base Laplace estimation. More precisely, the probabilities $p(c)$ and $p(x_i|c, \mathbf{x_p}(X_i))$ are estimated as follows.

$$p(c) = \frac{n_c + 1}{t + k},$$

$$p(x_i|c, \mathbf{x_p}(X_i)) = \frac{n_{ic} + 1}{n_c + v_i},$$

where t is the total number of training instances, k is the number of classes, v_i is the number of values of attribute X_i, n_c is the number of instances in class c, n_{ic} is the number of instances in class c, and with $X_i = x_i$ and $\mathbf{X_p}(X_i) = \mathbf{x_p}(X_i)$. Note that n_{ic} is essentially the number of instances in class c and with $X_i = x_i$ in the data associated with node X_i.

For the example in Figure 2, the probabilities are estimated as follows.

$$p(C = a|Pri = a, Sec = r) = \alpha p(C = a)P(Pri = a|C = a)p(Sec = r|C = a, Pri = a)$$
$$= \alpha \frac{10 + 1}{110 + 2} \times \frac{10 + 1}{10 + 2} \times \frac{0 + 1}{10 + 2} = 0.0075\alpha$$

$$p(C = r|Pri = a, Sec = r) = \alpha p(C = r)p(Pri = a|C = r)p(Sec = r|C = r, Pri = a)$$
$$= \alpha \frac{100 + 1}{110 + 2} \times \frac{1 + 1}{100 + 2} \times \frac{1 + 1}{1 + 2} = 0.0117\alpha$$

After normalization, $p(C = a|Pri = a, Sec = r) = 0.39$. Similarly, we can get $p(C = a|Pri = a, Sec = a) = 0.61$, which means that $E_2 = \{Pri = a, Sec = a\}$ will be ranked higher than $E_1 = \{Pri = a, Sec = r\}$, just as we expect.

The resulting model is called *probabilistic inference trees (PITs)*, because probabilities are computed from probabilistic inference based on Equation 3. There are a few main points for PITs that we need to notice.

1. It is obvious that the class probability in a PIT based on Equation 2 and 3 would be different from the one based on the fraction of instances in class c. In addition, the classification based on Equation 1 and 3 could also be different from the one given by the traditional decision tree (use the most common class). This point will be verified by the experiments in Section 4, which show that the accuracy of the classifier (PIT) based on Equation 1 and 3 is significantly higher than the classifier (C4.4) based on the most common class.

Table 1. Description of the data sets used in the experiments

data set	Size	Number of Attribute	missing value	Class
Letter	20000	17	N	26
Mushroom	8124	22	Y	2
Waveform	5000	41	N	3
Sick	3772	30	Y	2
Hypothyroid	3772	30	Y	4
Chess End-Game	3196	36	N	2
Splice	3190	62	N	3
Segment	2310	20	N	7
German Credit	1000	24	N	2
Vowel	990	14	N	11
Anneal	898	39	Y	6
Vehicle	846	19	N	4
Pima Indians Diabetes	768	8	N	2
Wisconsin-breast-cancer	699	9	Y	2
Credit Approval	690	15	Y	2
Soybean	683	36	Y	19
Balance-scale	625	5	N	3
Vote	435	16	Y	2
Horse Colic	368	28	Y	2
Ionosphere	351	34	N	2
Primary-tumor	339	18	Y	22
Heart-c	303	14	Y	5
Breast cancer	286	9	Y	2
Heart-statlog	270	13	N	2
Audiology	226	70	Y	24
Glass	214	10	N	7
Sonar	208	61	N	2
Autos	205	26	Y	7
Hepatitis Domain	155	19	Y	2
Iris	150	5	N	3
Lymph	148	19	N	4
Zoo	101	18	N	7
Labor	57	16	N	2

2. In a PIT, all the instances falling into the same leaf still have the same class probability and classification based on Equation 1, 2, and 3. However, we can build a large tree no longer to worry about overfitting and unreliable probability estimation caused by the small sample size for leaves, since we now use the probabilities along the path from root to leaf to estimate the class probabilities, instead of only using the probabilities in a leaf.

3. Note that pruning is not needed in a PIT and its classification could be the same as the pruned tree. So overfitting can be naturally handled in a PIT without pruning.

The learning algorithm for PITs is simple and depicted as follows.

Algorithm. PIT(D)
Input: A set **D** of training instances.
Output: A probabilistic inference tree.
1. Using C4.5 without pruning to learn a decision tree **T**.
2. **for** each leaf L in **T**
      Compute the class probabilities for L using Equation 3 and 2
      Compute the class label for L using Equation 1 and 3
3. Output **T** in which each leaf has a class label and class probabilities.

Once a PIT is built, the testing process is similar to the traditional decision tree. Given a test instance E, we sort E down to a leaf and use the class label and class probabilities in the leaf as E's classification and class probabilities.

4   Experiments

We conduct experiments in Weka [14] to compare PITs to the state-of-the-art decision tree learning algorithms. In our experiments, we used AUC (the area under the Receiver Operating Characteristics curve) [8] to evaluate the quality of rankings generated by a classifier. The AUC of a classifier on a data set with two classes is computed using the following formula.

$$\hat{A} = \frac{S_0 - n_0(n_0 + 1)/2}{n_0 n_1}, \qquad (4)$$

where n_0 and n_1 are the numbers of negative and positive instances respectively, and $S_0 = \sum r_i$, where r_i is the rank of the i_{th} positive instance in the ranking. Multi-class AUC is calculated by M-measure in [4].

The average AUC and accuracy on each data set was obtained by using 10-fold stratified cross validation 10 times, and then the two-tailed t-test with a confidence level of 95% was conducted to compare each pair of algorithms.

We used 33 UCI data sets selected by Weka [14] that represent a wide range of domains and data characteristics. A brief description of the properties of the data sets is in Table 1. The data sets are sorted in terms of their sizes. Numeric attributes are handled by the decision tree itself. Missing values are processed using the mechanism in Weka, which replaces all missing values with the modes and means from the training data.

Table 2 and 4 show the accuracies and AUC of the algorithms on each data set, respectively. The abbreviations used in the tables are described as follows.

PIT: the algorithm proposed in this paper.
C4.5: the traditional decision tree learning algorithm [11].
C4.4: the improved decision learning algorithm designed for ranking [10].

LingYan: the learning algorithm proposed by Ling and Yan [6]. Though they indicated the LingYan algorithm is not sensitive the confusion factor setting.

Table 2. Experimental results on accuracy

Data Set	PIT	C4.5	C4.4	LingYan
Letter	88.12±0.72	88.03±0.71	87.44±0.76 •	50.29±2.94 •
Mushroom	100.00±0.00	100.00±0.00	100.00±0.00	99.41±0.27 •
Waveform	75.36±1.93	75.25±1.90	74.99±1.88	78.62±1.98 ○
Sick	98.87±0.58	98.81±0.56	98.81±0.54	94.81±0.91 •
Hypothyroid	99.66±0.29	99.58±0.34	99.57±0.35	93.69±0.50 •
Chess-End-Game	99.40±0.39	99.44±0.37	99.45±0.40	89.26±1.87 •
Splice	93.80±1.29	93.94±1.31	89.94±1.99 •	93.58±1.63
Segment	96.78±1.22	96.79±1.29	96.62±1.24	36.93±3.76 •
German-Credit	70.08±3.50	71.13±3.19	68.32±4.05	72.67±2.58 ○
Vowel	81.57±4.11	80.08±4.34 •	81.29±4.19	55.80±5.53 •
Anneal	98.35±1.02	98.57±1.04	98.66±1.11	76.50±0.85 •
Vehicle	71.96±4.14	72.28±4.32	71.53±4.34	39.12±9.32 •
Pima-Indians-Diabetes	73.97±5.36	74.49±5.27	73.85±5.42	73.00±4.09
Wisconsin-breast-cancer	94.88±2.64	94.89±2.49	94.01±2.98	93.76±3.17
Credit-Approval	84.59±3.90	85.75±4.01	79.64±4.69 •	84.94±3.89
Soybean	92.65±2.73	92.55±2.61	92.37±2.75	71.24±6.05 •
Balance-scale	79.56±3.50	77.82±3.42 •	78.22±3.79	83.84±3.58 ○
Vote	95.90±2.77	96.27±2.79	94.38±3.22	95.72±2.81
Horse-Colic	84.24±5.53	83.28±6.05	79.89±6.30 •	83.69±6.36
Ionosphere	90.12±4.12	89.74±4.38	89.94±4.35	86.15±5.09 •
Primary-tumor	40.83±6.47	41.01±6.59	38.76±7.00	35.25±5.34 •
Heart-c	76.28±7.20	76.64±7.14	75.28±7.37	76.90±6.77
Breast-Cancer	72.01±6.80	75.26±5.04	68.85±7.73	70.64±2.15
Heart-statlog	78.07±8.01	78.15±7.42	76.85±7.94	80.56±6.93
Audiology	76.31±6.96	76.69±7.68	72.65±7.71 •	55.72±7.40 •
Glass	68.10±9.61	67.63±9.31	66.78±10.17	51.64±8.61 •
Sonar	73.85±9.65	73.61±9.34	73.61±9.20	73.35±9.37
Autos	79.08±9.95	78.64±9.94	80.18±9.56	63.95±10.88•
Hepatitis	78.64±10.44	77.02±10.03	75.15±11.60	79.84±5.08
Iris	94.80±5.24	94.73±5.30	94.20±5.74	94.40±5.82
Lymph	74.02±10.30	75.84±11.05	73.40±10.48	76.77±10.24
Zoo	93.41±7.28	92.61±7.33	93.41±7.28	93.59±7.05
Labor	80.40±13.83	81.23±13.68	82.90±13.35	79.63±13.00

○, • statistically significant improvement or degradation

Table 3. Summary of the accuracy results

	C4.5	C4.4	LingYan
PIT	2-31-0	5-28-0	15-15-3
C4.5		6-27-0	15-16-2
C4.4			13-15-5

We observed that using the percentage of the subset as the confusion factor is slightly better than the original parameter 0.3. Thus, we used the new confusion factor in our comparison.

Table 4. Experimental results on AUC

Data Set	PIT-B	PIT	C4.4	LingYan	C4.4-B
Letter	99.73±0.07	98.96±0.16 •	98.11±0.23 •	96.96±0.31 •	99.66±0.08 •
Mushroom	100.00±0.00	100.00±0.00	100.00±0.00	100.00±0.00	100.00±0.00
Waveform	94.94±0.69	91.07±1.01 •	88.27±1.34 •	93.50±0.91 •	94.69±0.74 •
Sick	99.24±1.28	98.81±1.58	99.04±1.31	97.97±2.17	99.28±1.33
Hypothyroid	99.23±2.16	94.73±4.59 •	93.91±5.31 •	99.57±0.97	98.90±3.06
Chess-End-Game	99.96±0.06	99.93±0.08	99.95±0.06	96.19±1.13 •	99.97±0.05
Splice	98.92±0.46	98.76±0.51	97.68±0.81 •	98.19±0.68 •	98.61±0.57 •
Segment	99.80±0.20	99.48±0.40 •	99.46±0.44 •	97.44±0.85 •	99.77±0.29
German-Credit	75.69±4.38	71.79±4.57 •	67.85±4.83 •	74.36±4.65	74.10±4.49 •
Vowel	99.45±0.36	96.32±1.36 •	92.75±2.61 •	95.23±1.15 •	99.43±0.41
Anneal	93.59±5.72	92.82±5.70	92.58±6.62	93.05±4.75	93.72±5.96
Vehicle	92.32±1.98	90.27±2.46 •	89.38±2.59 •	80.82±3.58 •	92.13±1.98
Pima-Indians-Diabetes	82.03±5.25	79.29±5.63 •	78.43±5.80 •	79.43±5.51	81.58±5.31 •
Wisconsin-breast-cancer	98.98±1.00	98.11±1.63 •	98.12±1.61 •	97.64±2.14 •	99.01±0.99
Credit-Approval	92.79±3.18	91.28±3.58 •	88.10±3.93 •	91.23±3.80 •	91.86±3.48 •
Soybean	99.28±1.08	98.86±1.33 •	98.09±1.65 •	98.33±0.77 •	98.89±1.29
Balance-scale	84.99±3.72	82.05±5.45	81.89±5.12	76.91±5.89 •	85.92±3.37 ∘
Vote	98.48±2.01	97.81±2.44	97.62±2.44	96.00±3.95 •	98.44±1.99
Horse-Colic	88.62±6.45	86.76±6.75	83.88±7.25 •	84.45±7.32 •	87.55±6.83
Ionosphere	96.77±3.25	92.53±5.42 •	92.50±5.52 •	91.83±5.56 •	96.85±3.24
Primary-tumor	74.39±2.67	73.09±2.86 •	69.14±3.33 •	73.58±3.11	73.13±3.09 •
Heart-c	83.83±0.58	83.42±0.66 •	83.30±0.66 •	83.34±0.76 •	83.81±0.57
Breast-Cancer	66.42±10.49	63.35±10.07	59.75±9.72 •	64.44±11.14	64.43±10.35
Heart-statlog	88.94±5.95	84.94±6.71 •	84.12±7.35 •	87.90±6.45	88.72±6.05
Audiology	69.50±1.60	66.87±2.36 •	65.76±2.38 •	68.95±1.88	69.59±1.52
Glass	89.13±4.36	83.39±5.37 •	80.95±5.44 •	81.05±6.63 •	88.30±4.96
Sonar	87.22±8.62	79.04±10.00•	79.14±10.32•	80.13±9.96 •	87.50±8.37
Autos	95.47±1.93	92.82±3.17 •	89.98±4.01 •	91.89±3.02 •	95.28±2.17
Hepatitis	84.32±12.83	77.80±13.87•	75.94±14.26•	75.35±17.44	83.79±13.34
Iris	98.15±3.42	97.49±3.37	97.45±3.52	97.38±3.41	98.23±3.36
Lymph	88.35±3.41	86.24±5.03	85.75±4.75	86.53±4.44	88.17±3.50
Zoo	80.29±6.46	80.52±5.92	80.45±6.35	84.58±4.71 ∘	80.76±6.61
Labor	94.96±11.67	86.02±16.01	86.29±16.27	89.46±15.23	95.15±11.07

∘, • statistically significant improvement or degradation

C4.4-B: the C4.4 algorithm with bagging.
PIT-B: the PIT algorithm with bagging.

Table 2 and 4 show the accuracies and AUC of the algorithms on each data set, respectively. Table 3 and 5 show the results of the two-tailed t-test, in which each entry $w/t/l$ means that the algorithm in the corresponding row wins in w data sets, ties in t data sets, and loses in l data sets, compared to the algorithm in the corresponding column.

Table 5. Summary of the AUC experimental results

	PIT	C4.4	LingYan	C4.4-B
PIT-B	20-13-0	23-10-0	17-15-1	7-25-1
PIT		15-18-0	7-22-4	0-17-16
C4.4			5-20-8	0-10-23
LingYan				1-15-17

Now, we summarize the highlights of accuracy results briefly as follows:

1. PIT is competitive with C4.5(2 win and 0 loss).
2. PIT performs better than C4.4 (5 wins and 0 loss).
3. PIT significantly outperforms the LingYan algorithm (15 wins and 3 loss).

The following is the highlights of AUC results briefly:

1. PIT performs significantly better than C4.4 (15 wins and 0 loss).
2. PIT outperforms slightly the LingYan algorithm (7 wins and 4 loss).
3. PIT-B performs better than C4.4-B (7 wins and 1 loss).

In summary, our experimental results show that PITs perform well in both classification and ranking. Overall, it is among the best in the decision tree learning algorithms compared in this paper.

5   Conclusions

In this paper, we pointed out that traditional decision trees have an inherent obstacle to achieving both accurate classification and ranking, and proposed to overcome this issue from probabilistic perspective. Experiments show that our new model outperforms or is competitive with the state-of-the-art decision tree learning algorithms in both classification and ranking. Our work provides a new model for the applications in which both accurate classification and ranking are desired.

One key observation in our new model is that each internal node in a decision tree can represent a conditional probability distribution that can be used to estimate the class probability for leaves by using the product rule in probability theory. In our current work, we used frequency-based Laplace estimation to estimate the distribution for each internal node. Apparently, more sophisticated approach can be done in this step. This is one direction for our future work.

References

1. Bauer, E., Kohavi, R.: An Empirical Comparison of Voting Classification Algorithms: Bagging, Boosting, and Variants. Machine Learning, **36(1-2)** 1999 105-139
2. Buntine, W.: Learning Classification Trees. Artificial Intelligence Frontiers in Statistics. Chapman Hall, London (1991) 182-201
3. Ferri, C., Flach, P. A., Hernndez-Orallo, J.: Improving the AUC of Probabilistic Estimation Trees. Proceedings of 14th European Conference on Machine Learning. Springer (2003) 121-132
4. Hand, D. J., Till, R. J.: A simple generalisation of the area under the ROC curve for multiple class classification problems. Machine Learning **45** (2001) 171-186
5. Kohavi, R.: Scaling Up the Accuracy of Naive-Bayes Classifiers: A Decision-Tree Hybrid. Proceedings of the Second International Conference on Knowledge Discovery and Data Mining (KDD-96). AAAI Press (1996) 202-207
6. Ling, C. X., Yan, R. J.: Decision Tree with Better Ranking. Proceedings of the 20th International Conference on Machine Learning. Morgan Kaufmann (2003) 480-487

7. Pazzani, M., Merz, C., Murphy, P., Ali, K., Hume, T., Brunk, C.: Reducing mis-classification costs. Proceedings of the 11th International conference on Machine Learning. Morgan Kaufmann (1994) 217-225
8. Provost, F., Fawcett, T.: Analysis and visualization of classifier performance: comparison under imprecise class and cost distribution. Proceedings of the Third International Conference on Knowledge Discovery and Data Mining. AAAI Press (1997) 43-48
9. Provost, F., Fawcett, T., Kohavi, R.: The case against accuracy estimation for comparing induction algorithms. Proceedings of the Fifteenth International Conference on Machine Learning. Morgan Kaufmann (1998) 445-453
10. Provost, F. J., Domingos, P.: Tree Induction for Probability-Based Ranking. Machine Learning **52(3)** (2003) 199-215
11. Quinlan, J. R.: C4.5: Programs for Machine Learning. Morgan Kaufmann: San Mateo, CA (1993)
12. Symth, P., Gray, A., Fayyad, U.: Retrofitting decision tree classifiers using kernel density estimation. Proceedings of the Twelfth International Conference on Machine Learning. Morgan Kaufmann (1996) 506–514
13. Su, J., Zhang, H.: Representing Conditional Independence Using Decision Trees. Proceedings of the Twentieth National Conference on Artificial Intelligence (AAAI-05). AAAI Press(2005) 874-879.
14. Witten, I. H., Frank, E.: data mining-Practical Machine Learning Tools and Techniques with Java Implementation. Morgan Kaufmann (2000)
15. Zhang, H., Su, J.: Conditional Independence Trees. Proceedings of the 15th European Conference on Machine Learning (ECML2004), Springer(2004) 513-524

Parameter Estimation of One-Class SVM on Imbalance Text Classification

Ling Zhuang and Honghua Dai

School of Engineering and Information Technology, Deakin University,
221 Burwood Highway, VIC 3125, Australia
lzhu@deakin.edu.au, hdai@deakin.edu.au

Abstract. Compared with conventional two-class learning schemes, one-class classification simply uses a single class for training purposes. Applying one-class classification to the minorities in an imbalanced data has been shown to achieve better performance than the two-class one. In this paper, in order to make the best use of all the available information during the learning procedure, we propose a general framework which first uses the minority class for training in the one-class classification stage; and then uses both minority and majority class for estimating the generalization performance of the constructed classifier. Based upon this generalization performance measurement, parameter search algorithm selects the best parameter settings for this classifier. Experiments on UCI and Reuters text data show that one-class SVM embedded in this framework achieves much better performance than the standard one-class SVM alone and other learning schemes, such as one-class Naive Bayes, one-class nearest neighbour and neural network.

1   Introduction

One-class classification problem becomes of special importance in recent machine learning research. One essential difference between one-class and conventional classification is that in one-class learning, it is assumed that only the target class information is available. In other words, in the classifier training process, instances from the target class are used and there is no information about its counterpart. The boundary between the two classes has to be estimated from data of the only available objects. Thus, the task is to define a boundary around the target class, such that it encircles as many target examples as possible and minimizes the chance of accepting outliers.

One-class classification is practically significant in many real world applications. For example, in order to classify sites of "interest" to a web surfer, the sites that are of interest are regarded as the positive instances. However, those "non-interest" ones are normally difficult or expensive to obtain and define. In such cases, one-class classification is the better solution.

Applying one-class classification to imbalanced data is a relatively new research direction, although some work has already been done [1, 2]. Due to the imbalance characteristics of the data, the conventional classifier tends to have

L. Lamontagne and M. Marchand (Eds.): Canadian AI 2006, LNAI 4013, pp. 538–549, 2006.
© Springer-Verlag Berlin Heidelberg 2006

a bias towards the majority class. The advantage of the one-class classifier is that by discarding the distractive majorities, the "space" where minority data resides could be better determined. In [2], empirical results also show that on heavily-unbalanced data, one-class classifier achieves much better performance than the two-class ones.

With the employment of one-class learning on the target class, the information of the other class is typically discarded, or wasted. However, will these available information be helpful in other aspects? The goal of this paper is to investigate these possibilities. We propose a general framework which applies one-class classification to imbalanced data. The majority instances are not involved in the classifier training procedure. But it is utilized to help in tuning the parameters of one-class SVM. Experimental results show that with the assistance of the majority class, the overall performance is improved and the accuracy rates on minority and majority class are more balanced.

2   Background

In this section, we will briefly introduce the original one-class SVM as an important background knowledge for this paper. One-class SVM was first proposed in [3] to estimate the probability density function where the data set is drawn from. As stated in [3], the problem one-class SVM aims to solve is:

Suppose a data set is drawn from an underlying probability distribution P. Estimate a "simple" subset S in the input space such that the probability that a test point drawn from P lies outside of S equals a priori specified value between 0 and 1.

The solution to this problem is to estimate a function f that is positive on S and negative on the complement. In other words, in [3], they developed an algorithm which returns a function f that takes the value $+1$ in a "small" region capturing most of the training data points and -1 elsewhere. Their strategy could be summarized to two steps:

- Map the data into a feature space corresponding to an appropriate kernel function.
- Separate the mapped vectors from origin with maximum margin.

Let $x_i (i \in [1, l])$ denote the training examples labeled as the positive class, and $\Phi : X \longrightarrow H$ be a kernel map which transforms the data into an inner product space H. Common kernel functions include linear, sigmoid, polynomial and gaussian kernels. We employed the gaussian kernels only in this paper which has the advantage that the data are always separable from the origin in feature space [3]. The gaussian kernel is given as follows:

$$k(x, y) = e^{-||x-y||^2/c}$$

The problem of separating the data set from the origin is essentially the problem of optimizing the following quadratic programming problem:

$$min \frac{1}{2}||w||^2 + \frac{1}{vl}\sum_{i=1}^{l}\xi_i - \rho$$

$$s.t.(w \cdot \Phi(x_i) \geq \rho - \xi_i,$$

$$i = 1, 2, ..., l,$$

$$\xi_i \geq 0$$

If w and ρ solve this problem, then the decision function $f(x) = sign((w \cdot \Phi(x)) - \rho)$ will be positive for most training points x_i.

Note that $v \in (0, 1]$ is a significant parameter in one-class SVM. It is an upper bound on the fraction of outliers, that is, training points outside the estimated region. It is also a lower bound on the fraction of support vectors. In other words, the value of v indicates the size of region function f covers. The smaller value v has, the bigger size the estimated region will be. The ideal solution is to find a smaller region covers more fraction of the training points. Thus, the value of v is one factor we need to take into consideration in the parameter estimation process.

3   Related Work

One-Class SVM has been applied to document classification in [1]. In their paper, besides the original one-class SVM, they also proposed an extended version which is called the "outlier" methodology. In the outlier methodology, not only the origin is assumed as in the negative class, but also the data points which are "close enough" to the origin. To identify the "outliers", they made such an assumption: if a document shares very few words with the chosen feature subset of the dictionary, that is, the corresponding document vector has few non-zero entries, this document is not a good representative of the class and can be treated as an outlier. Hence, by counting the number of non-zero elements in a document vector and if it is less than a threshold, the document is labeled in the negative class. In [1], the threshold was decided empirically. However, the theoretical foundation for this approach is not very strong and the empirical method to determine the threshold is not convincing. The major contribution of [1] is that they have done extensive tests on various classification algorithms with different document representations such as binary representation, frequency representation, tf-idf representation and Hadamard representation. In particular, they tested the SVM algorithms with several kernel functions, including linear, polynomial, sigmoid and radial basis kernels. The results achieved on the Reuters data set show that the one-class SVM is more robust to smaller categories. However, it is very sensitive to the parameters and choice of kernel.

The outstanding performance of one-class SVM applied to data with heavily unbalanced class proportions is reported in [2]. This paper investigates the impact of re-balancing on imbalance data set for SVM classifiers. The extreme case is to ignore the majority examples in the learning procedure, which is exactly the one-class SVM classifier. Experiments on one high-dimensional real world data and low-dimensional synthetic data with noise prove that there is a consistent pattern of decreasing performance with increasing proportion of negative class instances. On the Reuters data set, when removing the most frequent features, the drop in performance for 2-class SVM models is much larger than the one-class one. The intuitive explanation as given in [2] is: if the learner uses the minority class only, the "corner" where minority data resides is properly determined. However, the minority class is "swamped" by the majority class. Hence, once the majority instances are added, the SVM solution becomes suboptimal. All these indicate that one-class classification does have potential to be superior to the normal classifier on imbalance data. However, in their work, they only considered the linear kernel for SVMs and the important parameter selection issue is hardly mentioned.

One-Class SVM has appeared in many applications such as anomaly network traffic detection [4], relevant sentence extraction [5], image retrieval [6]. Some work has also been done on estimating the generalization performance [7] and by using the generalization performance as the objective function, [8] employed the generic algorithm to optimize the training model, i.e., select the best parameter setting of the kernel and v.

4   Algorithm Description

4.1   Motivation

Imbalance classification could be roughly divided into two categories according to the class distribution. The first type might be considered as anomaly detection. In this case, the majority class is well-sampled based on a certain probability distribution. But it is impossible to sample the minority due to their randomness. Conversely, in the other situation, we are able to sample the minority class quite well. However, the size of majorities are so huge that it is unlikely to draw a proper distribution from it. For example, in text classification, when we are targeting to classify articles relating to a specific topic "football", we first select all those ones about "football" to constitute the positive class and regard those ones not on "football", i.e, "non-football" as the negative. However, the number of "non-football" articles is definitely much larger than the "football" ones, since they could include anything else, such as traveling, cooking, movies etc. The definition of "non-football" is an ambiguous concept and instances belong to it are extremely difficult to sample due to their diversities.

Normal classifiers generally perform poorly on imbalanced datasets, whether the data belongs to category one or two. Most of classifiers are designed to generalize from training data and output the simplest hypothesis that best fits the data. This is based on the principle of Occam's razor. With imbalanced data, the simplest hypothesis is often the one that classifies almost all instances as the majority class. This is a very common situation when apply most normal classification algorithms to imbalance data. One-class classification has been proven to be superior to the normal classifiers empirically and theoretically in [2].

In one-class imbalance classification, the minority class is specifically targeted. As mentioned in Section 2, a function f is estimated to be positive on the minority instances and negative on the others. However, this approach is not appropriate for imbalance data fit in category 1. Note that in this category, the minority class could not be well-sampled. This problem is beyond the scope of this paper and we will only consider the imbalanced data described in category 2, especially on text data.

The advantage of one-class classification on imbalance data is that by discarding the majority information during training procedure, it is no longer a distraction for the classifier. However, this creates another problem: will the classifer overfit the training minority class? Another issue we consider is the parameter selection problem in SVM. SVM is very sensitive to the parameters. Besides the different set of kernel parameters, one-class SVM has the additional one v as introduced in Section 2. To solve these problems, we propose a general framework to apply one-class classification on imbalance data. In this framework, the majority instances are not used in training the classifier. However, they are utilized in estimating the generalization performance and tuning the classifier parameters. In this paper, although we only focus on the one-class SVM methodology with the gaussian kernel, this proposed framework could be easily adapted to other one-class classifiers, such as one-class neural network, one-class nearest neighbor.

4.2 One-Class Classification Framework

The one-class classification framework is divided into three stages:

1. Training Stage.
2. Estimation Stage.
3. Adjustment Stage.

Figure 1 illustrates the detailed procedure with the employment of one-class SVM classifier. In the first stage, to construct the classifier, normally an initial parameter setting needs to be given. Generally this initial setting is chosen randomly. The classifier is trained from the minorities, i.e., the target class in the training set. Based upon the hypothesis induced in the first step, the performance is evaluated utilizing BOTH minority and majority data. This is the estimation stage. Finally at the adjustment stage, with the generalization performance as the objective function, the parameter settings are adjusted to achieve better results. This optimization process will repeat recursively and stop while the "best" parameter setting is selected.

Generalization performance estimation of a classifier is one of the key tasks in learning process. There are several generic performance estimators, including training error, hold-out testing, bootstrap, cross-validation and leave-one-out. The most popular method is cross-validation. Among the various versions of cross-validation estimator, the leave-one-out estimator is shown to be almost unbiased [9]. The general leave-one-out estimator is described as follows: From the training instances $S = ((x_1, y_1), \ldots, (x_n, y_n))$, the first instance is removed. The remaining instances $S^1 = ((x_2, y_2), \ldots, (x_n, y_n))$ are used for training, producing a classification rule h_L^1. This rule is tested on the held out instance (x_1, y_1). This process is repeated for all training examples. The generalization performance is measured by these test results.

We employed the leave-one-out estimator due to its high reliability. However, we revise the leave-one-out estimator accordingly due to the speciality of this framework. Note that the majority instances are not involved in the training procedure. Thus, when estimating the classification performance on majorities, or negative class, the classifier is first constructed on the entire minorities. Then each majority instance is tested. This estimation is a fast process since the classifier only needs to be constructed once. On the other hand, when estimating the performance on minorities, or positive class, the standard leave-one-out estimation is utilized. Since the number of minorities is generally small, this process is also fast comparing to normal leave-one-out estimations.

The overall performance is measured upon the accuracy of both positive and negative classes. In the experiments of this paper, g-metric is used as the performance measurement. We will introduce g-metric in Section 5.2.

4.3 Parameter Search Algorithms

Grid search is a straightforward approach. In grid search, a uniform grid is defined in the parameter space. Then points in each of the grid are evaluated and the global optimum is found in this space. The coarseness of the grid determines the quality of the solution and the efficiency of the search.

Grid search has been widely used in SVM parameter selection. Although lots of effort has been spent in parameter search for SVM, grid search is still regarded as the most reliable approach. The only problem is its high computational demands. Even moderately high resolution searches can result in a large number of evaluations and unacceptably long run times. In this paper, we will also employ grid search as the basic search method.

The idea of parameter selection based on design of experiments(DOE) was first proposed in [10]. This approach basically is to start with a very coarse grid covering the whole search space and iteratively refine both the grid resolution and search boundaries, keeping the number of samples at each iteration roughly constant.

A combination of three-level experiment design with the two-level experiment design constitutes the sampling pattern in our experiment design search method. The three-level design is also written as a 3^k factorial design. It means that k factors are considered, each at 3 levels. Similarly, the two-level design is to consider k factors at 2 levels. In a two parameter space, if each parameter is considered as one factor, this approach will produce thirteen solutions($3^2 + 2^2 = 13$). Please note that when we select the points, we first discretize each parameter space by dividing it into three or two equal-length sections. In this paper, the middle point of each section is chosen as the representative for each level.

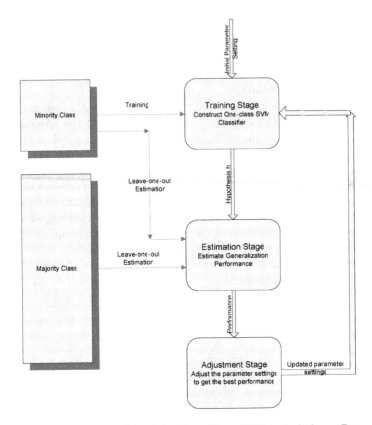

Fig. 1. Framework of Applying One-Class SVM to Imbalance Data

Table 1. UCI Dataset Description

Dataset	Positive Insts.	Negative Insts.	Ratio	Attribute
Segment1	330	1980	1:6	19
Glass7	29	185	1:6	9
Letter26	734	19266	1:26	16
Abalone19	32	4145	1:130	8

Table 2. Reuters-21578 ModApte Dataset Description

Data set	Money-fx	Grain	Crude	Trade	Interest	Ship	Wheat	Corn
#+Training	475	371	330	369	347	197	212	181
Ratio(+:-)	1:19.2	1:24.9	1:28.1	1:25.2	1:26.7	1:47.8	1:44.3	1:52.1

In each search iteration, the system evaluates the classifier performance at the sampled points, i.e., with the selected parameter settings. The one with the best performance will be chosen and the search space is refined around it. Currently in our experiment, we half the parameter range after each iteration. However, this could be adjusted accordingly. If the new search space could center around the best point without going outside the original boundary, that is the best choice. Otherwise, the new search range will start from or end to the closest original bound and then extend to the other half section. This process is repeated as many times desired or once the points in the refined search space could not improve the previous performance any more.

5   Experimental Results

5.1   Data Set

Four UCI datasets are used first to evaluate the performance of different search algorithms. They are abalone(19), letter(26), glass(7) and segment(1). The number in the parentheses indicates the target class we chose as the positive. All the other classes are regarded as negative. Table 1 summarizes the details of each data set with respect to the number of positive and negative instances, positive-to-negative ratio and the number of attributes.All the attributes in these four data sets are continuous variables and scaled to either $[-1, 1]$ or $[0, 1]$. The first two data sets are slightly imbalanced with the ratio $1 : 6$ and the last data set(abalone) is the most imbalanced one with a very high ratio $1 : 130$.

Another real world data set we used is *Reuters-21578* Modified Apte Split. This benchmark text collection contains 9603 documents in the training set and 3299 documents in the test set. We preprocessed the documents using the standard stop word removing, stemming and converted the documents to high-dimensional vectors using TFIDF weighting scheme. In order to reduce the size of the term set, we discarded terms which appear in less than 5 documents and the total number of terms extracted finally is 6362. We have chosen 8 topic categories for evaluation in the experiments. They are all mildly imbalanced and Table 2 summarizes their details. It lists, for each specific topic, the number of positive documents(#+Training) and the positive-to-negative ratio in the training set.

5.2   Evaluation Measurement

The g-metric means suggested by Kubat et. al. [11] is employed to evaluate classifiers on highly imbalanced datasets. The calculation of g-means metric is as follows:

$$g = \sqrt{acc + *acc-}$$

where $acc+$ indicates the sensitivity metrics and $acc-$ the specificity. Sensitivity is defined as the accuracy on the positive instances(true positives/(true positives + false negatives)), and specificity is defined as the accuracy on the negative instances(true negatives/(true negatives + false positives)).

Another popular evaluation measurement we employed is F_1 measure. The calculation is defined based on the precision and recall:

$$F_1 = \frac{2 \times recall \times precision}{recall + precision}.$$

5.3   Results

UCI Dataset. First of all, we compared the accuracy of parameter search algorithms on the small UCI data sets. Table 3 lists the g-metric mean accuracy rates. Table 4 gives more details of the search performance by listing the accuracy rate on positive and negative class respectively. The reason for doing this is to further investigate the classification performance on different classes. From Table 3, it is clear that the search algorithm based on the experiment design achieves the best overall performance. If we look into the details as Table 4, we will find that apparently, experiment design search did improve the accuracy rate on positive minority class compared to grid search. However, the accuracy rate on negative majority class of experiment design search is slightly worse than the grid search. From the definition of experiment design search, we could see that the advantage of it is that it could sample the parameter space in a better way. By increasing the grid resolution in each iteration, the search space is refined.

Another series of experiments is to test with and without the assistance of majority instances in the estimation stage. When it is without the majority instances, it is similar as standard one-class SVM. The negative class is discarded and only minority class is considered in the process. The leave-one-out estimation is only performed on minority instances. Only accuracy rate on minority is taken into consideration when evaluating the classifier performance, since no other information is available.

Table 5 lists the comparison results. An interesting common phenomenon is that in the "without" case, one-class SVM does achieve excellent performance on the positive minority class. However, this is accompanied by very poor recall rate on negatives. However, when the negative majorities are considered in the estimation stage, although the accuracy rate decreases slightly on the positives, the performance on majorities is improved. In situations where performance on both class is equally important, our approach is a better solution for more balanced results.

Table 3. Search Algorithm Comparison(G-metric)

Dataset	Grid Search	Experiment Design Search
Segment	0.799	0.921
Glass	0.722	0.781
Letter	0.866	0.909
Abalone	0.583	0.635

Table 4. Search Algorithm Comparison(Recall on P/N class)

Dataset	Grid Search		EDS	
	P	N	P	N
Segment	0.667	0.957	0.94	0.903
Glass	0.552	0.946	0.724	0.843
Letter	0.869	0.863	0.895	0.924
Abalone	0.438	0.777	0.594	0.679

Table 5. Comparison(Recall on P/N class) with and without the negative instances

Dataset	GS With		GS Without		EDS With		EDS Without	
	P	N	P	N	P	N	P	N
Segment	0.667	0.957	0.667	0.957	0.94	0.903	0.913	0.897
Glass	0.552	0.946	0.758	0.551	0.724	0.843	0.828	0.741
Letter	0.869	0.863	0.932	0.513	0.895	0.924	0.990	0.192
Abalone	0.438	0.777	0.688	0.551	0.594	0.679	0.75	0.458

Results on Real-World Text Dat. Based on the first section of our experimental work, we selected the experiment design search as the default search
approach. We compared our method on Reuters21578 text collection with the
results published in [1]. To the best of our knowledge, [1] is the first work to
apply one-class SVM on document classification. However, they discarded the
negative class information and in their experiments, they only considered the
impact of various document representation on classification performance, nor
the parameter selection in one-class SVM. Table 6 shows the comparison details.
The evaluation measurement is F1 measure. The algorithms we compared with
include the standard One-class SVM(RBF kernel, binary document representation), Outlier-SVM(Linear kernel, binary document representation), Neural
Networks, one-class Naive Bayes, one-class Nearest Neighbour(Hadamard document representation) and Prototype Algorithm(tf-idf document representation).
According to [1], the listed F1 results are the best among various document
representations and parameter settings. As we could see, in most of the cases,
our approach achieves much better results than the standard one-class SVM and
the other approaches. This further proves that a good set of parameters for SVM
does have a huge impact on the classifier performance.

Table 6. Comparison of standard One-class SVM(OC), Outlier-SVM(OS), Neural Net-
works(NN), Naive Bayes(NB), Nearest Neighbour(NN2), Prototype Algorithm(P) and
our Improved One-Class SVM(I-OC)

Dataset	OC	OS	NN	NB	NN2	P	I-OC
Money	0.514	0.563	*0.642*	0.493	0.468	0.484	0.550
Grain	0.585	0.523	0.473	0.382	0.333	0.402	*0.742*
Crude	0.544	0.474	0.534	0.457	0.392	0.398	*0.715*
Trade	0.597	0.423	0.569	0.483	0.441	0.557	*0.634*
Interest	0.485	0.465	0.487	0.394	0.295	0.454	*0.609*
Ship	*0.539*	0.402	0.361	0.288	0.389	0.370	0.427
Wheat	0.474	0.389	0.404	0.288	0.566	0.262	*0.647*
Corn	0.298	0.356	0.324	0.254	0.168	0.230	*0.542*

Time Complexity. There are two major factors which affect the running time
of our approach. The first one is the size of training set. Since the classification algorithm is one-class classification, only the positive instances are used in

the training procedure. Hence, the size of positive instance influences the construction time of classifier. The larger size of positive minority class, the longer running time it will be.

Another important factor which will have huge impact on the time complexity is the search algorithm. It is a conflicting situation since when we do the parameter selection, the more parameter settings we tried, the more likely we will find the better ones. At the same time, it will also cost longer running time. Therefore, a search algorithm which could find a relatively better parameter setting quickly is the suboptimal solution.

The basic idea behind these search algorithms are actually the same. It is to find an appropriate sample pattern in the search space so that the estimation procedure could locate the best point in an effective and efficient way. Grid search is an exhaustive search which makes it very inefficient. However, it is also the safest solution for this problem. In the grid search, the resolution of the parameter space determines the running time. In our experiments, the parameter ranges are $v \in (0,1)$ and $\log(\gamma) \in [-15,3]$. For a very coarse grid of 10×18, the parameter settings need to be tested is 180. The grid resolution in this case is $0.1 \times 1 = 0.1$. Please note here this is the size of one grid in the parameter space. One point in this grid is selected randomly to represent it for estimation purpose.

In our current experiment design search, after each iteration, the grid resolution is doubled and the bounds shrunk. At each iteration, in total 13 points are sampled and tested. To repeat this process 10 times, $13 \times 10 = 130$ points are tested and the size of final grid is $0.1 \times 1.8 = 0.18$. Note here this is the block size inside which we will further sample data points. Compare to the grid search, the resolution is much higher and the number of points need to be evaluated is reduced.

6   Conclusion

In this paper, we propose a general framework for one-class classification on imbalance data. In this framework, only minority class is engaged in training the classifier but both majority and minority instances are utilized in estimating the generalization performance of constructed classifier. Using the generalization performance as the measurement, a set of best parameters are selected. Experimental results prove that this framework with the one-class SVM achieves much better accuracy results than the standard OC-SVM and other one-class learning schemes. In addition, from a series of accuracy test with or without the participation of majority class in the estimation stage, we find that with the majorities the classifier is able to achieve more balanced results on positive and negative classes.

Our future work will be focused on investigating more one-class classification algorithms within this framework. Although in this paper we only considered one-class SVM with gaussian kernel, it is possible to be extended to more one-class learning schemes. Another important issue is the parameter search algorithms. A better way to search for the best setting is to let the classification performance converge to a optimal value rather than do a exhaustive search.

References

1. Manevitz, L.M., Yousef, M.: One-class svms for document classification. Journal of Machine Learning Research **2** (2001) 139–154
2. Raskutti, B., Kowalczyk, A.: Extreme re-balancing for svms: a case study. SIGKDD Explorations **6** (2004) 60–69
3. Scholkopt, B., Platt, J.C., Shawe-Taylor, J., Smola, A.J., Williamson, R.C.: Estimating the support of a high-dimensional distribution. Neural Computation **13** (2001) 1443–1471
4. Tran, Q.A., Duan, H., Li, X.: One-class support vector machine for anomaly network traffic detection. In: Proceedings of the 2nd Network Research Workshop of the 18th APAN. (2004)
5. Kruengkrai, C., Jaruskulchai, C.: Using one-class svms for relevant sentence extraction. In: Proceedings of the 3rd International Symposium on Communications and Information Technologies (ISCIT-2003). (2003)
6. Chen, Y., Zhou, X.S., Huang, T.S.: One-class svm for learning in image retrieval. In: Proceedings of the International Conference in Image Processing (ICIP'01). (2001)
7. Tran, Q.A., Li, X., Duan, H.: Efficient performance estimate for one-class support vector machine. Pattern Recognition Letters **26** (2005) 1174–1182
8. Tran, Q.A., Zhang, Q., Li, X.: Evolving training model method for one-class svm. In: Proceeding of 2003 IEEE International Conference on Systems, Man & Cybernetics (SMC 2003). (2003)
9. Lunts, A., Brailovskiy, V.: Evaluation of attributes obtained in statistical decision rules. Engineering Cybernetics_ (1967) 98–109
10. Staelin, C.: Parameter selection for support vector machines. Technical Report HPL-2002-354R1, Hewlett-Packard Company (2003)
11. Kubat, M., Matwin, S.: Addressing the curse of imbalanced training sets: one-sided selection. In: Proc. 14th International Conference on Machine Learning, Morgan Kaufmann (1997) 179–186

MITS: A Mixed-Initiative Intelligent Tutoring System for Sudoku

Allan Caine and Robin Cohen

David R. Cheriton School of Computer Science
University of Waterloo, Waterloo, Ontario, Canada N2L 3G1
{adcaine, rcohen}@cs.uwaterloo.ca

Abstract. In this paper, we propose a model called MITS — Mixed Initiative Intelligent Tutoring System for Sudoku. Extrapolating from theory for tutoring in scholastic subjects, and tutoring in the game of chess, we develop a model for tutoring the game of Sudoku using a mixed-initiative paradigm. Moreover, our aim is to design a system which not only proposes moves to make but also gives advice on why a particular move ought to be made. We operate in a decision-theoretic framework that measures the benefits and costs of interacting with students who are learning the game. The tutor will take the initiative to interact when the student lacks knowledge and is making moves that have low utility. But it will also interact when the student takes the initiative to elicit further input on the game he or she is trying to play. We illustrate our graphic user interface prototype and take the reader through a sample session. As a result, we present a system that is useful not only to gain insight into how to tutor students about strategy games but also about how to support mixed-initiative interaction in tutorial settings.

1 Introduction

Sudoku is a game, developed in Japan and recently made popular in North America, that consists of trying to fill in empty cells in a partially completed 9×9 grid, with a clear set of rules about the possible entries in a cell (the numbers 1 to 9) and the conflicts to avoid when completing cells (only one of any number in any one column, row and particular 3×3 blocks of the grid). It can be viewed as a kind of constraint-satisfaction problem that is accessible to the game player, and yet, not always trivial to solve. A Sudoku board solved by pencil and paper is illustrated in Figure 1.

In this paper, we propose a model called MITS — Mixed-Initiative Tutoring System for Sudoku. The promotion of mixed-initiative interaction was encouraged as early as 1970 [1] and has been reinforced more recently with projects that have implemented mixed-initiative designs (e.g. [2]). Extrapolating from a theory for tutoring in scholastic subjects and motivated by some methods used in a strategy-based system for tutoring the game of chess [3], we develop an architecture to enable tutoring a student for an entire game of Sudoku. We provide for mixed-initiative interaction during the tutorial session, where either the system (tutor) or the user can take the initiative to direct the tutorial session.

We begin with an initialization phase where the tutor strictly controls game play in an effort to characterize the player's skill at playing Sudoku. After the initialization phase

L. Lamontagne and M. Marchand (Eds.): Canadian AI 2006, LNAI 4013, pp. 550–561, 2006.
© Springer-Verlag Berlin Heidelberg 2006

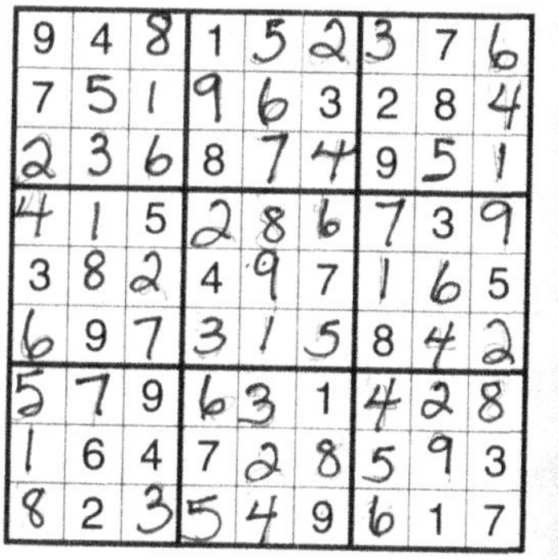

Fig. 1. A solved Sudoku Puzzle

is complete, we allow a student to try to complete a Sudoku game board, with the tutor "looking over the student's shoulder." The aim of the tutor is to both suggest cells in the grid for the student to fill in and to provide commentary on moves that the student has chosen to make (trying to assign a value to a grid position), in an effort to have the student learn more general strategies that will enable the completion of the entire game board. In our mixed-initiative setting, the user can as well solicit input from the tutor, when he or she is unclear either about the best move to make or the reason why their previous attempts have not been successful.

Within the field of mixed-initiative systems, one challenge is how to develop algorithms for a system to reason about when to initiate interaction with a user, in order to improve the expected utility of the actions to be taken. One particularly useful decision-theoretic model is presented in [4]. In this model, the benefits of interacting are weighed against the costs (e.g. bothering the user). In addition, the expected utility of the actions emerging from an interaction with a user have to be tempered by an estimation of whether the user has the knowledge that is being solicited, and whether he or she is likely to even understand what is being requested. In essence, user modeling becomes a critical factor in the decisions about when to initiate interaction.

When designing an intelligent tutoring system, one of the overall aims is to enable the student to learn sufficiently well so that he or she can in fact operate fairly independently, in the future. And yet, the tutor should not sit idle if the student is making errors, while attempting to learn. As a result, we can still apply a decision-theoretic model such as the one in [4]; we need to revisit, however, what it means when the student's attempted actions are reducing the overall expected utility. This is in fact a signal that interaction should take place. And we also need to revisit what to do when it does not appear to be important to interact and yet the student is requesting more guidance. Again, in this case, interaction should be initiated.

The model that we present has the following important features: i) it demonstrates how to tutor a student for an entire game; ii) in contrast with some other systems to tutor students about games, it provides for a strategy graph to be completed dynamically online; iii) it provides an architecture for managing mixed-initiative tutoring; iv) it shows how to adjust a standard algorithm for reasoning about interaction in mixed-initiative systems, when the context is one of tutoring and the aim of teaching the student is also important to achieve; and v) it provides insight into the game of Sudoku and the essential elements of this game to consider, when addressing the challenge of tutoring this particular game.

2 Background

According to Freedman [5], an intelligent tutoring system has four parts: a model of the domain, a model of the student, a model of the learning environment, and a teaching model. The model of the domain is what is being taught. The model of the student is a representation of the student by the tutor in the computer system. The model of the learning environment is essentially the user-interface. Finally, the teaching model is a representation of how the material is taught to the student. These important elements are retained in our proposed architecture for tutoring students in the game of Sudoku.

We also take as a starting point some research on the topic of teaching students about endgames of chess, the UMRAO system [3]. This system includes two major components: the Expert and the Tutor. The Expert is responsible for selecting the specific game board to be played and generating the strategy graph — a graph of all the possible next moves from a given game board position. Attached to each node is an explanation of the move. The Tutor uses the strategy graph to evaluate the moves made by the student, providing feedback and suggesting future moves to attempt. UMRAO incorporates as well a graphical interface that displays both the game board being considered and a the running feedback from the Tutor.

UMRAO is a valuable starting point for our research to develop a tutoring system for Sudoku, but it has a number of shortcomings that we attempt to address in our model, as follows: i) it has no explicit student model. Instead, Gadwal *et al.* [3] claim that the student is modeled in terms of the strategy graph — the level of play demonstrated in that graph can serve to characterize the student as novice or expert; ii) UMRAO cannot switch its interpretation of the student's abilities during a tutoring session; as such it cannot adapt during the game play; and iii) the strategy graph that represents how to correctly play the game is computed off-line because of the great deal of time needed to compute it.

We elected to study a game that was less open-ended than chess, Sudoku, where the student's moves could be interpreted in terms of a small fixed number of possible strategies. We wanted to emphasize the opportunity for interaction during the tutoring session and to explore the circumstances under which interaction should take place, based on a modeling of the current state of the student. As such, we made sure that the student model is updated with each move to reflect the abilities of the student. In contrast to UMRAO, our strategy graph displays what is allowable as the next move in the game (see Figure 3). We update the strategy graph only when the student has made an acceptable move; the graph reflects the student's progress in solving the Sudoku puzzle. While the student model reflects what the student knows and understands, the strategy graph reflects what the student has solved. In the end, the interaction provided in the system depends on the student and the state of the game and is adjusted as the student becomes more skillful in playing the game.

3   Our Proposed Model: MITS

Our proposed game tutor is given in Figure 2. We call it MITS for **M**ixed **I**nitiative Intelligent **T**utoring **S**ystem for Sudoku. While MITS is similar to the UMRAO model of Gadwal et al. [3], MITS is also different in many important respects.

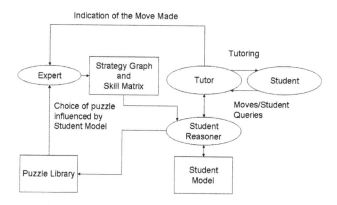

Fig. 2. Our Proposed Model

The strategy graph is now reasonable to compute *on-line* (while in UMRAO this is done off-line). Like UMRAO, the Expert is responsible for computing the strategy graph, but choosing the puzzle is the responsibility of the student reasoner operating on the student model compared to UMRAO where the Expert chooses the puzzle endgame.

The Tutor is relieved of any responsibility of reading the strategy graph. Rather, the Tutor is focused entirely upon a dialogue with the student. Instead, the strategy graph is read by the student reasoner. The student reasoner selects that part of the Sudoku puzzle that it wishes the tutor to focus upon *when the tutor is taking the initiative*. The student reasoner makes its selection based upon that part of the puzzle which exemplifies the strategy for which it has the least information about the student's performance, or where it appears important for the student to have more exposure to a poorly understood strategy.

On the other hand, *when the student is taking the initiative*, the tutor will communicate the move made by the student to the student reasoner. The Expert will reply with information about the correctness or incorrectness of the move.

When a move is confirmed as being made, the move is reported to the Expert. Incorrect moves do not update the strategy graph; MITS interacts with the user to correct the move. With each correct move, the Expert updates the strategy graph. The new strategy graph is now visible to the student reasoner. The tutoring process can continue with up-to-date information.

3.1   Mixed Initiative System

Generally, the tutor will first take the initiative and strictly control the solving of the puzzle in an effort to impart some initial knowledge to the student (see Section 3.4). As more moves are made by the student and witnessed by the student model, the student reasoner can develop a prediction of the success rate of the student solving a Sudoku puzzle without assistance from the tutor. As the probability that the student can solve the puzzle without assistance rises, the student reasoner will instruct the tutor to allow the student to take the initiative. Even while the student is taking the initiative, the system will continue to monitor the student's performance. If the student's performance should degrade during unassisted play, the tutor can resume assisting the user.

Because we are using a mixed-initiative paradigm, we have the problem that the Tutor needs know when to intervene and offer help, and when to permit the user to play without assistance. We argue that the model of Fleming and Cohen [4] can be easily incorporated into MITS. Their model is suitable because there are only four strategies that can be used in solving a Sudoku puzzle. For the sake of brevity, we label these strategies $s_1 \ldots s_4$. In particular, the strategies are:

- **Rows and Columns.** s_1 We look at the numbers in the current rows and columns and determine what must be left by a process of elimination;
- **Blocks.** s_2 This strategy is like s_1 except that we look at the 3×3 block to eliminate possibilities;
- **Pointing Pairs.** s_3 In this strategy, we look for pairs of numbers in the same row, column, or block which then cannot be possibilities in any other cells of that row, column, or block; and
- **Block-Line Reduction.** s_4 In this strategy, we compare the values needed in a particular block to the values needed in any row or any column which intersects that block. We will illustrate this technique in the sample session (see Section 4).

In accordance with their model [4], a cost-benefit analysis is conducted to determine if assistance should be given by the Tutor. In general, if the benefit of giving assistance exceeds the cost, the Tutor gives assistance.

The benefit of giving assistance for move j using strategy i is given by the equation

$$B_{j,i} = [1 - P_{\text{UK}}(s_i)][P_{\text{UU}}(s_i) + (1 - P_{\text{UU}}(s_i))P_{\text{UMU}}(s_i)]\Delta EU_j \qquad (1)$$

where an explanation of the variables used in Equation (1) follows.

While play is underway, the student reasoner witnesses the answers provided by the student in the empty cells. For each cell, one of the strategies would have been employed by the student. Consequently, the student model can keep a simply tally:

$$P_{\text{UK}}(s_i) = \frac{\# \text{ of times strategy } s_i \text{ was used correctly}}{\# \text{ of times strategy } s_i \text{ was used}} \qquad (2)$$

for $i \in 1 \ldots 4$, and thus keep a running probability of each strategy where $P_{\text{UK}}(s_i)$ is the probability that the student has the knowledge of strategy i. The use of the factor $1 - P_{\text{UK}}(s_i)$ in Equation (1) is opposite to the use in [4]: the benefit of giving advice is inversely related to the probability that the student already knows strategy i.

Furthermore, $P_{\text{UU}}(s_i)$ is the probability that the student would understand the advice given for strategy s_i and $P_{\text{UMU}}(s_i)$ is the probability that the student could be *made* to understand the strategy s_i. At the outset, MITS does not know if a student would understand the advice given or if it would be able to *make* the student understand the advice given. So, these probabilities are initialized to 0.5. These probabilities would be adjusted, up and down, with actual experience as the student interacts with MITS and makes correct or incorrect moves. As illustrated in further detail in Section 4, explaining a strategy occurs when MITS takes the initiative to direct a user to fill a particular square and a detailed explanation occurs when the student is provided with additional hints for filling a square. The probabilities are calculated as:

$$P_{\text{UU}}(s_i) = \frac{\text{\# times strategy } s_i \text{ was explained and understood}}{\text{\# of times strategy } s_i \text{ was explained}}, \tag{3}$$

and, in the event that the initial explanation was not understood,

$$P_{\text{UMU}}(s_i) = \frac{\text{\# times } s_i \text{ was explained in detail and understood}}{\text{\# of times } s_i \text{ was explained in detail}}, \tag{4}$$

for $i \in 1 \ldots 4$.[1]

The expected utility for a particular board state j is computed as,

$$EU_j = \frac{\text{\# of cells known unambiguously}}{81} \tag{5}$$

where the number of cells known unambiguously means *known unambiguously to the Expert*. A unambiguous cell means that for some strategy s_i the cell's value can be determined. An ambiguous cell means that no strategy currently exists to solve the cell. When moving from board state j to $j + 1$, we define

$$\Delta EU_{j+1} \equiv EU_{j+1} - EU_j \tag{6}$$

Simply put, ΔEU is a measurement of the extent to which a particular move advances the game towards the solution if $\Delta EU > 0$; or the extent of a digression from the solution if $\Delta EU < 0$. It is also possible for $\Delta EU = 0$, which means that the move failed to disambiguate any other cells. In brief, Equation (1) suggests that: i) it is beneficial to interact if the student lacks knowledge and either would understand or could be made to understand the strategy that needs to be explained; and ii) it is more beneficial to interact about moves that resolve more of the game board.

Cost would be measured as follows,

$$C_i = C_{\text{simple explanation of } s_i} + (1 - P_{\text{UU}}(s_i))C_{\text{detailed explanation of } s_i} \tag{7}$$

for some strategy $i \in 1 \ldots 4$. The costs $C_{\text{simple explanation of } s_i}$ and $C_{\text{detailed explanation of } s_i}$ would be each set on a scale $(0, 1]$ and would be in proportion to the difficulty of explaining the strategy to the user. Some of the four strategies are easier to explain than others.

Under this approach, an explanation would be given if $B_{j,i} > C_i$ for some plausible move j and strategy i. However, because of the manner in which we have defined expected utility, EU, we must make an exception to the ordinary cost-benefit rule

---

[1] The strategy used is determined by reference to the Sudoku Skill Matrix, which will be discussed in Section 3.3.

whenever $\Delta EU_j < 0$ for some move j made by the student during unassisted play. If $\Delta EU_j < 0$, then the benefit calculated according to Equation (1) will be negative. Since the cost is always non-negative, the cost-benefit rule is never met under these circumstances. Yet, whenever $\Delta EU_j < 0$, the student has committed an error and Tutor must intervene to correct the improper play.

The ultimate goal of the student model is $B_{j,i} \leq C_i$ for every plausible move j and strategies i from the current board state. This means that the student is playing Sudoku independently. Yet, we cannot uncompromisingly apply the rule $\Delta EU_j > 0$ and $B_{j,i} > C_i \ \forall i, j$ plausible moves and strategies as a condition of giving advice. Consider that case where the student *wants* advice when the student is playing independently. For example, the student may be playing a puzzle at a high level of difficulty and has managed to "get stuck." In this case, the tutor computes $m = \text{argmax}_j (B_{j,i} - C_i) \ \forall i, j$ plausible. The focus of discourse will now revolve around move m, which has the least net cost to the student model and the greatest probability of being understood by the student.

Finally, expected utility has one other advantage. Suppose that MITS wants to compute the best possible move m^*. The best possible move is computed easily as $m^* = \text{argmax}_j (\Delta EU_j) \ \forall j$ moves plausible from the current board state. This calculation would be useful in cases where the student wants to know where is the next and best move but does not desire or need an explanation of the strategy for finding the solution for that cell.

3.2   Sudoku Strategy Graphs

Sudoku Strategy Graphs (SSG's) are straightforward to read. A typical strategy graph is given in Figure 3(a). A cell with a single large number means that the cell was either an initial clue or it has been subsequently and correctly solved out by the student. A cell with one small number means that the cell is unambiguous, and, for the current board state, the cell can be solved out. If a cell in the SSG has two or more small numbers, the cell is ambiguous. The numbers appearing in the cell are the current possibilities, but the actual answer is unknown. A student who attempts to solve out an ambiguous cell is in fact committing an error.

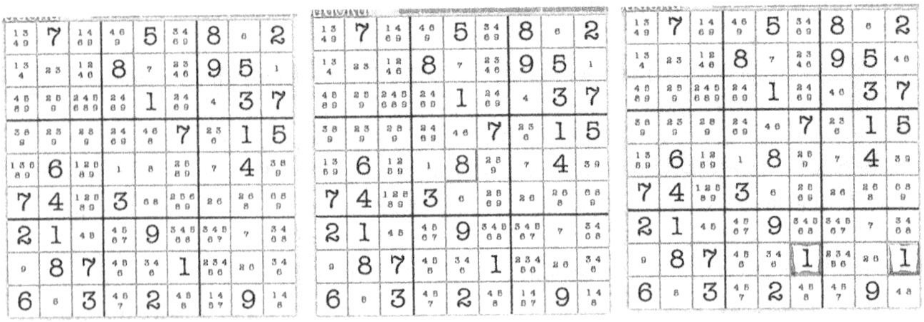

(a) First board Position   (b) SSG after an "8" is played   (c) SSG after a "1" improperly played in i8
in cell e5

Fig. 3. Sudoku Strategy Graphs

By convention, the columns of the strategy graph a labeled with letters with "a" on the left to "i" on the right. The columns are numbered from 1 to 9 with 1 at the top and 9 at the bottom.

Using Equation (5), the expected utility for the SSG in Figure 3(a) is $EU_1 = \frac{38}{81} = 0.469$. Suppose the player plays an 8 into square e5 — the centre cell of the centre block as illustrated in Figure 3(b). Therefore, $EU_2 = \frac{39}{81} = 0.482$. For that particular move, $\Delta EU = \frac{39-38}{81} = 0.012$.

As well, an SSG can become contradicted. Suppose a player plays "1" in cell i8 from the board state in Figure 3(b). The strategy graph that would result is illustrated in Figure 3(c). This play is improper because "1" is not a possibility for cell i8, because a "1" already appears in cell f8. So, we have $EU_3 = \frac{36}{81} = 0.444$ and $\Delta EU = \frac{36-39}{81} = -0.037$. So, we can indeed see how $\Delta EU < 0$ is indicative of an improper move; the SSG is therefore not updated. The Tutor should take the initiative and correct the student's play.

3.3   Sudoku Skill Matrix

It is not enough for the Expert to simply draw up the SSG. It must also compute the Sudoku Skill Matrix (SSM). The SSM is a 9×9 matrix each entry of which is an integer from 0 to 4. The numbers 1 to 4 indicate the strategy (or skill) that the student must use to solve the given position on the Sudoku board. If the Expert assigns a zero to any entry of the SSM, the zero signifies that either the cell has already been solved out, or that the cell is ambiguous and any attempt to solve the cell would be premature. The SSM related to Figure 3(a) is given in Figure 4.

Potentially, there might be more than one strategy available for solving out a cell in the Sudoku board. So, the programmer will need to provide for storage for additional integers in each cell. In the case of multiple strategies, we must consider two cases: the tutor has the initiative and the student has the initiative.

If the tutor has the initiative, then the strategy i will be selected such that $P_{UK}(s_i)$ is a minimum. Consequently, Equation (1) is maximized all other things being equal. The tutor will be focused upon the strategy that the student knows the least.

0	0	0	0	0	0	0	2	0
0	0	0	0	4	0	0	0	4
0	0	0	0	0	0	4	0	0
0	0	0	0	0	0	0	0	0
0	0	0	4	1	0	1	0	0
0	0	0	0	0	0	0	0	0
0	0	0	0	0	0	0	1	0
4	0	0	0	0	0	0	0	0
0	1	0	0	0	0	0	0	0

Fig. 4. A Sudoku Skill Matrix for the SSG in Figure 3(a)

If the student has the initiative, the problem is more complex because the issue of *plan recognition* arises. If the student gives the right answer, the tutor does not know which strategy the student used. The tutor could query the user to find out, but queries following a *proper* move might be viewed as an annoyance to the user. We take the view that it would be better to simply not trouble the user even though the probability $P_{UK}(s_i)$ will not be updated for that play. On the other hand, if the user supplies the wrong answer, the tutor can re-take the initiative and choose the strategy i such that $P_{UK}(s_i)$ is minimized over all plausible strategies. The tutor has moved the focus of discourse to the strategy least understood by the user.

3.4 Initializing the Student Model

There are two ways in which a student model can be initialized. The student can provide the parameters, or the system can develop the model during play. We take the position that the latter approach is best.

The user is modeled using 12 probabilities $P_{UK}(s_i)$, $P_{UU}(s_i)$, and $P_{UMU}(s_i)$ for $i \in 1\ldots 4$. We concede that the user *might* be able to provide the four probabilities $P_{UK}(s_i)$ provided that the user actually understands the strategies $s_1 \ldots s_4$. The danger is that the user might believe incorrectly that they understand a strategy and overestimate one or more or the probabilities $P_{UK}(s_i)$.

Until a sufficiently large sample of moves is witnessed by the student model, these probabilities cannot be used. However, the student reasoner can keep game play under strict tutor control selecting a variety of possible moves as the subject of discourse which exemplifies all four strategies $s_1 \ldots s_4$. Once a sufficiently large sample of moves is obtained by the student model, the mixed initiative model can be brought on-line and used actively.

We have already suggested that the eight other probabilities $P_{UU}(s_i)$ and $P_{UMU}(s_i)$ should be all initialized to 0.5. MITS cannot anticipate how well its discourse with the student will fare. Likewise, since the student has yet to interact with MITS, the student cannot anticipate how well he or she will understand the MITS' advice. So, it makes no logical sense for the student to provide those probabilities to the student model.

Unlike UMRAO, the student reasoner recommends the next puzzle to be played. In UMRAO, the Expert makes the decision. To account for this difference, the puzzles would be ranked by their level of difficulty. The difficulty level of a Sudoku puzzle is a function of the number of ambiguous cells from the first board state. The number of ambiguous cells can be determined from the puzzle's first strategy graph.

MITS would start a new student off with a puzzle having the least degree of difficulty advancing the student upwards to the most difficult puzzle. When a puzzle is solved, it would be recorded by the student model to prevent the puzzle from being selected again. The student model would also store the level of difficulty of the last solved puzzle for reference in making future puzzle selections.

Finally, once a student wishes to stop playing, the variables used in the student's model would be saved to a disk file for later retrieval. The variables are the 12 probabilities together with a list of the solved puzzles and the level of difficulty of the last solved puzzle. Consequently, students who have already used MITS would not need to go through the initialization procedure again.

4   A Sample Session

MITS as illustrated in this section is a *prototype* only. So far, we have worked out the generation of the strategy graph. So, the Expert of Figure 2 has been largely programmed. We also have a repertoire of sample puzzles, the Puzzle Library. The Tutor and the Student Model are still in development. So, the discourse shown in the following illustrations is simulated. On the other hand, the graphical user interface is quite real.

One of the dangers of a mixed initiative system is that the student may ask unexpected questions or abruptly change the focus of discourse. For our purposes, we believe that Freedman's [2] paper is quite relevant here. First, Freedman suggests asking short specific questions rather than open-ended ones. In our model, we would propose to ask questions like: "What is the value in cell i9?" The question is short and specific. A poor question to ask in the context of our model might be, "Why is finding the solution to i9 the best strategy?" The question is too open-ended.

Second, Freedman suggests that the computer's turn in the conversation should always conclude with a request. So, in our model, it would be a mistake to simply end the

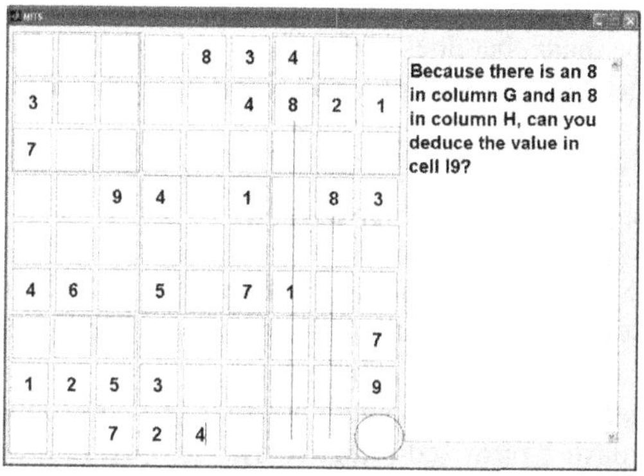

(a) Sudoku GUI — Move #1 Detailed Explanation

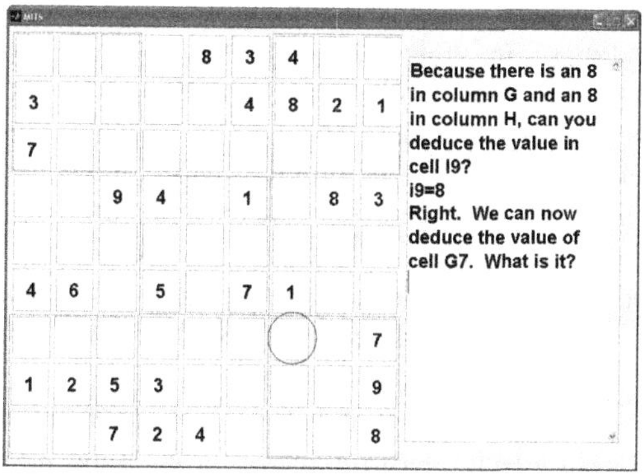

(b) Sudoku — Move #2 Simple Explanation

Fig. 5. The MITS Graphical User Interface

computer's turn with an explanation of the strategy and never ask a question. Instead, our tutor explains *why* the solution to a particular cell can be found, and then asks the user for the answer. Even though this dialogue model appears to be restrictive, Freedman concludes that this is not so. A specific and on-task discussion is preferred by users to an open-ended and incoherent dialogue with an ITS.

The learning environment is illustrated in Figure 5(a). We have opted for a simple GUI patterned after UMRAO. The playing board is to the left; the discourse window to the right. In Figure 5(a), the Tutor has taken the initiative and is testing the user. The test concerns strategy s_4, Box-Line Reduction. Since there is an 8 in each of columns g and h and the columns intersect the block in the lower right, the user ought to be able to conclude that the value in cell i9 is an 8. We call this a detailed explanation (refer to Equation (4)) because the Tutor specifically names the other cells needed in making the logical deduction that i9 is "8.". Detailed explanation occurs during initial tutoring.

Assume that the user correctly plays 8 in cell i9. Now the tutor shifts the focus of discourse to cell g7. This is a test of another variation of strategy s_4. Here, the student must recognize that there exists a 2 in each of rows 8 and 9, *and* a 2 in column h. So, it follows that g7 is 2. The Tutor is trying to ascertain if the student can use what was learned in board Figure 5(a) to solve cell g7 in board Figure 5(b). We call this a simple explanation (refer to Equation (3)), because the Tutor merely indicates where the move ought to be made, but does not explain the logic. If the student cannot determine the value of the cell, then the Tutor will resort to a detailed explanation similar to Figure 5(a).

5   Conclusions and Further Research

In developing MITS, a system for tutoring a student about Sudoku, we have designed an architecture to support mixed-initiative interaction during tutoring, with a student being modeled and advised about an entire game.

We have been able to introduce some innovative changes to the model of Fleming and Cohen for the design of mixed-initiative systems [4], in order to apply it to the problem of intelligent tutoring. Providing for a model of whether a user understands or can be made to understand, when engaged in dialogue, leads to a tutorial system that tracks the understanding of the student, based in part on past attempts. In addition, the need to ensure that we are also enabling learning serves to adjust the decisions about interaction in the mixed-iniative model.

The domain of Sudoku is generally helpful for investigating mixed-initiative tutoring because there is an intuitive interpretation of the expected utility of a move, in terms of the ability to disambiguate any open cells in the grid. We are then able to make use of this term of expected utility to critique the actions of the student, leading to intervention from the tutor when the student lacks knowledge and is following paths that have low utility.

In contrast with others designing systems to tutor students about games (e.g. [6, 7]), we therefore focus less on techniques for capturing what the student is learning, emphasizing instead the task of reasoning about interaction. Our approach to intelligent tutoring also differs from others (e.g. [3]) in that it builds the strategy graph on-line and combines this with the student model, to advise the Tutor about when to interact in order to facilitate successful completion of the game board for this student. And whereas some researchers have also investigated a mixed-initiative design for intelligent tutoring, the efforts have been focused on distinct topics, such as how to predict when the student will take the initiative [8].

There are several avenues for future research. In particular, developing a more sophisticated student reasoner and a more detailed student model would both be helpful, in order to deliver more customized tutoring to the student. For instance, the reasoner could identify patterns of difficulty in a student's strategy graph, in order to predict values for the $P_{UU}(s_i)$ and $P_{UMU}(s_i)$ variables manipulated in the formulae. Another suggestion is to estimate more precisely the value of certain factors, such as the expected number of interactions to explain a given strategy, by analyzing the student's current knowledge and past behaviour. The suggestion of allowing for either very basic or more detailed commentary, when advising a student, is yet another area where more intelligent algorithms may be designed, mapping a certain range of values of student modeling factors with a proposed level of detail, for the interaction.

References

1. Carbonell, J.R.: AI in CAI: An artificial-intelligence approach to computer-assisted instruction. IEEE Transactions on Man-Machine System **MMS-11** (1970)
2. Freedman, R.: Degrees of mixed-initiative interaction in an intelligent tutoring system. In: AAAI 1997 Spring Symposium on Computational Model for Mixed-Initiative Interaction. (1997)
3. Gadwal, D., Greer, J.E., McCalla, G.I.: Tutoring bishop-pawn endgames: an experiment in using knowledge-based chess as a domain for intelligent tutoring. Applied Intelligence **3** (1993) 207 – 224
4. Fleming, M., Cohen, R.: A user modeling approach to determining system initiative in mixed-initiative ai systems. Proceedings of User Modeling 2001 (2001)
5. Freedman, R.: What is an intelligent tutoring system? Intelligence **11(3)** (2000)
6. Manske, M., Conati, C.: Modelling learning in an educational game. In: Proceedings of AIED 2005. (2005)
7. Baena, A., Belmonte, M., Mandow, L.: An intelligent tutor for a web-based chess course. In Burusilovsky, P., Stock, O., Strapparava, C., eds.: Lecture Notes in Computer Science. Volume 1982/2000. (2000)
8. Beck, J., Jia, P., Sison, J., Mostow, J.: Predicting student help-request behavior in an intelligent tutor for reading. In: Proceedings of User Modeling 2003. (2003)

Author Index

Lecture Notes in Artificial Intelligence (LNAI)